Travellers of the World Revolution

Travellers of the World Revolution

A Global History of
the Communist International

Brigitte Studer

Translated by Dafydd Rees Roberts

VERSO

London • New York

This English-language edition published by Verso 2023
First published in German as *Reisende der Weltrevolution*
© Suhrkamp Verlag Berlin 2020
© Brigitte Studer 2023
Translation © Dafydd Rees Roberts 2023

All rights reserved

The moral rights of the author have been asserted

1 3 5 7 9 10 8 6 4 2

Verso
UK: 6 Meard Street, London W1F 0EG
US: 388 Atlantic Avenue, Brooklyn, NY 11217
versobooks.com

Verso is the imprint of New Left Books

ISBN-13: 978-1-83976-801-9
ISBN-13: 978-1-83976-803-3 (UK EBK)
ISBN-13: 978-1-83976-804-0 (US EBK)

British Library Cataloguing in Publication Data
A catalogue record for this book is available from the British Library

Library of Congress Cataloging-in-Publication Data
Names: Studer, Brigitte, author. | Roberts, Dafydd, translator.
Title: Travellers of the world revolution : a global history of the
   Communist International / Brigitte Studer ; translated by Dafydd Rees
   Roberts.
Other titles: Reisende der Weltrevolution. English
Description: London ; New York : Verso, 2023. | "First published in German
   as Reisende der Weltrevolution © Suhrkamp Verlag Berlin 2020"--Title
   page verso. | Includes bibliographical references and index. | Summary:
   "The Communist International was the first organized attempt to bring
   about worldwide revolution and left a lasting mark on twentieth-century
   history. Acclaimed historian Brigitte Studer offers a new and
   fascinating account of this transnational organization founded in 1919
   by Lenin and Trotsky and dissolved by Stalin in 1943, telling the story
   through the eyes of the activists who became its 'professional
   revolutionaries'"-- Provided by publisher.
Identifiers: LCCN 2023009895 (print) | LCCN 2023009896 (ebook) | ISBN
   9781839768019 (hardback) | ISBN 9781839768033 (ebook)
Subjects: LCSH: Communist International--History. |
   Communism--History--20th century.
Classification: LCC HX11.I5 S842813 2023 (print) | LCC HX11.I5 (ebook) |
   DDC 324.1--dc23/eng/20230322
LC record available at https://lccn.loc.gov/2023009895
LC ebook record available at https://lccn.loc.gov/2023009896

Printed and bound by CPI Group (UK) Ltd, Croydon, CR0 4YY

For Vincent

Contents

Preface	xi
Introduction	1
Revolution and Organization	4
Local Beginnings of a Global Project	8
Revolution as an Employment	13
The Global in the Local	19
Women, Men and the Revolutionary Self	23
Situated Action	29
Sources and Structure	33
1 Moscow 1920: Revolutionary Rendezvous	41
Through the Allied Blockade to Soviet Russia	44
Revolutionary Enthusiasm and the Experience of Transnational Solidarity	52
The Search for Shared Principles and a Common Language	60
Revolutionaries of a New Type?	69
2 Baku and Tashkent: The Revolution Goes East	74
The 'Oppressed Peoples of the East'	76
Force of Arms, Force of Propaganda: Exporting the Revolution	80
Modernity *and* Tradition?	90
Daily Life in the Early Days of the Comintern Apparatus	95

3 Berlin: Bridgehead in Europe and
   Hub of Transnational Circulation ... 102
   Transfers of Money and Knowledge ... 104
   An Early Comintern Agent and His Team ... 109
   Interacting Apparatuses ... 118
   An Organ of Party Control in the West ... 122
   The Working Day on a Foreign Mission ... 126
   A Rigorous System of Coordination and Supervision ... 130

4 Berlin, Cultural Capital of International Communism ... 141
   Cosmopolitan Intellectuals ... 142
   Changing Personnel Policy ... 148
   Euphoria and Sadness, Integration and Isolation ... 155
   Between Ascesis and Bohemia ... 167
   A Communist Entrepreneur ... 174
   Avant-Garde Culture and Prop-Art ... 184

5 Paris, Brussels, Berlin: Anti-Imperialism and
   Transcolonial Networks ... 189
   Anticolonialism Reaches the Metropole ... 192
   China: New Epicentre of the World Revolution ... 204
   Building Global Anticolonial Solidarity ... 211
   From Anticolonialism to Anti-Imperialism ... 214
   Mobilizing Friends and Sympathizers ... 219
   Coordination with the Eastern Department ... 232
   'Negro Workers': The Internationalization of the International ... 235

6 Guangzhou and Wuhan: On Missions
   for the Comintern in China ... 242
   Disunion and Deadlock ... 244
   In the New Capital ... 251
   Communicating the Line ... 256
   Departure and the Political Consequences of the Debacle ... 265

7 Shanghai: The Perilous Life of the Comintern Agent ... 275
   Rallying Point for Professional Revolutionaries ... 277
   Smashing of the Comintern Network ... 283
   Conspiracy as an Occupation ... 292
   Sowing Confusion ... 296
   Improvised Cooperation Between Apparatuses ... 304
   A Communist Enclave amid the Foreign Concessions ... 309

8 Cities of Refuge: Paris, Basel, Zurich, Moscow	320
Paris: A Disorganized Effort to Rebuild the Apparatus	323
Basel and Zurich: Precarious Safety	344
Moscow: Caught in the Trap	362
9 The Last Big Mission: Barcelona, Madrid, Albacete, Valencia	378
Advent of the Comintern Representatives	382
Solidarity with the Spanish Republic . . . and the Revolution	386
Recruitment and Conveyance of Volunteers	392
Establishment of a Military Base in Albacete	403
(Proto-)Humanitarian Aid	409
Security and Surveillance in Spain	420
Fatigue and Conflict among the Comintern Advisers	431
10 Conclusion: A Life with Bags Packed	441
Conditions, Duties, Job Requirements	442
Personality Types, Career Opportunities and Cadre Policy	444
Violence and Imprisonment	446
Political Commitment: Gains and Losses	449
Stalin and the Transformation of the Comintern	453
The Dead on Leave: The Great Massacre	456
Aftermath	457
A Brief Epilogue: The Survivors	460
Index	467

Preface

When, in 1980, I decided to make Rosa Grimm the subject of the dissertation I had to write for my *licence*, as the master's was then still called in French-speaking Switzerland, I had no idea how this would shape my life. Born Rosa Schlain to a Jewish family in Odessa, Grimm had been, with Rosa Bloch, one of the women most prominently active in the Swiss labour movement during the First World War. One of the founder members of the Communist Party of Switzerland (KPS), she then worked for a time for the Communist International in Moscow. My interest in women's history thus led me to the history of international Communism – both fields considered somewhat exotic in those days. After completing my studies, I received an offer to work on the edition of the Jules Humbert-Droz papers. In addition, I planned to write a PhD thesis on the activities of women in the public sphere in Switzerland in the interwar period. However, the two research areas proved too demanding to be carried out simultaneously. So I concentrated on the history of communism and wrote a thesis on the ties between the KPS and the Comintern. It was in that connection that I visited the Moscow archives in 1990; successive research projects in the history of Communism and Stalinism then saw me frequently return in the years that followed the end of the Soviet Union, before I abandoned the field for a decade to turn my attention elsewhere. About ten years ago, however, my interest in the Comintern was rekindled, with the emergence of transnational and actor-centred perspectives in history suggesting that there was still much that remained to be said on the subject. Published in English in 2015, a first book on the world of the foreign Communists resident in Moscow in the 1930s was generally well received, though one reviewer noted that it raised the question of *why* these people should have bowed to the demands of Stalinism. This prompted me to extend the field of investigation, both temporally and geographically, filling in the background by studying the life-courses of a representative group of individuals and in doing so grasping something of the world-spanning aspect of a unique political experiment: the attempt to change the future for the better through systematic, coordinated and rationally conceived action on a global scale.

No scholarly endeavour can be brought to a worthwhile conclusion without the engagement of colleagues. I was able to present my first thoughts on the project at an international workshop organized by Paolo Capuzzo at the University of Bologna, and then to discuss them further at a conference organized by Silvio Pons in Rome and at Ioana Popa and Ioana Cirstocea's seminar at the École des Hautes Études en Sciences Sociales [School for Advanced Studies in the Social Sciences] (EHESS) in Paris. I am most grateful for the ideas and suggestions put forward at that early stage. Oleksa Drachewych's invitation to join his panel at the Association for Slavic, East European & Eurasian Studies convention held in Boston in 2018 then forced me to structure my thoughts more clearly, even if in the end I had to pull out at relatively short notice on account of pressure of work.

Wolfram Adolphi, Gleb Albert, Silvia Berger Ziaudin, José M. Faraldo, Heiko Haumann (to whom I owe special thanks for his friendship and long collaboration on different projects), Sonja Matter, Roman Rossfeld, Bernhard Schär and Martin Wagner all read and offered critical comments on individual chapters, while Victor Magalhaes Strazzeri de Araujo read the entire manuscript in an early draft. I am grateful to them for their many suggestions for improvement; for any remaining errors of fact or interpretation I must accept sole responsibility. I owe much, as well, to informal discussion with colleagues and friends. Sabine Dullin offered me much food for thought in the course of our close collaboration, in 2016, as editors of the special isssue of *Monde(s)* on Communism in transnational perspective, and I would also take this opportunity to thank the authors who contributed. I was in regular contact with Andrée

Lévesque; we encouraged each other as we worked on our articles, each passing on tips to the other about new and relevant publications. Jean-François Fayet, Kevin Morgan, Claude Pennetier and Bernard Pudal also provided their quota of inspiration in our many friendly discussions. I learnt a great deal about global history approaches from Stephan Scheuzger, notably in the course of the seminar we jointly ran on 'The most International of Internationals: the Global History of the Comintern' and from his always cogent contributions to our regular departmental seminar. I also have to thank Alain Chatriot, who most kindly copied a file in the French national archives, saving me a journey to Paris, and Natalia Akhramovich, who found files for me at the Comintern archives in Moscow when they turned out to be unexpectedly needed in the course of writing. Magali Delaloye helped me decipher a sheaf of papers in barely legible Cyrillic handwriting found in one Moscow personnel file, while Katharina Hermann helped with some translations. For suggestions regarding documents, publications, images and biographical data I am indebted to Bernhard Bayerlein, Elife Biçer-Deveci, Stefanie Brander, Marco Buttino, Harald Fischer-Tiné, Wladislaw Hedeler, Andreas Herbst, Thomas Kampen, Dainis Karepovs, Reinhart Müller, Claudio Natoli, Claude Pennetier, Marc Perrenoud, Julia Richers, John Riddell, Carmen Scheide, Joanna Simonow, Miin-Ling Yu and Alexander Vatlin. Stephen Smith provided me with an unpublished paper, while Patrick Karlsen sent me a digital copy of his biography of Vittorio Vidali before the book became available at our university library, together with two pictures of Vidali. My warmest thanks go to them, as they do to Yvonne Hirdman, who most kindly sent me two pictures of her mother, Charlotte Stenbock-Fermor, and to Vera Blaser, Timo Probst and Therese Dudan, who provided invaluable assistance as I was researching and writing the book. Damiana Salm's punctilious copy-editing much improved the German manuscript, while my translator Dafydd Roberts has been assiduous in dispelling any remaining obscurities or ambiguities. My thanks go to both. At Verso, I am grateful to Dan O'Connor. It is thanks to Sebastian Budgen's initiative that the book can be published in English.

Not the least of my debts is owed to Pietro Boschetti, endlessly patient over supper or Sunday breakfast as I complained of difficulties with my research or waxed enthusiastic about some discovery in library or archive, and ever ready for detailed discussion of the issues that arose.

Also helpful, in her own very particular way, was Miss Tinguette, whose close interest in my labours was reflected in her inclination to lie down on whatever I was reading at the time. Negotiations over her departure afforded me much-needed breaks from work.

The broad geographical span of the Comintern's activities has necessitated recourse to primary and secondary sources in a variety of languages, and where not indicated otherwise the translations (into German) were the author's own. Chinese names have been romanized in accordance with the Pinyin system, with the exception of those already well known in older forms, such as Chiang Kai-shek (Jiang Jieshi in pinyin) or Sun Yat-sen (Sun Zhongshan).

Introduction

'Revolutionary' was what Manabendra Nath Roy wrote under 'occupation' when in 1921 he filled in the questionnaire the Comintern – the Communist International – issued to all foreign Communists who came to Moscow.[1] Like thousands of others, Roy was employed by the Comintern as a salaried official. He was thus one of the elite of inter-war Communism, engaged in a historically unique political experiment in seeking to apply rational analysis and sophisticated and complex organization to the conception, preparation and execution of a global revolution. Born the son of a Brahmin in Arbelia, not far from Calcutta, Roy was a radical anticolonial activist who had discovered Marxism and Communism in his quest for weapons in the struggle for Indian independence. With Evelyn Trent, his first wife, he had taken part in the Second World Congress of the Comintern in Moscow in 1920 and thereupon entered the service of international Communism. As he would write later, 'since 1919, when I left for Europe with my wife . . . we have lived and travelled in most of the European countries, writing, studying, organising and making propaganda for the liberation of India.'[2]

---

1 *Anketa* (questionnaire) by M. N. Roy, Moscow, 31 January 1921, RGASPI 495/213/18.
2 Letter from Manabendra Nath Roy to the French Ligue des droits de l'Homme et du citoyen protesting his expulsion from France, Luxembourg, 1 February 1925, appended to Evelyn Roy, 'Indian Political Exiles in France', *Labour Monthly* 7:4, April 1925, 205–10.

His activities would also take him to Uzbekistan and China, and back and forth to the Soviet Union, always in illegality and under permanent threat of imprisonment or deportation, and once back in India he would be tried behind closed doors and sentenced to a long term of imprisonment.[3]

This study looks at the working lives and everyday circumstances of the professional revolutionaries directly employed or otherwise funded by Moscow, dispatched on missions they hoped would help bring about the revolutionary transformation of social and political relations. Why did people like M. N. Roy and Evelyn Trent take up careers as global professional revolutionaries, at risk of imprisonment, torture, or death? Why did they choose an uncertain, nomadic life without any of the comforts or security afforded by conformity? How was it that they threw themselves so completely into the life of the Comintern? 'A revolutionary', wrote the novelist and former Communist Manès Sperber, 'is a man [sic] who will stake everything he owns, that is to say the present, on a single number, in the hopes that the ball in the roulette wheel will stop at that one number and he'll win the future. From a common-sense point of view that is so idiotic it makes one want to cry. But to a gambler

---

3 Roy was never able to complete his memoirs, which cover only the early years of his work for the Comintern: Manabendra Nath Roy, *Memoirs*, Delhi: Ajanta, 1984. There are many studies of Roy's life, the most exhaustive being Sibnarayan Ray, *In Freedom's Quest: A Study of the Life and Works of M. N. Roy, 1887–1954*, 4 vols, Kolkata: Minerva/Renaissance, 1998–2007. A detailed overview of the socioeconomic background and of Roy's earlier years as a Bengali nationalist terrorist when he also committed robberies as acts of revolutionary fund raising and was wanted by the police as a Bengali 'nationalist terrorist', is given by Suchetana Chattopadhyay, 'Being "Naren Bhattacharji"', in Vijay Prashad, ed., *Communist Histories* 1, New Delhi: LeftWord Books, 2016, 29–71. Kris Manjapra, *M. N. Roy: Marxism and Colonial Cosmopolitanism*, New Delhi: Routledge, 2010, is another study, though criticized for the unclarity of its central category in Stephan Scheuzger, 'Readings of Cosmopolitanism: Revolutionaries' Biographies in the Intersections of Marxism and Anti-Colonialism in the Interwar Period', *Monde(s): histoire, espaces, relations* 10, 2016, 151–66. Also useful, despite being more strongly focussed on Roy's post-Comintern years than the title might suggest, is John Patrick Haithcox, *Communism and Nationalism in India: M.N. Roy and Comintern Policy, 1920–1939*, Princeton, NJ: Princeton University Press, 1971. On Evelyn Roy, née Trent, see the short and unfortunately somewhat confused study by Narisetti Innaiah, *Evelyn Trent alias Shanti Devi, Founder Member of Exile Indian Communist Party* [sic], Hyderabad: Booklinks Corporation, 1995. Reference to both can be found in Gene D. Overstreet and Marshall Windmiller, *Communism in India*, Berkeley: University of California Press, 1959.

it seems quite normal, for whatever he may happen to possess is for him a stake and not a fortune.'[4]

From the distance of our own individualistic present, such total engagement belongs to another world. For Roy, on the other hand, the Comintern represented a promising political option in his struggle against India's British masters. For this international organization was not only the first thoroughly organized attempt at worldwide anti-capitalist revolution, it was also the pioneer of a global, anticolonial, antiracist and anti-imperialist politics. In the ferment that followed the First World War it offered the various national liberation movements in colonial, and what the Comintern called 'semi-colonial' territories, not merely an ideology of emancipation but material, organizational and personal resources. After their seizure of power in 1917, the Bolsheviks had published the secret agreements under which the European powers had carved up among themselves the as yet uncolonized regions of the globe, and in the manifesto of the founding Congress of the Comintern, in 1919, Lenin and Trotsky had proclaimed the forthcoming liberation of 'the colonial slaves of Africa and Asia'.[5] The young Soviet state had proclaimed peoples' right to self-determination from the start. The Finns and Estonians were the first to act upon this, declaring their independence, but, as their territories were objects of contention between warring Whites and Reds, they had to fight for their freedom.

The emancipatory and internationalist worldview embodied by the Comintern also offered other social groups – workers, of course, but also women, Blacks, and young people – possibilities of identification, meaning and action. Communism offered a new sense of belonging in which ethnic, national or social origin, and even gender, were, in some respects, unimportant. To the Communists, internationalism meant more than the abolition of borders and the abandonment of an outdated nationalism. It was part of doing away with capitalism, of putting an end to class society, colonialism, racism and women's oppression.

---

4 Manès Sperber, *Like a Tear in the Ocean: A Trilogy* [1949–1952], vol. 3, *Journey Without End*, trans. Constantine FitzGibbon, New York: Holmes & Meier, 1988, 16.

5 John Riddell, ed., *Founding the Communist International: Proceedings and Documents of the First Congress, March 1919*, New York: Pathfinder Press, 1987, 227–8.

Revolution and Organization

The revolutionaries more readily took on the challenge of this collective political adventure because the goal already seemed to be in sight. The fall of tsarism and the Bolshevik seizure of power in November 1917 (or October 1917, as the Julian calendar had it) seemed to mark the beginning of a new age.[6] The 'Ten Days That Shook the World' – title of the renowned first-hand report by American journalist John Reed[7] – had turned Russia into the laboratory of a vast revolutionary project that was already playing out over a sixth of the globe. In the wake of the Russian Revolution, historically new practices of emancipation began to emerge. In Europe and elsewhere, the legitimacy of existing power relations was thrown into question, prompting, says the historian Geoff Eley, a transnational, Europe-wide moment of democratization.[8] Regarding the Revolution's effects elsewhere in the world, other authors have similarly spoken of an 'internationalist moment'.[9]

The revolutionary flood that followed 1917 came in several waves before the failure of the German revolution in 1923 saw it ebb. In Finland, civil war broke out following the country's declaration of independence from Russia. In Germany, the November Revolution brought about the abdication of the Kaiser. In Austria-Hungary, the Dual Monarchy collapsed, as did the similarly multi-ethnic Ottoman Empire further east. Mass strikes, insurrections and the formation of workers' and soldiers' councils in Poland, Austria and Germany culminated in 1919 in the proclamation of soviet republics in Bavaria and in Hungary, the factory and land occupations of Italy's 'Biennio Rosso', the Irish declaration of independence, and mutiny by French

---

6 For a concise overview of the revolution's dramatic consequences in urban and rural Russia and the response to them abroad, see Heiko Haumann, ed., *Die Russische Revolution 1917*, Cologne: Böhlau-Verlag, 2016.

7 John Reed, *Ten Days That Shook the World*, New York: Boni & Liveright, 1919.

8 Geoff Eley, 'Cultural Socialism, the Public Sphere, and the Mass Form: Popular Culture and the Democratic Project, 1900 to 1934', in David E. Barclay and Eric Weitz, eds, *Between Reform and Revolution: German Socialism and Communism from 1840 to 1990*, New York: Berghahn Books, 1999, 315–40, at 319.

9 Ali Raza, Franziska Roy and Benjamin Zachariah, eds, *The Internationalist Moment: South Asia, Worlds and World Views, 1917–1939*, New Delhi: Sage, 2015.

sailors in the Black Sea.¹⁰ There was ferment beyond Europe as well. In the United States, prolonged race riots alarmed the white governing class, while business was threatened by strikes. In Korea and China, there were mass demonstrations against Japanese colonialism and European imperialism. Europe, however, also saw pogroms, the expulsion of whole populations, and the emergence of counterrevolutionary forces and paramilitary formations prepared to use violence. More than four million people died in the armed conflicts of the post-war period.¹¹

While this wave of protest, unrest, rebellion, insurrection and revolution was indeed driven by the workers, the classical revolutionary subject of Marxist theory (even if many were in uniform), hitherto politically and socially marginalized forces also entered upon the stage, notably women and young people. Artists, women architects, journalists, lawyers, shopgirls and housewives all radicalized. As historian Jörn Leonhard puts it, there was a 'global revolution of rising expectations'.¹² The historically rare convergence of interest between social groups that emerged in the train of the worldwide shockwave released by the Russian Revolution is only comprehensible if one understands '1917' as marking the confluence of the radical critique of the contradictory process of enlightenment, industrialization and Western modernity with radical currents and liberation movements, ideas and practices from the 'global South'.¹³ The Bolsheviks made themselves the voice of class struggle, the spearhead of the workers' movement, but also supported the demands of left feminists, anticolonial activists and national liberation movements, seeking to promote a sense of the 'we' despite the diversity.

---

10 On the revolutionary events of 1919 across the globe, see Jean-François Fayet, '1919', in Stephen Smith, ed., *The Oxford Handbook of the History of Communism*, Oxford: Oxford University Press, 2014, 109–24.

11 Robert Gerwarth, *The Vanquished: Why the First World War Failed to End, 1917–1923*, London: Allen Lane, 2016.

12 Jörn Leonhard, '1917–1920 and the Global Revolution of Rising Expectations', in Stefan Rinke and Michael Wildt, eds, *Revolutions and Counter-Revolutions: 1917 and Its Aftermath from a Global Perspective*, Frankfurt a. M.: Campus, 2017, 31–51.

13 For an account along these lines, though from a Eurocentric perspective, see Matthew Rendle, 'Making Sense of 1917: Towards a Global History of the Russian Revolution', *Slavic Review* 76:3, 2017, 610–18, at 618.

The political situation in 1919 confirmed Lenin in his belief that the Great War would lead to civil war, opening the road to revolution.[14] Yet speed was of the essence, he thought. The revolutionary flood that had swept Europe after 1918 threatened to recede just as quickly. The radical forces were divided into small splinter groups, while the mass of the working class still remained loyal to the parties of the Second International. Without the support of Europe's working class, Lenin believed the Soviet regime would be unable to survive. For him, the October Revolution was only a prologue. The Bolsheviks thus set their hopes on a revolution in Germany, from which others would follow. The establishment of the Communist International in Moscow in March 1919 accordingly represented a deliberate attempt by the Bolshevik leadership to unite the forces of revolution in a new, third International. There were in Moscow only three delegates from foreign Communist parties, and, of these, only the delegate of the German party carried any political clout. Communist parties outside the Soviet Union were still rare. The founding congress thus mostly attracted the representatives of small radical groups and the left wings of social-democratic parties.[15] The word 'Communism' itself was hardly ever uttered. Only in March 1918 had the Russian party renamed itself the All-Russia Communist Party (Bolsheviks) – abbreviated in Russian as VKP(b). The first revolutionary groups to emerge from the war had called themselves Spartakus (in Germany) and Gruppe Forderung (in Switzerland). To adopt the title 'Communist Party' was to declare solidarity with the Bolsheviks, as did the Communist Party of Germany in late 1918, before it ever joined the Communist International. Indeed, Hugo Eberlein, the party's representative at the 1919 congress, was given an imperative mandate to vote against the founding of the

---

14 On the Bolsheviks' thinking on war and civil war, see Silvio Pons, *The Global Revolution: A History of International Communism, 1917–1991*, trans. Allan Cameron, Oxford: Oxford University Press, 2014.

15 No complete official record of the Congress exists, testimony to the scarcity of the resources available to the Bolsheviks. Scholarly editions of the proceedings have been based on the typescripts of individual speeches, what minutes are available, German-language reports on the Congress and the expanded Russian version of the proceedings published in 1933 by the Marx-Engels-Lenin Institute in Moscow: Wladislaw Hedeler and Alexander Vatlin, eds, *Die Weltpartei aus Moskau: Der Gründungskongress der Kommunistischen Internationale 1919; Protokoll und neue Dokumente*, Berlin: Akademie Verlag, 2008; Riddell, *Founding*.

organization as premature. Rosa Luxemburg, brutally murdered by paramilitaries shortly after the founding conference of the German party, feared that a body in which the Bolsheviks were the only mass party would be subordinate to them – as indeed proved to be the case. She was not, however, against the establishment of a new International in principle, wanting only to wait for the emergence of Communist parties in Western Europe.

While the founding of the new International was contentious, it nonetheless answered to something in the spirit of the times. The old social democracy was worn out, and the future organization of the workers' movement was very unclear. At the Second World Congress of the Comintern, which met in Moscow in late July and early August 1920, the right social democrats were the only working-class force not to be represented, by an observer at least. Radical leftists, anticolonial 'terrorists', feminists and members of anarchist groups and national liberation movements all came. The phase of enchantment was not over, the yearning for world revolution was still strong.[16] The Congress had been given the task of steeling the recently founded International ideologically and endowing it with a proper organizational structure. For the new organization needed cadre and a global network. In the words of its first president, Grigori Zinoviev, the Communist International had to be turned from 'an organ of propaganda and agitation' into a 'fighting organization'.[17]

The Second World Congress not only determined how the Comintern would function but also laid the basis for the global organization of revolutionary activity. If the capitalist world order were to be destroyed and a world revolution brought about through armed insurrection, a political and administrative apparatus and a global network had to be constructed. To the Bolsheviks and their allies, it was clear that – given the longer timescale it seemed they now faced – their self-imposed task called for professional revolutionaries with a solid theoretical grounding and good practical skills. The mighty enemy could not be overcome by spontaneous actions, but only through the intervention of a

---

16 For the Soviet side of this, see Gleb Albert, *Das Charisma der Weltrevolution: Revolutionärer Internationalismus und frühe Sowjetgesellschaft, 1917–1927*, Cologne: Böhlau-Verlag, 2017.

17 Cited in Pierre Broué, *L'histoire de l'Internationale communiste 1919–1943*, Paris: Fayard, 1997, 153.

hard-hitting, well-trained and coordinated avant-garde. The masses too had to be ideologically prepared. Such a transnational endeavour required organization, clear directives and resources in the form of money, know-how and personnel.

Local Beginnings of a Global Project

Founded in 1919 with world revolution as its declared goal, only to be dissolved without fanfare by Josef Stalin in 1943, the Communist International developed a historically distinct form of political engagement that stood in the tradition of the European workers' movement yet was in many ways unique. It formulated a new political grammar, a distinctive set of rules for a new form of collective, radical engagement. Its means to this were a strictly disciplined organization, a network in part underground and in part triumphantly public, directed and coordinated by an Executive Committee (ECCI).[18] In the Comintern, the different facets of Communism came together: an international political programme with a utopian dimension, cross-border political organization and a territorially based political regime that had its own interests to pursue.

The Comintern was founded as a fighting organization, an entrepreneur of revolution, but rapidly grew into a bureaucratic institution called by its own actors the *apparat*. This polysemously metaphorical German and then Russian term can mean both 'instrument' (and so means to an end) and well-oiled 'machine' (run by operatives or cadre). It could be

---

18 On the often reorganized Comintern apparatus, see Grant M. Adibekov, Elena N. Shachnazarova and Kirill K. Shirinia, *Organizatsionnaia struktura Kominterna 1919–1943* [The Organizational Structure of the Comintern, 1919–1943], Moscow: Rosspen, 1997. A list of the different elements of the ECCI network, of which there were more than 100, together with a good many subsidiary organizations, is to be found in Bernhard H. Bayerlein, 'Das neue Babylon: Strukturen und Netzwerke der Kommunistischen Internationale und ihre Klassifizierung', *Jahrbuch für Historische Kommunismusforschung*, 2004, 181–270. See also Peter Huber, 'The Central Bodies of the Comintern: Stalinization and Changing Social Composition', in LaPorte, Morgan and Worley, eds, *Bolshevism*, 66–88; Niels Erik Rosenfeldt, *The 'Special' World: Stalin's Power Apparatus and the Soviet System's Secret Structures of Communication*, vol. 2, Copenhagen: Museum Tusculanum Press, 2009; and Brigitte Studer, 'Die Kominternstruktur nach dem 7. Weltkongress: Das Protokoll des Sekretariats des EKKI über die Reorganisierung des Apparates des EKKI, 2. Oktober 1935', *Internationale wissenschaftliche Korrespondenz zur Geschichte der deutschen Arbeiterbewegung* 31:1, 1995, 25–53.

said that the Bolsheviks, for reasons of efficiency, turned to a permanent bureaucratic apparatus and an employed staff to control a machinery intended to bridge the gap between those who gave the orders and those who executed them. As is well known, a bureaucracy in any event develops with time a distinctive logic of its own, in which self-preservation can come to take precedence over its original goals. Force of circumstance saw the ECCI quartered in Soviet Russia, the only country that had undergone a successful revolution and could therefore serve as a secure base for revolutionaries from all over the world, at least until the German revolution should take place. This, however, gave the Bolsheviks, as the party governing the country that bore most of the financial burden, the right to five voting members of the Executive, as compared to the one vote each granted to the ten to thirteen larger parties represented on the committee.[19] It was the Bolsheviks, too, that made the ECCI into a permanent body. While the German Communist Paul Levi had proposed regular meetings every three months, Zinoviev had opposed such routinism in the name of permanent readiness for action. For him, the ECCI was the 'international general staff of the fighting proletariat'. It was 'an epoch of revolutionary struggle'. The ECCI – locus of micro-struggles with macro-political effects – was, however, able to meet only irregularly, as even its permanent members were not always in Moscow, either from personal disinclination or on account of their many responsibilities in their own parties. The Third World Congress of 1921 thus decided to employ three permanent, salaried secretaries. On the suggestion of the Russian party, these were the Hungarian Mátyás Rákosi, the Finn Otto Kuusinen and the Swiss Jules Humbert-Droz – all representatives of small or banned parties with negligible revolutionary prospects, whose seasoned revolutionaries were thus wasted in their own countries. Their interlocutor would be Russian Osip Piatnitsky, channel of communication with the Soviet party and the Soviet authorities, and vice versa.

With its worldwide networks, many front organizations and eighty or so Communist parties, the Comintern in all its diversity presents a considerable challenge to historians. Until well into the 1970s, and in

---

19 Despite the existence of a further ten alternate members, these numbers proved insufficient as early as 1921, given the growth in the number of sections, and the membership of the committee was expanded to twenty-four.

many cases even longer, historical work on the International did not go beyond a basic institutional approach, the focus falling on political ideology, political strategy, organizational form and the identification of actors. Who the historical actors were, how many members Communist organizations really had, how the Comintern apparatus developed and the location of its offshoots across the world: such information is absolutely essential for any history of international Communism, of that there is no doubt. Comprehensive overviews have, however, been few.[20] (The case is quite different as regards individual parties.[21]) Yet a perspective confined to organizational technique, organizational history and organizational sociology led to a narrowing of research that would be criticized by Karl Schlögel, the great champion of the spatial turn in history, in an interview some years ago. For, he explained, 'the Comintern is of course a cultural phenomenon of the very first order, in some ways a community of fate [*Schicksalsgemeinschaft*] defined by the Great War period yet at the same time very much tied to, and intimately familiar with, different local circumstances.'[22]

In recent years the field has, however, seen major changes. One might cite first the advent of cultural, experiential, subjectivity- and actor-centred perspectives. These have shown that to be a Communist

---

20 Broué, *Histoire*; Kevin McDermott and Jeremy Agnew, *The Comintern: A History of International Communism from Lenin to Stalin*, Basingstoke, UK: Palgrave Macmillan, 1996; Alexandr Vatlin, *Komintern. Idei, resheniia, sud'by* [The Comintern: Founding, Programme, Actors], Moscow: Rosspen, 2009, available in German translation as *Die Komintern. Gründung, Programmatik, Akteure*, Berlin: Dietz, 2009; Serge Wolikow, *L'Internationale communiste: Le Komintern ou le rêve déchu du parti mondial de la révolution*, Ivry-sur-Seine: Éditions de l'Atelier, 2010. For a brief overview, see Alexander Vatlin and S. A. Smith, 'The Comintern', in Steve A. Smith, ed., *The Oxford Handbook of the History of Communism*, Oxford: Oxford University Press, 2014, 187–94. See also Mikhail Narinsky and Jürgen Rojahn, eds, *Centre and Periphery: The History of the Comintern in the Light of New Documents*, Amsterdam: Internationaal Instituut voor Sociale Geschiedenis, 1996; Tim Rees and Andrew Thorpe, eds, *International Communism and the Communist International, 1919–1943*, Manchester: Manchester University Press, 1998. And, for the whole century, with a focus on the role of the Soviet state, Pons, *Global Revolution*.

21 Summing up the vast body of existing research, see Matthew Worley, ed., *In Search of Revolution: International Communist Parties in the Third Period*, London: I.B. Tauris, 2004.

22 Karl Schlögel, 'Über Räume und Register der Geschichtsschreibung: Ein Gespräch mit Karl Schlögel', *Zeithistorische Forschungen/Studies in Contemporary History* 1:3, 2004, 396–413, at 353.

was not a matter of political conviction alone but involved one's entire lived experience. Members of the international Communist movement of the inter-war period constituted a distinctive lifeworld, a global community joined by a common language and common practices. Behind this lay a form of life and a mode of conduct acquired through schooling and practice – this being even more markedly so in the time of Stalin's revisions and tergiversations. The Stalinization of the Comintern was thus not only a matter of political control and surveillance but also had its cultural and subjective concomitants.[23] The varied kinds of biographical writing generated by Communist institutions were not only a means to bureaucratic surveillance, but also a medium of self-constitution.[24] Scholarship has been infused with new energy by the postcolonial critique of the Eurocentrism of established perspectives and the emergence of subaltern studies, which prompted attention to the elective affinities between Communism, anticolonialism and anti-imperialism in the wake of the October Revolution.[25] Most recently, interest has turned toward the Comintern's efforts to bring class and race together in the 'Negro question' – a term the organization used without any negative connotation.[26] Further

---

23 Brigitte Studer and Heiko Haumann, eds, *Stalinistische Subjekte: Individuum und System in der Sowjetunion und der Komintern, 1929–1953/L'individu et le système en Union soviétique et dans le Comintern, 1929–1953/Stalinist Subjects: Individual and System in the Soviet Union and the Comintern, 1929–1953*, Zurich: Chronos, 2006; Gina Herrmann, 'The Spanish Civil War and the Routes of Stalinization', in LaPorte, Morgan and Worley, *Bolshevism*, 167–87; Brigitte Studer, *The Transnational World of the Cominternians*, trans. D. R. Roberts, Basingstoke, UK: Palgrave Macmillan, 2015; Lisa Kirschenbaum, *International Communism and the Spanish Civil War: Solidarity and Suspicion*, Cambridge: Cambridge University Press, 2015.

24 Claude Pennetier and Bernard Pudal, eds, *Autobiographies, autocritiques, aveux dans le monde Communiste*, Paris: Belin, 2002; Pennetier and Pudal, *Le sujet communiste: Identités militantes et laboratoires du 'moi'*, Rennes: Presses universitaires de Rennes, 2014; Brigitte Studer, Berthold Unfried and Irène Herrmann, eds, *Parler de soi sous Staline: La construction identitaire dans le communisme des années trente*, Paris: Éditions de la MSH, 2002.

25 Kasper Braskén, *The International Workers' Relief, Communism, and Transnational Solidarity: Willi Münzenberg in Weimar Germany*, Basingstoke, UK: Palgrave Macmillan, 2015; Fredrik Petersson, *Willi Münzenberg, the League Against Imperialism and the Comintern, 1925–1933*, 2 vols, Lewiston, NY: Queenston Press, 2013; Raza, *The Internationalist Moment*; Holger Weiss, ed., *International Communism and Transnational Solidarity: Radical Networks, Mass Movements and Global Politics, 1919–1939*, Dordrecht: Brill, 2016.

26 Hakim Adi, *Pan-Africanism and Communism: The Communist International, Africa and the Diaspora, 1919–1939*, Trenton, NJ: Africa World Press, 2013; Holger

stimulus has come, thirdly, from the transnational turn and the development of global history.²⁷ These have raised new questions, for example, how the spatial ordering of actor groups is reflected in their political programmes or technical projects. As a result, organizational and personal networks, infrastructural interconnection and financial transfers have come to attention alongside the circulation of ideas and practices.²⁸ In this field, however, there still remains a great deal to be done. The same can be said regarding Comintern policies on women and gender, so far treated only in individual articles and chapters rather than any monographic study.²⁹

Nor has there been much work on the historically specific community of fate represented by those who made revolution their vocation and for whom political engagement meant employment by the

---

Weiss, *Framing a Radical African Atlantic: African American Agency, West African Intellectuals and the International Trade Union Committee of Negro Workers*, Leiden: Brill, 2014; Oleksa Drachewych, *The Communist International, Anti-Imperialism and Racial Equality in British Dominions*, London: Routledge, 2019; Oleksa Drachewych and Ian McKay, eds, *Left Transnationalism: The Communist International and the National, Colonial, and Racial Questions*, Montreal: McGill–Queen's University Press, 2019.

27 David Mayer, 'Weltrevolution, Stalinismus und Peripherie: Die Kommunistische Internationale und Lateinamerika', in Karin Fischer and Susan Zimmermann, eds, *Internationalismen: Transformation weltweiter Ungleichheit im 19. und 20. Jahrhundert*, Vienna: Promedia/Südwind, 2008, 171–92; Joachim C. Häberlen, 'Between Global Aspirations and Local Realities: The Global Dimensions of Interwar Communism', *Journal of Global History* 7:3, 2012, 415–37; Sabine Dullin and Brigitte Studer, 'Introduction – Communisme + transnational: L'équation retrouvée de l'internationalisme, premier XXᵉ siècle', *Monde(s): histoire, espaces, relations* 10, 2016, 9–31, as well as the rest of the special issue 'Communisme transnational'. Our introductory essay is available in English as 'Communism + Transnational: The Rediscovered Equation of Internationalism in the Comintern Years', *Twentieth Century Communism* 14, 2018, 66–95.

28 Josephine Fowler, *Japanese and Chinese Immigrant Activists: Organizing in American and International Communist Movements, 1919–1933*, New Brunswick, NJ: Rutgers University Press, 2007; Constance Margain, 'L'Internationale des gens de la mer, 1930–1937: Activités, parcours militants et résistance au nazisme d'un syndicat Communiste de marins et dockers', doctoral thesis, Université du Havre, 2015, and the same author's 'The International Union of Seamen and Harbour Workers, ISH 1930–1937: Interclubs and Transnational Aspects', *Twentieth Century Communism* 8, 2015, 133–44.

29 Studer, *Transnational World*, 40–58, chapter on 'The New Woman'; Lisa Kirschenbaum, 'The Man Question: How Bolshevik Masculinity Shaped International Communism', *Socialist History* 52, 2017, 76–84; Brigitte Studer, *Von der 'Neuen Frau' zur Neuen Frauenbewegung: Emanzipationskonzepte auf Zeitreise*, Vortragsreihe des Zentrums für Zeithistorische Forschung Potsdam, des Centre Marc Bloch und der Bundesstiftung zur Aufarbeitung der SED-Diktatur, zeitgeschichte-digital.de/.

Comintern. The professional revolutionaries who worked for the Third International and its many front organizations are the subject of this book, whose focus is on those who travelled on its behalf.

Revolution as an Employment

Sometimes taken in a moment of enthusiasm, sometimes the culmination of a much longer political involvement in the workers' movement, the decision to work for the Comintern was life changing. These activists became salaried employees with a determinate role in a rapidly differentiating institution with a distinctive division of labour, a role that might nonetheless quickly change in response to administrative requirements or a shift in political line. Revolutionary enthusiasm could thus lead to an alternative career, as part of a corps of like-minded people. The increasing professionalization and bureaucratization of the Comintern brought new duties: to account for oneself, to report on the work one had done to a hierarchy whose own business was to supervise and control these things. As with any other employer, there were budgets to adhere to, expenses to file, information to be passed on, professional standards and rules to comply with. Given this employer's particular business, there were special precautionary measures to be followed, the so-called 'rules of conspiracy' for work in illegality, but also in legality – rules that would later be taught on courses at the International Cadre School but which the first Comintern employees had to learn on the job. That meant, notably, not using your own name but one or more pseudonyms when on mission or at one's place of assignment, and so travelling with false passports, writing in code, or communicating by encrypted telegram, enclosing letters in a double envelope and sending them to a cover address from which they would be forwarded to the intended destination. Depending on the degree of illegality, it might also mean meeting secret party members or other Comintern representatives only at secure locations, checking to see whether the police were following or whether anyone might be eavesdropping. In his highly autobiographical novel, *Life's Good, Brother*, the Turkish writer Nâzım Hikmet, one of the first students at the Communist University of the Toilers of the East (KUTV in its Russian acronym), recounts how at a May Day parade in Moscow a man sought to photograph Japanese students who had travelled incognito to the Soviet Union. This set off a considerable commotion, as the students rushed at this supposed (or indeed real) member of the Japanese secret police, smashed his camera and beat him up before he was taken away by militia officers.[30] Even where not a question of survival, all members were expected to keep party matters confidential, and Comintern staff, like other members, were meant to know only as much about the functioning of the organization as they needed for their own work – an obligation that extended as well to private life. In Hikmet's case, this meant unhappily hiding from his Russian partner, the emancipated Anushka, that he was soon to be sent back to Istanbul on Party business.

The history of international Communism is not just the story of the power of an ideal, a mental conception. Without the material basis represented by the Comintern, the countless public activities, international campaigns and clandestine networks would have been inconceivable, let alone maintained across almost a quarter of a century. This book thus offers a somewhat different history of the Comintern, a history of the Comintern as place of work. Its approach is therefore multiply selective. First, it looks at key moments in interwar history; second, it focuses on the major nodes, the places where for a time the organization more particularly concentrated its world-revolutionary activities; and, third, it adopts an actor-centred perspective. Central to the picture it draws are individual members of the Comintern apparatus and their experiences. That wonderful storyteller Amitav Ghosh, who holds a doctorate in social anthropology from Oxford, once distinguished in an interview between doing history and telling a tale:

> There is a huge difference between writing a historical novel and writing history. If I may put it like this: history is like a river, and the historian is writing about the ways the river flows and the currents and crosscurrents in the river. But, within this river, there are also fish, and the fish can swim in many different directions. So, I am looking at it from the fish's point of view and which direction the fish

---

30 Nâzım Hikmet, *Life's Good, Brother: A Novel*, trans. Mutlu Konuk Blasing, New York: Persea Books, 2013 [1967], 99–100.

swims in. So, history is the water in which it swims, and it is important for me to know the flow of the water. But in the end I am interested in the fish. The novelist's approach to the past, through the eyes of characters, is substantially different from the approach of the historian.³¹

Ghosh is right, of course, to say that the novelist and the historian work in different ways; but he is wrong to claim that the historian is not interested in the fish, the historical actors. And this also because, unlike the water in which the fish swim, the history in which men and women are immersed is of their own making. There can be water without fish, but without people there is no history but natural history.

The exposition here in fact follows the careers of individuals, men, and women, from holders of high political office to lowly and almost unknown junior staff, from long-serving party functionaries to up-and-coming young cadre. For the Comintern apparatus consisted of far more than such well-known and high-ranking officers as Georgi Dimitrov, Palmiro Togliatti and Walter Ulbricht. There were very many different kinds of jobs to be done, both at Comintern headquarters in Moscow and at its outposts abroad. International delegations and political missions likewise called for a wide range of skills. As well as emissaries holding plenipotentiary powers (euphemistically called advisers), there were instructors charged with specific ancillary tasks, often technical or organizational; couriers, often women, who maintained communications, smuggling money and information across borders, or from one place to another; the senior staff of local outposts; agents of the OMS, the Comintern's top secret International Liaison Department, which served as the Bolshevik party's operational arm abroad; the journalists employed by Comintern newspapers and periodicals based outside the Soviet Union. All these short-term or more-or-less permanent deployments needed secretaries, translators and interpreters, radio technicians, cipher clerks, informal collaborators, informants, sometimes even military experts. Delegations abroad often consisted of representatives

---

31 Mahmoud Kooria, 'Between the Walls of Archives and Horizons of Imagination: An Interview with Amitav Ghosh', *Itinerario* 36:3, 2012, 7–18, at 9. Ghosh made his name with a trilogy on the colonial history of Asia, a fiction set in the 1830s, not long before the outbreak of the First Opium War.

of different organizations, such as the Red International of Labour Unions (Profintern), the Youth International (KIM), the short-lived Women's International, or Workers' International Relief, to name only the most important of the bodies making up the planetary system of international Communism. Comintern responsibilities could also be assigned to officers of local parties. Furthermore, someone like the German cultural entrepreneur Willi Münzenberg could work on behalf of the Comintern, which provided him with financial support. The same went occasionally for artists, writers, filmmakers and photographers. The Comintern's workforce was numerous and varied, much more diverse than had been realized until recently.

Before the opening of the Russian archives, some 800 Comintern functionaries were known by name.[32] Today the more-or-less complete database compiled by a German-Russian research team has some 30,000 entries for people all over the world who worked for the Comintern in some capacity at one time or another. Slightly less than a sixth of these were women. Around a quarter were of Russian or Soviet origin.[33] On average, some 400 to 500 people worked at any one time as part of the Comintern apparatus in Moscow, a number that might at times reach as high as 800. Collective biographical studies have provided a first insight into the sociology of this group and provided more precise detail about their roles and the division of labour within the Comintern apparatus.[34]

---

32 Branko Lazitch and Milorad Drachkovitch, eds, *Biographical Dictionary of the Comintern*, new edn, Stanford, CA: Hoover Institution Press, 1986.

33 The database includes 28,689 persons, of whom 4,410 – around 16 per cent – are women. On this, see Michael Buckmiller and Klaus Meschkat, eds, *Biographisches Handbuch zur Geschichte der Kommunistischen Internationale: Ein deutsch-russisches Forschungsprojekt*, Berlin: Akademie-Verlag, 2007, which includes the database on CD-Rom. My own research has revealed that the database is not entirely complete.

34 José Gotovitch et al., *Le Komintern: L'histoire et les hommes*, Paris: Éditions de l'Atelier, 2001; now available as a database on CD-Rom accompanying Serge Wolikow, *L'Internationale communiste, 1919–1943: Le Komintern ou le rêve déchu du parti mondial de la révolution*, Ivry-sur-Seine: Éditions de l'Atelier, 2010; Hermann Weber and Andreas Herbst, eds, *Deutsche Kommunisten: Biographisches Handbuch 1918 bis 1945*, Berlin: Dietz, 2008; Lazar Jeifets, Victor Jeifets and Peter Huber, *La Internacional Comunista y America Latina, 1919–1943; Diccionario Biografico*, Moscow: Instituto de Latinoamérica de la Academia de las Ciencias, 2004; Kevin Morgan, Gideon Cohen and Andrew Flinn, eds, *Agents of the Revolution: New Biographical Approaches to the History of International Communism in the Age of Lenin and Stalin*, Oxford: Peter Lang, 2005; Buckmiller, *Biographisches Handbuch*; Bernard Pudal and Claude Pennetier, *Le souffle d'Octobre 1917: L'engagement des communistes français*, Ivry-sur-Seine: Les Éditions de l'Atelier, 2017.

The actors who figure in the following chapters thus represent only a small sample from among this body of professional revolutionaries. Around 320 Comintern employees are identified by name and feature in the narrative here, though the focus falls mainly on some two dozen key individuals and their contacts, a group of people whose transnational careers traverse the historical space and time of the Comintern and whose paths repeatedly cross at different places in the world. Among them are the Germans Hilde Kramer (later a British citizen), Willi Münzenberg and Babette Gross, Margarete Buber-Neumann, Heinrich Kurella and his partner, the Countess Charlotte Stenbock-Fermor – born Charlotte Schledt in Estonia – and Ruth Werner, née Kuczynski, together with the aforementioned M. N. Roy and his successive partners, most notably the American Evelyn Trent; Virendranath Chattopadhyaya, another Indian; Jakov Reich, born in Lemberg (today's Lviv) in Galicia; the Hungarian Gyulá (Julius) Alpári; Jules Humbert-Droz and his wife Jenny, from French-speaking Switzerland; the Italian Tina Modotti, an emigrant to the USA who later moved on to Mexico, and her partner Vittorio Vidali; the American Agnes Smedley, who in the 1920s and 1930s lived in Germany, China and the Soviet Union; and the Russians Mikhail Borodin and Elena Stasova.

In a number of cases, their commitment did not survive the successive changes of political line. Expulsions and resignations were frequent events in Communist organizations. There were also many who did not survive the Stalinist terror of the 1930s, whose extent and modes of repression are now much better understood. More than half the members of the party cell at the ECCI (to which the members of foreign parties also belonged) found themselves arrested between January 1936 and April 1938[35] – thus bringing to an abrupt end the careers of many of those portrayed here.

---

35 Friedrich I. Firsow, 'Die Säuberungen im Apparat der Komintern', in Hermann Weber and Ulrich Mählert, eds, *Kommunisten verfolgen Kommunisten: Stalinistischer Terror und 'Säuberungen' in den kommunistischen Parteien Europas seit den dreißiger Jahren*, Berlin: Akademie-Verlag, 1993, 37–51, at 50. Evidence has since emerged of cooperation between the Comintern and the NKVD, though the extensive literature on the Terror in the Soviet Union includes few works dealing directly with the Comintern: Aleksandr Vatlin, 'Kaderpolitik und Säuberungen in der Komintern', in Weber, *Terror*, 33–119; William J. Chase, *Enemies Within the Gates? The Comintern and the Stalinist Repression, 1934–1939*, Russian documents trans. Vadim A. Staklo, New Haven, CT: Yale University Press, 2001.

Commitment to the Comintern was never 'self-explanatory', each decision only making sense in its specific context. Not a few of the revolutionary 'generation of 1920' had already rejected a bourgeois plan of life before 1914; the war and the political turmoil of 1917–19 radicalized them still further.[36] Often despite their own reservations, they then found themselves carried away by the allure of the Bolsheviks. It is this 'generation of 1920' that serves as the basis for this study. They provided the apparatus with its first, and, with certain exceptions, its longest-lasting cadre, thus supplying the underpinnings of the Comintern's global political project. In contrast to the customary focus on Lenin, Trotsky, Zinoviev and other world-famous figures, attention is also paid here to the middle- and low-ranking employees, these last being mostly female assistants, secretaries, translators, couriers, etc. It does not, however, propose a 'history from below' in the sense of the history of an anonymous, oppressed and disregarded group. All the figures considered here belonged to the Comintern apparatus and its transnationally circulating elite, even if they occupied different positions in the hierarchy.

The historical actors chosen to stand at the centre of this study are intended to reflect the early diversity of the Comintern's staff, in terms of age, sex and social or regional origin.[37] The choice further fell on those who had as long as possible a transnational career with the Comintern. In addition, their work had to take them to the shifting regional and political nodes of Communist activity in the inter-war period. Finally, care was taken to ensure that they were so far as possible involved in the most important, core areas of Comintern activity, and that their paths frequently intersected. Given their political and numerical dominance in the early days of the Comintern, it is 'Western' employees (from Europe or the Soviet Union) who provide the material for this study, bringing their own perspectives to bear on political situations and local party officers in the places to which they were sent. As well as analytical focus, practical considerations also played a role. Further, to grasp the complexity of human action, the choice had to fall on actors

---

36 On the rejection of bourgeois life, see, for example, Georg Lukács, 'Gelebtes Denken, 1970–1971', in *Autobiographische Texte und Gespräche: Werke Bd. 18*, ed. Frank Benseler and Werner Jung, Bielefeld: Aisthesis, 2005, 199–223, at 204.

37 Biographical details are provided in the relevant chapters.

whose lives were as well documented as possible. The matter of sources cannot be reduced, however, to survival and accessibility: they also had to be chosen in relation to the author's language skills.

All in all, what will be presented here is less a collective biography proper than a number of intermittently intersecting biographies woven together in a single, contextually informed narrative.[38] Not since Pierre Bourdieu's structuralist critique of biography as a genre, at the latest, has anyone harboured the illusion that a human life represents a coherent and purposeful whole crystallized around a personal name.[39] In the cases under consideration here, the very names are often uncertain. Several made use of many dozen pseudonyms. Some appear in the historical record only under a pseudonym, while others changed their official names in the course of time. Lives are fragmented, all the more so those of the figures dealt with here, who not only often changed name, country and activity but also frequently found themselves challenged in their very identity as Communists by the successive changes in the Comintern's political line. The biographical approach adopted here will be contextual, with individuals' conduct explained in terms of the cultural practices prevailing in the milieu. To tell this story, it will thus be necessary to draw on theoretical perspectives and methodological approaches from recent social history, cultural history, the history of everyday life and the history of practice, as well as sociology and political science, and, not least, the history of gender, with its early sensitivity to the hierarchical organization and distribution of powers. And not only this: the account also adopts a transnational- and global-historical perspective.

The Global in the Local

The twentieth century knew of no other organization or social movement so international in its rhetoric, so transnational in its practice, so

---

38 Giovanni Levi, 'Les usages de la biographie', *Annales ESC* 44:6, 1989, 1325–36, distinguishes between modal biography, in which the features of a group are captured through a single representative figure, limit-case biography, hermeneutic biography and the contextual biography (1330–1) essayed here.

39 Pierre Bourdieu, 'L'illusion biographique', *Actes de la recherche en sciences sociales* 62/3, 1986, 69–72.

global in its ambitions. A British, French or Dutch Communist was thus expected to fight colonialism everywhere, including at home. The revolution was to be global, not sectoral, not confined to one country or one continent. The Third International practised and promoted an internationalization that ran contrary to the general development of nation states. At a time when most industrialized countries were tightening migration policy, it opted for a policy of ignoring, of getting around and fighting against, political borders. The Comintern's networks promoted a transnational mode of life among its functionaries, people who spent years, if not decades, travelling to and fro between countries and continents, crossing and recrossing frontiers, most often in clandestinity. That this situation has only recently found conceptual reflection in the human sciences is to be explained, first of all, by the domination of the field by traditional political history. It is also no doubt due to the difficulty of coming to grips with the Comintern's extensive, dense but also labile networks in their complex spatio-temporal ramification, especially given the pace of events and the sheer number of highly mobile actors involved. The abundance of interconnected contexts, from local to national to international, calls for a multi-scalar perspective sensitive to Jacques Revel's *jeux d'échelles*, in which the different levels are not separate but slip smoothly one into another. In such a perspective, there is no predetermined hierarchy of levels of observation such that the local level is explained by reference to the regional, the national or the international. It is rather assumed that 'each historical actor participates to one degree or another in various processes (hence within various contexts) of different dimensions and at different levels, from the most local to the most global.[40]

The two key terms of the transnational and global turns in history thus prove pertinent to the analysis of the Comintern: 'transnational' reflecting its cross-border networks and the careers of actors who moved between different countries;[41] 'global' evoking the spatial interconnectedness and reciprocal constitution of the different actors' activities (or the character of their ideal goals, at any rate), even if the comrades

---

40 Jacques Revel, 'Microanalysis and the Construction of the Social', trans. A. Goldhammer, in Jacques Revel and Lynn Hunt, eds, *Histories: French Constructions of the Past*, New York: New Press, 1996, 492–50, at 501.

41 See also Michael David-Fox, 'The Implications of Transnationalism', *Kritika: Explorations in Russian and Eurasian History* 12:4, 2011, 885–904.

themselves talked not of global but of world revolution. The older 'international' retains its importance as a concept in the sources. Actors were guided in their action by 'internationalism', sometimes rhetorically intensified as 'revolutionary' or 'proletarian' internationalism. 'Internationalism' was indeed a key term for the Comintern, though its meaning varied over time.[42] Internationalism or 'international solidarity' were continuously created and reproduced through practices of social togetherness, everyday behaviour, friendship networks and work relationships. Or, as David Featherstone has it, through 'dynamic practices' that forged solidarity between different locations.[43] International solidarity required a geography of connections that linked political activity, generally only ever local, with other, transnational, levels of action.

In adopting a global and transnational approach, it must not be forgotten that however universal the Comintern's political message and agenda, its activities were local.[44] The Comintern's action was not 'simply limitless',[45] and even less can its history be that. While this study adopts a global perspective, it deliberately focuses on specific places and prioritizes certain themes. Simply stated, it deals with global actors, cities, and moments. Rather than a linear, chronological narrative, let alone a systematic overview, in touching on the three revolutions that followed the Russian – the German, the Chinese and the Spanish – it focuses on the most important moments of global internationalization in the history of the Comintern: moments of flux, moments of compressed eventuation. These moments could vary in duration. While the three

---

42 On the different aspects of the meaning of internationalism for the Bolsheviks around 1917, see Albert, *Das Charisma*, 22–5, and the same author's 'International Solidarity With(out) World Revolution: The Transformation of "Internationalism" in Early Soviet Society', *Monde(s): histoire, espaces, relations* 10, 2016, 33–50.

43 David Featherstone, *Solidarity: Hidden Histories and Geographies of Internationalism*, London: Zed Books, 2012. On internationalism as practice, see also Talbot C. Imlay, *The Practice of Socialist Internationalism: European Socialists and International Politics, 1914–1960*, Oxford: Oxford University Press, 2018, 1–16, at 12; and Braskén, *International Workers' Relief*, 8.

44 This is also the argument of Bernhard H. Bayerlein, Kasper Braskén and Holger Weiss, 'Transnational and Global Perspectives on International Communist Solidarity Organizations: Introduction', in Weiss, *International Communism*, 1–27, at 15.

45 Stefan Berger and Holger Nehring, 'Introduction: Towards a Global History of Social Movements', in Berger and Nehring, eds, *The History of Social Movements in Global Perspective: A Survey*, Basingstoke, UK: Palgrave Macmillan, 2017, 1–35, at 7.

finally unsuccessful revolutionary processes in question extended over several years, there were also global events that took place over much shorter times, such as the Second World Congress or the Baku Congress, which, even if they did not bring together people from all over the globe, nonetheless caused a global stir, their effects continuing to resound throughout more or less the whole of the twentieth century. To these temporal emphases correspond changing spatio-locational foci of political activity. The study attends exclusively to 'global cities', the hotspots of worldwide revolution – key nodes on international networks and meeting places of revolutionary activists – that stood at the centre of contemporary international attention. These might be metropoles like Berlin or Paris, but equally places that gain their historical significance from the concentration there of Comintern agents and activities. The choice of places and moments has further allowed consideration of the political orientations and modes of political action specific to them: as for example the appeal to the Muslim world in Baku, the establishment of extraterritorial outposts in Berlin, clandestine activity in Shanghai, and international solidarity in Spain.

The Comintern emissaries and others who are the object of this multiperspectival study travelled between these nodes, halting as their work required. Their nomadic life, now here, now there, afforded them little in the way of settled existence or fixed expectations. Least of all was it the result of their own free choice, and travel for them was no passport to self-discovery. They moved on when instructed to do so by the Comintern or when compelled by the forces of repression. The organization's agents travelled abroad, or found themselves posted to their home countries, on instructions from above, and remained in regular contact with those who instructed them, by letter, telephone or telegram, even if distance and time did sometimes pose problems. They had a job to do and responsibilities to discharge. They had false identities to assume, and regular changes of name to accustom themselves to. Yet so long as their political convictions held firm and they did not doubt what they did, they could feel that they belonged to a secret fellowship committed to a higher cause, whatever the internal disputes.

Travel was, for them, an aspect of work, one that called not only for great personal commitment and courage in the face of danger, but also for language skills, cultural adaptability, organization, discretion, negotiating ability and tolerance of frustration. What is more, these cross-border workers served as go-betweens or mediators between two and sometimes more revolutionary contexts or spheres of Comintern activity, with all the manoeuvring that might involve. They might, for instance, have to sell new political positions or directives adopted in Moscow or by the local party. Sometimes they would have to act as bridge-builders between opposing fractions or groups. And increasingly often, invested with Moscow's authority, they had to purge a party of its oppositionists, real or supposed. In the late 1920s, their missions in many cases involved the removal of entire leaderships for recalcitrance, a goal generally achieved only with great difficulty and at the cost of considerable losses in terms of membership. And, in all of this, they had always to translate the changing conceptions embodied in the party line into another language, in a different context. The difficulties they encountered – their experience of the task – will be one of the topics of this study, as will the role of friendship and personal relationships in the construction of networks and teams. How were they able to make use of the new knowledge they gained from their contacts at the local level in their dealings with their employer, the ECCI? And vice versa: How could the ECCI in Moscow exert control at a distance over its representatives abroad? What then were the limits to networking and mobility?

Women, Men and the Revolutionary Self

Work for the Comintern made great demands on the individual. Not only was the body totally engaged, but a considerable part of the self too had to be invested in one's activity. While other occupations do not necessarily call for personal belief in the logic of the employing institution, the Comintern required absolute loyalty of its employees. Not only students at the international cadre schools but all who worked for the organization had to continuously adjust their own ideas and representations to the realities of the social world that was the Comintern.

In return, as Claude Pennetier and Bernard Pudal have argued, party cadre who had graduated to the Comintern hierarchy found themselves possessed of greater 'political capital' than ordinary party members. They had authority, an authority derived from their place in the apparatus.[46] These professional revolutionaries formed an elite based not on wealth, income or socio-occupational status, but on their membership of a small group bound together, despite permanent conflict and competition, in service to a higher cause. But who rose to such positions? What were the qualifications beyond revolutionary credentials and a certain theoretical competence?

While roles assigned in the organization did indeed depend on the size of the party of origin, the most influential factor in this respect was gender: it was significantly harder, when not impossible, for women to gain recognition as representatives of the working class, from either a local party or the Comintern. Communist organizations operated a clear hierarchy of relevance in terms of the embodiment of the revolutionary subject. The Russian-German Communist Rosa Meyer-Leviné – born Rosa Broido, widow both of Eugen Leviné, the leader of the Munich Soviet Republic shot in 1919, and of Ernst Meyer, a former leader of the German Communist Party who died of illness in 1930 – reported the following reaction by her second husband: 'I have on many occasions been told that one must distinguish between the value to the revolution of organized and unorganized workers. I was once carried away by the sight of a big demonstration. "Too many housewives, maids and young people", said Ernst, unmoved.'[47] This sociopolitical ordering principle also governed the Comintern's recruitment policy, and is thus reflected in the sources and in the historical research reliant upon them, which often uncritically treats men as 'important' actors, women as merely secondary. On reading many studies, one finds oneself compelled to observe, in an echo of Alfred Hitchcock's film title, 'the ladies vanish'. A gender-historical perspective is thus absolutely necessary if the views and attitudes of the historical actors are not to be inherited by the historian. Otherwise, there is a danger of reproducing the gender skew of the past in one's own historical object of research, in a kind of historiographical mimicry, thus redoubling the exclusion of women.

---

46 Claude Pennetier and Bernard Pudal, 'La volonté d'emprise: Le référentiel biographique stalinien et ses usages dans l'univers communiste, éléments de problématique', in Pennetier and Pudal, eds, *Autobiographies, autocritiques, aveux*, 15–39.

47 Rosa Meyer-Leviné, *Im inneren Kreis: Erinnerungen einer Kommunistin in Deutschland 1920–1930; Herausgegeben und eingeleitet von Hermann Weber*, Cologne: Kiepenheuer und Witsch, 1979, 231.

To use the language of Pierre Bourdieu, these first Comintern operatives doubtless brought with them embodied behavioural dispositions, in the shape of their readiness to commit themselves, to make a personal investment in a collective project.[48] Highly structured and disciplined, centralized and at the same time distributed network-fashion across a multiplicity of sites, the Comintern's organizational form and modus operandi were something new to the founding generation: they had much to learn. What they did bring with them, on the other hand, was 'activist capital', to use the term of Frédérique Matonti and Franck Poupeau.[49] Those who travelled to Moscow in 1920 were no political novices: even if many of them were young, they already had political experience, in the Zimmerwald movement and the small radical groups that emerged after 1917, or in the social democratic parties among whose critics they now numbered. They were consequently possessed of political knowledge and technical know-how. They knew how to lay out a leaflet, how to address a gathering, to draw up notes for a speech, how to argue in committee, how to compose an article, how to prepare an action, how to mobilize people, how to acquire the knowledge called for by political activity (legal, economic or otherwise). Individuals did of course differ. Not all had read the Marxist theorists. Age and gender especially were associated with different possibilities and experiences of political action. The great majority of delegates to the Second World Congress were under forty years of age. Women, who, before the First World War, still had no right to vote in any European country other than Finland and Norway, made up a little more than a tenth of the delegates – a very small minority, admittedly, and one that would remain small, despite the Comintern's professed belief in women's emancipation, but still a very rare thing. No more than social origin or class were nationality, regional or ethnic origin a reason for exclusion. The Comintern did, however, emerge from the workers' movements and progressive forces of 'the West', and representatives from colonial territories were few at first.[50]

---

48 Pierre Bourdieu, *Outline of a Theory of Practice*, trans. Richard Nice, Cambridge: Cambridge University Press, 1977, 72.

49 Frédérique Matonti and Franck Poupeau, 'Le capital militant: Éssai de définition', *Actes de la recherche en sciences sociales* 155:5, 2004, 4–11.

50 John Riddell, ed., *Workers of the World and Oppressed Peoples, Unite! Proceedings and Documents of the Second Congress, 1920*, 2 vols, New York: Pathfinder, 1991, vol. 1, 8–9.

Given the professionalization of the Comintern apparatus, the knowledge acquired through everyday practice and reading would soon be insufficient. To draw new forces into the international political struggle, and to equip them with a standardized body of knowledge, the first two international cadre schools were opened in Moscow in 1921: the Communist University of the Toilers of the East (KUTV) mentioned earlier, and the Communist University of the National Minorities of the West (KUNMZ). In 1925, as hopes grew of a revolution in China, the Sun Yat-sen Communist University of the Toilers of the East was set up in Moscow as a specialist institution for young Chinese, though it did not long survive. In 1926, lastly, these were joined by the International Lenin School, primarily intended for party members from Europe, North America, Latin America and Australia. The hopeful rising generation were no longer to be instructed in the sometimes heterodox ideas of the individual parties, but in accordance with a centralized, Russian-inspired curriculum.[51]

---

51 The literature on the international cadre schools is now quite considerable. One of the first researchers to have access to the archives was Leonid G. Babitschenko, 'Die Kaderschulung der Komintern', *Jahrbuch für historische Kommunismusforschung*, 1993, 37–59. Studies have tended to focus on particular nationalities: on the Swiss, see Brigitte Studer, *Un parti sous influence: Le Parti communiste, une section du Komintern, 1931 à 1939*, Lausanne: L'Âge d'Homme, 1994, 230–49; on Swiss, Germans and French, Brigitte Studer, 'Penser le sujet stalinien', in Pennetier, *Le sujet communiste*, 35–57, the same author's *Transnational World*, 90–108, and Brigitte Studer and Berthold Unfried, *Der stalinistische Parteikader: Identitätsstiftende Praktiken und Diskurse in der Sowjetunion der dreißiger Jahre*, Cologne: Böhlau, 2001; on the Irish, Barry McLoughlin, 'Proletarian Academics or Party Functionaries? Irish Communists at the International Lenin School, Moscow, 1927–1937', *Saothar: Yearbook of the Irish Labour History Society*, 22, 1997, 63–79; on South Africans: Irina Filatova, 'Indoctrination or Scholarship? Education of Africans at the Communist University of the Toilers of the East in the Soviet Union, 1923–1937', *Paedagogica Historica* 35:1, 1999, 41–66; on the French, Serge Wolikow and Jean Vigreux, 'L'école léniniste internationale de Moscou: Une pépinière de cadres communiste', *Cahiers d'histoire* 79, 2000, 45–56; on the Germans and the Austrians, Julia Köstenberger, 'Die Geschichte der Kommunistischen Universität der nationalen Minderheiten des Westens, KUNMZ in Moskau 1921–1936', *Jahrbuch für historische Kommunismusforschung*, 2000/2001, 248–303; Köstenberger, 'Die Internationale Lenin-Schule, 1926–1938', in Buckmiller, *Biographisches Handbuch*, 287–309; Köstenberger, *Kaderschmiede des Stalinismus: Die Internationale Leninschule in Moskau und die österreichischen Leninschüler und Leninschülerinnen*, Vienna: LIT, 2016; on the British, Gideon Cohen and Kevin Morgan, 'Stalin's Sausage Machine: British Students at the International Lenin School, 1926–37', *20th-Century British History* 13:4, 2002, 327–55; on the Chinese, Alexander V. Pantsov and Daria A. Spichak, 'New Light from the

In taking up their new employment, the actors at the centre of this book put all their labour and their time at the disposal of the Comintern. But they gave up much more than this, as will be shown. Their nomadic lifestyle saw them not infrequently jeopardize family life, personal relationships, career and sometimes health, bodily integrity or even life. To account theoretically for what one might thus call a 'total' engagement, a concept such as individual 'belief' is inadequate. For the commitment of the first generation of Comintern operatives was determined not only by behavioural dispositions acquired through personal experience but also by the transnational rise of radical social movements.[52] The close of the First World thus saw the emergence of a group of people for whom, despite their very diverse origins, a collective political project became a new life focus, a lived reality. In the Comintern, they created a social space that corresponded to their individual behavioural dispositions and, in turn, supported and validated their political activities. That this social space was stratified and exhibited an asymmetry between the Bolsheviks and other members of the group they simply accepted.

Rather than thinking of political engagement, as is commonly done, only in terms of personal costs and material sacrifice, one also has to take account of the compensations or rewards it offers, as political scientist Daniel Gaxie has argued.[53] For women, political engagement opened up a historically new field of action and self-realization. Of value to both sexes might be the feeling of taking part in history and the sense of standing up for one's own ideas. So, finding a place for oneself in the public realm could meet needs for self-assertion and self-valorization. Such engagement could also bring with it the acquisition of skills and knowledge. Some Comintern employees also had agendas of their own

---

Russian Archives: Chinese Stalinists and Trotskyists at the International Lenin School in Moscow, 1926–1938', *Twentieth-Century China* 33:2, 2008, 29–50; on the Americans, Kirschenbaum, *International Communism*, 15–51.

52 The rather broad notion of 'cadre' proves insufficiently differentiated given the division of labour and associated hierarchy within the Comintern apparatus. Furthermore, its military connotations tend to leave little conceptual or methodological room for the agency of those concerned. In what follows, I shall therefore generally employ such terms as 'functionary', 'employee' or 'staff'.

53 Daniel Gaxie, 'Rétributions du militantisme et paradoxes de l'action collective', *Schweizerische Zeitschrift für Politikwissenschaft/Revue suisse de science politique/Swiss Political Science Review* 11:1, 2005, 157–88.

to pursue, and for them the organization supplied resources in the way of know-how, funding, networks, contacts and collaborators. For writers and artists who associated with the Comintern as fellow-travellers and the journalists and photographers of the Comintern press there were also sometimes professional advantages (where Communist organizations were operating legally) or a particularly gratifying way of plying one's trade. The question that needs to be asked, however, is whether there were contradictions or splits between actors' political and individual agendas.

Not least important, employment by the Comintern also offered a space of social integration, a place of recreation, comradeship, friendship and sexual relationship. In the early, enchantment phase, costs seemed irrelevant in comparison, especially given the boundarilessness of the identification.[54] Things might change, however, as work became routine, the collective doubted the value of one's contribution, lack of success brought disappointment, or one had difficulty with the political line. At such times, other objects of affective investment (such as family or previous occupation) could come into competition with work for the Comintern. This too will be looked at in the chapters that follow. What personal costs and constraints were Comintern employees prepared to accept? What personal legitimation and coping strategies did they mobilize? Were there conflicts between their political beliefs and their personal philosophies, their political engagement and their family relationships, between party loyalty and critical distance? With this, notions such as loyalty, suspicion and betrayal come into play. How did commitment continue when enchantment was over? Here, Howard Becker's idea of the 'side-bet', the spin-off from commitment, proves helpful.[55] Without their necessarily being aware of it, Becker notes, actors' commitment can (in time, at least) embroil them in unforeseen obligations and dependencies, as for example through the adoption of the group's cultural norms, breach of which entails sanctions. In the social world of the Comintern, to leave the party was to betray the cause; so-called

---

54 See also Brigitte Studer, 'Communism as Existential Choice', in Silvio Pons and Stephen Smith, eds, *The Cambridge History of Communism*, vol. 1: *World Revolution and Socialism in One Country, 1917–1941*, Cambridge: Cambridge University Press, 2017, 503–25, at 511–14.

55 Howard S. Becker, 'Notes on the Concept of Commitment', *American Journal of Sociology* 66:1, 1960, 32–40.

renegades were cut off socially and often defamed, later even persecuted. Materially, for Comintern employees, expulsion from the party meant loss of income.

The stronger the commitment, the greater the danger that resignation or expulsion provoked an existential crisis. To cite Manès Sperber once again: 'Only through one door does one take leave of the revolution; it opens on nothingness.'[56] The 'nothingness' could be the void left by the cessation of activism and the loss of self-image it brought. For the Communist identity, or perhaps better, sense of belonging, found expression in continuous activity framed by the norms and practices of the Comintern, from which the former member was now cut off.

Situated Action

While drawing on experiential history and on transnational and global approaches, this study also finds inspiration in the history of practice, whose analytical armamentarium has been considerably refined by French authors over recent years.[57] This French history of practice makes critical borrowings from Italian microhistory, Bourdieusian sociology, historical anthropology, science studies and pragmatic linguistics. It draws too on the history of everyday life, as it has been shaped in particular – though with different approaches, objects and frames of reference – by two outsiders, the essentially uncategorizable freelance scholar Michel de Certeau with his *Arts de faire,* or 'ways of doing', and Alf Lüdtke, to whom institutional recognition came only belatedly.[58] Rather than taking 'things' as given – whether space, domination or the

---

56 Manès Sperber, *Wie eine Träne zum Ozean: Romantrilogie*, Munich: dtv, 1983 [1961; first pub., in French translation, 1949–53], 459, the sentence here being very inadequately rendered in the English translation cited elsewhere: Sperber, *The Abyss*.

57 Simona Cerutti, 'Histoire pragmatique, ou de la rencontre entre histoire sociale et histoire culturelle', trans. Sami Bargaoui, *Tracés: Revue de sciences humaines* 15, 2008, 147–68; Francis Chateauraynaud and Yves Cohen, 'Présentation', in Chateauraynaud and Cohen, eds, *Histoires pragmatiques*, Paris: Éditions EHESS, 2016, 9–28.

58 Michel de Certeau, *L'invention du quotidien*, vol. 1: *Arts de faire*, Paris: Gallimard, 1980, published in English as *The Practice of Everyday Life*, trans. Steven Rendall, Berkeley: University of California Press, 1984; Alf Lüdtke, *Alltagsgeschichte: Zur Rekonstruktion historischer Erfahrungen und Lebensweisen*, Frankfurt a. M.: Campus, 1989.

working class – they inquired into what people did and its performative effects. A second, crucial line runs from Bourdieu's renegade pupil Luc Boltanski and co-author Laurent Thévenot and their book *On Justification: Economies of Worth* to the historian Bernard Lepetit, a scholar who died far too young and whose own contribution to the history of practice is considered to be one of the chief foundations of the practice-centred approach to the writing of history.[59] The analytical focus here falls on the questions of how historical actors create social structures through their interactions, how they negotiate with institutions, what room for manoeuvre they enjoy and what use they make of it. From such a practice-centred perspective, a society, a social structure, or an institution is the ever-changing resultant of the human action that it in turn informs. For the history of Communism, and of Stalinism in particular, which, almost more than any other history, is prone to the temptation to explain things from the end backwards, and in which actors' agency tends to be forgotten in the face of the power of institutions, this proves to be a fruitful approach. For a practice-centred approach, the situated nature of action means that the course of events must be explained in terms of its own unfolding, that it gains its meaning in the course of action (rather than its meaning being given *a priori*).[60]

Boltanski and Thévenot speak of the different 'economies of worth' that in varying contexts determine or at least frame the logic of individual action and behaviour – but always as individually appropriated, or indeed circumvented if not contested, hence Lepetit's invocation of a 'semantics of the situation'.[61] Like the other two, he takes it that historical actors act knowingly in so far as they have the capacity to evaluate the situation. They must, however, find their bearings in the first place, which not all can do equally well. For 'norms and taxonomies are plural' and, given this, they cannot be analysed in terms of pure imposition,

---

[59] Luc Boltanski and Laurent Thévenot, *Les économies de la grandeur*, Paris: PUF, 1987, revised and expanded as *De la justification: Les économies de la grandeur*, Paris: Gallimard, 1991, available in English as *On Justification: Economies of Worth*, trans. Catherine Porter, Princeton, NJ: Princeton University Press, 2006; Bernard Lepetit, 'Histoire des pratiques, pratique de l'histoire', in Lepetit, *Les formes de l'expérience: Une autre histoire sociale*, Paris: Albin Michel, 1995, 9–22.

[60] Lepetit, 'Histoire des pratiques', 14.

[61] Ibid., 14.

Introduction 31

but rather represent for actors a set of reference points by which to situate themselves and resources to be mobilized under the constraint of the situation.'[62] Actors must thus conduct themselves in accordance with context, adopting those tactics that are 'appropriate'. To do this, they must mobilize and put to use their knowledge, their cultural and material resources and their interpretative competence. As Simona Cerutti also insists, the social world – and so the world of action – is an interpretative world. Action and interpretation cannot be separated.[63] While the historian knows how things turned out in the end, the actors at the time did not. One therefore has always to ask what logic the actors are following and how they not only justify but also legitimate their actions.

Communism, however, was like few political movements in the way it set itself up as supreme authority over the norms and practices of social and political life.[64] With its adoption of the concept of the vanguard party, its quickly established routines of work and the institutionalization of a bureaucratic apparatus, the Comintern helped create the conditions for this (which of course does not imply any process of compulsion). Under Stalin, this ascendancy took on a new aspect, as with his writings on 'Leninism' he increasingly promoted himself as the authority on theory. At the time of the Second World Congress, debates were open to all who wished to contribute, even if Lenin and Trotsky enjoyed greater political authority than other Marxist theorists. In creating 'Marxism-Leninism', however, Stalin prescribed an analytical method and in doing so gained a means of control over possible interpretations. Argument gradually came to be confined to the translation of theory into practice, discussion limited to the interpretation of political directives rather than debating the political line and its abrupt changes.[65] Students at the Comintern's international schools learnt to eschew all doctrinal deviation, being trained instead in the application of theory. In their 'academic characterizations', these would be praised for their

---

62 Ibid., 20.
63 Cerutti, 'Histoire pragmatique', 156.
64 Yves Cohen, 'La pratique des praticiens', in Chateauraynaud, *Histoires pragmatiques*, 105–45, at 109.
65 Bernard Pudal, *Prendre parti: Pour une sociologie historique du PCF*, Paris: Presses de la FNSP, 1989, 207.

ability to 'draw the necessary conclusions from practice'.[66] Like those students, Comintern employees had to learn the ways of going about things and the cultural codes of the normative space they now inhabited.

In taking up the language of the Comintern, entering into relationships or situating themselves in the period, they did of course make use of what Michel de Certeau called 'tactics', the art or skill of those who do not possess power or authority, or, in the case of Comintern functionaries, those whose powers were increasingly limited.[67] They complied, but knew how to make use of loopholes in certain circumstances.[68] From a practice-centred point of view, it is necessary to consider actors' room for manoeuvre, which not only altered over time but could also be modified by entering into other social spaces. The itinerant Comintern operatives under study here shifted between different contexts. Travel or the move to a foreign city brought an encounter with sometimes alien cultural norms.[69] Operatives sent abroad thus participated in more worlds than that of their employer alone. Though they owed loyalty to the latter, their distance from Moscow and their navigation between different contexts offered them new openings and new possibilities of action. The supposedly totally closed system of the Comintern proves in their case to be an illusion, if such were the intent behind the idea of a centralized, disciplined and homogeneous organization. In addition, their local knowledge gave them an advantage over the decision-makers in Moscow, who depended on their reports and analyses.

How far they were able to exploit this is one of the questions that will be considered here, but in doing so a further qualitative change in the control exercised by Stalin must be taken into consideration. The political space for organized opposition shrank visibly before collapsing entirely in the face of Stalin's preference for repression as a technique of government.[70] What began in the Comintern in 1928 as a global wave of

---

66 See Studer, *Transnational World*, 90–107.
67 De Certeau, *L'invention*, 60. See also Gabrielle M. Spiegel, 'Introduction', in Spiegel, ed., *Practicing History: New Directions in Historical Writing After the Linguistic Turn*, New York: Routledge, 2005, 16–17.
68 De Certeau, *L'invention*, xlvi.
69 Madeleine Herren, 'Transkulturelle Geschichte: Globale Kultur gegen die Dämonen des Eurozentrismus und des methodischen Nationalismus', *Traverse* 2, 2012, 154–69.
70 Cohen, 'La pratique', 128.

mass expulsions for political deviation ended in the second half of the 1930s in the massacre of very many of those members of the Comintern who lived in the Soviet Union, a massacre that did not stop at the borders of the 'Workers' Fatherland'. In the face of irrational and baroque accusations, tactical play demanded an almost inhuman capacity for discursive accommodation. In many cases, however, this was not enough to escape death. Only those who were beyond the reach of the Soviet secret police, the People's Commissariat for Internal Affairs (the NKVD), had the option of 'exit',[71] though its long arm could sometimes stretch far beyond Soviet territory.

Sources and Structure

The historian does not enjoy the artistic license that a novelist like Amitav Ghosh can allow himself with regard to his historical materials. Gaps cannot be filled with imagination. Every statement must find support in the sources, which enjoy the power of veto. As has been outlined above, this history of the Comintern as workplace follows a variety of its employees as they go about their jobs in different places and different political contexts. The multiple perspective adopted requires the analysis of a great diversity of source materials whose results then need to be knitted together.

This book could not have been written without long years of research in the more than a million-and-a-half files of the Russian Archive of Socio-Political History (RGASPI) in Moscow. This holds (alongside the Soviet party archive) the records of the Comintern, contained for the most part in Fonds 495 with its 234 *opisi* and 138,545 files. The vast body of material generated by the 'report-production machine' that was the Comintern covers the ECCI and its leading organs (e.g. the Presidium, the Political Secretariat, the Political Commission of the Political Secretariat, the Small Commission, the Little Bureau and the personal secretariats of the ECCI Secretaries and the Cadre Department) from 1919 to 1943. It also contains the records of the different departments, the regional secretariats, the thirteen ECCI plenums, correspondence

---

71 Albert O. Hirschman, *Exit, Voice and Loyalty: Responses to Decline in Firms, Organizations and States*, Cambridge, MA: Harvard University Press, 1970.

with individual Communist parties and the personal files of ECCI staff (14,852 files). In addition, Fonds 489 to 494 contain the minutes of the seven World Congresses, Fonds 545 documents relating to the Spanish Civil War and the International Brigades, while Fonds 533 to 543 cover subsidiary or mass organizations such as Communist International Youth, the Profintern and International Workers' Relief.

As well as records pertaining to political-institutional matters, many personal files were also consulted: these are biographical files such as are familiar to any administration, but in the Soviet context one also finds within them much autobiographical material.[72] These dossiers can turn out to be extremely comprehensive. In them one finds the questionnaires issued by the ECCI, CVs drawn up by the subjects themselves, official evaluations and diverse correspondence and other materials relating to the subject. Complementing these, and sometimes just as important, are the memoirs, autobiographies, diary notes and letters of Comintern employees, so-called renegades or otherwise. These types of records offer access to the experiential and emotional aspects of the history, echoes resounding through time whose meaning can only be made comprehensible through contextualization and careful assessment of the sources. While diary entries and letters offer insight into the sometimes complex processes whereby actors situated themselves amid day-to-day political events and newly promulgated discursive regimes, these retrospective records have to be read as means of self-validation as the writer's interpretations of the world shift with time and place. Whatever the differences between these types of records, the narratives they contain can also be understood as acts in a social transaction in which it is always a question of bringing 'self' and 'world' into a certain accord.[73] Such narratives generally also offer an idea of the form and scale of revolutionaries' personal investment in the project. In any event, these types of sources need to be approached critically, as must the biographies of the actors dealt with here, bearing in mind who was considered to be notable and thus worthy of biography.

---

72 Studer, *Parler de soi*; and Studer, *Transnational World*, 73–89; Pennetier, *Autobiographies* and *Le sujet communiste*.

73 On speech act theory, see John Langshaw Austin, *How to Do Things with Words*, Oxford: Clarendon Press, 1975. For an application of this theoretical approach, see Brigitte Studer, 'Liquidate the Errors or Liquidate the Person? Stalinist Party Practices as Techniques of the Self', in Studer and Haumann, *Stalinistische Subjekte*, 197–216.

Other indispensable resources have been published collections of source material on the history of the Comintern in Germany, China and Spain, and the literature on individual topics and regions.[74] Also essential were the debates, theses and resolutions of the early World Congresses and the Baku Congress, now published in their entirety with accompanying scholarly apparatus.[75] For my own approach, the wealth of work on the highly ramified structure of the Comintern and its many reorganizations provided an important basis for understanding and categorizing individual action. Where called for, research was also carried out at various other archives, among them the Swiss Federal Archive in Bern and the Archives Nationales in Paris. And in closing, mention must be made of the data banks and biographical dictionaries covering Comintern cadre compiled by different teams of researchers.

The exposition here follows the activities and interactions of a number of actors in the relational field constituted by the Comintern, with its fluctuating power relations and different spatial orders. The leading roles change with each chapter, bringing further characters into focus. Sometimes these are people who supposedly carried out ancillary tasks in the thousands-strong world of the Comintern: the women, for example, who carried out discreet infrastructural or logistical duties or served as secretary to their husband or partner, and who were thus collectively indispensable to the functioning of the Comintern apparatus.

These professional revolutionaries were required to adopt party lines and political emphases that changed over time. While the idea of internationalism prompted their initial commitment and pervaded their

---

74 Hermann Weber, Jakov Drabkin and Bernhard H. Bayerlein, eds, *Deutschland, Russland, Komintern*, 2 vols, Berlin: de Gruyter, 2013–14; Mechthild Leutner et al., eds, *KPdSU(B), Komintern und die national-revolutionäre Bewegung in China: Dokumente*, vols 2–4, Münster: LitVerlag, 1998–2006; Ronald Radosh, Mary R. Habeck and Grigory Sevostianov, eds, *Spain Betrayed: The Soviet Union in the Spanish Civil War*, New Haven, CT: Yale University Press, 2001. The literature this study relies on will be noted in the different chapters, by theme and regional focus.

75 Riddell, *Founding*; *Workers of the World*; *To See the Dawn: Baku, 1920 – First Congress of the Peoples of the East*, New York: Pathfinder, 1993; *Toward the United Front: Proceedings of the Fourth Congress of the Communist International, 1922*, Leiden: Brill, 2011; *To the Masses: Proceedings of the Third Congress of Communist International, 1921*, Leiden: Brill, 2015. On the 1920 Congress, see Vatlin's account with accompanying documentary sources: Alexander Vatlin, *Das Jahr 1920: Der Zweite Kongress der Kommunistischen Internationale*, trans. Wladislaw Hedeler, Berlin: BasisDruck, 2019.

ongoing political activity, its meaning soon changed, as has already been noted. Other political foci, such as anticolonialism and antifascism might be prioritized at different times and places, work sometimes falling, indeed, to individual groups or even persons. The chapters thus focus on a series of places, or more precisely, cities, that exemplify the work of the Comintern at different times and under different policies.

The first chapter looks at Moscow in the summer of 1920, when more than two hundred official delegates from East and West assembled there to consider the foundation of a new international. Moscow in 1920 was the material and symbolic birthplace of a worldwide revolutionary movement. It was a meeting point for numerous political activists from all over the globe, young revolutionaries and long-serving politicians, anticolonial campaigners and trade union leaders from the imperialist countries, who brought with them their different ideas about organizing the radical transformation of the existing order. In Moscow, this 'Generation of 1920' encountered the Bolshevik leadership, who were successful revolutionaries and soon-to-be rulers over a vast national territory. Moscow became for revolutionaries the whole world over the centre of a wide network, a pole of international political reference, a hub of global circulation, a safe haven.

The second chapter deals first with the Baku Congress of 1920, another moment of global encounter and transfer, before moving on to consider a different approach to the revolutionization of Asia. Following the debate on anticolonialism at the Second Congress, the Bolsheviks in September that same year convened in Baku a 'Congress of the Peoples of the East', the first of its kind. Given the darkening of the revolutionary horizon, the call for world revolution had to ring out beyond the industrialized nations of Europe and North America. The Bolsheviks hoped to harness the desire for national self-determination to the struggle against capitalism. Furthermore, they sought to export the notion of women's emancipation to the Muslim world by propagandizing for gender equality. In another approach to colonial liberation, the Bolsheviks set up in Tashkent a short-lived bureau and a military training school to prepare for an armed expedition to India, an experiment in the 'export of revolution' that was very soon abandoned, in part on account of the geopolitical relationship of forces, in part on account of the lack of willing volunteers. In closing, the chapter looks at the Comintern operatives who returned to Moscow after Soviet Russia's revolutionary excursions to the East, who, together with their colleagues from all over the world, now had a common workplace and residence in the new Comintern headquarters and in the Hotel Lux, respectively.

The third chapter follows the Comintern's efforts to set up an extraterritorial outpost and logistical hub in Western Europe. For the Russian revolutionaries Berlin was a alternative organizational centre, for the new Soviet state both a diplomatic and economic door onto the West and a locus of revolutionary leverage to help secure its own continued existence. In the early years after the war, Germany and its capital represented the future of the revolution in Europe, and the Comintern expected to soon move its headquarters there. To facilitate the movement of cadre, funds and directives, the Comintern set up in Berlin a multichannel logistics and communication hub. From there extended a network that reached not only the other capitals of Europe but also the Americas and many colonial lands. Between congresses and plenums in Moscow, Berlin served as a meeting point and communications centre for the whole organization. Over time, there were changes in both the type of functionaries posted there and the tasks they were charged with, with accompanying changes in the circumstances of their work.

The fourth chapter also plays out in Berlin. Until the Nazi takeover, the German capital was also the main European centre of Comintern cultural operations. The city was not only the gateway to the Soviet Union, but also the site of a brisk artistic and cultural exchange between East and West. Published in Berlin, *Inprekorr* was the Comintern's most important newspaper, and alongside it the organization operated or financially supported many other publishing and film production projects. The relative anonymity of the metropolis made it easier to maintain the cover of illegally resident operatives and the secrecy of clandestine activities. While Berlin did not witness a revolution, despite Communist preparation for a 'German October', it was nonetheless a gathering place for revolutionaries from all over the world.[76] The Comintern organs and the Communist media established there employed a transnational staff who found in the city a thriving, left-inflected cultural life.

---

76 On the failed revolution in Germany, see the documents in *Deutscher Oktober 1923: Ein Revolutionsplan und sein Scheitern*, ed. Bernhard Bayerlein et al., Berlin: Aufbau-Verlag, 2003.

The fifth chapter is devoted to the construction of an anticolonial network on European soil, a network whose external links reached North and South America, Asia and parts of Africa. The episode reveals the difficulties but also the successes of Communist anticolonial policy. Communist organizations acted on their programmatic commitments in this field only on the initiative of individual activists, who first had to overcome their own organizations' resistance to committing scarce human resources to political support for distant struggles. In addition, anticolonial activists, mostly operating in clandestinity and often living in precarious circumstances in the European metropoles, had always to reckon on police surveillance and the possibility of imprisonment and deportation, while the challenge to the imperialist world order they represented prompted international cooperation between the police authorities of the imperialist states. The networked activity of the Comintern's operatives nevertheless succeeded in creating a cosmopolitan, transethnic space embracing Berlin, Paris, Brussels, London and Moscow – a space of solidarity, material, personal and imaginative – that is surely historically unique in its scale and ambition.

The sixth chapter shifts the focus from Moscow and the capitals of Western Europe to the colonial territories, and more particularly to China, whose situation the Comintern understood as 'semi-colonial', the next great hope of the world revolution. In cooperating with the Guomindang, the most important national-revolutionary force, the Soviet Union and subsequently the Comintern worked to draw that country into the Communist sphere of influence. The emissaries despatched to Guangzhou (then known in the West as Canton) and Wuhan enjoyed official status as advisers. Their task was no easy one in China's politically complex and militarily unstable situation. The directives from Moscow were contradictory and all the more difficult to implement as the members of the Chinese party had their own agenda to pursue and the Comintern representatives disagreed among themselves.

The seventh chapter stays in China, but focuses now on Shanghai. That port city dominated by the Western powers had an essential place in the ramified spatial geography of the Comintern apparatus. Although Communist activity almost came to a standstill for a time following the slaughter of Communists in April 1927, the end of the decade saw the Comintern rapidly rebuild its clandestine apparatus, re-establishing the network linking its Shanghai centre to surrounding countries. Its representatives ran great dangers, however. Police surveillance and the penetration of cover saw operations interrupted time and time again, until in 1931 the arrest of a series of key personnel as a result of internationally coordinated police action brought Comintern activities to almost a complete halt. To protect the false identities of those arrested, the Comintern launched a large-scale, worldwide campaign. The chapter shows how very great a capacity for mobilization the Comintern apparatus enjoyed and also – contrary to official assessments and the common assumption of historical scholarship – how closely the Comintern was in fact involved with Soviet intelligence.

The eighth chapter follows Comintern employees as they fled the Nazi takeover of power in early 1933. What mattered now was to save what could be saved. Preparations for such a catastrophe, which brought the collapse of the Comintern agencies installed in Berlin and other cities, had been completely inadequate, its consequences culpably underestimated even long after. Escape had thus to be improvised, often exposing Comintern employees to great danger. For comrades in the countries where they now sought refuge, their plight represented one more call on their international solidarity. For many, the episode only strengthened their commitment to antifascist resistance – if only from a distance – and to rebuilding the apparatus that had been destroyed. Not all succeeded, however, in finding more or less legal refuge in a West European country. For those who thought they would find a safe haven in the 'Workers' Fatherland', the outbreak of the Terror in 1935 saw Moscow turn out to be a trap, and many figured among the victims of Stalin's wholesale attack on the cosmopolitan milieu of the Comintern.

The ninth chapter is devoted to Spain, the last great revolutionary hope of the inter-war period, which in 1936–39 became the emblematic arena of antifascist struggle, attracting many fighters for freedom, democracy and social justice. Civil war and revolution also saw the Iberian Peninsula become the locus of the Comintern's last great mobilization, and with that the last rendezvous of the mostly already widely travelled Comintern personnel. As in Germany and China, the two earlier foci of revolutionary hope, they were accompanied by Soviet intelligence officers and Red Army cadre, but were also now under obvious surveillance by agents of the NKVD. In this theatre of war, to their customary role in advising and supporting the local Communist party were added not only military functions but also a humanitarian mission of unprecedented scope, albeit guided by political considerations. Politically, they now had to cooperate with social democratic, anarchist and bourgeois democratic forces, while at the same time seeking to maintain control over such alliances. Furthermore, antifascism and international solidarity had to be accompanied by 'vigilance' against Trotskyists and other critical forces. All in all, this would prove to be too much to ask.

1
Moscow 1920: Revolutionary Rendezvous

Once, I looked up from my typewriter to see a middling-sized man in a black lustre jacket come out of the conference hall. I couldn't see his face, but the figure and the clothing seemed familiar to me from pictures. My heart almost stopped still, and I asked the young woman next to me: 'Isn't that Lenin?' She confirmed the fact, without any special enthusiasm. For me, it was the high point of my life so far. And although afterwards I saw Lenin often, and from much closer, it's that moment when I just saw his back that today remains engraved in *every detail* on my memory. —Hilde Kramer, *Rebellin in München, Moskau und Berlin*

In 1920, there arrived in Moscow a young translator and shorthand writer, a founding member at the age of eighteen of Erich Mühsam's Vereinigung Revolutionärer Internationalisten Bayerns (Union of Revolutionary Internationalists of Bavaria), and since late 1918 a member of the KPD who, during the Bavarian Soviet Republic, had acted as a courier, distributed false passports and written reports for the *Rote Fahne*, and who had just escaped conviction on a charge of aiding and abetting high treason. Also a Bengali who had once been sought as a terrorist and who would go on to become a globe-trotting top official of the Comintern; a former pastor from the Swiss Jura who would very soon be appointed secretary to the Comintern and settle in Moscow with his family; a Dutchman who in conditions of secrecy had set up a

Communist party in Indonesia; an uneducated worker from Thuringia who would soon become the Comintern's greatest propagandist and one of the most important of German press magnates; and an American journalist, a Harvard graduate, an eye-witness who had written the first history of the Russian Revolution; and very many others.

All of them possessed activist capital, skills and knowledge acquired in the course of political activity.[1] Political builders, they had all been involved in setting up the first Communist parties in their countries of permanent or temporary residence: Hilde Kramer (1900–1974) in Munich; M. N. Roy (1887–1954) in Mexico; Jules Humbert-Droz (1891–1971) in Switzerland; Hendricus (known as 'Henk') Sneevliet (1883–1942) in Indonesia; Willi Münzenberg (1889–1940) in Bern and Berlin; John Reed (1887–1920) in the USA . . .[2] And all of them had travelled to Moscow to attend the Second World Congress of the Communist International. The young Hilde Kramer had come from Berlin on the orders of Comintern emissary Mikhail Borodin (1884–1951).[3] She would serve as a German-English translator at the congress and as assistant to Karl Radek, alongside Angelica Balabanova (1878–1965), one of the two secretaries serving the gathering. Borodin, whom she describes as looking like 'one's idea of a Russian grand duke, with his slightly greying beard and long fur-trimmed coat',[4] had organized delegates from half the world. In Mexico, in the character of the supposedly Romanian Peter Alexandrescu, he had won to the Communist cause Manabendra Nath Roy (1887–1954) and Evelyn Trent Roy (1892–1970), who had fled there to escape the risk of imprisonment in the USA, and also the young New Yorker Charles Phillips, black sheep of a well-off

---

1 Frédérique Matonti and Franck Poupeau, 'Le capital militant: Essai de définition', *Actes de la recherche en sciences sociales* 155:5, 2004, 4–11.

2 The dates of birth and death of Comintern figures are given on their first mention.

3 Lavar Kheifetz and Victor Kheifetz, 'Michael Borodin: The First Comintern-Emissary to Latin America', *International Newsletter of Historical Studies on Comintern, Communism and Stalinism* 2:5/6, 1994/95, 145–9, and 3:7/8, 1996, 184–8; Gene D. Overstreet and Marshall Windmiller, *Communism in India*, Berkeley: University of California Press, 1959, 25. No satisfactory scholarly biographical study of Borodin yet exists: Dan N. Jacobs's *Borodin: Stalin's Man in China*, Cambridge, MA: Harvard University Press, 1981, is tendentious and was written without access to the Russian archives.

4 Hilde Kramer, *Rebellin in München, Moskau und Berlin: Autobiographisches Fragment 1900–1924*, ed. Egon Günther and Thies Marsen, Berlin: BasisDruck, 2011, 80–1. The fur turned out to be sable!

Jewish family. The pacifist and conscientious objector Jules Humbert-Droz attended as the representative of the left wing of the Swiss Social Democratic Party. Willi Münzenberg – a man 'of middling stature, with a pale and somewhat lopsided face', a 'gifted orator and brilliant organizer' who in 1915, amid the Great War, had organized an international youth conference in Bern, and who in November 1918 had found himself expelled from Switzerland to Germany – arrived as president of the newly created Young Communist International.[5] John Reed, the fearless American journalist and eyewitness to the events of the Russian Revolution (described in his book *Ten Days That Shook the World*), represented one of the two mutually hostile American parties that were applying to join the Comintern.

In Moscow, the Bolsheviks set about converting the historically unique convergence of different political tendencies into a set of shared goals, and to marshal together their supporters and representatives from across the globe. Revolution was no abstract idea; if it were to be realized it had to be embodied. For this, the attendees had first to agree on what Communism was and how a revolutionary, i.e. Communist, party should function. For those present, these labels were not as fixed and indisputable as they were later to become. How could the multiplicity of political agendas be unified? How could local concerns be formulated in a universal language? How were global aspirations to be realized? How were the working masses to be reached, if Communist organizations represented only a small minority? And how from spontaneous riots, strikes and uprisings, from splinter groups and the radical fringes of social democratic mass organizations, could one build a worldwide, combat-ready organization of professional revolutionaries? Above all: how was the Comintern to appeal to, and hence harness, contemporary radical energies? Such questions were essential to the Comintern's Second World Congress in Moscow. Discussion of that event will draw on both the minutes of the congress and on the substantial body of historical research now available, but will not confine itself only, or even primarily, to matters of ideology or organizational structure. For while these are essential to any understanding of the Comintern, my

---

5 This description of Münzenberg is from Paul Thalmann, *Wo die Freiheit stirbt: Stationen eines politischen Kampfes*, Olten and Freiburg in Breisgau: Walter-Verlag, 1974, 10.

particular interest here is in participants' personal responses. At least a dozen participants in the Second World Congress of the Comintern have given their own accounts of events.[6] How did they maintain their universal enthusiasm for the October Revolution when faced with the material conditions of everyday life in a starving Russia? How was the Bolshevik leadership's dominance over all other congress delegates justified? What expectations did they have of their commitment to the Communist International? These are the kinds of questions chiefly dealt with in this chapter.

Through the Allied Blockade to Soviet Russia

The year since its foundation in 1919 had seen substantial growth in the Comintern's membership, with the adhesion of a number of mass

---

6 Among individuals' accounts of their experience of the Second World Congress are Angelica Balabanoff, *My Life as a Rebel*, New York: Greenwood Press, 1968 [1938]; Walther Bringolf, *Mein Leben: Weg und Umweg eines Schweizer Sozialdemokraten*, Bern: Scherz, 1965; Ludovic-Oscar Frossard, 'Mon journal de voyage en Russie', published by the French Communist paper *L'Internationale*, 1921; Jules Humbert-Droz, *Mémoires*, vol. 1, *Mon évolution du tolstoïsme au communisme, 1891–1921*, Neuchâtel: A la Baconnière, 1969; Hermann Knüfken, *Von Kiel bis Leningrad: Erinnerungen eines revolutionären Matrosen 1917–1930*, Berlin: BasisDruck, 2008 [from a manuscript composed after the Second World War]; Kramer, *Rebellin*; Denis Peschanski, ed., *Les carnets de Marcel Cachin, 1917–1920*, vol. 2, ed. Gilles Candar, Brigitte Studer and Nicolas Werth, Paris: Editions du CNRS, 1993; Willi Münzenberg, *Die dritte Front: Aufzeichnungen aus 15 Jahren proletarischer Jugendbewegung*, Berlin: Litpol, 1978 [1930]; J. T. [John Thomas] Murphy, *New Horizons*, London: John Lane/The Bodley Head, 1941; Alfred Rosmer, *Moscow Under Lenin*, trans. Ian H. Birchall, New York: Monthly Review Press, 1972; Manabendra Nath Roy, *Memoirs*, Delhi: Ajanta Publications, 1984 [1964]; Victor Serge, *Memoirs of a Revolutionary*, trans. Peter Sedgwick, New York: New York Review Books, 2012 [1951]; Charles Shipman, *It Had to Be Revolution: Memoirs of an American Radical*, Ithaca, NY: Cornell University Press, 1993. There are also accounts by other authors then well-disposed to the Bolsheviks and present in Moscow: Max Barthel, *Vom roten Moskau bis zum Schwarzen Meer*, Berlin-Schöneberg: Internationaler Jugendverlag, 1921; Max Barthel, *Die Reise nach Rußland*, Berlin: Verlag der Jugend-Internationale, n.d.; Max Barthel, *Der Rote Ural*, Berlin: Internationaler Jugendverlag, 1921; Alexander Berkman, *The Bolshevik Myth: Diary 1920–1922*, New York: Boni & Liveright, 1925; Louise Bryant, *Mirrors of Moscow*, New York: Thomas Seltzer, 1923; Emma Goldman, *My Disillusionment in Russia*, Garden City, NY: Doubleday, Page & Co., 1923; Pierre Pascal, *En Russie rouge*, Paris: Librairie de l'Humanité, 1921.

socialist parties, among them the Italian Socialist Party with its 264,000 members, which had gained admission to the new International, with flying colours, a few days after the First Congress.⁷ Also attending the Second Congress were representatives of Europe's social democratic parties, there to sound out the intentions of the Bolsheviks and assess the relationship of forces, while from the other end of the left spectrum came radical left groups and individuals of anarchist, syndicalist and revolutionary bent. Also present were representatives of the national-revolutionary liberation movements that had invested their hopes in the new international. The contours of this novel political venture were still unclear. This being so, and because the Russian Revolution was the only one to survive while the Bavarian and Hungarian Soviet Republics had fallen, it seemed to show the way forward. In the summer of 1920 – the Congress ran from 19 July to 7 August – Moscow was the place to be for revolutionaries from all over the world.

Not all succeeded in reaching Petrograd in time for the opening of the Congress. Civil war and blockade meant taking roundabout and sometimes hazardous routes. The south of the country was still in the hands of Denikin's army, while Makhno's forces made Ukraine unsafe. In addition, Poland and Soviet Russia were at war. In the Far East, the way was barred by the Japanese army, which occupied part of Siberia, though a number of Chinese and Japanese delegates managed to travel through Mongolia.

Forbidden to travel by their own governments or refused transit visas by Germany, most delegates made the journey illegally. The American John Reed, one of the few foreigners to have been involved in the October Revolution, passed himself off as a seaman, transiting Germany under a false name. The Frenchman Alfred Rosmer (1877–1964), one of a number of delegates to have left an account of their journeys, travelled from Paris to Milan and from there to Berlin via Vienna and Prague, before making for Stettin, then still part of Prussia, where he took ship for Reval (today's Tallinn, capital of Estonia), before travelling by train from there to Petrograd. The journey took six weeks.⁸ The American Charles Francis Phillips, later and better known as Charles Shipman,

---

7 The figure is for 1920: Pierre Broué, *Histoire de l'Internationale communiste 1919–1943*, Paris: Fayard, 1997, 96.
8 Rosmer, *Moscow*, 18–37.

had been in Europe since December 1919, having arrived there from Mexico, where he had been one of the founding members of the Communist Party. Under the name of Jesús Ramírez, he had travelled with Comintern emissary Mikhail Borodin, making a comfortable voyage from Veracruz via Havana to La Coruña in northwestern Spain. Roy, too, was a member of the delegation, which took rooms at the grand Hotel Palace in Madrid. From there they laid the foundations for the Spanish Communist Party.[9] While Borodin left for Amsterdam only three weeks later and Roy and his wife went on to Berlin, 'Ramírez' stayed in Spain, charged with mobilizing comrades for the Second World Congress. By June, it was time for him too to make the journey to Berlin, not leaving Barcelona for Paris but making a detour to Genoa as a revolutionary tourist: 'Exciting things were happening in Italy; militant workers were seizing factories, and I hoped to get a feel for the situation *en passant*.'[10]

Jules Humbert-Droz and Walther Bringolf (1895–1981), the two Swiss delegates, whose memoirs also recount their difficult journeys, had also to make illegal border crossings. Humbert-Droz succeeded in sneaking out of Basel to reach nearby Lörrach on the German side of the border only on his second night-time attempt. The young comrade who helped him and who would soon embark on a transnational revolutionary career of his own was Basel's Fritz Sulzbachner (1897–1980), a member of the radical socialist youth organization known as the Jungburschen, whose leader, until his expulsion from Switzerland in November 1918, had been Willi Münzenberg. A young man 'full of ideas', Münzenberg was the one who with his youth organization had succeeded in bringing 'the Swiss party movement . . . an essentially local movement . . . onto demonstrations for international causes', in the words of his friend and mentor, the Zurich physician Fritz Brupbacher (1874–1945).[11] The years since the end of the war had seen the Basel group establish a durable smuggling network that ferried revolutionaries and their literature across the border between Switzerland and

---

9 Shipman, *It Had to Be Revolution*, 92–3. See also Antonio Elorza and Marta Bizcarrondo, *Queridos Camaradas: La Internacional Comunista y España, 1919–1939*, Barcelona: Editorial Planeta, 1999, 19–21.

10 Shipman, *It Had to Be Revolution*, 97.

11 Fritz Brupbacher, *60 Jahre Ketzer: Selbstbiographie*, reprinted as '*Ich log so wenig als möglich*', Zurich: Verlagsgenossenschaft, 1973 [1935], 245.

Germany.¹² Once in Germany, they could travel to Berlin by train. From Frankfurt, Humbert-Droz sent his wife Jenny a postcard: 'All going well. Elsi.'¹³ In Berlin, however, he had to wait before continuing his journey. Yet, as he told Jenny, 'Since seeing James and knowing that efforts are being made to ensure a speedy onward passage I am reassured and can wait with patience.'¹⁴ The 'James' he refers to was Jakov Reich (1886–1955), also known as 'Comrade Thomas', head of the West European Secretariat (WES) and the Bolsheviks' unofficial representative in the West.¹⁵

The German capital was an important hub for those travelling to Moscow. Manabendrah Nath Roy and Evelyn Trent had been waiting there several months to continue their journey, being accommodated, according to 'Ramírez', who arrived there later, 'in a very superior rooming house' on the Kurfürstendamm.¹⁶ The couple had most probably left Mexico in January in order to attend the Second World Congress as delegates, he for the Mexican Communist Party, with full voting rights, she – under the pseudonym Santi Devi – for India, with consultative status only.¹⁷ In Berlin, where they had arrived in March 1920 after a stopover in Spain, they had made contact with representatives of the German Communist Party and with the Indian Revolutionary Committee, though they did not succeed in meeting its leading figure, Virendranath Chattopadhyaya, known as Chatto (1880–1937), as he was away in Stockholm.¹⁸ While in Berlin, Roy drew up, together with his wife and Abani Mukherji (1891–1937), an Indian Communist manifesto that however attracted no more than their own three signatures.

---

12 Thalmann, *Wo die Freiheit stirbt*, 19–22.
13 Humbert-Droz, *Mon évolution*, 356–7.
14 Ibid., 358.
15 On this, see chapter 3.
16 Shipman, *It Had to Be Revolution*, 96.
17 They left in December 1919, according to Overstreet and Windmiller, *Communism in India*, 27. As against this, the confirmation of their appointment as the delegates of the Mexican party – in the sardonically conceived names of Roberto Allén and Helen B. de Allén – by José Allén, general secretary of the Executive Committee, is dated 12 January 1920, RGASPI 495/213/277. Roy made use of a host of pseudonyms, among them V. García, Roberto Allen y Villagarcía, Richards, Dr Mahmud, Manuel Méndez, Dr Banerji, Roberts, C. A. Martin, and later, on his mission to China, Johnson.
18 Roy, *Memoirs*, 294. On their activity in Mexico see Daniela Spenser, *Stumbling Its Way Through Mexico: The Early Years of the Communist International*, translated by Peter Gellert, Tuscaloosa: The University of Alabama Press, 2011.

Like Roy, Mukherji had transferred his anticolonial and revolutionary allegiance from nationalistic terrorism to the Communist International and was likewise making his way to the Second World Congress.

'Ramírez' seems to have spent quite an agreeable week in Berlin while waiting for his Swedish visa. He got to know the twenty-year-old Hilde Kramer, five years his junior, by whom he was evidently very taken, describing her as a 'tall, statuesque beauty'. The attraction must have been mutual: 'Hilda and I had a convulsive three-day affair, which we resumed during my next visit to Berlin. Among other things she taught me quite a bit of German.'[19] It is interesting to find such details in memoirs, showing as they do that the revolutionary period that followed the First World War was a time of easy-going emancipation in sexual matters for the young women of the Communist movement too, as they allowed themselves the freedoms that had traditionally been reserved to men. Hardly a year earlier, in a letter to a former teacher, the young Hilde Kramer had expressed her decisive rejection of bourgeois values: 'You ask about my fiancé, raising the question of matrimony. But I am not at all thinking of getting married. I need no official stamp to make a life for myself... We reject marriage in principle. If at some point we no longer get on, we want to be able to separate without bitterness and without the involvement of the authorities.'[20]

The political situation in Berlin was difficult, however. The police arrested any foreign Communists they found and had them deported. The young Serb Voja Vujović (1897–1936) – an officer of France's Jeunes Socialistes, who, in passing through Switzerland, stayed with the Humbert-Droz family and had carelessly arranged to meet other young comrades in a café, among them Willi Münzenberg, himself sought by the police – promptly found himself arrested and locked up for a few days.[21] The somewhat older Humbert-Droz was more circumspect, confining himself to his room for the twelve days he had to wait before

---

19 Shipman, *It Had to Be Revolution*, 98.

20 Letter from Hilde Kramer to her former teachers, Fräulein Fischer and Fräulein Koch, Stadelheim, 16 July 1919, in Christiane Sternsdorf-Hauck, ed., *Brotmarken und rote Fahnen: Frauen in der bayrischen Revolution und Räterepublik 1918/19*, Frankfurt a. M.: Neuer ISP-Verlag, 1989, 105–6, at 106.

21 Humbert-Droz, *Mon évolution*, 358; Münzenberg, *Die dritte Front*, 314–15; Sean McMeekin, *The Red Millionaire: A Political Biography of Willi Münzenberg, Moscow's Secret Propaganda Tsar in the West*, New Haven, CT: Yale University Press, 2003, 90.

they could continue their journey. On 12 July he and some two dozen comrades of various nationalities were eventually able to board at Stettin the ship that Jakov Reich had just managed to charter.[22] Among the passengers were a four-strong delegation from the USPD (Unabhängige Sozialdemokratische Partei Deutschlands), visiting Moscow as observers to find out more about the new International, and Paul Levi (1883–1930) and Eduard Fuchs (1870–1940), representing the German Communist Party and the Spartakusbund, respectively.[23] Also travelling were two journalists from *Le Phare*, the international French-language Communist journal founded by Jules Humbert-Droz, whose later careers could not have been more different: Lucien Laurat (1898–1973), a young Viennese of Czech parentage – born Otto Maschl – would join the internal party opposition in 1927–28, while the Bulgarian Stojan Minev (1889–1959), whose true name was Ivanov-Minej and who had studied medicine in Geneva, there coming into contact with the Zimmerwald Left, was a member of Stalin's private office from 1927 to 1929 and then held a variety of posts of responsibility within the Comintern until its dissolution in 1943. Also on board was the barely twenty-year-old Hilde Kramer, a fluent speaker of French and English in addition to her native German. Following her involvement in the failed Bavarian Soviet Republic, she had joined the staff of the Comintern's West European Secretariat in Berlin. She too travelled on false papers.[24]

A two-and-a-half-day voyage brought them all to Reval (Tallinn). The Soviet government had concluded its first treaty with Estonia, and this required that the port be open to those travelling on to Russia. Yet, as Hilde Kramer recalled, 'The Estonian authorities did not allow the ship to dock, and while negotiations over our onward journey went on we lay in the roads off Reval, amid a fierce storm, and all of us seasick.'[25] They then had to travel to Narva on the Russian-Estonian border. From there they went, first by motorboat and then on a requisitioned train of antiquated sleeper and restaurant cars, to Petrograd and thence to Moscow, where the Congress that had opened in the old capital was now again in session. Also travelling by ship from Stettin to Nerval were the

22 Humbert-Droz, *Mon évolution*, 358.
23 Bringolf, *Mein Leben*, 76.
24 Kramer, *Rebellin*, 88–90.
25 Ibid., 90. Bringolf, on the other hand, mentions a British naval vessel that was stationed in the port: *Mein Leben*, 78.

Germans Willi Münzenberg and Ernst Meyer (1887–1930), the Swiss Siegfried (Sigi) Bamatter (1892–1966), the British Communist John T. Murphy (1888–1965), with an eventful journey through the Netherlands, Germany and Denmark already behind him, and the youth representative from France, Aron Goldenberg (1896–1993), son of a Romanian-Jewish family. They had good weather but were being smuggled in among repatriated Russian prisoners of war.

Roy had more luck. Armed with a recommendation from Victor Kopp, the representative of the Russian Soviet Federative Socialist Republic in Berlin, 'Helen and Roberto Allén' travelled to Reval on the Russian passenger ship *The Soviet*,[26] together with the wife of Jacques Sadoul (1881–1956), the French military envoy to Russia, who had fought alongside the Bolsheviks and played a part in setting up the Red Army – a journey Roy would remember as 'pleasant and uneventful'.[27] What he does omit to note in his memoir is that his partner was with him as well. Together with 'Ramírez', who had crossed to Reval from Sweden, the couple were among the very first to arrive at the hotel allocated to those attending the Congress.[28]

Even earlier arrivals in Moscow were the two delegates of the Kommunistische Arbeiterpartei Deutschlands (KAPD), who had hijacked a cargo boat. Antiparliamentary, Council Communist and syndicalist in orientation, the KAPD was the fruit of one of the earliest splits in the party, being formed by the Left Opposition expelled from the KPD in April 1920. In an endeavour to bring together the widest range of revolutionary forces, the Bolsheviks had invited them to the Second World Congress alongside Paul Levi's KPD. Wanting to reach Moscow before the Congress opened, in order to correct what they took to be false characterizations of their organization, and so unwilling to wait for the West European Secretariat to arrange for their travel together with the other delegates, the KAPD's two representatives – the shipbuilder and seaman Jan Appel (1890–1985) and the Expressionist writer Franz Jung (1883–1963) – decided to make their way to Russia under their own steam.[29]

---

26 Personal files of Evelyn Roy, RGASPI 495/213/277 and M. N. Roy, RGASPI 495/213/18.

27 Roy, *Memoirs*, 307.

28 Shipman, *It Had to Be Revolution*, 105.

29 Jan Appel and Franz Jung, 'Bericht der nach Moskau entsandten Delegation' [9 July 1920], in *Das Exekutivkomitee der 3. Internationale und die Kommunistische*

With the help of their comrade Hermann Knüfken (1893–1976), who was employed on a trawler, they hijacked the vessel, arriving in Murmansk on the first of May. From there, they travelled via Petrograd to Moscow, where they had their first talks with the Little Bureau of the Executive Committee of the Communist International, and also with Lenin. Rather than argue with them, the latter gave them the manuscript of the German translation of his pamphlet *'Left-Wing' Communism: An Infantile Disorder* to read. 'What for us were principles, were for the Russians tactics,' Knüfken would write later of their irreconcilable difference of opinion.[30] The two delegates left again before the Congress even opened, though Knüfken stayed until October. He then travelled back to Germany via Norway, as a courier for the Comintern, only to be arrested and sentenced to five years' imprisonment for robbery, mutiny and kidnapping. On his early release in May 1923, he went back to the Soviet Union, where he became head of the International Seamen's Club in Leningrad.[31]

A rather more comfortable journey was had by the two French Social Democrats, Marcel Cachin (1869–1958) and Louis-Oscar Frossard (1889–1946). Provided with a visa for Germany through the good offices of the USPD, they were able to get to Moscow much quicker. To Cachin's annoyance, however, the Bolsheviks paid them little attention,[32] though other delegates, such as the Italians, were received with great pomp. Cachin, in fact, was seen as an incorrigible chauvinist. Unlike most others attending, he enjoyed only an institutional legitimacy, rather than the activist credibility that came from opposition to wartime political truce, participation in revolutionary uprisings or the building of Communist organizations. John Reed, indeed, found it thoroughly unacceptable that he should have been allowed into the country.[33] Willi Münzenberg, who argued forcefully at the Congress against the admission of the social democratic parties, was still fulminating at

---

Arbeiter-Partei Deutschlands, Berlin: Verlag der KAPD, 1920, 3–6, also available at web.archive.org.

30 Knüfken, *Von Kiel*, 118.

31 Hans Manfred Bock, *Syndikalismus und Linkskommunismus von 1918 bis 1923: Ein Beitrag zur Sozial- und Ideengeschichte der frühen Weimarer Republik*, Darmstadt: Wissenschaftliche Buchgesellschaft, 1993 [1969], 251–6. On the hijacking and the three comrades' experiences in Moscow, see Knüfken, *Von Kiel*, 84–124.

32 Cachin, *Carnets*, 434.

33 John Riddell, ed., *Workers of the World and Oppressed Peoples, Unite! Proceedings and Documents of the Second Congress, 1920*, vol. 1, New York: Pathfinder, 1991, 33.

Arthur Crispien and Wilhelm Dittmann, the two representatives of the right wing of the USPD, when he came to write his memoirs in 1930, describing them as 'plaster statues of saints that no-one had remembered to put away'.[34] There was, then, no question of unity among all those assembled. Despite the Bolshevik leadership's charm offensive vis-à-vis the big European socialist parties, the political differences of the war years rumbled on, only too easily bursting into flame again.

Revolutionary Enthusiasm and the Experience of Transnational Solidarity

Like the rest of the country, Moscow in 1920 was marked by the years of world war, civil war and War Communism. The economic situation was dire. Industrial production had reached a nadir, in some sectors being no more than 10 to 20 per cent of pre-wartime levels. Living conditions were dreadful, the population impoverished, their clothes shabby. There was little to eat, and there were beggars everywhere. As the foreigners arriving in Petrograd for the Congress would note in due course, the chairs in the Winter Palace were missing their leather, stripped off to make shoes.

In Moscow, the delegates were housed in a hotel specially renovated for the purpose, the Delovoi Dvor, located on a quiet side street not far from Kitai-gorod, its furnishing apparently determined by Trotsky personally. This was meagre but functional: a bed, a desk and two chairs. And on the first floor was a large dining hall. Although the hotel had been disinfested prior to delegates' arrival, bed bugs were still a problem – a plague that afflicted all Russia in those days, the subject of constant complaint by foreigners, both then and later.[35] While the visitors were certainly accorded special treatment, this was far from meeting Swiss standards, as Walther Bringolf noted.[36] Luck was with those who were lodged near the Italian delegation, who generously allowed them to share in their copious provision of wine and salami. Material conditions, though, were a secondary matter to delegates, who experienced

---

34 Münzenberg, *Die dritte Front*, 323.
35 Rosmer, *Moscow*, 39; Knüfken, *Von Kiel*, 115–16.
36 Bringolf, *Mein Leben*, 79

them as no more than a temporary inconvenience. The real question was nothing less than the construction of a new world, at least for those who looked forward passionately to a revolutionary future. Perceptions varied with political commitments. Sceptical social democrats like Dittmann criticized Russian backwardness. Willi Münzenberg recalled that he would have 'gladly thrown the fellow off the balcony' on hearing him grumble about the bathtub at the hotel. 'They went on all day about the poor sanitation and saw during their visit only the battered façade of the building.'[37] For many of the delegates, it was the first time they had travelled so far. Others, like John Reed, who had lived through the October Revolution, knew Moscow already. The atmosphere was electric, says Alfred Rosmer in his memoirs, charged with excited expectation, resonant with keen debate. Rosmer speaks of a 'true spirit of comradeship' among those present,[38] swept up in a wave of solidarity that transcended national and ethnic boundaries. Roy, too, emphasizes in his memoirs the significance of the congress as a place of encounter and new friendships.

Not without a certain naivety, the young Hilde Kramer wrote to a friend in Berlin, recounting her experience:

> Of course, it's difficult for a Central European to adjust to Asian conditions, but all these outward things are overridden by the shared idea that all of us here are working for. It is just so lovely to see the Red Flag fly over an imperial palace and a Communist Congress in the throne room developing theses on the advancement of world revolution. Despite the blockade, the Russians are very well informed about political and social conditions in other countries and immediately get the right handle on emerging problems. The Third International has grown immeasurably over the space of a year. Last year, at the first, founding congress, it was a little propaganda group, in which the all-important European states were hardly represented. This time, the congress is an assembly of revolutionary leaders from nearly every country on earth. Here there are no distinctions of nationality or race. English and Indian delegates discuss together the question of their common liberation. A Polish delegate makes a long and enthusiastic

---

37 Münzenberg, *Die dritte Front*, 323.
38 Rosmer, *Moscow*, 44.

speech saluting Soviet Russia's victory over Poland and enjoining another campaign against his country.[39]

Kramer's Polish delegate was referring to the Russo–Polish War that had begun in 1919. While the Congress met, the Red Army was advancing on Warsaw, and the delegates attentively followed its progress, displayed on a large map. The Bolshevik leadership, Trotsky and Radek excepted, believed that with the support of the Red Army the Polish workers would rise up against the bourgeoisie. In this they underestimated the importance of the national question, for the Russians were seen as invaders rather than as liberators. The Red Army was brought to a halt before Warsaw and then beaten back, bringing to an end the attempt to export the revolution to the West by force of arms.

Delegates' enthusiasm was nourished too by other factors. Many would remember the impressive cultural productions laid on for their entertainment. As the historian Gleb Albert has shown, the Bolsheviks understood the Comintern congresses held under the auspices of the young Soviet state to be world-historic events, and they were reported in great detail by the state and party press.[40] The presence of foreign delegates not only lent prestige to their hosts, the Soviet leadership, but also represented, for ordinary members of the party and its youth organization, a living symbol of the proletarian internationalism of which they had such great hopes. The festivities organized in honour of the delegates were thus also equally aimed at the domestic population.

The opening ceremony of the congress, held in Petrograd on 19 July, was notably impressive. The delegates were enthralled by the rousing welcome they received from the massed ranks of attendees, solemn addresses were given, a memorial for the fallen of the Revolution took place on the Marsovo Pole (Field of Mars), a fireworks show was held on the Neva, while the streets, the main square (Palace Square, then known as Uritsky Square) and the Smolny Institute were bedecked with flags and hung with banners. 'Red flags everywhere, and everywhere the

---

39 Letter from Hilde Kramer to 'Friedel', Moscow, 22 August 1920, reprinted in Kramer, *Rebellin*, 138–44, at 142–3.

40 Gleb Albert, '"Verehrte Komintern!" Dritte Internationale als politisches Symbol und charismatische Institution im frühen Sowjetstaat', *Jahrbuch für Historische Kommunismusforschung*, 2013, 17–38.

sound of the Internationale,' Hilde Kramer wrote to her friend in Berlin. 'And all this despite the prevailing misery, which can hardly by imagined by those elsewhere.'[41]

Willi Münzenberg later described the people of the city as suffused by a 'tremendous mass consciousness' and 'proud of what has been accomplished and achieved'. He was not the only one to be greatly impressed by the mass performance – 'Of the Two Worlds' – staged on the steps of the Petrograd Stock Exchange.[42] He speaks of 20,000 participants, while the ever-sceptical Cachin offers the likely more realistic estimate of 3,000. Max Barthel, who had witnessed the dress rehearsal, and who was still full of enthusiasm for Soviet developments (though the 1930s would see him transfer his allegiance to the Nazis), reckoned on 5,000: 'Workers and women from the factories, schoolchildren from the drama sections of the Proletkult and the workers' clubs, actors and actresses from the Petrograd Theatre, sailors, regiments of Red soldiers and boisterous squadrons of Red cavalry'.[43] The audience, for its part, has been estimated as anything up to 80,000.[44] Devised by Maxim Gorky, the scenes performed depicted the history of humanity since 1848 as a class struggle between workers and bourgeoisie. The first part featured the publication of the *Communist Manifesto* and the creation of the Paris Commune, the second the betrayal of the Second International on the

---

41 Letter from Hilde Kramer to 'Friedel', Moscow, 22 August 1920, reprinted in Kramer, *Rebellin*, 138–44, at 142–3.

42 The mass performance best known to the literature is 'The Storming of the Winter Palace', staged on the third anniversary of the October Revolution: Inke Arns, Igor Chubarov and Sylvia Sasse, eds, *Nikolai Evreinov: 'The Storming of the Winter Palace'*, Zurich: Diaphanes, 2016; and it is possible that the 'Forward to the World Commune' of July 1920 was the same piece. See the description in Platon Kerzhentsev, 'The Successes of the New Theater', in Arns, *Nikolai Evreinov*, 167–76, an essay originally published in Russian in 1923, 'Uspekhi novogo teatra', in Kerzhentsev, *Tvorcheskii teatr*, Petrograd: Gosizdat, 1923, 135–46. See also Gleb Albert, *Das Charisma der Weltrevolution: Revolutionärer Internationalismus und frühe Sowjetgesellschaft, 1917–1927*, Cologne: Böhlau Verlag, 2017, 318; Karl Schlögel, *Petersburg: Das Laboratorium der Moderne, 1909–1921*, Munich: Fischer, 2002, 464–7; James von Geldern and Richard Stites, eds, *Mass Culture in Soviet Russia: Tales, Poems, Songs, Movies, Plays and Folklore, 1917–1953*, Bloomington: Indiana University Press, 1995, 29–32.

43 Cachin, *Carnets 1917–1920*, 571; Barthel, *Die Reise nach Rußland*, 29.

44 Kerzhentsev, 'The Successes', 170. Other figures are given in Gleb Albert, *Das Charisma*, 318, which estimates 4,000 lay performers and an audience of 45,000.

outbreak of war in 1914, the third the advent of the 'Russian Commune' with the Revolution of 1917 and the defence of the Soviet Republic. The spectacle climaxed with the appearance of the 'world proletariat' and resounding shouts of welcome to the delegates of the Third International, accompanied by the singing of the *Internationale* – for Rosmer 'an act of faith that made a worthy conclusion to a day full of emotion'.[45] Münzenberg was evidently much taken by the critical depiction of the social democrats, writing that the 'Kautskyans and leaders of the Second International' had stood anxiously between the working classes and the bourgeoisie and then gone to ground as soon as the Revolution broke out:

> Red flags rise nameless out of the masses, bands of wounded join the crowd of workers, the din of the hammers becomes louder, more threatening, more compulsive. Workers press forward against the terraces [where the bourgeoisie are assembled], the police arrive, the social democratic theorists vanish, the first shots are fired, suddenly from around the corner there appears an armoured car with armed sailors and red flags flying – the sailors of Kronstadt hastening to the aid of the workers.

Later he writes of the spectators' reaction:

> All this at night, around 2 a.m., with red flags waving greetings from the Winter Palace, the warships on the Neva displayed the Soviet star, wonderfully lit up, and a hundred thousand workers filled the streets to witness the sight. It was like a dream. As the armoured car with the red sailors approached, we delegates rose to our feet, whooping, gesticulating, at a loss for what to do with our enthusiasm.[46]

The show went on, in fact, even longer than Münzenberg remembered, until four in the morning. Even Cachin was led to comment in his diary that 'the whole day gave an impression of strength, grandeur,

---

45 Rosmer, *Moscow*, 68.
46 Münzenberg, *Die dritte Front*, 320–21.

organization'.⁴⁷ To the astonishment of those present, he even clapped as the patriotic socialists were mocked and reviled.⁴⁸

The formal opening of the Congress in Petrograd, together with supporting programme and gala dinner, cost the hosts 20 million roubles.⁴⁹ 'Techniques of hospitality' were not an Intourist invention.⁵⁰ In Moscow, where the Congress eventually met, the delegates were woken each morning by a soldiers' choir singing outside the hotel. Cachin was smitten, finding it 'superb'.⁵¹ Hilde Kramer, M. N. Roy and Charles Shipman later recalled their emotion at hearing the bells of the Kremlin clock ring out the Internationale.⁵² The delegates were offered the opportunity to visit factories, where they were each time enthusiastically welcomed by the waiting workers. They took part in many public meetings and other public events, where they would be expected to speak, or to embody international proletarian solidarity by their mute presence. Hermann Knüfken tells of one such mass demonstration on Red Square, a send-off for the soldiers of the Red Army on their way to the Polish front:

> The foreign delegates were to inspect the massed ranks of troops. As soon as we set off down the line, the bands began to play the Internationale. The sight of the various delegates in their fine suits must have caused a stir among the poorly clothed soldiers. I must admit, my heart beat for these worker and peasant soldiers who would in a few days be at the front, to defend the young RFSR, or bring the idea of international proletarian solidarity to Western Europe on the tips of their bayonets. (That's what I was thinking!).⁵³

Another event, held in honour of the Comintern in Moscow, saw perhaps as many as 250,000 attend.⁵⁴ As in the case of the soldiers, their presence

---

47 Cachin, *Carnets 1906–1947*, 571.
48 Albert S. Lindemann, 'Socialist Impressions of Revolutionary Russia 1920', *Russian History* 1:1, 1974, 31–45, at 41.
49 Alexander Vatlin, *Das Jahr 1920: Der Zweite Kongress der Kommunistischen Internationale*, trans. Wladislaw Hedeler, Berlin: BasisDruck Verlag, 2019, 69.
50 The concept is from Sylvia R. Margulies, *The Pilgrimage to Russia: The Soviet Union and the Treatment of Foreigners, 1924–1937*, Madison: University of Wisconsin Press, 1968.
51 Cachin, *Carnets 1917–1920*, 588.
52 Kramer, *Rebellin*, 95; Roy, *Memoirs*, 350; Shipman, *It Had to Be Revolution*, 103.
53 Knüfken, *Von Kiel*, 126–7.
54 Albert, '"Verehrte Komintern!"', 30.

was not always voluntary, factory staffs often being obliged to attend by management or by party officials. In return, they got a day off with pay, with a ration of food also generally being distributed at the event.[55]

If they wanted, foreign delegates were provided with tickets for cultural events. They would often be impressed by the sheer scale and heroics of these cultural offerings, and most especially by the experience of community they afforded. Avant-garde, though, was something else, and by no means loved by all. Walther Bringolf was especially keen. He visited the Tretyakov Gallery, saw Gorky's *The Lower Depths* (though this was performed in Russian, he knew the play almost by heart), attended a performance of *Carmen* and also a summer concert. This last particularly impressed him, as the Moscow Symphony Orchestra played without a conductor – one of the democratic experiments of the period of War Communism.[56]

Delegates who arrived some time before the congress opened were also able, if they wished, to take advantage of the voyage down the Volga laid on in the first half of July. In eight days or so, this journey of over 3,000 kilometres, which also featured a number of excursions, took them to Saratov, from whence they returned to Moscow by train – a journey via Tambov, the industrial city of Tula, and Ivanovo, which itself took three or four days. In their contemporary notes or later recollections, those who travelled speak of the lasting impression made by the beauty of the landscape and express their enthusiasm at the warm welcome offered by a mobilized population.[57] Where popular euphoria was muted, this was explained in terms of Menshevik sympathies.[58] The hot summer days, however, saw some just go and swim in the Moskva River, behind the Kremlin, where they discovered, to the consternation of some, that Russians of both sexes bathed naked.

It seems unlikely, though, that most delegates ever became truly aware of Soviet Russian living conditions under War Communism. Victor Serge

---

55 Simon Pirani, *The Russian Revolution in Retreat 1920–24: Soviet Workers and the New Communist Elite*, London: Routledge, 2008, 35; Albert, *Das Charisma*, 312–21.

56 Bringolf, *Mein Leben*, 91–2. Stites discusses the conductorless orchestra movement of the 1920s, (*Persimfans* in its Russian acronym) in his work on utopian revolutionary practices, though he dates its emergence to 1922: Richard Stites *Revolutionary Dreams: Utopian Vision and Experimental Life in the Russian Revolution*, Oxford: Oxford University Press, 1989, 135–40.

57 Cachin, *Carnets*, 520–55.

58 Albert, *Das Charisma*, 506.

(1890–1947), a Belgian journalist and writer of Russian parentage, a former anarchist whose real name was Victor Kibalchich, who had joined the Russian Communist Party in 1919 and who would later join the Left Opposition, certainly didn't think so, noting in his memoirs:

> The only city the foreign delegates never got to know (and their incuriosity in this respect disturbed me) was the real, living Moscow, with its starvation rations, its arrests, its sordid prison episodes, its behind-the-scenes racketeering. Sumptuously fed amidst universal misery (although, it is true, too many rotten eggs turned up at mealtimes), shepherded from museums to model nurseries, the representatives of international socialism seemed to react like holiday-makers or tourists within our poor Republic, flayed and bleeding from the siege.[59]

He thought little better of those who later attended meetings of the Comintern-affiliated trade union international:

> On the whole, the foreign delegates were a rather disappointing crowd, charmed at enjoying appreciable privileges in a starving country, quick to adulate, and reluctant to think. Few workers could be seen among them, but plenty of politicians. 'How pleased they are', Jacques Mesnil remarked to me, 'to be able to watch parades, at long last, from the official platform!'[60]

It was not that delegates and other attendees were simply taken in by the charm of Potemkin villages. Rather, if they saw hunger, poverty or imprisonment, many of them rationalized these as the inevitable difficulties of a regime still in the process of establishing itself and consolidating the Revolution. Serge described this attitude as 'a novel variety of insensitivity: Marxist insensitivity'.[61]

Even so, congress delegates were chiefly occupied in discussion, negotiation and the reading and writing of reports. Before, after, and during the congress, they gathered together for lengthy special commission meetings, plenary sessions, informal discussion groups and

---

59 Serge, *Memoirs*, 121.
60 Ibid., 171.
61 Ibid., 121.

spontaneous discussions in the Kremlin corridors, on the streets or at the hotel. Lenin and Trotsky were especially concerned to get serious work done and did not tolerate unpunctuality, as we learn from Alfred Rosmer, a delegate of anarcho-syndicalist background:

> One morning, already gone ten o'clock, we were still at the hotel when a message reached us saying that Lenin reminded us that the meeting was due to begin at ten at the Kremlin. There is no need to say that we were somewhat abashed as we sat down round the table. We had acquired bad habits from Zinoviev and Radek; they were always somewhat behind the timetable.[62]

Despite all their differences and points of contention, the congress represented for many a first experience of internationalism in practice.

The Search for Shared Principles and a Common Language

After repeated delays, the Congress finally opened on 23 July, at the Kremlin, where the redundant imperial throne found a new role as a coat stand. Despite the difficulties of travel, it was attended by 217 delegates from 37 countries, 10 of them Asian, representing in total 67 different organizations. More than 30 delegates came from 'oppressed nations' such as China, the Dutch East Indies, India, Ireland, Korea, Mexico, Iran and Turkey.[63] Of those with full voting rights, 124 represented Communist parties, and 31 non-Communist organizations. Twelve delegates represented youth organisations.[64] Given the incompleteness of the data, any sociological analysis of delegates to the 1920 Congress can only be approximate. According to John Riddell, some two-thirds of the 176 delegates for whom information is available were under 40 years old. The youngest, the Russian Lazar Shatskin (1902–1937), one of the officers of the Youth International, was no more than 18. Only 12 delegates were older than 50. It is worth noting, in terms of the later development of the

---

62 Rosmer, *Moscow*, 74.

63 Riddell, *Workers of the World*, 38; Robert J. C. Young, *Postcolonialism: An Historical Introduction*, Oxford: Blackwell, 2001, 130.

64 Günther Nollau, *Die Internationale: Wurzeln und Erscheinungsformen des proletarischen Internationalismus*, Cologne: Verlag für Politik und Wirtschaft, 1959, 52.

Comintern and the Soviet Union, that the coming year would see at least 20 delegates join the (left) Communist Opposition of Leon Trotsky (1879–1940) and 13 would join the Right Opposition around Nikolai Bukharin (1888–1938). And of the foreign delegates, three-fifths would abandon the Comintern by 1933.

By 1943, when Stalin dissolved the organization, only a quarter were still members. Of those who were not, a horrifically high proportion had fallen victim to the terror of the late 1930s. Of seventy-six delegates then living in the Soviet Union, only thirteen (less than a fifth) did not suffer death or imprisonment.[65] Data on gender are lacking; the credentials committee made no special note, and there has been little later research. It can be said, however, that women represented a small minority. John Riddell gives a figure of nineteen female delegates, without offering any further information.[66] Of those women cited by name in the proceedings of the Congress, seven came from Soviet Russia, the others from Norway, Sweden, Germany, Great Britain, Denmark, Austria and Czechoslovakia. Photographs and other sources, however, indicate that other women were also present at the congress. Only delegates, however, were officially counted and listed in the proceedings. The landscape of memory too is socially ordered: no report or memoir records the presence of Hilde Kramer, the shorthand-typist with a gift for languages; only the speakers on the podium were worthy of remembrance. The same goes for contemporary outsiders and later historians. Of the leading figures of the congress, only Jenö ('Eugen') Varga (1879–1964), an émigré who had taken refuge in Soviet Russia after the fall the Hungarian Soviet Republic in 1919, seems to have paid any attention to Hilde Kramer. She recalls that he spoke to her and asked her why she smoked, and that he was a 'friendly and congenial character'.[67]

The congress, which like all Communist meetings was extremely prolific of words and paper, could not, however, have taken place without the work of a host of ancillaries, responsible for what in the language of the Comintern were called 'technical' tasks. They worked beside the platform and in the wings. 'My days are spent in the conference hall, at the little table directly beneath the speakers' platform,' Kramer writes. 'I

---

65 Riddell, *Workers of the World*, 9.
66 Ibid., 8.
67 Kramer, *Rebellin*, 102.

hardly had time for a cup of tea or a bite to eat, or to exchange a word or two with the many people I knew.'[68]

These administrative, secretarial and linguistic roles were chiefly if not almost exclusively fulfilled by women, in accordance with the traditional and still prevalent sexual division of labour. Even Hilde Kramer, who in her 1920 questionnaire described her occupational background as 'intellectual', had no input whatsoever into the political proceedings.[69] All this despite the fact that Communist organizations were committed to women's emancipation. As in the Second International, roles at every level, including the highest leadership, were in principle open to women members. In the years following the First World War, women's participation in political parties on an equal basis with men was more the exception than the rule. To that extent, the Communist organizations offered women what was still a novel opportunity for political, indeed public, activity. Yet the gulf between possibility and actuality was wide, and this was equally true in Soviet Russia. The male gaze had not somehow been automatically abolished, as witnessed, for example, by Victor Serge's description in his memoir of M. N. Roy's companion Evelyn Trent as 'a statuesque Anglo-Saxon woman who appeared to be naked beneath her flimsy dress'.[70] He omits to mention that she was an official delegate and the representative of British India on the congress's Colonial Commission.[71]

To return to the infrastructure of the congress: according to Hilde Kramer, 'technical preparations for the congress were very inadequate. Above all, we lacked interpreters and stenographers'. She goes on: 'There were only two interpreters for the speeches, a man whose name escapes me, and Angelica Balabanova, both fluent in French and German, the two languages of the congress.'[72] That they 'effortlessly

---

68 Ibid., 98.
69 Anketa – Fragebogen – Enquête – Questionnaire (then still printed in four languages, though later in Russian only) of Hilde Kramer, n.d. [1920], RGASPI 495/65a/8878.
70 Serge, *Memoirs*, 124.
71 Overstreet and Windmiller, *Communism in India*, 27.
72 Kramer, *Rebellin*, 93. Not known for her modesty, Angelica Balabanova nevertheless described herself, in her own memoirs, published in 1938, as 'the only translator available for the Congress': Angelica Balabanoff, *My Life as a Rebel*, Bloomington: Indiana University Press, 1973, 274 – the name is variously transliterated as Balabanoff and Balabanova.

translated from any language into any other', as Hermann Knüfken remembers, must surely be something of an exaggeration.[73] The man whose name Kramer forgot must have been Jules Humbert-Droz from Switzerland. In actual fact, any number of multilingual delegates must have acted as interpreters into different languages at meetings of the congress's special commissions. Most Soviet representatives, in any event, gave their speeches in one or other of the (initially) two official languages of the congress, whether the German that nearly all the Bolshevik leaders spoke, or French. Only after the forceful protest of the English-speaking delegates, who went so far as to boycott a whole day of proceedings, was interpretation into English provided. Interpretation was not simultaneous but sequential, bringing with it much delay. While it caused much stress and fatigue to polyglot delegates, interpreting also brought responsibility, and with it, power: they could indeed influence the course of debate. According to some delegates, Angelica Balabanova, who had left Russia in the 1890s to study in Brussels, Leipzig, Berlin, Rome and Switzerland, was quite unscrupulous in exploiting her position. Her fanciful translations often went on significantly longer than the original speech.[74] Resolutions, motions and delegates' written position papers, on the other hand, were typed up in four languages – German, Russian, French and English – by the secretarial staff. A shorthand record of debates was kept in German, French or Russian, as the case might be. As was noted in the 1921 edition of the proceedings, there were two shorthand writers for German (the Comintern's working language in the 1920s), one for French and none for English.[75] The German-speaking shorthand writers were Hilde Kramer, who really only acted as a relief, and a widely travelled Russian woman named Evnina, who seems to have been fluent in all the congress languages. She had been seconded to the congress by her boss, Georgy Chicherin, people's commissar for foreign affairs.[76]

Expectations ran high among those attending. Zinoviev (whom Hilde Kramer found pompous and who made an unfavourable impression on

---

73 Knüfken, *Von Kiel*, 113.
74 Humbert-Droz, *Mon évolution*, 365; Knüfken, *Von Kiel*, 127.
75 Cited in Riddell, *Workers of the World*, 61.
76 Kramer, *Rebellin*, 94.

most of his contemporaries, especially women[77]) opened the proceedings, observing that this was a great historical event. The congress had to settle the most important questions facing the Communist International. For those present, the subject of their debates was no less than the political future of humanity, which would lose all meaning in the absence of a proletarian world revolution. Opinions differed, however, on how this was to be accomplished and what such a revolution should look like.

The Bolsheviks, in this respect, were well prepared and had divided the work up between themselves, in the manner of a general staff. Lenin, Trotsky, Radek, Bukharin and Zinoviev each took responsibility for one major topic on which a position had to be formulated and a resolution adopted. The first thing to be done was to define the role and mode of operation of the Communist parties. Three texts were involved in this: the Statutes, the 'Theses on the Role of the Communist Party in the Proletarian Revolution' and the especially hotly debated 'Conditions for Entry into the Communist International'.[78] The chief point of contention with regard to this last was the admission of parties of the Second International that had expressed an interest, such as the USPD – described by one delegate as a 'party of government' – the French and Italian Socialist Parties, and also the Swiss and other social democratic parties. For the Bolsheviks and their allies in other countries, these parties and their leaders were 'opportunists' and traitors to the cause. It was in these, however, that the mass of workers was organized. The big social democratic parties, for their part, were of two minds. Despite reverses, the political situation in 1920 was still favourable to the Bolsheviks and the Third International. Did they not risk political isolation by not joining the new international? The USPD had after all sent

---

77 Ruth Fischer nevertheless credits him with a certain oratorical power of persuasion: Fischer, *Stalin und der deutsche Kommunismus*, vol. 1, Berlin: Dietz Verlag, 1991 [1950], 190–1. This must in fact have been so, as witnessed by Zinoviev's speech to the USPD party conference in Halle in October 1920, which was decisive in persuading the majority of the membership to transfer to the KPD, making the latter a mass party for the first time.

78 On this, see Report on the Statutes, with Discussion, of 4 August 1920, Riddell, *Workers*, vol. 2, 671–94, and the text of the Statutes themselves, ibid., 694–9; 'Role and Structure of the Communist Party', Riddell, *Workers*, vol. 1, 190–200, and the Discussion of 23–24 July 1920, ibid., 141–210; 'Theses on the Conditions for Admission', vol. 2, 765–71, and Discussions of 29–30 July, vol. 1, 291–419, and 6 August 1920, vol. 2, 732–65.

four delegates to Moscow; the French Socialist Party two, and the Italians another two, one of them their long-serving leader and editor of *Avanti*, Giacinto Menotti Serrati (1872–1926). The only one of these parties to have formally pronounced in favour of joining the Third International was the Italian, and Serrati thus opposed the exclusion of party leaderships that had supported a political truce during the war, which would threaten a split in his party. For some, this simply meant that he was unwilling to break with reformism.

Indeed, this was precisely the point on which the Bolsheviks and indeed very many other delegates were inflexible. The Twenty-One Conditions finally adopted were to serve, in Zinoviev's words, as a 'bulwark against centrism'.[79] The seventh condition thus declared point blank that 'parties that wish to belong to the Communist International have the obligation of recognising the necessity of a complete break with reformism and "centrist" politics' and that this break be effected 'in the shortest possible time'. The congress further required of aspirant member parties that they call a special congress as soon as possible to confirm adherence to the Conditions; that they adopt the principles of democratic centralism (freedom of discussion until the moment of decision, unconditional discipline thereafter, combined with a hierarchical and centralized decision-making structure) and accordingly agree to be bound by decisions of the World Congresses and of the Executive Committee of the Communist International; ensure that at least two-thirds of the membership of their central committees and other important bodies consist of comrades who even before the Second Congress had supported joining the Communist International, and that those who rejected the Statutes and the Twenty-One Conditions be expelled from the party. The thirteenth condition further required Communist parties operating in conditions of legality to effect regular purges of the membership, to rid themselves of 'petty-bourgeois elements'. These provisions would later serve as tools for the exclusion of Stalin's opponents and critical and oppositional forces more generally. They certainly led to fierce debate at the congress. USPD delegates Crispien and Dittmann argued for longer discussions between their party and the new International, while the Italian Serrati, as we have seen, disagreed

---

79 Jane Degras, ed., *The Communist International 1919–1943: Documents*, vol. 1, Oxford: Oxford University Press, 1956, 166.

with the immediate expulsion of leading figures of the Second International. Serrati argued that the key criterion for admission should be the will to revolution. In that respect, the Russians were ahead and the workers of other countries should emulate them. However, the Congress ought not to be a schoolteacher giving out good and bad marks. His fellow Italian Amadeo Bordiga (1889–1970), the Dutchman David Wijnkoop (1876–1941) and even Switzerland's Humbert-Droz took a very different position, calling rather for the conditions to be made even more rigorous. In the end, the Conditions of Admission, which arrived at their final number only in the course of the debate, were adopted with only two votes against (these being Crispien and Dittmann of the USPD).

The Statutes likewise debated at the Congress laid down the how the Communist International was to work:

> The new international association of workers is established for the purpose of organising common action between the workers of various countries who are striving towards a single aim: the overthrow of capitalism, *the establishment of the dictatorship of the proletariat* and *of the international Soviet Republic,* the complete abolition of classes and the realisation of socialism, *as the first step to communist society.*[80]

How then was this to be done? One means to it was the adoption, in contrast to the two preceding internationals, of a highly centralized organizational structure and the creation of a single, global Communist Party, a world party of the revolution. This being so, individual Communist parties would only be sections of the new international association of workers, rather than self-subsistent organizations. With certain exceptions, contacts between individual Communist parties had to take place through the ECCI in Moscow, a centralization of communications that in practice strengthened the hand of the Russian party. For those involved at the time, however, it was essentially a matter of efficiency, the ECCI serving a kind of switchboard mediating transnational solidarity and cooperation. As the preamble to the Statutes declares: 'The organisation of the Communist International is directed towards securing for the workers of every country the possibility, at any

---

80 'Statutes', in Riddell, *Workers*, 696–7.

given moment, of obtaining the maximum of aid from the organised workers of the other countries.'

For the Communists, the revolutionary working class could only achieve victory through an unrelenting struggle against the bourgeoisie, what Lenin conceived of as a European or indeed international civil war.[81] This required of them a quasi-military discipline (the Twelfth Condition), for repression by the class enemy was the normal and expectable context of political activity. To protect against this, it would be necessary, they decided, to establish parallel organizational structures, legal and illegal.

The congress had in addition to decide on two tactical questions, though the answers given to them would soon be turned into key principles of Communist analysis and activity. The year 1920 had seen the prospects of imminent civil war (understood as a necessary stage on the path to socialist revolution) become uncertain, and it was necessary to adjust to a somewhat longer time frame. If there was to be war, the self-appointed avant-garde had to rally the masses to the cause. Concretely, they faced a double problem: First, what was their attitude to be to parliamentary work? And second, how were they to relate to the trade unions, most of which were in social democratic hands? Positions on these matters were to some extent diametrically opposed. Council Communist and Left Communist groups, such as the small Communist party (the 'Altkommunisten') around Jakob (Joggi) Herzog (1892–1931) in Switzerland, or the larger Kommunistische Arbeiterpartei Deutschlands (KAPD) in Germany – emphatically rejected any participation by Communists in the 'bourgeois' institution of parliament or in 'reactionary' trade unions. Lenin, the cunning tactician, had, however, prepared the ground for the debate by the publication just before the congress of his *'Left-Wing' Communism: An Infantile Disorder*. Bolstered by the Bolsheviks' political success, in this he had not only advocated the need for 'strictest centralisation and iron discipline' but also taken a stand against what he took to be the politically immature radicalism that failed to recognize realities in its desire to skip the necessary intermediate stages on the path to the conquest of power. At the present time, it

---

81 For an extensive discussion, see Silvio Pons, *The Global Revolution: A History of International Communism, 1917–1991*, trans. Allan Cameron, Oxford: Oxford University Press, 2014.

was impossible to renounce engagement in 'bourgeois parliaments' and 'reactionary' trade unions. Until the masses were ripe for revolution, it was the task of revolutionaries to fill these old forms with new content. However, although all delegates found a copy of Lenin's short, hastily translated essay in their hotel rooms, his arguments were fiercely contested at the Congress. As Charles Shipman observed ironically in his memoir: 'If ultra-leftism was a disease, then a lot of the arriving delegates had caught it – myself included. We had never dreamed it was possible to be "too left".'[82] Alfred Rosmer, too, noted that this insistence on the tactical was something new.[83] On the question of parliamentarism, a majority of the British delegation rejected participation. And according to Amadeo Bordiga, the 'bourgeois' institution of parliament no longer had any justification in the age of soviets, of workers' councils. Bukharin, who opened the debate, argued, like Lenin, for the propagandistic use of this political platform to educate the proletarian masses. Jules Humbert-Droz found himself convinced by Lenin's essay and the arguments of Bukharin, with whom he would soon become close friends, abandoning his anti-parliamentarist inclinations and finally voting with the Bolsheviks.[84]

Such pragmatism also won through in the matter of trade unions. John Reed was indeed appalled at the idea that a Communist might be involved in the American Federation of Labor (AFL), and his attitude was shared by others such as Jack Tanner (1889–1965), representing the British shop stewards' movement. It was Karl Radek, whom John Reed and Alfred Rosmer both thought lacked any trade union experience,[85] who put the Bolshevik case. He argued in favour of participation in the existing trade unions as a means of drawing the mass of workers to the side of the Communists. That the Russian organizers of the congress were not able to simply impose their ideas is evident from the resolution finally adopted, which reflects a somewhat unbalanced compromise. While it alludes to factory committees, it sees the existing trade unions as considerably more important. It was agreed, too, to set up a committee to prepare for a congress of 'red trades unions', a decision that by

---

82 Shipman, *It Had to Be Revolution*, 108.
83 Rosmer, *Moscow*, 44 and 53.
84 Humbert-Droz, *Mon évolution*, 369.
85 Broué, *Histoire*, 174; Jean-François Fayet, *Karl Radek (1885–1939): Biographie politique*, Bern: Peter Lang, 2004, 341.

1928 would have far-reaching consequences, with the establishment in Germany of the Revolutionäre Gewerkschaftsopposition (Revolutionary Union Opposition), marking a turn towards Communist-aligned unions.

Revolutionaries of a New Type?

The Second Congress of 1920 thus laid down the pattern to which members of the Communist Party would be expected to conform and determined the political principles that individual Communist parties had to follow. The 'Russian' party, with its immense revolutionary prestige, served as a model. While others had not advanced so far, or had failed in their revolutions, the Bolsheviks had won power. They had lessons to teach. As Victor Serge put it concisely in his memoirs: 'The Russians led the dance, and their superiority was so obvious that this was quite legitimate.'[86] Hilde Kramer would justify the dominance of the 'Russian comrades' in similar terms: 'Despite my naivety, it was clear to me then that the congress was under not only the organizational but also the political control of the Russians, something I found entirely natural.'[87] Like most other delegates, Kramer was bewitched by the Bolsheviks, but she was by no means blind. Immediately after the closure of the congress, she wrote to her friend in Berlin:

> At the Congress one saw quite clearly what great figures hold the fate of this country in their hands. Lenin and Trotsky and several other great Russian revolutionaries represented the Russian Communist Party and outshone all other delegates. Only a decade ago they might have been minor authors in Switzerland, like many of the delegates, and now, as a result of the experience of revolution, as a result of struggle, of many years working to realize their ideas, they have become giants, with whom none of the revolutionary avant-garde who assembled here could remotely compare themselves.[88]

---

86 Serge, *Memoirs*, 124.
87 Kramer, *Rebellin*, 102.
88 Ibid., 138–9.

Behind this, however, was a great labour of persuasion. 'The Russians seemed incapable of exhaustion by discussion,' British delegate John T. Murphy noted in his memoirs.[89] This had its effect on him, too; having arrived a revolutionary syndicalist, he left Moscow a Communist:

> My experience in Russia as well as the discussions had shown me the real meaning of the struggle for political power . . . It was this which led me to a complete revaluation of political parties. Instead of thinking that a Socialist Party was merely a propaganda organisation for the dissemination of Socialist views I now saw that a real Socialist Party would consist of revolutionary Socialists who regarded the party as the means whereby they would lead the working class in the fight for political power.[90]

The Bolsheviks championed at the Second Congress what they believed the Civil War had taught them.[91] Their party discipline, inspired by the model of military command, had now to be adopted by the Comintern. In political practice, however, things were more complicated. When Congress found it difficult to agree on a principle, details were in many cases left to smaller party organs to determine. This could still lead to considerable conflict, for, despite the appeals to discipline, party members and individual sections could not just be directed from above. The whole history of the Comintern is thus a history of conflict, difference and dissidence, and the departure, indeed, not just of individuals but of whole parties. Not the least important evidence of this is the high number of delegates to the 1920 Congress who left the International over the following decade, while the number of victims of terror among them, previously noted, suggests that the extreme homogeneity of the 1930s, such as it was, was largely achieved through repression and physical annihilation.

In Moscow in 1920, this was but a distant and unknown future. Delegates had their minds set on one thing only: revolution. And not they alone: in those days the Comintern still attracted Marxist

---

89 Murphy, *New Horizons*, 151.
90 Ibid., 160.
91 Alexander Vatlin, *Die Komintern: Gründung, Programmatik, Akteure*, Berlin: Dietz, 2009, 41.

intellectuals, revolutionary syndicalists, suffragettes, social democrats, anarchists and adventurers. Its borders were still porous.

Hilde Kramer worked for the Comintern Secretariat in Moscow for four months, but gradually became homesick, even though she 'had made friends with Willi Münzenberg, Max Barthel and a number of other young comrades'.[92] So, she goes on to write, she 'got in touch with Comrade Mirov who was a kind of director of travel for the Communist International. He was a little man, with a narrow, pointed face and an ironic smile. As I had come to Russia without papers and didn't even have a name, Mirov started by naming me 'Gretchen Müller'.[93]

Delegates did not always have an easy return journey. Indeed, not all of them got home safely, three young Frenchmen and their ferryman being drowned when they attempted to make the crossing from Murmansk in a small fishing boat, so as to evade the Allied blockade. Two Greek delegates were probably killed by the fishermen they hired to get them home, while two Turks were murdered on arrival, drowned by the police in the Sea of Marmara.[94] The Norwegian delegate Augusta Åsen (1878–1920), for her part, suffered a fatal accident in the Soviet capital, while the American John Reed, who joined the delegation to the Baku Congress, likely caught the typhus there from which he died Moscow on 19 October. Hilde Kramer made the journey as a courier for the Comintern, with a counterfeit passport and a false identity as a former governess. She crossed from Russia to Finland with a trainload of repatriated prisoners of war, the 800 Hungarian soldiers and 200 German officers being accompanied by a number of civilian internees. There they all had to wait a long time in a Red Cross camp for the arrival of a ship. Once on board, she says, she handed her large suitcase over to a representative of the International Seafarers' Union, who would smuggle her luggage and her dollars through customs in Stettin. After the international encounters at the congress in Moscow, this was another instance of practical international solidarity.

---

92 The worker-poet Max Barthel (1893–1975) was in the early 1920s an enthusiastic Communist, before becoming a social democrat and finally turning to National Socialism in 1933.
93 Kramer, *Rebellin*, 107.
94 Broué, *Histoire*, 183–5.

The Second World Congress of the Comintern that had so urgently developed the organizational and political principles of world revolution had lasted twenty-five days. Unlike the founding congress of 1919, which had been able to get through its business in only four, it had called for extensive advance preparations, many ancillary commissions and numerous written submissions. In the weeks that followed, the shorthand record was worked up into an official minute of proceedings. Hilde Kramer and Evnina were responsible for the transcription, working under enormous time pressure. Writing up only the French and German took two months. It was a difficult job, some of the record being fragmentary or hardly legible. The timetable was not the only pressure, for the Bolsheviks responded to Evnina's insistence that she would work only in exchange for a passport by stationing a 'Red Guard with fixed bayonet' outside the door of the room where they worked in the foreign ministry. 'This astonished us', Kramer reports, 'as in those days one was not accustomed to such thuggish behaviour towards comrades.'[95]

While the work of the congress assumed that revolution was imminent, there were also signs of pragmatic adjustment to a changing political situation. The congress issued no call to armed uprising, but called on Communist parties to participate in parliaments and trade unions, a shift towards the 'conquest of the masses' that heralded the turn that would be formalized at the Third Congress.

For the present, however, it was a matter of closing up ranks, building a powerful organization and finding the best means of effective communication at the global level. The international revolutionary organization had to provide its members with guidelines for disciplined political activity. 'The Comintern is not an organization in which it is enough to send postcards to one another,' said Radek.[96] The first priority was the establishment of a network of professional revolutionaries with the requisite technical knowledge. The Bolsheviks and their allies were clear that if the revolutionary horizon had now receded, then the Comintern required a political and administrative apparatus if it were to fulfil its tasks. A revolution, one might say, would have to be professionally organized, and the Bolsheviks thus

---

95 Kramer, *Rebellin*, 95.
96 Cited in Fayet, *Radek*, 356.

formed a body of functionaries that developed and issued political and technical quality standards.[97]

For the Bolsheviks, organization was indispensable to the success of the undertaking. The professionalization and globalization of the revolution was not just a political-ideological programme but was also the most important condition for the survival of Soviet Russia itself. That this would have to change with Europe's return to political stability from 1924 on was neither inevitable nor foreseeable. It was a development that likewise transformed the relationship of Communist parties abroad to the Soviet Union. Once focus and platform for a worldwide internationalist project, the Soviet Union became the territorial basis for the political project of the Communist parties, the guarantor of their national existence and the legitimating exemplar of their worldview and their struggle. But before any of this happened, a select number of delegates to the Second Congress would travel on to the East, hoping to find in Baku new allies for the revolution.

---

97 Yves Cohen, 'Circulatory Localities: The Example of Stalinism in the 1930s', *Kritika: Explorations in Russian and Eurasian History* 11:1, 2010, 11–45, at 43.

2
Baku and Tashkent: The Revolution Goes East

In the summer of 1920, the signs were still encouraging. In Germany, a general strike in March had averted the counterrevolutionary Kapp Putsch; in Italy, workers had demonstrated their readiness for struggle in factory and land occupations. Yet the window of opportunity was already beginning to close again. Zinoviev's prediction in May 1919, that the whole of Europe would be Communist within a year, had not come true. The strategy needed readjustment, with the opening of an Eastern front of the world revolution in response to growing radicalization in Asia and the Middle East – as Trotsky had proposed a year earlier.[1] Even as revolution in Europe had kept the Communists waiting, anticolonial and national independence movements had sprung to life in Turkey, Iran, India, China and many other countries. Delegates from 'colonially oppressed nations' in Asia and also Latin America had come to Moscow seeking support for their struggle. The year 1920, then, saw the beginning of a perceptible West-to-East shift in the Comintern's strategic orientation. How anti-imperialist revolution and national liberation might be combined was the subject of intense debate at the Second World

---

1 Letter from Trotsky, dated 5 August 1919, published in Iakov S. Drabkin et al., eds, *Komintern i ideia mirovoi revoliutsii: Dokumenty* [The Comintern and the Idea of World-Wide Revolution: Documents], Moscow: Nauka, 1998, 145–50. See also *The Trotsky Papers 1917–1922*, vol. 1, ed. Jan M. Meijer, The Hague: Mouton, 1964, 620–9.

Congress. What should a 'geopolitics of subversion and solidarity' spanning Europe and Asia look like?[2] How were imperialist countries to relate to colonial and semi-colonial countries – the latter being those that weren't formally colonies but were, nonetheless, under Western dominance? Who constituted the revolutionary force where a proletariat had not yet developed? And how could the emancipation of women of the East be reconciled with respect for the beliefs, customs and the national and cultural institutions of the 'toiling Muslims of Russia and the East'?[3]

The Bolsheviks had no intention of stopping at the theoretical or programmatic. Seeking to put anti-imperialist struggle into practice, in June 1920 they made a radio appeal to the 'workers and peasants of the Near East', one of the first times the new technology was used to mobilize nationalist and revolutionary freedom fighters. It included an invitation to attend an anti-imperialist congress to be held in Baku in September 1920. Another step was the marshalling of a group of Indian revolutionaries in Tashkent, with a view to an armed intervention in India. The effort to integrate the 'East' into the Comintern's sphere of revolutionary activity is discussed in this chapter with reference to the first congress of the 'Peoples of the East', held in Baku, and the first attempt to revolutionize Asia through military intervention. As will become clear, this encounter between East and West was rife with misunderstanding on both sides, in no way dispelled by the Bolsheviks' adoption of the language of Islam or the appropriation of Communist language by local actors whose primary interest was national and cultural independence. The chapter concludes with an inside look at what was then probably the only place in the world where Communist party members could feel absolutely secure: the city of Moscow and, within it, the Hotel Lux. That was where those involved in the ventures of Baku and Tashkent returned at the end of their mission, there to be reunited with other delegates to the Second World Congress who had

---

2 Karl Schlögel, 'Über Räume und Register der Geschichtsschreibung: Ein Gespräch mit Karl Schlögel', *Zeithistorische Forschungen/Studies in Contemporary History* 1:3, 2004, 396–413, at 353.

3 John Riddell, ed., *To See the Dawn: Baku, 1920—First Congress of the Peoples of the East*, New York: Pathfinder, 1993: 'Declaration of Soviet Government on Rights of Peoples of Russia', 247–9, and 'Appeal to All Toiling Muslims of Russia and the East', 250–2.

likewise joined the staff of the Comintern, so becoming functionaries of the world revolution.

The 'Oppressed Peoples of the East'

Lenin had already drafted theses on the national and colonial questions two months before the Second World Congress, submitting them to its National and Colonial Commission and circulating them in advance among delegates.[4] In doing so, he used the broad but poorly defined concept of 'oppressed peoples'. The Comintern had finally, he argued, to fulfil a task that had been criminally neglected by the Second International: the provision of practical support to the revolutionary liberation movements of dependent and disenfranchised peoples, such as the Irish, or the American Negroes, and the colonies (Thesis 9). Formulations like this sought to establish common ground not only with colonized countries but also with those suffering national or racial oppression anywhere. In 1920, however, the 'Negro question' – as the issue of the domination of Blacks by whites was then generally termed – had not yet appeared on the congress agenda. This would happen only with the Fourth World Congress of 1922, which also saw Black delegates present for the first time, among them the Surinam-born Otto Huiswoud (1893–1961) and the Jamaica-born and internationally renowned poet Claude McKay (1889–1948). There were no African American representatives – indeed no Black representatives at all – at the Second World Congress of 1920. It was, in fact, the American John ('Jack') Reed, representing the American party on the ECCI, who stepped into the breach, writing Lenin a note asking whether the moment had not come to say something about the question of America's Black community. In his own speech, he underlined their importance for the class struggle. He understood the 'Negro question' first and foremost as governed by the economic, that is, as a class question. In his view, Black people were especially exploited proletarians and racism a particular form of class oppression. He therefore identified the

---

4 Edward Hallet Carr, *The Bolshevik Revolution, 1917–1923*, vol. 3, Harmondsworth, UK: Penguin Books, 1977, 253–62; Manabendra Nath Roy, *Memoirs*, Delhi: Ajanta Publications, 1984 [1964], 365.

oppression of Black people as oppression by capitalism and imperialism – both equally the enemies of white proletarians.[5] The notion of linking Black peoples' global struggle for freedom with the global struggle of all oppressed peoples against colonialism and capitalism was later expanded upon by the theses of the Fourth World Congress – theses to which the American delegate 'Sasha' – Rose Pastor Stokes (1879–1933, born Rose Harriet Wieslander in a shtetl of the Russian Empire) – had contributed. These postulated an intercontinental dimension to the Black liberation struggle – a viewpoint originating from Black revolutionaries from the West Indies rather than the Comintern. They also took into account the particular discrimination experienced by the Black community, calling – in the sixth and final section – for political and social equality for Blacks.[6]

The discussion in 1920 chiefly focussed on Asia, however, this being due, first and foremost, to the intervention of M. N. Roy. He was probably the most prominent figure among the delegates from 'colonially oppressed nations', and the one most closely watched by the British intelligence services.[7] According to Hilde Kramer, he was also one of the

---

5 John Riddell, ed., *Workers of the World and Oppressed Peoples, Unite! Proceedings and Documents of the Second Congress, 1920*, vol. 1, New York: Pathfinder, 1991, 224–8. Reed spoke in similar vein at the Baku Congress. See the Congress transcript in Riddell, *To See the Dawn*, 149–54.

6 Linking the categories of class and race, and likewise those of class and gender, continued to create problems for the Comintern. At the Fourth World Congress, Clara Zetkin (discussing women's rights) and Huiswoud (discussing the 'Negro question') brought in the 'psychological' aspect, i.e. the idea that racism and the subordination of women were forms of oppression independent of capitalism and imperialism that would not simply disappear if those were overcome. The years that followed, however, did not see the Comintern formulate a theory that took these forms of discrimination into account. See John Riddell, ed., *Toward the United Front: Proceedings of the Fourth Congress of the Communist International, 1922*, Leiden: Brill, 2011, 800–7, and more particularly 801 and also 839. For a concise critical presentation of the 'Negro question' in the Comintern through to 1928, see Stephan Scheuzger, *Der Andere in der ideologischen Vorstellungskraft: Die Linke und die indigene Frage in Mexiko*, Frankfurt a. M.: Vervuert Verlag, 2009, 89–92. In the 1930s, however, some women Communists did adumbrate the beginnings of an intersectional theory: Brigitte Studer, *Von der 'Neuen Frau' zur Neuen Frauenbewegung: Emanzipationskonzepte auf Zeitreise*, Vortragsreihe des Zentrums für Zeithistorische Forschung Potsdam, des Centre Marc Bloch und der Bundesstiftung zur Aufarbeitung der SED-Diktatur, zeitgeschichte-digital.de/.

7 Sir David Petrie, who took over as director of the Indian government's Intelligence Bureau in 1924, published a striking study of Communism in India in 1927, focussing

most attractive of revolutionaries: she described him as 'one of the most impressive manifestations of the masculine' she had ever encountered. 'In summer he frequently went barefoot, in sandals, and wore short-sleeved shirts, allowing the beauty of his hands and feet to be admired.' Not that she was in love with him, as such – for her it was simply 'an aesthetic pleasure to contemplate him'.[8] Like most anticolonial revolutionaries at the time, he lived in exile. Born Narendra Nath Bhattacharya, this son of a large, impoverished Brahmin family from near Kolkata had joined the Swadeshi Indian liberation movement, a clandestine organization that adopted violence as a revolutionary method, as Roy himself recorded in his handwritten autobiography for the Comintern.[9] He had been arrested for the first time at the age of twenty, and had left India in 1915, on the run from the British police and in search of weapons. This quest took him to Indonesia, Korea, Vietnam, the Philippines, China and Japan, from where, in 1916, he took a boat to California. In Palo Alto, he met his future wife, Evelyn Trent, at Stanford University. He also came into contact with pacifist and anti-imperialist circles and with Indian nationalist adherents of the Ghadar Party. Early in 1917, he and Evelyn moved to New York, joining the lively Indian diaspora and anti-colonial scene of the US East Coast. The pair fled the USA when that country entered the war, Roy fearing arrest in connection with the Hindu-German Conspiracy case the American authorities brought against Indian nationalists, under pressure from Britain. In Mexico City, with the Russian Mikhail Borodin – earlier, under the alias Brantwein, the Comintern's emissary in the United States – he founded the Mexican Communist Party (a rival, in fact, to a previously existing Communist party). It was this Mexican party that Roy subsequently represented at the Comintern congress.

Roy had been asked by Lenin to draw up a supplement to his own draft theses. The congress's National and Colonial Commission

---

principally on Roy but also attending closely to Evelyn Roy's activities: Sir David Petrie, *Communism in India, 1924–1927,* ed. Mahadevaprasad Saha, Calcutta: Editions Indian, 1958 [1927]. Many biographies of Roy use this as a source, even though the details are not always substantiated.

8 Hilde Kramer, *Rebellin in München, Moskau und Berlin: Autobiographisches Fragment 1900–1924*, ed. Egon Günther and Thies Marsen, Berlin: BasisDruck, 2011, 85–8.

9 Personal file of Manabendra Nath Roy, handwritten curriculum vitae in English, RGASPI, 495/213/18.

– whose secretary was Henk Sneevliet ('Maring'), from the Netherlands – therefore had two sets of theses to consider. (Like Roy, Sneevliet was first and foremost an anticolonial activist, attending the congress as the representative of the Indonesian party, which he had founded.) In his theses, Roy highlighted the importance, for the future of world revolution, of national revolutionary uprisings in Asia. After all, he argued, it was only thanks to the profits from its colonies that British capitalism had been able to sustain itself during the First World War. And it was only thanks to the colossal revenues flowing into the metropolis from the colonies that British workers, and the labour aristocracy in particular, enjoyed an elevated standard of living. This took the edge off class conflicts and pacified the workers, at the cost, however, of 'enslaving the hundreds of millions of inhabitants of Asia and Africa'.[10]

The difference between Roy's and Lenin's draft theses did not lie in this understanding of imperialism. On the contrary, Roy's theses were very close to Lenin's theory of imperialism of 1916.[11] Yet, although explicitly described as not a counterproposal to Lenin's, they did represent a significant tactical adjustment, evidenced in the two authors' divergent attitudes to collaboration with local bourgeois-nationalist forces. While Lenin was prepared, in some instances, to accept the leadership of radical nationalist elements in the struggle against colonizers and European imperialism, Roy categorically rejected any alliance between Communist movements and national bourgeoisies. According to Roy, the latter were not to be trusted and would betray the revolution. In the end, the National and Colonial Commission agreed on a compromise: Lenin's original formulation regarding the possibility of collaboration with 'bourgeois-democratic' forces was retained, while collaboration with 'national-revolutionary' forces was encouraged. The forms such collaboration might take remained open, however, as did the role to be accorded to the narrow but politically aware class of urban workers in relation to the significantly more numerous but politically less articulate peasantry.[12]

---

10 Cited in Riddell, *Workers of the World*, vol. 1, 219.

11 Lenin's *Imperialism, the Highest Stage of Capitalism* was written in Zurich in 1916 and published in 1917.

12 On the editing of M. N. Roy's draft theses on the national and colonial questions, see Riddell, *Workers of the World*, vol. 2, 846–55.

More recent research from a postcolonial perspective has highlighted another, strategic dimension to the debate.[13] Roy, who had found himself exasperated by the nationalist insularity of the 'average proletarian revolutionary' when he spent time in Berlin on his way to the Congress,[14] was arguing for the possibility of shifting the revolutionary subject from Europe to Asia. The revolutionary potential of the colonial world was quite as great, he asserted. And he went further still, arguing that anticolonial revolution in Asia was a precondition for world socialism. Yet for most members of the National and Colonial Commission, such questioning of the privileged role of the European working class was a step too far, and they therefore amended the relevant passages in the final version of the theses.[15] Only after 1921/22 – at the Third and Fourth World Congresses of the Comintern – were national liberation movements declared to be as important for socialism as was the class struggle in Europe.[16]

The Baku Congress, which took place after the Second World Congress, from 1 to 8 September 1920, was a first step towards forming an alliance with the world's national and colonial liberation movements, signalling the Comintern's new, globalizing aspirations.

Force of Arms, Force of Propaganda: Exporting the Revolution

Baku had not been chosen by chance. The region was home to substantial oil reserves – a resource urgently needed by the young Soviet Russia. (Though the oil well installations were in a lamentable state, according to Alfred Rosmer, the city itself was very picturesque.[17]) In April that year, the Red Army had driven the foreign troops out of Azerbaijan and

---

13 Robert J. C. Young, *Postcolonialism: An Historical Introduction*, Oxford: Blackwell, 2001, 131–2.

14 Roy, *Memoirs*, 306.

15 Riddell, *Workers of the World*, vol. 2, 848.

16 Minkah Makalani, 'Internationalizing the Third International: The African Blood Brotherhood, Asian Radicals and Race, 1919–1922', *Journal of African American History* 96:2, 2011, 151–78. See the transcripts in John Riddell, ed., *To the Masses: Proceedings of the Third Congress of Communist International, 1921*, Leiden: Brill, 2015, and Riddell, *Toward the United Front*.

17 Alfred Rosmer, *Moscow Under Lenin*, trans. Ian A. Birchall, New York: Monthly Review Press, 1982, 88.

declared the Caucasian city the capital of the Azerbaijan Soviet Socialist Republic. It was the only city in the region to have a significant working class with revolutionary experience, while it also offered a gateway to Islam and to the 'East' in the wider sense, standing as it did between the Middle East and Central Asia, or, as Rosmer put it more simplistically, 'on the border between Europe and Asia'.[18] The city's proximity to the disintegrating Ottoman Empire was a factor as well. In the years immediately following the First World War the globe was being reconfigured as the colonial powers hastened to divide up the spoils, and Soviet Russia had every interest in being close to the action.[19]

The decision to call this congress 'of the peoples' was taken by the Council of People's Commissars in June 1920 and confirmed at an ECCI meeting in July.[20] The summons was initially addressed to the

---

18 Rosmer, *Moscow*, 86.

19 On the Sovietization of Central Asia, see the early research of Hélène Carrère D'Encausse, *Islam and the Russian Empire: Reform and Revolution in Central Asia*, Berkeley: University of California Press, 1988; Marco Buttino, *La rivoluzione capovolta: L'Asia centrale tra il crollo dell'impero zarista e la formazione dell'URSS*, Naples: L'Ancora del Mediterraneo, 2003; and more recently Adeeb Khalid, 'Communism on the Frontier: The Sovietization of Central Asia and Mongolia', in Silvio Pons and Stephen A. Smith, eds, *The Cambridge History of Communism*, vol. 1, *World Revolution and Socialism in One Country 1917–1941*, Cambridge: Cambridge University Press, 2017, 616–36. Adeeb Khalid disagrees with interpretations that see the Soviet Union as merely the continuation of the Russian Empire dressed up in ideological guise, emphasizing, as the key distinction, the idea of a common Soviet citizenship as opposed to legal differentiation along ethnic lines. See Adeeb Khalid, 'The Soviet Union as an Imperial Formation: A View from Central Asia', in Ann Laura Stoler, Carole McGranahan and Peter C. Perdue, eds, *Imperial Formations*, Santa Fe, NM: School for Advanced Research Press, 2007, 113–39.

20 On the Baku Congress: one of the first mentions of it in the West, discussed in terms of 'Islamic backwardness', comes from the British writer H. G. Wells, in *Russia in the Shadows*, London: Hodder & Stoughton, 1920. Wells had not been in Baku himself, but had seen a film about it in Moscow. Particularly interesting is Stephen White, 'Communism and the East: The Baku Congress, 1920', *Slavic Review* 33:3, 1974, 492–514. See also Edith Ybert-Chabrier, *Le premier congrès des peuples de l'Orient, Bakou (1er–8 septembre 1920)*, Paris: EHESS, 1984; Edith Chabrier, 'Les délégués au Premier Congrès des Peuples d'Orient, Bakou (1er au 8 septembre 1920)', *Cahiers du monde russe et soviétique* 2:1, 1985, 21–42; Somaz Rustamova-Tohidi, 'The First Congress of the Peoples of the East: Aims, Tasks, Results', in Mikhail Narinsky and Jürgen Rojahn, eds, *Centre and Periphery: The History of the Comintern in the Light of New Documents*, Amsterdam: Internationaal Instituut voor Sociale Geschiedenis, 1996, 74–80; Alp Yenen, 'The Other Jihad: Enver Pasha, Bolsheviks, and Politics of Anticolonial Muslim Nationalism During the Baku Congress 1920', in T. G.

'Enslaved Popular Masses of Persia, Armenia and Turkey' but was soon thereafter expanded to include the more distant nations of India and China. Yet even as national liberation movements were emerging in Turkey, Persia ('Iran' from 1935 onward) and China, the Bolsheviks were in the process of abandoning the 'right of national self-determination' that had been one of their key slogans, as they set about reintegrating the former tsarist colonies of Central Asia.[21] More than 3,000 delegates were expected in Baku; some 2,000 arrived, representing thirty-seven nationalities and ethnic groups. The fifty-five women attending were heavily outnumbered by the men.[22] The majority of delegates came from the Caucasus and Central Asia, Turkey, Persia and the Arab world. India was represented by just fourteen people; China by eight. This despite the efforts of the organizing committee, directed chiefly by Elena Stasova (1873–1966) and Grigory Ordzhonikidze (1888–1937), both Old Bolsheviks and subsequently close associates of Stalin. The tough and demanding Stasova, 'Comrade Absolute', had been a party member since 1898 and had taken over as secretary of the Central Committee in 1917, a role from which she was ousted in the spring of 1920. In July, she was instead appointed secretary of the Caucasian Bureau of the Russian Communist Party. Ordzhonikidze, who took part in the defeat of Denikin's White Army during the civil war, had been head of the Caucasian Bureau since 1920.

The delegations were diverse in make-up, a mix of Communists, anarchists and radical nationalists of all stripes.[23] The majority came from Soviet territories, sent by individual regions. Pan-Islamic

---

Fraser, ed., *The First World War and Its Aftermath: The Shaping of the Middle East*, London: Gingko Library Press, 2015, 273–93. From the Soviet perspective, see Grigorii Z. Sorkin, *Pervyi s"ezd narodov Vostoka* [The First Congress of the Peoples of the East], Moscow: Nauka, 1961.

21 On the complex inter-ethnic relations of Central Asia and the conflicts between Russian settlement policy, national independence movements and local aspirations to modernization, see Buttino, *La rivoluzione capovolta*, and Khalid, 'Communism on the Frontier'.

22 The numbers vary with the source: Sorkin, *Pervyi s"ezd*, 20–1, states that there were 2,050 names on the attendance lists, but the shorthand record lists only 1,891: Riddell, *To See the Dawn*, 22 and 204–7; Chabrier, 'Les délégués'.

23 Michael Weiner, 'Comintern in East Asia, 1919–39', in Kevin McDermott and Jeremy Agnew, eds, *The Comintern: A History of International Communism from Lenin to Stalin*, London: Palgrave, 1996, 158–90, at 162.

delegations were especially well represented. At a time when the colonial powers were dividing up the Middle East between them, the Bolsheviks sought to make use of the upsurge of anticolonial Islamic nationalism to strengthen their own hand. An invitation had even been extended to Enver Pasha, who was agitating for a new caliphate. In the end, he was not given an opportunity to address the Congress, but he clearly enjoyed high levels of respect among the Muslim delegates. Many of the delegates had rather flimsy credentials as activists – just over half were party members, and many of those were members in name only. After all, as Persian delegate Mir Ja'far Javadzadeh (1892–1947) observed at the Third World Congress, in the East, in Turkey or Persia, any nationalistic leader could establish a Communist party in order to expand their own power base. And, in this party, they would very quickly be appointed president of the Central Committee.[24] In contrast to this somewhat casual approach to the invitation of delegates, the Comintern had sent its most senior officers, chairman Grigory Zinoviev, secretary Karl Radek, and committee member Béla Kun (1886–1938), who had just returned from Germany. They were accompanied by the Frenchman Alfred Rosmer, the American John Reed, Jan 'Jansen' from the Netherlands (1890–1942, real name Jan Proost) and Tom Quelch (1886–1954) from Britain, all four of them as anticolonial representatives of the colonial empires. Their journey in a specially chartered train – which stopped in Rostov and several cities of the Caucasus – took five days. The delegates saw a land devastated by civil war, a destruction they blamed on the White forces alone. At the same time, they wanted to make the most of this exceptional opportunity. John Reed, in particular, was clearly able to enjoy the journey 'the way a young American can', as Rosmer put it. Every time they stopped, he reports, Reed rushed out of the train and bought up great armfuls of the fruit-sellers' wares. And when they stopped beside the Caspian, he would run down to the water and dive in.[25] Once arrived in the city of Baku, the Western delegates found the hot, humid climate oppressive. For those who had become 'Muscovites' – as Rosmer described himself and the other travellers – the heat was

---

24 Riddell, *To the Masses*, 323.
25 Rosmer, *Moscow*, 87.

clearly difficult to cope with.[26] Not that this prevented Reed from buying silk fabrics during the breaks – including 'some unique items', as he informed his comrade Rosmer, encouraging him to do likewise. When Rosmer replied that he did not have the money, Reed apparently suggested that he ask Zinoviev for the roubles he ought to be entitled to as a member of the Executive Committee.[27]

M. N. Roy had refused to take part in 'Zinoviev's circus'. As he saw it, there were as yet no truly revolutionary organizations in the East, and so the Congress could be no more than an exercise in agitation. Of Reed he remarked that the idea had appealed to his poetic temperament and lively imagination.[28] Roy, on the other hand, preferred to travel direct to Tashkent. In that Muslim-majority city, a centre of Islamic culture that was under the Red Army's control, the Comintern had decided to establish a Central Asian Bureau under the joint leadership of Roy and two Russians, Georgi Safarov (1891–1942) and Grigory Sokolnikov (1886–1938). (A second office was also opened at Irkutsk in Siberia – with a subsidiary outpost in Vladivostok – under the leadership of Boris Shumyatsky [1886–1938], an Old Bolshevik and former railway worker who had lived in exile in China and Argentina for a number of years. In 1921, it briefly became the nerve centre of the newly established telegraphic connection between Moscow and Shanghai.[29])

While the overarching objective of the Baku Congress was the opening of a broad anti-British front in the East, the goal of the revolutionary centre established in Tashkent was more immediate: as historian Juri Tichonow has it, it was to gain access to British India via the 'Afghan corridor'. Revolution was to be brought to India by military means, with an armed expedition across the country's border with Afghanistan, an area where the British colonial power was at its most

---

26 Ibid., 87.
27 Ibid., 88.
28 Roy, *Memoirs*, 391–2.
29 Bernhard H. Bayerlein, 'Das neue Babylon: Strukturen und Netzwerke der Kommunistischen Internationale und ihre Klassifizierung', *Jahrbuch für Historische Kommunismusforschung*, 2004, 181–270, at 228; Jérémie Tamiatto, 'Des révolutionnaires entre deux mondes: Trajectoires croisées de Grigori Voitinsky et Henk Sneevliet en Chine (1920–1923)', *Monde(s): histoire, espaces, relations* 10, 2016, 51–68, at 63–4; Branko Lazitch and Milorad M. Drachkovitch, *Lenin and the Comintern*, vol. 1, Stanford, CA: Hoover Institution Press, 1972, 415.

vulnerable.[30] In Tashkent, Roy drew on politicized young Muslims who had left British India to assemble the revolutionary nucleus of an Indian CP. His plan was to form a liberation army whose arrival would spark armed rebellion across India. 'I had no intention of leaving Moscow without being amply provided with the sinews of war – material to make a revolution. I had failed in a similar attempt in the Far East. Then the Germans duped us. This time, I wanted to succeed. The Russian Bolsheviks were reliable allies.'[31] He set off from Moscow, accompanied by a Red Army detachment, with two trainloads – heavily guarded throughout the seven-day journey – of arms, munitions, state-of-the-art field equipment, even dismantled aircraft, as well as gold and cash in various currencies. He took with him, too, a letter from the ECCI, written in French, signed by Bukharin, then deputy chair of the ECCI presidium, and his secretary Mikhail Kobetsky (1881–1937), and authenticated with the Comintern stamp, stating that he had been sent to Tashkent 'pour mener l'action en Orient' (to lead the campaign in the East). The document required all Soviet and Party organizations and all civilian and military institutions to offer Roy every assistance.[32]

Living conditions in Tashkent were spartan and not without danger. During these years of War Communism, the city and the surrounding region were convulsed by intense political conflict, with violent confrontations between Russian workers and soldiers, the local Soviet and representatives of Moscow on the one hand and the local Muslim population on the other. It was a conflict between city and countryside: food supplies were very scarce and rations unequally distributed; brigades sent out to requisition grain turned the starving peasants against the regime; and cotton production, the basis of the region's wealth, had more or less ground to a halt. The region was still under threat from Basmachi insurgents and the Party's authority was weak. Emissaries from Moscow were unable to restore order, prompting the Central Executive Committee to send in a top-level team of around a hundred

---

30 Juri Tichonow, 'Die Komintern und der 'afghanische Korridor' 1919–1943', in Michael Buckmiller and Klaus Meschkat, eds, *Biographisches Handbuch zur Geschichte der Kommunistischen Internationale: Ein deutsch-russisches Forschungsprojekt*, Berlin: Akademie Verlag, 2007, 310–28. See also Roy, *Memoirs*, 390–476.

31 Roy, *Memoirs*, 395.

32 'Certificat', Moscow, September 1920, RGASPI 495/213/18.

people, called the Turk Commission, at the end of November 1919, yet even this did not bring about the stability they were seeking to achieve.[33] The climate was brutally hot in summer, bitterly cold in winter. As Roy later recounted, it snowed soon after he arrived in the city (accompanied by his wife – a fact he does not mention). Almost all the houses were pretty much uninhabitable. Roy and his team were accommodated in a two-storey building on the main street, opposite the central park. The electricity lines had been destroyed. In place of furniture there were piles of dust-covered Persian carpets, which they used as beds. 'The electric connection was restored; but the burst water-pipes could not be replaced by new ones. So washing, not to mention bathing, remained a problem. Water drawn from the well could not be heated.'[34] The train service was intermittent and supplies therefore unreliable and scarce, the meagre store of fuel being reserved for military and official vehicles.

> Fuel was the scarcest commodity . . . The kitchen fire of the big city was fed with small rations of the tough gnarled roots of shrubs which grew on the surrounding steppes. We were privileged to receive a special ration which was big enough to keep the kitchen fire burning for longer hours than needed to cook two meals a day . . . Except when in bed, warmed with piles of thick woollen carpets, all the members of my personal staff congregated in the basement to sit around the kitchen stove. Perhaps for the sake of dignity, I refused to shift my office to the kitchen; but the brave resolution gave way as the winter advanced and temperature inside the house fell below the freezing point.[35]

Roy describes the food, deficient in both quantity and quality, in minute detail. Their ration consisted of black bread, rice, mutton, apple tea and grapes. 'The *pièce de resistance* of each meal was rice or *kasha* (a dark brown coarse grain) cooked in rancid mutton fat with some lumps of meat. Brightened up with tiny bits of carrots, the evil smelling and ugly

---

33 See Jeff Sahadeo, *Russian Colonial Society in Tashkent, 1865–1923*, Bloomington: Indiana University Press, 2010 [2007].
34 Roy, *Memoirs*, 431.
35 Ibid., 431–2.

looking thing was called 'pilaf'.³⁶ Only grapes were available in abundance. 'On the whole', he recalled, 'it was a life full of hardships, but also of great promise.'³⁷

Meetings of the Comintern's Central Asian, or Turkestan, Bureau took place once a week, attended by Roy, together with Sokolnikov and Safarov. The bureau was headquartered in the former Russian Imperial Bank, an elegant red stone building. According to Roy's memoirs, the role of leader fell to him: 'The other two members of the Bureau having additional responsibilities of more exacting nature, the charge of directing its activities virtually devolved upon me, although I had declined to assume it formally as the chairman.'³⁸ The task of making contact with revolutionary elements in the surrounding countries and igniting revolutionary movements proved difficult.³⁹

Roy's plan was to arm the 'revolutionary groups' in the Pashtun tribal region on the Indian–Afghan border, place himself at their head, and invade the Punjab province of British India from Afghanistan. The Soviet government and the Comintern leadership agreed to the scheme – on Trotsky's orders, 25,000 guns were sent to Turkestan for the use of Indian insurgents.⁴⁰ As part of the plan, Roy set up a school to train Indian revolutionaries in military command, which likely attracted more than a hundred volunteers. They came from among the Muslims from British India who had emigrated to Afghanistan as part of the Hijrat movement, and then come to Tashkent in response to the Bolsheviks' appeal to oppressed and colonized peoples. They were instructed in political doctrine, drilled, trained in the use of machine guns and artillery, and even taught to fly.⁴¹ In Tashkent, too, on 17 October 1920, Roy, together with his wife Evelyn and a small group of Indian émigrés, founded the Communist Party of India. The founding document bore seven signatures. Two of the signatories were women: Santi Devi (Evelyn Trent Roy) and Rosa Fitingov, originally from Russia. The latter, a party member since 1918 and employed in Lenin's private

---

36 Ibid., 432.
37 Ibid., 432.
38 Ibid., 433.
39 Ibid., 433–4.
40 Tichonow, 'Die Komintern', 312.
41 Hubert Evans, 'Indian Revolutionary Organizations in Central Asia', *Central Asian Review* 16:4, 1968, 322–7, at 325.

office, was working for Roy as a translator. In 1920, she had met and married Abani Mukherji from Bengal. Mukherji, who had taken part in the Second World Congress as a non-party-affiliated delegate and later represented Indian revolutionaries in Baku, was also a signatory.[42] Another, Muhammad Shafiq (1900–?), who later used the pseudonym 'Raza' at the Comintern's Fifth World Congress, was appointed secretary. Like others, he had first migrated to Kabul, but had been inspired by Bolshevik propaganda to make his way to Tashkent.[43] Roy had met him at the Second World Congress in Moscow, where the two had got on well.[44]

Roy returned to Moscow as early as January 1921, while Mukherji remained in Tashkent until the military school closed in May. Preparations for the Third Comintern Congress, scheduled to take place from 22 June to 12 July 1921, were in full swing. Roy attended as the emissary of the Indian Communist Party, tasked with securing recognition as a section of the Comintern of the party he had helped found in Tashkent.[45] For the journey to Moscow, the secretary of the Turk Bureau provided him with the written authorization necessary to send official coded telegrams. The document also required that 'party, military, civilian and other organisations and the railway administration lend Comrade Roy their full support throughout his journey'.[46]

Yet Roy's return to Moscow was motivated by more than the upcoming Congress. While he had been in Central Asia, contact had been made between Chatto and the Comintern, via the Soviet foreign ministry. Following this, the Indian Revolutionary Committee from Berlin had come to Moscow – sending a seven-strong delegation that included

---

42 In the 1930s, Mukherji devoted himself exclusively to his academic work as an Indologist at the Oriental Institute of the USSR Academy of Sciences. He was arrested in June 1937 and shot for supposedly being a member of the 'Moscow Centre'.

43 Maia Ramnath, *Haj to Utopia: How the Ghadar Movement Charted Global Radicalism and Attempted to Overthrow the British Empire*, Berkeley: University of California Press, 2011, 210.

44 M. Naeem Qureshi, 'From Pan-Islamism to Communism: The Russian Connection of the Indian *Muhajirin*, 1920–1924', *Journal of South Asian and Middle Eastern Studies* 32:1, 2008, 30–61, at 45; Sibnarayan Ray, *In Freedom's Quest: A Study of the Life and Works of M. N. Roy, 1887–1954*, vol. 1, Kolkata: Minerva, 1998, 106–7.

45 Mandate to M. N. Roy 'as delegate to the Third Congress of the Communist International of the Indian Communist Party', Tashkent, issued by party secretary Muhammad Shafiq, n.d., RGASPI 495/213/18.

46 Certificate, Russian, RGASPI 495/213/18.

Chatto's partner, the American (and future writer) Agnes Smedley (1892–1950) – to discuss what financial and operational support the Comintern might be able to offer, which might well have involved the IRC's official recognition as the Comintern's Indian section. For Roy, this was a most alarming prospect, for the Comintern allowed only one section per country. And, for him personally, this would also mean a weakening, if not indeed the loss, of his position as the Comintern's great Indian specialist. In the event, negotiations with Chatto's group broke down after four months – an outcome for which Roy bore no responsibility, but which came as something of a relief to him, nonetheless.[47]

There was another reason as well for Roy's departure from Tashkent. His mission to establish a revolutionary base in Afghanistan had failed. The notion that India might be revolutionized by a corps of hastily trained military cadre had proved illusory. For the thirty-three-year-old Roy, this also meant abandoning the idea that revolution was a matter of getting hold of weapons. The lesson he drew from the experience, as he records in his memoirs, was that the revolution needed not soldiers but politically aware revolutionaries in the form of trained cadre: 'The army of revolution should be first trained politically.'[48] The key reason for the debacle, however, lay elsewhere, in the Soviet government's efforts to normalize relations with London. As Soviet foreign minister Chicherin told the *New York Times*, Soviet Russia had only pursued a policy of world revolution in the early months, in the context of war; now that time had passed. Comintern policy and his country's policy, he declared, were no longer identical.[49] In order to secure a trade deal with Great Britain in March 1921, the Soviets had had to agree to the cessation of Comintern activity against British India and the dissolution of the Tashkent Bureau – a volte-face that local actors said 'dealt a fatal blow' to their work.[50] As a result, the Comintern shifted its activity further

---

47 Nirode K. Barooah, *Chatto: The Life and Times of an Indian Anti-imperialist in Europe*, New Delhi: Oxford University Press, 2004, 157–77. Cf. Roy, *Memoirs*, 477–85.

48 Roy, *Memoirs*, 529.

49 Quoted in Paul Dukes, *The USA in the Making of the USSR: The Washington Conference 1921–22 and 'Uninvited Russia'*, London: RoutledgeCurzon, 2004, 62.

50 The words of two members of the Baku council, quoted in Stephen White, 'Colonial Revolution and the Communist International, 1919–1924', *Science and Society* 40:2, 1976, 173–93, at 177.

east. The following year, in early 1922, it organized the First Congress of the Toilers of the Far East; more cautiously, this took the form of a closed event held in Moscow and Petrograd. Discussions focussed on Mongolia, China and Korea, the countries from which the majority of the 150 delegates came (7 of them women). By contrast, there were just 2 delegates from India, Roy and Abani Mukherji – and they were both living in Soviet Russia at the time. A second Far Eastern congress was never held.

Modernity *and* Tradition?

With the Baku Congress, the Bolsheviks were looking to mobilize Great Britain's enemies in the Middle East and Central Asia – a fact that had by no means escaped the British authorities. Seeking to hinder the participation of Turkish and Persian delegates, Britain deployed not only naval forces but an aircraft whose bombs killed two Persian delegates and wounded several others. The anti-imperialist thrust of the event was given dramatic and striking expression at the very start, with a show trial staged on Freedom Square featuring formally dressed and highly decorated effigies of Lloyd George, Alexandre Millerand and Woodrow Wilson. When these were eventually set alight, bundles of British pound notes tumbled from their pockets as they burned. Another public event was the solemn interment of the twenty-six people's commissars of the first regional Soviet, captured and executed by the British during the war. The new Soviet government also organized gatherings intended to win over the local population, no easy undertaking as the frequently insensitive, even brutal, behaviour of the representatives of Bolshevik power struck the local population as 'colonial', as Taspolad Narbutabekov (?–1938) put it in his speech to the Congress.[51]

Hardly had they arrived in Baku than the Western delegates were called to make their way to the city theatre, where they were awaited by a large and colourful crowd dressed in 'all the costumes of the East'. Speeches had to be translated into multiple languages and were

---

51 Riddell, *To See the Dawn*, 116–23, in particular 119. See also Carrère D'Encausse, *Islam*, 165–6; Rustamova-Tohidi, 'The First Congress', 77.

repeatedly interrupted by frenetic applause. John Reed, who could speak a certain amount of Russian, was particularly well received when he asked the audience how they thought 'Baku' was pronounced in English, and answered: 'It's pronounced "oil"!'[52]

The diverse nations and ethnicities – and so languages – represented at the Baku Congress posed a dual problem of translation for the organizers. First, speeches were given in Russian, Turkish, Farsi, Turkmen, Chechen, Uzbek and Komi, but it was impossible to provide translations into all these languages. Official translations were thus limited to Russian, Azeri Turkish and Farsi, excluding many participants from the debates. Second, it very soon became apparent that communication across cultural differences was a challenge. Certainly, the Congress opened up the possibility of being a Bolshevik and a Muslim at the same time. Zinoviev, for example, drew on the language of Islam in calling for a 'holy war' against British imperialism, against the 'robbers and oppressors'.[53] In the long run, though, conflicts inevitably arose between the secular worldview of the Communists on the one hand, and the religious traditions and customs and the national and cultural institutions of the Muslim peoples on the other. In their call to the Congress, the Bolsheviks had promised to uphold cultural traditions, though they now expected them to be abandoned in important respects. This contradiction, even at this point, did not escape the British secret service: 'Many violent speeches were made, but the general effect was in many cases spoiled by large numbers of the Moslem representatives going outside to say their prayers.'[54] The paths of Pan-Islamism and Bolshevism would soon diverge.[55]

Such tensions were especially apparent in connection with the issue of women's rights. This despite the fact that a Muslim women's movement had begun to emerge in certain areas of the Islamic world and the existence of movement for Islamic reform that included the

---

52 Rosmer, *Moscow*, 87, translation of the first direct quote modified.
53 Riddell, *To See the Dawn*, 78.
54 Quoted in White, 'Colonial Revolution', 181.
55 Tichonow, 'Die Komintern und der "afghanische Korridor"', 310–28; Yenen, 'The Other Jihad'. Especially critical of the Communists' 'pan-Islamic flirtations' is Mohammed Nuri El-Amin, 'The Role of International Communism in the Muslim World and in Egypt and the Sudan', *British Journal of Middle Eastern Studies* 23:1, 1996, 29–53, at 39.

emancipation of women as an integral element of its modernizing programme.⁵⁶ These were both essentially urban phenomena, however, involving élites and intellectuals. For the Comintern, on the other hand, women's emancipation was an uncontested core principle, still actively promoted at this time.⁵⁷

In Baku, however, it was only on being pressured by the women present that Zinoviev proposed that three women be elected to the congress presidium and that two persons of each sex be chosen to take the chair. Two women also addressed the plenary meeting. The Turkish feminist Naciye Hanim warned delegates that there would be no liberation but only ruin for their countries if they, the 'men of the East' continued in their indifference to women's fate. She presented a five-point programme: equal rights, the creation of local women's rights committees, equal access to education and to state institutions, the unconditional abolition of polygamy, and full equality of rights in marriage. According to the minutes, she was met with tumultuous applause. She was followed by Bibinur from Turkestan (today's Kazakhstan), who spoke in Turkic and lamented the reclusive existence of Muslim women, asserting that 'we, the women of the East, are exploited ten times worse than the men'.⁵⁸ Both women insisted in their speeches on the autonomy of the struggle for women's rights. In recognizing these rights, Communism had found a new ally in feminism. In Hanim's words: 'In recognizing that we have equal rights, the Communists have reached out their hands to us, and we women will prove their most loyal comrades.'⁵⁹

However, the immediate political results of the Baku Congress fell far short of what had been hoped, a stable alliance with the anti-British forces of the Islamic world failing to materialize. In many cases, it was the Bolsheviks' practices of political organization rather than their

---

56 Adeeb Khalid, *The Politics of Muslim Cultural Reform: Jadidism in Central Asia*, Berkeley: University of California Press, 1998.

57 Adrienne Edgar points to the ambivalent and unintended boomerang effects of Bolshevik policy on the emancipation of women in the Muslim republics of Central Asia, in 'Bolshevism, Patriarchy and the Nation: The Soviet "Emancipation" of Muslim Women in Pan-Islamic Perspective', *Slavic Review* 65, 2006, 252–72. On the shortcomings of Communist emancipation policy, see Brigitte Studer, 'Communism and Feminism', *Clio* 41:1, 2015, 139–52.

58 Riddell, *To See the Dawn*, 204–8; her full name is not known.

59 Ibid., 206–7; Young, *Postcolonialism*, 142.

Communist ideology that had appealed to the nationalist leaders of the East. Within a year, a number of the Central Asian Muslim leaders would be lining up on the anti-Bolshevik side. Yet the impact of the congress should not be underestimated; it did after all lay the basis for the integration of new groups with the struggle of the workers' movement. The Comintern had earlier concentrated on the notion of class; with the congress, it took on board the concepts of gender, race and ethnicity, and the interactions between them. By proactively ensuring women a role at the Baku Congress, the Comintern clearly signalled the importance it accorded to the emancipation of Muslim women, and of women in traditional-patriarchal societies in general. In the process, the Comintern also made women the subjects of their own liberation. Referring to the Second International Conference of Communist Women in a speech to the Third World Congress of the Comintern in 1921, Clara Zetkin forcefully pointed out to her comrades the broader significance of that event:

> Comrades, it would perhaps be tempting and seductive for some to view the appearance of delegations from the Near and Far East simply from an aesthetic viewpoint. But the women delegates personified more than the exotic, unusual, and fairy-tale character of the Orient. The conference experienced a powerful historical moment, unforgettable and undying in its significance. For what was the significance of the appearance of women's delegations from the East? It told us that the Eastern peoples have begun to awaken and enter into struggle ... Comrades, the fact that women of the East came to us shows the exceptionally wide-reaching significance of the Third International's revolutionary struggle. It is the first, and until now the only organisation that truly inspires the hopes and the trust of the Eastern peoples. It is the first International to embrace all humankind. The International shall be the human race – the entirety of humanity.[60]

The Baku Congress also for the first time declared the Comintern's solidarity with the 'oppressed peoples' of the world. While addressed to the 'Peoples of the East', it represented more than a turn to Asia, as reflected

---

60 Riddell, *To the Masses*, 783–4.

in the enthusiastic comment of the Jewish autodidact, Bolshevik and Orientalist Mikhail N. Pavlovich (1871–1927), one of the organizers of the event: 'All Communists – Russian, French, British, Italian, and so on – have now become Asians and are resolved to help every revolutionary movement in the East and in Africa.'[61] This broader conception of the struggle also included among the oppressed the peoples of Mexico and the Caribbean who suffered under US domination, as John Reed emphasized in his speech. Zinoviev even went so far as to improve upon the Communist Manifesto with the slogan 'Workers of all lands and oppressed peoples, unite!' The appeal issued by the Congress to the workers of Europe, America and Japan showed, furthermore, that the traditional hierarchical division between East and West was coming undone. The workers of Great Britain, the USA, France, Italy, Japan, Germany and other countries were urged to listen to the representatives of the peoples of the East, who had pledged to rise up and help the workers of the West in their fight, and expected fraternal aid in their own struggle in return.[62]

In concrete terms, it is from this point onward that the Comintern began to allocate institutional resources to the revolutionary struggle in the colonial and so-called semi-colonial nations. The congress set up a Council for Propaganda and Action, which had forty-seven members, of whom two were women. One of these was Khaver Shabanova-Karayeva (1901–1958), just nineteen years old at the time, who, despite her youth, had already undertaken medical training and gained an impressive record of political and military experience. She had joined the Party at the age of seventeen, served in the Red Army, and had since 1920 been organizing revolutionary women in Azerbaijan. Shabanova was imprisoned for a time in 1937, during the Great Terror, but was later readmitted to the Party.[63] The second woman was the experienced and widely travelled Elena Stasova. Based in Baku, the Council for Propaganda and Action was very active from the start. It published the congress transcripts in Farsi, Turkish and Arabic, produced the

---

61 Riddell, *To See the Dawn*, 164–5. On Pavlovich, see Michael Kemper, 'Red Orientalism: Mikhail Pavlovich and Marxist Oriental Studies in Early Soviet Russia', *Die Welt des Islams* 50:3, 2010, 435–76.

62 'Appeal to the Workers of Europe, America, and Japan', in Riddell, *To See the Dawn*, 234–41, here 240.

63 Riddell, *To See the Dawn*, 332.

newspaper *Peoples of the East*, which appeared in both Russian and Turkish, and produced many books and pamphlets. One source gives the figure of 1,270 pieces of literature sent out over a period of just two weeks, 433 in Farsi, 176 in Turkish.[64] During the first ten weeks alone, it recruited 170 political instructors and propaganda coordinators. Finally, a cadre school was established, whose first fifty students completed their training in January 1921.[65] Yet only a year later, both the council and the cadre school in Baku – so far from Moscow – were closed down.[66] This was followed by the closure in Tashkent of both the Central Asian Bureau and Roy's Indian military school. As already discussed, their fate had become inevitable, given wider events.

Daily Life in the Early Days of the Comintern Apparatus

The responsibilities of the Council for Propaganda and Action were in fact transferred to the Comintern's Eastern Bureau in Moscow, whose first leader was Karl Radek. The role later fell to Grigori Voitinsky (1893–1953), who in 1920 had been sent to China as the Comintern's first emissary in that country. In December 1922, following the Fourth World Congress of the Comintern, the Eastern Bureau was officially tasked with coordinating Communist activities in all regions of the world under Western domination – which meant North Africa and the Middle East, South Asia, South-East Asia and Latin America.[67] Those students from Tashkent whom Roy regarded as serious revolutionaries – a minority – would now be trained at the Communist University of the Toilers of the East (KUTV) in Moscow, opened at the end of 1921. Roy understood the name adopted for the institution to be a sign that

---

64 Ibid., 30 and 202–20.

65 It is not known whether there were female students among them. Nor is it known whether the Egyptian students notified to the Comintern in July 1921 by local party leaders Husni al-'Urabi and Joseph Rosenthal were still able to go to Baku or instead went directly to the KUTV in Moscow. Their journey, though, was funded by the ECCI: Rami Ginat, *A History of Egyptian Communism: Jews and Their Compatriots in Quest of Revolution*, Boulder, CO: Lynne Rienner Publishers, 2011, 63 and 73.

66 M. Naeem Qureshi, *Pan-Islam in British Indian Politics: A Study of the Khilafat Movement, 1918–1924*, Leiden: Brill, 1999, 227; Carr, *Bolshevik Revolution*, vol. 3, 269.

67 Serge Wolikow, *L'Internationale communiste: Le Komintern ou le rêve déchu du parti mondial de la révolution*, Ivry-sur-Seine: Les Éditions de l'Atelier, 2010, 36.

his theses on the colonial question were now to be implemented in practice: the cadre for any revolutionary movement in the colonies could only come from among the toiling masses, not the bourgeoisie.[68] M. N. and Evelyn Roy were also among the KUTV's first lecturers, as American journalist Ernestine Evans reported. By then a member of the ECCI, Roy would recall in his memoirs that 'teaching at the Communist University did not require more than a few hours a day'.[69] In this initial phase, the university's educational aspirations seem to have been relatively modest. As Evans noted, the course taught by Evelyn Roy consisted 'in [her] reading aloud in English to eighteen Indian boys chapters from Raymond William Postgate's *Revolutions from 1789–1906*'.[70]

The first Indian students (none of them female) initially stayed at the Hotel Lux, as no other accommodation was available. This hotel turned Comintern hostel would, however, soon become the exclusive residence of the Comintern's staff in Moscow, among them Evelyn and M. N. Roy and other delegates to the Second World Congress. The impressive building stood on one of the main thoroughfares, at 36 Tverskaia Ulitsa (Tverskaya Street) in the city centre. Prior to its confiscation by the fledgling Soviet government, the hotel had belonged to a wealthy bakery entrepreneur named Filippov. He had built above his Moscow shop, at the turn of century, what was for those days a relatively luxurious hotel, with an annexe in the inner courtyard for guests of less importance.[71] This hierarchical distinction perdured: during the Terror, the wives of prisoners had to move into the ill-lit annexe. The bakery still survived, and next to it was a restaurant that would serve as a canteen for revolutionaries from all over the world. The hotel had originally five floors; later, when it became too cramped, another was added. With more than

---

68 Roy, *Memoirs*, 537.
69 Ibid., 552–3.
70 Quoted in Maia Ramnath, *Haj to Utopia: How the Ghadar Movement Charted Global Radicalism and Attempted to Overthrow the British Empire*, Berkeley: University of California Press, 2011, 143; Kumari Jayawardena, *The White Woman's Other Burden: Western Women and South Asia During British Colonial Rule*, New York: Routledge, 1995, 232.
71 Ruth von Mayenburg, *Hotel Lux: Mit Dimitroff, Ernst Fischer, Ho Tschi Minh, Pieck, Rakosi, Slansky, Dr. Sorge, Tito, Togliatti, Tschou En-lai, Ulbricht und Wehner im Moskauer Quartier der Kommunistischen Internationale*, Munich: C. Bertelsmann-Verlag, 1978, 20.

300 rooms, the building had an ornate façade and a recessed entrance flanked by two weighty columns. Alfred Rosmer, who also entered the service of the Comintern following the Baku Congress, as a member of its presidium, and who would spend the next year in Moscow, was distinctly unenthusiastic when his transfer to the hotel was announced. Compared to his rooms at the Delovoi Dvor, he regarded the Lux as noisy and impractical. And he disliked the overall architectural style: 'A huge monster of a building, where everything was in bad taste – the façade, the furniture, the remnants of the "luxury" that had given the hotel its name.'[72]

Not everyone was so critical. Jules Humbert-Droz remembered his time at the Lux with mixed feelings, while Roy recalled the place with great enthusiasm. Humbert-Droz had been appointed one of the ECCI's three permanent secretaries following the Third World Congress, and moved into the Lux in the summer of 1921, along with his wife, Jenny, and daughter, Zou. They would stay there for ten years, during which time the family grew from three to four with the birth of a son. Although Humbert-Droz had initially turned down the role, having eventually accepted it he was brimming with anticipation as he started his work in Moscow: 'A thrilling, hopeful life opened up before me.'[73] One of his first jobs, however, went well beyond the standard brief of a Comintern secretary. Together with Dutch artist Jan Jansen, safely returned from Baku, he was tasked with ridding the Lux of its unwanted guests: delegates who had not wanted to leave after the Congress was over, and the Russian women who had offered themselves as 'wives' and were now living with them in the hotel. Due to the elaborate tenant protections in place, getting rid of them at first proved somewhat problematic. Finally, though, the Swiss-Dutch pair seem to have succeeded in their purge. Now that there was more space in the Lux, Jenny and Jules Humbert-Droz reaped the benefit, moving into two connecting rooms on what was then the top floor of the hotel. From there they had a view over Moscow rooftops and Tverskaya Street itself. Jenny wrote delightedly to her mother, in the Neuchâtel region of the Swiss Jura:

---

72 Rosmer, *Moscow*, 92.
73 Jules Humbert-Droz, *Mémoires*, vol. 1, *Mon évolution du tolstoïsme au communisme, 1891–1921*, Neuchâtel: À La Baconnière, 1969, 436.

> It's much quieter here, better heated, and brighter: a proper little apartment of our own. The front door opens onto a little vestibule . . . which has two doors, one leading to the bathroom with a washbasin and toilet, the other to a large room lit by three windows. The three beds and washstand are hidden behind a screen. The wardrobe, with a mirror, is set slightly at an angle, dividing the room in two, the other part functioning as a dining room, with a large table and a chaise longue. I've set up my electric cooker by the window, on a little table that serves very well. A door from this room leads to the study, which occupies the south-eastern corner of the building. It is furnished with a desk, a little typewriting table, a sofa, two armchairs and a glazed cabinet that does as a bookcase.[74]

These living conditions were positively luxurious compared with those of other residents, and above all, those of most Muscovites. The Humbert-Droz family even had their own cooking facilities, which meant they did not have to use the communal kitchen with its inevitable squabbles.[75] In 1921, when the Lux had just 160 residents, such living conditions were still possible. Yet, as the Comintern apparatus expanded, the hotel filled up and was soon overcrowded. Four years later, more than 600 people lived there.[76]

Bedbugs and rats were, in consequence, a constant plague. According to Jenny Humbert-Droz, the body developed an immunity to bedbug bites over time, but these pests were permanent residents at the Lux. The food, by contrast, got better as time passed. At first, the Comintern employees received a *paëk* (ration) for their evening meal consisting only of black bread, rancid butter and hard-boiled eggs, which were mostly well past their best. The *paëk* contained cigarettes, too, which the Humbert-Droz family traded for milk with peasants on the street.[77] The food only improved in the New Economic Policy (NEP) period, when private businesses were again tolerated.

---

74 Letter published in Jules Humbert-Droz, *Mémoires*, vol. 2, *De Lénine à Staline: Dix ans au service de l'Internationale communiste, 1921–1931*, Neuchâtel: À La Baconnière, 1971, 14–15.

75 For more detail on living conditions in the Lux, see Mayenburg, *Hotel Lux*.

76 Minute of the inter-departmental consultation on improving the work of the apparatus, Moscow, 30 November 1925, RGASPI 495/46/3.

77 Humbert-Droz, *De Lénine*, 14.

Roy recalls that the hotel restaurant at that time offered soup, a main course with meat and a dessert for the evening meal, which was taken late in the afternoon.

Although the Comintern's standard six-hour working day was genuinely revolutionary, the practice of working in the evenings as well quickly became widespread. Both Jules Humbert-Droz and M. N. Roy mention this extension of their hours.[78] Then, at around eleven in the evening, the telephones in the hotel rooms would start ringing as the residents of the Lux invited each other to midnight suppers. Alcohol flowed freely on these occasions, it seems – with the new salaries of the NEP period (around 500 roubles for Comintern functionaries) money was not a problem. In the early years, wage differentials were still low. Before 1934, Soviet society had a maximum salary for party members, the party maximum; this was subsequently abolished, allowing greater financial differentiation.[79] Comintern wages followed the same pattern.[80]

The partying often continued into the early hours, despite complaints from the occasional 'kill-joy', as Roy reports.[81] At times like this, even the privileges enjoyed by members of the ECCI, the Presidium and the Secretariat – being chauffeur-driven, for example, at a time when cars were difficult to get hold of – signified little. All in all: 'Whoever had the opportunity to live in the Hotel Lux in those early days of the Revolution must cherish the memory as one of the richest experiences of his life.'[82] M. N. and Evelyn Trent Roy stayed in Soviet Russia until 1922, then moved to Berlin, where they continued their anticolonial activities under the auspices of the Comintern.[83] The British Colonial Office, which followed Roy's every move, attributed this change of location to the Soviet government's efforts to tone

---

78 Ibid., 18; Roy, *Memoirs*, 558.

79 Sheila Fitzpatrick, *Everyday Stalinism: Ordinary Life in Extraordinary Times; Soviet Russia in the 1930s*, New York: Oxford University Press, 1999, 102.

80 Brigitte Studer, *The Transnational World of the Cominternians*, trans. D. R. Roberts, Basingstoke, UK: Palgrave Macmillan, 2015, 70.

81 Roy, *Memoirs*, 562.

82 Ibid., 563.

83 They both took part in the Third World Congress of the Comintern, 22 June–12 July 1921, as delegates for Mexico and India respectively: Grant M. Adibekov, Elena N. Shakhnazarova and Kirill K. Shirinia, *Organizatsionnaia struktura Kominterna 1919–1943*, Moscow: Rosspen, 1997, 39.

down its Eastern propaganda following the conclusion of the Anglo-Soviet Trade Agreement.[84]

The policy of openness towards Muslim jihad pursued by Zinoviev and Radek in Baku provoked criticism in some quarters. According to Angelica Balabanova, Roy was not alone in not taking the Congress seriously: John Reed, a member of the ECCI, described it as a 'farce'.[85] The presence of Enver Pasha, one of the architects of the Armenian genocide, gave rise to criticisms within European parties. The Swiss Communist Rosa Bloch (1880–1922) complained to Zinoviev, and that same year he had to defend his approach at the German party's unification congress in Halle. In Tours, too, at the founding congress of the PCF, the Bolsheviks were criticized for their 'opportunism' in Baku.[86] There was hardly anything Socialist about a call to 'holy war', observed Louise Bryant, John Reed's widow. Enver Pasha had simply served as a means of exerting pressure on the British to lift their blockade.[87]

Bryant was undoubtedly right to emphasize the Bolsheviks' foreign policy calculation, yet this was only one side of the coin. The anticolonial activists were also to some extent following their own agendas. In the very first years after the Revolution, the Bolsheviks still saw no incompatibility between securing their own borders and extending the revolution across the globe. By 1920, however, the interests of the Soviet government as the representative of a state and the interests of the Communists organized within the Comintern no longer necessarily coincided, and contradictions began to appear. Thereafter, the modernization – or, more accurately, the Sovietization – of Central Asia became once again a primarily intra-Soviet concern. And the export of the revolution beyond the Soviet border proved more difficult than expected. In Turkey, Kemal Pasha's nationalist movement – supported by the Comintern – was victorious, but the Communist Party found itself banned, while the revolutionary movement in Persia was utterly

---

84 Daniel Brückenhaus, *Policing Transnational Protest: Liberal Imperialism and the Surveillance of Anticolonialists in Europe, 1905–1945*, Oxford: Oxford University Press, 2017, 253, n.125.
85 Balabanoff, *My Life as a Rebel*, New York: Greenwood Press, 1968 [1938], 281.
86 Chabrier, 'Les délégués', 31; Yenen, 'The Other Jihad', 288–9.
87 Louise Bryant, *Mirrors of Moscow*, New York: Thomas Seltzer, 1923, 158.

defeated. In the years that followed, those who had represented the Western, imperialist nations at Baku turned their attention to other battles. The First Congress of the Toilers of the Far East remained a small, internal event, and a one-off, without any sequel.[88] Roy's project of launching a national revolution in India by military means, from a base in Soviet territory, had also proved a false hope.

At the same time, however, the Comintern did offer Roy a means of pursuing the liberation of India. With its turn to the colonized world, the Second World Congress of 1920 broadened the field of struggle: Europe was no longer to be the sole focus. The Baku Congress, more of a mass meeting than a genuine working congress, showcased this approach to great effect, in terms of propaganda. Yet at that time the Bolsheviks' 'revolutionary East' extended only as far as the former tsarist territories in the Caucasus and Central Asia and their neighbouring states, areas strategically important in the civil war. China was not yet part of the picture, even if the Russian party had sent Voitinsky there as an emissary, in April 1920. China, unlike India, Japan and the Indonesian island of Java, was seen as a sleeping giant. It was only after 1921, when the Chinese Communist Party was founded, that the 'revolutionary East' came to extend as far as China, which then fell within the Comintern's sphere of responsibility.[89]

Yet the Baku Congress was more than a 'farce'. It gave the delegates 'of the East' a platform to draw attention to their demands and even to express public criticism of the 'colonial' policy pursued by the Bolsheviks' representatives in Turkestan. The Congress also provided an arena for the expression of feminist demands that would remain equally relevant a century later. It would be several years, however, before colonial issues were addressed once again, at the Brussels Congress of 1927. Meanwhile, Roy continued to pursue his goal – aided by the Comintern – but now by different means.

---

[88] 'John Sexton: The Congress of the Toilers of the Far East', an interview by Selim Nadi, historicalmaterialism.org; originally published in French as 'Le congrès des travailleurs d'Extrême-Orient: entretien avec John Sexton', at revueperiode.net.

[89] Carr, *Bolshevik Revolution*, vol. 3, 621; Tamiatto, 'Des révolutionnaires', 55.

3
Berlin: Bridgehead in Europe and Hub of Transnational Circulation

'All eyes are on Germany, waiting for the German revolution,' Hilde Kramer wrote from Moscow on 22 August 1920, to her friend Friedel in Berlin. 'All eyes are on the German workers, wondering whether they will allow the passage of Entente troops and munitions through Germany, to be used against Soviet Russia.'[1] Thanks to its political importance for the future of the Revolution, and with it, that of Soviet Russia, the years of the Weimar Republic saw Germany come to play a key role in the Comintern's international network. It was also, in the twenties, one of the major arenas where the very definition of Communism was fought over. At issue in those debates was by no means only the echo in the KPD and the Comintern of the struggles over the political direction of the Russian party. The close of 1918 had seen the creation in Germany of one of the very first Communist parties outside Soviet Russia, which had very rapidly grown to become the biggest party in the Comintern, bar the Russian.[2] The fall of the capitalist system

---

1 Hilde Kramer, *Rebellin in München, Moskau und Berlin: Autobiographisches Fragment 1900–1924*, ed. Egon Günther and Thies Marsen, Berlin: BasisDruck, 2011, 138–44, at 143.

2 Among accounts of the history of the KPD under the Weimar Republic are Hermann Weber, *Die Wandlung des deutschen Kommunismus: Die Stalinisierung der KPD in der Weimarer Republik*, 2 vols, Frankfurt a. M.: Europäische Verlagsanstalt, 1969 – the standard work, which, however, takes a purely institutional approach. A more socially and culturally oriented overview is Eric D. Weitz, *Creating German Communism, 1890–1990: From Popular Protests to Socialist State*, Princeton, NJ: Princeton University

seemed then to be only days or weeks away, the failure of the November Revolution no more than a temporary setback.

Politically and culturally vibrant, the city of Berlin had many attractions. As the historian Karl Schlögel notes: 'No city was so closely linked to Moscow as Berlin.'[3] On the absorption of surrounding municipalities in 1920, its population rose to almost 3.9 million, and in 1925 it hit 4 million. This made Berlin the largest industrial city in Europe and the third largest city in the world after New York and London. With its historically strong workers' movement, the city offered great freedom. The KPD and its many mass organizations were omnipresent: in parliament, on the street, and in cultural life. In addition, thanks to relatively loose controls, Berlin was a place of refuge for revolutionaries from elsewhere persecuted and driven into exile. Furthermore, Germany was the first of the great powers to have recognized the Bolshevik government, and the Weimar government had much closer links with the Soviet regime than any other. Among those regularly in and out of the Soviet Embassy and its many dependencies were not only the leaders of the KPD and the 'hundreds of German party members who became paid employees of the various Soviet agencies in Germany',[4] but also representatives of the German authorities. The police, however, kept an eagle eye on the doings of the Communists, both legal and illegal.

The subject of this chapter is the construction in Berlin of a Comintern outpost to enable political liaison with the West. It begins with an account of the Comintern's efforts to set up the West European Secretariat (WES). Information channel, organizational fulcrum and port of call for all emissaries travelling through the German capital, the WES was active from 1919 to 1925. Its relative independence and poor coordination with the Soviet presence in Berlin (which included not only the embassy but also the largest International Liaison Department [OMS] post abroad) soon brought it into conflict with the Comintern leadership. After a two-year absence, the Comintern made a new attempt in 1927, with the establishment of the West European Bureau (WEB), with much

---

Press, 1997, which gives greater emphasis to internal differences and the intransigence of the membership, but generally ignores the role of the Comintern.

3 Karl Schlögel, *Das russische Berlin: Ostbahnhof Europas*, Munich: Hanser, 2007, 180.

4 Ruth Fischer, *Stalin and German Communism: A Study in the Origins of the State Party*, Cambridge, MA: Harvard University Press, 1948, 503.

clearer lines of political control. The following chapter will look at how these bodies operated, and at the people who ran them and worked for them.

Transfers of Money and Knowledge

In the first years after the October Revolution, the Soviet Union was still isolated on the international stage. The Allied blockade hindered not just travel to Russia but also all communication with the exterior. Yet communication was essential if the Revolution was to spread. The newly established ECCI thus decided on 14 April 1919 to set up an international communications and propaganda apparatus based on a number of outposts abroad.

The most important of these was the Western European Secretariat in Berlin, created in November 1919. At its head was Jakov Reich, known in Germany as 'Comrade Thomas', who was employed in the Propaganda Section of the Executive Committee of the Supreme Soviet when he was given the task of establishing a bridgehead in the West to facilitate relations with newly emerging Communist organizations.[5] These he was to supply with materials for agitation and propaganda, financial support, political advice and instruction in the basics of clandestine political activity. Communication was not, however, one-way. The Bolsheviks had urgent need of information from abroad. They needed books, newspapers and reports on political and socioeconomic developments in other countries. Their activities on behalf of the revolution called for knowledge, and they invested great resources in getting it.

Our own knowledge of the Western European Secretariat we owe in the first place to Jakov Reich himself, who, in exile in Prague in 1935 and under pressure of time, told Menshevik historian Boris Nicolaevsky about his activities on behalf of the Comintern in Berlin. Other sources have since become available in the Russian archives, confirming and

---

5 On Reich and his work at the WES, see Markus Wehner and Aleksander Vatlin, '"Genosse Thomas" und die Geheimtätigkeit der Komintern in Deutschland 1919–1925', *IWK* 29:1, 1993, 1–19, reprinted in Alexander Vatlin, *Die Komintern: Gründung, Programmatik, Akteure*, Berlin: Dietz, 2009, 247–72. Sources differ on the year of his death, given as either 1954 or 1955, though the latter seems more probable.

expanding upon Reich's account.⁶ They show that the fabulous quantities of cash and diamonds said to have been given to the Comintern's travelling representatives were not just one of the countless legends to have grown up around the Comintern and its doings. Before he went to Berlin, Reich says, he was given a million roubles in Swedish and German currency by Jakub Hanecki (1879–1937), a Polish Communist and economic expert whose name is often found Russified as Yakov Ganetsky. The son of an industrialist, whose real name was Fürstenberg, in 1919 he was chairman of the Russian State Bank and one of the Comintern's financial wizards. He also took Reich to an underground treasure chamber in the Palace of Justice, inviting him to take with him as many of the valuables stored there as he could carry. Reich took diamonds, believing that gold would take up more space. Hanecki advised him to sell off the diamonds a few at a time, rather than all in one go, advice that Reich later followed. For the cash, he provided a receipt, though none was seemingly required for the diamonds.⁷ Babette Gross (1898–1990), who joined the Young Communist League in 1921 and the party a year later, also speaks of these kinds of financial transfers in the early years of the Comintern, in her biography of her partner Willi Münzenberg:

> Because foreign currency was then in very short supply in Russia, the Russian Politbureau had asked the Cheka for several sacks of confiscated diamonds. They were handed to trusted Communists for their work abroad. Münzenberg successfully smuggled this small fortune – stitched in the cuffs of his jacket – through all controls. In Berlin he handed the stones over to Thomas who arranged for his middlemen to convert them into cash.⁸

While we do not know whether or not Reich gave a receipt for the diamonds, the fact of his having taken them was certainly recorded by

---

6 Boris Nicolaevsky, 'Les premières années de l'Internationale communiste: D'après le récit du "camarade Thomas", recueilli, introduit et annoté par Boris Nicolaevsky', in Jacques Freymond, ed., *Contributions à l'histoire du Comintern*, Geneva: Librairie Droz, 1965, 1–28; Wehner and Vatlin, '"Genosse Thomas"'.

7 Nicolaevsky, 'Les premières années', 12–13.

8 Babette Gross, *Willi Münzenberg: A Political Biography*, trans. Marian Jackson, East Lansing: Michigan State University Press, 1974, 99.

Jan Antonovich Berzin (1881–1938), briefly secretary to the ECCI, who noted on 18 August 1919 that Reich had been given valuables worth 300,500 roubles as well as Swedish and Austrian crowns and German and Finnish marks and an unspecified amount in bills of credit (*kreditnye bilety*).[9]

Reich arrived in a Berlin vacillating between left and right in the wake of the Treaty of Versailles. According to Victor Serge, who was sent there from Moscow two years later, together with his wife and son, a sense of imminent collapse prevailed. Corruption was rife, and vast new wealth and direst poverty lived cheek by jowl. Everything was for sale, even a residence permit as a supposed Pole. Only the Social Democrats believed in a future for capitalism, says Serge, but they had, in any event, lost the youth, who were either socialists or nationalists.[10] Soviet Russia was, in fact, in fashion.[11] Not only in women's dress, where open-necked shirt, boots and shingled hair were popular, but also in speech. As Ruth Fischer reports, the Berlin organizational secretary was ironically known as 'Kartothekowitsch' (Card-filo-vich, rendered into English).[12]

Whatever money might have been received from Russia, the resources of the West European Secretariat were initially modest. It did not even have a telephone connection to Moscow.[13] Communications were maintained by courier. One courier is mentioned in several of the sources, a certain Slivkin, an expert in clandestine operations and illegal border-crossing whose identity remains unknown today. The sources also show that, in this initial period, the transmission of funds to those Western revolutionaries who enjoyed the favour of the Bolsheviks inspired great ingenuity and much improvisation. The gold, jewellery and precious stones the Russian government wished to send, via the Comintern, to Communist parties or splinter groups abroad had to be

---

9 ECCI reports on expenditure on Communist parties and sympathizing movements in individual countries, April–August 1919, RGASPI 17/84/31, published in German in Hermann Weber, Jakov Drabkin and Bernhard H. Bayerlein, eds, *Deutschland, Russland, Komintern*, Part II, vol. 1, *Dokumente, 1918–1943*, Berlin: de Gruyter, 2014, 92–4, in Russian in Iakov Drabkin, Leonid Babichenko and Kirill Shirinia, *Komintern i ideia mirovoi revoliutsii: Dokumenty*, Moscow: Nauka, 1998, 150–2.

10 Victor Serge, *Memoirs of a Revolutionary*, trans. Peter Sedgwick, New York: New York Review Books, 2012 [1951], 187–8.

11 Schlögel, *Das russische Berlin*, 182.

12 Fischer, *Stalin*, 324.

13 Ibid., 135.

physically carried from one place to another, crossing borders and evading customs controls along the way. They could be sewn into sleeves, though 'objects of value, and diamonds more particularly' could also be secreted in leather soles.¹⁴ One also had to avoid always using the same couriers, who might otherwise attract attention. Foreign delegates, Comintern employees and even repatriated prisoners of war would thus be called upon. Slip-ups of one sort or another would still happen, however. Not all those chosen proved reliable, some making off with the valuables entrusted to them. Not all couriers, it would seem, were committed to the Revolution, either. So it was that the WES complained in May 1920 that 'the kinds of imbecile we get as couriers, it's beyond a joke', asking the ECCI 'not to send any old idiot here'. Not only were these messengers careless about keeping secret addresses secret, they also expected to be fed and lodged before being put safely on the train.¹⁵

One of Jakov Reich's responsibilities was the distribution of funding. In those days, when the Russian revolutionaries were still unstinting in their support for a German revolution still expected any day, they privileged the Spartacists and their successors in the German Communist Party above all other Communist or leftist groups in Western Europe or the Americas,¹⁶ and Reich was the one who supplied them with Bolshevik money. The sums were considerable: between April and August 1919 the Comintern received more than 7 million roubles from the Central Committee of the Bolshevik Party, one and a half million of which it sent abroad. The remainder was chiefly devoted to running the three departments of the Comintern itself, variously located in Moscow, Petrograd and Kiev.¹⁷

Reich was, however, chiefly occupied with propaganda and organization, for the furtherance of the revolution required the dissemination of the ideas and lines of action being formulated in Moscow. The WES

---

14 Letter from Comintern administrative secretary Gustav Klinger to Elena Stasova, Moscow, 18 August 1919, RGASPI 17/84/31, published in Weber, *Deutschland*, vol. 2, 94–5.

15 RGASPI 499/1/5, cited in Barry McLoughlin, Hannes Leidinger and Verena Moritz, *Kommunismus in Österreich 1918–1938*, Innsbruck: StudienVerlag, 2009, 125.

16 Note from Jan Berzin to Zinoviev, Moscow, 28 August 1919, RGASPI 495/18/5, published in Weber, *Deutschland*, vol. 2, 95–6.

17 ECCI reports on expenditure on Communist parties and sympathizing movements in individual countries, April–August 1919, RGASPI 17/84/31, published in German in Weber, *Deutschland*, vol. 2, 92–4.

printed and distributed the Comintern's newspapers and pamphlets. To this end, Reich acquired Verlag Carl Hoym in the port city of Hamburg, which would serve as the Comintern's publishing house. It was later joined by Frankes-Verlag in Leipzig. This was the above-board side of his activity. As many as 25,000 copies of *Kommunistische Internationale*, the German edition of the official Comintern newspaper, would be printed, with Russian, French and English editions produced in shorter runs. Between 1920 and 1922, the partly colour-illustrated *Russische Korrespondenz* provided news of Soviet Russia. The considerable costs were met by the Comintern, and, in the last analysis, by the Russian state. In 1921, publishing costs ran as high as 10 million marks, while revenues stood at around half a million.[18] At the time of the Russo–Polish War of 1920, Soviet Russia made every effort, in terms of propaganda, to prevent French military matériel reaching Poland. And, during the Volga famine of 1921–23, which affected 20 million people, the same energy was put into supporting aid for Russia. This campaign Lenin entrusted to Willi Münzenberg, whom he knew from his time in Zurich, a move intended in part to make up for the loss of the Youth International, whose headquarters were transferred to Moscow in 1921.[19]

Reich also had logistical responsibilities. One of the missions assigned to the WES was the development of an infrastructure that would allow contact and exchange among what was still, in 1919–20, a still fragmented array of grouplets and parties. That meant establishing secure channels of communication with each country, to enable the passage not only of money and information, propaganda material and ECCI directives, but also personnel. Thanks to Reich's organizational talents, the Comintern's many representatives were generally able to travel from one country to another without coming to official attention. Nikolai N. Lyubarsky (1887–1938), who had worked with Reich at the Soviet mission in Berne, could thus be despatched to Vienna in the summer of 1919, and from there sent on to Italy under the name 'Carlo Niccolini'. Alexander Abramovich (1888–?) was a Russian from the Odessa region

---

18 Vatlin, *Die Komintern*, 254.
19 Münzenberg himself would write, years later, that Lenin sought thereby to assuage 'the bitterest disappointment of my life', Letter from Münzenberg addressed to 'Dear Comrade' [Stalin], Paris, 20 July 1933, RGASPI 495/205/7000.

whom Reich had very likely also got to know in Switzerland, the two of them having been members of the Socialist Party there. Abramovich, a member of the Munich Soviet government in April 1919, was one of the Comintern's first instructors in Western Europe, active in Berlin under the name 'Albrecht', and afterwards in Czechoslovakia and France (where he was imprisoned) under the Polish name 'Zalewski'. Reich's multifaceted activity was thus, for the most part, clandestine, and, for cover, he sold books and art from a shop located, according to Babette Gross, in Berlin's Leibnizstraße.[20] There, in the back room, he received couriers and other go-betweens.[21]

An Early Comintern Agent and His Team

Who then was this Jakov Reich? A number of memoirs describe him in very similar terms, a sign not so much of the authenticity of the recollection as of the intertextuality of autobiographical writing. Karl Retzlaw (1896–1979) remembered him as 'chubby, of middling height'.[22] Babette Gross, for her part, describes him as 'small, rotund and known in party circles as "Fatty"', adding, however, that he was 'always immaculately dressed' and 'a true master of conspiracy' who 'was not arrested once during his year of activity for the WEB [the WES, in fact – B. S.]. He 'distributed money and false papers, provided illegal accommodations and served as a forwarding agent for secret mail'.[23] Hilde Kramer, who in 1919 was working for the Communist writer and journalist Wilhelm Herzog after fleeing Munich, and then poached for the WES by Mikhail Borodin (probably in early 1920) writes that 'Borodin introduced me to James Thomas, secretary of the famous WEB, the West European Bureau of the Communist International [still then the WES], who was looking for a German–English translator. James was a small, plump man, a Pole

---

20 On the other hand, Paul Thalmann of Switzerland, who needed money and false papers for his journey to the Soviet Union in 1922, gives Feurigstraße in Schöneberg as the address: Paul Thalmann, *Wo die Freiheit stirbt: Stationen eines politischen Kampfes*, Olten and Freiburg in Breisgau: Walter Verlag, 1974, 39.
21 Gross, *Münzenberg*, 93.
22 Karl Retzlaw, *Spartakus, Aufstieg und Niedergang: Erinnerungen eines Parteiarbeiters*, Frankfurt a. M.: Verlag Neue Kritik, 1976 [1972], 196.
23 Gross, *Münzenberg*, 93.

by birth, called 'Chubby' by the few comrades I knew.' She too credits him with great skill in clandestine work.

> No-one knew where he lived. His staff met him in cafés or restaurants, and through his hands passed the famous Russian roubles with which the Russians supported the West-European communist parties. It was he, too, with the help of his secret suppliers, who provided the false passports, fake visas and everything else that was required to travel illegally over every European border. All correspondence with the Comintern passed through his hands.[24]

Reich, or 'Comrade Thomas', is a colourful but elusive historical figure, who, like nearly all those operating in clandestinity, left only fragmentary traces. He represents a type of Comintern employee associated with the organization's early period and very rarely found later. He was a professional revolutionary and bon viveur, with something too of the conman about him, who shifted easily between worlds and between countries, between the comforts and enjoyments of bourgeois life and commitment to the revolution. Like many revolutionaries of his time, Reich was a polyglot. As well as Polish, he spoke Russian, English, French and German. Born in Lemberg (today's Lviv) in 1886 – the city then being part of the Habsburg Empire, and capital of Austrian Galicia – at the age of nineteen he moved to Warsaw, where he joined an underground socialist organization and was reportedly involved in bomb attacks.[25] After the failure of the 1905 Revolution, he fled, through Germany, to Switzerland. In Zurich, together with like-minded comrades, he experimented with explosives in an improvised chemical laboratory. He also studied education, helped establish a newspaper, and was a member of the Social Democratic Party and also of an organization of freethinkers. He was then married to Berta Brutzkus (1887–1965), a Jewish doctor from Memel (today's Klaipeda, in

---

24 Kramer, *Rebellin*, 82.

25 Hermann Weber and Andreas Herbst, eds, *Deutsche Kommunisten: Biographisches Handbuch 1918 bis 1945*, Berlin: Dietz, 2008, 710-11; and Pierre Broué, *Histoire de l'Internationale Communiste 1919–1943*, Paris: Fayard, 1997, 93–4. Various details about Reich's time in Switzerland can also be found in Regula Bochsler, *'Ich folgte meinem Stern': Das kämpferische Leben der Margarethe Hardegger*, Zurich: Pendo Verlag, 2004, and Ina Boesch, *Gegenleben: Die Sozialistin Margarethe Hardegger und ihre politischen Bühnen*, Zurich: Chronos Verlag, 2003.

Lithuania), and their daughter Hanna would be born in Zurich in 1914. On the outbreak of war, he was mobilized into the Austrian army, but was discharged a year later with heart problems. Reich then returned to Zurich, where he worked as a teacher while also being active in international socialist youth organizations under the pseudonyms James Gordon, James Reich and Thomas. He was in close contact with Russian émigrés, notably with Grigory Zinoviev, then also an exile in Switzerland.

Thanks to his good relations with the Bolsheviks, he found employment at the Soviet diplomatic mission, which opened in Berne in May 1918, where as head of the press office he was responsible for propaganda. His articles and information bulletins were printed by Promachos Verlag in nearby Belp,[26] but it was not he, as many have claimed,[27] who set up the press, but the brothers Fritz and Hans Jordi.[28] They had begun printing socialist literature in 1916, though collaboration with the Soviet mission brought them big orders and connection to an international distribution network. So it was that pamphlets by Lenin, Trotsky, Radek, Lunacharsky and others were printed in Switzerland, and that a publication by the Third International's French group in Moscow reached the francophone countries via Belp.[29]

However, under Allied pressure, the Soviet mission was expelled from Switzerland on 12 November 1918. Reich himself was able to remain in the country, until he too, after a short spell of imprisonment, was deported to Russia, together with others associated in one way or another with the mission, on a train carrying returning prisoners of war.[30] In March, he took part in the founding congress of the Comintern. Eventually, in the autumn of 1919, he left Moscow for Berlin, as the 'permanent plenipotentiary representative of the Communist International for Western Europe'.

Reich could carry out his various clandestine operations only with the help of reliable collaborators. He was helped in selecting these

26 Peter Collmer, *Die Schweiz und das Russische Reich 1848–1919: Die Geschichte einer europäischen Verflechtung*, Zurich: Chronos, 2004, 452.
27 See Weber and Herbst, *Deutsche Kommunisten*, 710–11.
28 Bernard Degen and Julia Richers, eds, *Zimmerwald und Kiental: Weltgeschichte auf dem Dorfe*, Zurich: Chronos, 2015, 168–70.
29 Marie-Cécile Bouju, 'Le livre comme arme de propagande: Le cas des relations entre le Service d'éditions de l'Internationale communiste et la France (1919–1939)', *Communisme* 97/8, 2009, 7–23.
30 Collmer, *Die Schweiz*, 467.

comrades by Karl Radek, an old acquaintance from his time in Switzerland, who since late 1918 had been living illegally in Germany as the Bolsheviks' representative in that country, and who on 31 December had attended the founding congress of the German Communist Party, a fusion between the Spartacist League and small left radical groups.[31] Jailed on 12 February 1919, following the failure of the revolution, he spent more than a year in Berlin's Moabit prison. Thanks to the special privileges accorded to him, Radek was, however, able to keep up exchanges with the outside world, the Bolsheviks' somewhat murky Swiss financier, Carl Vital Moor (1852–1932), a *bon viveur par excellence*, serving as his intermediary.[32] According to Ruth Fischer (1895–1961), in 1924–25 the first woman to preside over a Communist party, the German government considered Radek to be a valuable channel of communication with the new Bolshevik government in Russia.[33] Born Elfriede Eisler, Fischer was a German brought up in Vienna who had become Austrian by marriage, and had joined as Member No. 1 on the formation of the Communist Party of German Austria in late 1918,[34] but had been living in Berlin since September 1919.

Like Reich, Radek, whose real name was Sobelsohn, came from Lemberg (Lviv) in Galicia. Home to Polish, Ukrainian and Yiddish-speaking populations, at different times and to varying extents ruled by Russia, Poland and Austria-Hungary, the region was at the turn of the century a hotbed of revolutionaries. For them, then, nationality was something determined not by place of birth but by accidents of political history, and borders were very evidently a function of changing political relationships of forces. Both Reich and Radek were members of Lemberg's Jewish minority and familiar with the existential insecurity that came with anti-Jewish discrimination and pogroms. Both had been forced into exile on account of their political activities, and both had very early committed themselves to the Bolshevik cause. A bourgeois

---

31 On Karl Radek, see Jean-François Fayet, *Karl Radek (1885–1939): Biographie politique*, Bern: Peter Lang, 2004.

32 Leonhard Haas, *Carl Vital Moor 1852–1932: Ein Leben für Marx und Lenin*, Zurich: Benziger Verlag, 1970, 236–9.

33 Fischer, *Stalin*, 206; see also Schlögel, *Das russische Berlin*, 263–6.

34 Gabriella Hauch, '"Eins fühlen mit den Genossinnen der Welt": Kampf- und Feiertage der Differenz; Internationale Frauentage in der Ersten Republik Österreich', in Heidi Niederkofler, Maria Mesner and Johanna Zechner, eds, *Frauentag! Erfindung und Karriere einer Tradition*, Vienna: Löcker, 2011, 60–105, at 68–69.

plan of life was thus never on the cards. The crossing of borders – not only spatial and political, but also social – was part of their lives.

Thanks to the personal connections of his old comrade in struggle, Radek, 'Comrade Thomas' was very quickly able to build up a team of capable assistants equally devoted to the cause. Employed at the illegal bureau were Fanny Jezierska (1887–1945), the former bookkeeper Werner Rakov (1893–1937) ('Felix Wolf', and in Soviet Russia also 'Vladimir Bodganovich Kotlov'), soon replaced by Karl Gröhl (1896–1979), and Ruth Oesterreich (1894–1943).

They all had, already, much revolutionary experience and enjoyed the kudos, as activists, that went with it. The daughter of a Jewish businessman, Fanny Jezierska had been born in the eastern part of what was then Russian-occupied Poland.[35] At home, she had spoken primarily Russian and German, Polish rather less. At the age of sixteen, she had gone to France and then Switzerland; she moved on to Germany around 1909, where she joined the Social Democratic Party. She was an engineer by profession, a highly unusual occupation for a woman at that time. Between 1914 and the spring of 1918 she was employed in that capacity by AEG Telefunken, before joining the staff of the Russian Embassy in Berlin, which enabled her to become more politically active again. In the spring of 1915, she had joined the International Group in the SPD, from which then emerged the Spartacus Group formed around Rosa Luxemburg. After the November Revolution of 1918, Jezierska worked as Luxemburg's secretary, but also did work for Karl Radek. It must have been he who recommended her to Jakov Reich when the latter started to set up the West European Secretariat. In any event, she worked for Reich from November 1919 until the autumn of 1920. She writes in a document in her personal file that she was employed at the 'West-European Secret Comintern'.[36] Given her linguistic abilities and her local knowledge, she was likely employed as a liaison officer, a role she later played in Italy, ensuring liaison between the Communists and the Socialists from 1921 on. Her tasks at the WES would then have been broadly similar to her responsibilities in Rome, in whose cafés she

---

35 For her biography, see Ottokar Luban, 'Fanny Thomas-Jezierska (1887–1945): Von Rosa Luxemburg zu Gramsci, Stalin und August Thalheimer – Stationen einer internationalen Sozialistin', *Jahrbuch für Historische Kommunismusforschung*, 2003, 286–319. Jezierska added the surname Thomas only in 1935, on her marriage in France.

36 Cited in Luban, *Fanny*, at 298.

regularly held meetings with Antonio Gramsci (1891–1937) and Angelo Tasca (1892–1960), as she would with Jules Humbert-Droz when he was the Comintern emissary in Italy in 1924.[37] On such occasions, reports would be exchanged, ECCI instructions communicated, news passed on to the comrades in Moscow. It is quite possible, too, that Jezierska would have been responsible in Berlin for paying out the money that came from Moscow.

Werner Rakov, another member of the team around Reich, was the second-born of three Russian brothers who all ended up working for the Comintern in one capacity or another.[38] He had entered Germany together with Radek on 24 December 1918, in the guise of an Austrian prisoner of war. There, he set up a publishing house in Hamburg on the Comintern's behalf. In late 1920, he was appointed an 'informant to the Little Bureau of the Comintern', a role for which there is no documentary trace until after the Third World Congress, which chiefly involved supplying Radek with personal reports on the situation in Germany, and most especially about doings at KPD headquarters. This to the considerable irritation of the party's leadership, which had already complained to the ECCI when Reich had been doing it. These reports were sent to Moscow by secret courier. Rakov also served 'Thomas' as his contact with the Central Committee of the KPD, as also with the Soviet Embassy and the OMS – the Comintern's International Liaison Department – and was also very likely already working for the Soviet secret service. In 1922, after a warrant was issued for his arrest, he worked primarily for the Soviet mission in Vienna, where he set up, on behalf of the Red Army's Fourth Department, the military intelligence service later to be known as the GRU, a network of agents to cover the Balkans. On returning to Germany, he established the equally secret intelligence service of the German party, the so-called 'N-Apparat'.

His successor at the WES was Karl Gröhl (who changed his surname to Retzlaw in 1953), a former bronze caster and tool grinder, an active participant in the November Revolution in Berlin and then joint police commissioner and people's commissar for the interior under the

---

37 Jules Humbert-Droz, *Mémoires*, vol. 2, *De Lénine à Staline: Dix ans au service de l'Internationale communiste, 1921–1931*, Neuchâtel: À La Baconnière, 1971, 256.

38 Markus Wehner, 'Kaderkarrieren der Weltrevolution: Die deutsch-russische Geschichte der Brüder Rakow', *IWK* 30:1, 1994, 29–67.

Munich Soviet Republic. Under the name 'Karl Friedberg', Gröhl built the KPD's clandestine apparatus and a paramilitary force (understood by the Party as a self-defence organization) known as the Proletarische Hundertschaften (Proletarian Hundreds), which, in 1924, would become the Rote Frontkämpferbund (Alliance of Red Front Fighters).[39] For Reich, he was the official manager of Carl Hoym Verlag and unofficial liaison with both the Central Committee of the KPD and the OMS post at the Soviet Embassy. In his memoirs, Gröhl notes, very much in passing, that

> Apart from the work at the publishing house, there were other matters to be dealt with. Party members from other countries would come to Berlin, under cover or otherwise, who wished to go on to Moscow but whose papers were not good for the onward journey, or who did not wish their papers to show their journey to Moscow when they returned home. For these travellers, papers and visas had to be produced. Later, after the resumption of diplomatic relations between Russia and Germany, requests for visas and support made to the Russian embassy in Berlin would be passed on to Thomas for assessment, who in turn often turned them over to me for checking.[40]

Comrade Thomas's third close collaborator was his secretary Ruth Oesterreich, a member of the socialist movement since earliest youth, who had joined the KPD in 1919.[41] She married Reich and had a daughter by him. (It is not known when Reich and his first wife Bertha divorced. She came with him to Berlin, and worked there as a doctor until 1931, when she went to Moscow to join the staff of the health ministry, taking her daughter with her.) Oesterreich, who sometimes went by the name 'Ruth Gebhardt', maintained contact with those employed outside the illegal office, such as Hilde Kramer, and indeed Karl Retzlaw. 'The translation work would be delivered to me by James's wife, Ruth Oesterreich', writes Kramer, 'in a café, usually somewhere between Nollendorfplatz and the Kaiserallee, and we'd make an

---

39 The SPD too had a paramilitary force, the Reichsbanner Schwarz-Rot-Gold.
40 Retzlaw, *Spartakus*, 221–2.
41 For her life, see Birgit Schmidt, *Wer war Ruth Oesterreich? Auf den Spuren einer vergessenen Sozialistin,* Lich: Verlag Edition AV, 2011.

appointment to meet in another café, where I would hand over my work, receive my fee, and be given more work to do.'[42] Meetings with Karl Retzlaw took place in public space, on the streets or elsewhere in the open air, presumably to ensure maximum variation, though two women friends meeting in a café would have been less likely to draw attention than an encounter between a married woman and a man not her husband.[43]

In May 1921, the Russian Elena Stasova – 'Comrade Fritzmann' – joined the team. She had been despatched to Germany under a false name to provide support to the KPD apparatus but had in fact been asked by the OMS to keep an eye on the Comintern's financial affairs, monitoring in particular the way that Comrade Thomas dealt with the millions entrusted to him. (She may officially have been a replacement for Fanny Jezierska, who was recalled to Moscow in the autumn of 1920 and who worked for Litvinov in the People's Commissariat for Foreign Affairs before being sent to Rome for reasons of health.) In a somewhat feebly coded communication, Béla Kun, then the ECCI emissary in Germany, introduced Stasova to Wilhelm Pieck as Comrade Extaso from Sovdepia (the Soviet Union).[44] To gain a residence permit, she contracted a marriage of convenience with the bookbinder and KPD member Ernst Wilhelm[45] – an arrangement evidently engineered by 'Thomas', and one also resorted to by Ruth Fischer, who had become Austrian upon her first marriage, to avoid her expulsion from Germany in 1922. From July 1922, then, Stasova officially resided in Berlin-Charlottenburg as Lydia Wilhelm, and was employed as a 'bookkeeper' at 'retailer' Reich's bookshop. Following the establishment of International Red Aid at the Fourth World Congress in November 1922, she took on responsibility for the German section[46] – an indication of the multiple roles played by such functionaries of the early Comintern.

---

42 Kramer, *Rebellin*, 82.

43 Retzlaw, *Spartakus*, 220.

44 Letter from Béla Kun, ECCI emissary in Germany, to Wilhelm Pieck, Berlin, 10 May 1921, RGASPI 495/293/15, published in Weber, *Deutschland*, vol. 2, 156–7.

45 The marriage was ended in 1924.

46 Nikolaus Brauns, *Schafft Rote Hilfe! Geschichte und Aktivitäten der proletarischen Hilfsorganisation für politische Gefangene in Deutschland, 1919–1938*, Bonn: Pahl-Rugenstein, 2003, 27–8.

Around this small core, Comrade Thomas constructed an extensive network. Among its members in the early days were KPD officers Paul Levi and August Thalheimer, together with Willi Münzenberg for the party youth organization, while Eduard Fuchs was cashier.[47] There were also connections with the Soviet Embassy, which was housed in a palatial 101-room building on Unter den Linden, one of Berlin's most important thoroughfares. The embassy was open to German comrades, or to their officeholders at least. In the early days, the staff of Willi Münzenberg's Internationale Arbeiterhilfe (IAH – Workers International Relief) were able to lunch at the canteen established in a wonderful room in one of the wings. Nearby were the Intourist travel agency, and, until 1935, the Soviet trade mission. As many as 1,200 were employed at this complex in the years before 1933. The embassy also had a guest-house at Kronprinzenufer 10, which accommodated the many intellectuals, artists and writers who came to Berlin for readings, exhibitions and so forth, though its most important users, it would seem, were the many couriers and other agents of the Comintern and its sections, and indeed of the Soviet intelligence services, as they travelled back and forth between Moscow and the cities of Europe.[48]

One of Comrade Thomas's most important and trusted collaborators was the Pole Mieczyslaw Warszawski (1882–1941), known as Bronski, whom he knew from the days of the Soviet mission in Bern. Bronski afterwards joined the staff of the Soviet Embassy in Berlin, to be expelled from there in 1919, only to return to Germany soon afterwards as a liaison agent. The most important contact, however, and not for Reich alone, was 'Mirov' (Alexander Abramov, 1895–1937); officially secretary to the press department of the Soviet Embassy, which gave him diplomatic immunity, and unofficially head of the Berlin outpost of the ECCI's International Liaison Department. 'Through his hands passed all the threads of the conspiratorial activities of both the Narkomindel [the Soviet foreign ministry] and the Comintern,' says Babette Gross.[49] Overseas liaison also passed through the OMS's European head office.

---

47 According to Broué, *Histoire*, 94; Weber and Herbst, *Deutsche Kommunisten*, 595.

48 Schlögel, *Das russische Berlin*, 155–6.

49 Personal file, RGASPI 495/205/6083; Gross, *Münzenberg*, 130. See also, despite its doubtful reliability, Walter Krivitsky, *In Stalin's Secret Service*, New York: Enigma Books, 2000 [1939], 47.

For security reasons, it sometimes served as a staging-post for Moscow's correspondence with colonial territories.[50] It handled more than correspondence, however; the liaison service also conveyed such things as the banners that in the 1920s were regularly exchanged between KPD cells and party groups in Soviet workplaces or army.[51] In 1926, 'Mirov' was recalled to Moscow, where – testimony to his competence – he was appointed operations director of the OMS under Osip Piatnitsky (1882–1939). From 1929 to 1932, the head of the OMS's Berlin office would be Solomon Mikhelson-Manuilov, alias Max Ziese, known as 'Max' or 'Uncle Max'.[52]

Interacting Apparatuses

The different apparatuses were interlocking, but also in competition. The centralization embarked upon by Moscow in late summer 1920 did not see the WES closed, like the other international bureaux, but it did lose its autonomy and some of its functions. While it survived as the Comintern's Berlin office, it was explicitly stripped of any political role. In addition, Reich was sidelined by the appointment in 1921 of August Guralsky (1890–1960), a leading member of the Comintern apparatus, as the Comintern's emissary at KPD headquarters. Guralsky, who had been born Abraham Heifetz, and who had joined the Bolsheviks from the Bund in 1919, then also used the pseudonyms 'August Kleine' and 'Lepetit' (though twenty others are also known). Reich was now only responsible for publishing and other technical-administrative tasks, notably managing the OMS presence in Berlin.[53] Reich and Stasova were under the direct

---

50 Depending on the circumstances, such mail might also go through Paris. Letter from Avigdor, in Egypt, to his wife Charlotte Rosenthal, who worked for the Comintern in Moscow, 13 March 1928, cited in Rami Ginat, *A History of Egyptian Communism: Jews and Their Compatriots in Quest of Revolution*, Boulder, CO: Lynne Rienner Publishers, 2011, 161.

51 Gleb Albert, *Das Charisma der Weltrevolution: Revolutionärer Internationalismus und frühe Sowjetgesellschaft, 1917–1927*, Cologne: Böhlau-Verlag, 2017, 474.

52 Josephine Fowler, *Japanese and Chinese Immigrant Activists: Organizing in American and International Communist Movements, 1919–1933*, New Brunswick, NJ: Rutgers University Press, 2007, 88.

53 Letter from Comrade Thomas to KPD national headquarters, 29 August 1920, RGASPI 499/1/3, in Weber, *Deutschland*, vol. 2, 123–4.

supervision of Guralsky, and soon found themselves also answering to 'Mirov'. The extensive technical responsibilities of the WES – postal communications, the creation of documents, travel arrangements for comrades sent to or from Moscow, the organization of secure accommodation and meeting places for ECCI representatives, legal and illegal, the maintenance of maritime communications with Russia, England and the USA, the organization of illegal border-crossings into the neighbouring states of France, Holland, Austria, Switzerland and Czechoslovakia, communications with the French and other Communist parties – were now transferred to the Berlin office of the OMS.[54] As Stasova protested, 'in practical-organizational terms', this led to a duplication of effort.[55]

Furthermore, the performance of the OMS in Berlin was poor, as was reported to Moscow in October 1921 by Boris Souvarine (1895–1984), appointed by the ECCI Presidium to inspect the work of the Berlin 'subsidiary'. His own passport was such an obvious forgery that it would be safer to have no papers at all.[56] (The Comintern's passport practices would still suffer glitches in later years. When Comintern secretaries Jules Humbert-Droz and Dmitri Manuilsky (1883–1959) were in Berlin together in 1927, they noticed with dismay that they had both been issued with exactly the same forged passport![57]) But he was able to report, back in Moscow, that the OMS had now established a functioning communications link with the French party. Special couriers travelled between Paris and Berlin three times a month, and another courier could be mobilized in case of need, while a special channel was available for large quantities of material.[58]

Undetected by the police, and this at the height of the repression that followed the failed attempt at revolution in 1923, Reich also played a double role in the management of the Comintern's publishing activities.[59] The conflict over responsibilities with the OMS continued, until Reich was summoned to Moscow in the spring of 1925 and stripped of

---

54 Plan of work for the representative of the International Liaison Department (OMS) and the Comintern's budgetary commission in Germany, [Moscow], before 1 August 1923, RGASPI 495/293/31, published in Weber, *Deutschland*, vol. 2, 287–90.
55 Ibid.
56 Cited in Branko Lazitch, 'La formation de la section des liaisons internationales du Komintern (OMS), 1921–1923', *Communisme* 4, 1983, 65–80, at 75.
57 Humbert-Droz, *De Lénine*, 291.
58 Lazitch, *La formation*, 76.
59 Wehner and Vatlin, '"Genosse Thomas"', 15–18.

all his responsibilities by the ECCI. The reasons for this were many. A number of contemporaries allude to his political sympathies: according to Babette Gross, Reich was an admirer of Trotsky, and Karl Retzlaw identifies him as an early opponent of Stalin.[60] Furthermore, his patron in Moscow had been Karl Radek, already stripped in 1924 of all his roles in the Comintern and in the Russian party for being a follower of Trotsky. Zinoviev's star, too, was on the wane: in October 1926, he would be removed from the presidency of the Comintern.[61] The ongoing conflict between the WES and the OMS also had a part in it. And, last but not least, the bureaucratization of the Comintern had rendered Reich's style of work an anachronism. The lack of bookkeeping had been a thorn in the side of the Comintern's new treasurer (and head of the OMS), Osip Piatnitsky – the son of a Jewish family from today's Lithuania, whose real name was Tarshis – ever since the latter's appointment.[62] Already in 1921, he had accused Reich of embezzlement, but failed to prevail in the face of the support offered by Zinoviev, Radek and Bukharin. A specially appointed commission of inquiry headed by Soviet ambassador Nikolay Krestinsky (1883–1938) concluded that, while Reich had been negligent in his management (waiting too long, for example, before exchanging German marks for another currency at a time of inflation), there had been no actual wrongdoing.[63]

Reich's purchase in July 1924 of another publishing house, which soon ran into debt, threatening political consequences for the Comintern, led to a new investigation into Comrade Thomas's activities. In the meantime, Piatnitsky's influence in the Comintern had grown, not only because he took his responsibilities extremely seriously, but because he held the purse-strings, as Roy laconically observes in his memoirs. So great was the treasurer's influence, in his eyes, that he called him the 'evil genius' of the International.[64] This time, Reich's case came before the

---

60 Gross, *Münzenberg*, 176; Retzlaw, *Spartakus*, 222.
61 This was a decision not of the ECCI but of the Central Committee of the Russian party: Fayet, *Radek*, 565.
62 Grant M. Adibekov, Elena N. Shakhnazarova and Kirill K. Shirinia, *Organizatsionnaia struktura Kominterna 1919–1943* [The Organisational Structure of the Comintern, 1919–1943], Moscow: Rosspen, 1997, 25.
63 Wehner and Vatlin, '"Genosse Thomas"', 13–14. Krestinsky was Soviet ambassador to Germany from October 1921 to 1930.
64 Manabendra Nath Roy, *Memoirs*, Delhi: Ajanta Publications, 1984 [1964], 520 and 523.

International Control Commission, which, in turn, set up a subcommittee to examine all his publishing activities. It turned out that Reich had never been a member of a Communist party. The fact that he did not belong to the KPD was due to the rules for underground operation that Piatnitsky had issued to the Comintern's employees in publishing. But Reich had never joined the Russian party, either – still possible in the 1920s, but not for very much longer with the growth of cadre control.

The WES was thus abolished in 1925. The Comintern's decision also accommodated the complaints of the KPD, which had repeatedly complained about WES employees' interference in German party affairs and their reporting to Moscow. By this they meant not only Thomas but also Stasova, and earlier Rakov. That same year, Stasova returned to Moscow, where she worked in the information office of the Central Committee before taking on a leading role at International Red Aid (abbreviated as MOPR in Russian) in 1928.[65] Ruth Oesterreich, the secretary to the WES, had found work for the Soviet trade agency while Reich was in Moscow, where she would stay until the end of 1929. Reich, now calling himself Arnold Rubinstein, worked until 1935 as an employee of the Berlin office of the Soviet publisher Mezhdunarodnaya Kniga, while also pursuing his own projects as a private scholar. His publications included a large-format, two-volume illustrated history of the Russian Revolution published by Münzenberg's Neue Deutsche Verlag in late 1928. This contained a contribution by Leon Trotsky, who had been expelled from the Russian party a year earlier. Despite its great size, the first edition of 35,000 copies was a notable success.[66] After a posting to Paris, their former colleague Rakov was sent to the USA, presumably to coordinate Soviet clandestine operations there, in the character of a philosophy student at Columbia University. He would return to the Soviet Union in 1927. Hilde Kramer too found a place for herself in the extensive network of Communist undertakings. From January 1926 she was able to work in the press office of International

---

65 Stasova was one of the few Old Bolsheviks in Moscow to die a natural death. For biographical details, see Barbara Evans Clements, *Bolshevik Women*, Cambridge: Cambridge University Press, 1997, 288. In her autobiography, Stasova passes in silence over her five years in Berlin: Jelena Stassowa, *Genossin Absolut: Erinnerungen*, Berlin: Dietz Verlag, 1978.

66 Rolf Surmann, *Die Münzenberg-Legende: Zur Publizistik der revolutionären deutschen Arbeiterbewegung 1921–1933*, Cologne: Prometh Verlag, 1983, 90.

Red Aid. Karl Gröhl (Retzlaw) officially remained managing director of the Comintern's Carl Hoym publishing house until 1926, when he was arrested for his activities as head of the KPD's secret apparatus and sentenced by the German courts to two years' imprisonment. Following an amnesty, he worked until 1933 as the manager of the Neue Deutsche Verlag.

An Organ of Party Control in the West

Of course, the Comintern could not for long do without representation and direct communications with Berlin. With 'Bolshevization' – the imposition of the Russian party's strict discipline on all other sections – Moscow's need for control over Communist parties – 'Comparties' as they were known in Comintern-speak – only increased. In the second half of the 1920s, Berlin was *the* city where oppositional currents of all kinds were to be found. Among these were the so-called 'Compromisers', who rejected the social-fascism line but not the predominance of the Russian party, and various left-wing groups associated with the emergence of Trotskyism and of the KPD opposition (KPD-O), sometimes termed the party Right. This was headed by Heinrich Brandler (1881–1967), and his followers were also called Brandlerites.[67]

Over the years that followed, the former employees of the WES would become oppositionists who – like many other party members at the time – rejected the ultraleft course. Stasova, who had been ordered back to the Soviet Union in the mid-1920s, and who had earlier played an important role in combatting the Left Opposition and later the United Opposition within the KPD, was an exception in this regard. As a 'disciplined comrade', as she described herself, she always followed the party line.[68] In 1929, Hilde Kramer and Ruth Oesterreich, together with Hilde's

---

67 On the history of the 'Right' Opposition, see Theodor Bergmann, *'Gegen den Strom': Die Geschichte der KPD (Opposition)*, Hamburg: VSA, 2001; on the 'Left' Opposition, Marcel Bois, *Kommunisten gegen Hitler und Stalin: Die Linke Opposition der KPD in der Weimarer Republik; Eine Gesamtdarstellung*, Essen: Klartext-Verlag, 2014; also M. Bois, 'Opposing Hitler and Stalin: Left Wing Communists after Expulsion from the KPD', in Ralf Hoffrogge and Norman Laporte, eds, *Weimar Communism as Mass Movement 1918–1933*, London: Lawrence & Wishart 2017, 150–69.

68 See her letter to Vyacheslav Molotov asking to be allowed to remain in Germany, 17 April 1925, in Weber, *Deutschland*, vol. 2, 442–3.

friend Cilly Geisenberg (1895–1963), were expelled from the KPD as 'right-deviationists' [sic]. Oesterreich joined the leadership of the KPD-O and worked as an administrator at the Arbeiterpresse cooperative, publishers of the daily *Arbeiterpolitik*.[69] Fanny Jezierska, too, joined the KPD-O after returning to Berlin from Moscow in late 1928 or early 1929. The same was true of Comrade Thomas, who joined the KPD-O in 1929. Brandler was an old confidant who had always supported him when he was under investigation by the Comintern. In 1932 or thereabouts, however, he switched to the left-wing Sozialistische Arbeiterpartei Deutschlands (Socialist Workers' Party of Germany) and maintained contacts with Trotsky's son.[70]

Such a break with the KPD meant the loss of employment. In late 1929 or early 1930, Ruth Oesterreich gave up her job at the Soviet trade agency because, as one of her acquaintances wrote, 'she was so badly harassed that she left'.[71] Hilde Kramer, on the other hand, was dismissed. Karl Gröhl broke with the KPD in 1933, joining the Left Opposition. At that time, however, the move to opposition did not necessarily mean the rupture of all personal relationships. Fanny Jezierska, for example, kept up old friendships from her time in the KPD and the Comintern, as with Angelo Tasca and Clara Zetkin. She also continued to correspond regularly with Fritz (1874–1945) and Paulette Brupbacher (1880–1967) of Switzerland, even visiting them several times in Zurich, despite the fact that Fritz was expelled from the Swiss CP in 1933, on account of his 'anti-Marxist, anarchist attitudes'.

Since the mid-1920s, the question of how to best to handle intra-party factional struggles so as to bind Communist parties more strictly to the political line had been a topic of debate in the Comintern. The time of bricolage and improvisation was over. A new office was required in the West, staffed by tested and disciplined cadre. The ECCI expected a great deal from the establishment of this liaison office, whose tasks would be clearly outlined by Comintern Secretary Jules Humbert-Droz in his memoirs: 'The effort of the far-left Trotskyists to form an international fraction called for . . . closer ties

---

69 Bergmann, *Gegen den Strom*, 210; Schmidt, *Wer war Ruth Oesterreich?*, 27.
70 Pierre Broué, *Trotsky*, Paris: Fayard, 1988, 658.
71 Letter from Alexandra Ramm-Pfemfert to Trotsky, Berlin, 6 May 1930, cited in Schmidt, *Wer war Ruth Oesterreich?*, 27–8.

between the parties and a more thorough and objective surveillance of the Trotskyists' activities.'[72]

While the fight against opposition groups was one goal of the new liaison office, another was better coordination of international campaigns and actions and improved communication with individual parties. Even in the second half of the 1920s, postal communications between the ECCI in Moscow and other countries were sometimes poor. In a 1925 internal consultation on organizational and technical problems, which saw an unusually high degree of plain speaking, the question of how well the resolutions would be implemented on the ground took a large place. More attention had to be paid to the inner life of parties, it was said. According to the Finn Mauno Heimo (1894–1937), a former law student and long-standing, extremely capable chief administrator of the ECCI Secretariat,[73] 'No party can be considered Bolshevik until it is in a position to ensure that its decisions are monitored.'[74]

The establishment of a new liaison and control body in the West occupied the Comintern leadership for a long time. Only Berlin was ever considered as a location, the key decision being taken by the ECCI Political Secretariat on 13 April 1927. But how was the future Western European Bureau (WEB) to operate? Paradoxically enough, a decentralized and federal structure was initially proposed for this instrument of centralization, to be directed by a committee made up of seven to nine representatives of European CPs.

So far as possible, meetings would be held alternately in the most important countries of Central and Western Europe, while day-to-day business would be looked after by offices in London, Paris, Berlin and Vienna, each with its own manager.[75] Yet such a scheme ran counter to the political objectives of the project, and the choice thus fell on a centralized organ that enjoyed extensive decision-making powers while

---

72 Humbert-Droz, *De Lénine*, 287.

73 Heimo occupied a number of other key roles between 1924 and 1937, becoming responsible, for example, for the Cadre Department in 1936. In 1937, however, he and his wife, an American of Latvian extraction, who had come to the Soviet Union as a translator with the American Relief Administration (ARA) during the famine of 1921, were arrested and shot.

74 Minute of the consultation of the different departments on improving the work of the apparatus, 30 November 1925, RGASPI 495/46/3.

75 ECCI Presidium, The Creation of an ECCI West European Secretariat, n.d., RGASPI 495/18/569.

also being obliged to provide Moscow with regular and comprehensive reports on its activities – an obligation by then already familiar to all the Comintern's organs and party sections. The organization chart was strictly hierarchical and structured by area of work. The Institute for World Economy and World Politics (the Varga Bureau), which collected statistical material and economic data on the West and on the Communist parties, previously based at the Soviet trade mission in Berlin, was also incorporated into the WEB. Set up by the Comintern and the Russian party, the institute had been run since 1921 by the economist and researcher on German imperialism Jenö 'Eugen' Varga (1879–1964, real name Jenö Weiss).[76] He had been travelling regularly back and forth between Moscow and Berlin, but this long-time member of the ECCI was now asked to return to Moscow, being appointed head, in 1926, of the International Agrarian Institute there – a move that may have been intended to keep him under closer watch, without losing his outstanding economic and statistical skills – and he and his family would leave Berlin definitively in the autumn of 1927.[77]

The only person to really criticize the idea of dealing with the weaknesses of the Moscow apparatus by the creation of a new structure was the German Alfred Kurella (1895–1975), then deputy head of the Agitprop department in Moscow and still a highly combative Communist. Kurella, whose younger brother Heinrich also worked for the Comintern, had been one of the founders of the Young Communists in Germany. He was regularly sent to Italy, Czechoslovakia and the Scandinavian countries on behalf of the Communist Youth International, and he had spent 1924–26 in France, setting up the party school in Bobigny. In the early 1930s, he would work for the Münzenberg apparatus in Berlin and give introductory courses on Marxism-Leninism at the Marxist Workers School (MASCH). In December 1927, when the WEB had begun to operate on a trial basis, Kurella, in hospital recovering from an operation, submitted a critical memorandum to the Commission for the Reorganization of the ECCI Apparatus. Unless the weaknesses of the Moscow apparatus were eliminated, he said, the WEB stood no

---

76 Gerhard Duda, *Jenö Varga und die Geschichte des Instituts für Weltwirtschaft und Weltpolitik in Moskau 1921–1970: Zu den Möglichkeiten und Grenzen wissenschaftlicher Auslandsanalyse in der Sowjetunion*, Berlin: Akademie-Verlag, 1994.

77 Jules Humbert-Droz met him in Berlin in September or early October 1927, shortly before his departure: Humbert-Droz, *De Lénine*, 290.

chance of success: 'The current unsatisfactory situation of the ECCI apparatus has to be overcome if the plan for a Western European Bureau is to be maintained. A WEB alongside a weak, disoriented Moscow apparatus will lead to an impossible situation.'[78]

The Working Day on a Foreign Mission

By then, however, the new outpost had already begun its work. Although the Communist parties would only approve the proposal at the Ninth ECCI Plenum the following February, the office opened in the autumn of 1927.[79] Jules Humbert-Droz was one of the first of the Comintern staff to be posted to Berlin, and this immediately after his summer holiday, which he had spent in Switzerland, rather than on the Black Sea, as was his usual habit, a break that had apparently not proved very restful. From a letter to his wife, Jenny, we learn that he arrived in Berlin two days before his thirty-sixth birthday, so on 21 September.[80] After a first night at a hotel, the German comrades had billeted him with a worker's family, whose address he could not give her, on account of security. He suggested therefore that she should write to him via the OMS. His instructions were to support Manuilsky, already resident in Germany as an ECCI instructor with the KPD, under code name 'Marian'.[81] It was the latter, then, who also had charge of the WEB during this first phase.

The two of them now had to organize the work, dividing responsibilities between themselves. The WEB was very evidently a bureaucratic agency. As Humbert-Droz reported to Jenny, he was washed and dressed by eight every morning, was provided with three rolls and an 'unspeakable' coffee by his landlady, and then sat at his table reading newspapers and magazines and drafting articles and other documents until one. He then went, with Manuilsky – 'Manu' he calls him in his letters – 'to the city centre' for lunch. The two of them then went to the

---

78 Alfred Kurella, from the Botkin Hospital, Memorandum to the Commission on the Reorganization of the ECCI Apparatus, 8 December 1927, RGASPI 495/46/12.

79 The ECCI Presidium took the final decision on the creation of the WEB in August 1927 at the latest: Weber, *Deutschland*, vol. 2, 577.

80 Humbert-Droz, *De Lénine*, 288.

81 On this, see Hoppe, *In Stalins Gefolgschaft*, 47–55.

office (though where that was, he never says), where they were visited by those who needed to speak or meet with them. 'We have our meetings and appointments at the office. We also read our documents there, and then at six in the evening we leave.'[82] He and Manuilsky would then generally take a stroll in the Tiergarten and have a bite to eat together before returning home between nine and half past. It was all very dull, he added. With the prospect of revolution having receded and everyday routine having taken over, revolution lost its romance for the professional revolutionaries.

Visiting comrades, rare moments of conviviality, and the opportunity to travel broke the monotony and boosted flagging spirits. One unexpected arrival was 'Ercoli' – Palmiro Togliatti (1883–1964) – then head of the Italian Communist Party's Paris office. According to Humbert-Droz, this former teacher of economics at a private school had organized a party school in the Swiss Jura for some twenty Italian comrades, and when discovered by the police they had to come to Berlin to complete their studies. Manuilsky and Humbert-Droz immediately recruited 'Ercoli' to their team, arranging that he should spend three or four days in Berlin every month. Another visitor to Berlin was the Italian-born Victorio Codovilla (1894–1970), whose youthful antimilitarist activities had led him to emigrate to Argentina, where he had taken Argentinian citizenship; now with the Comintern, he was regularly dispatched to Latin America, first as a regional specialist (*referent*) and from 1927 as an employee in the ECCI's Latin American and the British-American regional bureaux.[83]

One of Humbert-Droz's first missions outside Germany saw him travel to Brussels. On his return, he sent Jenny an enthusiastic report:

> I have just spent three days in Brussels, at a meeting of the Central Committee of the Belgian Communist Party. It's this kind of work that makes me realize the usefulness of the West European Bureau. The personal contact, the ability to intervene on all these questions at the CC, is a much better way of correcting mistakes and of guiding and stimulating a party's activities than any letter from Moscow. It's

---

82 Humbert-Droz, *De Lénine*, 289.
83 Ibid., 291.

much less bureaucratic, more vital, and above all we gain a much better knowledge of the parties' circumstances and needs.[84]

He was plainly much less enthusiastic about the work in Berlin. It was freewheeling, without plan or organization: 'We work without any directing idea, frantically and chaotically moving from one thing to another. What is more, technical resources are so poor that the work is even less productive than in Moscow. Only visits to parties yield anything of use.'[85] Though he endorsed the chief object of his labours, the struggle against the 'Trotskyist opposition', he was nevertheless critical of the Comintern's methods. Writing again to Jenny, and requesting that his observations should be passed on to his friend Bukharin, general secretary of the Comintern and chair of the ECCI Political Secretariat, and to Otto Kuusinen (1881–1964), the long-serving Finnish ECCI secretary, he complained that the Russian party and the Comintern did not publish the Opposition's documents: 'When I speak to workers and loyal party activists on the provinces, I see that this incomprehensible silence, this way of publishing only excerpts and brief quotations from the Opposition creates an atmosphere favourably disposed to them. And our party leaderships don't know how to respond to this.'[86]

In Paris on a mission, Humbert-Droz found himself arrested and confined for five months in the inappropriately named La Santé prison, subject to a harsh regime unlike that of the political prisoners. 'No newspapers, no books, no light', as he wrote to his wife on toilet paper, so that she could warn Stepanov and Piatnitsky that the Parisian liaison agent's cover had likely been blown. He asked her to arrange that money be sent to him from his salary, so that he could pay for proper food, or otherwise get International Red Aid to meet the cost.[87] Only in early 1928 was he able to return to Moscow, his work in Berlin probably being covered in the meantime by Kuusinen.[88]

The WEB's importance to the Moscow leadership is underlined by the appointment of Manuilsky, a member of the ECCI Presidium since 1924, a member of the Political Secretariat since 1926, and, after

---

84 Ibid., *De Lénine*, 290.
85 Ibid., 291–2.
86 Ibid., 292.
87 Ibid., 298–9; direct quote on 298.
88 Ibid., 304.

Zinoviev's fall from power, the Soviet party's chief mouthpiece in the Comintern. He would, however, leave Berlin in late January 1929. As well as the technical staff – the *Maschinistinnen* or 'operatives' as the secretaries and stenographers were known in Comintern-language, a host of Communist functionaries also worked at the bureau at one time or another. By April, the Latvian Wilhelm (properly Vilgelm or Vilhelms) Knorin (1890–1939), who went by the code-name 'Tischler' in Germany, had taken over. He was a man of the apparatus, already well experienced in the rooting out of oppositionists. He would be succeeded by Georgi Dimitrov (1882–1949), appointed his deputy a month before. The latter was likewise a long-serving member of the Comintern apparatus, who had had to flee his native Bulgaria as the organizer of the failed September Uprising of 1923. He then moved between Belgrade, Vienna and Moscow, acting for the Comintern in a variety of roles, notably as head of the Balkan Communist Federation. Instructed to oversee the expulsion of KPD oppositionists Heinrich Brandler and August Thalheimer (1884–1948), he had arrived in Berlin in late 1928. In Moscow, many were glad to see the back of him, as he was known for his inflexibility. He was, however, considered a loyalist, having already helped impose discipline on the Bulgarian party.[89] The spring of 1929 also saw the secretariat of the Balkan Communist Federation, which Dimitrov still headed, shifted from Vienna to Berlin. There, Dimitrov adopted a series of false identities. In 1929, he represented himself as Dr Rudolf Hediger, a Swiss writer, like many other Comintern functionaries operating in illegality adopting a liberal profession as cover. At the WEB, he used the code-name 'Helmuth'.

Secretary to the bureau, from May 1929, was Richard Gyptner (1901–1972), who arrived directly from Moscow. For his code-names he chose the historically redolent and hardly modest 'Alaric' and 'Magnus'.[90] Among the other staff, according to an internal document of 1929, were the Austrian Richard Schüller (1901–1957), who came from the Youth

---

89 Aino Kuusinen, *Der Gott stürzt seine Engel*, Vienna: Molden, 1972, 74, the relevant passage being omitted from the English translation cited elsewhere (Kuusinen, *Before and After Stalin*). For Dimitrov's life, see Marietta Stankova, *Georgi Dimitrov: A Biography*, London: I.B. Tauris, 2010.

90 Richard Gyptner, 'Das Westeuropäische Büro der Kommunistischen Internationale (1928–1933): Erinnerungen an Georgi Dimitroff', *Beiträge zur Geschichte der deutschen Arbeiterbewegung* 3, 1976, 481–9.

International; the German Hermann Remmele (1880–1939), who between 1929 and 1932 stood alongside Ernst Thälmann (1886–1944) and Heinz Neumann as a leader of the KPD; and the Frenchman Henri Barbé (1902–1966), who after graduating from the Lenin School in Moscow acted as head of the PCF between April 1929 and 1931 – these last two being Stalin's men in their respective parties. The second half of 1928 saw the Frenchman Jacques Duclos (1896–1975) act as liaison with his party, though he may have been replaced at times by Jacques Doriot (1898–1945). In 1932–33, it was the German Fritz Heckert (1884–1936) who played the same role with respect to the KPD. Advisers on important matters were Klemens Gottwald (1896–1953), a member of the ECCI Presidium, and Togliatti.[91] The year 1929 had also seen the arrival in Berlin of the Czech Bohumír Šmeral (1880–1941). A lawyer by trade, he had been head of the ECCI's Balkan Secretariat in Moscow since 1926. The ECCI had now appointed him as the Comintern's representative on the International Secretariat of Willi Münzenberg's League Against Imperialism, while also making him a member of the WEB in order to ensure coordination.[92]

A Rigorous System of Coordination and Supervision

The WEB did not replace the advisers from Moscow. In the meantime, these had also been sent to individual parties, to ensure the implementation of directives and to keep Moscow informed about their internal affairs. The practice of sending ECCI members or other emissaries with plenipotentiary powers, or the instructors assigned to deal with more specific, technical tasks, was not made official until the Third and Fourth Comintern Congresses, but it went back longer than that. Visits from ECCI members were from the very first part of the transnational exchanges between Comintern sections. Among the earliest such 'advisers' were August Guralsky, Stojan Minev (who went by the names

---

91 Minute no. 1 of the 30 July 1929 meeting of the commission set up by the Senioren Konvent ['council of elders' or steering committee] of the Tenth Plenum to evaluate the work of the ECCI and its apparatus, RGASPI 495/46/15.

92 Fredrick Petersson, *Willi Münzenberg, the League Against Imperialism and the Comintern, 1925–1933*, Lewiston, NY: Queenston Press, 2013, 1014–15. On the League Against Imperialism, see chapter 5.

'Lebedev' or 'Lorenzo Vanini' when in Germany and France between 1921 and 1926) and the Georgian Vissarion 'Beso' Lominadze (1897–1934), code-name 'Albrecht'. In the KPD, ECCI representatives got under each other's feet, so many were there. This might also happen in other countries much less politically significant to the Comintern, but as witnessed by the case of Switzerland, they were not a permanent presence in the smaller sections, but were mainly sent in times of crisis.[93]

In the early days, the Comintern relied mainly on polyglots from the Baltic or other Eastern European states, often of Jewish extraction, among them Communists in exile from Hungary or the Balkans, though a number of Germans also figured among its emissaries. According to Aino Kuusinen (1886–1970), a Finn and one of the few women to serve the Comintern as an instructor, the ECCI gradually built up a transnational team of some forty people who could be called on for such missions abroad, 'known collectively as "international cadre"'.[94] The despatch of an emissary had always to be approved by the ECCI Little Commission, and, after the debacle in France in early 1921, when Zalewski's arrest had led to further arrests and his chequebook had served to fuel the idea of 'Moscow gold', the Comintern avoided sending Russians as representatives.[95]

With a staff of its own, the WEB now had the authority to appoint its own instructors, emissaries or plenipotentiary representatives. This represented a form of rationalization, given that it was geographically closer and in better touch with the parties of Western Europe than was distant Moscow. The Comintern assigned one 'Henrykowski' (the Pole Saul Amsterdam, 1898–1937) to the WEB as an instructor. There is also mention of a 'Turner' and a 'Sorge' 'for a while longer', though it is entirely unclear whether this last was the later 'master spy'.[96] In late

---

93 Brigitte Studer, *Un parti sous influence: Le Parti communiste, une section du Komintern, 1931 à 1939*, Lausanne: L'Âge d'Homme, 1994, 191–210.

94 Kuusinen, *Before and After Stalin*, 58–9. See also the ECCI minutes of 15 March 1932, RGASPI 495/19/435.

95 The scandal led to the ECCI appointing an ad hoc commission to investigate the incident, Branko Lazitch and Milorad M. Drachkovitch, *Lenin and the Comintern*, vol. 1, Stanford, CA: Hoover Institution Press, 1972, 162.

96 Minute no. 1 of the meeting on 30 July 1929 of the commission established by the Senioren Konvent of the 10th Plenum to evaluate the work of the ECCI and its apparatus, RGASPI 495/46/15. 'Turner' was one of the pseudonyms of Franz Freihaut of Vienna (1902–?), who also called himself Anton Gruber, and while at the Lenin School in the

1927 or early 1928, the Swiss Edgar Woog (1889–1973, who went by 'Alfred Stirner' and 'Numa') was posted to the WEB.[97] A speaker of five languages – German, French, Spanish, English and Russian – Woog was already an experienced Comintern functionary. He had emigrated in 1920 to Mexico, where he had set up the Communist youth organization, and had been elected to the ECCI as the Latin American representative. In 1922, he was employed in the ECCI's Information Department. A qualified librarian, and made responsible for the library and archives, he was regularly sent abroad as an ECCI representative, as for example to the Netherlands in 1923 and to Mexico in 1927. In 1924 he became a member of the powerful International Control Commission, serving as its secretary from 1925 to 1927. Yet the demands of the post did not suit him. In 1925, showing all the signs of what today one would call burnout, he asked to be allowed to return to Switzerland. He was physically exhausted and wanted more involvement in practical political work, something not available to the Comintern's foreign employees in Moscow. And finally, he also wanted time for further theoretical study.[98] A second Swiss, Siegfried (Sigi) Bamatter, who joined the WEB in 1928 and worked there for about a year, was also an old-established apparatchik. Someone of humble background who had worked in a variety of unskilled jobs in Switzerland, France and England, mastering several languages in doing so, he had likewise begun his political career as the founder of a Communist youth organization. He very soon joined the secretariat of the Communist Youth International, from whence he moved on to the Organization Department of the Comintern in 1925. The 1920s he spent mostly in Moscow, being often sent on missions

---

mid-1930s, Franz Stojan. The same pseudonym was later also used by the renowned historian and economist Jürgen Kuczynski (1904–1997), who only officially joined the KPD in 1930. It is unclear whether the Sorge in question was Richard Sorge, but the latter was a long-time member of the KPD who also became a member of the VKP(b) in 1925. Between late 1924 and late 1925 he acted as Manuilsky's secretary. In 1929, in any event, he was in Germany for a short period, following a mission to England, likely on behalf of the OMS, before returning to Moscow the same year. It would appear that, from 1929 on, he worked exclusively for the GRU, the Soviet Union's military intelligence service.

97 Minutes of the ECCI Political Secretariat, Moscow, November 1927, RGASPI 495/19/426.

98 Stirner to the Secretariat of the Communist International, Moscow, 4 March 1925, RGASPI, copy in Schweizerisches Sozialarchiv, Ar 140.40.1.

abroad (including a visit to China in 1925, as well as work as an organizational instructor in France, Belgium, England, Luxemburg, the Netherlands and the USA). Finally, in 1932, the WEB saw the arrival of the two Bulgarians, Blagoi Popov (1902–1968) and Vasil Tanev (1897–1941), who, within a year, would be arrested alongside Dimitrov, accused of responsibility for the Reichstag Fire.

The WEB also served to distribute the money sent from Moscow to the West. This had been the responsibility of the OMS, but the Political Secretariat decided on a change in 1928, after several of the OMS's local centres disregarded the requirements of security. Rather than using Russian couriers, funds for Communist parties abroad would now be sent with 'foreign comrades' operating from the WEB and its eastern counterpart in Irkutsk.[99] The casualness that characterized the handling of money matters in the early days of the Comintern had now given way to a sometimes contested budgetary rigour. The ECCI had established a Budget Commission in 1921, at the time of the Third World Congress, and it was this that decided the financial support to be made available to the parties and how it was to be distributed, as well as supervising the finances of the parties more generally. The WEB exercised a parallel control via its own Audit Commission, presided over by Hugo Eberlein (1887–1941), the KPD's chief finance officer and head of its commercial operations, and the Comintern's man in Germany.[100] The different departments of the Comintern, its sections abroad, the Youth International and other such organizations now had to submit their funding requirements for the coming year. The Comintern's senior administrators then drew up an annual budget, which had to be approved by the Politburo of the CPSU. The process was by no means without frictions, hardly surprising given the complexity of the Comintern apparatus and the organization's dependence of the Russian party. There were continual complaints from the departments: in the words of Comrade M. M. Kivilovich, a former lawyer now head of the Comintern administration, 'the budget is too small, so that departments are compelled to

---

99 Niels Erik Rosenfeldt, *The 'Special' World: Stalin's Power Apparatus and the Soviet System's Secret Structures of Communication*, vol. 2, Copenhagen: Museum Tusculanum Press/University of Copenhagen, 2009, 232.

100 Plan of work for the representative of the International Liaison Department and the Comintern's budgetary commission in Germany, Moscow, before 1 August in Weber, *Deutschland*, vol. 2, 287.

abstract funds from other heads to cover their expenses'.[101] Difficulties also arose from the fact that the Russian party only approved the budget after a long delay, that for calendar year 1927, for example, being approved only on 24 January.[102] However, in addition to its regular operating budget, the Comintern was also granted additional resources to meet particular demands. On 2 February 1928, the Politburo of the CPSU thus approved an extra allocation of 6,368,010 roubles, while 500,000 gold roubles were to be set aside as a reserve, in preparation for election campaigns in Poland, France, Germany, England and the USA.[103]

By then, detailed regulations had also been introduced for the remuneration and expenses of ECCI delegates and others posted abroad. In 1927 they were entitled to 'rail travel by upholstered carriage (with couchette) (2nd class abroad), 1st class travel on steamers', but 'the use of international sleeping cars is not covered'. Monthly salary was fixed as follows: Germany, $160; Sweden, $120; Switzerland, $150; Austria, $120; Czechoslovakia, $120; England, $170; America, $170; Italy, $120; Balkan countries, $120 and Spain, $135. (Average monthly pay in Germany in 1927 was around 150 Reichsmark, while $160 was worth some four times as much as this, more than the maximum pay of a skilled worker).

For short missions, a daily rate was paid, to cover meals, hotel accommodation and minor out-of-pocket expenses. This was normally $3, though $4 was payable in countries with a higher cost of living, such as the United Kingdom and the United States and sometimes France and Germany.[104] How long the rates given here remained valid is unknown. The Comintern's financial determinations were always dependent on budget, and generosity of provision could not always be maintained. In 1925, for example, the separation allowance payable in respect of family members left behind and unable to work was abolished.

It was also laid down that 'wives have no claim to a daily allowance', a provision that makes it clear that these roles were expected to go to men.

---

101 Minute of the consultation of the various departments on improving the work of the apparatus, 30 November 1925, RGASPI 495/46/3.

102 Decision of the Politburo of the CPSU, 24 January 1927, referred to in Weber, *Deutschland*, vol. 2, 552.

103 Minute no. 8 (Sonder-Nr. 8) of the meeting of the Politburo of the VKP(b), 2 February 1928, RGASPI 17/162/6, cited in Weber, *Deutschland*, vol. 2, 599.

104 Instruction on the payment of ECCI delegates and those sent on mission by the ECCI, 4 March 1927, RGASPI 495/18/596. It is not entirely clear whether Germany and France were not at some point struck out of this document.

This finds confirmation in the rarity of women so engaged. Apart from Aino Kuusinen, mentioned earlier, who travelled to Japan on behalf of the Comintern, few women are known to have served as ECCI-appointed instructors abroad. One was the Romanian Anna Pauker (1893–1960), the daughter of a rabbi and earlier a teacher of Hebrew, who was in Paris from 1930 to 1932 as a member of a multimember Comintern delegation. Another was the Russian Anna Razumova (1899–1973), likewise a former teacher, who in 1927–28 was an instructor with the Women's Secretariat in China, and possibly also in Vietnam. She later spent several years in Paris as the ECCI's representative on the French Communist Party's Colonial Commission, and, from November 1936 to April 1937 she was active in Spain. Finally, Grete Wilde (1904–1943), who came from a working-class Berlin background, was sent to Turkey in 1931, to spend almost four years there before becoming a political specialist in the ECCI Cadre Department, under the name 'Greta [Erna] Mertens'. Active in a similar capacity for the Communist Youth International (CYI) was the German Olga Benario (1908–1942), who later took the name of her partner Luís Carlos Prestes (1898–1990), and who became famous for her dramatic and tragic story. Her father was a Munich lawyer and she herself worked as a shorthand typist. After freeing her lover Otto Braun from prison in Berlin, in a film-worthy operation organized by the intelligence department of the KPD, and then escaping with him to the Soviet Union, she received military training in Moscow. As an instructor for the CYI, she completed several assignments in England and France between 1930 and 1932. In late 1934, she travelled to Brazil as a bodyguard for Prestes. The failure of the Communist uprising of 27 November 1935 saw her arrested and extradited into the hands of the Gestapo, to die in the gas chamber at the Bernburg euthanasia centre during the Second World War.[105] The Czech dressmaker Marie Schramm-Ehrlich (b. Reichenberg, 1908–?) also worked as an instructor for the CYI. She was active in Austria from May 1934, in the wake of the February Uprising, under the names 'Hilde Herbst' and 'Magda'. Mention should also be made of the Italian Tina

---

105 Benario has been the subject of a number of biographies and films, and has also inspired an opera and a dance piece. Her first biographer was the German Communist Ruth Werner (see chapter 7): Werner, *Olga Benario: Die Geschichte eines tapferen Lebens*, Berlin: Neues Leben, 1961. See also Fernando Morais, *Olga: Revolutionary and Martyr*, New York: Grove Press, 1990.

Modotti (1896–1942), who made a name for herself as a photographer in Mexico, who was sent on secret missions to a number of European countries in 1933 and 1936 and who lived there in illegality for even longer. As an instructor for International Red Aid, she travelled to Poland under cover in 1932, taking donations, and very likely to Portugal in 1933 and Spain in 1935. As one of the people in charge of International Red Aid's West European office, she also spent considerable time in Paris. During the Spanish Civil War, she worked for Red Aid in Madrid, Valencia, Albacete and Barcelona.[106]

The powers and duties of the WEB were extensive. Through its cadre of instructors, the WEB was to systematically monitor the work of the individual sections, 'in order to determine how they are implementing the ECCI's directives and resolutions'. It was also 'to furnish the Political Secretariat with regular, brief reports'. It would also be its responsibility, where necessary, to coordinate the activities of the West European parties. To this end, transnational connections between Communist parties were to be strengthened. 'Under the overall supervision of the WEB', the French party was to concern itself with the affairs of the Belgian, the German party those of the Austrian, and the Italian those of the Spanish. In addition, British and American CPs were 'to make every effort to provide real assistance to the movement in India over the next six months'.[107] Its responsibilities for supervision and coordination of West European Communist parties would see the WEB call representatives to Berlin to explain their policies, pulling them back into line where necessary, and organize secret international get-togethers or inter-party conferences where required. So, for example, on 16 May 1929, the WEB held a meeting that brought together thirteen Communist parties and also representatives of the Communist Youth International and the Red Trade Union International to discuss preparations for a day of anti-war activities.[108]

The intensity of contact can be illustrated by an example. When, in the years between 1928 and 1932, the Swiss party had reservations about the Comintern's new political line, Gyptner travelled to Switzerland on

---

106 On Modotti, see in particular chapter 9.
107 Proposals on improving the work of the leading organs of the ECCI and of the apparatus [Tenth Plenum of the ECCI, July 1929], RGASPI 495/46/15.
108 Gyptner, 'Das Westeuropäische Büro', 485.

at least seven occasions, sometimes staying a considerable time. Dimitrov and at least eight other representatives were likewise sent to Switzerland on various occasions.[109] While this shows the power of the WEB, it also reveals its limits: such interventions in the affairs of Communist parties did not always meet with success. Its representatives were sometimes received only unwillingly, and their criticisms and attempts at control felt to be unwarranted interference. They might then be met with varying degrees of passive resistance.[110] Even with the whole authority of the ECCI behind them, the efforts of WEB's emissaries to Switzerland at first came to naught. Only by organizing a coup and replacing the entire party leadership was the Swiss party brought into line. This gained the WEB no friends, as witnessed by the comments of leading Swiss cadre.[111]

A look at the WEB's doings over eight days in November 1928 reveals the degree of effort put into its supervision and control of the European parties. Over this short period, the WEB received oral reports from staff or instructors on the parties of Germany, Czechoslovakia, Norway and Austria, and written reports on those of Belgium (two), Yugoslavia, Sweden and Denmark. That same week saw a staff member despatched to Austria, another to Romania and another again to France, Belgium and Britain. Pierre Semard (1887–1942), general secretary of the French PCF from 1924 to 1928, and until 1931 also a member of the ECCI, committed to attend the Czechoslovak party congress at Christmas; Hermann Remmele, a former leader of the Germany party and now a member of the ECCI, agreed to attend the Norwegian. Furthermore, the WEB appointed one staff member as its representative on an antifascist committee, and assigned another to review the Comintern periodical *Inprekorr*. It instructed Thälmann to keep a closer watch on Workers' International Relief, where money had seemingly disappeared. Also present on the schedule, the planned meeting with Italian comrades about an antifascist congress did not materialize, a problem typical of illegal work, as the leadership of the PCI, now banned in Italy, went back and forth

---

109 Studer, *Un parti*, 194–206.
110 Ibid., 77–90, 191–209; Hoppe, *In Stalins Gefolgschaft*, 92–6.
111 Studer, *Un parti*, 46–61. In other parties, too, there was a dismissal of 'right-deviationist' leaderships on the initiative of Comintern representatives taking advantage of Moscow's symbolic capital, as for instance in the Australian party in 1929.

between France and Switzerland, being underground in both countries and pursued by the police.[112]

Emissaries coming from Moscow would call on the way at the WEB and obtain more precise information about the parties they were to visit. In Berlin, they would thus be able to work out the details of their mission with the relevant local Comintern representatives. Unlike in the early years of the Comintern, everyone now travelled under pseudonyms with matching false papers.[113] The rules provided that they were to be given a contact address, where they would be met and taken onward, and they knew neither the address of the Wilhelmstrasse headquarters, disguised as a publishing house, nor the other ten or so secret addresses – apartments or offices – maintained in the city. Such security measures applied in principle to every appointment or group meeting.[114]

The reality, however, was very different. Even the most high-ranking officials sometimes neglected the rules. So it was that in August 1931 the always highly conscientious Piatnitsky had to admonish Dimitrov for having included the full names and addresses of Comintern agents in an unencrypted letter.[115] Of, course, this was not simply a matter of individual carelessness. Strict separation between legal and illegal Communist operations and between official and unofficial Soviet institutions could not always be ensured, even in a big city like Berlin. According to an undated document analysing relations between the OMS and the WEB, these were far too public and too close in terms of personal relationships. It seems, too, that people in the KPD knew far too much about the WEB. The report observes that the German party always used the same apartment for its meetings with the WEB, and that the connections between the OMS and the Soviet Embassy were far too obvious. The errors were attributed to 'democratic illusions about German democracy and police'.[116] This indeed gave those involved a sense of security that would turn out to be misplaced, but in the 1920s the catastrophe of 1933 was as yet unforeseeable.

---

112 Reports to Moscow by 'Alarich' (Richard Gyptner), Berlin, 21 and 28 November 1928, RGASPI 495/19/212.
113 Studer, *Un parti*, 194.
114 Gyptner, 'Das Westeuropäische Büro', 488.
115 Stankova, *Georgi Dimitrov*, 102–3.
116 Organizational failures and shortcomings in the work of the WEB and its auxiliary organs, n.d., RGASPI 499/1/34.

Both the German and Austrian police were in any case aware of Dimitrov's political activities, although they never moved to arrest him, being in fact ignorant of the true significance of his role.[117] Letters and other materials seized when the premises of the League Against Imperialism were searched on 31 December 1931 revealed to the police the WEB's presence in Berlin, but they were however unable to establish a connection with Dimitrov.[118]

In the 1920s, Berlin stood alongside Moscow as international Communism's second centre of global operations. It served as the link between Moscow and the West, the centre of the radial network uniting the Communist organizations of Europe and beyond. It functioned as a hub for the movement not only of people and money, of periodical publications and propaganda material, but also of information and ideas. The city was scattered with secret apartments and lodging houses. The West European Secretariat, the OMS post at the imposing Soviet Embassy with its capacious guesthouse, and later the WEB, were all detached elements of the Comintern apparatus. Not included under this category were the local offices of the Profintern, the Communist Youth International and the Krestintern, which stood in similar relation to their own organizations.

Even after the failure of the German Revolution of 1923 and the displacement of revolutionary hopes to the East, Berlin remained the most important outpost for the Comintern and the young Soviet Union. The Moscow–Berlin axis would not become less important for the Communist movement and the now stabilizing Soviet Union – on the contrary. If Comintern representatives travelled to Berlin in the early 1920s to prepare a revolution, in the second half of the decade they did so to exert control over the many oppositional groups that had emerged inside the KPD. Thanks to the strength of that party and its privileged position within the Comintern, the Comintern's strategy was decided just as much in Berlin as it was in Moscow, and with it the future of the world revolution and of the Soviet Union itself. This brought with it a change in the mix of work. While the WES served above all for agitprop

---

117 Stankova, *Georgi Dimitrov*, 103.
118 Friedrich Firsov, 'Georgi Dimitroff und das Westeuropäische Büro der Komintern', *Beiträge zur Geschichte der Arbeiterbewegung* 6, 1973, 935–46, at 937.

and the communication of information, the priority of the WEB – the second attempt at a permanent bridgehead in Europe – was control over its own ranks, and in this it was more or less successful. If the KPD leadership complained about the reports that Reich sent to Radek, the sources also reveal that the emissaries and instructors sent by the WEB were not always well received by the Communist parties.

Styles and methods of work also changed with the Comintern's new orientation: the improvisation of the early years soon gave way to the rigours of systematic reporting. Though the head of the WES could still refuse to keep proper books, those who ran the WEB had to account for every expenditure and every trip, recording all contacts with party representatives, attendances at party congresses, visits to Berlin by the officials of foreign parties, encounters with illegal operatives and all work meetings, providing statistical reports covering all these things to the Comintern. This brought an explosion in the volume of work facing the officials who had to check, evaluate and file such reports. At Moscow headquarters, they often just piled up unread in a corner.

By 1924, Stalin had formulated the theory of 'socialism in one country', which made the continued existence of the Soviet Union the guarantor of the world revolution, and not the other way round, as had been the case before. And it was not just the Russian state that was digging in for the long haul. The Comintern, too, became institutionalized, turning into an apparatus with fixed structures and rules. As it did so, it developed a bureaucracy with its own logics of self-preservation and control. From then on, Communist activity in Berlin would concentrate on longer-term objectives: supporting international revolutionary networks and the corresponding channels of communication, legal and illegal; producing, printing, and distributing agitational and informational materials; developing an underground and even an armed apparatus; supporting class-struggle actions and the propagandistic mobilization of new party members and fellow-travellers.

4
Berlin, Cultural Capital of International Communism

Berlin was not just the location of the Western European Bureau (WEB), the Comintern's most important office abroad, and home to many Soviet institutions. The city also acted as the central hub for the global circulation of information. Before 1933, a substantial part of the Comintern's press operations were based there. Subsidized by the Comintern, Willi Münzenberg had built up a media consortium that included not only illustrated magazines, daily newspapers, publishing houses and book clubs, but also film production and distribution facilities. A decision by the Third World Congress in 1921 had also seen the establishment in Berlin of a new publication to stand alongside the theoretically oriented *Kommunistische Internationale,* to bring news of the Comintern's activities to a broader public.[1] This newsletter, named *Inprekorr* (short for *Internationale Pressekorrespondenz: Für Politik, Wirtschaft und Arbeiterbewegung* – International Press Correspondence: For Politics, Economics and the Labour Movement), first appeared in September 1921, in German, French and English, and would be published later, at different times, in Swedish, Spanish, Czech, Hungarian and Italian). *Inprekorr* was another Comintern institution that employed a transnational, cosmopolitan staff, and another extraterritorial space of Communist world-revolutionary activity – one of many such globally networked enclaves in which German and foreign Communists worked

---

1 Implemented by a decision of the Little Bureau of the ECCI, 13 August 1921.

together on their shared political project. How did the Comintern's multinational migrant workforce fit into the vibrant life of 1920s Berlin in general, and into the highly ramified network of Communist social and cultural institutions in particular?

Cosmopolitan Intellectuals

The *Inprekorr* writers were all leading comrades of the Communist parties. According to one former employee, the Hungarian Irén Komját-Rona (1895–1982), who went under the names of 'Olga', 'Nora' and 'Frau Stein', the newsletter soon had a roster of 188 correspondents in 31 different countries. Among them were Evelyn and M. N. Roy, and in 1927–28 Fanny Jezierska, who reported on the situation in Italy.[2] Only in the Soviet Union, and only from 1933 onward, did *Inprekorr* have its own permanently stationed special correspondent, the Hungarian László Boros (1895–1938).[3] Editorial offices and press were both in Berlin, where, with only one interruption, the newsletter was able to publish legally until the Nazi takeover in 1933. Working conditions, however, were not ideal, as Boris Souvarine reported to Moscow in October 1921, after being sent on a visit of inspection by the ECCI Press Department. The editorial team, which at first numbered only four, did not have its own office, but shared that of the *Rote Fahne*. And only the German Franz Dahlem (1892–1981) had legal status. The three foreign members of staff – Victor Serge, the Hungarian Gyulá (Julius) Alpári (1882–1944) and the Frenchman Robert Petit (1893–1951) – were still awaiting identity documents and therefore at risk of being picked up by the police during one of their frequent raids on the premises of the *Rote Fahne*. What was more, postal communications were poor, and there was too little 'material' from the Soviet Union, by which Souvarine

---

2 Gene D. Overstreet and Marshall Windmiller, *Communism in India*, Berkeley: University of California Press, 1959, 42; Ottokar Luban, 'Fanny Thomas-Jezierska (1887–1945): Von Rosa Luxemburg zu Gramsci, Stalin und August Thalheimer – Stationen einer internationalen Sozialistin', *Jahrbuch für Historische Kommunismusforschung*, 2003, 286–319, at 302.

3 Iren Komját, *Die Geschichte der* Inprekorr, *Zeitung der Kommunistischen Internationale (1921–1939)*, Frankfurt a. M.: Verlag Marxistische Blätter, 1992, 6 and 90.

seemingly meant directives from the Comintern.⁴ In 1923, when the KPD and the Communist press found themselves banned following the failed uprising in Hamburg, the editorial office moved temporarily to the more sedate Vienna. The Austrian capital was, at that time, a refuge for many persecuted revolutionaries, notably from Eastern and South-Eastern Europe and Italy. Among them were Georgi Dimitrov, head of the Balkan Secretariat, and Antonio Gramsci, who arrived in late 1923, to live there as 'an industrious and Bohemian exile, late to bed and late to rise' until April 1924, when his election to parliament allowed him to return to Italy.⁵ Another was Georg Lukács (1885–1971), former deputy people's commissar for education, forced into exile in Vienna after the fall of the short-lived Soviet Republic of Hungary. With its Soviet Embassy and secret service station, the OMS station that opened in March 1922, and a subsecretariat of the Young Communist International, the city of Vienna was at times a Communist 'Little Berlin', and *Inprekorr* could also be published there legally. But Berlin remained important even during this period of exile, as direct contact with Moscow was possible only from there.⁶

Inprekorr's return to Berlin in 1926 saw the concomitant establishment of a branch of the Comintern's own press agency, the Telegraphenagentur Inprekorr. In 1925, 70,000 gold roubles were provided in support to *Inprekorr*, while the ECCI, the Profintern and the MOPR (International Red Aid) each contributed 10,000 gold roubles for the setting up of the telegraphic agency. (For comparison: From the Comintern's total budget of 4.1 million gold roubles, the ECCI received 270,000 gold roubles, the German CP a little more than a million, the Swiss CP 10,000, the Mexican CP 1,000.)⁷ *Inprekorr* and the

---

4 Boris Souvarine, report to Zinoviev from Berlin, 16 October 1921, cited in Branko Lazitch, 'La formation de la section des liaisons internationales du Komintern (OMS), 1921–1923', *Communisme* 4, 1983, 75.

5 Victor Serge, *Memoirs of a Revolutionary*, trans. Peter Sedgwick, New York: New York Review Books, 218–19. In 1924 Gramsci was known to the Vienna police as the 'press officer of the Russian mission': Barry McLoughlin, Hannes Leidinger and Verena Moritz, *Kommunismus in Österreich 1918–1938*, Innsbruck: StudienVerlag, 2009, 112.

6 Komját, *Geschichte der Inprekorr*, 25.

7 Decision of the Politburo of the CC of the Russian CP on the funding of Communist parties, Moscow, 24 December 1924, RGASPI 17/162/2, published in Hermann Weber, Jakov Drabkin and Bernhard H. Bayerlein, eds, *Deutschland, Russland, Komintern*, vol. 2, Berlin: de Gruyter, 2014, 411–14.

Telegraphenagentur were now housed at KPD headquarters, first at 38 Rosenthalerstraße, and from November 1926 in the massive Karl-Liebknecht-Haus on the Bülowplatz (today the Rosa-Luxemburg-Platz), which assertively declared its politics on giant banners hung on the façade. This housed the central committee of the German party, the Berlin-Brandenburg-Lausitz-Grenzmark district office, the editorial office of the *Rote Fahne*, and the central committee of the German Young Communists. There was also a bookstore, a shop selling the uniform of the Roter Frontkämpferbund and a printshop. *Inprekorr* also had its despatch department there, and a statistical office which drew up a monthly report on the use of Telegraphenagentur articles in Communist publications across the world.[8]

The newsletter's Berlin office was in 'daily telephonic communication with Vienna, Prague, London, Paris, Stockholm and Moscow', reports Margarete Buber-Neumann (1901–1989), who worked for *Inprekorr* from April 1928 to June 1932.[9] Intercontinental communications (e.g. with China or the United States) were effected by teleprinter, post or courier. For security reasons, the official editors were comrades holding German citizenship, while the staff were 'a mixed bag'.[10] The combined editorial offices of newsletter and agency employed more than a dozen journalists and translators, together with 'technical', that is, administrative personnel, for the most part women. They worked days and nights in alternate weeks, and much coffee was therefore consumed.[11]

Publisher and director of the newspaper was the Hungarian Gyulá (Julius) Alpári, who most often went by the names 'Ami' and 'Richard Mannheim'. He kept the job for nineteen years, a rarity if not a record at the Comintern! His nomadic life typified the condition of flight and exile shared by many East European Jewish comrades of his generation, a life of hiding from the police, of bed and breakfasts and rented rooms,

---

8 Komját, *Geschichte der Inprekorr*, 27.

9 Four-page, typewritten curriculum vitae, written in Moscow on 22 September 1936, RGASPI 495/205/1612. See also Margarete Buber-Neumann, *Von Potsdam nach Moskau: Stationen eines Irrwegs*, Stuttgart: Deutsche Verlags-Anstalt, 1957, 124. Until the mid-1930s, the author called herself Margarete or Grete Buber, thereafter Margarete Neumann.

10 Buber-Neumann, *Potsdam*, 124.

11 Ibid., 150.

of borders crossed illegally. Only 1920s Berlin would offer, at times, a certain safety. At the age of eighteen, Alpári had been expelled from his Jewish school for making Marxist propaganda. He joined the Social Democrats in 1901 and aligned himself with the socialist internal opposition before joining the Hungarian Communist Party in 1919. Following the failure of the Hungarian Revolution, in which he served as deputy people's commissar for foreign affairs, he had to leave the country, whereupon the Comintern sent him to Czechoslovakia as an instructor. There, under the name 'Marmorstein', he instigated a general strike, another grand failure. While still posted to Czechoslovakia, he took part in the Third World Congress of the Comintern in 1921, and then moved to Berlin as editor-in-chief and administrator of *Inprekorr*, spending the years 1923 to 1926 in Vienna before returning to Berlin. During that time, he travelled regularly to Moscow to cover the news and to attend meetings. So it was, for example, that he attended the Twelfth Plenum of the ECCI in 1932, together with his colleague Heinrich Kurella (1905–1937, called 'Schief'). In 1927, he spent some time in the United States, presumably in connection with the international campaign to save Sacco and Vanzetti. Alpári seems to have dealt with his exiled condition, exacerbated at times by illegality, by a compensatory stability of private life and living habits. These last were, it is said, 'so bourgeois and pernickety that no-one would ever have guessed that that he was working directly for the Comintern in Moscow'.[12] Victor Serge described him unflatteringly as 'a bloated, artful, and well-informed individual' with a noncommittal attitude that was intended to ensure him, even in illegality, a steady career as a functionary.[13] However that may be, Alpári certainly sought steadiness in his staff. He 'preferred to employ married couples', writes Irén Komját, 'believing that this made for a more harmonious atmosphere, as there would be no wife waiting impatiently at home for a spouse working late at night'.[14] During his time in Vienna, Alpári made a further argument in support of this preference. Accused by his compatriots of profiteering from the Comintern by paying himself double and employing his wife at the same time, he defended himself as follows: 'To my knowledge, the Party . . . has no ban on the employment

---

12 Ibid., 124.
13 Serge, *Memoirs*, 191.
14 Komját, *Geschichte der Inprekorr*, 28.

of husbands and wives. Be that as it may, a semi-legal enterprise that is harried from country to country needs reliable comrades with good language skills. A ban of this kind could not possibly be applied to such enterprises.'[15]

And *Inprekorr* did indeed employ an unusually high number of couples. Irén and Aladár Komját [Korach], Friedrich [Fritz] and Marie Runge (1893–1961, 1895–?) and Hans and Mireille Glaubauf (1901– 1942, 1905–2000), succeeded each other on the German edition, which in 1927 also saw the arrival of Heinrich Kurella, first as translator, then as editor,[16] who would be joined in the 1930s by his companion Countess Charlotte Stenbock-Fermor (1906–1966). The English edition (*Inprecor*) employed Bertha Braunthal (1887–1967), older sister of the Viennese Social Democrats Alfred and Julius Braunthal, while her English husband William Clark had charge of it; the Swedish had the Smolans. One of the few to live alone was the Newcastle-born Englishwoman and German citizen (Ethel) Maud Parlow-Hutchinson (1880–?), who worked as a translator.[17]

The Sudeten German Fritz Runge and the Hungarian Aladár Komját formed part of the permanent core of the team. The former was responsible for administration and finance and saw to correspondence, the latter was head of editorial. Among the journalists were Josef Gruen of Vienna, known as 'Pepi', whom Margarethe Buber-Neumann describes as 'tall and highly strung' but 'tending rather to plumpness' and 'highly critical of the policy of the KPD leadership'. One of his favourite sayings, it seems, was: 'Even the KPD will be unable to prevent the masses from coming to it in the long run.'[18] Another permanent member of staff, as a journalist in Vienna and Berlin, was the László Boros mentioned earlier, another acquaintance of Alpári's from the days of the Hungarian Soviet Republic, when Boros had been head of the propaganda department of the Young Workers' Association at the People's Commissariat for Popular

---

15 Cited in McLoughlin et al., *Internationaler Kommunismus*, 239.

16 According to his personal file, which features an autobiography of 1924 reproduced in part in Yvonne Hirdman, *Meine Mutter, die Gräfin: Ein Jahrhundertleben zwischen Boheme und Kommunismus; Aus dem Schwedischen von Nina Hoyer*, Berlin: Insel Verlag 2011, 334–6.

17 Komját, *Geschichte der Inprekorr*, 28.

18 Buber-Neumann, *Potsdam*, 125.

Passport photograph of the twenty-year-old Hilde Kramer, attached to a party questionnaire in her personal file in Moscow (RGASPI).

The Russian Mikhail Borodin, who helped found the Communist parties of Mexico and Spain as he travelled through those countries.

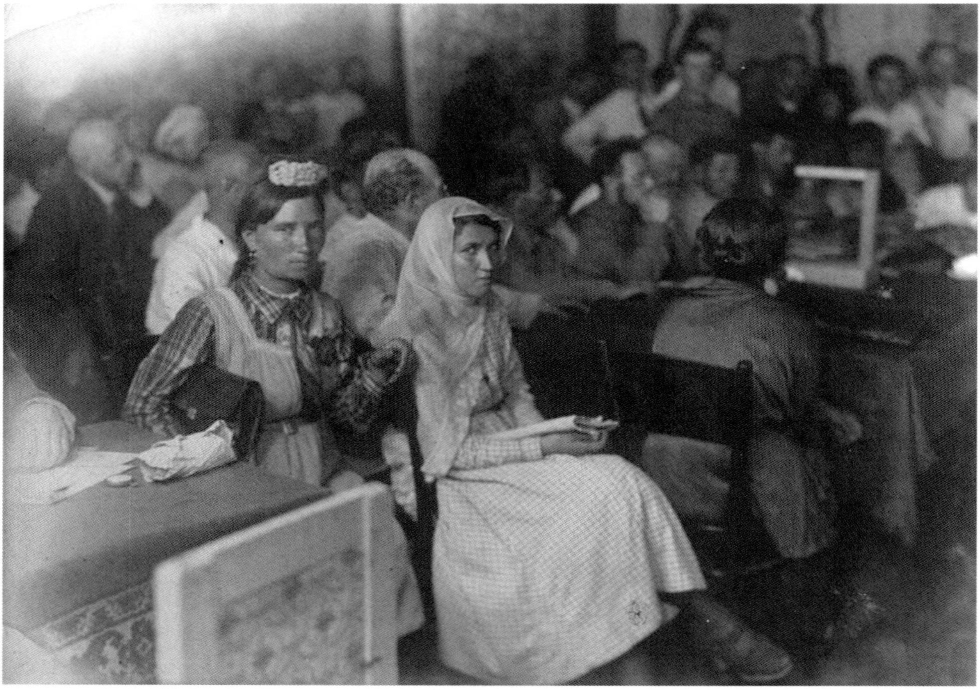

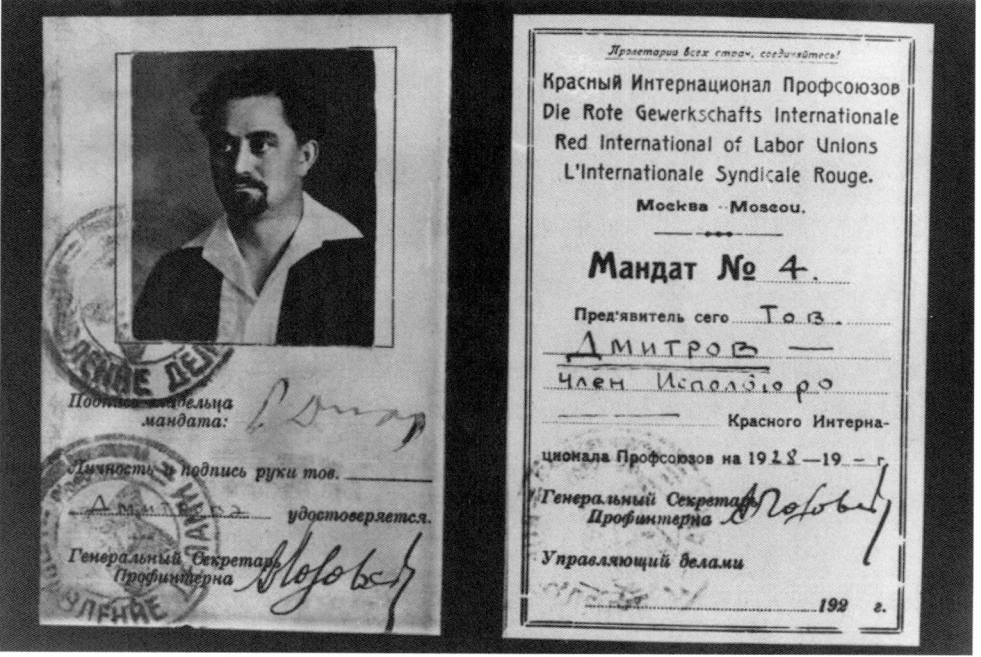

Bibinur and the nineteen-year-old Khaver Shabanova-Karayeva on stage alongside the presidium, between and behind them the Russian orientalist Mikhail N. Pavlovich, one of the organizers of the congress; at the table with beard and glasses is Karl Radek (Bibliothèque de la Ville, La Chaux-de-Fonds).

Подпись владельца мандата:

Личность и подпись руки тов. ______ удостоверяется.

Генеральный Секретарь Профинтерна

Пролетарии всех стран, соединяйтесь!

Красный Интернационал Профсоюзов
Die Rote Gewerkschafts Internationale
Red International of Labor Unions
L'Internationale Syndicale Rouge.
Москва - Moscou.

Мандат № 4.

Пред'явитель сего Тов. Дмитров — член Исполбюро

Красного Интернационала Профсоюзов на 1928—19 — г.

Генеральный Секретарь Профинтерна

Управляющий делами

192 г.

Credentials for 1928 issued to 'Cde Dimitrov' by the Red International of Labor Unions, or Profintern.

Education. From Autumn 1924 to April 1929, the Austrian Paul Friedländer (1891–1941) was also a member of the editorial team, first in Vienna and then in Berlin, after which he became editor-in-chief of *Welt am Abend*, one of Münzenberg's newspapers. Michel Dieschbourg (1899–1965, pseudonym Michel 'Hollay') of Luxembourg joined the editorial team in 1926, spending a short time in Vienna and Berlin, first for the French edition and from 1931 for the German. Dieschbourg was a former medical student who had given up his studies to work as a journalist at France's *Humanité*; he had been expelled from France in 1925, despite being married to a Frenchwoman and having two children with her. Night editor at the telegraphic agency from 1926, joining in Vienna and moving then to Berlin, was the Irishman and British subject Edward Fitzgerald (1902–1966), cover name 'Edward Gerhardt', the husband of Hilde Kramer. He had been brought to Berlin by the Kommunistischer Jugendverlag in 1923 to edit the English version of *Kommunistische Jugendinternationale*, the German-language newspaper of the Communist Youth International, together with the organization's pamphlets. When he saw the writing in question, he was horrified, as Hilde Kramer recalls in her memoirs:

> All the material had first been translated from Russian into German, the political jargon simply being taken over from one language to the other, and the resulting English was not only ugly but in many cases barely comprehensible. This Communist 'thesis language', originating in Moscow, was to be found in all communist publications. Our new colleague [Fitzgerald] fought a fierce battle against it.[19]

The documentary evidence, however, shows that he lost the war. The importance he accorded to language is reflected in his embarking on a writing career on his own account in 1928, which might explain Buber-Neumann's remark that 'one had the impression that he saw his work at *Inprekorr* as merely a means of earning a living, to which there was no need to commit oneself body and soul'.[20] Such an attitude was considered petty-bourgeois in Comintern circles, and she says of the

---

19 Kramer, *Rebellin*, 116–17.
20 Buber-Neumann, *Potsdam*, 126.

commitment of the *Inprekorr* staff more generally: 'If it was necessary to work overtime, we naturally stayed in the office beyond regular working hours. We were bound not by a contract of employment but by a common cause.'[21]

Given the good relations between Germany and the Soviet Union, *Inprekorr*'s journalists faced no legal impediment to their work,[22] but any foreign staff did have to have their papers in order. This Fitzgerald would learn to his cost. Issued in Moscow in 1924, his passport was considered invalid by both the British and the Germans, leaving his right of residence in question and him under permanent threat of deportation. This equally applied to his wife, Hilde Kramer, at a time when the women of most countries lost their original nationality on marrying a foreigner. This was likewise the case in France, where the French Communist Mireille Gaillard had lost her French citizenship on marriage to the Austrian Hans Glaubauf, a doctor in political science whom she had met in Moscow. In 1931, both were expelled from France; they went to Berlin, where she worked for *Inprekorr* while he wrote for *Freunde der Sowjetunion*, though he may have made occasional contributions to the Comintern's publication.

Changing Personnel Policy

A look at the *Inprekorr* staff reveals that the 'internationals', that is, those in Berlin who worked for the Comintern in any capacity, were connected among themselves in a multiplicity of ways. Those in the city who devoted their lives 'full-time to the victory of the world revolution' (Buber-Neumann) represented a small elite compared to the mass membership of the KPD. They were not isolated, however, but moved in an environment peopled by other Communists and sympathizers. The party was divided, riven by fierce political disputes and personal enmities, but members knew each other and had friends in common. The

---

21 Ibid., 150.
22 See Alpári's regular invitations to ministerial receptions for the foreign press and the communication of 13 December 1932 from the foreign press association addressed to Alpári at Moritzstrasse 17, Berlin SW 42, in connection with a police press card, in the Julius Alpári papers at Zurich Central Library: Nachlass Julius Alpári, SGA Ar.10.10.2.

internationals would also meet elsewhere – in Zurich, for example, where in 1934 Margarete Buber-Neumann and her partner Heinz Neumann were in hiding at the same time as Heinrich Kurella and Charlotte Stenbock-Fermor.

But it was in Moscow, above all (with its Hotel Lux and its Comintern headquarters no great distance from the Kremlin) that members of this dispersed international elite would come across each other, and Margarete, Heinz, Heinrich and Charlotte would certainly find themselves there in 1935–37.[23] Those who worked for the newsletter and the telegraphic agency were often enough already related in some way. *Inprekorr*'s typist, Fite (originally Frida) Kaetzler (1898–1956), a laboratory assistant by profession, was a friend and indeed a half-sister of sorts of Hilde Kramer's. The orphan Hilde had been fostered from the age of ten by Fite's mother, Gabriele Kaetzler, who was already looking after an ailing husband and six children of her own at her home near Munich. There she had enjoyed a free-thinking and permissive upbringing. Along with her sister Wise (Luise), who had been an employee of the Soviet Russian telegraphic agency ROSTA in Berlin at the time of the Spartacus Uprising, her sister Fite and her mother Gabriele, Hilde had been involved in the Bavarian Soviet Republic, with Hilde herself having a central role. Communism, then, was a family affair. 'You can never be radical enough,' said one of the sisters.[24] All four were arrested by 'White Guards' in early May, but then released for lack of proof. Shortly afterwards, they all moved to Berlin. Margarete Buber-Neumann's political destiny, too, was connected to the family. Born to aristocratic parents in Berlin in 1872, and disowned on account of her socialist and soon Communist sympathies, Gabriele Kaetzler had met Buber-Neumann in 1920, when that young woman was working at the Kinderhilfe (a municipal after-school centre) in Berlin-Schöneberg, and it was her account of the Bavarian Socialist Republic that finally spurred Buber-Neumann to join the Communist movement.[25] Alpári selected his team on the basis

---

23 See chapter 8.
24 On the four women's political involvements, see their correspondence of this period in Christiane Sternsdorf-Hauck, ed., *Brotmarken und rote Fahnen: Frauen in der bayrischen Revolution und Räterepublik 1918/19*, Frankfurt a. M.: isp-Verlag, 1989, excerpt at 79.
25 Buber-Neumann, *Potsdam*, 126, and *Kriegsschauplätze der Weltrevolution: Ein Bericht aus der Praxis der Komintern 1919–1943*, Stuttgart: Seewald Verlag, 1967, 75.

of personal acquaintance, choosing people he knew and trusted. Komját he knew from intellectual circles in Budapest in the early days of the Hungarian party and the time of the Hungarian Soviet Republic,[26] Runge from his exile in Czechoslovakia in 1920. It would seem that Alpári even felt a certain fatherly responsibility towards his staff. That, at least, is what is suggested by Margarete Buber-Neumann, whom he angered by asking her about her relationship with Heinz Neumann, with whom she had just fallen in love.[27]

Recruitment to the WEB offers a strong contrast to the 'spontaneous growth' of the *Inprekorr* and WES teams, its staffing being decided by the ECCI in Moscow. An initial list featured several names against each post, the final choice being determined by the availability of those concerned. The absence of women is striking, when compared to the situation at *Inprekorr*, though even there senior posts were confined to men. Another characteristic of the 'candidates' is their closeness to the apparatus in Moscow. The WEB would be staffed by proven Comintern *apparatchiki* who had already gone through a number of political turns. Their political capital lay in their bureaucratic experience and loyalty to the party line – two 'qualities' that were to be put to use in Berlin. The much smaller WES, on the other hand, had been staffed by the improvisational revolutionaries of the early days (an origin shared, indeed, by some of the WEB's bureaucrats). The late 1920s would see them repudiate the Comintern policy that those at the WEB represented and worked to promote. This the latter did in so satisfactory a manner that most of them survived the purges in the Soviet Union (though even they did not always escape untouched) and were able to make careers in their national parties on the dissolution of the Comintern: Dimitrov in Bulgaria, Gyptner in the DDR, Bamatter in the Soviet Union, Schüller in Austria and Woog in Switzerland.

Jules Humbert-Droz, who would remain employed by the Comintern until his expulsion from the party in 1943, probably represents a special case. His bad humour during his short interlude in Berlin – 'The food is as bland as only German cuisine can make it', 'Films in the West are so

---

26 In his novel *Optimisták* (The Optimists), Ervin Sinkó, who would marry Komját's then mistress, portrays the wedded but unfaithful poet as a member of the Budapest's circle of left-wing intellectuals, writers and artists at the time of the Soviet Republic of 1919.

27 Buber-Neumann, *Potsdam*, 160.

stupid that I can't sit through to the end'[28] – cannot be attributed to separation from family alone. As an ECCI secretary, it was not the first time he had been sent to another country, on his own, for some considerable period. And not much later, when, as Comintern representative 'Luis', he spent three months in Latin America – on the occasion of the first conference of Latin American revolutionary trade unions, held in Montevideo, and the first conference of Latin American Communist parties, held in Buenos Aires – his letters struck a very different tone. He found the atmosphere much more relaxed than in Moscow. On the other hand, he did not want to stay, despite being urged to do so by Victorio Codovilla, now Comintern-appointed head of the Latin American Secretariat in Montevideo. It was too far away from political events and decision-making, news from Moscow and Berlin coming through only in dribs and drabs, and he needed to know how things were developing politically.[29] Behind his ill temper in Berlin, in fact, was his dissatisfaction with the ultraleft policy imposed since 1928 and the shrinking of internal democracy in the Comintern, and, on top of that, his uncertainty about breaking from it. In this time of doubt and uncertainty regarding his political and organizational commitment, the 'costs' of the Comintern emissary's life in illegality – separation from family, poor accommodation or boring, routine work – seemed higher.[30] Humbert-Droz had always advocated cooperation with the Social Democrats, and he was a supporter of Bukharin, who was just about to go down to defeat in the factional struggle with Stalin. In the years that followed, Humbert-Droz would become close to the so-called 'Compromisers', a current he was supposed to battle against while at the WEB. Returning from Latin America, he found himself publicly reprimanded – for his silence on the new political line – by Manuilsky, at a session of the Tenth Plenum of the ECCI in July 1929. In response, he made a written statement to the ECCI. 'In order to prevent any

---

28 Typical remarks from a letter to his wife Jenny: Jules Humbert-Droz, *Mémoires*, vol. 2, *De Lénine à Staline: Dix ans au service de l'Internationale communiste, 1921–1931*, Neuchâtel: À La Baconnière, 1971, 288–92.

29 Humbert-Droz, *De Lénine*, 376–94. See also André Lasserre and Bernhard H. Bayerlein, eds, *Archives de Jules Humbert-Droz*, vol. 4, *Engagements à travers le monde: Résistances, conciliations, diffamations*, Zurich: Chronos Verlag, 2001, 455–7.

30 Daniel Gaxie, 'Rétributions du militantisme et paradoxes de l'action collective', *Swiss Political Science Review* 1:1, 2005, 157–88, at 177–8.

misunderstanding, I wish to state my position.' As a member of the Communist Party of Switzerland (Humbert-Droz had never joined the VKP(b), something not even required of Comintern secretaries at the time) he declared that his earlier dissent had reflected the position of his own party: 'When, following the Sixth World Congress, I expressed my disagreement with a number of decisions by the Presidium, I did so in complete accordance with the political line and the decisions of my party.' Now that the Swiss party had swung behind the Comintern line,[31] so would he: 'I defer.' He was now a loyal follower of ECCI policy.[32]

How true this was, or, to put it another way, to what extent Humbert-Droz may have secretly collaborated with the Compromisers, is unclear. He was, in any event, several times called to account for himself before organs of the Comintern, but nonetheless managed to retain a role in the Comintern and the Party (even if in not so exalted a position as Comintern secretary).[33] He was not alone in finding himself in more or less silent opposition to the turns of the 1920s and 1930s. We know that Fritz Brupbacher, *enfant terrible* of the Swiss party, spent a week in Berlin in January 1930, with his wife Paulette, in order to meet with leading members of the Berlin opposition around Heinrich Brandler.[34]

When the Wittorf Affair became public in the autumn of 1928, most of the *Inprekorr* editorial team were sympathetic to the 'Compromisers', according to Buber-Neumann.[35] John Wittorf had embezzled party funds and KPD leader Thälmann had covered up for his friend; when all became known, Thälmann was removed from his post by the Central Committee. The *Inprekorr* staff were happy at this victory for the 'Compromisers', with only the shrewd Alpári urging restraint until

---

31 It had, however, required the intervention of more than a half-dozen emissaries or instructors despatched from the WEB and the ECCI, among them Dimitrov, Gyptner and Eugen Fried, to get the Swiss party to drop its opposition to the social-fascism line: Brigitte Studer, *Un parti sous influence: Le Parti communiste, une section du Komintern, 1931 à 1939*, Lausanne: L'Âge d'Homme, 1994, 46–55 and 194–202.

32 Jules Humbert-Droz, Statement to the Executive Committee of the CI, 15 July 1929, RGASPI 495/18/738.

33 On Humbert-Droz's contacts with the 'Compromisers', see Lasserre and Bayerlein, *Archives de Jules Humbert-Droz*, vol. 4.

34 Karl Lang, *Kritiker, Ketzer, Kämpfer: Das Leben des Arbeiterarztes Fritz Brupbacher*, Zurich: Limmat Verlag, 1976, 300–1.

35 Buber-Neumann, *Potsdam*, 127.

Moscow's decision was known. And Thälmann was indeed reinstated as party chairman over the heads of the KPD leadership, in a victory for the Stalinist 'party left'. Given their political sympathies, the team would be suspicious of the relationship that later developed between Margarete (or Grete) Buber, as she was then still called, and Heinz Neumann, a confidant of Stalin's. The two met in 1929, and they were in a relationship from August onward. Kurella is reported not to have minced his words: 'You friends with that Stalinist? Nice taste you have!'[36] For the ambitious, highly intelligent and eloquent Neumann had been sent to Berlin in 1928 specifically to neutralize the 'Compromisers'. He was one of the few Germans who spoke Russian, one of the reasons, says Ruth Fischer, for his rapid rise since 1924. Another, in her opinion – here again, not entirely uncoloured by resentment – was that he followed Stalin 'like an admiring puppy that had found its new master'.[37] Despite Neumann's involvement in Fischer's dismissal from the party leadership in the mid-1920s, she credits him with courage for his lonely opposition, in 1931–32, to Stalin's policy of toleration of the National Socialists then rising in Germany.[38] Neumann was so self-confident that the following story was told about him in the Comintern: 'During a Comintern meeting with representatives of the Chinese Communist Party, the interpreter suddenly went missing. Heinz Neumann stepped in and fluently translated the speaker's remarks into Russian, to everyone's great astonishment. Asked afterwards how he had learnt Chinese so quickly, he replied, laughing, "Well, what else could he have said?"'[39]

Born in Berlin on 6 July 1902, the elder child of a bourgeois Jewish family, Neumann gained a reputation as a political *Wunderkind*. At the early age of eighteen, he had already embarked on university studies in philology, only to abandon them a few semesters later in favour of his

---

36 Ibid., 160. Although the precise qualification as 'Stalinist' that Buber-Neumann recalls is surely anachronistic, the animus towards Neumann is entirely plausible.

37 Ruth Fischer, *Stalin and German Communism*, Cambridge, MA: Harvard University Press, 1948, 405.

38 Fischer, *Stalin*, 446.

39 Ruth von Mayenburg, *Hotel Lux*, Munich: Piper, 1991 [1978], 131. Further evidence of either fluency or excessive self-confidence is Neumann's use of the name Giovanni Costa when he arrived in Vienna in early 1925: McLoughlin, *Kommunismus in Österreich 1918–1938*, 107.

activities with the KPD.⁴⁰ In 1922, he spent six months in prison for illegal political activities, time he used to learn Russian. He then enjoyed a rapid rise through the party, not only in Germany, where he was taken under August Thalheimer's wing, but also in the Comintern, a rise however interrupted at times on account of the risky roles he took on and a certain reputation for opportunism. Sought by the police in 1924, he fled to Vienna, where he was arrested and deported to the Soviet Union. In Moscow, in 1925, he became the German party's representative at the Comintern. One of the few foreigners to have direct access to Stalin, he was a keen advocate of Bolshevization. Thälmann's reinstatement saw him catapulted into the leadership of the KPD, where he acted as the leader's *éminence grise*, writing his speeches and articles. From 1928 to 1932, he was also editor-in-chief of the *Rote Fahne*, the German party newspaper, and, from 1930 to 1932, he sat in the Reichstag as part of the Communist parliamentary group. Heinrich Kurella's barbed comment to Margarete Buber was perhaps, however, not entirely politically motivated, for his personal file reveals that he had earlier been in a relationship with her. At a party meeting in Moscow, so the shorthand minute records, he declared that 'Comrade Neumann's wife is my ex'.⁴¹

There were also social differences between the two groups of Comintern functionaries. While most WEB staff were former workers, the *Inprekorr* journalists were, for the most part, graduates or professionally qualified. An educated man who occasionally gave somewhat theatrical expression to his love of German poetry, Alpári had already worked as a journalist and newspaper publisher before the First World War. Grün had been a journalist for the *Rote Fahne* in Vienna before 1926, while Runge had worked for the Social Democratic newspaper *Vorwärts* in Reichenberg until 1922. Komját had studied law before giving it up for poetry and journalism, his Futurist-Constructivist poetry soon finding a place in workers' publications. Fitzgerald came from a poor background, but would publish the first of a series of novels in 1938. Kurella was the son of an educated middle-class family of

---

40 In the record of his interrogation by the Zurich police on 9 December 1934, following his arrest, Neumann is said to have said that he had studied philosophy. This might, however, be an error of transcription by someone who had misheard or to whom the term 'philology' was unfamiliar; see chapter 8.

41 Minutes of the party group meeting, Moscow, 28 September 1936, RGASPI 495/205/6202-2; see also Hirdman, *Meine Mutter*, 414.

conservative inclinations, but had attended a progressive local-authority school as a boarder. His father was a doctor, his mother a member of the Polish minor nobility. He, too, had begun by studying law only to give it up in favour of politics and journalism. These people's education was also reflected in their knowledge of languages, Kurella being fluent in English and Russian,[42] Komját speaking Italian and very good German as well as the Hungarian in which he published his literary work, while Alpári added German and Russian to his native Hungarian, his German, however, being marked by such a pronounced accent that 'you could think he was making fun of himself'.[43]

Euphoria and Sadness, Integration and Isolation

The introduction of emergency rule and the collapse of the Grand Coalition saw treason charges against *Inprekorr* proliferate. As its legally responsible editor, Heinrich Kurella was jailed for a year in 1931, to be followed in 1932 by Max Gohl (1886–1951) – in reality, the sales manager and packer, according to Buber-Neumann. State repression intensified with the 'Third Period' increase in Communist militancy on the one hand and the growing weight of the National Socialists on the other. The most spectacular instance was the 'Blutmai', the 'Bloody May' of 1929. As the KPD marched on May Day in defiance of a ban by Berlin's Social Democratic police chief Karl Zörgiebel, the police moved in with batons and water cannon. The conflict escalated as the day wore on, and in the evening the police fired on residential buildings where the red flag was displayed. In response, the KPD called a general strike. The police then moved in on working-class neighbourhoods, searching house-to-house and making many arrests. In total, 30 civilians were killed and around 200 injured. More than a thousand were arrested, of which only one in ten proved to have any relationship with the KPD, direct or indirect. In reality, working-class neighbourhoods' traditional class solidarity in the face of the police had played a central role in the resistance to them, even at this

---

42 He filled out in Russian the 1934 questionnaire in his personal file, RGASPI 495/205/6202.
43 Buber-Neumann, *Potsdam*, 124.

time of 'social Fascism'.⁴⁴ In their violent clashes with the Nazis, the Communists could not generally count on police protection, and relied rather on their own stewards, in the shape of the Rote Frontkämpferbund and its successors.⁴⁵ The Swiss Communist Mentona Moser (1874–1971), who worked for the banned Rote Hilfe (the German section of International Red Aid) in Berlin between 1929 and 1933, while being officially employed by the Arbeiterkult record shop, describes in her memoirs the darkening atmosphere and intensifying police surveillance. The growing general anxiety also affected the KPD's commercial operations, the record shop, at least, being increasingly often visited by detectives or undercover spies in search of such 'prohibited items' as recordings of Communist battle songs. This meant that 'many customers no longer dared come into the shop, the tills rang ever more infrequently, and creditors became ever more pressing'.⁴⁶ From her apartment on the Bülowplatz, Moser watched, horrified, the violence on the streets below, as the police went after demonstrators.⁴⁷

Increasingly often, National Socialists attacked known Communists and persons of Jewish appearance. At the artists' colony on Laubenheimerplatz, home to Heinrich Kurella and his partner Charlotte as well as many other Communists and party sympathizers, the summer of 1932 saw the residents organize their own defence association in the face of the now numerous Nazi attacks. The writer and journalist Gustav Regler, a member of the party since 1929 and another resident of the artists' colony, later recorded his scepticism: 'People used to say that our block was a well-organized fortress; in reality an NCO and four men could have cleaned out every apartment.'⁴⁸

---

44 Ibid., 153. The consequent deepening of the division between the KPD and the SPD is also described in Axel Weipert, *Das Rote Berlin: Eine Geschichte der Berliner Arbeiterbewegung 1830–1934*, Berlin: Berliner Wissenschaftsverlag, 2013, 202–4.

45 On the role of inter-party physical violence in political conflict in the late Weimar Republic, see Eve Rosenhaft, *Beating the Fascists? The German Communists and Political Violence, 1929–1933*, Cambridge: Cambridge University Press, 1983; and Pamela E. Swett, *Neighbors and Enemies: The Culture of Radicalism in Berlin, 1929–1933*, Cambridge: Cambridge University Press, 2004.

46 Mentona Moser, *Ich habe gelebt*, Zurich: Limmat Verlag, 1986, 225.

47 Ibid., 224.

48 Gustav Regler, *The Owl of Minerva: The Autobiography of Gustav Regler*, trans. Norman Denny, London: Rupert Hart-Davis, 1959, 147.

Alpári was therefore extremely careful about security and demanded strict discipline of his staff. They were to avoid demonstrations and rallies if there were any risk of these deliberate provocations leading to a clash or an intervention by the police. There were many demonstrations. Important gathering points or meeting places were the Kösliner Straße in Wedding, the Kliems Festsäle function rooms on the Hasenheide in Neukölln, the playing fields in the Treptower Park, the Lustgarten park on Museum Island, the Sportpalast indoor arena and, of course, the Liebknechthaus, the KPD's own headquarters.[49] Alpári himself never attended mass meetings, not even the massive May Day parades.[50] He therefore missed out on the motivating power of the big events at which the party demonstrated its strength by physically occupying urban space, mobilizing members and sympathizers for future activity. Such emotionally charged collective exercises could also win new members. The experience of togetherness, the sense of merging into a single, collective body of fighting proletarians, has been described by those who were there as both euphoric and empowering. That was indeed the effect the organizers of large-scale rallies and demonstrations intended. They did not just call for international solidarity but constantly celebrated the international character of the movement through symbolic practices. The countless red flags were one element, as was the raised fist as sign of allegiance and declaration of war on the class enemy. International solidarity was also evoked by the exchange of banners between party cells in Germany and their Soviet counterparts – in the 1920s a phenomenon whose scale sometimes overwhelmed the party officials who had to deal with it.[51] Choreographed movements and increasingly paramilitary discipline were intended to demonstrate the martial determination of a physically and symbolically unified and powerful body of workers, and their willingness to sacrifice themselves for the cause. In doing so, the Communists 'reversed the sign' of the

---

49 Karl Schlögel, *Das russische Berlin: Ostbahnhof Europas*, Munich: Hanser, 2007, 199. See also the list of meeting-places at 207–8.

50 Komját, *Geschichte der Inprekorr*, 55.

51 For an extensive treatment of this international practice, see Gleb Albert, *Das Charisma der Weltrevolution: Revolutionärer Internationalismus und frühe Sowjetgesellschaft, 1917–1927*, Cologne: Böhlau-Verlag, 2017, 470–95. See also Ulrich Eumann, *Eigenwillige Kohorten der Revolution: Zur regionalen Sozialgeschichte des Kommunismus in der Weimarer Republik*, Frankfurt a. M.: Peter Lang, 2007, 176, and more generally on the symbolism of the Red Flag, 173–8.

worker's body, signifier no longer of low social status but of self-identification with a proletariat conceived in the most positive of terms.

Especially effective in this respect was music, connecting Communists across borders. The Swiss Theo Pinkus, who completed his apprenticeship at Rowohlt in Berlin in 1927 before going on to work for Münzenberg's *Arbeiter Illustrierte Zeitung* (*AIZ*), felt himself 'at last among comrades' when the Internationale was sung at his first Communist meeting.[52] The stirring words and urgent rhythms of such compositions as the *Kominternlied* [Song of the Comintern] promoted a fighting mood and a sense of international solidarity. Its complex but exciting music was the work of Hanns Eisler (1898–1962), who in the winter of 1925 had moved from Vienna to Berlin, where his elder siblings Ruth (Fischer) and Gerhart (1897–1968) already lived, the first having just then lost the leadership of the KPD, the second being associate editor of the party newspaper, the *Rote Fahne*. Years after abandoning his Communism, Arthur Koestler was still full of praise for Eisler's music: 'These songs . . . were at the same time sentimental, stirring and didactic. They were the only successful works of popular art that the European Communist movement has created, the beginnings of a revolutionary folklore.'[53] Extolling the heroism of the international class struggle and promising victory despite all setbacks, the *Song of the Comintern*'s dramatic and martial lyrics were composed by Franz Jahnke and Maxim Vallentin:

> Quit the machines, go out proletarians! At the double, quick march! . . . We shall conquer the world! . . . Our best have died in the struggle . . . New fighters, come up comrades! . . . We are the storm troops of justice to come. . . . In Russia, workers' arms were victorious! They did it, and we shall too! Come, soldiers of the Revolution!

The same martial tenor characterizes the *Solidaritätslied* [Song of Solidarity] written towards the end of the Weimar Republic, to words by Bertolt Brecht. With its call for all to unite, 'black, white, brown, yellow',

---

52 Diary entry for 29 September 1927, cited in Rudolf M. Lüscher and Werner Schweizer, *Amalie und Theo Pinkus-de Sassi: Leben im Widerspruch*, Zurich: Limmat Verlag, 1987, 80.

53 Arthur Koestler, *The Invisible Writing*, New York: Macmillan, 1954, 40.

it was explicitly anticolonialist and antiracist, reflecting the turn to radical anti-imperialism that came with the 'Third Period' analysis adopted by the Comintern in 1928.[54]

The everyday experience of Comintern officials was often less inspiring, their illegality calling for much routine and great caution in their contact with others. Yet contrary to the myth of the lone Comintern agent, many of those active internationally were married or had long-term partners. Their missions, however, often imposed lengthy separations. There were affairs and a notably high number of changes of partner. (One who had multiple affairs was Georgi Dimitrov.[55]) The example of M. N. Roy's partner Evelyn Trent shows how the nomadic and dangerous life they led exacted its costs, and the role gender played in this. In principle, Communist organizations regarded women as equal members, but in practice, without the deliberate adoption of corrective measures, the socially prevailing hierarchical difference between the sexes continued to influence perceptions and practices. Though single women were more likely to be seen as independent political actors, the Comintern tended to treat wives as appendages to their husbands, assigning them roles as their assistants.[56] Especially when the man was a prominent activist, the woman's political activity would be overshadowed by his, as happened in the case of M. N. and Evelyn Trent Roy. While his political activities had official status, as those of a member of the ECCI apparatus, her own remained for the most part informal and unofficial and her relationship to the Comintern was mediated through him. Roy became one of the few non-European members of the ECCI at the Third Comintern Congress of 1921. In 1926, he was appointed to the Presidium, the Secretariat and the Orgburo. With the reorganization of the ECCI apparatus (to structure its work on a regional basis), he was made head of the regional secretariat for America and Canada, and within that

---

54 The emotionally unifying power of the themes of struggle and solidarity is discussed in connection with this song in Eric D. Weitz, *Creating German Communism, 1890–1990: From Popular Protests to Socialist State*, Princeton, NJ: Princeton University Press, 1997, 255–6.

55 Marietta Stankova, *Georgi Dimitrov: A Biography*, London: I.B. Tauris, 2010, 99 and 103–4.

56 Brigitte Studer, *The Transnational World of the Cominternians*, trans. D. R. Roberts, Basingstoke, UK: Palgrave Macmillan, 2015, 40–58.

secretary of the Japan subgroup [*sic*]. He was also a member of the regional secretariat for England, Ireland, Holland, Australia and South Africa, and within that secretary and head of the subgroup on British and Dutch India.[57] The following year, overburdened with work, he was relieved of responsibility for the recently established British-American secretariat, but was additionally appointed a member of the Eastern Secretariat, dealing with China, Mongolia and Persia, as well as Syria, Palestine, Egypt and other Arab lands.[58] Evelyn Trent Roy, on the other hand, lacked the symbolic capital of a role in the apparatus. Women were not rejected for such positions, they were simply not considered. Such political invisibility also had its counterpart in memory: Roy's memoirs make no mention at all of his first wife.[59]

Yet Evelyn Trent – a Stanford graduate and a feminist, intelligent, multilingual and already politically active in California – had social, cultural and activist capital of her own. After meeting on the Palo Alto campus in 1916, the two had moved to New York together, where they got married, before travelling to Mexico under false names, in 1917, to escape the attentions of the New York police, who were targeting Indian nationalists. In Mexico, on the urging of Mikhail Borodin, they jointly founded a Communist party, within which Evelyn set up a women's group. They had journeyed to Communism together, but the British colonial authorities would attest to Evelyn's more solid knowledge of Marxism: 'Mrs Roy ... is said to be a cleverer and more capable Communist than Roy himself.'[60]

Evelyn was by no means only Roy's partner, but a political actor in her own right. She came to her own political decisions and played a

---

57 Distribution of work among the secretaries of the ECCI and the creation of regional secretariats, Moscow, 1926, RGASPI 495/46/7.

58 Decision of the Political Secretariat on the composition of the regional secretariats, Moscow, 8 July 1927, RGASPI 495/18/596. The following year saw him relieved of his functions after publicly criticizing Comintern policy, ECCI decision of 28 September 1928, RGASPI 495/20/762.

59 It could certainly be argued, however, that Roy was seeking instead to protect his former wife during the age of McCarthy.

60 Sir David Petrie, *Communism in India, 1924–1927*, ed. Mahadevaprasad Saha, Calcutta: Editions Indian, 1958 [1927], 335. Director of the Intelligence Bureau of the Government of India since 1924, Petrie wrote this report for the use of 'officers of the British Government, in India and abroad, whose duty was to carry on espionage against communist and revolutionary nationalists' (Introduction, iii).

significant role among Indian revolutionary nationalists. Under the name Santi Devi, she wrote numerous articles about the revolutionary and nationalist anticolonial movements in India for *Inprekorr* and other Communist publications, covering, for instance, the Bombay textile workers' strike of 1924. She was the editor of *The Vanguard* (later *Masses of India*), founded in Berlin in 1922 as the journal of the émigré Communist Party of India, to which she contributed many articles on India and what she considered to be the idealist politics of the Ghandian movement, whose critical arguments have been judged by some authorities to be 'among the best to be found in the Communist literature'.[61] Several of these would be published in 1923 in a volume jointly edited with M. N. Roy.[62] Like him, she taught at the Communist University of the Toilers of the East on its foundation in Moscow in 1921. In May that year, she visited Britain on the Comintern's behalf, travelling under a false name on a Mexican passport. Arrested by the British police, she was deported to Mexico but sneaked off the ship in Cuba and made her way back to Europe.[63] Sometimes together, sometimes apart, Roy and she resided in Berlin, Tashkent, Moscow, Zurich and Paris before their eventual separation. The hardships and strains of such a life only became too much for her when they broke up, separating in the summer of 1925 and divorcing in the autumn of 1926.[64] This revealed the equality they supposedly enjoyed in both their working relationship and their private life to have been an illusion. Writing the following spring to Henk Sneevliet ('Maring'), a fellow campaigner against imperialism whom she had known since the Second World Congress of 1920 – and who would himself leave the Communist Party only two months later – she wrote:

---

61 Overstreet and Windmiller, *Communism in India*, 510–11. An altogether more positive judgement of Ghandi's movement was given by Agnes Smedley, in a long newspaper article emphasizing the great strengths of the Indian National Congress and the success of its sexual equality policy: Ghandi's movement had made 'the greatest contribution to women's awakening': 'Die Frau in Indien', *Neue Zürcher Zeitung* 1256, 12 August 1925, 9–10.

62 M. N. Roy and Evelyn Roy, *One Year of Non-Cooperation from Ahmedabad to Gaya*, Calcutta: Communist Party of India, 1923.

63 Daniel Brückenhaus, '"Every Stranger Must Be Suspected": Trust Relationships and the Surveillance of Anti-Colonialists in Early Twentieth-Century Western Europe', *Geschichte und Gesellschaft* 36:4, December 2010, 523–66, at 543–6.

64 The British authorities took Evelyn Trent's return to the USA to be another mission for the Comintern, though there is no evidence for this: Petry, *Communism*, 140.

'I was so weary of being hunted from place to place, from country to country, of having to hide and always to be surrounded by a terrible fog of suspicion and fear, and to have others suspect and fear me.'[65] The dramatic tone of her words reflects the life she had lived, marked not only by arrests and deportations but by factional struggles among campaigners. In London, she was accused of embezzlement following her failed attempt to contact the Indian-born British Communist Shapurji Saklatvala (1874–1936), one of the two members of the CPGB elected to parliament in 1922. And M. N. Roy was accused of being an informer by his former friend and fellow-campaigner Abani Mukherji.[66]

While the Indian exile groups, like many others, were divided and riven by personal animosities, the effects could sometimes be drastically different as between men and women, on account of the differences in the way they were perceived as political actors. Since women in politics were rarely accorded the symbolic power invested in men, their position was weaker and more vulnerable. Politically active women with a high-profile partner would always be associated with him, their own political activities being relegated, as it were, to the private sphere. Should the relationship break up, the power differential would be revealed undisguised. In a politically active couple, it was the man to whom the political role would fall, and, in case of conflict, there was a tendency to assign private motives to women's behaviour. Roy's memoirs offer an example. In them, he attributes his conflict with Chatto to the latter's companion Agnes Smedley alone, retrospectively projecting his own negative feelings onto a woman and so preserving the illusion of a spotless solidarity between men. According to Roy, Smedley's character, life choices and whiteness made her political commitment to the 'Indian cause' questionable. He crudely describes her as 'hysterical – a pathological case' and as 'a fanatical hero-worshipper'. And 'when she espoused the Indian cause, she seemed to believe that to fall in love with famous Indian Revolutionaries would be the

---

65 Evelyn Roy, letter to Henk Sneevliet, 13 March [1927], transcribed from a copy in the Evelyn Trent Collection, Hoover Institution Archives, Stanford University, available on line at marxists.org. This correspondence is extensively cited in Sibnarayan Ray, *In Freedom's Quest: Life of M. N. Roy*, vol. 2, *The Comintern Years 1922–27*, Kolkata: Minerva, 2002, 165–75.

66 Brückenhaus, '"Every Stranger Must Be Suspected"', 551.

expression of her loyalty to India.'⁶⁷ It was she, evidently, who stood between the two men: 'Chatto wanted to meet me and cultivate my acquaintance, but Smedley stood in the way'. Chatto, on the other hand, he described as 'a very intelligent and energetic man'. His behaviour when the Indian Revolutionary Committee came to Moscow in 1921, to negotiate its admission to the Comintern, had, however, astonished him: 'I expected to find in him a valuable colleague in the revolutionary work. Therefore his attitude of unconcealed hostility puzzled me very much.' For this he blamed Smedley, thus excluding from all consideration his own dealings with his rival: 'His attitude in Moscow was largely the result of the influence of Agnes Smedley.' And last, but not least, he remarks that it was presumptuous in Smedley, as a non-Indian, to wish to present the Indian case.⁶⁸ Roy's commitment to the revolution did not automatically make him a feminist. As Roy apparently confided to Sneevliet, 'he did not like the combination of wife and politician'. After they broke up, Evelyn Trent wondered whether the asymmetry in their relationship, to which she had committed herself entirely as his wife, prioritizing her partner's personal freedom and political commitments, was not the result of his having been brought up in a 'patriarchal environment'. Taking a critical view of relationships between the sexes in the Communist Party and, as one may read between the lines, of mid-1920s developments in the Comintern, she adds that perhaps his behaviour was that of a man 'thrust too abruptly into a degenerate, post-revolutionary environment'.⁶⁹

Flight and arrest were also a recurrent feature in Evelyn Trent Roy's life. In early 1924, when Roy was expelled from Germany, the couple

---

67 Roy, *Memoirs*, 484. An interpretation more alive to the agency and political contribution of these women can be found in Kumari Jayawardena, *The White Woman's Other Burden: Western Women and South Asia During British Colonial Rule*, New York: Routledge, 1995.

68 Roy, *Memoirs*, 487–8. It should be noted that Roy's rivalry with Chatto may not have been solely political: it is possible that he was, in fact, the rapist presented in fictional guise in Smedley's autobiographical novel *Daughter of Earth* (1929). This suspicion is raised in both Purnima Bose, 'Transnational Resistance and Fictive Truths: Virendranath Chattopadyaya, Agnes Smedley and the Indian Nationalist Movement'; in Babli Sinha, ed., *South Asian Transnationalisms: Cultural Exchange in the Twentieth Century*, London: Routledge, 2012, 46–65, at 58; and Ruth Price, *The Lives of Agnes Smedley*, New York: Oxford University Press, 2005, 61 and 440.

69 All quotes from Ray, *In Freedom's Quest*, vol. 2, 171.

travelled to France via Switzerland, arriving in Annecy and then Paris.[70] While Roy was in Moscow attending the Fifth World Congress, she continued to publish the *Vanguard* newspaper and act as leader of the Comité Pro-Hindou, chaired by Henri Barbusse, which she had established to support the cause of Indian independence.[71] In early 1925, both of them were arrested and while Roy was deported to Luxembourg, she was able to remain in Paris. For Trent, the break with Roy also meant the end of her involvement with the Comintern (though not with the left, which she continued in her capacity as a journalist in the USA). She had put up with the nomadic life, the Comintern's internal political surveillance and the atmosphere of mutual mistrust so long as involvement in the International made sense. Sneevliet would no doubt understand: as the founder of the Indonesian CP (and thus an 'enemy' of his own government) and as a Comintern emissary in China, he had risked great personal dangers before breaking with the Comintern in 1927 and soon after founding a new socialist party, eventually joining the Trotskyist Left Opposition in 1933.

Given the gender relations prevailing in the Comintern, Evelyn Trent Roy had adapted her life to her husband's political activity. In her 1926 letter of farewell, she declared that she had given up everything for him – her home, her social circle and her former friends – and now 'nothing was left'.[72] As she confided to Sneevliet, she had committed herself to a cause she still believed in, but to which she no longer had any personal connection: 'If I had ever been in India, or could ever go there, it might have been different, but always it had been pure theoretical abstraction to me. The only living link was my husband. When this link was broken,

---

70 Overstreet and Windmiller, *Communism*, 68–9. The Roys were presumably assisted in Switzerland by the Ghadar network, on which see Harald Fischer-Tiné, 'The Other Side of Internationalism: Switzerland as a Hub of Militant Anti-Colonialism, c. 1910–1920', in Patricia Purtschert and Harald Fischer-Tiné, eds, *Colonial Switzerland: Rethinking Colonialism from the Margins*, Basingstoke, UK: Palgrave Macmillan, 2015, 221–58.

71 On the Comité Pro-Hindou, see Brückenhaus, *Policing*, 109; and Overstreet and Windmiller, *Communism in India*, 74.

72 Direct quote from Kris Manjapra, *M. N. Roy: Marxism and Colonial Cosmopolitanism*, Delhi: Routledge, 2010, 76. Evelyn Trent did, however, stand up for Roy when he was arrested in India in 1931, keeping in contact with Roy's then wife, Ellen Gottschalk. On this campaign, see Sibnarayan Ray, ed., *The World Her Village: Selected Letters and Writings of Ellen Roy*, Calcutta: Ananda, 1979.

only the abstraction remained, and I was so tired of abstract theories.'[73] Even so, the end of the relationship would cost Roy as well, the historians Overstreet and Windmiller dating to this period the decline of his influence in India.[74]

Roy soon embarked on another relationship, though it is not known exactly when. However, when he travelled to China as a Comintern emissary in early 1927, he was accompanied by his new companion, Luise Geissler (1899–1973).[75] She was, like him, an employee of the Comintern, but it is only as Roy's partner that she has been paid any attention in the literature. This despite the fact that she too had very likely been assigned political tasks in China, if only as Roy's secretary.[76] That this was indeed so is suggested by the fact that the Little Commission granted her a month of paid leave on her return from China, with Roy, on 30 September 1927. Luise Geissler – or Luise Scheller, as she was known after her marriage to the Swiss Hans Walter Scheller – had come to Communism as a young woman, at the time of the Bavarian Soviet Republic. She was the daughter of a civil servant in the Bavarian foreign ministry and a free-spirited mother of Sinti and Roma extraction. Having joined the USPD at the age of seventeen, she became a member of the Munich branch of the Spartacist League in February 1919. Under the Soviet Republic, she worked for the Action Committee, its highest governmental body, and found herself arrested following the violent intervention of central government forces on 4 May. Accused of high treason and assistance to fugitives, after four months in pretrial detention she was released for lack of evidence and deported to Switzerland. That a native German could be expelled from the country was the result of the patriarchal character of the prevailing legal provisions regarding marriage and citizenship. On marrying Hans Walter Scheller, a student at the Munich Academy of Art, in 1918, Geissler had lost her German citizenship, obliging her to take the nationality of her Swiss husband.

---

73 Evelyn Roy, letter to Henk Sneevliet, 13 March [1927].
74 Overstreet and Windmiller, *Communism in India*, 80–1.
75 See chapter 6.
76 The biographical information that follows derives from Geissler's records in the Comintern archive, RGASPI, 495/65a/10679, among the ECCI personal files. She receives no attention at all in the literature, with the exception of her time with Roy. Robert North, who interviewed her as a contemporary witness, asked only about Roy. Somewhat more interest is shown by Sibnarayan Ray, *In Freedom's Quest: A Study of the Life and Works of M. N. Roy, 1887–1954*, vol. 2, Kolkata: Minerva, 2002, 260–2.

That marriage did not last, however, and they divorced in 1921. From September 1919 to December 1920, Geissler lived in Zurich, where she joined the Social Democratic Party and worked for a number of employers as a shorthand typist, among them Fritz Platten (1883–1942) and the party Left, which sought its adherence to the Third International. She then moved to Vienna, where she worked for the secretariat of the Austrian CP until the summer of 1921. In August, she was in Moscow, a Comintern employee and a resident, with many interruptions, of the Hotel Lux. She worked first for the Hungarian Mátyás Rákosi at the ECCI Secretariat, then at the Press Department, the Czech Secretariat, the Balkan Secretariat, the Central European Secretariat and the ECCI Presidium. In Moscow, she lived for a short time with the German-Russian Max Levien (1885–1937), one of the leaders of the Bavarian Soviet Republic, who had studied for his doctorate in Munich. He succeeded in escaping to Vienna and started working for the Comintern apparatus in June 1921. Luise Geissler returned to Germany in the spring of 1922, working in the trade union department of the KPD as a stenographer and typist. In November, she returned to Moscow, where she acted as stenographer and shorthand typist at the Fourth World Congress. Some six months later, the KPD asked for her back, this time to work for the party's secret military apparatus. This led to her being 'badly compromised' in the so-called Cheka Trial, as the KPD's representative on the ECCI later reported, forcing her return to the Soviet Union. This did not prevent her from holidaying in the Netherlands in October 1924, on a false passport provided by the OMS. In Moscow, she joined the Russian party, before going back to Germany in April 1925 and travelling in September from there to the United States. During the year she spent there, she was involved with the German Bureau of the Workers' Party and the American Negro Labor Congress and was also secretary of a District Factory Nucleus, as she notes in a handwritten curriculum vitae of July 1926. With the 'assent' of the US party, she returned to the Comintern apparatus in Moscow in May 1926, as secretary of the Czech Secretariat, now using the name Schuman. It was in Moscow, most probably, that she met Roy.

Between Ascesis and Bohemia

Housing was often problematic. The 'conspiratorial' restrictions on those operating in illegality only rarely allowed them to rent an apartment in their own names. Frequent changes of address were therefore the rule.[77] Accommodation was generally found with comrades or sympathizers, or sublets secured through volunteer intermediaries of middle-class background. After 1929, Jakov Reich used for his contact address an apartment at Waghäuseler Straße 19 in Wilmersdorf that belonged to the doctor Minna Flake, a former member of the KPD who had left it for the KPD-O, but he actually lived with Ruth Oesterreich at Aroser Allee 189/III in the borough of Reinickendorf, part of a workers' housing scheme built in the 1920s that provided small but modern apartments with heating and running water.[78] Margarete Buber-Neumann, who lived alone in a large apartment, without her two daughters, following her divorce, recalls putting up Dimitrov and his first wife, Ljubica Ivošević, for a time in accordance with a 'secret' arrangement with the party,[79] though when this was exactly, she does not say. It must, however, have been before the end of 1928, for by then Ivošević was in a psychiatric institution in Moscow, and committed suicide in May 1933. During his time with the WEB, Dimitrov lived some of the time with his lover, Ani Krueger, and some of the time as a lodger with a family in Steglitz. Rarely can he have lived as comfortably as he did during his six weeks in Vienna in 1930, when the son of the industrialist Knopp put the family's large apartment at his disposal.[80] Even someone like Münzenberg lived until the age of thirty-seven in a state of permanent makeshift, 'in offices, travelling, escaping from the police, in hotels and coffee houses'. Only a furnished room with a working-class family whose address no-one knew afforded him a private retreat from time to time.[81] Hilde Kramer and Edward Fitzgerald were

---

77 As it was for Victor Serge and his family: Serge, *Memoirs*, 190.

78 Birgit Schmidt, *Wer war Ruth Oesterreich? Auf den Spuren einer vergessenen Sozialistin*, Lich: Verlag Edition AV, 2011, 27.

79 See her curriculum vitae of 22 September 1936, which, however, gives no details of the 'secret' arrangement. More detail is found in Buber-Neumann, *Potsdam*, 137–47.

80 McLoughlin et al., *Internationaler Kommunismus*, 426.

81 Babette Gross, *Willi Münzenberg: A Political Biography*, trans. Marian Jackson, East Lansing: Michigan State University Press, 1974, 186.

likewise constantly on the move, for lack of both money and suitable accommodation. Charlotte Stenbock-Fermor and Heinrich Kurella first lived together at his sister Tania's before they found their own apartment. December 1932 saw them installed at the Wilmersdorfer artists' colony on Laubenheimerplatz (Ludwig-Barnay-Platz from 1963), in the 'Red Block' built between 1927 and 1930. Other party members lived there too: the journalist Arthur Koestler (1905–1983), who had moved to Berlin in 1930; the journalist Gustav Regler, who had come to Berlin in 1929 with his second partner Marieluise Vogeler, daughter of the painter Heinrich Vogeler; Alfred Kantorowicz (1899–1979), then editor of the *Vossische Zeitung*, and his wife, the Munich actress Frieda (Friedel) Wolf-Ferrari, née Ebenhoech (1905–1968); the Adlerian psychotherapist and later writer Manès Sperber (1905–1984); the Jewish-Polish architectural student Karola Piotrkowski (1905–1994), previously in a relationship with Kantorowicz and now with Ernst Bloch, when she moved there in 1931; the journalist Susanne Leonhard (1895–1984), a founding member of the KPD, who had been head of the press department at the Soviet Embassy in Vienna in 1920–22, together with her son Wolfgang. In his autobiography their comrade Gustav Regler observes of this Bohemia that 'they were cheap apartments and yet hardly anyone paid their rent, neither the salaries nor the so-called income of the liberal professions being sufficient'.[82]

With the exception of Susanne Leonhard, these intellectuals were recent party members. Manès Sperber had joined the KPD in 1927. Ernst Bloch had presumably done so at some time in the 1920s, though when is a matter of dispute. Regler joined in 1929, Friedel and Alfred Kantorowicz in 1930, Koestler in 1931 and Karola Bloch in 1932. While these last-minute additions to the ranks may seem surprising in retrospect, there were a number of reasons why it should have been so. First, the image of the Soviet Union among progressives had improved, and that to the point of idealization, probably thanks to the tenth anniversary celebrations of the Russian Revolution masterminded by Münzenberg, whose propaganda offensive met with a great response. According to his report to the ECCI, the circulation of the *Arbeiter Illustrierte Zeitung* reached an unprecedented 350,000 on that occasion. Many workers' delegations had travelled to Moscow for the

---

82 Regler, *The Owl of Minerva*, 143.

celebratory congress and mass meetings with many international guests had drummed up enthusiasm in Germany.[83] Second, the economic crisis of 1929 added to the lustre of the 'Workers' Fatherland'. Compared to the dramatic unemployment in the capitalist countries, the Soviet Union could seem a workers' paradise, a factor not only for working-class people but also for more socially aware artists and intellectuals. Third, many were driven to act by contemporary political developments. Karola Bloch had hesitated at first to join the party, 'but the dangerous political situation in Germany called for a disciplined struggle against the Nazis, and I believed that only the KPD could carry it forward', as she would write in her memoirs.[84] (Fanny Jezierska, a member of the KPD opposition, had a very different judgement on the party's capacity for political action. In a letter of December 1931 to her Zurich friend Fritz Brupbacher, she wrote: 'The situation here becomes ever more threatening, the Nationalists [sic] speak openly of their intentions, nowhere are preparations for resistance being made. Not even among the Communists, who as ever limit themselves to ultra-left talk and dread any action – for fear of jeopardizing the five-year plan.'[85]

When Münzenberg and his partner Babette Gross – Margarete Buber-Neumann's older sister – eventually rented a place of their own in 1926, they did not take a whole apartment but only a number of rooms in a bourgeois villa on Berlin's Tiergarten, at In den Zelten 9a (today John-Foster-Dulles-Allee 10). This belonged to the sexologist Dr Magnus Hirschfeld, himself a Social Democrat, but quite open to Communism. Soon they were joined on the same floor by other Comintern employees. Among them was Heinz Neumann, Margarete's future partner, now back from Moscow, and possibly, for a short period in 1928 or 1929, Roy and Luise Geissler, the latter Lu to her friends.[86] Münzenberg, who had also been a member of the

---

83 Kasper Braskén, 'Celebrating October: The Transnational Commemorations of the Tenth Anniversary of the Soviet Union in Weimar Germany', in Jean-François Fayet, Valérie Gorin and Stéfanie Prezioso, eds, *Echoes of October: International Commemorations of the Bolshevik Revolution 1918–1990*, London: Lawrence & Wishart, 2017, 76–105.
84 Karola Bloch, *Aus meinem Leben*, Pfullingen: Verlag Günther Neske, 1981, 69.
85 Luban, *Fanny Thomas-Jezierska*, 309.
86 Buber-Neuman, *Potsdam*, 132; Jayawardena, *The White Woman's Other Burden*, 241; written communication from the Zurich City Archives, 26 September 2017.

Reichstag since 1924, used these rooms as offices for himself and his staff as well as his home. There preparations were made for the Brussels Congress of the Anti-Imperialist League and meetings were held with illegal foreign visitors.[87] There was a constant coming and going: 'Emissaries came from Moscow; Dimitrov met his Balkan representatives there.'[88] Yet the house was by no means suitable for conspiratorial activities. Hirschfeld's Institute of Sexology stood right next door, and visitors to the exhibition housed there often wandered through the corridors of the villa, also full of objects from Hirschfeld's collection. Münzenberg's apartment was, in fact, the talk of the Comintern.[89]

The institute also served as the headquarters of the World League for Sexual Reform, founded in Copenhagen in 1928. One member of its International Committee was Fritz Brupbacher, Münzenberg's friend and mentor from his time in Switzerland, who in late 1921 had accompanied him on one of the first transports of food to starving Russia. *Enfant terrible* of the Swiss Social Democrats and after 1921 of the Swiss Communist Party, this independent-minded workers' physician of anarchic inclinations campaigned alongside his wife, Paulette Raygrodski, the daughter of Belarusian Jews and likewise a doctor, for popular access to contraception and abortion. Both were in close contact with left reformers in Weimar, among them Hirschfeld and the renowned German sex educator Max Hodann, and published regularly in Germany's Communist press.[90] Even when Brupbacher was expelled from the Swiss party in February 1933, he and Münzenberg kept up their friendship. Before 1933, the Brupbachers must often have stayed

---

87 On the Brussels Congress, see chapter 5.
88 Gross, *Münzenberg*, 186–7.
89 The house was no conspiratorial, 'need-to-know' secret within the party, although Hirschfeld's institute next door was also used as a base by the military-political apparatus of the KPD: Bernd Kaufmann et al., *Der Nachrichtendienst der KPD 1919–1937*, Berlin: Dietz, 1993, 279.
90 Among the works by Fritz Brupbacher published by Münzenberg's Neuer Deutscher Verlag in 1930 was his little book *Liebe, Geschlechtsbeziehungen und Geschlechtspolitik* [Love, Sexual Relations and Sexual Politics]. On the couple's sex education activities, see Lina Gafner, *'Mit Pistole und Pessar': Sexualität im Blick des Brupbacher-Kreises – zwischen revolutionärer Gesellschaftskritik und hygienischem Reformprojekt im Zürich der 1920er- und 1930er-Jahre*, Nordhausen: Traugott Bautz, 2010.

with Münzenberg and Gross. Paulette was a member of the central committee of Workers' International Relief and contributed to the Communist women's magazine *Der Weg der Frau*, one of Münzenberg's stable of periodicals.

In Comintern circles in the 1920s, one thus finds co-existing a bohemian and artistic avant-garde on the one hand and bourgeois family structures and habits of life on the other, despite the demands of illegal activity. This paradox was especially pronounced in Weimar Germany and its capital, Berlin. While some, such as the Alpáris and the Komjáts, had more or less stable marriages (Komját's affairs notwithstanding), living with their children, their everyday life, as we have seen, was nonetheless marked by the uncertainties of exile and the dangers that accompanied their political commitments. When Irén Komját gave birth to her first son, in Italy in 1920 – the second followed in 1923, in Berlin – her husband was in jail and the family was deported shortly afterwards. For many, however, circumstances made it impossible to bring up their children. On getting involved in the hectic life of Willi Münzenberg, Babette Gross, for example, gave her son Peter – born in 1923, from her first marriage – to her parents in Potsdam. Her sister Margarete left her two daughters with her in-laws following her divorce, when she immersed herself in Communist activity and the left-wing artistic milieu of Berlin.

Open relationships were not uncommon among the younger party members who had come to politics in the revolutionary years that followed the First World War, or later under the Weimar Republic. The intense debates on sexual reform, women's emancipation and the ending of the patriarchal family; the campaigns against the ban on abortion (Section 218 of the Criminal Code), essentially led by the KPD, and the criminalization of homosexuality (Section 175), in which the party was actively involved; the establishment of counselling centres for adolescents and young adults and the availability of contraceptives: all these contributed to a liberalization of sexual practices and to changes in the relationship between the sexes. Young Communist women and the women of the urban party elite were receptive to the notion of the New Woman, independent and confident, who took her life into her own hands. They demanded not only economic independence but also sexual autonomy, believing that the modern couple relationship had to be based on friendship and erotic affinity rather than on female dependence.[91] Already in 1920, writing under the name Elfriede Friedländer – the surname being that of her first husband – Ruth Fischer had published a pamphlet on Communist sexual ethics.[92] In it she attacked 'capitalist sexual hypocrisy', demanded the same sexual freedom for women as for men, rejected bourgeois marriage as an oppressive institution, for women most particularly, and argued for the collective upbringing of children. In the avant-garde and Communist circles of the capital, homosexuality was tolerated when not entirely accepted, while unmarried sex, brief affairs and abortion became commonplace among heterosexuals. 'Marriages' would not be 'legally registered', couples forming and living together without formality, as did Margarete Buber and Heinz Neumann, for example. Partners took the relationship between man and woman to be something to be built together, an object of shared reflection. A good example is offered by Hilde Kramer's friend Cilly Geisenberg and her French lover Albert Vassart (1898–1958). Both were opponents of the party's Third Period line. Geisenberg, who had worked for a party publishing house in the early 1920s and then for International Red Aid from 1924, was expelled from the KPD in 1929, alongside Hilde Kramer, while Vassart remained a member, though the early 1930s saw him lose his leadership positions in the PCF for a time. Their correspondence of the late 1920s, when one was in Berlin, the other in Paris, illustrates the efforts then made to rationalize intimate relationships in terms of 'comradely marriage'.[93] When Hilde was at a loss at the fact that Edward Fitzgerald had fallen in love with a young woman, not even a Communist, yet did not want to break with her, Cilly told her lover Albert, who was able to provide

---

91 Atina Grossmann, 'German Communism and New Women: Dilemmas and Contradictions', in Helmut Gruber and Pamela Graves, eds, *Women and Socialism, Socialism and Women: Europe Between the World Wars*, New York: Berghahn Books, 1998, 135–68; Grossmann, 'Continuities and Ruptures: Sexuality in Twentieth-Century Germany: Historiography and its Discontents', in Karen Hagemann and Jean H. Quataert, eds, *Gendering Modern German History: Rewriting Historiography*, New York: Berghahn Books, 2007, 208–27.

92 Elfriede Friedländer, *Sexualethik des Kommunismus: Eine prinzipielle Studie*, Vienna: Verlagsgenossenschaft Neue Erde, 1920.

93 On the comradely couple that has its basis not in self but in service to the collective, see Dagmar Reese, 'Die Kameraden: Eine partnerschaftliche Konzeption der Geschlechterbeziehungen an der Wende vom 19. zum 20. Jahrhundert', in Dagmar Reese et al., eds, *Rationale Beziehungen? Geschlechterverhältnisse im Rationalisierungsprozeß*, Frankfurt a. M.: Edition Suhrkamp, 1993, 58–74.

Hilde with an explanation. People had many facets, and in a couple relationship it was not inevitable that one would love all of them all at the same time. Hilde's husband was obviously still attracted to her intellectually, but not physically just then. He urged Hilde to objectify her feelings. She should think about what she loved about him, whether she could tolerate his partial infidelity, and whether she wanted to fight for the relationship.[94]

Among the *Inprekorr* staff, Heinrich Kurella and Charlotte Stenbock-Fermor can serve as an example of the love relationship free of bourgeois convention. Alfred Kurella's younger brother Heinrich had joined the Communist Youth at nineteen and was only twenty-two when taken on by *Inprekorr* in 1927 (apparently on the recommendation of his brother Alfred). Like others of his generation, he enjoyed an uninhibited sexual life. Theo Pinkus, his equally young friend, tells how Heinrich snatched away the girl he was himself keen on in the Communist Youth and spent the night with her. 'I wasn't jealous, I admired him if anything. He was more uninhibited than I in all these things.'[95] Kurella's personal file reveals that he had first been married to a Russian woman with whom he had one child. It was around 1930 that he met Charlotte, then in her mid-twenties and only two years younger than he. A German-speaking Romanian with a mother from French-speaking Switzerland, born in Dorpat (Estonia) and brought up in Bukovina and Germany, Charlotte (née Schledt) had been married to the Latvian Count Stenbock-Fermor for a year. The couple frequented progressive artistic circles in Berlin and took part in Berlin's lively nightlife, but they soon came into contact with Communists. Both were politicized and joined the Rote Hilfe in 1931. In her Comintern questionnaire of 1934, Charlotte wrote: 'In 1931 I became a member of the R.H. I wanted to join the party then, but Stenbock held me back, saying that we could better work for it outside. I unfortunately allowed myself to be convinced.'[96] She did not join the KPD until the following year, when she

---

94 Extracts from this correspondence are published in Bernard Pudal and Claude Pennetier, 'L'auto-analyse d'un dirigeant communiste et d'un couple communiste: Albert Vassart et Cilly Geisenberg-Vassart', in Pudal and Pennetier, eds, *Le sujet communiste: Identités militantes et laboratoires du 'moi'*, Rennes: Presses universitaires de Rennes, 2014, 105–38, here 130–2.
95 Lüscher and Schweizer, *Amalie und Theo Pinkus-De Sassi*, 100.
96 Hirdman, *Meine Mutter*, 251.

also got divorced. In the meantime, she had begun a relationship with Heinrich Kurella, who was and would remain a friend of her husband's. All three of them would go out together, and, for a time, they had a ménage à trois.

A Communist Entrepreneur

Berlin was the headquarters of Willi Münzenberg's media consortium, which ranged from film production (Mezhrabpom-Russ) and distribution (Prometheus) to publishing, a book club (Universum Bücherei) and mass magazines. Münzenberg was an exceptionally talented player in the media attention economy. He also succeeded in combining the new artistic forms of the age with agitation and propaganda on behalf of the Comintern.[97] Described by the Swiss police as a 'fanatic',[98] Münzenberg was a dedicated, though not heartless, businessman: he did not hesitate to speculate on the stock market to finance his businesses,[99] while often taking on comrades who had become unemployed.

His most innovative product was the *Arbeiter-Illustrierte-Zeitung* (The Workers' Pictorial Newspaper), known as the *AIZ*. By the time Hitler came to power, it enjoyed a circulation of half a million. For a time in the early 1930s, it had a woman editor, Lilly Korpus (later Becher, 1901–1978). In 1929, Alfred Kurella took on the job, alongside his agitprop activities on behalf of the International Committee of the Friends of the Soviet Union. What was distinctive about the *AIZ* was its new aesthetics and visual language, with John Heartfield photomontages and the new genre of journalism that was photoreportage. Münzenberg believed that the image was the best way to reach non-Communist (and indeed Communist) readers. Because even if one were not inclined to read, one would look at a picture. Berlin was thus

---

97 On the agitprop activities of the KPD, see also Fischer, *Stalin*, 606–25.
98 Hans Ulrich Jost, *Linksradikalismus in der deutschen Schweiz 1914–1918*, Bern: Verlag Stämpfli, 1973, 49.
99 Jean-Michel Palmier, 'Einige Bemerkungen zu den Propagandamethoden Willy Münzenbergs', in Tania Schlie and Simone Roche, eds, *Willi Münzenberg, 1889–1940: Ein deutscher Kommunist im Spannungsfeld zwischen Stalinismus und Antifaschismus*, Frankfurt a. M.: Peter Lang, 1995, 35–58, at 55, n.13.

the site of production of a certain image of Russia, at the origin of a vast, worldwide circulation of images.[100] The *AIZ* also published photos from across the world, such as the Italian photographer Tina Modotti's pictures from Mexico in 1928. By then already living in Moscow, in March 1932 she would publish a programmatic article in the magazine of the Berlin branch of Rote Hilfe, entitled 'Photos als Waffe der RH-Agitation' [Photos as a Weapon of Red Aid Agitation].[101] In it she approaches photography not as an art form but as a medium that allows the 'objective' reproduction of reality, thus helping to document the hardships and injustices of capitalism. She does, however, argue for the distinctive qualities of the visual image and recommends that photographs not only be used to illustrate text but also be allowed to speak for themselves.

Thanks to Münzenberg's imagination and unremitting energy, Communist parties around the world saw the KPD as a model in its implementation of the injunction to use 'propaganda as a weapon'. In a decade, he had built up the second largest media group in Germany. According to the publishing plan drawn up for 1929/30 by the Agitprop Department of the Comintern, 17 per cent of the 800 titles published worldwide were German, followed by English and French on 10 per cent each.[102] However, despite Münzenberg's efforts to maintain editorial independence, the Communist press – and so his publications – fell under the Comintern's Agitprop Department, headed by Béla Kun from 1924.[103] Communist newspapers and publishing houses could not exist without the International's financial support. Communist parties' political activities also required money and, given that the Comintern apparatus by no means had access to unlimited resources, the parties were always complaining of the lack of it. Nevertheless, the Comintern and

---

100 Schlögel, *Das russische Berlin*, 184.

101 Tina Modotti, 'Photography as a Weapon', trans. Berndt Ostendorf, in 'Notes & Reviews', *History of Photography* 18:3, 288–96, at 289. See also Modotti's earlier (bilingual) article: Tina Modotti, 'Sobre la fotografía / On Photography', *Mexican Folkways* 5:4, October/December 1929, 196–8.

102 Marie-Cécile Bouju, 'Le Livre comme arme de propagande : Le cas des relations entre le Service d'éditions de l'Internationale communiste et la France (1919–1939)', *Communisme* 97/8, 2009, 7–23.

103 Report by Béla Kun to the meeting of the Commission on the Improvement of the Work of the Apparatus with the Agitprop Department, 12 November 1925, RGASPI 495/46/3.

the Soviet state that ultimately provided the money were generous in their support. According to a financial report of 27 October 1931, drawn up by Francesco Misiano (1884–1936), then the representative of Workers' International Relief in the Soviet Union, the Neue Deutsche Verlag received 7,500 of its 11,000 dollars of monthly costs in subsidy from Moscow. On this basis, Sean McMeekin estimated in his biography of Münzenberg that the WIR's financial support to the press amounted to 60 to 70 per cent of operating costs.[104]

The *AIZ* had its own distribution network, which also extended abroad, notably to other countries with German-speaking populations, and in 1928 the French CP launched a similar product, the illustrated *Nos Regards: Illustré mondial du travail* (called *Regards* from 1932). With the Neue Deutsche Verlag, founded in 1924 with his partner Babette Gross as managing director, Münzenberg created one of the most important left-wing publishing houses of the Weimar Republic, and among the journals he founded or came to control were *Der Arbeiterfotograf, Der Weg der Frau, Welt am Abend, Film und Volk, Eulenspiegel* and, from 1931, the daily newspaper *Berlin am Morgen*, which soon attracted 60,000 subscribers. In addition, the Neue Deutsche Verlag, which had a sales operation of its own, sold the magazines *Literatur und Weltrevolution, Internationale Literatur* and *Das neue Rußland*.

That Münzenberg was very much the businessman was remarked on by his contemporaries. Margarete Buber-Neumann, the 'little sister' (as Münzenberg called her) of his partner Babette Gross, says of him: 'He seemed less a revolutionary than a manager, and as this stocky, broad-shouldered man kept the employees in his numerous offices in constant activity, proceeded anything but democratically at meetings and extracted the last drop of work out of his staff, I could understand why he was dubbed an "entrepreneur" in the party.'[105] The characterization was meant literally, but the term is equally appropriate in its figurative, sociological sense. He was a political 'entrepreneur' as opposed to the 'successors' who created nothing new.

---

104 Sean McMeekin, *The Red Millionaire: A Political Biography of Willi Münzenberg, Moscow's Secret Propaganda Tsar in the West*, New Haven, CT: Yale University Press, 2003, 350, n.35.
105 Buber-Neumann, *Potsdam*, 195.

Berlin, Cultural Capital of International Communism 177

'He alone?' – The question that Brecht's 'reading worker' raises regarding the Great Men taken to be the agents of history is equally applicable to Münzenberg. By the early 1920s already, Münzenberg had a chauffeur, a bodyguard (who also served as factotum) and a private secretary.[106] He had a car bought for the office, first an open Chevrolet, afterwards a huge Lincoln limousine. While most other Communist functionaries strove to acquire the habits of the 'proletarian', Münzenberg blithely ignored such expectations. He cultivated a way of life all his own, working almost non-stop but going away for a break now and then, making time for visits to the theatre or cinema, and not at all spurning fine food. Always in a hurry, he kept going on coffee. On the other hand, he neither smoked nor drank. If necessary, he would take a very uncommunist taxi.[107] For him, time was not money but something to be used efficiently; what was at issue was the result, the advancement of the cause.

When historians like Sean McMeekin express disbelief at Willi Münzenberg's style of work and manner of life, denouncing them as 'bourgeois', their judgements are based both on a very impoverished conception of the revolutionary and on a misunderstanding of how Communist organizations functioned.[108] Any manager of a business group, such as Münzenberg was, relies on a host of subordinate staff, including personal assistants. At the same time, the work of party and Comintern officials was subject to norms of efficiency, and their expenses were regulated and regularly checked. The Comintern's businesses faced the same laws of the market as did their capitalist counterparts. Unlike the latter, however, they were subsidized and did not have to yield a profit, nor did they allow the personal enrichment of those in charge.[109]

---

106 Koestler, 'Vorwort', in Gross, *Münzenberg*, 10.
107 Gross, *Münzenberg*, 146; Buber-Neumann, *Kriegsschauplätze*, 262.
108 In his biography, Sean McMeekin moralizes about these aspects of Münzenberg's lifestyle and indeed embroiders upon them, stating, for instance, that he was shaved and manicured daily by a personal barber. For this he cites Stephen Koch, *Double Lives: Stalin, Willi Münzenberg, and the Seduction of the Intellectuals*, London: HarperCollins, 1995, 8 and 12, while remarking in a footnote that Koch provides no attribution or reference, *The Red Millionaire*, 204–7 and 347.
109 The articles of association of the Aufbau-, Industrie- und Handels-AG, the IAH subsidiary that handled the film business, specified that the shareholders had, as individuals, no claim to a share of the company's profits: introduction to the reprint of *Zeitschrift Film und Volk: Organ des Volksfilmverbandes, Februar 1928–März 1930*, Cologne: Verlag Gaehme, 1975, 8.

Münzenberg's diary was packed. He maintained regular contact with intellectuals, artists, politicians and other persons of importance, who did not necessarily belong to the Communist milieu and therefore laid store by 'bourgeois' manners and a well-groomed appearance. Furthermore, political violence was an ever-present possibility in the last years of the Weimar Republic, so a bodyguard was hardly a needless luxury for such a high-profile and vulnerable figure.

Münzenberg occupied an exceptional position. Alongside his media group, Münzenberg also had his own organization, Workers' International Relief. He had built this up over the 1920s, and that with the authority of Lenin, who in 1921, in time of famine, had charged him with organizing humanitarian aid for Soviet Russia. He thus had his own apparatus in parallel with that of the KPD, in contravention of the Comintern's organizational principles. In theory, a national party exercised control over all Communist organizations and activities in that country. In reality, however, there were parallel Comintern structures that were not accountable to a national party but stood in a supervisory relation to them. The Comintern leadership's own discontent at Münzenberg's autonomy is revealed by a communication addressed to the WIR by Georgi Dimitrov in 1931, when he was in Berlin as head of the Western European Bureau: 'It is absolutely necessary to put an end to the present practice ... that Münzenberg has everything under his personal control and operates with staff answerable only to him.'[110] Yet, sometimes to the annoyance of German party leaders, Münzenberg repeatedly succeeded in obtaining Comintern funding for his projects. Some of these were even self-supporting and – at least as far as the press was concerned – significantly more successful than the KPD's own ventures.

With the crash of 1929 it became increasingly difficult to keep Communist businesses afloat financially. In the autumn of 1932, Münzenberg sought to make money by buying a share in a German cigarette company. The party leadership, however, was unhappy at the way he had acted 'on his own authority'. The Business Department of the KPD therefore vetoed the signature of a contract already signed by the

---

110 Cited in Kasper Braskén, 'Willi Münzenberg und die Internationale Arbeiterhilfe (IAH) 1921 bis 1933: Eine neue Geschichte', *Jahrbuch für Forschungen zur Geschichte der Arbeiterbewegung* 11/3, 2012, 57–84, at 82.

counterparty, insisting that Münzenberg call off the deal. He, however, defended his action, submitting to Ernst Thälmann a nine-page typewritten memorandum explaining his business model. 'I have always made it my special endeavour to overcome such [financial] difficulties on my own without recourse to those sources that would otherwise be called upon.'[111] In the economic crisis, the cigarette industry was one of the few still to make a profit. As an intelligent entrepreneur, Münzenberg had also found out what the political competition was up to: other parties had also invested in cigarette manufacturing, notably the NSDAP with their Sturm cigarette, which yielded a monthly net profit of 150,000–200,000 marks. He also pointed out the advantages to the Communist press of having the party's cigarettes advertised in its newspapers. A particularly strong argument, he thought, was the support that would be afforded to the USSR through the use of Soviet tobacco, and he called on Communist parties to promote Soviet exports. Likely intending to make it clear to the KPD leadership that the matter was no longer entirely in their hands, he added that 'Comrade X' ('well known' to Thälmann) and the Hamburg and Berlin offices of the Soviet Union's Export Department had already expressed their support. These, of course, were arguments the KPD could not counter, for they were ideologically effective.

Münzenberg had also commissioned a series of portrait cigarette cards, 'Heads of the Workers' Movement'. It was a way of making propaganda, he said, just as the bourgeois forces did. The Business Department did not see things in quite the same way, imposing its veto on the names of Karl Radek, Max Hölz, Willi Münzenberg (!) and Hermann Remmele. For Radek, like Hölz and Remmele (who had already been accused of 'factionalism') was now considered an unreliable element. Münzenberg, though, was not inclined to give in, and sent his nine-page memorandum to Piatnitsky. It was for the Comintern to decide. Yet by late December 1932, no decision had been taken in Moscow. Misiano thus submitted to the Political Commission of the Politsecretariat of the ECCI a request that the CC of the KPD be instructed to take no decision

---

111 Memorandum from Willi Münzenberg to Ernst Thälmann, Berlin, 29 November 1932, RGASPI, 495/205/7000. Two days earlier, he had written in a short letter to a comrade in Berlin that in accordance with the agreement struck 'over there', i.e. in the Soviet Union, he had done everything to re-establish the 'old working relationship and comradeliness', letter to 'Dear Comrade' of 27 November 1932, RGASPI, 495/205/7000.

in Berlin before the ECCI had considered the matter.[112] When it came, shortly before Hitler's takeover, it was, in any event, too late.

Münzenberg's success might be said to be in large part due to his personnel policy. In the first place, he had in his partner Babette Gross and the personal secretary, chauffeur and bodyguard/factotum earlier mentioned a small group of close collaborators. Münzenberg would have been unable to deal on his own with all the demands he made of himself, and he always worked in a team. In this, the central role was played by Babette Gross, his closest and most long-standing collaborator, who supported him in everything he did and always accompanied him on his travels. This daughter of a Potsdam brewery manager was a tall woman, described by contemporaries as an elegant figure. Arthur Koestler attests not only to her 'classical features', but also to her great efficiency, in her 'unobtrusive, unruffledly polite way'. Outwardly, the 'cool and patrician' Babette Gross and the 'burly former factory apprentice' Willi Münzenberg presented a striking contrast. Yet they radiated such 'visible harmony' that they gave the 'impression of a couple perfectly attuned to one another'.[113] After graduating from high school, Babette had worked as governess to one of the emperor's grandchildren. In 1921, she joined the Young Communists in Frankfurt am Main, entering the party a year later.[114] In 1922, she began work at the IAH office before becoming managing director of the Neue Deutsche Verlag, the 'heart of the IAH business empire', in 1924.[115]

Second, Münzenberg practised a personal solidarity in the real world, which created a network of solidarity around him. He mostly engaged people with whom he was friends or who were otherwise close to him. One example is his sister-in-law Margarete Buber-Neumann, who found work in various Münzenberg enterprises after she separated from her husband: as a shorthand typist at the Universum Bücherei in early 1927, then for a time in the office of the German section of the Anti-Imperialist League in the wake of the Brussels Congress, and then in advertising

---

112 Francesco Misiano to the Political Commission of the Politsecretariat of the CI, Moscow, [*illegible*] December 1932, RGASPI 495/205/7000.
113 Koestler, 'Vorwort', 10.
114 Personal file, RGASPI, 495/205/6083.
115 Rolf Surmann, *Die Münzenberg-Legende: Zur Publizistik der revolutionären Arbeiterbewegung, 1921–1933*, Cologne: Prometh Verlag, 1983, 84.

sales for the newspapers.[116] They were notably often trusted acquaintances from his early days in politics in Switzerland, and the importance that Münzenberg attached to the comrades his youth can be seen in his choice of Francesco Misiano and Hans-Heinrich Itschner to fill two important posts in Moscow.

A native of Calabria, Misiano had been an employee of the Italian state railway.[117] As secretary of the railway workers' union in Turin, he was jailed in 1915 for trade union and antiwar activity. To avoid conviction as a deserter, in 1916 he fled to Zurich, where he worked for the Italian Socialist Party and edited its weekly *L'Avvenire del Lavoratore*. In 1919 he was arrested on the occasion of the Spartacus uprising in Berlin, and on his release he returned to Italy, where he was elected to the chamber of deputies that same year, and he then became one of the founders of the Italian Communist Party. The Fascists were then beginning to spread terror through violence. Jules Humbert-Droz, who in January 1921 attended the Congress of Livorno as a delegate of the left of the Swiss Socialist Party, recalled that Misiano would only venture onto the streets protected by a bodyguard: 'The fascists were after his blood.'[118] Münzenberg and the five-years-older Misiano knew each other, then, from Switzerland, where Münzenberg had been head of the Youth Secretariat. Together, they had founded the Youth International, which was close to the Zimmerwald Left. In 1921, Münzenberg brought Misiano to Berlin to work for the IAH, but Misiano would soon be spending more time in Moscow as a representative of the Central Committee of the IAH and the head of its Russian section. There, on Münzenberg's instructions, he set up Mezhrabpom-Russ (Mezhrabpom-Film from 1928). This German-Russian film production company was based at the IAH's Russian office at 3 First Tverskaia-Iamskaia Street,

---

116 Personal file, and more particularly the curriculum vitae of 22 September 1936, RGASPI 495/205/1612. See also Buber-Neumann, *Potsdam*, 107, and ibid., *Kriegsschauplätze*, 306.

117 For biographical detail on Misiano, see Claudio Natoli, 'Francesco Misiano e il Soccorso Operaio Internazionale', *Studi storici* 37:4, October/December 1996, 1227–55; Branko Lazitch and Milorad M. Drachkovitch, *Biographical Dictionary of the Comintern*, new edn, Stanford, CA: Hoover Institution Press, 1986, 319–20; and *Historisches Lexikon der Schweiz* online at hls-dhs-dss.ch/.

118 Jules Humbert-Droz, *Mémoires*, vol. 1, *Mon évolution du tolstoïsme au communisme, 1891–1921*, Neuchâtel: À La Baconnière, 1969, 397. Humbert-Droz mistakenly spells the name as 'Missiano'.

outside the city centre. It was an important channel of cultural transfer between the two countries, though rather an expensive one. Its few commercial successes, such as Vsevolod Pudovkin's *Mother* and Iakov Protazanov's *Aelita, Queen of Mars*, were not enough to cover the costs of production and distribution.

Even in difficult times, Münzenberg would be loyal to his staff, as witnessed by later developments in the Soviet Union. With the First Five-year Plan in 1928, the Soviet state increased its control over film production, and 1930 saw the first attempt made to bring Mezhrabpom-Film under the aegis of Soyuzkino, the centralized Soviet film administration, headed by Boris Shumyatsky, a strict adherent to the party line. Although Münzenberg succeeded in maintaining Mezhrabpom-Film as an 'independent proletarian franchise under the responsibility of the CC of the *Arbeiterhilfe*', all production plans now had to be approved by Soviet institutions.[119] In 1933, Soyuzkino was given control over film exports and imports. To ensure political control, Mezhrabpom-Film saw a Russian manager imposed, who, in the growing paranoia about political enemies, accused Misiano of 'conciliationism'. Misiano was then subjected to a protracted political investigation, which soon came to extend to the other founders of the Youth International. The affair saw Misiano condemned for 'political errors' by the Political Commission of the ECCI,[120] while the International Control Commission accused him of 'financial conduct not beyond reproach' and of supporting the 'unprincipled struggle in the Italian party'.[121] In the summer of 1935, the Soviet authorities decided to close the IAH and incorporate its national sections into International Red Aid, starting with its Moscow office. Misiano was dismissed, the 'liquidator' appointed being the Swiss Karl Hofmaier, ironically enough another comrade of Münzenberg's from the early years of the Youth International in Switzerland.[122] Formally, Misiano was allowed to resign, which he did on 22 August 1935, the day

---

119 Braskén, 'The International Workers' Relief', 164–6, quote at 166.

120 On this, see Studer, *Transnational World*, 118–19.

121 Written communication from Albert Müller to the Cadre Department re. Willi Münzenberg, Moscow, 15 September 1936, RGASPI 495/205/7000.

122 Letters from Karl Hofmaier to Piatnitsky, Moscow, 3 July 1935, and to Dimitrov, Moscow, 13 September 1935, in RGASPI 495/91/211. See Brigitte Studer, 'Ein Prozess in Rom und seine Wiederholung in Moskau: Der Fall des Schweizer Komintern-Instrukteurs Karl Hofmaier', *Jahrbuch für historische Kommunismusforschung*, 1994, 254–74.

after the close of the Seventh World Congress of the Comintern. Münzenberg, who attended the Congress under the name of 'Max', was still in Moscow, and two days later wrote his friend and former employee a reference of sorts, in which he thanked him for his 'loyal, tenacious and effective' work for the IAH. He went on to add that 'if, despite all the difficulties, the IAH enjoys today the position it does, it is thanks in particular to your contribution'.[123] Misiano, who would have liked to return to party work – an idea rejected as 'inopportune' by Togliatti, in the name of the Italian delegation to the Seventh World Congress[124] – had to remain in the Soviet Union. He fell seriously ill soon after, dying almost a year later, on 16 August 1936, at the age of only fifty-two. That was a month after Mezhrabpom was officially closed down by the Russian authorities. Had he not died, he would most likely have faced imprisonment or worse.

Hans-Heinrich Itschner (1887–1962), who, in Moscow in the mid-1920s, had assisted Münzenberg with preparations for the Brussels Congress, was someone else Münzenberg knew from the circle around Fritz Brupbacher, back in his Zurich days. In 1917, Itschner, a typesetter by training, was one of the founders of the anti-authoritarian and anarcho-syndicalist 'Forderung' group, from which emerged, in 1919, the Altkommunisten who in 1921 would join together with the Socialist Party Left to form the Communist Party of Switzerland. By then, Itschner was already in Moscow. For after the November Riots of 1917, which saw a police officer killed, he fled to Soviet Russia to escape prosecution for 'subversive activities' (the publication of a leaflet), travelling via France and Spain. In Moscow, he represented the Swiss Communist Party during the early years of the Comintern. He then worked for the Comintern in a number of roles, including a spell in the translation department, and was sent as an emissary to various European countries. In the mid-1920s, he joined the Moscow office of the IAH, serving Münzenberg as a go-between with the Eastern Department in important matters that he wanted to negotiate directly with Kuusinen or Roy. In 1925 the IAH sent him to Beijing to set up a section in China. This task he shared with another Swiss, Siegfried Bamatter, and a 'Russian

---

123 Letters and documents in RGASPI, 538/3/172 and 538/3/174.
124 Natoli, 'Francesco Misiano', 1253–4.

Comrade'.¹²⁵ He continued to live in Moscow until 1931, when he returned to Switzerland, where he was soon expelled from the party, thereafter turning back to anarchism.

Avant-Garde Culture and Prop-Art

Berlin was also a laboratory of modernity in another respect. The city's cultural life and nocturnal entertainments saw the mixing of social milieux, if not of left and right.¹²⁶ Communist Party members encountered progressive intellectuals, artists, journalists, directors, actors and musicians in pubs, at the theatre performances and, last but not least, in meeting halls. Margarete Buber-Neumann, who had returned to Berlin from the provinces after a failed marriage, plunged 'with enthusiasm . . . into the political and cultural maelstrom of the big city'. She wanted to 'let the mighty current I felt all around me carry me to a new, a better time'.¹²⁷ There were evenings of intellectual discussion, lectures on Marxism, readings of avant-garde literature. Comintern employees from other countries also enjoyed the lively intellectual and artistic life of the city, some of them becoming energetic contributors to it. M. N. Roy, for example, was a regular participant in the Karl Korsch circle.¹²⁸ Aladár Komját, whose conception of culture was close to that of the Proletkult, was involved in the Union of Proletarian-Revolutionary Writers. His dramatic poem on 'Hamburg's October' was translated into German and performed by agitprop groups in the Weimar Republic.¹²⁹

---

125 Fredrick Petersson, *Willi Münzenberg, the League Against Imperialism and the Comintern, 1925–1933*, Lewiston, NY: Queenston Press, 2013, 134.
126 Joachim Häberlen, *Vertrauen und Politik im Alltag: Die Arbeiterbewegung in Leipzig und Lyon im Moment der Krise 1929–1933/38*, Göttingen: Vandenhoeck & Ruprecht, 2013.
127 Buber-Neumann, *Potsdam*, 121.
128 Manjapra, *M. N. Roy*, 40.
129 Sabine Kebir, 'Aladár Komját, 1891–1936) – ein unbekanntes Mitglied des BPRS', *UTOPIE kreativ* 102, 1999, 72–5. For a concise overview of the relationship between Communism and the German avant-gardes and its reflection in art theory and aesthetics, see Ben Fowkes, 'Communism and the Avant-Garde in Weimar Germany', in Ralf Hoffrogge and Norman Laporte, eds, *Weimar Communism as Mass Movement 1918–1933*, London: Lawrence & Wishart 2017, 220–39.

'Life in Berlin [at the end of the 1920s] was full of a tremendous, almost feverish activity', wrote Mentona Moser. Jokingly called the Red Millionaire, this wealthy Swiss heiress, the daughter of a father who had made money in tsarist Russia and a mother from an aristocratic German family, was so captivated by the city that in 1929 she decided to close down her household in Zurich and move to the German capital with her ailing eighteen-year-old son, who would attend a school of film and photography there. Her daughter, two years older, would go to ballet school and later become a painter. 'Musicians, painters, poets, writers, actors and revolutionary fighters worked [together]. Almost every week, demonstrations would march through the streets, the unemployed demanding 'Work and Bread!', Young Communists, worker athletes, Red Front Fighters, the band in front . . . Thälmann, Hermann Remmele, Willi Münzenberg and Maria Reese were some of those who spoke in the overcrowded halls' – Reese (1889–1958) being a writer who publicly abandoned the SPD for the KPD in 1929.[130] And Moser goes on enthusiastically: 'Even the Sportspalast couldn't hold the crowds . . . In the theatres there were performances of *Revolte im Erziehungshaus* . . ., *Cyankali* . . . The Theater am Nollendorfplatz in the West End, also known as the Piscator Theatre, put on Ernst Toller's *Hoppla wir leben*, a combination of film and drama . . . The performances often inspired so much enthusiasm that at the end the audience would stand up and sing the *Internationale*.'[131]

Red Berlin also had its own clubs, variety shows and revues. At Dessauerstraße 2, there was the Klub Roter Stern of Berlin's Soviet colony, where German Communists would meet staff of the Soviet embassy, trade representation and other more or less official Soviet institutions. The three-storey building boasted gymnasium, canteen, library, reading room, club meeting room, orchestra rehearsal room, a large auditorium for theatre and film performances and a sizeable exhibition space.[132]

Agitprop groups like the Rote Sprachrohr, the Rote Sprechchor, Roter Wedding and Rote Raketen (Red Megaphone, Red Chorus, Red Wedding

---

130 In 1933, however, she disassociated herself from Stalinism, becoming close to Trotskyism for a time.
131 Moser, *Ich habe gelebt*, 219–20.
132 Schlögel, *Das russische Berlin*, 156–7.

– named for the former Berlin borough – and the Red Rockets) remained in close cultural contact with the Russian avant-garde while it still existed. In their performances, they employed a new type of music, *Kampfmusik* – music for [revolutionary] struggle – developed by composers such as Hanns Eisler and distributed on record by the KPD's Arbeiterkult business. Communist and sympathizing 'cultural and intellectual workers' – a new term emphasizing their proximity to the proletariat – formed a dense and highly active network. Director Erwin Piscator staged Bertolt Brecht's *Lehrstück* or 'learning play' *The Measures Taken*, criticized even then for its argument that the revolutionary end justifies the means. John Heartfield, famous for his photomontages, was responsible for the set design. The composer, Eisler, also wrote music reviews for *Die Rote Fahne* and taught at the Marxistische Arbeiterschule (MASCH), a Communist adult education institute that attracted 20,000 to 25,000 students each year. As did Albert Einstein, the educational campaigner Käte Duncker, 'Reporter on the Rampage' Egon Erwin Kisch, educator Edwin Hoernle, Swiss architect Hannes Meyer, sexologist Wilhelm Reich, writer Ludwig Renn, sociologist and sinologist Karl August Wittfogel and many others. Developments in its curriculum ran counter to the changing party line.[133] For while the 'Third Period' policy established a bulkhead between the Communists and other working-class organizations, the MASCH also directed its efforts to non-party workers and grassroots members of the Social Democratic Party. From 1929, the course offerings were extended to cover matters of everyday life and cultural and leisure activities. Now, in addition to theoretical and practical knowledge about the capitalist economy, class struggle, the history of the revolutionary labour movement, social policy and the operation of works councils, the Communists also offered gymnastics, English, health advice and shorthand, while guided tours of museums and paddle-steamer excursions also featured on the programme.[134] The more political courses continued to be offered, of course. One course

---

133 Gabriele Gerhard-Sonnenberg, *Marxistische Arbeiterbildung in der Weimarer Zeit, MASCH,* Cologne: Pahl-Rugenstein, 1976.

134 Carsten Krinn, '"... der Klassenkampf erlaubt selten die Anstellung eines Schwimmlehrers": Zwischen Emanzipation und Edukationismus; Lehren aus der Schulungsarbeit der Weimarer KPD', in Janek Niggemann, ed., *Emanzipatorisch, sozialistisch, kritisch, links? Zum Verhältnis von, politischer Bildung und Befreiung,* Berlin: Karl Dietz Verlag, 2012, 23–34.

might deal with 'militarism, Fascism, imperialism', another with 'the growth and decline of British imperialism'.[135] These were explicitly aimed at the numerous representatives of colonial countries, the Chinese, Indian and African diaspora in Berlin. In attending Hermann Duncker's courses at MASCH, antiracist activists of the Liga zur Verteidigung der Negerrasse (the League for the Defence of the Negro Race) like the Cameroonian Joseph Ekwe Bilé (1892–1959), came into contact with Indian, Asian and Arab revolutionary nationalists and also with Berlin's Communist intelligentsia.[136]

Countless Comintern employees lived in Berlin. They might work for years in this 'little Moscow', as secret emissaries, instructors, office staff, accountants, journalists, editors, translators, couriers, photographers or artists, or indeed in a variety of other roles. While the personnel of 'political' bodies (the WES and the WEB) changed in character over time, this was less the case at the 'technical' *Inprekorr*. Those who staffed the WEB were predominantly men (in the more senior roles, at least) who had received their political schooling in Moscow. The careers of WES staff, on the other hand, had been marked by involvement in the early revolutionary movements around the First World War and the exile this often entailed. Those who worked for *Inprekorr* were of the same stamp, the publication employing revolutionaries from many European countries and working with a global network of correspondents.

Thanks to the size of the German capital and the intensity of its political conflicts, the Comintern employees based there could enjoy a rich cultural life and a wealth of social interaction. For many, the city was also a waiting room or halting place before proceeding on their mission. In Berlin they received travel instructions, foreign exchange and passports – or perhaps Moscow's approval for a new project, like Nguyen Ai Quoc – better known as Hô Chi Minh – who spent several months in Berlin in late 1927 and early 1928, waiting for the go-ahead and the funds for his trip to Siam.[137]

---

135 Gerhard-Sonnenberg, *Marxistische Arbeiterbildung*, 172.
136 Robbie Aitken and Eve Rosenhaft, *Black Germany: The Making and Unmaking of a Diaspora Community, 1884–1960*, Cambridge: Cambridge University Press, 2013, 209.
137 Thanyathip Sripana, 'Tracing Hô Chí Minh's Sojourn in Siam', *Southeast Asia Studies* 2:3, 2013, 527–58, at 536; Gross, *Münzenberg*, 197 (though no date is given).

Berlin in the years of the Weimar Republic was not only the most important centre of international Communist activity, it was also the place where new and radical forms of life and art were developed and explored. It was then a global city: its aura as the second centre of world revolution survived the failure of the German uprising of 1923, and it retained its magnetic draw until the Nazi takeover. The city was home and meeting-place not only to countless avant-garde artists but also to the most active and the most persecuted revolutionaries of Central and Eastern Europe. Last but not least, Berlin was an important hub in the intensive circulation between European capitals, linking Paris, Brussels and London, while also offering temporary shelter to anti-imperialist, antiracist and anticolonialist revolutionaries such as Roy. The international networks that they maintained connected Europe with Asia, Africa and Latin America, enabling an intercontinental flow of people, things and ideas through both conventional and clandestine channels.

5
Paris, Brussels, Berlin: Anti-Imperialism and Transcolonial Networks

'Europe is not the World': this was Roy the anticolonial activist and Comintern functionary writing in *Inprekorr* in late 1924, vexed by the Eurocentrism of the European workers' movement.[1] Despite the truth of his objection, colonialism itself had Europe at its centre, so anticolonial politics were thus not a matter for the colonies alone but also concerned the metropolitan countries. In them were to be found many anticolonial revolutionaries, intellectuals and freedom fighters, come to seek a living or an education or to escape colonial repression at home. These students and workers in the metropoles quickly formed networks and had formed revolutionary organizations of their own even before the Comintern's emphatic return to the colonial question following the political setbacks in Europe.

Focussing on the places where such anticolonial revolutionaries and intellectuals lived and worked – women a small minority among them – this chapter looks at the cities of Paris, Brussels and Berlin.[2] Any

---

1 *International Press Correspondence* 90, 31 December 1924, 1045, cited in Edward Hallett Carr, *Socialism in One Country 1924–1926*, vol. 3, Harmondsworth, UK: Penguin Books, 1972, 640.

2 The Swiss cities of Geneva, Lausanne and Zurich, too, were frequented by anticolonial activists, even before the First World War: Harald Fischer-Tiné, 'The Other Side of Internationalism: Switzerland as a Hub of Militant Anti-Colonialism, c. 1910–1920', in Patricia Purtschert and Harald Fischer-Tiné, eds, *Colonial Switzerland: Rethinking Colonialism from the Margins*, Basingstoke, UK: Palgrave Macmillan, 2015, 221–58. There, however, the Communist Party presence was much weaker than in the

narrower a geographical scope could hardly do justice to the topic, with the high mobility of anticolonial activists alone necessitating the adoption of a multilocal approach. Given their uncertain status as regards citizenship and right of residence, intensifying police surveillance that sometimes extended across national borders often saw prominent activists forced to move in haste. European capitals thus offered anticolonial activists persecuted in their home countries only temporary havens, and this volatility might see leaderships repeatedly shift their base of operations.

In January 1924, Roy, together with his wife Evelyn Trent Roy, thus found themselves expelled from Germany, where they had lived more or less regularly since August 1922, under a variety of different names, publishing the newspaper *The Vanguard* and finding there a fixed point of sorts in a life of exile and constant travel. The two of them then settled for a short while in Paris, until Roy was once again expelled, forcing him to look for safety in Moscow. Before finally returning to India in November 1930, he made one last attempt, in Berlin in 1928, to settle in a European capital. Like Roy in their constant, more-or-less illegal movement between European capitals, the representatives of national liberation movements, the employees of the Comintern or Communist anticolonial organizations, and sympathizing or fellow-travelling academics, journalists and artists formed a multinodal network, their shuttling between countries and cities in the attempt to escape state surveillance and repression paradoxically strengthening transnational networking between members of national-revolutionary organizations.[3]

What follows offers a sketch of the cosmopolitan space constructed between Berlin, Paris, Brussels, London and Moscow – more or less closely interconnected sites of internationalist activity each also networked with the world beyond Europe. Crucial to anticolonial

---

cities mentioned. On the European activities of Netherlands-based Indonesian anticolonialists, see Klaas Stutje, *Campaigning in Europe for a Free Indonesia: Indonesian Nationalists and the Worldwide Anticolonial Movement, 1917–1931*, Copenhagen: NIAS Press, 2019.

3 On the expansion of police surveillance of anticolonial activists in Western Europe in the years between the wars, see Daniel Brückenhaus, *Policing Transnational Protest: Liberal Imperialism and the Surveillance of Anti-Colonialists in Europe, 1905–1945*, Oxford: Oxford University Press, 2017.

activists' turn to the Comintern was the distinctive historical moment that followed upon the end of the First World War, the imperial world order being put into question with the emergence of the League of Nations, on the one hand, and the stabilization of the young Soviet state on the other. And, while the League failed to deliver on hopes for an end to colonial rule, the Comintern made this its goal. Each national section was to have its own country's colonial empire in its sights, while in Weimar Germany, which the Treaty of Versailles had stripped of its colonial possessions, there developed a particularly close connection with China, in a movement embracing the Comintern, Chinese revolutionaries and left-liberal and progressive intellectual and artistic circles.

After earlier attempts, first in London and then in Paris, had failed on account of the stricter police surveillance there, the second half of the 1920s saw the Comintern make Berlin the chief nexus of its anticolonial activities outside the Soviet Union. Through it flowed the financial aid it provided to Japanese, Korean, Chinese, Indian, Persian, Egyptian and Cameroonian anticolonial and radical revolutionary groups, the conspiratorial knowhow of the Comintern apparatus and of the mighty German Communist Party proving to be particularly useful in this regard. It was Münzenberg who was chiefly responsible for pulling together the many different threads of anticolonial activity. In this he made use of networks of his own, exceptionally rich and extensive even by Comintern standards, drawing in the most prominent of anticolonial activists. In 1925, he began to make preparations for the biggest event ever staged in pursuit of the International's anticolonial policy, the Brussels Congress of February 1927, intended to bring together revolutionary activists from Europe, Asia, Africa and North and South America. And in the League Against Imperialism and Colonial Oppression that emerged from it he created an organization whose reach extended from Asia in the East to Latin America in the West. Berlin also served as organizational centre for the international congress of 'Negro workers' eventually held in Hamburg in July 1930, the British authorities having made it impossible to stage it in London.[4] This

---

4 'Negro' is the term used in the sources, as it is in the names of organizations such as the International Trade Union Committee of Negro Workers or the Liga zur Verteidigung der Negerrasse [League for the Defence of the Negro Race], which despite their racist connotations today – connotations they did not have for the Comintern – will be given here as they were used, without scare-quotes.

marked the beginning of a brief period of intense activity that sought to bring together activists of African origin not only as members of an exploited class but also as a 'race', a period, too, that witnessed a real internationalization of the International.

After examining the Comintern's strategy for the struggle against colonialism and imperialism, this chapter goes on to look at how it went about setting up a transimperial activist network that would operate under its aegis.[5] The focus will fall primarily on the practical and personal aspects of this 'intercolonial internationalism' – an internationalism that sought 'to rethink the proletariat and proletarian revolution beyond the white working class'.[6]

Anticolonialism Reaches the Metropole

The eighth of the twenty-one conditions of admission adopted by the Comintern in 1920 required Communist parties whose bourgeoisie held colonial possessions or oppressed other nations to actively (and not merely rhetorically) support colonial liberation movements and to engage in domestic struggle against the imperialism of their own ruling classes.

This, of course, particularly concerned the British and French Communist parties, but the Comintern considered their efforts in this regard to be inadequate, occasioning heavy criticism. The Comintern's colonial policies, indeed, faced a number of difficulties in the early years. They were hard to sell not only to the general public but also among its own ranks. Furthermore, agitation against the colonial policies of the British or French governments was met with particularly severe repression, while Communist organizations found themselves politically isolated in the United Front period, the social democrats refusing any

---

5 A plea for attention to entanglements between empires is made in Daniel Hedinger and Nadin Heé, 'Transimperial History: Connectivity, Cooperation and Competition', *Journal of Modern European History* 16:4, 2018, 429–52. On the transimperial entanglements of science, see Bernhard C. Schär, 'From Batticaloa via Basel to Berlin: Transimperial Science in Ceylon and Beyond Around 1900', *Journal of Imperial and Commonwealth History*, 2019, 1–33.

6 Minkah Makalani, 'Internationalizing the Third International: The African Blood Brotherhood, Asian Radicals and Race, 1919–1922', *Journal of African American History* 96:2, 2011, 151–78, at 154.

cooperation with them.⁷ And in 1923, what is more, the PCF had to concentrate its forces on the international campaign against the French occupation of the Ruhr.

Roy's efforts to build a Communist party in India from the outside, following the fiasco of the armed expedition, could count on financial and logistical support from the Comintern, but could expect little if anything from Europe's own Communist parties, as opposed to a few individual comrades. He therefore acted largely on his own initiative. Although his endeavour never really took shape, he spared no efforts to smuggle propaganda materials into India, with the help of seafarers. Had he travelled there himself, he would immediately have been arrested by the British authorities, who had been after him since the war and had since issued a warrant for his arrest in connection with the Cawnpore [Kanpur] Bolshevik Conspiracy Case of 1924.⁸ And, given the rigorous postal censorship, there would have been no point in Roy trying to send *The Vanguard*, the newspaper he produced together with his wife, Evelyn,⁹ or any other Communist materials, to India in the conventional fashion. He therefore relied on the Profintern's early contacts with Asian seafarers and dock workers to send his propaganda materials by ship from Hamburg, Rotterdam or Marseille, using a variety of landward channels, the route sometimes passing through Switzerland.¹⁰ In this, he could not always be very choosy about his collaborators. So it was, then, that in 1923, and perhaps also the year before, he worked with Simon Sabiani, a Marseille businessman and politician with close ties to

---

7 In Germany, for example, the SPD banned its members from joining the IAH. Social democratic parties everywhere rejected proposals for a united front.

8 'A conspiracy to establish throughout British India a branch of a revolutionary organisation known as the Communist International with the object of depriving the King of the Sovereignty of British India': Gene D. Overstreet and Marshall Windmiller, *Communism in India*, Berkeley: University of California Press, 1959, 67; and Carr, *Socialism in One Country*, vol. 3, 680. On British repression against Indian revolutionaries in India and elsewhere, see Kris Manjapra, 'Communist Internationalism and Recognition', in Kris Manjapra and Sugata Bose, eds, *Cosmopolitan Thought Zones: South Asia and the Global Circulation of Ideas*, Basingstoke, UK: Palgrave Macmillan, 2010, 159–77, at 170–1.

9 Evelyn Trent Roy's contribution to her husband's work is most often ignored in the literature, though it is at least alluded to in Narisetti Innaiah, *Evelyn Trent alias Shanti Devi, Founder Member of Exile Indian Communist Party* [sic], Hyderabad: Booklinks Corporation, 1995, 24.

10 Brückenhaus, *Policing*, 132.

the criminal underworld, who was briefly a member of the PCF before later becoming a fascist and a collaborator. By the time the police put an end to the operation in the autumn of 1923, Roy had been able to send more than a thousand copies of his paper to Colombo, and from there to Pondicherry (today's Puducherry).[11] This French enclave on the Indian subcontinent was particularly important, because the British censors had no say there. Not, at least, until they finally succeeded in arranging cooperation with the French authorities, whereupon Roy's two contacts there were unmasked.[12] Nevertheless, Roy did succeed in smuggling *The Vanguard* and its successor *The Masses of India* into the country over the following few years. Going by the specimens confiscated by the British police, they were sent in some numbers, for at least 4,274 were seized in the second half of 1926. *Inprecor*, too, was regularly intercepted by customs at Indian ports, the seizure of 1,753 copies in May 1925 representing a notable success.[13]

The Bolshevization of the Comintern in 1924 saw an increase in the attention and resources devoted to the colonial question, and in the middle of that year the Eastern Department of the ECCI decided to establish an International Colonial Bureau. It would be headed by M. N. Roy, recently elected to the ECCI and even made a candidate member of the Presidium at the Fifth World Congress and then at the height of his

---

11 Jonathan Hyslop, 'Guns, Drugs and Revolutionary Propaganda: Indian Sailors and Smuggling in the 1920s', *South African Historical Journal* 61:4, December 2009, 838–46. The author does show, however, that the seafarers involved were not truly revolutionaries but considered themselves rather to be traders. On Sabiani, see Paul Jankowski, *Communism and Collaboration: Simon Sabiani and Politics in Marseille, 1919–1944*, New Haven, CT: Yale University Press, 1989. With the advent of the Third Period, both Comintern and Profintern sought to strengthen their anticolonial networks, to this end setting up in 1930 the International Union of Seamen and Harbour Workers, on which see Constance Margain, 'The International Union of Seamen and Harbour Workers (ISH) 1930–1937: Interclubs and Transnational Aspects', *Twentieth Century Communism* 8, 2015, 133–44; Holger Weiss, 'The International of Seamen and Harbour Workers – A Radical Labour Union of the Waterfront or a Subversive World Wide Web?', in Weiss, ed., *International Communism and Transnational Solidarity: Radical Networks, Mass Movements and Global Politics, 1919–1939*, Dordrecht: Brill, 2016, 256–317.

12 Brückenhaus, *Policing*, 136.

13 Sir David Petrie, *Communism in India, 1924–1927*, ed. Mahadevaprasad Saha, Calcutta: Editions Indian, 1958 [1927], 114–16. On the harsh repression of Communist activity in India see Ali Raza, *Revolutionary Pasts: Communist Internationalism in Colonial India*, Cambridge/UK: Cambridge University Press, 2020, chapter 6.

Comintern career.¹⁴ The original plan was to establish the Colonial Bureau in London. Not only was British imperialism the Soviet Union's chief enemy, but Britain also hosted the greatest number of immigrants from the colonies, notably Africans and Caribbeans, making London a particularly obvious choice.¹⁵ The British policing of activists from the colonies made this impossible, however, as it would have put Roy himself in great danger. Which is why the Comintern decided in favour of Paris, the French capital in any case having a non-European population of around 100,000 in the inter-war period.¹⁶

The aftermath of the First World War saw 1,600 Chinese – though only 50 of them women – arrive in France, to establish themselves in Paris and other European capitals, notably Brussels and Berlin. They were representatives of the work-study movement that had emerged in reaction to the decision of the Versailles Peace Conference to assign the former German concession of Kiautschou [Jiaozhou] to Japan rather than return it to China, an anti-Confucian cultural movement being transformed as a result into a movement of national liberation from foreign imperialism. By appropriating Western culture and technology, its activists sought to 'save China'.¹⁷ Known as the May Fourth Movement, it formed part of a wave of revolt against the imperial

---

14 Mustafa Haikal, 'Das Internationale Kolonialbüro der Komintern in Paris', *Jahrbuch für Historische Kommunismusforschung*, 1993, 126–30.

15 Anticolonial activists were not rare among seafarers in the ports of London, Cardiff and Liverpool: Susan D. Pennybacker, *From Scottsboro to Munich: Race and Political Culture in 1930s Britain*, Princeton, NJ: Princeton University Press, 2009, 3 and 5.

16 Michael Goebel, *Anti-Imperial Metropolis: Interwar Paris and the Seeds of Third World Nationalism*, Cambridge: Cambridge University Press, 2015, 10.

17 On the New Culture Movement, see the classic study by Hans K. Van de Ven, *From Friend to Comrade: The Founding of the Chinese Communist Party 1920–1927*, Berkeley: University of California Press, 1991; and the more recent Shakhar Rahav, *The Rise of Political Intellectuals in Modern China: May Fourth Societies and the Roots of Mass Party Politics*, Oxford: Oxford University Press, 2015. On the Chinese in Europe, Marilyn Avra Levine, *The Found Generation: Chinese Communists in Europe during the Twenties*, Seattle: University of Washington Press, 1993; Paul Bailey, 'The Chinese Work-Study Movement in France', *China Quarterly* 115, September 1988, 441–61. For their migration to France and also on the considerable numbers of workers the French Empire recruited in China during the war, see Annie Kriegel, 'Aux origines françaises du communisme chinois', in *Communismes au miroir français: Temps, cultures et sociétés en France devant le communisme*, Paris: Gallimard, 1974, 55–93, and on gender relations more particularly, 81.

world order that spread that year to other colonial countries and also to what the Comintern called the semi-colonial countries, such as Egypt, Korea, Vietnam and India. It was a time when Bolshevism appeared to many to present an alternative path to national independence.[18] The young Chinese who had come to Europe encountered industrial work and discovered Marxism while remaining in contact with fellow campaigners still in China, their awareness of developments there and their experience in Europe combining to lead many of them to the Comintern.

Cosmopolitan Paris was also refuge, residence and crucible of experience to anti-imperialist migrants from the Maghreb, sub-Saharan Africa, Vietnam and Latin America. While the capitals of France and Britain were the two cities in Europe with the greatest numbers of foreign residents in the years between the wars, these represented a higher proportion in Paris than they did in London. How many came from colonies, even the French authorities did not know exactly,[19] not only because the numbers fluctuated constantly, while many were in France illegally, but also because the categorial distinctions between foreigners in general on the one hand and colonial workers or *protégés* on the other, or between Asians, Chinese and Vietnamese, were variable and uncertain. A police report of 1927 estimated that there were 2,500 to 3,000 Vietnamese in Paris, while official figures for the number of Chinese for the year before ranged from 2,800 to 3,600, depending on the administrative authority responsible. A conservative estimate put West Africans in the Paris region at around 5,000 in the late 1920s, while those from the French West Indies and Martinique were French citizens and so not counted. With only 500 members, the Indian community was quite small in comparison.[20] Only a small proportion of any of these ethnic groups were anticolonial activists, though the percentage is likely to have been higher in the German capital, which was less cosmopolitan than Paris and attracted hardly any workers, but rather colonial political activists. As the great metropolis of a country that no longer had any colonies after the Treaty of Versailles, its imperial past had made

---

18 Erez Manela, *The Wilsonian Moment: Self-Determination and the International Origins of Anticolonial Nationalism*, New York: Oxford University Press, 2007, 196.
19 On the statistical uncertainties, see Goebel, *Anti-Imperial Metropolis*, 21–32.
20 Ibid., 26–7 and 31.

it a magnet and refuge for many. It was particularly attractive to Indian activists, as Germany had supported India's anticolonial movement with money and weapons during the First World War, in accordance with the notion that 'my enemy's enemies are my friends', and likewise tolerated anti-British exiles in the years after the war. As a result, 500 Indian independence activists are estimated to have been resident in Berlin.[21] Like many of the Chinese, they mostly came to Germany as students. The country is believed to have hosted several thousand anticolonial activists in the decade following the First World War, with most living in the capital.[22] On the other hand, Black migrants to Germany were very few. Until the late 1920s, post-war arrivals were predominantly West Africans from former German colonies, who numbered no more than a few dozen.[23] Their rights of residence and social status were precarious, Africans being neither ordinary foreigners nor entitled to German citizenship.

Another argument in favour of locating the Colonial Bureau in Paris was that Roy and his wife Evelyn were already resident there. With the Berlin police on their trail, the two of them had fled Germany in early 1924, moving to Zurich, where they managed to publish *The Vanguard*.

21 Under British pressure, Indians were, however, kept under close surveillance by the German foreign office: Nirode K. Barooah, *Chatto: The Life and Times of an Indian Anti-Imperialist in Europe*, New Delhi: Oxford University Press, 2004, 187–95.

22 Many studies of Indian emigrant populations unfortunately lack precise figures: Benjamin Zachariah, 'Indian Political Activities in Germany, 1914–1945', in Joanne Miyang Cho, Eric Kurlander and Douglas T. McGetchin, eds, *Transcultural Encounters Between Germany and India: Kindred Spirits in the 19th and 20th Centuries*, New York: Routledge, 2013, 141–54. According to the KPD newspaper *Die Rote Fahne*, some 5,000 persons of Asian or African origin lived in Berlin in the mid-1920s, some 4,000 of whom it described as 'genuine anti-colonialists': cited in Mustafa Haikal, 'Die Liga gegen Imperialismus und für nationale Unabhängigkeit, 1927–1937)', unpublished paper, international conference on the History of the Communist International held at IISH, Amsterdam, in 1992, 18. Barooah (*Chatto*, 247) gives the same figure of 5,000, referring to students and political refugees, while Manjapra ('Communist Internationalism', 166) gives the figure of 4,000 anticolonial activists in Berlin, though neither gives precise dates or details of sources. For a concise overview of the different ethnic/national groups present, see Nathanael Kuck, 'Anti-Colonialism in a Post-Imperial Environment – The Case of Berlin, 1914–33', *Journal of Contemporary History* 49:1, 2014, 134–59.

23 The Comintern did not begin to work with the Black community in Germany until the late 1920s, as shown by Robbie Aitken and Eve Rosenhaft, *Black Germany: The Making and Unmaking of a Diaspora Community, 1884–1960*, Cambridge: Cambridge University Press, 2013, 194–230, esp. 195.

The move was probably arranged with the help of the Swiss lawyer and parliamentarian Christian Hitz (1883–1954), a Communist who would work as legal adviser to the Soviet trade delegation in Berlin in the early 1930s, until the Nazis came to power, and who was a close friend of Roy's. He certainly used Hitz's postal address for his correspondence.[24] Only two months later, however, in the face of intensive police surveillance in Switzerland, the Roys moved to Annecy and eventually to Paris. There they hoped to be granted asylum under the recently elected left-republican Herriot government. Soon afterwards, Roy travelled to Moscow for the Fifth World Congress. After the usual stop-off in Berlin, he was back in Paris in August 1924, embarking immediately on an investigation of anticolonial politics in France that concluded in proposals for action.[25] He noted great organizational and political fragmentation, which the creation of the Colonial Bureau office would help correct. All things considered, he thought, Paris could well serve as the centre of international anticolonial struggle.

Another member of the Colonial Bureau, alongside Roy, was August Guralsky, the ECCI representative to the PCF. This veteran Comintern emissary had already done a stint in Paris in 1921, before being posted to Germany, where, as a member of the ECCI mission, he promoted the failed uprising of 1923. Having escaped, he was redeployed to France in 1924–25, one of his tasks there being to deal with the influence of Boris Souvarine, a figure close to Trotsky who had criticized bureaucratic centralism. In addition, he was to ensure the selection of a loyal PCF delegation to the Fifth World Congress.[26] A third member of the Colonial Bureau was Jacques Doriot, youthful head of the Fédération des Jeunesses Communistes, whose meteoric rise had seen him become, at the age of twenty-three, a member of the ECCI presidium, a deputy in the French National Assembly and, more recently, head of the PCF's colonial commission. In an account written upon his death – he was by then a fascist and a collaborator – Victor Serge, who had met him while working for *Inprekorr* in Berlin in 1922, described

---

24 Sibnarayan Ray, *In Freedom's Quest: Life of M. N. Roy*, vol. 2, *The Comintern Years 1922–27*, Kolkata: Minerva, 2002, 59.

25 Overstreet and Windmiller, *Communism in India*, 68–9 and 73.

26 Appointed head of the ECCI's Latin American Secretariat in 1929, he was sent to Brazil, Argentina and Chile. It was he who established the South American Bureau in Buenos Aires in 1930.

him as 'a young man wearing glasses, ruddy-faced, sturdy, with a firm mouth and a modest air . . . He was known as an excellent militant of the Young Communists, a good speaker and with plenty of guts.'[27] Yet another was Clemens Palme Dutt (1893–1975), a man of Indian-Swedish descent and the British party's India expert. All four knew each other already from Moscow. Roy and Palme Dutt had also met in Berlin in July 1923, when the latter had stopped off for several months in the German capital, on the way back from Moscow to London. During that time, Palme Dutt had worked with Roy, who was head of the Comintern's Indian section.

This, then, was a high-powered team. In practice, however, relations between Roy and Palme Dutt were difficult, on account of the conflict between Roy and Clemens's elder brother and close confidant Rajani Palme Dutt (1896–1974), who was then living in Brussels together with his Estonian wife Salme Dutt, née Murrik (1888–1964),[28] and who sought to influence the bureau's work. The elder Palme Dutt's views on Communist strategy in India were, however, diametrically opposed to Roy's. Roy opposed any collaboration with the Indian National Congress while Rajani Palme Dutt supported it.[29] And the fact that Clemens Palme Dutt apparently did not turn up to the bureau's first meeting in early September 1924 likely had not helped matters.[30]

In late October, the bureau was sent 2,600 dollars from Moscow to cover its activities. A fifth of this was allocated to technical staff and publications, but the money had arrived very late and soon ran short, given the scale of the work to be done. A plan drawn up that same month envisaged a whole series of activities: the preparation of a conference of French colonial workers; the establishment of a school to train revolutionary agitators, trade union organizers and party workers in the colonies; the preparation of an international congress of students from the

---

27 Victor Serge, 'In a Time of Duplicity: The Case of Doriot' [journal entry, 23 February 1945], *New International*, March/April 1950, 115–21.

28 In the early 1920s, she had acted as informal ECCI representative in Great Britain.

29 On R. Palme Dutt's positions on India and his relationship with Roy, see his biography by John Callaghan, *Rajani Palme Dutt: A Study in British Stalinism*, London: Lawrence & Wishart, 1993, 86–94.

30 According to the generally well-informed police report by Sir David Petrie, *Communism*, 59.

colonies in Europe; the publication of a formally independent anticolonial political magazine to be published in English and French; the development of a concrete plan for the reorganization of activities in the French colonies.

Although informed by the concentrated Indian expertise of the International Colonial Bureau and the Eastern Department of the ECCI, the work of the Colonial Bureau mainly concerned France and its North African colonies. Thanks to the collaboration of the PCF and its now centralized and reorganized colonial commission, on which the ECCI was represented by the Russian Anna Razumova, the Colonial Bureau successfully implemented two of the items on its ambitious programme during its short existence: the establishment in Paris of a school to train party workers for the North African colonies, and the organization in the same city of a regional conference for workers from the colonies resident in France.[31] Despite the criticisms of the Comintern, the French party did have some organizational successes to its credit. It had succeeded in gaining influence over the Union Intercoloniale (UIC), founded in 1921, which brought together anticolonial activists from Asia, Africa and the French West Indies.[32] In 1922, it began publishing the monthly newspaper *Le Paria* – whose title, meaning 'The Pariah', reflected the outsider status of colonial immigrants, who enjoyed few if any rights. The paper called for equality with the citizens of metropolitan France and an end to police brutality in the colonies; territorial independence, on the other hand, was of less concern. With a circulation of between 1,000 and 4,000, *Le Paria* reached as far as Saigon, Shanghai, New York, Porto-Novo, Lima and Hamburg.[33] In total, thirty-six issues were published.

---

31 Philippe Dewitte, *Les mouvements nègres en France 1919–1939*, Paris: L'Harmattan, 1985, 106–7, though the author makes no mention of the Comintern's Colonial Bureau.

32 On the Union Intercoloniale (earlier the Comité pour l'Union Intercoloniale) and its newspaper *Le Paria*, see Claude Liauzu, *Aux origines des tiers-mondismes: Colonisés et anticolonialistes en France 1919–1939*, Paris: L'Harmattan, 1982, 105–36; as well as Dewitte, *Les mouvements nègres*, 95–122, and the more recent Michael Goebel, '"The Capital of the Men without a Country": Migrants and Anticolonialism in Interwar Paris', *American Historical Review* 121:5, 2016, 1444–67, and Goebel, *Anti-Imperial Metropolis*, 187–99.

33 In 1922, the print run was 1,000: Dewitte, *Les mouvements nègres*, 101. In Lima, it has to be said, there was only one subscriber: Goebel, *Anti-Imperial Metropolis*, 288.

The UIC was a training ground for anticolonial revolutionaries and Communist party cadre. The Algerians Hadj Ali Abdelkader (1883–1949) and Messali Hadj (1898–1974), the Vietnamese Nguyên Ai Quôc (Hô Chi Minh) and the Senegalese Laminé Senghor (1889–1927) all took their first steps in politics there. Nguyên Ai Quôc, the delegate of 'Indochina' at the founding congress of the PCF and soon a member of its colonial commission,[34] had been one of its founding members. As he would later explain, it was reading the theses on the national and colonial question adopted at the Second World Congress that made him a Communist.[35] The UIC did not only represent a demand for civil rights; by repeatedly drawing parallels and making comparisons between the different colonies, it also bound the colonized peoples together in a common space of solidarity, while also emphasizing the unity between the workers of metropole and colonies.

Dealings with British Communist Party, which Roy, with India in mind, had already accused of inaction on the colonial question at the Fifth World Congress, proved to be less positive. The criticism was repeated in several letters he sent from Paris to Grigori Voitinsky, then head of the ECCI's Eastern Department. He had also developed a plan of work that called on the British party to immediately send at least three British comrades to India, to set up a colonial committee in London (with his wife Evelyn as a member), and to try and draw large parts of the Labour Party and the unions into the anticolonial struggle.[36] Roy's complaints had an effect: on 22 December 1924 and 13 January 1925, the ECCI Secretariat discussed the International Colonial Bureau. It decided to expand its powers, conferring on it a 'monitoring

---

34 At first called the *Comité d'études coloniales*, it was only in September 1924, with the reorganization and centralization brought about by the Bolshevization of the party that it became the *Commission coloniale centrale*: Liauzu, *Aux origines*, 229; Dewitte, *Les mouvements nègres*, 106.

35 Alain Ruscio, '"L'agitateur annamite Nguyen Ai Quoc": Ho Chi Minh à Paris, 1917 à 1923', *Revue du centre d'étude d'histoire et de sociologie du communisme* 28, 1990, 6–16, at 9–10; Sophie Quinn-Judge, *Ho Chi Minh: The Missing Years, 1919–1941*, Berkeley: University of California Press, 2003, 31; Levine, *Found Generation*, 166. On the politicization of Vietnamese migrants in Paris, see also Pierre Brocheux, 'Une histoire croisée: l'immigration politique indochinoise en France, 1911–1945', *Hommes & Migrations* 1253, 2005, 26–38.

36 Haikal, 'Das Internationale Kolonialbüro', 128–9.

and coordinating role' with regard to the colonial commissions of the British and French parties.³⁷

It never came to that, however. As a result of British government pressure, Roy was arrested on 30 January 1925 and deported to Luxembourg. It had apparently not been an easy task for the French police charged with the task, as deprecatingly noted by Sir David Petrie, director of the Intelligence Bureau of the Government of India: 'Considerable difficulty has been experienced in locating Roy – who covered his tracks cleverly in Paris – in order to serve on him the order of expulsion.'³⁸ Roy was escorted to the frontier immediately upon his arrest, which Evelyn Trent Roy, who was not allowed to speak to her husband before his expulsion, described as a clear indication of Franco-British cooperation: 'The fact that he was sent to Luxembourg only shows that a country was selected where his abduction by British Secret Police would be an easy matter.'³⁹ In this, she was right, but in order to counter suspicions that the French police had acted under British orders, Roy was deported on the grounds that he had entered France on a forged Mexican passport.⁴⁰ Thanks to his wife's efforts, there was public protest against Roy's expulsion, news of which even reached Great Britain. The Comité Pro-Hindou that the French-speaking Evelyn Roy had just helped to found, with the Communist writer Henri Barbusse as secretary, and which assembled a whole swathe of French intellectuals, sent a letter of protest to the French government, accusing France of bowing to the 'imperialist exigencies' of Great Britain. Roy's detention was a violation of human rights. What was at issue was a 'crime of opinion', for Britain pursued Roy wherever he went not because he was a Communist, but because he sought independence for his country.⁴¹ The UIC too protested, holding a meeting in March that attracted some 400 people, to hear speeches by Laminé Senghor, Nguyên Ai Quôc and Hadj Ali Abdelkader among others.⁴²

---

37 Ibid., 129.

38 Petrie, *Communism*, 59.

39 Evelyn Roy, 'Indian Political Exiles in France', *Labour Monthly* 7:4, April 1925, also available at marxists.org.

40 Brückenhaus, *Policing*, 136.

41 *L'Humanité: journal socialiste quotidien*, 14 April 1925, front page [daily newspaper of the PCF]. The letter of protest was also published in Britain: Henri Barbusse, 'The Roy Case: A Protest', *Labour Monthly* 7:3, May 1925, 294–5, also available at marxists.org.

42 Goebel, *Anti-Imperial Metropolis*, 160.

Roy's expulsion from France brought an abrupt end to the bureau's activities, as a lack of suitably qualified cadre meant no replacement could be found. Roy himself had escaped the British police in Luxembourg and was now in Berlin. This was a difficult time for him. Lacking the legitimacy that came with grassroots engagement and political responsibility in the field, Roy now saw his position as the Comintern's Indian policy expert and liaison with the movement in India come under threat. The British party, whose two leading India specialists, Shapurji Saklatvala and Palme Dutt, were no friends of his, had sent a representative to India and thereupon accused Roy of complete failure, having found not the slightest trace of an Indian Communist party. Roy, in turn, described the British party's claim to leadership in matters of India policy as 'imperialist'. A unification conference held in Amsterdam on 11 and 12 July, with Roy and his wife Evelyn, on the one hand, and representatives of the British party and of various Indian groups on the other, was to resolve the dispute over jurisdiction. This was chaired by Sneevliet, a good friend of both Roy and Evelyn's.[43] As the historians Overstreet and Windmiller put it laconically: 'Roy, who had previously complained to the Comintern that the British Communists were not doing enough to organize the revolution in India, protested at Amsterdam that they were doing too much.'[44] The conflict would seem to have abated after the meeting, at least to the extent that responsibility for India within the Comintern ended up shared, though historians' accounts differ.[45]

Roy was, in any event, limited in his ability to act, being unable to visit India or Great Britain without finding himself arrested, and in Germany, too, he was persona non grata. He therefore went to Moscow,[46] a train journey that in those days took fifty hours.[47] While Evelyn Trent Roy remained in Paris and the couple separated, Roy stayed in the Soviet

---

43 Overstreet and Windmiller, *Communism in India*, 74–6; Carr, *Socialism in One Country*, vol. 2, 684.

44 Overstreet and Windmiller, *Communism in India*, 75.

45 Overstreet and Windmiller argue that agreement was reached with the British CP (*Communism in India*, 76), while Carr concludes that the Comintern ordered a transfer of responsibilities from Roy to the British party (*Socialism in One Country*, vol. 2, 684–5).

46 Overstreet and Windmiller, *Communism in India*, 74 and 76.

47 Karl Schlögel, *Das russische Berlin: Ostbahnhof Europas*, Munich: Hanser, 2007, 53.

capital until early 1927, working for the ECCI's Eastern Secretariat.[48] In that role, he was Münzenberg's contact person in connection with the colonial policy of the IAH, and for a long time indeed his hierarchical superior in the variably ramified structure of the Comintern apparatus.

China: New Epicentre of the World Revolution

While the Colonial Bureau in Paris was intended to coordinate and strengthen the anticolonial activities of the Communist parties of Europe's imperial powers, more extensive projects were also being contemplated by the Comintern's leading bodies. In September 1924, the ECCI Secretariat envisaged the creation of an anticolonial world organization to fight imperialism, a nonproletarian organization that would both bring together the Communist organizations of the colonies and the oppressed nationalities and bring broader layers under the Comintern's influence.[49]

The idea, however, would be turned into reality not by the Comintern in Moscow but by the dynamic Willi Münzenberg and his IAH (Workers' International Relief) in Germany, the central apparatus seemingly proving incapable of doing so. In good bureaucratic logic, the ECCI set up a commission, but no action followed. Yet the context was extremely favourable. In many parts of the world that would later be counted as the Third World and today the Global South, matters had reached boiling point. In late 1924, an anti-British uprising broke out in the Sudan. In 1925, the war against the Spanish colonialists in the Moroccan Rif, which had been going on since 1921, took on an international dimension when France joined in the conflict. In Syria, the Druze rose against French mandatory rule. Revolution broke out in China. In 1926, the Indonesian Communist Party launched an uprising against the Dutch, which was brutally suppressed. In 1927, Augusto Sandino led a rebellion against the occupation of Nicaragua by US military forces.

---

48 Sometimes 'Eastern Department', depending on the source: Bernhard Bayerlein, 'Das neue Babylon: Strukturen und Netzwerke der Kommunistischen Internationale und ihre Klassifizierung', *Jahrbuch für Historische Kommunismusforschung* [2004], 181–270, at 222.

49 Haikal, *Die Liga*, 11–12.

Münzenberg would succeed in uniting anticolonial and anti-imperialist forces, until then fragmented and scattered among cities and continents. He was certainly no great innovator: his talent lay rather in taking up political ideas that were in the air but which others shied away from realizing, because they required great organizational skill, unflagging perseverance and extraordinary personal powers of persuasion. These things he had in great measure. In addition, he had the ability to make use of his contacts in a politically productive way, and to develop still further the ideas of others. These would all play a role in the creation of the League Against Imperialism and Colonial Oppression in 1927. Münzenberg's initiative was not the first of its kind. E. H. Carr alludes to the launch of a League Against Imperialism by Chinese parliamentarians and representatives of left organizations at a public meeting held in Beijing in July 1924. This called for a common struggle of all the oppressed peoples of Asia and Africa against the imperialist powers of Great Britain, France, Japan and the USA.[50] At this point, the Communist Chinese in Germany, fewer than fifty of whom were German party members (two of them women),[51] sent representatives to the IAH congress held in October 1924 to ask for aid to their country. Presumably as a result of contacts between Chinese and Latin American students in Paris, the Communist Liga Antiimperialista de las Américas (LADLA; known in English as the All-America Anti-Imperialist League) was founded in Mexico City in 1925. It aimed, in particular, to combat the military and economic dominance of the USA over South and Central America and the Caribbean.[52]

Münzenberg's anticolonial activities reflected activist proposals but also responded to directions from Moscow. In 1924, the IAH's central committee decided to set up a section in China and sent two

---

50 Carr, *Socialism in One Country*, vol. 3, part 2, 703.

51 Thomas Kampen, 'Chinese Communists in Austria and Germany and Their Later Activities in China', *Asian and African Studies* 11:1-2, 2007, 21-30.

52 On the history of the LADLA, see Daniel Kersffeld, *Contra el imperio: Historia de la Liga Antimperialista de las Américas*, Mexico City: Siglo XXI, 2012; Ricardo Melgar Bao and Mariana Ortega Breña, 'The Anti-Imperialist League of the Americas between the East and Latin America', *Latin American Perspectives* 35:2, 2008, 9-24; Jürgen Mothes, *Lateinamerika und der 'Generalstab der Weltrevolution': Zur Lateinamerika-Politik der Komintern*, Berlin: Dietz, 2010, 139-42; and also the memoirs of Charles Shipman, *It Had to be Revolution: Memoirs of an American Radical*, Ithaca, NY: Cornell University Press, 1993, 154-7.

representatives there for the purpose, not long after an aid organization called Hands Off China had been formed in the Soviet Union.[53] It was that same year that Vladimir Mayakovsky wrote his combative poem *Hands Off China!*, in which he called on the Chinese 'coolies' to revolt and chase the colonizers out of the country. 'Hands off China!' was its repeated refrain, addressed to the 'pirates of the world'.[54] The slogan spread throughout the globe, being taken up in many languages. In November 1924, a short-lived 'Hands Off Egypt' association was formed in Baku,[55] and, from 1927, the same form of slogan would be used in support of the Nicaraguan liberation struggle by the '¡Manos fuera de Nicaragua!' committees of Mexico and South America and the 'Hands Off Nicaragua' committees of the United States. In December 1924, the Comintern authorized the IAH to initiate solidarity campaigns with China, Japan and other countries whose masses had not yet attained class consciousness but were engaged in struggles for national liberation.[56] At the Fifth ECCI Plenum of March–April 1925, the Soviet leadership declared the situation in the East to be objectively revolutionary, while noting a certain stabilization in Germany and Europe. Comintern sections were thus asked to strengthen their ties with non-Communist organizations. Kuusinen then fleshed out the new orientation at the Sixth ECCI Plenum in March 1926. Henceforward, the task was to mobilize sympathizers and invest in the development of 'mass organizations'. As he put it, an entire 'solar system' of organizations and smaller committees had to be created around the Communist parties.[57] The

---

53 This continued in existence until 1928, when the CC of the All-Union Communist Party (Bolsheviks) decided on its closure: Mechthild Leutner et al., eds, *KPdSU(B), Komintern und die Sowjetbewegung in China*, vol. 3, part 1, *1927–1931* (Münster: LitVerlag, 2000, 629.

54 Cited in Alexander Lukin, *The Bear Watches the Dragon: Russia's Perceptions of China and the Evolution of Russian–Chinese Relations Since the Eighteenth Century*, London: Routledge, 2015 [2003], 99.

55 Carr, *Socialism in One Country*, vol. 3, 668.

56 Kasper Braskén, *The International Workers' Relief, Communism, and Transnational Solidarity: Willi Münzenberg in Weimar Germany*, Basingstoke, UK: Palgrave Macmillan, 2015, 146; Haikal, *Die Liga*, 13. On the campaign in the United States, see Josephine Fowler, *Japanese and Chinese Immigrant Activists: Organizing in American and International Communist Movements, 1919–1933*, New Brunswick, NJ: Rutgers University Press, 2007, 54–7.

57 Extracts from the Resolution of the Sixth ECCI Plenum on the Development of Methods and Forms for Consolidating Communist Party Influence on the Masses, in

Sixth Plenum also dealt specifically with China for the first time, passing a resolution drafted by the Far Eastern Commission under Roy's presidency.[58]

Events in the spring of 1925 had brought China abruptly to the attention of the Western public. On 30 May, Shanghai's international police opened fire on demonstrating Chinese students, killing thirteen of them. This sparked a general strike in Shanghai and numerous anti-British and anti-Japanese strikes across the country. The strike movement swelled rapidly, bringing with it a vast increase in membership of the Chinese Communist Party. It was particularly strong in the city of Guangzhou (Canton), the Guomindang's new seat of government from July. It was the first major protest movement to demand national independence alongside better conditions for workers in the foreign-owned factories. For the Soviet party, China moved to the centre of the world revolution, as its Fourteenth Congress declared that December. Mediated by Chinese students in Europe, these events marked the beginning of a broad, anti-imperialist movement of support for China in Western capitals.

Thanks to the Chinese 'worker-students', branches of the Chinese Communist Party were created in Europe – not only in France, but also in Germany and Belgium, where certain students expelled from France had settled.[59] During the period of hyperinflation, German cities offered at least the advantage of cheap housing and a low cost of living. The transnational discussion and education network established between

---

Degras, *Communist International*, vol. 2, 265–8; Babette Gross, *Willi Münzenberg: A Political Biography*, trans. Marian Jackson, East Lansing: Michigan State University Press, 1974, 181.

58 Excerpts in Degras, *Communist International*, vol. 2, 275–9.

59 On Chinese students and revolutionaries in Berlin, see Mechthild Leutner, ed., *Deutsch-chinesische Beziehungen 1911–1927: Vom Kolonialismus zur 'Gleichberechtigung'; Eine Quellensammlung*, Berlin: Akademie Verlag, 2006, 414–18, which includes an estimate of their number as 500 at its highest in 1924, falling only a year later to around 300 (416); Roland Felber and Ralf Hübner, 'Chinesische Demokraten und Revolutionäre in Berlin (1900–1924) und Chinesische Demokraten und Revolutionäre in Berlin (1925–1933)', *Wissenschaftliche Zeitschrift der Humboldt Universität* 37:2, 1988, 148–72; Thomas Kampen, *Chinesen in Europa – Europäer in China: Journalisten, Spione, Studenten*, Gossenberg: OSTASIEN Verlag, 2010; Weijia Li, 'Otherness in Solidarity: Collaboration Between Chinese and German Left-Wing Activists in the Weimar Republic', in Qinna Shen and Martin Rosenstock, eds, *Beyond Alterity: German Encounters with Modern Asia*, New York: Berghahn Books, 2014, 73–93.

these Chinese Communist groups functioned through couriers and personal contacts. It helped train a number of cadres who would later become famous, including Zhu De (1886–1976) and Zhou Enlai (1898–1976). After studying first in Japan and then in France, England and finally Germany, Zhou Enlai spoke several European languages and, thanks to his upper-class background, possessed both enough money for travel and the talent for political leadership he came to show in the May Fourth Movement of 1919. As head of the Guomindang's European office and the person responsible for coordinating the work of Chinese Communists in Europe under the CCP's United Front policy, he commuted back and forth between Berlin and Paris. In Berlin, he had an apartment in Charlottenburg. Thanks to the efficacy of the network and the efforts of Zhao Shiyan (1901–1927), the various party and youth cells united in 1922 to form the European Section of the Chinese Communist Party.[60] This adopted a formal organizational structure and founded its own newspaper entitled *Shàonián* (Youth), which in 1924 became *Chiguang* (Red Light). Under the United Front policy of its parent party in China, it likewise collaborated in Europe with the Guomindang, which had set up a secretariat in Berlin in 1925. The ECKP also developed close contacts with Moscow relatively early on, apparently receiving financial support from the Comintern through Wilhelm Pieck (1876–1960), a member of the Orgbüro (Organizational Bureau) of the KPD. More than forty members of the ECKP subsequently undertook a training course at the Communist University of the Toilers of the East. The Comintern connection also enabled such comrades to return to China via Moscow.[61] For revolutionaries, this was not only more discreet, but also safer than by routes on which they faced arrest by the colonial powers.

Inspired by Chinese nationalists and revolutionaries, only a minority of whom were Communists, numerous protests and solidarity events were staged in Germany and other European countries, as also in the United States, under the slogan 'Hands Off China'. They were supported by the IAH and the national sections of the Comintern. As Münzenberg wrote to Zinoviev, by July 1925 more than a thousand events (indoor meetings, protest rallies and public demonstrations)

---

60 Levine, *Found Generation*, 137–58.
61 Ibid., 170.

had already taken place. He estimated that around 5 million people worldwide had attended.⁶²

To achieve such a success (somewhat overestimated as it might be) Münzenberg had been energetic in his propaganda. In June, he had launched the first issue of the multilingual *Bulletin für China / For China / Pour la Chine*,⁶³ news from that country coming to him via Francesco Misiano, his man in Moscow. Münzenberg did not hesitate to use film as a medium of agitprop, something highly unusual in the labour movement at that time, cinema being mostly thought to be 'rubbish'. Münzenberg, however, did not wish to leave this 'weapon' to the class enemy.⁶⁴ As early as December 1922, he had put his conception of film as a medium of propaganda into practice in setting up a limited company to buy the German distribution rights to Soviet films. This IAH subsidiary thus enjoyed a monopoly on Soviet films in Germany. To produce films on his own account, he also established his own Russian-based production company, Mezhrabpom-Russ, and a little later the film rental and distribution company Prometheus. *Das Dokument von Shanghai* [*Shankhaiskii dokument*; 'The Shanghai Document'] by Russian director Iakov Bliokh, a film intended to provide anti-imperialist 'counter-information' on China, was, however, produced by the state film company Sovkino and not completed in time for the 'Hands Off China' campaign.⁶⁵ The German premiere of this silent film was therefore staged in Berlin on 28 October 1928, as a private screening for the left-wing though non-party Volksfilmverband [People's Film Association], at the Tauentzien Palast on Nürnbergerstrasse, the leading cinema of the commercial UFA film conglomerate with almost a thousand seats, being shown to the general public only a fortnight later. The size of the cinema reflects the

---

62 On this campaign see Braskén, *International Workers' Relief*, 141–61, at 156, and on the meetings in France, Levine, *Found Generation*, 187–92. For the China campaigns of the British left: Tom Buchanan, *East Wind: China and British Left, 1925–1976*, New York: Oxford University Press, 2012.

63 Braskén, *International Workers' Relief*, 149.

64 Willi Münzenberg, *Erobert den Film! Winke aus der Praxis für die Praxis proletarischer Filmpropaganda*, Berlin: Neuer Deutscher Verlag, 1925. His conception of political agitation is developed in Münzenberg, *Propaganda als Waffe*, Paris: Carrefour, 1937.

65 Thomas Tode, 'Filmic Counter-Information: A Few Highlights from Film History', trans. A. Derieg, available at tranversal.at.

enthusiasm for China that gripped the Western world and Germany more especially in 1925.

That enthusiasm found expression too in scholarship and literature. Inspired by the May Thirtieth Movement, in 1926 the sinologist Karl August Wittfogel (1896–1988) – a member of the Frankfurt Institute for Social Research and a member of the KPD, though later, in the United States, a virulent anti-Communist – published the study *Das erwachende China* [Awakening China] an account of the history and present-day situation of the country. The following year, the Communist writer F. C. Weiskopf wrote an epic poem on the fall of the Canton Commune. Already a recognized novelist, the youthful Anna Seghers looked at this worldwide solidarity with the Chinese Revolution in her kaleidoscopic novel *Die Gefährten* (1932), showing in doing so, according to Siegfried Kracauer in the *Frankfurter Zeitung* of 13 November 1932, the 'unity of a movement that spans the world'.[66] Based on the experiences of Gerhart Eisler, who worked for the Comintern in China between 1928 and 1931, Brecht's didactic play *The Measures Taken* (1930) would be set to music by Eisler's brother, Hanns Eisler, playwright and composer discussing not only the music but also the text over weeks of conversations.[67] China enjoyed a new salience in the Soviet Union, too. In 1929, the Russian play *Roar, China!* had its German premiere in Frankfurt; based on a true story, it denounced the oppression of the Chinese people by the American and British imperialists.[68] The work of Sergei Tretyakov (1892–1937) and directed by internationally renowned Vsevolod Meyerhold was also performed in Japan, England, Poland and the United States. In 1930, it was produced in Berlin.

Building without delay on this mounting wave of sympathy, Münzenberg worked with young Chinese activists to organize a broad-based 'Hands Off China' solidarity congress, held in Berlin in mid-August 1925, variously said to have attracted between six hundred and a thousand people. Among them were many women, according to police reports. Foreign delegates came from Austria, France, Great Britain and

---

66 Li, *Otherness*, 73–93; and Li, *China und die China-Erfahrung in Leben und Werk von Anna Seghers*, Oxford: Peter Lang, 2010, Kracauer quote at 52.

67 Li, *China*, 52.

68 On the history of the play *Roar, China!* (a title which derives from the Baku manifesto of 1920) see Katerina Clark, *Eurasia without Borders: The Dream of a Leftist Literary Commons, 1919–1943*, Cambridge/Mass.: The Belknap Press, 2021, 206–11.

Paris, Brussels, Berlin: Anti-Imperialism and Transcolonial Networks 211

Czechoslovakia, and representatives of the Profintern (the Red Trade Union International) and the Krestintern (the Communist farmers' international) were also present. Last but not least, there were also twelve invited guests from China, one of whom gave the opening speech. Münzenberg had as usual succeeded in obtaining the endorsement of a wide range of figures and organizations beyond the Communist left, from the German League for Human Rights to the Quakers to a leading champion of anarchism. In gathering such signatures, Münzenberg was able to make use of a fat address book that held the details of the diverse roster intellectuals, academics, trade unionists, artists and writers to whom he regularly turned, people who – in his own words – had given him 'a blank power of attorney, as it were' – a power that Münzenberg exploited shamelessly.[69]

Building Global Anticolonial Solidarity

This campaign of solidarity with 'suffering China' was only the beginning of Münzenberg's anticolonial and anti-imperialist activities. As the historian Kasper Braskén has shown, it sparked a transformation in the way the relationship between Europe and Asia, between the German and Chinese proletariat, was understood.[70] The international solidarity invoked by the IAH was at first asymmetrical: while German workers were portrayed as strong and autonomous, the Chinese figured essentially as in need of their assistance, an image that isolated representations of active resistance could not dispel. The narrative focussed on the suffering of the Chinese people, reflecting, admittedly, the function of an aid campaign primarily intended to collect money. Yet it gave only the scantest expression to the interdependence of struggles in metropole and colonies propounded by the Comintern at the congresses of 1920 (Moscow and Baku) and 1922 (Irkutsk and Moscow).

Münzenberg's initiatives via the IAH helped remedy this lack and so establish a more balanced relationship between East and

---

69 Said at a meeting of the KPD Politburo, 1 February 1927, and cited in Haikal, *Die Liga*, 14.

70 Braskén, *International Workers' Relief*, 150–1.

West. On the one hand, he soon went beyond the organization of aid campaigns, by setting humanitarian goals in the context of open political support for national liberation struggles. On the other, he strove to replace unilateral Western solidarity with the people of the colonies with a true collaboration with their organizations effected through permanent structures. The process he set in motion can be characterized as a shift from proletarian internationalist philanthropy to a transnational anti-imperialist politics. Through a series of projects, his anticolonial efforts eventually led to the formation of a trans-imperial network. With the establishment of the League Against Imperialism and Colonial Oppression, he would bring anticolonial politics to the metropole, into the heart of empire. This was something around which bourgeois-progressive, national-revolutionary, left-wing socialist and Communist forces could unite, answering to the model of the non-party-affiliated mass organization called for by the Comintern – to be kept, of course, as far as possible under Communist control! Central to Münzenberg's overall plan was the idea of a big anticolonial congress. This would require much preparatory work, not only in terms of organization, but in obtaining the funding and therefore the approval of the ECCI.

Münzenberg's first step, at the end of 1925, was to set up a committee 'against the atrocities in Syria'. In accordance with the new line, the committee did not limit itself to humanitarian appeals but also explicitly hailed the Syrian liberation struggle. It was thus significantly more political in its activity than the China campaign had been.[71] The committee also enabled Münzenberg to make contact with the Arab world for the first time, through the Syrian, Palestinian and Transjordanian students in Berlin.[72] Further contacts in the colonies were provided by 'Karl Müller' (a code-name mainly used by the

---

71 On this committee and Münzenberg's subsequent anticolonial activities, see Fredrik Petersson, *Willi Münzenberg, the League Against Imperialism and the Comintern, 1925–1933*, 2 vols, Lewiston, NY: Queenston Press, 2013); Braskén, *International Workers' Relief*, 141–61.

72 Gerhard Höpp, 'Arabische Periodika in Deutschland. Initiatoren und Zielsetzungen, 1915–1929', in *Ibn an-Nadīm und die mittelalterliche arabische Literatur: Beiträge zum 1. Johann Wilhelm Fück-Kolloquium*, Wiesbaden: Harrasowitz Verlag, 1996, 136–43, at 142. The target of fifty signatures of notable figures in support of the committee was not achieved, only forty-four being obtained.

Swiss Hans-Heinrich Itschner) at the IAH's Moscow office. However, the Syria Committee did not last long, the lack of stable and reliable structures at the Syrian end making the transfer of material aid impossible. But, as the British Colonial Office correctly assessed in December 1925, it enabled Münzenberg and the IAH to strengthen connections between the European lefts.[73]

Against this background, Münzenberg was able to assemble for a first meeting, on 10 February 1926, not only anticolonial activists and representatives of left-wing organizations from Germany, but also foreign delegates from different parts of the world. This initial event took the form of a conference, but its goal was far-reaching: it was not just a matter of setting up another committee. Rather, the League Against Colonial Oppression was intended to serve as the foundation for an anticolonial movement in Germany. And, as Münzenberg explained at the conference, his intentions were more ambitious yet. The future would see the organization of regular international congresses that would be global in their impact. These would not only denounce the colonial policy of the imperialists but explore new ways of fighting it through solidarity between the international proletariat and the anticolonial movements.[74]

To prepare for the first anticolonial congress, an international organizing committee was officially formed, composed of a large number of important figures from colonial national liberation movements, the pacifist movement and left social democracy. In practice, however, it was Münzenberg's deputy and confidant Louis Gibarti (1895–1967) and Virendranath Chattopadhyaya (Chatto) who set about the planning. Chatto's partner, Agnes Smedley, was also informally involved, bringing her into contact with Berlin's Chinese revolutionaries and sparking her interest in China as the next candidate for an anti-imperialist revolution and a future model for India:

> Many middle-class Chinese revolutionaries had fled to Europe and the Soviet Union. I had made friends with a few of them and had edited a book by one. Virendranath had tried to unite all subjected Asiatic people behind the Chinese Revolution, and I had become

---

73 Petersson, *Münzenberg*, vol. 1, 160.
74 Ibid., vol. 1, 179–82.

involved. To the turmoil of German life was now added a new element, the Chinese Revolution.[75]

She did not, however, attend the Brussels congress herself.[76]

From Anticolonialism to Anti-Imperialism

On 10 February 1927, after almost a year of intense preparations, Münzenberg was able to officially open the First Congress Against Colonial Oppression and Imperialism at the Palais Egmont in Brussels.[77] This imposing building in the heart of the Belgian capital belonged to the municipality, and was made available following negotiations with Emile Vandervelde, the country's foreign minister and leader of the Belgian Socialist Workers' Party. It was, however, a condition of the congress's being held in Brussels that there be no denunciation of Belgian colonialism, though the choice of location was nonetheless symbolically powerful, Belgium being among the leading imperialist powers after the First World War.

The congress opened with the reading of letters and telegrams of solidarity from figures not in attendance (Albert Einstein, Mahatma Gandhi and Romain Rolland, among many others). The elderly British

---

75 Agnes Smedley, *Battle Hymn of China*, London: Victor Gollancz, 1944 [1943], 23.

76 Ruth Price, *The Lives of Agnes Smedley*, New York: Oxford University Press, 2005, 153–4. The author speculates that Smedley was perhaps held back by the fact that the congress would be attended both by Chatto and by Bakar Ali Mirza, with whom she was having a tumultuous affair at the same time.

77 On this see the proceedings of the congress, minuted by Louis Gibarti and published by Münzenberg's publishing house: *Das Flammenzeichen vom Palais Egmont: Offizielles Protokoll des Kongresses gegen koloniale Unterdrückung und Imperialismus, Brüssel, 10.–15. Februar 1927*, ed. Liga gegen Imperialismus und für nationale Unabhängigkeit, Berlin: Neuer Deutscher Verlag, 1927. The congress and its preparation, together with the League Against Imperialism and Colonial Oppression that emerged from it, are discussed in great detail in Petersson, *Willi Münzenberg*, vol. 1, 175–390. See also Peter Martin, 'Die Liga gegen koloniale Unterdrückung', in Ulrich van der Heyden and Joachim Zeller, eds, '. . . Macht und Anteil an der Weltherrschaft': Berlin und der deutsche Kolonialismus, Münster: Unrast Verlag, 2005, 261–9, and more recently the collection of contributions on the participant countries and their leaders: Michele Louro, Heather Streets-Salter, Carolien Stolte and Sana Tannoury-Karam, eds, *League against Imperialism: Lives and Afterlives*, Leiden: Leiden University Press, 2020.

Labour MP George Lansbury, who would arrive late, also expressed support in this way. Contrary to expectations, the congress was a great success. Even the organizers were surprised by the positive response to their invitations, Münzenberg reported to the ECCI.[78] A total of 174 delegates attended, representing 134 organizations or political parties from 34 different countries. The majority of the delegates, 104 of them, came from the colonies, though most of these lived in Europe. 'Münzenberg was in his element', noted his partner. 'He moved easily among the crowd, one of his staff always by his side to interpret for him.'[79]

Among the delegates was Julio Antonio Mella, born Nicanor McParland (1903–1929), a former law student in Havana and one of the founders of the Cuban Communist Party, who had had to flee to Mexico when the dictator Gerardo Machado came to power; there, together with Tina Modotti, later his partner, he had led the '¡Manos fuera de Nicaragua!' campaign. As delegate of the Liga Antiimperialista de las Americas, he represented Mexico, Cuba, Panama and Colombia. From Switzerland came two of Münzenberg's old acquaintances from his time in Zurich, Willi Trostel (1894–1942) and the physician Max Tobler (1876–1929), the latter secretary and afterwards president of the Swiss section of International Red Aid. From Great Britain came Ellen Wilkinson of the Independent Labour Party (ILP), from Germany the left-wing pacifist writers Ernst Toller and Karl August Wittfogel, from the USA Manuel Gómez representing the All-America Anti-Imperialist League (which existed there only on paper) and Roger Baldwin, founder of the American Civil Liberties Union. From France came the feminist pacifist Gabrielle Duchêne, representing the International Women's League for Peace and Freedom and Henri Barbusse, Münzenberg's man in Paris during the preparations for the congress. At the centre of attention, however, stood colonial representatives such as Jawaharlal Nehru of India, who was accompanied by his wife; the two South Africans Josiah Tshangana Gumede, president of the African National Congress, and James La Guma, its secretary; the Indonesian Mohammad Hatta (future vice-president of the independent Republic of Indonesia); the Haitian writer Carlos Deambrosis Martins; the Senegalese Laminé

---

78 Petersson, *Münzenberg*, vol. 1, 288.
79 Gross, *Münzenberg*, 190.

Senghor, representing the Ligue de défense de la race nègre (League for the Defence of the Negro Race); Messali Hadj representing the Étoile Nord-Africaine (North African Star); and many more. Numbering about thirty, the Chinese representatives to the congress formed the largest group, alongside the Germans. Other delegates came from Palestine, Syria, Egypt, Mexico, Venezuela, Vietnam, Japan, Korea, China, Iran (then still Persia) and from North and sub-Saharan Africa. They met anticolonial delegates representing the imperial powers – British, French, Belgians, Dutch and American – and others from Western countries that did not themselves have colonies but nonetheless participated economically in the colonial system – Austrian, Swiss, Czechoslovak and Italian. The congress was also unusually diverse in its political composition, bringing together anticolonial nationalists of various stripes, pacifists, human rights defenders, left-wing social democrats and trade unionists (who did not wish to abandon anticolonialism to the Communists) and, of course, Communists. Babette Gross describes the striking diversity of those present: 'Hindu princes, Kuomintang generals, leaders of Asian freedom movements and trade union officials ... met with politicians from the liberal, Socialist and Communist camps of Europe and America for the first time.'[80] What she does not mention, however, are the differing motives of those who attended, and the now documented presence of British and French police spies alongside an informer for the German Foreign Office.[81]

Together with the many declarations of sympathy, the assembly of such a great number of delegates of differing political hues, representing almost every continent (with the exception of Australia and Oceania) generated an almost euphoric mood, cleverly promoted by symbolic stagings of fraternization between the representatives of colonized and colonizers. One such moment was the handclasp between the Briton Fenner Brockway, general secretary of the ILP, and Liao Huanxing (1895–1964), European representative of the Guomindang's Central Executive Committee. This gesture that brought everyone to their feet in thunderous applause was, however, by no means spontaneous. As Brockway later revealed in his autobiography, Münzenberg had

---

80 Gross, *Münzenberg*, 188–9.
81 Brückenhaus, *Policing*, 142–3. See this too for the growing cooperation between French and British police on the one hand and the German police on the other.

whispered to him as he mounted the podium: 'End your speech by a declaration of unity with the Chinese workers and peasants.'[82] When he did, he suddenly found a Chinese comrade stood next to him with outstretched hand, and took it in his own.

Another high point was a speech by Laminé Senghor.[83] Emaciated by tuberculosis, this former French soldier, one of the 200,000 conscript *tirailleurs sénégalais*, delivered a fierce indictment of imperialism, which he described as an inhuman system of domination that would never bring civilization to the colonies. He denounced its abuses, its exaction of forced labour and the generalized injustice that he himself had suffered, being denied as a Senegalese the same military pension as the French veterans. When it came to work, they were French, but when it came to rights, they were just 'negroes'. He ended his speech with a forceful invocation of international solidarity and a call for the end of every form of oppression that imperialism, a product of capitalism, exercised both against the inhabitants of the colonies and against workers elsewhere:

> Those who suffer under colonial oppression over there must join hands and stand side by side with those who suffer the misdeeds of imperialism in the metropoles. They must wield the same weapons and destroy the universal evil that is none other than world imperialism! Comrades, it must be destroyed and replaced by the union of free peoples. No more slaves![84]

For Willi Münzenberg, the optimistic, even euphoric mood of the congress offered an unmissable propaganda opportunity, and he took advantage of the occasion to have several of these anticolonial campaigners appear in Berlin, arranging a longer lecture tour through Germany

---

82 Fenner Brockway, *Inside the Left: Thirty Years of Platform, Press, Prison and Parliament*, London: George Allen & Unwin, 1942, 167.
83 'Der Freiheitskampf der Neger', in *Das Flammenzeichen vom Palais Egmont*, 113–17.
84 The speech was issued as a pamphlet in June that same year by the publishing house of the PCF: Laminé Senghor, *La violation d'un pays*, Paris: Bureau d'Éditions, 1927, and is cited here as reprinted in Laminé Senghor, *La violation d'un pays et autres écrits anticolonialistes*, présentation de David Murphy, Paris: L'Harmattan, 2012, 63. See also David Murphy, 'Tirailleur, facteur, anticolonialiste: La courte vie militante de Laminé Senghor (1924–1927)', *Cahiers d'histoire: Revue critique* 126, 2015, 55–72.

for some. At the close of the congress, then, a number of the delegates travelled on – or back – to Berlin by train. Among them were most of the executive committee of the newly established league, and, it would seem, nearly every member of the Chinese delegation, either because they lived there or because they wished to return to China via Berlin and Moscow.

Münzenberg and Babette Gross – who for some time had had their own apartment near the Zoo – thus ended up inviting the delegates for an evening party. Also there was Babette's sister Margarete, who recalls the occasion in her memoir, speaking of 'a colourful medley of races: Negroes, Chinese, Mohammedans'.[85] Among them were Laminé Senghor, Manuel Gómez, Mazhar Bey el Bakri from the Berlin headquarters of the Syrian insurgents, George Lansbury, Beso Lominadze, a Kabyle from the Rif, as well as many others. English served as the lingua franca. The only one 'who had not the slightest trouble with understanding or even speaking a foreign language was Willi Münzenberg'.[86] He relied on his translator and interpreter Käthe Güßfeld (1899–?), employed at the IAH secretariat in Berlin since 1924, who had earlier carried out missions in England and France on behalf of the OMS, and who would emigrate to the Soviet Union in 1927, to eventually die in the Gulag. The gathering soon became animated, and people began to sing political songs, as Margarete goes on to tell, nearly all of them Communist and in many different languages, including, of course, the Internationale. The younger guests, among whom were Margarete herself and the thirty-year-old Georgian Lominadze, then moved on to the popular hits of the day and began to tell jokes, amid much laughter. This shocked the sixty-year-old South African Gumede so much that he complained to Münzenberg: such things were unworthy of true fighters. When Münzenberg then asked them to quieten down, the younger generation took their leave to plunge into Berlin's nightlife elsewhere.

---

85 Margarete Buber-Neumann, *Von Potsdam nach Moskau: Stationen eines Irrwegs*, Stuttgart: Deutsche Verlags-Anstalt, 1957, 97.

86 Ibid., 100.

Mobilizing Friends and Sympathizers

Communists were actually better represented at the Brussels Congress than they would have seemed to be on paper. Sen Katayama, for example, attended as a representative of the Japanese labour movement, but he was in fact the head of the ECCI's unofficial representation and leader of the Communists' secret fraction or party group at the Congress.[87] Senghor was a member of the French Communist Party. 'Manuel Gómez', officially delegate of the All-American Anti-Imperialist League, was also unofficially head of the American Communist delegation. He was, in fact, Richard Francis Phillips and also head of the Profintern's Latin America office in New York, regularly sent on missions to Mexico, Nicaragua, Peru, Cuba and other countries of the region. Münzenberg knew him from the Second World Congress of the Comintern. 'Gómez' worked under many pseudonyms: Frank Seaman, Jesús Ramírez, David Tanner, Manuel Díaz de la Peña and José Rocha among others, while he published his memoirs under the name Charles Shipman. Following the Brussels Congress, of which he said in retrospect that it had not 'accomplished anything',[88] he became secretary, in Chicago, of the American section of the League Against Imperialism. He would be elected to the ECCI at the Sixth World Congress, but expelled from the party in 1932. Karl August Wittfogel was likewise a member of the KPD, since 1920. In the run-up to the congress, he had worked with Münzenberg, in great haste, to draft the resolutions to be presented to it. And there were many others.

Münzenberg had, of course, also mobilized his own trusted acquaintances and others sympathetic to the goals of the Comintern and its sections. That is not to say that such people simply followed the party line or could easily be manipulated. What in retrospect seems the astonishing social diversity of the Communist delegates at the congress, in terms of both occupation and form of political engagement, shows how widespread was the appeal of the ideas of 'colonial liberation' and 'anti-imperialist struggle'. Communism was often only a vehicle for such ideas, a means of turning them into action. Fellow-travellers kept company with the party only so long as they found themselves reflected

---

87 Petersson, *Münzenberg*, vol. 1, 275.
88 Shipman, *It Had to Be Revolution*, 162.

in its politics. Ellen Wilkinson, for example, left the CPGB in 1924, while remaining close to the party. Gabrielle Duchêne and Roger Baldwin, then becoming close to the party, did not allow themselves to be recruited into the organization and took different positions on many political issues.

The example of Senghor himself shows that joining the party did not necessarily mean abandoning the capacity to think and act for oneself. Adherence almost always involved a complex transaction between party and member, from which both hoped to gain advantages. Laminé Senghor had experienced racism in his own body. Married to a white Frenchwoman, he was denied help to return home after the war. It was his marriage, he wrote, that first showed him how deep racism ran.[89] He joined the UIC in late 1924, at a time when North Africans had largely replaced Asians in the organization, though Africans from south of the Sahara were rare indeed. His almost instantaneous elevation to the Executive Committee clearly indicates how the PCF felt the need to better reflect the diversity of the colonial world. For the party, he became the embodiment of transcolonial solidarity. In 1925, Senghor stood at the forefront of a campaign against France's involvement in the Rif War in general and its unlawful use of mustard gas in particular.[90] It was there that this postman from the poverty-stricken working-class and immigrant neighbourhood of the Goutte-d'Or, just east of Montmartre, discovered his talent for oratory. When he tired of his position as the African alibi of the Communist Party, he founded his own organization to defend the interests of Africans, the Comité de Défense de la Race Nègre (CDRN, the Committee for the Defence of the Negro Race), in March 1926. A year later this became the Ligue de defense de la race nègre (LDRN), which Senghor founded with Tiemoko Garan Kouyaté (1902–1942), a former primary school teacher from French Sudan (now Mali) and also a member of the PCF.[91] The term *nègre* – 'negro' – was deliberately chosen. For Senghor, influenced by Marcus Garvey, the

---

89 Murphy, *Tirailleur*, 55–72.

90 On this campaign by the PCF, though lacking any mention of Senghor and highly critical of the party's inconsistency in matters of antiracism and anticolonialism, see David H. Slavin, 'The French Left and the Rif War, 1924–25: Racism and the Limits of Internationalism', *Journal of Contemporary History* 26:1, 1991, 5–32.

91 In 1942, Kouyaté was arrested in France by the Nazis; it is unclear whether he was shot or died in a concentration camp.

terms 'coloured' or 'black' represented categories introduced by imperialism so as to divide and rule. *Nègre*, on the other hand, designated the mass of the oppressed who refused to cooperate with the imperialist, capitalist system.[92] With the founding of the CDRN, Senghor said goodbye to the belief in abstract intercolonial solidarity, yet without abandoning its transnational dimension. Internationalism remained an important value, as would soon be shown by his cooperation with Germany's Liga gegen koloniale Unterdrückung (League Against Colonial Oppression). While Senghor's move away from the Communist Party expressed a certain disillusionment with a Communism that had not overcome its Eurocentrism, it also echoed a turn in anticolonial policy in the wider pro-Communist sphere, the Comintern having adopted in 1926 a new line that promoted the formation of liberation movements on a national basis.[93]

The new political line was also evident in the name and politics of the League Against Imperialism and National Oppression, which now called for the independence of the colonies rather than only an end to the oppression of their inhabitants. Without the consolidation of anti-imperialist forces initiated at the Congress with the establishment of the league, the unity achieved might well have remained ephemeral. Münzenberg, however, had already planned a permanent organizational form, the establishment of the League Against Imperialism figuring as item 16 on the conference programme. It would exist for ten years, with sections in dozens of countries, not only in Great Britain, Germany, the Netherlands and France, but also outside Europe, in the United States, South Africa, Cuba, Brazil . . .

The league was as diverse in political and ethnic complexion as the congress had been. At the time, it offered a unique platform to organizations that saw transnational action as the means to combat

---

92 Murphy, *Tirailleur*, 66. On the semantics and Marcus Garvey's influence on Senghor, see also Brent Hayes Edwards, *The Practice of Diaspora: Literature, Translation and the Rise of Black Internationalism*, Cambridge, MA: Harvard University Press, 2003.

93 Among the organizations that thus emerged from the UIC were the Étoile Nord-Africaine in the Maghreb, and the Parti annamite de l'indépendance (Annamite Independence Party), in reality a section of the PCF, in Vietnam. See Céline Marangué, *Le communisme vietnamien (1919–1991): Construction d'un Etat-nation entre Moscou et Pékin*, Paris: Presses de Sciences Po, 2012, and Marangué, 'Le Komintern, le Parti communiste français et la cause de l'indépendance algérienne (1926–1930)', *Vingtième siècle: Revue d'histoire* 131, 2016, 53–70.

internationalism and colonialism. 'The whole world is on the move', proclaimed the league's founding manifesto, 'and the smallest impulse in any of its parts has a mighty echo in immeasurable realms.'[94] Among its patrons appeared the names of the 'usual suspects', familiar figures such as Henri Barbusse, Albert Einstein and Madame Sun Yat-sen (Song Qingling) from the Guomindang, who would later continue to work with the Communists after the Guomindang Left's break with the Comintern. The political spectrum represented on the General Council ranged from the Italian Catholic trade unions to the Étoile Nord-Africaine, the Philippine Independence Association, the Central Council of the All-China Federation of Trade Unions, the Women's International League for Peace and Freedom, and the Soviet trade unions.

The league's Executive Committee, presided over by George Lansbury (soon to be replaced by another Briton, James Maxton), whose work, however, was directed in practice by the Dutch trade union leader Edo Fimmen, was similarly politically heterogeneous in make-up. Of the seven other members, only three were Communists (if we except Albert Marteaux, the Belgian socialist MP, who joined the Communist Party only in the 1930s), Willi Münzenberg and Liao Huanxing among them, the others representing liberation movements in Indonesia, Latin America and India. Given the great distances involved, however, day-to-day decision-making was in the hands of league's international secretariat, the small team of committed full-timers based in Berlin, thus leaving Willi Münzenberg and the two secretaries, Chatto and Liao Huanxing, in effective charge of the doings of the league. Münzenberg, the unofficial leader, not only enjoyed the symbolic power of his charisma but also had a monopoly of dealings with the Comintern in Moscow and the KPD's central committee in Berlin.

Münzenberg again turned to old acquaintances and other trusted figures in staffing the newly founded organizations. One such was Fritz Sulzbachner, who, in 1926, under the name Fritz or Federico Bach, was seconded from the IAH to work at the international secretariat of the League Against Colonial Oppression at Bambergerstrasse 69 in Berlin

---

94 'Manifest an alle unterdrückten Völker und Klassen, Manifest des Brüsseler Kongresses gegen den Imperialismus', in *Das Flammenzeichen vom Palais Egmont*, 243–54, at 247.

and, the following year, that of its successor, the League Against Imperialism and National Oppression. Münzenberg knew him from his youth in Switzerland. The son of a working-class family in Basel and employed as a clerk in the post office there, he had joined the central committee of the Jungburschen, the Social Democratic youth organization that Münzenberg had founded in 1917. Paul Thalmann, another member of the group, describes him as 'very much the bohemian anarchist, but in a serious way'. He was 'extremely well-read and good at languages'. Indeed, according to Thalmann, he had a 'particular interest in psychoanalysis, and he knew his way around Freud, Reich, and Jung. It was through him that we were introduced to the literature of the German Left.'[95] A member of the left wing of the Social Democratic Party, Sulzbachner was elected to the nine-member central committee on the foundation of the Communist Party of Switzerland.[96] He married the daughter of Otto Rühle, a Spartacist, Council Communist and author of numerous socio-educational studies, who was, at that time, one of the few on the left who sought to marry Marxism and psychology.

In the summer of 1927, Sulzbachner travelled to Mexico as Münzenberg's representative and correspondent of the *Arbeiter Illustrierte Zeitung*. In autumn 1928, writing as 'F. Bach', he reported on one of his trips to Nicaragua in an article headed (in German) 'With the Rebel General Sandino, with numerous photographs by the American journalist Carleton Beals'.[97] The paper also used pictures by the then already well-known photographer Tina Modotti. A member of the Mexican CP since the autumn of 1927 and an activist with the Münzenberg-associated ¡Manos fuera de Nicaragua! Committee, she saw it as her responsibility to document the party's struggle. Unlike Carleton Beals's pictures, her photograph *Child in Sombrero* was published on the front page of the *AIZ* without a credit. Worse yet, pictures of hers were not only not credited to her, as a woman

---

95 Paul Thalmann, *Wo die Freiheit stirbt: Stationen eines politischen Kampfes*, Olten and Freiburg in Breisgau: Walter-Verlag, 1974, 11.

96 Peter Stettler, *Die Kommunistische Partei der Schweiz 1921–1931*, Bern: Francke Verlag, 1980, 41.

97 'Bei dem Rebellengeneral Sandino: Originalbericht von F. Bach für die AIZ mit bisher unveröffentlichten Aufnahmen von Carleton Beals, dem ersten Journalisten, der den Führer der Kämpfe um die Unabhängigkeit Nicaraguas in seinem Lager aufsuchte', *Arbeiter-Illustrierte-Zeitung*, [October or November 1928], 8–9.

photographer, but were captioned 'Original photos by our special reporter F. Bach on mission in the Americas'.[98] In Mexico, 'Bach' met with the Italian Vittorio Vidali (1900–1983). The two knew each other, having met in the early 1920s, when Vidali had entered Germany illegally, found himself arrested, and had been helped to escape by Sulzbachner and other members of the Young Communists.[99] By the end of the decade, however, the Comintern was engaged in a furious struggle against 'right opportunists', who had to be purged from the party, a task that Vidali was charged with as Moscow's representative in Mexico. As Sulzbachner refused to subordinate the ¡Manos fuera de Nicaragua! Committee to the Comintern's ultraleft line (which demanded that Sandino break off relations with the Mexican government), he and others were expelled from the Mexican CP in late 1929 – an event that Vidali took credit for in a letter to another comrade, claiming it as a victory against 'the agents provocateurs of the bourgeoisie in our own ranks'.[100] The 1930s saw Sulzbachner settle in Mexico, where he became a professor of economics, he and his wife being followed there by her parents. He remained close to Swiss-German artistic circles throughout his life; his brother Max was a recognized painter and later co-founder of Gruppe 33, a group of antifascist artists in Basel.

Another former member of the Jungburschen employed by Münzenberg was Otto Schudel (1902–1979), also from Basel, who having completed a commercial apprenticeship worked at the league's secretariat from 1927 to 1930. In 1929, Münzenberg sent him to Geneva to persuade delegates to the ILO's International Labour Conference to attend the League's Frankfurt Congress after their own event was over. Straightforward lobbying evidently also formed part of Münzenberg's armamentarium.

Friendship, and so trust, also played a role in the construction of Münzenberg's anticolonial activist network. To organize the large-scale

---

98 They appeared in the issue of 14 March 1928: Christiane Barckhausen, *Auf den Spuren von Tina Modotti* Kiel: Agimos, 1997, 193. Modotti was not the only inter-war woman photographer sometimes left uncredited by her publishers; on this, see Irme Schaber, *Gerda Taro, Fotoreporterin: Mit Robert Capa im spanischen Bürgerkrieg*, Marburg: Jonas Verlag, 2013.

99 The episode is recounted in the CV submitted to the Comintern by Vittorio Vidali, Moscow, 28 January 1932, RGASPI 513/2/36.

100 Patrick Karlsen, *Vittorio Vidali: Vita di uno Stalinista (1916–56)*, Bologna: Il Mulino, 2019, 146.

international anticolonial congress he had in mind and to gather well-known names representative of the various currents, he first mobilized his friends among the anticolonial intellectuals and revolutionaries living in Germany, so extending his reach both locally and transnationally. Among them were Liao Huanxing of China, Chatto from India, and Ahmed Hassan Mattar of Sudan (1904–1985, spelt Matar or Matari in some sources). As secretary of the Guomindang's European office in Berlin, Liao consolidated the existing good relationship with Chinese students. Chatto, through his Verein der Inder in Zentraleuropa (Union of Indians in Central Europe) and thanks to the addresses he had from the days of his Indian News and Information Bureau, funded by Borodin and operational until 1925, made contact with revolutionaries in India. And Mattar, finally, did the same for the Arab world, through his connections with the Egyptian nationalists who met at Berlin's Zaglulist Club and his own extensive international network.[101]

Liao had come to Berlin to study in 1922.[102] A member of the Chinese Communist Party, he brought news from the Central Committee to the Chinese party's local leadership in Paris and Berlin. Like his friend Mao Zedong (1893–1976), he was a native of Hunan Province.[103] In 1923, he transferred his membership from the Chinese to the German party, as required by the Comintern regulations. He spoke better German than did most other Chinese Communists in Germany, and married a German Communist, Dora Dombrowski, with whom he had a son.[104] In late 1923, he became leader of the party cell in Berlin. In 1924, after Zhou Enlai returned to China to take a political post at the Guomindang's military academy, he became one of the leaders of the Chinese

---

101 Petersson, *Münzenberg*, vol. 1, 166–7. On Mattar's life see Daniel Kersffeld, 'Más allá de las fronteras: Ahmed Hassan Mattar y su activismo entre África y Sudamérica', *Culture & History Digital Journal* 11:2, December 2022. Contacts between the ECCI and the Arab world, however, went back further: see Rami Ginat, *A History of Egyptian Communism: Jews and Their Compatriots in Quest of Revolution*, Boulder, CO: Lynne Rienner Publishers, 2011, which focuses on the role of Jewish figures.

102 The spelling of the name varies in both the sources and the literature, appearing as Liau Hansin, Liao Khuan'sin, Liau Gunzin or Liao Gongxing.

103 Thomas Kampen, 'Liao Huanxing oder Tang Xingqi: Für KP und Kuomintang in Berlin', *Das neue China*, June 2001, 29–31.

104 In 1950, she was still living in the Soviet Union: Permit for Dora Liau-Dombrowski and her son Gert Mindju to leave the Soviet Union for Berlin, minute no. 111/50, meeting of the Secretariat of the CC of the SED of 31 May 1950, Bundesarchiv, DY 30/J IV 2/3/111.

Communists in Germany. Employed by the sociologist and sinologist Karl August Wittfogel, a member of the Frankfurt Institute for Social Research, he helped him with his research on Sun Yat-sen.[105] While officially the representative of the Guomindang, Liao was at the same time acting on behalf of the CCP and the Comintern.[106] Under the pseudonym Tang Xhinshe, he wrote for the German Communist press and for the Comintern publications *Die Kommunistische Internationale* and *Inprekorr*, and also translated Chinese articles into German. As Iren Komját recalls, he was incredibly idealistic in his motivation, sparing himself no effort.[107] From 1925 to 1927, Liao also worked for Jenö Varga's statistical office at the Soviet trade agency in Berlin, where he was responsible for data on China,[108] but found himself dismissed as a result of Comintern budget cuts.[109] That same year, the break between the Guomindang and the Chinese Communist Party in April 1927 also saw Liao lose his position at the Guomindang's Berlin office.

Liao was well connected in Berlin. He evidently knew Anna Seghers, who portrayed him in her novel *Die Gefährten* as a young Chinese who migrates to Germany at his elder brother's behest, to learn as much as possible for the sake of the revolution, and there grows into the role of responsible and self-sacrificing revolutionary. Similarly described by Babette Gross as 'young and eager',[110] Liao was

---

105 Sun Yat Sen, *Aufzeichnungen eines chinesischen Revolutionärs*, trans. G. Iversen, ed. K. A. Wittfogel, Vienna: Agis-Verlag, 1927.

106 Levine, *Found Generation*, 226; Thomas Kampen, 'Deutsche und österreichische Kommunisten im revolutionären China (1925–1949)', *Jahrbuch für Historische Kommunismusforschung*, 1997, 88–104, at 23.

107 Iren Komját, *Die Geschichte der Inprekorr: Zeitung der Kommunistischen Internationale (1921–1939)*, Frankfurt a. M.: Verlag Marxistische Blätter, 1992, 67.

108 Joachim Krüger, 'A Regular Chinese Voice from Berlin to Moscow: The China-Information of Liao Huanxing, 1924–1927', in Mechthild Leutner et al., eds, *The Chinese Revolution in the 1920s: Between Triumph and Disaster*, London: RoutledgeCurzon, 2002, 177–83.

109 Minute No. 1 on the question of the reduction of the apparatus, Moscow, 21 December 1928, RGASPI, 495/46/13; report to Moscow by Alarich, Berlin, 21 November 1928, RGASPI 495/19/212. The decision on the transfer of 'Comrade Varga's bureau' gave delayed effect to a decision by the Politburo of the CPSU of 25 August 1927 published in Hermann Weber, Jakov Drabkin and Bernhard H. Bayerlein, eds, *Deutschland, Russland, Komintern*, vol. 2, Berlin: de Gruyter, 2014, 577.

110 Babette Gross, *Willi Münzenberg: Eine politische Biographie*, Stuttgart: Deutsche Verlags-Anstalt, 1968, 197 [the relevant passage being missing from the English translation cited elsewhere].

a close friend of Münzenberg's. This saw him not only involved in the organization of the Brussels conference but also recruited by Münzenberg as one of the secretaries of the league that was founded there. Provided by Varga with an excellent testimonial (a 'trustworthy comrade' and an 'efficient' and 'satisfactory' employee[111]), he was also found a job at a business that Münzenberg was launching, a Chinese news agency in Berlin. Following the success of the congress and the foundation of the League Against Imperialism, Münzenberg wanted to strengthen his network of Chinese activists in Europe, while also making up for the loss of connections in China brought by the break with the Guomindang. By April, Münzenberg had put the idea to David Petrovsky (1886–1937), the former journalist who was the Comintern's representative in Berlin.

Born David Lipetz, Petrovsky had travelled to the United States on behalf of the Bund before the First World War, going by the name of Max Goldfarb, and then returned to Russia in 1917, where he worked for the Comintern. Under the pseudonym A. J. Bennett, he was sent to Great Britain, where he met his future wife, Rose Cohen. On his return to Moscow, he was regularly sent on missions to England and France, and in 1927 even to Germany, where he apparently used the code-name 'Isolde'. Petrovsky then passed Münzenberg's idea on to the ECCI Little Commission in Moscow, who gave their approval, on condition that Julius Alpári of *Inprekorr* have oversight of the agency that would be established at Friedrichstrasse 232.[112] The Comintern provided 3,500 marks a month for the first three months, to cover all expenses, a sum that was, however, nowhere near enough. Inadequate resources, the difficulty of getting enough reliable news from China to Berlin, the pressure of increasing police surveillance and, finally, personal differences between Liao, Münzenberg and Gibarti on the other, led to the closure of the agency some three and a half years later, in August 1927. In late 1928, Liao emigrated to Moscow with his wife. At first, he continued to work for the league, and also took part in its second and last congress, held in Frankfurt in 1929, but then transferred his party membership to the VKP(b), indicating that he definitely intended to remain in the Soviet Union.

---

111 Cited in Petersson, *Münzenberg*, vol. 1, 329 and n.417.
112 Ibid., 332.

The first secretary of the Anti-Imperialist League was Chatto. Margarete Buber-Neumann, who, as has been said, worked for the league for a short time in the wake of the Brussels Congress, described him as having been the 'soul' of the office. She was less complimentary about his appearance, perhaps, saying that he 'looked like an owl'.[113] Like Roy (with whom he was in constant competition) he came from a Brahmin family, though unlike Roy's people they were wealthy. His contemporaries describe him as polyglot, intelligent and erudite.[114] After studying at Oxford and the Middle Temple, he devoted himself to the struggle for Indian independence, living successively in London, Paris and Pondicherry. In 1914, he moved to Berlin, where he founded the Indian Revolutionary Committee. He then lived in Switzerland for a time until he was expelled, whereupon he travelled to Sweden. As a result, Roy missed Chatto when in Berlin in 1920, on his way to the Comintern's Second World Congress. In 1921, Chatto returned to Berlin, where, with financial support from Borodin, he opened the Indian Press and Information Office. Comintern records show that after its closure he was employed by Red Army intelligence in 1925–26.

Roy and Chatto's first encounter in Moscow in early 1921 had been fractious. In the dispute over who should be the Comintern's accredited India expert, Roy had won the day because the ECCI had more confidence in his group. The conflict between the two of them was not, however, only a matter of personal ambition. They also disagreed fundamentally regarding the formation of an Indian Communist Party, with Chatto rejecting Roy's establishment of a base in Tashkent and calling for a party to be set up inside India. In early 1926, when Chatto was contacted by Münzenberg and asked to attend a meeting in February to make preparations for an international anticolonial congress in Brussels, this was apparently done on Roy's recommendation, so it would appear that their relationship had improved.[115] Chatto was then teaching at an agricultural school outside Berlin.[116] He agreed, in any event, and took part in the conference that led to the

---

113 Margarete Buber-Neumann, *Kriegsschauplätze der Weltrevolution: Ein Bericht aus der Praxis der Komintern 1919–1943*, Stuttgart: Seewald Verlag, 1967, 306.

114 See Barooh, *Chatto*; and on his linguistic abilities, Smedley, *Battle Hymn*, 16.

115 Ray, *In Freedom's Quest*, vol. 2, 235, and vol. 3, part 1, *Against the Current (1928–39)*, Kolkata: Renaissance, 2005, 17.

116 Petersson, *Münzenberg*, vol. 1, 178.

establishment of the League Against Colonial Oppression. From then on, he would collaborate with Münzenberg in his anticolonial activities. In doing so, he relied on the assistance of his partner Agnes Smedley, who was always involved alongside him in his Indian endeavours – something she bitterly decried, following their separation, as the typically male exploitation of a female partner.[117]

It was thanks to Chatto that Nehru was persuaded to take part in the Brussels Congress and subsequently join the executive of the League Against Imperialism. As secretary of the league, in July 1928 Chatto launched the *Anti-Imperialist Review*, a quarterly magazine featuring articles on imperialism and the global resistance to what the first editorial called the 'double tyranny of foreign government and foreign capitalism' prevailing in the colonies.[118] That same year saw Agnes Smedley separate from 'Viren', as she called Chatto, and travel to China via Moscow. Chatto himself, who had secretly joined the party in 1927 (though he did not publicly identify himself as a member until late 1929 or early 1930), left Berlin for the Soviet Union in 1931. In this he followed Tina Modotti, who had made the same journey a year earlier, after only six months in Berlin. As a member of the Anti-Imperialist League in Mexico, the country from which she had been expelled as a Communist, she had been a regular visitor to the league's Berlin secretariat, where she made friends with Chatto, and so gave him as a reference when seeking employment with International Red Aid (MOPR) in Moscow.[119]

Münzenberg also had other friends among his collaborators, notably the Dutchman Edo Fimmen, not a Communist but, as general secretary of the International Transport Workers' Federation, one of the more important of his allies.[120] The two had known each other since August 1921, when Fimmen had come to Berlin, in his role as general secretary, to negotiate with the Russian Embassy the practical

---

117 Smedley, *Battle Hymn*.

118 *Anti-Imperialist Review* 1:1, July 1928, cited in Michele L. Louro, 'India and the League Against Imperialism: A Special "Blend" of Nationalism and Internationalism', in Raza Ali, Franziska Roy and Benjamin Zachariah, eds, *The Internationalist Moment: South Asia, Worlds and World Views 1917–1939*, New Delhi: Sage, 2015, 22–55, at 45. The author was the president of the league, the Scot James Maxton, pacifist, leader of the ILP, and member of parliament.

119 Letter to KPD, 're. Tina Modotti', signed D. V., Moscow, 29 January 1930, RGASPI 495/221/1605.

120 Gross, *Münzenberg*, 115.

arrangements for shipping aid to Soviet Russia. Since then, they had met, whenever Fimmen was in Berlin, at a 'small tavern' on Dorotheenstrasse 'frequented otherwise almost exclusively by East Elbian Junkers', to discuss events over good food.[121] Fimmen, eight years his senior, supported Münzenberg's anticolonial enterprises so long as the Comintern tolerated his united front policy. He took part in the preparatory work for the Brussels Congress, helping to forge contacts and opening the door to left social democratic and trade union circles and funders. Babette Gross describes him as deserving 'special credit' for the holding of the congress and the establishment of the League. 'Big and powerful, with a great shock of hair, Fimmen was very good at running the meetings. He translated proposals, smoothed troubled waters, conferred with Russian and other trade union representatives.'[122] Fimmen became vice president of the League Against Imperialism, but had to leave the organization following the change of political line at the Sixth World Congress of the Comintern in 1928, which rejected all cooperation with social democrats, no longer allies but 'agents of imperialism'. This did not, however, affect his relationship with Münzenberg, whom he later helped in his Paris exile, providing both material support and letters of recommendation to figures in the international labour movement. They would remain friends until Münzenberg's untimely death.[123]

Guided by friendship as it was, Münzenberg's recruitment policy was also attentive to practical requirements. These must likely have been to the fore in the case of Mattar, who worked in the colonial department of the IAH. Expelled from his home country by the British colonial authorities, this Sudanese journalist and anticolonial activist of Arab descent spent time in Marseille and London before settling in Tangier in 1924, where he involved himself in the struggle for the liberation of the Rif. After a stopover in Egypt, he travelled to Brazil on a propaganda mission for Abd el-Krim, president of the short-lived Republic of the Rif. In November 1925 he returned from Latin America to work as a newspaper correspondent in Europe, living in Marseille for a time and then reporting on the League of

---

121 Ibid., 155.
122 Ibid., 190.
123 Dieter Nelles, 'Eine neue Internationale – Edo Fimmen und Willi Münzenberg 1939/40', at muenzenbergforum.de.

Nations in Geneva before finally moving to Berlin, where he was recruited by Münzenberg.[124] He made his extensive network of contacts in the Arab world and North and West Africa available for the setting up of the Syria Committee, and later travelled to Tangier and Dakar, mobilizing his contacts there as part of the preparations for the Brussels Congress, which he attended himself as representative of the Kabyle of the Rif. Mattar worked for the IAW and the league for about two years.[125] On his expulsion from Germany in October 1927,[126] Münzenberg arranged for him to join the German delegation to the tenth anniversary celebrations of the October Revolution in Moscow. The expulsion order did not prevent Mattar from returning to League headquarters in Berlin for a while after his visit to the Soviet Union, before travelling again to Latin America on a propaganda tour on behalf of the Rif. He later gave up political activity, several times changing both name and personal circumstances.

The employment of Louis Gibarti, who joined Chatto in 1926 at the head of the Liga gegen Kolonialgreuel und Unterdrückung (League Against Colonial Atrocities and Oppression), must likewise have been motivated by merely practical considerations. He would be Münzenberg's most important collaborator in preparing the Brussels Congress and building the Anti-Imperialist League. Gibarti was a Hungarian named László Dobos, and he also used a number of other pseudonyms (among them Alfred Feller, Felix Gasbarra and Wladislaus Kaminski). He is one of those Comintern figures whose biographies are still marked by gaps and contradictions even today. According to a secret CIA memorandum released in 2011, he studied political science at Oxford and law and economics in Vienna and Budapest (where he received his doctorate) before becoming an artillery officer in the Austrian army during the First World War. During the Hungarian Soviet Republic of 1919, he took part in the fighting against invading Czech and Romanian

---

124 Dirk Sasse, *Franzosen, Briten und Deutsche im Rifkrieg 1921–1926: Spekulanten und Sympathisanten, Deserteure und Hasardeure im Dienste Abdelkrims*, Munich: R. Oldenbourg Verlag, 2006, 311–12; Gerhard Höpp, 'Die arabischen Nationalrevolutionäre in Berlin und die Liga', in Hans Piazza, ed., *Die Liga gegen Imperialismus und für nationale Unabhängigkeit 1927–1937*, Leipzig: Karl-Marx-Universität, 1987, 105–12. See also his autobiography, Ahmed Hassan Mattar, *Sindbad of the Sudan*, ed. Philip Oliver, Khartoum: n.p., 1968.

125 Haikal, *Die Liga*, 18–19.

126 Petersson, *Münzenberg*, vol. 2, 1008.

forces.[127] When exactly he began working for Münzenberg is unclear (as early as 1921, by some accounts). From 1926, together with 'Bach' and Mattar, he led the work of IAH's colonial department, which stood at the heart of all Münzenberg's anti-imperialist endeavours, where the Communists among the league's employees met as an organized fraction.[128]

Eloquent, efficient and highly adaptable, Gibarti proved indispensable to Münzenberg. It was he who made contact with anticolonialists around the world in advance of the Brussels Congress, sending out hundreds of invitations and corresponding with the organizations and individuals invited, and he also travelled to Brussels on Münzenberg's behalf to negotiate with the authorities there. His articles in the Liga's newspaper, *Der koloniale Freiheitskampf*, helped persuade anticolonial activists to take part in the Congress. He also sent copies of correspondence and other documents to Moscow, alongside the reports the Comintern insisted on. Yet by no means did Münzenberg simply leave him to his work; on the contrary, he checked every document before it was sent to Moscow. For it was Münzenberg who dealt with Moscow – that is, the ECCI and its Eastern Department.

Coordination with the Eastern Department

For the Comintern, and even more with the turn to Bolshevization, cultural and political diversity was of value only in terms of outward image. As a political institution, the Comintern was conceived as rigid, hierarchical structure that would maintain control over the political projects it initiated and the organizations it set up. The ECCI secretariat had thus instructed Münzenberg, as early as mid-1926, to convene an ongoing group that would coordinate the activities of all Communists involved in the preparation and conduct of the Brussels Congress, a group whose existence, however, was never to be made public. By late January 1927, the fraction had elected a leadership. In addition to

---

127 Memorandum. Subject: Ladilas Dobos, Louis Gibarti, Ladilas Dovosgas, Alfred Feller. The document is undated but marked 'Received from CIA 1/8/49': cia.gov/readingroom/document/0005632259.

128 Haikal, *Die Liga*, 18.

Münzenberg, this consisted of Walter Stoecker (1891–1939), a member of the Central Committee of the KPD (who would die in Buchenwald), a representative of the PCF, the Scotsman Arthur MacManus (1889–1927) representing the CPGB (though he would die not much later) and Petrovsky. This policy of intra-party coordination was maintained after the league was founded, and there was thus a Communist fraction on the league's executive, which agreed lines and tactics before each meeting.[129]

In fact, the ECCI and its Eastern Department were behind every key decision taken during the preparation of the Congress and thereafter. Willi Münzenberg did in the end succeed in gaining approval for idea of the Brussels Congress, a process reconstructed in detail by Mustafa Haikal and more recently Fredrik Petersson. Yet every step of the way had had to be negotiated with the Comintern leadership.[130] It was in August 1925 that Münzenberg submitted to Zinoviev his proposal to convene a 'comprehensive congress' of anti-imperialist forces, to which the Eastern Department initially responded negatively. This did not prevent him from making his first organizational preparations. On his regular visits to Moscow, he emphasized that, of course, he would do nothing without the Comintern's consent. When the Sixth Plenum of the ECCI, held in February–March 1926, issued its call to increase support to sympathizing movements, and more particularly those fighting colonial atrocities and the oppression of the 'peoples of the East', this allowed Münzenberg to present the apparatus with a fait accompli. The Eastern Secretariat thus learnt of the existence of the League Against Colonial Oppression only when he addressed them himself. Gibarti, for his part, assured them in a letter that the league was firmly under Communist control.

At the time, however, Moscow was still undecided as to whether an international anticolonial congress 'in Brussels or Amsterdam' was even desirable. While Roy supported the idea, Grigori Voitinsky, then deputy head of the Eastern Secretariat and regular ECCI emissary to China between 1924 and 1927, spoke against it. To deal with the matter, a five-person committee was set up, in the usual way, in March 1926, with one

129 Petersson, *Münzenberg*, vol. 1, 275–6.
130 Petersson, *Münzenberg*; Haikal, *Die Liga*. The account that follows is essentially based on the work of these two authors.

representative each from the Organization Department of the ECCI and the Central Committee of the KPD, another Comintern functionary, and the Hungarian József Pogány, alias 'John Pepper' (1886–1938).[131] Roy attended as its head, and that same month he was able to present a resolution to the ECCI Secretariat. This recommended adoption of Münzenberg's plan. Such a congress, it was suggested, might succeed, where the Comintern had failed so far, in contacting anticolonial activists. The point was to finally mobilize Europe's trade unions and 'bourgeois-liberal elements' in support of the 'colonies in struggle'. The resolution also underlined the need not to lose control of the movement, and to that end a member of the central committee of the KPD was to be actively involved in the preparations. A 'confidential preparatory committee' consisting of representatives of various European Communist parties was also to oversee the work of the League Against Colonial Oppression.

It is no wonder that Münzenberg radically disagreed: not only was his authority called into question, but the involvement of the various Communist parties, which would by no means escape attention, would seriously threaten the nonpartisan character of the undertaking. In the course of a short visit to Moscow in late May 1926, Münzenberg managed to fend off this approach by proposing instead that a 'reliable comrade' from the Eastern Secretariat be sent to Berlin. In this, two factors likely worked in his favour. On the one hand, the KPD leadership – with the exception of the two China campaigns of summer 1925 and spring 1927 – was hardly at all interested in the colonial question, Germany having no colonies and the party having numerous other priorities. It therefore failed to find a suitable comrade to take on this medium- to long-term assignment. And, on the other, the Moscow apparatus had become increasingly fearful of making political mistakes. The planned anticolonial congress had appeared at least twenty times on the agendas of the governing bodies of the ECCI (Presidium, Political Secretariat, Secretariat, Little Commission) and no fewer than five committees had been set up to deal with it, but decisions had been repeatedly delayed, passed on by one instance to another.

The IAH was then able to get on with organizing the Congress with very little external intervention, one factor being the high staff turnover

---

131 For Pogány's biography, see Thomas Sakmyster, *A Communist Odyssey: The Life of József Pogány / John Pepper*, Budapest: Central European University Press, 2012.

in the Eastern Secretariat. The lack of continuity of personnel made it difficult to maintain serious oversight of the project. In late June 1926, Voitinsky was sent to China, to take charge of the newly created Far East office in the face of growing difficulties with the Guomindang, to be replaced in Moscow by Fyodor Raskolnikov ('Petrov', 1892–1939). And, in early 1927, David Petrovsky replaced Roy,[132] who, on 11 January, was chosen by the Little Commission of the Political Secretariat to accompany Voitinsky and the Frenchman Jacques Doriot as Comintern delegates to the Fifth Party Congress of the Chinese CP.[133] Even a Münzenberg could not elude the radical change in political line marked by the Sixth World Congress, which had declared social democracy to be the chief enemy, if he wanted to continue to act politically within the framework of the Comintern.

'Negro Workers': The Internationalization of the International

The League Against Imperialism was one of the first victims of the new, Third Period policy, the ECCI demanding that it be cleansed of reformist and bourgeois-nationalist forces. The non-Communists – Nehru among them – left the league one by one, leaving it a purely Communist affair. With its hard-left turn, however, the Sixth World Congress also sharpened the struggle against racism, calling for nothing less than a 'Negro republic in America' and an independent South African republic for Blacks. Furthermore, it would be the task of Communist parties to organize the Black workers in unions, to mobilize them in the

---

132 That the report on the Brussels Congress was addressed to Jules Humbert-Droz indicates that responsibility for the matter had shifted again.

133 Minute no. 6 of the meeting of the Little Commission of the Political Secretariat of the ECCI, Moscow, 11 January 1926, in Leutner, eds, *KPdSU(B), Komintern und China, 1926–1927*, vol. 2, part 2, 785–7. Overstreet and Windmiller speculate that Roy was sent to China to remove him from India work, leaving the British CP a free hand in this respect (*Communism in India*, 94). Whether their hypothesis is correct it is impossible to say. However, the proposal that he be sent came – formally, at least – from Tan Pingshan (1886–1956), a member of the CC of the Chinese CP and of the Central Executive Committee of the Guomindang and a participant in the Seventh Plenum of the ECCI. Overstreet and Windmiller also suggest that he might have been sent to China to avoid the possibility of any clash between him and Chatto at the Brussels Congress (96).

anticolonial struggle and, above all, to win them to the party as members.[134] The Comintern set up a 'Negro Bureau' in the Eastern Department, while the Profintern launched an international information office for 'Negro workers' and, in July 1928, the newspaper *Negro Worker*.[135] What was called the 'Negro Question' also acquired a new urgency at the Frankfurt Congress of the League Against Imperialism, thanks to the interventions of the Black delegates of the CPUSA – George Padmore (1900–1959) and James W. Ford (1893–1957) – the representatives of France's Communist-aligned anticolonialist organizations, and a handful of participants from Africa. In Germany, the new line was reflected in a new interest in the Berlin's African population. With the assistance of the League Against Imperialism and of Kouyaté, secretary of the Paris-based Ligue de défense de la race nègre since Senghor's death and an important partner of Münzenberg's, who travelled on to Berlin following the Frankfurt Congress, a German league for the defence of the negro race was founded in September 1929. This was based at Friedrichstrasse 24, the offices of the League Against Imperialism and of Münzenberg's publishing house, the Neue Deutsche Verlag. Like the League Against Imperialism, the Liga zur Verteidigung der Negerrasse engaged in propaganda, political education and recruitment. To smuggle its materials into West Africa, it often made use of personal correspondence and family connections. With the support of the League Against Imperialism, it also organized training courses for future activists.

The driving force behind the Liga was the Cameroonian Joseph Ekwe Bilé, another protégé of Münzenberg's.[136] For people like Bilé, survival in depression-era Berlin was hard, Blacks generally being regarded as standing at the bottom of the racial hierarchy, making everyday life correspondingly more difficult for them than for anyone else. Although

---

134 John Callaghan, 'Storm over Asia: Comintern Colonial Policy in the Third Period', in Matthew Worley, ed., *In Search of Revolution: International Communist Parties in the Third Period*, London: I.B. Tauris, 2004, 18–37, at 29.

135 On the pan-African policy of Comintern and Profintern, see Holger Weiss, *Framing a Radical African Atlantic: African American Agency, West African Intellectuals and the International Trade Union Committee of Negro Workers*, Leiden: Brill, 2014.

136 On Bilé, see Robbie Aitken, 'From Cameroun to Germany and Back via Moscow and Paris: The Political Career of Joseph Bilé, Performer, "Negerarbeiter" and Comintern Activist (1892–1959)', *Journal of Contemporary History* 43:4, 2008, 597–616; and Aitken and Rosenhaft, *Black Germany*.

Bilé had studied architecture, he had to earn his living as an actor; the 1920s enthusiasm for jazz and all things American did mean there was a considerable demand for Black actors in films and variety. Bilé, who was a member of the league and who joined the KPD in 1930, quickly grew into his role as a Communist anticolonial activist. In early 1930, he had been successful in recruiting Black sailors in Bordeaux and Marseille on the Comintern's behalf, and he soon found himself very much in demand as a model activist among Germany's Communist organizations, a role that saw him regularly arrested. He appeared as a speaker at an anticolonial demonstration by the (Communist) Sozialistischer Schülerbund (Union of Socialist School Pupils) in December 1929, at a Communist trade union event in March 1931, and at the Anti-Imperialist Youth Conference held in Berlin on 30 May 1931, which also featured British and Indonesian speakers as well as Saklatvala of India.[137] In July 1930, he participated in the first international congress of 'Negro workers' in Hamburg. With only twenty attendees, it was no big event, but it was the first time that the most important African, Caribbean and Afro-American activists of the day had been brought together under the aegis of a Comintern organization. From that congress emerged the International Trade Union Committee of Negro Workers, the first institutional expression of the Comintern's efforts to organize African workers and to establish links between the African and Caribbean colonies and the centres of revolutionary activity in Europe. To strengthen these connections, some still rather weak, delegates to the Hamburg Congress were invited on a VIP trip to the Soviet Union, an established practice that La Guma and Gumede had taken advantage of after the Brussels Congress.[138] Bilé was one of those who went. On his return, however, he also criticized the one-sidedness of Communist social analysis: in his opinion, the question of race could not simply be subsumed under that of class.

For Münzenberg, Bilé nevertheless represented his best hope of establishing sections of the League Against Imperialism on the continent of Africa, and he promoted Bilé accordingly. He thus entrusted

---

137 Aitken and Rosenhaft, *Black Germany*, 291.
138 They were the first Black South Africans to visit the Soviet Union. On relationships between the two countries, see Irina Filatova and Apollon Davidson, *The Hidden Thread: Russia and South Africa in the Soviet Era*, Johannesburg: Jonathan Ball, 2013.

him, for example, with the campaign launched in 1931 in support of the Scottsboro Boys, nine Black American youths accused of the rape of two white women and who faced the possibility of the death penalty. In order to develop Bilé's potential to the full, Münzenberg tried to persuade the KPD to send him to the Soviet Union for training. However, the proposal met with opposition, both from the KPD leadership and from the Comintern's representative at the League, the Czech Bohumír Šmeral, who since 1930 had been keeping an eye on things on Moscow's behalf at the international secretariat in Berlin. Judged a 'conciliator' and 'deviationist' the year before, Šmeral was now overly cautious. Another negative factor was the growing tension between the Liga zur Verteidigung der Negerrasse and Chatto, who, with money always short, preferred to fund Indian rather than African activists.

Even so, in the autumn of 1930, Bilé and two other activists were selected for local cadre training, attending courses specially conceived for foreigners at the Deutsche Akademie für Politik and at the Marxistischen Arbeiterschule (there under Karl August Wittfogel, among others).[139] For a time, Münzenberg considered sending him to Cameroon, to recruit students for the Lenin School and the Communist University of the Toilers of the East. This the ECCI turned down on grounds of cost, but Münzenberg did not give up. In 1932, Bilé was finally allowed to attend the Communist University for eighteen months, where he went under the name of 'Charles Morris'. By the time he finished, the National Socialists had come to power in Germany, and Bilé settled in Paris, where the League Against Imperialism's international secretariat had been based since 1933, before moving on to London. By then, the initial enthusiasm for the league had long since dissipated. Chatto had emigrated to the Soviet Union in 1931, while Kouyaté had been expelled from the Communist Party, as had Padmore, in Paris since 1933. In 1934, Bilé too resigned from the French party. Willi Münzenberg, who gave up the leadership of the league on 9 September 1933, had long since turned to other tasks.[140]

~ ~ ~

139 Rosenhaft, 'From Cameroun', 606.
140 At Münzenberg's own request, the Political Commission of the Political Secretariat of the ECCI allowed him to resign as secretary to the league on 9 September 1933: Extract from minutes, RGASPI, 495/205/7000.

The Brussels Congress and its historical significance have for some time come in for growing scholarly attention, either in terms of its impact on the central figures of various national independence movements or its later influence on the Non-Aligned Movement.[141] A more direct historical effect can also be attributed to the congress, in that it brought together hitherto disparate political, national-revolutionary and nationalist groups and built bridges between nations and continents, strengthening global anticolonial forces.

The impetus for the construction of this space of international solidarity had come from radical intellectuals and anticolonial revolutionaries in Paris, Berlin and elsewhere, whose travels and whose exchanges with other colonial immigrants had often prompted an awareness of commonalities. This allowed the Comintern to build on existing nuclei and even already formally constituted organizations. But it was Münzenberg's organizational talent that raised local initiatives that were often confined to a national context to the transnational level and enabled the synthesis of their political demands. The Communist media entrepreneur and tireless activist was thus the person more responsible than any other for the development of the Comintern's colonial policy, which really took off in the mid-1920s. In this respect, he possessed advantages that Roy did not. Unlike Roy, forced into nomadism, Münzenberg enjoyed the security of legal residence and a fixed abode. As a member of the Reichstag, he also benefited from parliamentary immunity (so long as the KPD remained a legal political party). In addition, he acted within the space he sought to affect, while Roy had to intervene in Indian politics from afar.

What is more, Münzenberg, who stayed out of debates on the political line, always knew how to seize an opportunity, harnessing the native dynamics of different political currents and working patiently and persistently to get them to work together to the desired end. The Communists were not the first to enter the field of anticolonial struggle,

---

141 In addition to Petersson, with an emphasis on the transnational dimension of the history of decolonisation, see Louro, 'India', and Jürgen Dinkel, *Die Bewegung Bündnisfreier Staaten: Genese, Organisation, Politik (1927–1992)*, Oldenburg: De Gruyter, 2015, 35–44; in the context of the anticolonial *longue durée*, Vijay Prashad, *The Darker Nations: A People's History of the Third World*, New York: New Press, 2007; and from the perspective of the government security services, Brückenhaus, *Policing*, 139–68.

but, as Mustafa Haikal aptly put it, after 1925 they acted as the 'decisive ferment' that briefly transformed disparate political elements into a global if volatile whole.[142] This also required Münzenberg's ability to persuade the increasingly cautious Moscow-based leadership of the Comintern. Although the latter had sought from the start to maintain control over the Brussels Congress and the League Against Imperialism, these were for a short time exactly what they claimed to be, the manifestations of a movement open to liberal, bourgeois, national-revolutionary and social democratic forces.

Even if only a short-term success, this outcome was the fruit of Münzenberg's tireless commitment. A political workaholic, he always had several projects on the go at the same time, which might well yield synergies, but might equally lead to conflict and competition with other Comintern actors. When the Brussels Congress took place, Münzenberg was in the midst of preparations for the tenth anniversary of the October Revolution.[143] And when, on account of the Comintern's sectarian politics, the league went into decline after its Frankfurt Congress of 1929, he had already turned to antiracist organization. Münzenberg had the extraordinary ability to enlist existing political forces as local multipliers, to draw them in to his projects, and more generally to surround himself with an efficient and loyal staff. He knew how to use his network of acquaintances from early days in Switzerland, just as he was able to attract new cadre of exceptional quality. Yet he could never act without the consent and the financial support of the Comintern, on which he was both financially and politically dependent. The skill that he showed in the usually lengthy negotiations with Moscow headquarters was thus crucial. If need be, he could present the hierarchy with a fait accompli, and his evident success in propaganda and politics would for long protect him from the consequences of such an egregious breach of the rules.

Politically, the League Against Imperialism and National Oppression effected a shift from anticolonialism to anti-imperialism. Münzenberg's

---

142 Haikal, *Die Liga*, 1.

143 Kasper Braskén, 'Celebrating October: The Transnational Commemorations of the Tenth Anniversary of the Soviet Union in Weimar Germany', in Jean-François Fayet, Valérie Gorin and Stefanie Prezioso, eds, *Echoes of October: International Commemorations of the Bolshevik Revolution 1918–1990*, London: Lawrence & Wishart, 2017, 76–105.

initiative not only internationalized and globalized the hitherto regional liberation movements of continents far distant from each other, by highlighting what their struggles had in common; it also gave them a sharper political edge by promoting the demand for national independence. Not only symbolically but also practically, it imported the struggle from the colonies and 'semi-colonies' into the imperial metropoles.

The mid-1920s, then, saw the Comintern bring anticolonial politics in from periphery to centre. At the same time, it sought to promote its policy in the periphery, both in classical colonies and in countries like China, dominated by the imperialist powers. In early 1927, the Comintern thus sent to China a three-person delegation, headed by Roy, charged with ensuring the implementation there of the decisions of the Seventh ECCI Plenum.[144]

---

144 Instruction from the Political Secretariat of the ECCI to the ECCI delegation to China and instruction on the conduct of the Fifth Party Conference of the CPC, Moscow, 19 January 1927, in Leutner, *KPdSU(B)*, vol. 2, part 2, 812–14.

6

Guangzhou and Wuhan: On Missions for the Comintern in China

M. N. Roy's mission, to convey the decisions of the Seventh ECCI Plenum to the Fifth Congress of the Chinese Communist Party, came at a turning point in Chinese history, coinciding as it did with the Shanghai Massacre of April 1927 and the Guomindang's ensuing counter-revolutionary purge. The Chinese Revolution begun in 1925 had abruptly brought China to the forefront of international attention, the focus of revolutionary hopes worldwide. That space of the imagination found physical expression as the country became a transnational gathering-place for progressive journalists, radical intellectuals and, above all, professional revolutionaries, among them the agents despatched there by the Comintern and other Communist organizations, such as the Young Communist International, the Profintern (Red International of Labour Unions), International Red Aid or the Soviet intelligence services. In 1923, the Soviet Union had formed an alliance with the Guomindang, the National People's Party of China founded in 1912 by Sun Yat-sen (Sun Zhongshan). This 'united front' or 'bloc within' 'the only serious national revolutionary group in China' was established at the insistence of the Dutch Comintern emissary 'Maring' (Henk Sneevliet) after long, highly conflictual discussions both among Soviet diplomats and China specialists and in the ranks of the still minuscule Chinese Communist Party.[1] In

---

1 ECCI resolution on the relations between the Chinese Communist Party and the Kuomintang, Moscow, 12 January 1923, in Jane Degras, ed., *The Communist*

addition, the Soviet Union sent the Guomindang 2 million 'Mexican dollars' (gold roubles) each year and helped it set up the Whampoa Military Academy in Guangzhou (Canton).[2]

With all this came a steady stream of military and political advisers, emissaries, instructors and specialists sent to China by the Comintern and its affiliated organizations, and alongside them the diplomats and intelligence agents who worked for the Soviet Union. There might have been up to a hundred or so present at any one time, even more if one includes military personnel.[3] They were accompanied by the necessary technical and administrative staff: secretaries, couriers, radio operators, translators, coders and local employees. Like Roy, many did not come alone, but with wives or partners, and even children. Some stayed for years, while others had only short-term assignments. In any event, the advisers and specialists had to translate Comintern directives from Moscow in extremely complex and dangerous circumstances that were, on the whole, quite foreign to them. The country was torn apart by reactionary warlords, threatened by Japanese advances in the north-east and economically dominated by foreign powers, while social relationships in many places were still feudal. The advisers and specialists sent from Moscow might be funded with Soviet money, but many were operating illegally, and so under conditions of conspiracy. They also often encountered the obstinate resistance of their Chinese comrades; to see to the

---

International, vol. 2, *1923–1928*, London: Oxford University Press, 1960, 5–6. On Maring's influence, see Tony Saich, *The Origins of the First United Front in China: The Role of Sneevliet, Alias Maring*, Leiden: Brill, 1992, and Jérémie Tamiatto, 'Des révolutionnaires entre deux mondes: Trajectoires croisées de Grigori Voitinsky et Henk Sneevliet en Chine, 1920–1923', *Monde(s): histoire, espaces, relations* 10, 2016, 51–68.

2 Minute no. 53 of the meeting of the Politbüro of the CC of the RCP(B), Moscow, 8 March 1923, in *RKP(B), Komintern und die national-revolutionäre Bewegung in China: Dokumente*, vol. 2, *1920–1925*, ed. Russisches Zentrum für die Archivierung und Erforschung von Dokumenten zur Neuesten Geschichte et al., Paderborn: Ferdinand Schöningh, 1996, 256–7, at 256.

3 Mechthild Leutner estimates that at the high point of cooperation in 1926–27 there must have been well over a hundred: M. Leutner, 'The Communist Party of China (CCP), the Communist Party of the Soviet Union (CPSU) and the Comintern (CI) in the 1920s and early 1930s: Interactions between Cooperation and Defense', *Berliner China-Hefte / Chinese History and Society* 30, 2006, 41–55, at 43. Jean-François Fayet cites a document of January 1926 among Karl Radek's personal papers at the RGASPI, which says that 27 Soviet instructors and 19 technicians are to be sent to the Guomindang's national revolutionary army: *Karl Radek, 1885–1939: Biographie politique*, Bern: Peter Lang, 2004, 541.

implementation of Moscow directives was far from a matter of simply passing down orders from the centre. They also had to report back regularly to employers to whom they were at all times accountable – whether Comintern, Profintern, Young Communist International, Red Army intelligence or Soviet foreign ministry. In accordance with bureaucratic requirements, they had to draw up work plans and keep accurate records of expenses, even if, in reality, much remained improvised or neglected. Their position as mediators between two or more worlds was often uncomfortable. Very few could speak Chinese in either standard or local forms, while cultural differences didn't make communication any easier. And, once they had arrived, social realities turned out to be more intractable than had been imagined on the political drawing board.

The difficulties encountered by Soviet and Comintern envoys in Guangzhou and Wuhan – Guomindang strongholds and successive acting capitals of the Nationalist government – will be explored below. Roy and Borodin were expected to see to the implementation of an internally contradictory policy in an ever-changing politico-military situation, in a country engaged in a struggle for national liberation while also in the throes of a social, class-based revolution. We begin, however, by looking at the material expression of China's place in the Soviet Union's geopolitical sphere of interest on the one hand, and the Comintern's political sphere of interest on the other, in terms of flows of money and personnel during the first half of 1927. By then, the first stage of the Northern Expedition had been completed, extending the territory under the Guomindang's control far beyond the confines of its original base around the city of Guangzhou. The task was now to advance the revolution, both spatially and politically.

Disunion and Deadlock

As a prelude to his mission, Roy had been appointed to a committee of four charged with drafting a resolution on the organizational tasks of the Chinese party, based on the resolutions of the Seventh ECCI Plenum of November–December 1926.[4] As a member of another committee,

---

4 'Theses on the Situation in China by the Seventh Extraordinary Plenum of the Executive Committee of the Communist International', 22 November–16 December

he was also to formulate proposals for the organization by the Communist parties of Europe and the America of a campaign in support of the Chinese Revolution and against imperialist military intervention in China. That campaign was, however, only to be launched after the return of the Comintern delegation. Before leaving, Roy got in touch with Stalin, whom he then used to visit regularly in the Kremlin and to whom he had, according to his then partner, Luise Geissler, 'a sentimental attachment', probably because Stalin, like him, had rejected nonproletarian national liberation movements.[5] Roy wanted to check with Stalin exactly what he was expected to do, and the letter he wrote is in many ways instructive.[6] First, it shows how detailed was the knowledge about circumstances in China that circulated in Moscow, where they were very precisely informed about conflicts between Comintern officials in China, between Borodin and the Far Eastern Bureau, and between Voitinsky and the Central Committee of the Chinese Communist Party. Roy's knowledge was bolstered, too, by his contacts with Tan Pingshan (1886–1956), a member of the Political Bureau of the Chinese Communist Party who was then in Moscow, and Chinese party leaders such as the cultivated Cai Hesen (1895–1931), who had become a member of the ECCI Presidium in 1926. In his letter, Roy even makes himself a spokesman for Tan, putting the latter's suggestions to Stalin and urging him to 'have a personal conversation with Tan Pingshan as soon as possible'. Second, the letter shows how closely the Comintern's decision-making was entwined with that of the Soviet party. Referring to the drafting of directives for the Chinese party congress and Comintern representatives in China, Roy writes: 'I believe that the Politburo of the VKP(b) has already drawn up the directives. If that is

---

1926, in Robert C. North and Xenia Eudin, eds, *M. N. Roy's Mission to China: The Communist–Kuomintang Split of 1927: Documents*, trans. Helen I. Powers, Berkeley: University of California Press, 1963, 131–45.

5 His name appears many times in the register of visitors to Stalin for 1926: Sibnarayan Ray, *In Freedom's Quest: A Study of the Life and Works of M. N. Roy, 1887–1954*, vol. 3, part 1, Kolkata: Renaissance, 2005, 49–50.

6 Letter from M. N. Roy to J. V. Stalin, Moscow, 14 January 1927, in Mechthild Leutner et al., eds, *KPdSU(B), Komintern und die national-revolutionäre Bewegung in China: Dokumente*, vol. 2, *1926–1927*, part 2, Münster: LitVerlag, 1998, 788–9. [Though written in English, this has been published only in German translation, and is thus re-translated here. – *Trans.*] On Roy's personal admiration for Stalin, see North and Eudin, *Roy's Mission*, 128.

so, the work of the ECCI committee will be easier.' Third, the letter shows that while Roy was assigned to deal with the situation in China, he was still personally and perhaps primarily concerned with India, writing, in closing, 'For my part, I would like to discuss with you a plan for work in the East (Indonesia, India, etc.), separate from work in China.'[7]

In early February, the Politburo of the Soviet party had approved a budget of 9,000 roubles to cover the costs of the ECCI delegation to China. Their task would be no easy one amid China's political turbulence. The united front that the Chinese Communist Party had entered into with the Guomindang, at the urging of the Comintern, had been under threat since Chiang Kai-shek (Jiang Jieshi) had suddenly turned against the Communists on 20 March 1926. Furthermore, the theses adopted by the Seventh Plenum, which Roy had helped formulate, were themselves contradictory; the local representatives of the Comintern and the Soviet Union were divided in their opinions; and the Chinese party would not allow Moscow to simply impose a political line, as Roy – like earlier Comintern representatives – was soon to learn.

The best known of the advisers is probably the Russian Bolshevik Mikhail Borodin, born Mikhail Gruzenberg, who also used the pseudonyms Bankier, Brantwein, George Brown, Bao Luoding, the Englishman, Nikiforov and Kirill. Borodin was one of the earliest and most experienced of Comintern emissaries. He had been sent to China in September 1923, as Sun Yat-sen's personal political adviser, first representing the Russian party and then the Comintern as a whole,[8] before which he had been to the United States, Mexico, Spain, the Netherlands, Germany and Great Britain on the International's behalf. Borodin seems to have impressed his contemporaries by his personal presence and air of cultivation, the American Charles Shipman (in reality, Charles Phillips), who had gone to Mexico and Spain with him

---

7 Letter from M. N. Roy to J. V. Stalin, Moscow, 14 January 1927, in Leutner, *KPdSU(B)*, vol. 2, part 2, 788; written in English, the letter has been published only in German translation, and is thus re-translated here.

8 Edward Hallet Carr, *The Bolshevik Revolution, 1917–1923*, vol 3, Harmondsworth, UK: Penguin Books, 1977, 540. On Borodin's mission to China, see Dan N. Jacobs, *Borodin: Stalin's Man in China*, Cambridge, MA, Harvard University Press, 1981 (written, however, without the benefit of the Comintern archives); and Zhihong Chen, *Die China-Mission Michail Borodins bis zum Tod Sun Yatsens: Ein Beitrag zur Sowjetischen Chinapolitik in den Jahren 1923–25*, Hamburg: LitVerlag, 2000.

in 1919, saying of him years later, 'He had dignity, authority, intellect, culture, personal magnetism. And he knew a hell of a lot about socialists and revolution.'[9] The British engineer and trade unionist John T. Murphy, who had attended the so-called Amsterdam Conference, a meeting of West European revolutionary parties and organizations, and who came to know Borodin in the run-up to the Second World Congress of the Comintern, described him in very similarly positive terms long after he himself had left the party: 'He was a tall, well-built, black-haired, swarthy-complexioned man, an excellent linguist, thoroughly acquainted with the general literature and history of many countries and a professional revolutionary to boot.'[10] In *Les Conquérants* (1928), his novel about the Chinese Revolution in Guangzhou, published in English as *The Conquerors*, André Malraux portrays him as a 'man of action' who wore himself out in the service of the revolution in China, though Leon Trotsky, in a 1931 review of that novel, depicts him rather as a typical functionary, a creature of state and party bureaucracy who had no idea of revolution.

Trotsky was certainly wrong in one respect. While Borodin was indeed acting in the interests of the Soviet Union, which, under Stalin in the second half of the 1920s, wanted primarily to guarantee its own security, the life of a Comintern representative in China, especially during the years of the Chinese Revolution of 1925–27, was very far from being a matter of desk work. On the contrary, the job was dangerous. The Russian Vera Vishniakova Akimova, who worked as an interpreter for Borodin, recalled that

> even in peaceful times the lives of our advisers were far from safe. Borodin rode to the sessions of the Politburo of the Kuomintang CEC, right across the street, in a car with Mauser-bearing Chinese soldiers on the running-board. After all, it was right at the gates of this building that the killers of Liao Chung-k'ai [Liao Zhongkai] had lain in wait for him.[11]

---

9 Charles Shipman, *It Had to Be Revolution: Memoirs of an American Radical*, Ithaca, NY: Cornell University Press, 1993, 83.

10 J. T. [John Thomas] Murphy, *New Horizons*, London: John Lane/The Bodley Head, 1941, 88–9.

11 Vera Vladimirovna Vishniakova Akimova, *Two Years in Revolutionary China, 1925–1927*, trans. Stephen I. Levine, Harvard East Asian Monographs no. 40, Cambridge,

The brutal repression of a demonstration in Shanghai on 30 May 1925 had prompted the emergence of an anti-imperialist mass movement, supported by the Communists, that encompassed not only the cities but also the countryside. The peasants called for an agrarian revolution, but this conflicted with the interests of many of the Guomindang's generals. The Guomindang was a cross-class organization that included big landowners as well as landless peasants and urban proletarians, and when the Communists expropriated land in the territories they occupied and called on workers to strike, the bourgeois nationalist forces became alarmed, increasingly so as Communists began to occupy numerous positions of power in the government. Chiang Kai-shek, Sun Yat-sen's protégé and after his death his successor as head of the Guomindang, reacted by moving against them. On 20 March 1926, he had the Communist political commissars attached to his military units arrested and the Soviet advisers placed under house arrest, among them the top military adviser known by the nickname Vasily Blyukher or Blücher (1889–1938), who in China went under the pseudonyms 'Galin/Galen' and 'Uralsky'.[12] This was more than an unfriendly act, but it provoked no reaction from Moscow, where the Guomindang was still seen to offer the only possibility of a unified China, and cooperation with it was in no way to be jeopardized. In the summer of 1926, Chiang Kai-shek launched the Northern Expedition in order to defeat the warlords and so establish a national government. The campaign met with success, and when the Seventh ECCI Plenum convened it noted that half the country had already been liberated from the imperialists.

Neither Soviet advisers nor Chinese party leaders denied the need to unify the country and to centralize power, given the dominance of regional warlords and growing domestic militarization. It was in this context that the ECCI theses called on the Chinese Communists to further the social revolution. They were to strengthen the mass

---

MA: East Asian Research Center, Harvard University, 1971, 229 [*Dva goda v vosstavshem Kitae, 1925–1927*, Moscow: Nauka, 1965]. One of the three strongmen of the Guomindang, Liao Zhongkai had been close to the Communists.

12 Hans Van de Ven argues that without this coup by Chiang Kai-shek the Northern Expedition would have been postponed to a later date, as it did not eliminate but further intensified divisions within the Guomindang: *War and Nationalism in China, 1925–1945*, London: RoutledgeCurzon, 2003, 95–105. As we shall see below, Comintern representatives were also divided in their analysis of the coup. Blyukher himself would die in the Great Terror.

movement of the proletariat in the cities, promote class struggle in the villages with the call for an 'agrarian revolution' and build up a strong revolutionary army through political propaganda – a policy that saw party membership soar from the second half of 1926 to the spring of 1927.[13]

At the same time, the Chinese Communists were pressed by Stalin – inspired in this by Voitinsky – to conquer the Guomindang from within by allying themselves with the left wing and fighting against the right. This was a departure from Maring/Sneevliet's original conception of temporary cooperation between the two parties while the Communist Party was too weak on its own. The Chinese comrades were baffled by the contradiction, one of the founders of the CCP and its long-time leader, Chen Duxiu (1879–1942), shaking his head at a Politburo meeting held at Borodin's home in the spring of 1927 and saying, 'Earlier Zinoviev ordered us to help the bourgeoisie, and now Stalin tells us to carry out an agrarian revolution in the next twenty-four hours.'[14]

Chen Duxiu was among the Chinese party leaders who had been critical of the united front as early as 1924, and he now called for the Communists to withdraw from the Guomindang, which he believed to have lost any revolutionary role. His position was shared by party headquarters in Shanghai, but not at all by the party committee in Guangzhou, nor by Borodin, who had established himself at the Guomindang's headquarters. Political fault lines ran through not only the CCP Central Committee, but also the foreign advisers and emissaries. And, finally, there were also differences of opinion between the advisers, the authorities in Moscow and the Chinese Communists.[15] The decision to launch the Northern Expedition subsequently opened a divide between Borodin on the one hand and Voitinsky and 'Galin' on the other. While Borodin was involved in the planning of the Northern Expedition, Voitinsky, head of the newly established Far Eastern Bureau in Shanghai since June

---

13 In late 1926 the CCP had 20,000 members, and in April 1927 some 60,000, three times as many: Stephen A. Smith, *A Road Is Made: Communism in Shanghai 1920–1927*, Richmond, UK: Curzon Press, 2000, 168.

14 Cited in Alexander V. Pantsov, 'Comintern Activists in China: Spies or Theorists?', in Anne-Marie Brady and Douglas Brown, eds, *Foreigners and Foreign Institutions in Republican China*, London: Routledge, 2012, 93–108, at 96.

15 See the documents published in Leutner, *KPdSU(B)*, vol. 2, parts 1 and 2.

1926, viewed it as a political error.[16] The progress of the campaign, however, brought changes in these positions. Chen Duxiu, in his role as a member of the Far Eastern Bureau, moved closer to the initial, favourable attitude of the majority of the CCP Central Committee, while the Chinese party leadership gradually began to revise its unqualified support, moving closer to Voitinsky's critical position, while he in turn began to modulate his scepticism in view of the campaign's successes.[17]

January 1927 saw a debate within the Guomindang over the location of the acting capital. With the army's advances in the north, at the urging of Borodin and under pressure from its own left wing, in late 1926 the Guomindang's centre of government was moved from Guangzhou to Wuhan (a city at the confluence of the Yangtze and the Han, formed by the merger of the three cities of Hankou, Wuchang and Hanyang). Chiang Kai-shek refused to recognize the decision and attempted to install a counter-government in Nanchang.

The storming of the British Concession in Hankou by an angry mob, on 3 January 1927, was another event that led to differences between the Communists and the Guomindang and also among the foreign advisers themselves, in their assessment of the revolutionary potential of the political situation, though it did send a shock wave through the foreign community in Shanghai.[18] While this mass riot reinforced Borodin and the Left Guomindang in their determination to face down Chiang Kai-shek, Voitinsky and the Central Committee were more inclined to wait and see.[19] At the Far Eastern Bureau in Shanghai, however, such *attentisme* was considered opportunistic, and attributed to Voitinsky's influence. In a communication of 5 February 1927, M. N. Nasonov ('Charly') (1902–?), the Communist Youth International's representative at the Bureau, thus asked the ECCI to recall him. The party lacked a clear policy towards the petty bourgeoisie, he wrote. But 'Grig. V.

---

16 Letter to L. M. Karachan, 24 July 1926, in Leutner, *KPdSU(B)*, vol 2, part 1, 424–7. The decision that the ECCI should open a Far Eastern Bureau in Shanghai was taken by the Politburo of the Russian party on 25 March, the goal being to exercise closer control over the Chinese party, too lax in the way it went about things, in Soviet eyes: Smith, *A Road*, 126.

17 Leutner, 'The Communist Party of China', 50.

18 Smith, *A Road*, 154.

19 North and Eudin, *Roy's Mission*, 46–7.

[Voitinsky] cannot fight against this deviation because he himself is an "opportunist" (a person without an opinion), and if the party is to be educated in the fight against opportunism, the very first thing to be done is to replace him.'[20] The members of the Far Eastern Bureau were isolated, however, and the leadership of the Chinese party apparently avoided meeting them.[21]

In the New Capital

This was the situation as Roy left Moscow in February 1927. As he later put it laconically, referring to himself in the third person: 'It was generally known that he [Roy] had all along criticized the mess made in China. Now, he was sent to clear the mess at the eleventh hour.'[22] Roy did not travel alone, but was accompanied by his then partner, twenty-eight-year-old Luise Geissler from Munich. With him, too, went an acquaintance from his time in Paris, Jacques Doriot, head of anticolonial work at the PCF. Others who made the journey via Chita, Khabarovsk and Vladivostok were the seventy-year-old Briton Tom Mann (1856–1941), the American Earl Browder (1891–1973) – both members of a Profintern delegation to the Pan-Pacific trade union conference to be held in May – and the Tan Pingshan already mentioned, a member of the Central Committee of the CCP and of the

---

20 Published in Leutner, *KPdSU(B)*, vol. 2, part 2, 826–32, at 832.

21 Letter from A. E. Abramovich to I. A. Piatnitsky, Shanghai, 25 February 1927, in Leutner, *KPdSU(B)*, vol. 2, part 2, 842–8. Voitinsky had a meeting with Chiang Kai-shek in Jiujiang on 22–23 February: Note on discussions between G. N. Voitinsky and Chiang Kai-shek in Jiujiang on 22 and 23 February, in ibid., 850–2; cf. Steve Smith, 'Moscow and the Second and Third Armed Uprisings in Shanghai, 1927', in Mechthild Leutner et al., eds, *The Chinese Revolution in the 1920s: Between Triumph and Disaster*, London: RoutledgeCurzon, 2002, 222–43, at 224.

22 S. K. Vidyarthi [M. N. Roy], *China in Revolt*, Bombay: Vanguard Publishing Co., [1932?], 38. The book was first published in German by the publishing house of the Communist Party Opposition, as *Revolution und Konterrevolution in China*, Berlin: Soziologische Verlagsanstalt, 1930, and in English, under a pseudonym, only in 1932, according to John Patrick Haithcox in *Communism and Nationalism in India: M. N. Roy and Comintern Policy, 1920–1939*, Princeton, NJ: Princeton University Press, 1971, 360. It appeared later in an expanded edition, under Roy's own name, as *My Experiences in China*, Calcutta: Renaissance Publishers, 1938 and 1945, and *Revolution and Counterrevolution in China*, Calcutta, Renaissance Publishers, 1946.

Central Executive Committee of the Guomindang, who had taken part in the Seventh ECCI Plenum.[23] Zidor Stoljar (1900–1939?), who had already done 'work abroad' in the USA, Germany and Great Britain, came along as the group's secretary.

On 18 February 1927, Roy, Luise Geissler and Doriot arrived in Guangzhou. Straddling a river in southern China, this great, sprawling city would have struck them as alien, though Roy, perhaps, a little less than the others. This was not his first time in China, as he had visited on his way from Germany to California in 1916. Guangzhou did not offer the amenities that came with the long presence of foreign powers. There were very few foreigners indeed. Shortly after arriving in the city in October 1926, the young American journalist Rayna Prohme, who edited the Chinese nationalist newspaper the *Peking People's Tribune*, together with her husband, had written to an American friend: 'It's the dirtiest I've ever seen, and absolutely airless and flat – but I've never seen any place where there are so many things to look at and watch.' The alleys were so narrow that not even a sedan chair, much less a rickshaw, could get through. 'Everything is open to the eye. Women fixing dinners in the streets, peddlers cutting fish, butchers, merchants, weaving, a thousand kinds of shops, long pieces of cloth being dyed, washing clothes, and of course all the eating, nursing and latrine operations that are always open in China.'[24] While temperatures in subtropical Guangzhou would still have been tolerable in February, the same could not be said of the humidity, in which everything quickly went mouldy. In all likelihood, the travellers would have left Vladivostok on a Soviet steamer. In Guangzhou, they had to wait for over three weeks before going on to the new capital, Wuhan. The Fifth Party Congress of the CCP and the Pan-Pacific Trade Union Conference already mentioned were both to take place there. Roy, who used the pseudonym 'Johnson' on this mission to China, used the time to write articles for the international Communist

---

23 North and Eudin, *Roy's Mission*, 44, the account of the composition of the party being based on Robert North's interviews with Luise Geissler, conducted in Zurich in June 1958. Tan Pingshan, however, is not mentioned. On Browder's presence in China as the first general secretary of the Pan-Pacific Trade Union Secretariat, see Harvey Klehr, John Earl Haynes and Fridrikh Firsov, *The Secret World of American Communism*, New Haven, CT: Yale University Press, 1995, 42–5.

24 *Reporting the Chinese Revolution: The Letters of Rayna Prohme*, ed. Baruch Hirson and Arthur J. Knodel, London: Pluto Press, 2007, 43.

press – in order, he would write later, to persuade the Communists – in the face of great resistance – to publish a manifesto against Chiang Kai-shek, who was, for Roy, the embodiment of counter-revolution.[25] There was no train connection to Wuhan, and it had originally been planned that the group would fly, but mechanical problems made this impossible. There was no option but an overland trek through mountains and countryside, interspersed with passages by boat: a journey of almost a thousand kilometres, through villages and over mountain passes, that would take five weeks. This was a perilous undertaking, given the political and military instability.[26] We know, from the memoirs of the Russian translator and interpreter Akimova, who had made the same journey a little earlier, how difficult it was: after a short train journey, they would embark on a barge. To cross otherwise impracticable mountain ranges, the only means of transport was the palanquin, carried by Chinese porters over the steep and often slippery paths.[27] The group very likely took the same route as Borodin's wife, Fanni (or Fanja) Orluk and his youngest son, who had left Guangzhou two months earlier with officials of the nationalist government.

Roy knew Wuhan from his first trip to China. The conditions, though, were now quite different. As Luise Geissler later recalled, the party saw destroyed villages, devastated fields and villagers who had been hanged for their part in the struggle.[28] In his subsequent writings, however, Roy himself mentions only the revolutionary mass meetings with which they were welcomed on their way.[29]

On 3 April, the group finally arrived at Hankou, the port and commercial centre that was the most modern and important of the three cities merged together to form the new capital. It was home to a substantial foreign population, which, as in the port city of Shanghai, consisted for the most part of White Russian émigrés. Like Guangzhou, the city had a humid subtropical climate, though with a significantly colder winter.

---

25 Vidyarthi [M. N. Roy], *China in Revolt*, 46.
26 Haithcox, *Communism*, 64, referring to the author's correspondence with Luise Geissler.
27 Vishniakova Akimova, *Two Years*, 261–9.
28 North and Eudin, *Roy's Mission*, 59.
29 Vidyarthi [M. N. Roy], *China in Revolt*, 47; Sibnarayan Ray, *In Freedom's Quest: A Study of the Life and Works of M. N. Roy, 1887–1954*, vol. 2, Kolkata: Minerva, 2002, 265.

'Notoriously the worst climate in China', according to Rayna Prohme, who was there in late February 1927.[30] Most importantly, Hankou was one of the major centres of the broad social movement that had developed in China since 1926. Disputes and strikes proliferated in docks, textile factories, match factories, silk mills and shops, as workers fought for higher wages and shorter working hours. Trade union membership grew massively. Industrialists and other business owners complained of impending ruin.[31] Revolution seemed on the cards: the Wuhan government was at the height of its power, and the Chinese Communist Party, which had grown significantly, held the ministries of labour and agriculture. Almost all foreigners, men, women and children, had been evacuated. The British, Japanese and American governments had sent representatives to the city to negotiate with the new rulers over their concessions. In February and March, Britain had thus indicated its readiness to place its concession, occupied by workers in January, under temporary Chinese administration. Foreign military forces had, however, not withdrawn. The French had left their Annamite troops in the city, while large numbers of British and American warships were still at anchor in the river. The streets were filled day and night with naval police and sailors on leave, noted Vincent Sheean, an American journalist who was in Hankou in May and June.[32] Men now formed the vast majority of the local population, by a ratio of three to one.

The city was then a magnet for Communists, but also for progressives from all over the world, as Sheean also observed. They all wanted to see the Chinese Revolution with their own eyes. 'For a few months in 1927, a little more than half of the year, Hankow concentrated, symbolized and upheld the hope for a revolution of the world. Delegations came from all over Europe, Asia and America to see for themselves what constituted Hankow's success, the surprise and delight of a generation of thwarted Communists.'[33] The Comintern sent a host of people: the importance of the Chinese Revolution to the political future of the Soviet Union was evident even to the foreign, 'bourgeois' observer, as Sheean himself remarked. He noted that 'French Communists, German

---

30 *Reporting*, 72.
31 Harold Isaacs, *The Tragedy of the Chinese Revolution*, Stanford, CA: Stanford University Press, 1961 [1938], 208–9.
32 Vincent Sheean, *In Search of History*, London: Hamish Hamilton, 1935, 226.
33 Ibid., 242.

Communists, Hindoo Communists, British ILP people, and numerous agitators responsible for the Komintern gave the place a fine mixed flavour of international revolt ... Russians with ill-defined functions appeared and disappeared.'[34]

Like other 'Russian' advisers and technical staff working with the Guomindang, the Comintern and Profintern delegates were accommodated in the former Russian and German concessions in Hankou, whereas the government was installed in a modern building in the Chinese part of the city. Roy and his partner were put up in Borodin's large house, while Doriot found accommodation in a guesthouse, whose great advantage was a German landlady who did not check names or ask to see one's papers. The other foreign delegates to the Fifth Party Congress of the CCP who gradually arrived also took advantage of this, and among the residents were Voitinsky, head of the Far Eastern Bureau in Shanghai; his wife, who had travelled from Moscow as a member of the Profintern staff; and the Ukrainian Pavel Mif (1901–1938, 'Wilhelm'), head of the ECCI's Eastern Secretariat, a China expert who had served for a time as rector of Sun Yat-sen University.[35] They were all frequent guests at Borodin's, where other Comintern delegates and leaders of the Chinese party were regularly in and out, and where the journalist Rayna Prohme, too, was a frequent visitor. It was evidently Luise Geissler's job to act as hostess in place of Borodin's wife, captured by a warlord.[36] Comintern delegates and *Sovetniki* tried to keep a low profile, but Sheean the journalist only noticed them all the more: 'The beautiful carved-oak head of Manabendra Nath Roy, head of the Far Eastern section of the Comintern, could be seen across a restaurant table in effective contrast to the dishevelled pate of Jacques Doriot.'[37]

Borodin and Roy, who had founded the Mexican Communist Party together and who had since often encountered each other in Berlin and more especially in Moscow over the last few years, had met again on friendly terms, but soon found themselves in violent conflict.

---

34 Ibid., 243.
35 Vishniakova Akimova, *Two Years*, 282.
36 Ray, *In Freedom's Quest*, vol. 2, 266 and 273.
37 Sheean, *In Search*, 243.

Communicating the Line

Roy immediately embroiled himself in the political disputes about the Northern Expedition, the agrarian question and the Communists' attitude to the Guomindang. He did not, however, forget India: according to a British police source, he made contact with the Sikh community in Hankou and was later said to have distributed anti-British pamphlets among British Indian troops in Shanghai.[38] In Guangzhou, he criticized the Northern Expedition, warning that it was drawing the National Revolutionary Army into a war on two fronts, facing on the one hand the warlord armies in the North, and on the other the land and naval forces of the imperialists, concentrated in Shanghai.[39] During his weeks-long journey to Wuhan, events had accelerated: in mid-March, on the instructions of the Soviet Politburo, Borodin had convened the Third Plenum of the Guomindang's Central Executive Committee in Wuhan, which had taken the left turn the Soviet party had called for.[40] Chiang Kai-shek, however, had been conspicuous by his absence, as he moved towards Shanghai with his Nationalist troops.

In Wuhan, Roy and Doriot's ECCI delegation, together with Voitinsky from Shanghai, sought to bring their influence to bear on the Left Guomindang leadership. This was not easy, however, as Borodin refused to allow direct contact, given the great tensions of his own side, fearing that the Guomindang's Political Committee might witness the disagreement between him and the ECCI delegation (meaning Roy in particular). But how could the delegation prepare for the Chinese party congress without informing themselves at source? To solve the problem, the three Comintern representatives agreed at a meeting on 9 April to informally involve Borodin as an advisory member of the delegation, a decision that Roy and Doriot communicated to Moscow by telegram.[41]

---

38 Kris Manjapra, *M. N. Roy: Marxism and Colonial Cosmopolitanism*, Delhi: Routledge, 2010, 80.

39 North and Eudin, *Roy's Mission*, 50.

40 Excerpt from Minute no. 89 (*Sondernummer* 67) of the meeting of the Politburo of the CC of the CPSU, Moscow, 3 March 1927, in Leutner, *KPdSU(B)*, vol. 2, part 2, 853–6 and excerpt from Minute no. 90 (*Sondernummer* 68) of the meeting of the Politburo of the CC of the CPSU, Moscow, 10 March 1927, ibid., 868–70, at 868.

41 Minute of a meeting of the Comintern delegation, Hankou, 9 April 1927, in Leutner, *KPdSU(B)*, vol. 2, part 2, 893–6.

Roy, at this point, seems to have been in more conciliatory mood. On 12 April, he sent a telegram to Chiang Kai-shek from Wuhan. This was the day of the counter-revolutionary coup in Shanghai, though Roy did not yet know it. His telegram began by stating that the relocation to Nanjing of the scheduled meeting of the Central Executive Committee, as Chiang Kai-shek had demanded, would amount to no less than a split in the national-revolutionary front. Yet Roy, evidently, did not wish to burn all his bridges, as he declared himself willing, on certain conditions, to travel to Shanghai with Borodin for discussions with Chiang Kai-shek. This more emollient stance the journalist Harold Isaacs attributed to concern for the state interests of the Soviet Union, quoting a colleague from the *New York Times:* 'The Moscow leaders will do their utmost to restore Kuomintang unity, even at the sacrifice of the more extreme Communists.'[42]

Only ten days later did Chiang Kai-shek send a laconic reply that made no response to Roy's offer but merely regretted that 'Mr. Roy, delegate of the Third International' should have paid heed to one side only.[43] The offer, in any case, had been overtaken by events in Shanghai, which had led the Communists to break with Chiang. With the support of the All-China Federation of Trade Unions, the Chinese Communist leaders who remained in the city, Zhou Enlai among them, had started preparing for a general strike. Supposed to be the prelude to an armed uprising, it was to be launched when the national-revolutionary troops under Bai Chongxi got close to Shanghai. When these came to a halt outside the city, the insurgent forces in all their political and social diversity were left to fight the local warlords and British troops on their own. Only when they had prevailed did Chiang Kai-shek march into Shanghai and bring the city under his control. He then turned on his former allies and, with the help of criminal gangs – such as the 'Green Gang', which was closely connected to the local business elite, playing a key role in the city's corrupt economy – carried out a ruthless massacre of Communists and other social-revolutionary forces.[44]

---

42 Isaacs, *Tragedy*, 184.

43 Telegram from M. N. Roy to Chiang Kai-shek, Hankou, 12 April 1927, in Leutner, *KPdSU(B)*, vol. 2, part 2, 897–9; letter from Chiang Kai-shek to M. N. Roy, Nanjing, 22 April 1927, in Leutner, *KPdSU(B)*, vol. 2, part 2, 927–8.

44 The best accounts of the events in Shanghai in terms of the relationship between the Comintern and the Chinese party are in Smith, 'Moscow', and Smith, *A Road*, 145–208.

With the bloody coup of 12 April 1927, Chiang Kai-shek had taken an unequivocal position against social revolution, and with the proclamation of an alternative government in Nanjing on 18 April he also formalized his break with the Nationalist government of Wang Jingwei in Wuhan. Progressives around the world who had pinned their hopes on the Chinese Revolution were utterly dismayed, and even Chiang's son, a student at the Sun Yat-sen University in the Soviet Union, was outraged.[45] In *Inprekorr*, Liao Huanxing described Chiang as a 'traitor to the people',[46] while, a few years later, André Malraux's literary account of the conquest of Shanghai and the defeat of the Communists in his great novel *La Condition Humaine* (1933, published in English as *Man's Fate*), depicted it as a betrayal of the revolution.

The question that obviously arose for the Communist side after the April events was 'What now?' China policy presented a notable challenge for the Stalinist party leadership in its domestic struggle with the Left Opposition. Was it right to maintain the united front with the Guomindang? While Trotsky viewed the latter as a bourgeois formation and argued that the Communists should leave it, Stalin and the majority of the Russian party defended continued cooperation – Stalin could hardly admit that his policy of cooperation with the Guomindang had been a mistake and that his great opponent had been right. The reaction of the Russian party leadership and of the ECCI Plenum of May 1927 was to go on the offensive, Stalin and Bukharin tacitly adopting the demands of the Left Opposition. The tactic decided on was for the Chinese Communists to form a bloc with the Left Guomindang in the hope that the Left Guomindang would 'deal with' Chiang Kai-shek, as Liao Huanxing put it in *Inprekorr*, thus averting the need for a break.[47] Politically, the agrarian revolution was to be promoted and the urban labour movement strengthened. Furthermore, the Chinese party was to have its own armed forces. The Eighth Plenum characterized Chiang

---

45 Elizabeth McGuire, 'Sino-Soviet Romance: An Emotional History of Revolutionary Geopolitics', *Journal of Contemporary History* 52:4, 2017, 853–73, at 859. See also McGuire, *Red at Heart: How Chinese Communists Fell in Love with the Russian Revolution*, Oxford: Oxford University Press, 2017.

46 'Der Volksverräter Tschiang Kai Schek und die revolutionäre Kuo Min Tang', *Inprekorr*, 19 April 1927, 863–5.

47 'Die revolutionäre Kuo Min Tang wird auch mit Tschiang Kai Schek fertig werden', *Inprekorr* 29, April 1927, 947–8.

Kai-shek as a traitor and the Chinese bourgeoisie as counter-revolutionary, but, at the same time, insisted on the importance of maintaining the united front; it also called for the proletariat to gain hegemony over the national revolution, ending its telegram to the CCP with the exhortation, 'Long live the world socialist commune!'[48] But, as Vincent Sheean noted, 'the supreme characteristic of the Hankou experiment was that it was not Communist at all', for one couldn't conceive of an experiment in Communism in which private capital continued to circulate freely and the rule of the business class over the workers was maintained.[49] In reality, the Comintern's new policy simply resulted in a split in the Guomindang.

The Comintern representatives on the ground in China faced not only political but also military problems, as both Chiang Kai-shek and the Nationalist government in Wuhan sought to extend the areas under their control. What is more, Chiang's coup had made the foreign powers particularly aware of the weakness of the Wuhan government, the British foreign minister noting that the Nationalist government had lost the authority it had once enjoyed: 'It is at present little more than the shadow of a name.'[50] Shortly thereafter, Great Britain broke off diplomatic relations with the Soviet Union, accused of espionage following a search of the offices of the Soviet trade delegation in London, also home of the Arcos (All-Russian Co-operative Society) import-export business.[51] The British warships stationed on the Yangtze River clearly showed where the real power lay, and Roy's outrage at the fact that China's main commercial artery was under the control of 'imperialist guns' did nothing to alter that.[52] The economic and social situation in the part of the country under the control of the Wuhan government was also deteriorating. Economic blockade and increased military spending exacerbated class tensions and conflicts, reflected in discord and division within government. The peasant movement confiscated land and

---

48 Telegram from the Eighth Plenum of the ECCI to the CCP, 20 May 1927, in Leutner, *KPdSU(B)*, vol. 2, part 2, 974–5, at 975.
49 Sheean, *In Search*, 244.
50 Cited in Isaacs, *Tragedy*, 206.
51 Harriette Flory, 'The Arcos Raid and the Rupture of Anglo-Soviet Relations, 1927', *Journal of Contemporary History* 12:4, 1977, 707–23.
52 M. N. Roy, 'Imperialist Intervention in China', *Chinese Correspondence*, 1 May 1927, cited in Isaacs, *Tragedy*, 207.

strikes paralyzed production in the cities. Employers turned to lockouts, leaving 100,000 out of work as a result at the beginning of May, and twice as many four weeks later; speculators drove up food prices, and the banks refused to lend to peasants.[53] Their integration into the Guomindang, however, presented the Communists with a dilemma. So as not to threaten the interests of the 'Left' generals, who were largely landowners and entrepreneurs, these social struggles were supported in Communist rhetoric, but curbed in Communist practice: 'excesses' had to be avoided.

In this rapidly changing situation, the Comintern's representatives in China needed both analytical acumen and good judgement. Mediating between the Chinese comrades and the Comintern leadership, they found themselves in the midst of the action without really being part of it.[54] Both Roy and Borodin lived the life of expatriates, confined within their own circle: contacts with the Chinese population were explicitly restricted by the Comintern and the Soviet authorities, so that the Soviet Union could not be accused of political interference. Only the holders of the highest party or government positions had direct contact with them, though rumours about them circulated among ordinary members of the Chinese party.[55] They sometimes had to rely on the Communist press to make the Comintern's directives known. Their official role was to advise their Chinese allies, the Guomindang in Borodin's case, the CCP in Roy's. They had to pass on Moscow's directives and keep Moscow constantly informed about events in China, but depended on local Communists for their knowledge. These were often unwilling to divulge what they knew, and when they did they quite understandably presented matters from their own point of view. They also had their own opinions about Comintern envoys' intervention in their party affairs: a Chinese party cadre at the time described Roy's speeches as always 'grandiloquent'.[56]

Neither Roy nor Borodin spoke Chinese, and, in all likelihood, they communicated with each other in English. Borodin, who had

---

53 Isaacs, *Tragedy*, 208.
54 Leutner, 'The Communist Party of China'; Tamiatto, 'Des révolutionnaires'.
55 Wang Fan-hsi, *Chinese Revolutionary: Memoirs 1919–1949*, trans. Gregor Benton, Oxford: Oxford University Press, 1980, 41.
56 Zheng Chaolin, *Siebzig Jahre Rebell: Erinnerungen eines chinesischen Oppositionellen*, Frankfurt a. M.: ISP-Verlag, 1991, 164.

fled Russia after the revolution of 1905, had lived for the next eleven years in the United States, where he had established a school for immigrants. The elder of his two sons, both of whom were in China with him and his wife, spoke better English than Russian. Roy, for his part, wrote all his reports to Moscow, whether to the ECCI or to Stalin himself, in English. He also spoke Hindustani and Spanish, by his own account.[57] As a result, both he and Borodin relied on translators to communicate with the Chinese, and were thus also reliant on their competence and their loyalty, which might lie with the Chinese side, rather than the Soviet Union's. Borodin had a staff who prepared a daily summary of the Chinese and English press for him.[58] One of these, for a time, was the polyglot Nguyên Ai Quôc (Hô Chi Minh), who arrived in November 1924, following his training at the Communist University of the Toilers of the East. As well as Vietnamese, he spoke Mandarin and Cantonese, French, English, Russian and Thai, and among his other responsibilities was the education of his compatriots in Guangzhou – in those days a laboratory of revolution for young Vietnamese – and establishing contacts with Indochina.[59]

What Roy and Borodin knew of the situation in China had thus passed through multiple filters. Nor were they themselves the purveyors of a straightforward message: as has already been noted, the Comintern's directives were ambivalent, even contradictory. They were correspondingly difficult to put into practice, and much depended on interpretation. When clarification was requested from Moscow, the answers often arrived late, not only because a letter often took three to four weeks each way,[60] but also because the Comintern leadership was always overloaded with meetings and inquiries as reports piled up in their Moscow

---

57 M. N. Roy's personal file, RGASPI 495/213/18; that Borodin had little Chinese is also noted by Sheean, *In Search*, 226.

58 See the memoirs of Vishniakova Akimova, *Two Years*, 221–2.

59 Christopher E. Goscha, 'Pour une histoire transnationale du communisme asiatique: Les chevauchements sino-vietnamiens dans les mers du Sud', *Communisme* 2013, 21–46, at 29; Pierre Brocheux, *Ho Chi Minh: A Biography*, Cambridge: Cambridge University Press, 2011, 29–39. On Hô Chi Minh's activities in Guangzhou, see also Sophie Quinn-Judge, *Ho Chi Minh: The Missing Years, 1919–1941*, Berkeley: University of California Press, 2003, 69–115.

60 Letter from A. E. Abramovich to I. A. Piatnitsky, Shanghai, 25 February 1927, in Leutner, *KPdSU(B)*, vol. 2, part 2, 848–50, at 848.

offices. Cipher telegrams were cumbersome and suited only to brief communications.[61]

The leadership of the Chinese party did not simply give in and accept the imposition of a political line it had grave doubts about, especially as Roy and Borodin, the Comintern's own representatives, disagreed among themselves, as had become clear at the mid-April sessions of the Politburo. After the subsequent Central Committee meeting, Roy and Doriot somewhat discontentedly reported to Moscow that 'the Central Committee fought against the Comintern delegation, but reluctantly agreed in the end.'[62]

Charged with ensuring the implementation of the resolutions adopted by the Seventh Plenum, the Comintern representatives had to argue their case before the Fifth Congress of the CCP, held in Hankou between 27 April and 9 May 1927. And as expositions of the Comintern's political line always required references to the Marxist (or as Soviet-speak had it, 'Marxist-Leninist') classics, such argument called for a certain theoretical aptitude. In putting their respective positions to the Congress, Roy and Borodin disagreed over the role of the bourgeoisie. Borodin, who spoke first, argued for caution. The role of the bourgeoisie in semi-colonial countries had not yet been fully analysed in Marxist terms, and there was therefore insufficient clarity regarding 'the general aspect or particular detail of the concrete stages by which the bourgeoisie and bourgeois groups take their leave of the revolution.'[63] Therefore, he said, the Communists would continue to work with the Guomindang for a long while yet. Roy, who only got to give his report the following day, argued back without making explicit reference to Borodin. He advocated a revolutionary offensive by the peasants, whose organization had been presided over by CCP Central Committee member Mao Zedong since May; this would force the generals of the Left Guomindang to decide once and for all on which side they were on. He forcefully rejected the idea that the bourgeoisie had any anticapitalist, revolutionary role, referring to the Second World Congress of the Comintern and relying on the symbolic authority of Lenin:

---

61 Accompanying note from Fani S. Borodina, Guangzhou, 3 July 1926, in Leutner, *KPdSU(B)*, vol. 2, part 1, 335.

62 Telegram from J. Doriot and M. N. Roy to the Political Secretariat of the ECCI, Hankou, 20 April 1927, in Leutner, *KPdSU(B)*, vol. 2, part 2, 924–5, at 925.

63 Speech by G. N. Voitinsky at the Fifth Congress of the CCP, Hankou, 3 May 1927, in Leutner, *KPdSU(B)*, vol. 2, part 2, 944–54, at 948.

Neither in the theses nor in Lenin's speech was it said that the liberation movement in the colonies must develop inevitably as a purely bourgeois revolution thus creating conditions for the capitalist development of the colonies. The experiences of colonial revolutions from the time of this congress and the Chinese revolution, in particular, have demonstrated that in the process of the development of the revolutionary movement the national bourgeoisie deserts the revolution and even turns against it.[64]

The difficulty of drawing practical conclusions from such theoretical considerations was overcome in neither contribution, nor by any other speaker who addressed the matter, and so it is no surprise that the Congress's closing declaration proclaimed no more than the unification of all democratic elements under the banner of the Guomindang.

In Moscow there was very great concern about the situation in China and the mood within the delegation, with accusations of ineptitude flying about the ECCI. On the conclusion of the congress, then, Voitinsky and Roy were instructed to come back to Moscow to report. Roy, however, refused. If he travelled via Shanghai (the shortest route), he was at great risk of arrest by the British authorities. This was likely only one consideration, however, for he also made clear what he actually feared, that 'his invitation to Moscow [would] mean his release from work in China'. If that was so, he wrote to the Comintern, he would stay in China and permanently withdraw from political life.[65] At the beginning of May, this fear was premature, but it would become a reality only a few weeks later, when, on 22 June the Political Secretariat of the ECCI removed him from his post and appointed Heinz Neumann in his place.[66] In the meantime, events moved on.

That the congress had assented to the ambiguous and contradictory theses adopted by the Seventh Plenum did not at all mean that the Chinese party had accepted Roy's arguments. The contradictions that

---

64 'The Perspectives and the Character of the Chinese Revolution', M. N. Roy's report to the Fifth Congress of the Chinese Communist Party on the Theses of the Seventh Plenum of the ECCI, in North and Eudin, *M. N. Roy's Mission*, 216–30, at 221.

65 Minutes of a meeting of the Political Secertariat of the ECCI, Moscow, 11 May 1927, in Leutner, *KPdSU(B)*, vol. 2, part 2, 960–1.

66 Excerpt from Minute no. 30 of the closed meeting of the Political Secretariat of the ECCI, Moscow, 22 June 1927, in Leutner, *KPdSU(B)*, vol. 2, part 2, 1061–2.

arose from support for military action to expand the territory under Nationalist control on the one hand and the promotion of radical agrarian reform while maintaining a cooperative relationship with the Guomindang on the other hand remained unresolved. Nor were words followed by action, when that was exactly what Roy had urged. When, on 21 May, a Wuhan general carried out a coup d'état in Changsha, capital of Hunan province and a Communist stronghold, slaughtering some 20,000 Communists, Roy organized a counter-offensive with the help of local party forces. Given the passivity of the Wuhan government, he decided, in agreement with Blyukher, chief Soviet military adviser to the southern National Revolutionary Army and member of the Southern Bureau of the Chinese CP, to go over the head of the Chinese party leadership in moving onto the offensive and establishing a peasant army.[67] It may be that he himself visited the surrounding villages to mobilize the peasants.[68] Roy's plans for the storming of Changsha by peasant militias ended in a massacre when the Chinese party leadership (under Borodin's influence, he thought) called off the uprising.[69] To Roy, this policy represented nothing less than 'legalization of the counterrevolution'.[70] At the same time, Roy continued to do his utmost to persuade the Nationalist government to adopt more radical positions. He set his hopes on a split and a grassroots reorganization of the Guomindang around Wang Jingwei, president of the Nationalist government in Wuhan.[71] In this he received no support from Borodin, who, on the contrary, believed that such a move would shift the Left Guomindang to the right. The relationship between the two men was now at rock bottom. Roy reported to Moscow that the CCP was practically under Borodin's leadership and that Borodin did not take the Comintern delegation seriously.[72] He even suspected that Borodin did not forward his telegrams to Moscow, which had to go through him.[73] As Vincent Sheean noted of

---

67 Vidyarthi [M. N. Roy], *China in Revolt*, 59.
68 North and Eudin, *Roy's Mission*, 67.
69 On these events, see also Haithcox, *Communism*, 69.
70 Telegram from M. N. Roy to the Politburo of the CC of the CPSU(B), Hankou, 5 June 1927, in Leutner, *KPdSU(B)*, vol. 2, part 2, 1022–3, at 1023.
71 Vidyarthi [M. N. Roy], *China in Revolt*, 62.
72 Telegram from M. N. Roy to the Politburo of the CC of the CPSU(B), Hankou, 2 June 1927, in Leutner, *KPdSU(B)*, vol. 2, part 2, 1019–20.
73 Telegram from M. N. Roy to J. V. Stalin and N.I. Bukharin, Hankou, 17 June 1927, in Leutner, *KPdSU(B)*, vol. 2, part 2, 1035–7.

their relationship, '[T]he official representatives of the Komintern had no more love for him [Borodin] than had the official representatives of the Standard Oil Company.'[74]

To add weight to his recommendations, on 30 May Roy asked the ECCI for a 'telegram from Moscow urging action'.[75] On receiving this the following day, he showed it to Borodin, who was suffering an attack of malaria. Borodin was unimpressed, describing the instructions to dismiss the right-wing Guomindang generals and bring them before a revolutionary tribunal, to confiscate land and to mobilize the workers and peasants as 'absurd'.[76] Roy then showed the telegram to Wang Jingwei, believing that it would move him to act. It did not. The leader of the supposedly Left-Nationalist government, described by Sheean as 'the type of the fiery, romantic revolutionary', turned out to be a rational, calculating politician unwilling to take any risks.[77] The day he was removed as head of the ECCI delegation, Roy sent a telegram to Moscow explaining why he had shown Wang Jingwei the instructions: Wang had complained that he was not informed about Moscow's policy, and he, Roy, had feared that without further information Wang Jingwei could well come under reactionary influence, and that he had sought to prevent this. Finally, none of the contents of the telegram were secret and could have been shown to the Left Guomindang 'had we wanted to show them the danger from the right and the only way out'.[78] Borodin and Voitinsky, though, saw it very differently, and had already sent vehement complaints to Moscow.

Departure and the Political Consequences of the Debacle

What Borodin had feared now came to pass: the supposedly Left Guomindang generals went over to the anti-Communist camp and a

---

74 Sheean, *In Search*, 245.

75 Telegram from M. N. Roy to the Political Secretariat of the ECCI, Hankou, 30 May 1927, in Leutner, *KPdSU(B)*, vol. 2, part 2, 1015.

76 North and Eudin, *Roy's Mission*, 107.

77 Sheean, *In Search*, 252.

78 Telegram from M. N. Roy to the Politburo of the CC of the CPSU(B), Hankou, 22 June 1927, in Leutner, *KPdSU(B)*, vol. 2, part 2, 1038. Also, in similar terms, the telegram from M. N. Roy to J. V. Stalin and N. I. Bukharin, Hankou, 17 June 1927, in ibid., 1035–7, at 1036.

bloody repression was launched against Communists and militant peasants.[79] In July 1927, all Communists were expelled from the Guomindang and its army and the united front in China was at an end.

The ECCI was instructed by the Politburo of the Soviet party to immediately organize an international campaign of protest against the shooting of Communists in China. Stalin himself was furious. From his summer residence on the Black Sea, he berated his comrades Molotov and Bukharin for not keeping him informed (as if he had not been at all involved in policy-making regarding the CCP). He described the leadership of the Chinese party as incompetent, together with the Soviet advisers to the Guomindang and the Comintern representatives he called the 'nannies' of the Chinese Communists. He accused Roy of being the originator of the 'chatter about the "feudal bourgeoisie"'. And he ordered: 'Borodin and Roy and all the oppositionists obstructing our work there must be swept out of China. As a rule, we should send good cadre to China, not people we have no use for.'[80]

On 14 July, Bukharin announced in *Inprekorr* that the Wuhan government no longer played any revolutionary role.[81] Borodin was instructed to return to Moscow without delay, and the members of the Far Eastern Bureau were also ordered home. 'Galin' was to burn his papers. Roy was accused of breach of discipline and told to return to Moscow immediately. His departure was delayed, however, as he claimed that he could not travel via Shanghai on account of the British.

Borodin and Roy travelled in separate parties, a week apart. Borodin left on 27 July, following the release of his wife after almost four months of imprisonment. She returned to Moscow via Vladivostok, while he was joined on the 3,000-kilometre journey, which took them to Urga (Ulaanbaatar) via the Gobi Desert, by the American journalist and fellow-traveller Anna Louise Strong. From her account we learn that the first part was covered by train, accompanied by the bodyguard supplied

---

[79] The weakness of the left was remarked on by E. H. Carr, *Socialism in One Country 1924–1926*, vol. 3, Harmondsworth, UK: Penguin Books, 1972, 803. Roland Felber, however, goes further, arguing that there existed no Left Guomindang leadership, but only Left masses: R. Felber, 'A "Block Within" or a "Block Without"? Controversies on the CCP's Attitude Towards the Guomindang Before and After 20 March 1926', in Leutner, *Chinese Revolution*, 52–65, at 62–3.

[80] Letter from J. V. Stalin to V. M. Molotov and N. I. Bukharin, Sochi, 9 July 1927, in Leutner, *KPdSU(B)*, vol. 2, part 2, 1122–7, direct quote at 1126.

[81] Isaacs, *Tragedy*, 266.

by the Nationalist Government and the worker guards that always surrounded Borodin.[82] Their journey then continued by car through the desert: 'We took with us 220 boxes of gasoline, each containing ten gallons. We had five automobiles and five trucks. The plan was to abandon trucks as we used up their load of gasoline.'[83]

Roy and his partner followed in late July, likewise travelling by car, but with a rather smaller entourage. According to Luise Geissler, the Comintern had provided them with three large touring cars, with petrol reserves in drums at the sides. The drivers were GPU agents. They too travelled through the Gobi desert, a taxing journey. The days were scorching, the nights bitterly cold, which supposedly did not bother Roy but proved a trial for his partner.[84] They finally reached Moscow, via Urga, towards the end of August.[85]

Back in Moscow, Roy had to report on the situation in China and justify his actions, not only before the Eastern Secretariat but also before Political Secretariat of the ECCI and the committee it had set up 'to examine the case of Comrade Roy'.[86] It can be assumed that he blamed the defeat on the Chinese party leadership, which is what he did in his book *Revolution and Counter-Revolution in China*, published in 1930, not by a Comintern publishing house but by that of the Communist Opposition.[87] The leadership of the Chinese party had a 'mechanical conception of united front politics' and had failed to understand that it

---

82 Anna Louise Strong, *The Revolutionary Struggles from 1927 to 1935*, New York: Knight Publishing, 1935, 228–9; 3,000 km is the distance given by Strong, though the distance to Urga as the crow flies is only 2,000 km. She may have also counted the further 600 km she travelled to reach the Trans-Siberian railway, though Borodin would fly directly from Urga to Moscow.

83 Strong, *Revolutionary Struggles*, 255.

84 Ray, *In Freedom's Quest*, vol. 2, 297, the author relying here on an interview with Luise Geissler.

85 North and Eudin, *Roy's Mission*, 126. Overstreet and Windmiller write that Roy left Hankou on 8 August and arrived in Moscow only a few days later, which seems improbable: *Communism in India*, Berkeley: University of California Press, 1959, 98. In his memoirs, which North and Eudin say are not always reliable, Roy claims that he left a week before Borodin: *China in Revolt*, 64.

86 Shorthand record of the meeting of the Political Secretariat of the ECCI, Moscow, 14 October 1927, in Leutner, *KPdSU(B)*, vol. 2, part 1, 190–8, with Roy's interventions on 195–7.

87 Roy, *Revolution and Counter-Revolution in China*, Calcutta: Renaissance, 1946 [1930].

should have worked for a split in the Guomindang, 'along the line of the contradiction between the interests of the masses of its members and those of the feudal-bourgeois leading clique'.[88] On the other hand, he omitted to identify the Comintern's and Stalin's own error in enacting the policy, which must have helped him before the committee of inquiry. Although it described the fact that he had shown Wang Jingwei the contents of the telegram of 31 May as an 'organizational error', it found that in general he had taken a 'correct' political line 'on the main question of the agrarian revolution and the reckoning with the counter-revolutionaries'.[89] Stalin gave his consent to this 'proposed judgment'.[90]

In Moscow, Roy was as pugnacious as ever. While accepting that the telegram business was a mistake, he remained convinced that this in no way justified his recall. Words of advice and a reprimand would have been quite sufficient.[91] He also wrote a great deal. Between September 1927 and March 1929, he published seventeen articles in the *Inprekorr*. Though Roy's articles reflected the official Comintern line, this would only be after arguments with the editors.[92] There was, too, what was undoubtedly assigned as a test of loyalty, a pamphlet against the Trotskyist opposition, which, as historian Hans Piazza notes, 'did not match his style',[93] though said to be 'published with the author's permission'. In it, Roy describes his former comrades-in-arms – Rosmer, Souvarine, Radek and Karl Korsch – as well as, of course, Trotsky and the rest of the 'ultra-left oppositionists' and 'renegades', as

---

88 Ibid., 447.

89 Decision of the committee investigating the case of Comrade Roy, Moscow, n.d., RGASPI 495/213/18.

90 Proposals of the committee of the Political Secretariat of the ECCI investigating the matter of M.N. Roy, Moscow, 30 August 1927, in Leutner, *KPdSU(B)*, vol. 2, part 2, 1151–2. Handwritten note in Russian by Stalin 'Agreed'; Conclusions of the committee established by the Political Secretariat of the ECCI ... [*illegible*], 1927, RGASPI, 495/213/18.

91 Letter from M. N. Roy to the Political Secretariat of the ECCI, Moscow, 30 August 1927, in Leutner, *KPdSU(B)*, vol. 2, part 2, 1150.

92 Minute no. 51 of the meeting of the Political Secretariat of the ECCI, Moscow, 14 October 1927, in Leutner, *KPdSU(B)*, vol. 2, part 1, 190.

93 M. N. Roy, *Die internationalen Verbündeten der Opposition in der KPdSU*, Hamburg: Carl Hoym Nachf., 1928; Hans Piazza, 'Manabendra Nath Roy: Ein alter und bewährter Soldat in Indiens Freiheitskampf', in Theodor Bergmann and Mario Kessler, eds, *Ketzer im Kommunismus: 23 biographische Essays*, Hamburg: VSA-Verlag, 2003), 197–217, at 209.

'counter-revolutionaries'. One supposes that this was all to help legitimize his take on China policy, for he was chiefly occupied in writing a book about the Chinese Revolution and assembling a collection of his speeches and writings in China, both to be published under the aegis of the Comintern.⁹⁴ He would have liked to discuss the contents with Stalin, and wrote him at least three letters about it, though India was not forgotten either. 'I have some specific suggestions that I would like your opinion on. Please let me know when I can see you.'⁹⁵ Stalin's answer is not known, though it would seem that Roy did not visit. He was, however, commissioned to draft a resolution on the Indian question for the next ECCI Plenum.

In late October, Roy returned to Berlin, but not before meeting Nehru, in Moscow for the tenth anniversary of the Russian Revolution. In November, Trotsky and Zinoviev were expelled from the party. In December, Roy must, presumably, have attended the meeting of the General Council of the League Against Imperialism, having been allowed to resume his position of the Comintern's commission on the work of the League on coming back from China.⁹⁶ He would return to Moscow only once, in January–February 1928, to take part in the Ninth ECCI Plenum. There, at an informal conference of Comintern China 'experts', he met Heinz Neumann (alias 'Moritz'), his successor as ECCI representative in China.

The twenty-five-year-old Neumann had just returned from Guangzhou. In China, he and the twenty-nine-year-old Besso Lominadze (alias 'Werner'), likewise known among the comrades as one of Stalin's blue-eyed boys, had ousted the leadership of the Chinese party at the Comintern's behest,⁹⁷ the ECCI blaming defeat in China on the 'opportunistic deviations' of the old leadership.⁹⁸ After a certain

---

94 M. N. Roy, *Kitaiskaia revoliutsiia i Kommunisticheskii Internatsional: Sbornik statei i materialov* [The Chinese Revolution and the Communist International: A Collection of Articles and Documents], Moscow and Leningrad: n.p., 1929.

95 Letter from M. N. Roy to J. V. Stalin, Moscow, 16 September 1927, in Leutner, *KPdSU(B)*, vol. 2, part 2, 1154–5, direct quote on 1155.

96 Piazza, *Roy*, 206.

97 Deposed at the emergency party conference of 7 August 1927, Chen Duxiu was expelled from the party in 1929.

98 Resolution of the ECCI on the current situation of the Chinese Revolution, 14 July 1927, cited in Isaacs, *Tragedy*, 266, which relies on the English-language *Inprecor* of 28 July 1927.

amount of back and forth between Hankou and Shanghai, the two Comintern representatives had travelled to Guangzhou, where, having just arrived, they drafted an overly bold plan for an armed workers' uprising against the Guomindang troops in the city. Lominadze then returned to Moscow in November, his successor being the long-time Comintern emissary József Pogány (a.k.a. 'John Pepper').

With the benefit of his experience as people's commissar of war in the short-lived Hungarian Soviet Republic and one of the Comintern envoys sent to Germany to prepare the ill-fated March Action, Pogány spoke against the planned uprising, as did the local Soviet consul-general. However, the Politburo of the Soviet party and Stalin himself gave the go-ahead by telegram, though with a wording that left the responsibility to 'Moritz', i.e. Neumann: 'In view of the determined mood among the masses and the more or less favourable situation locally we have nothing against your suggestion and advise acting confidently and decisively.'[99] The undertaking failed radically, the uprising being bloodily suppressed in only three days, with 600 deaths and 5,700 more following in the aftermath.[100] To endow the venture with a certain revolutionary nobility, it was baptized the 'Commune of Canton' in Comintern-speak.[101] If mistakes had been made, the Ninth ECCI Plenum decreed, they were the responsibility of the Chinese party leadership. Roy, no longer a member of the Comintern at the time of writing, described it as 'the most tragic event in the entire history of the Chinese Revolution . . . the greatest mistake ever committed, because its bloody suppression was inevitable'.[102]

---

99 Telegram from Stalin, excerpted from Minute no. 139 (*Sondernummer* 116) of the meeting of the Politburo of the CC of the CPSU, 10 December 1927, in Leutner, *KPdSU(B)*, vol. 2, part 1, 236.

100 Brocheux, *Ho Chi Minh*, 41.

101 In 1928, a group of high-ranking cadre of the Comintern and of the Red Army published under a pseudonym a manual on armed insurrection that makes reference to the Canton Uprising: A. Neuberg, *Der bewaffnete Aufstand: Versuch einer theoretischen Darstellung*, ostensibly published by 'Otto Meyer: Zürich'. A French edition followed three years later: A. Neuberg, *L'insurrection armée*, Paris: Bureau d'Éditions, 1931. This was rapidly withdrawn from circulation, only to be reissued in 1934. Isaac erroneously states that Neumann was among the authors: *Tragedy*, 370. The work is available in English, with a foreword by the former Communist Erich Wollenberg, who was involved in its writing, as A. Neuberg, *Armed Insurrection*, trans. Quintin Hoare, London: NLB, 1970.

102 Roy, *Revolution*, 562.

According to the account of his later partner, Neumann himself only just managed to escape.¹⁰³ He was already wanted, with his picture on posters all over the city's walls. Dirty, his suit tattered, and with a three-day stubble on his chin, he had to bribe a rickshaw puller to take him to the gate of the foreign concession. From there, Neumann made for the port among the stream of Europeans taking their leave of bloody Guangzhou. A ship took him north, allowing him to take a train through Manchuria to reach the Soviet Union. Thanks to Stalin's protection, this terrible defeat that cost the lives of thousands of Chinese Communists did not affect Neumann's career. He and Lominadze were criticized as 'putschists' by a number of those attending the Ninth Plenum in February 1928, but it was Neumann who gave the presentation on China at the Sixth World Congress in July, a congress that took a sharp left turn. After February's plenum he had returned to Berlin, where, shortly afterwards, he reached the highest point in his career, an achievement not unrelated to his role in the elimination of Bukharin, against whom he and Lominadze had intrigued at Stalin's instigation. Appointed to the Political Secretariat of the KPD, he took over the party leadership with Ernst Thälmann and Hermann Remmele. At the Eleventh Plenum in March 1931 he was even co-opted to the ECCI Secretariat and made a candidate member of the ECCI Presidium. Official blame for the devastating defeat had once again been laid at the door of the CCP. That the united front with the Guomindang had not been a basic error by the Chinese party but had been reckoned pragmatically advantageous to both sides by the Comintern itself became sayable again only after the CCP had embarked on a new strategy in 1931, with the establishment of autonomous Soviet zones under Mao Zedong. In 1932, in her novel *Die Gefährten* (The Companions) the Communist Anna Seghers has one of her fictional Chinese remark that 'All the same, Sun Yat-sen . . . has made an alliance with Russia'. To which another retorts: 'What do you want to deduce from this? He hasn't allied himself with the Bolsheviks, but with a powerful empire that borders on ours.'¹⁰⁴ That such an alliance had made strategic sense under Sun Yat-sen but not any longer

---

103 Margarete Buber-Neumann, *Kriegsschauplätze der Weltrevolution: Ein Bericht aus der Praxis der Komintern 1919–1943*, Stuttgart: Seewald Verlag, 1967, 225.
104 This was also the analysis of Isaac, *Tragedy*, 49.

under Chiang Kai-shek was a self-criticism the Comintern did not venture to offer!

Roy's six-month mission to China marked the end of his Comintern career, so changing his life radically, not only in political but also in personal terms. After Stalin refused to receive him, he was elected to the ECCI Presidium one last time, at the Ninth Plenum of February–March 1928. His draft resolution was, however, not discussed. In fact, the Russian representatives on the ECCI suggested that he go to India, which meant nothing less than handing him over directly to the British police.[105] That same March, the Political Secretariat of the ECCI removed him from the leadership of the Communist fraction at the League Against Imperialism, and in September he lost his place in the Eastern Secretariat.[106] In the meantime, he had developed a serious ear infection and had had to travel to Switzerland to recover.[107] The journey was probably financed by his wealthy, upper-class friend Brajesh Singh, a member of the Indian Communist Party,[108] but it was Luise Geissler who hurried from Berlin to Moscow to help him.[109] Whether he really had to leave Moscow in haste and in secret, as she later claimed, or whether this was not rather a retrospective colouration in the light of the Great Terror, one cannot be sure.[110] Like all foreign Communists wishing to leave, however, he would have had to obtain an exit permit and secure the return of his passport from the Comintern, which he succeeded in doing with the help of his friend Bukharin, himself already in political trouble.[111] At the Sixth World Congress, which he was unable to attend due to his illness, Roy came under attack for his position on India, Kuusinen accusing him of taking an 'ultra-left, sectarian, Trotskyist line'.[112] This all came as an

---

105 Minute no. 3 of the meeting of the CPSU(B) delegation to the ECCI, Moscow, 22 February 1928, in Leutner, *KPdSU(B)*, vol. 2, part 1, 401–3.
106 Resolution of the ECCI, 28 September 1928, RGASPI 495/20/762.
107 Overstreet and Windmiller, *Communism in India*, 106.
108 Kumari Jayawardena, *The White Woman's Other Burden: Western Women and South Asia During British Colonial Rule*, New York: Routledge, 1995, 226.
109 Ray, *In Freedom's Quest*, vol. 3, 54.
110 North and Eudin, *Roy's Mission*, 128. Roy did however ask in a letter to an unnamed friend, 'Who told you I am having political difficulties? Nothing of the kind': Overstreet and Windmiller, *Communism in India*, 106.
111 Ray, *In Freedom's Quest*, vol. 2, 342–3.
112 *Protokoll des 6. Weltkongresses der kommunistischen Internationale*, Hamburg: Carl Hoym Nachf., 1928, 10, cited in Piazza, *Roy*, 211.

enormous shock to Roy. The congress's redefinition of the Comintern's political goals and the methods of achieving them robbed him of his role in the apparatus and with that diminished his political capital, plunging him into great mental and practical uncertainty. Everything he had committed himself to had been wiped away. In a letter to his friend, the British Communist Robert Page Arnot (1890–1986), he described himself as an 'outcast', completely in the dark about Comintern politics and his own future: 'I have not the slightest idea where I stand and what am I expected to do in the future. I presume that it is not desired that I should be pushed out of things altogether.' The Third Period policy struck him as 'insane'.[113] In a final attempt to save the enterprise of international Communism, he joined the Right Opposition, as many others did in early 1929, and wrote for its newspaper. In it, he denounced the 'arbitrary rule of the apparatus' and the dictatorship of the party bureaucracy, calling for a renewal of the Comintern. The Comintern responded by expelling him. Roy's exclusion was decided by the ECCI Presidium on 23 November 1929, 'in accordance with the resolution of the Tenth Plenum of the ECCI on the international situation and the tasks of the Communist International, Paragraph 9, and the resolution of the Presidium of the ECCI of 19 December 1928, according to which adherents of the Brandler organization cannot be members of the Communist International'.[114] This brought both a breach with his old comrades and the loss of his income. Roy sought nevertheless to maintain his contacts with the Indians in Berlin, which reignited his personal feud with Chatto. During these difficult months in the German capital, Roy hid behind the pseudonyms 'Roberto' and 'Villa Garcia' as he wrote his book *Revolution and Counter-Revolution in China*. He was supported, both financially and emotionally, not only by Luise Geissler but also by his new partner, Ellen Gottschalk (1904–1960), a polyglot German-Jewish Communist of US nationality, born in Paris and schooled in Cologne, who in the second half of the 1920s had worked as a secretary at the European Secretariat of the Krestintern (Peasant International) in Berlin, but who, like him, had become close to the KPD-O around 1929.[115] In late 1930, however, Roy

---

113 Letter from M. N. Roy in Berlin to R.P. Arnot in Moscow, 17 December 1928, RGASPI 495/213/18.

114 Excerpt from the minutes of the meeting of the ECCI Presidium, 23 November 1929, RGASPI 495/213/18.

115 Theodor Bergmann, *'Gegen den Strom': Die Geschichte der KPD (Opposition)*, Hamburg: VSA, 2001, 173 and 337–8. Gottschalk, however, gets no mention here!

returned to India alone, and illegally. The Damoclean sword under which he had lived for a decade and a half now fell: he was arrested on 21 July 1931 and spent the next six years in prison. His ex-partner Luise Geissler, with whom he had kept up a regular correspondence and who had not yet given up on him, followed him, uninvited, to India in May 1931. She succeeded in meeting him in secret but soon afterwards found herself arrested and deported to Germany as an undesirable alien.[116]

In late September 1932, Geissler left Berlin for Switzerland, where she still had contacts. Roy's old friend Dr Christian Hitz, formerly a legal adviser at the Soviet trade delegation in Berlin, helped her establish herself in Zurich, while an arranged marriage enabled her to gain Swiss citizenship once again. She worked for a time as a cashier at the Cornichon cabaret, successor to the Pfeffermühle that Erika Mann had co-founded in Munich and which had moved to Switzerland in 1933, and kept in touch with left-wing friends from the days of the Munich Soviet Republic, among them the playwright and revolutionary Ernst Toller.[117] She lived in Zurich with her younger sister Eva Geissler-Guaita (1900–1991), who had joined the Comintern as a 'technical secretary' in 1921, working mostly for the German section, and her sister's husband Armin Walter, a former volunteer in Spain. There she survived the Second World War, dying in 1973.[118] In this case, patriarchal marriage and citizenship rights served to protect the two sisters, who both continued to support the Indian struggle for independence.

---

116 Ray, *In Freedom's Quest*, vol. 2, 261, and vol. 3, 225–8.

117 Geissler maintained regular contact with Toller after 1932, as witnessed by their correspondence: *Ernst Toller: Briefe 1915–1939; Kritische Ausgabe*, 2 vols, ed. Stefan Neuhaus et al., Göttingen: Wallstein, 2018, 934–5, 971–2, 1283–4.

118 Written communication from residents' registration office, Zurich, 12 February 2018.

7
Shanghai: The Perilous Life of the Comintern Agent

The failure of the Chinese Revolution in 1927 represented a severe setback for the Chinese Communist Party (CCP), almost wiped out in the cities and forced into illegality, and the next few years saw China become the biggest recipient of assistance from International Red Aid. Some party members withdrew to the mountains, leading to the development of the 'soviet movement', which set out under the leadership of Mao Zedong to create territorial bases in central and southern China and a Red Army to go with them, thus beginning the militarization of Chinese Communism. Initial successes gave way to defeats in late 1932, with government troops pushing back the advances of the soviet movement. For the Guomindang, who had made Nanjing their capital, the CCP was now the chief domestic enemy, to be fought mercilessly. The Guomindang itself was divided by sharp disputes between various political and military forces, and this weakness, in turn, benefited a militaristic Japan, which occupied Manchuria in September 1931 and then attacked the Chinese quarters of Shanghai in January 1932. Fighting there continued until early May, when a ceasefire was agreed following the intervention of the League of Nations.

The break with the Guomindang saw Soviet advisers disappear and Comintern emissaries vanish from public sight, but this did not at all mean an end to Comintern activities in China. East and South East Asia had become too important, both for the international Communist movement and for the Soviet Union, not least because a Communist revolution in China would serve the USSR as a buffer against Japanese aggression. After the Guomindang's coup in 1927, the first thing that had to be done was to rebuild the structures of the Chinese party, now operating in illegality, and with them the party's organizing networks in the trade unions and the mass organizations, which meant training new cadre and recasting the work of propaganda. For all this, the anti-Communist repression of the following years would exact a high price. Finally, links to Bangkok and other cities, the focal points of international Communist activity in South East Asia, had to be re-established.

This chapter looks at the working lives of the Communists operating undercover in Shanghai around 1930. According to the Russian historian and China specialist Alexander Pantsov, the Comintern and its affiliated organizations had no fewer than fifty-three representatives active in China at one time or another between April 1920 and May 1943, most of them in that city. His list, which features only three women, was not complete, however, as more recent research has shown.[1] Shanghai stood at the centre of the Comintern's extensive, highly ramified apparatus in East and South East Asia, a network that even so essentially depended on a few key figures, and which was brought to its knees again in 1931 by the wave of arrests resulting from an international police operation coordinated between the colonial powers. The arrest of the supposed trade unionist Noulens and his wife, along with many other Communist functionaries, offers an insight into the Comintern's work under conditions of conspiracy, while the international defence campaign then launched highlights its capacity for worldwide mobilization. The event also illustrates the colonial powers' fear of Communism and the cooperation between a number of colonial police forces in South East Asia that this prompted. Second, the chapter looks at how the Comintern sought to limit the damage and again rebuild its apparatus. Third, it looks at the relationships between these foreign

---

1 Alexander V. Pantsov, 'Comintern Activists in China: Spies or Theorists?', in Anne-Marie Brady and Douglas Brown, eds, *Foreigners and Foreign Institutions in Republican China*, London: Routledge, 2012, 93–108, and also the documents published by the Russo-German research group under Mechthild Leutner and Michail Titarenko: Mechthild Leutner et al., eds, *KPdSU(B), Komintern und die Sowjetbewegung in China: Dokumente*, vol. 3, *1927–1931*, Münster, LitVerlag, 2000. On that project, see Mikhail L. Titarenko, 'The Joint Project on the RCP(B), Comintern and China', in Mechthild Leutner et al., eds, *The Chinese Revolution in the 1920s: Between Triumph and Disaster*, London: RoutledgeCurzon, 2002, 309–18.

comrades. In a Chinese city ruled by foreign powers, they enjoyed the privileges of foreigners, yet were always at risk. Bound together by danger and secrecy, they depended greatly on each other, while often being mutually distrustful. Finally, the chapter touches on the connections and collaborations between different types of Communist apparatus, between the Comintern, the Profintern and the Youth International on the one hand, and between these and Soviet intelligence on the other.

Rallying Point for Professional Revolutionaries

The heart of the Comintern apparatus in the city of Shanghai was the Far Eastern Bureau, established in June 1926, together with its associated OMS station. Funds destined for the Communist parties and youth organizations of China, Japan, Korea and Indonesia as well as Red Aid moneys for these countries went through the OMS in Shanghai. At various times, the bureau also had subsidiary offices in China, Japan and Korea, as well as in Taiwan, French Indochina, the Dutch East Indies, British Malaysia and the Philippines. After the disaster of April 1927 and the departure of the two Comintern emissaries, Borodin and Roy, the staff of the Far Eastern Bureau were also recalled to Moscow, leaving Comintern structures in the East to operate for some time on a very limited and fragmentary basis. It was not until 1929 that new cadre were sent to China, returning Shanghai to its position when 'Maring' had been active there in the early 1920s, as once again the Comintern's centre of communications and coordination in the Far East, where all information on revolutionary activity in the region was centralized.[2]

With its foreign concessions and its striking social contrasts, its ostentatious wealth and blatant poverty, Shanghai offered both anonymity and special protections for foreigners. A city of almost 3 million, in 1930 it was the economic and financial capital of China and the largest port in the country, and the third biggest financial centre in the world after New York and London. Domestic and foreign banks all had offices there, and movements of funds attracted barely any attention. Also,

---

2 On this, see Jérémie Tamiatto, 'Des révolutionnaires entre deux mondes: Trajectoires croisées de Grigori Voitinsky et Henk Sneevliet en Chine (1920–1923)', *Monde(s): histoire, espaces, relations* 10, 2016, 51–68.

there were hosts of foreign companies and their employees, offering Comintern organizations and their staff an ideal camouflage. What is more, Shanghai was well connected by post, telegraph and telephone and relatively easy to get to by ship, while visitors were not subject to visa or passport controls. All these together made the city a haven for shady activities; it was, for instance, the centre of the Chinese opium trade and more or less run by criminal gangs. At the same time, Shanghai was rich in cultural institutions, with cinemas, theatres and concert halls, and in places of entertainment, with a plethora of cafés, cabarets, dance halls and nightclubs.

Over 36,000 foreigners and nearly a million Chinese lived in the International Settlement, the British-dominated foreign enclave, while over 12,000 foreigners and almost half a million Chinese lived in the French concession.[3] These foreign enclaves were not subject to Chinese law or to any other regulation by the 'host country',[4] an extraterritoriality sharply criticized by left-wing intellectuals such as the renowned American journalist Edgar Snow[5] – and, of course, by the Communists – as an expression of colonial power relations. For, as the Moscow-born Austrian journalist and intermittent fellow-traveller Lili Körber acerbically noted, the 'whites in the motherland' sent there only 'their adventurers, their policemen, their merchants and their desperados'.[6] Even the German Communist Ursula Kuczynski (1907–2000), later known as Ruth Werner and later still as Ursula Hamburger, who lived in Shanghai with her husband, Rolf, from the summer of 1930, was filled with disgust: 'The dirt and poverty in which the coolies live are as appalling as the arrogance of the Europeans,' she wrote on 6 August 1931 in a letter to her brother Jürgen, already a well-known Communist

---

3 Frederic Wakeman, Jr, *Policing Shanghai 1927–1937*, Berkeley: University of California Press, 1995, 9.

4 On the life and atmosphere of the foreign enclaves in Shanghai and the reaction of these expatriate communities to the threat of revolution, see Nicholas R. Clifford, *Spoilt Children of Empire: Westerners in Shanghai and the Chinese Revolution of the 1920s*, Hanover, VT: Middlebury College Press, 1991.

5 Lois Wheeler Snow, ed., *Edgar Snow's China: A Personal Account of the Chinese Revolution Compiled from the Writings of Edgar Snow*, New York: Vintage Books, 1983, 21.

6 Lili Körber, *Begegnungen im Fernen Osten*, Budapest: Biblos Verlag, 1936, 178. She visited Shanghai in 1934.

economist in Berlin.⁷ For Western criminals or conspirators, however, this situation had its advantages, no fewer than fourteen states enjoying extraterritorial privileges: not only Great Britain, the United States, France and Italy, but also Belgium, Brazil, Denmark, Japan, the Netherlands, Norway, Portugal, Spain, Sweden and Switzerland.⁸ The Soviet Union had renounced its extraterritorial rights after the revolution, while Germany had lost its own with the Treaty of Versailles.

In 1928, the Comintern, Profintern, Communist Youth International, MOPR (International Red Aid) and Pan-Pacific Trade Union Secretariat had between them at least ten staff posted to Shanghai. Only one was a woman, the Lithuanian (or Pole?) Olga Mickiewicz (1889–1943), who represented the Profintern. March 1929 saw the Far Eastern Bureau reopen in the city with a four-person ECCI delegation. At its head was Ignacy Rylski (1893–1937) from Poland, whose real name was Jan Lubieniecki and who in China went under codenames 'Osten/Austin' and 'Paul'; his deputy was the German Gerhart Eisler ('Robert'). The other two members were the British seaman and trade unionist George Hardy (1884–1966), who just went by 'George' when undercover, and the Scot Alexander Massie (1905–1947, 'Burns') presenting the Youth International, who would stay for less time than the others. They were a diverse group. Apart from Hardy, who, together with his second wife, had been working in China for the Pan-Pacific Trade Union Secretariat since September 1927, first in Hankou and from the end of that year in Shanghai (before being sent to Hamburg and South Africa as president of the International of Seafarers and Harbour Workers), they lacked any experience of China.⁹ None of them spoke the language. For their

---

7 Ruth Werner, *Sonya's Report: The Fascinating Autobiography of One of Russia's Most Remarkable Secret Agents,* trans. Renate Simpson, London: Chatto & Windus, 1991, 65. For a collective portrait of the Kuczynskis – a family of Communist intellectuals – composed, regrettably, without recourse to the Soviet sources, see John Green, *A Political Family: The Kuczynskis, Fascism, Espionage and the Cold War,* London: Routledge, 2017.

8 Takeshi Onimaru, 'Shanghai Connection: The Construction and Collapse of the Comintern Network in East and Southeast Asia', *Southeast Asian Studies* 5:1, 2016, 115–33, at 118.

9 George Hardy, *Those Stormy Years: Memories of the Fight for Freedom on Five Continents,* London: Lawrence & Wishart, 1956. The author is very reticent about China, saying nothing about working undercover or the concrete circumstances of his work there, confining himself to anecdote and general observation and portraying above all the brutal social chasm between Chinese and foreigners.

information about the country and its politics, they relied on their rare contacts with the leaders of the CCP, on internal party documents, often translated only in part or with considerable delay, or simply on the press.[10] Local communications were thus dependent on the variable quality of the translators made available by the Chinese comrades, the Far Eastern Bureau having none of its own.[11] Misunderstandings arose not only from the difficulty of finding the right equivalent in one language for a term in the other, but also from terms' varying in meaning in differing contexts.[12] When, for example, the ECCI asked what the Chinese comrades meant when they said that they wanted to 'professionalize', a representative of the Far Eastern Bureau replied: 'This business of "professionalization" is very simple. There's nothing to worry about at all. It's just the idea that every comrade should be in employment and not depend on a party allowance, except of course when this is unavoidable. But why this is called "professionalization", God only knows.'[13] Contact with Moscow was maintained by post, which took several weeks, bringing great delay, or telegram, in sensitive cases sent in code. Documents from the Tenth ECCI Plenum of July 1929 trickled through only in late September and early October,[14] meaning that the bureau was late in implementing the new course in the Chinese party.

Initiated at the Sixth World Congress in 1928, the Comintern's left turn had been given a further twist by the Tenth Plenum. Outside the party, all members were now obliged to take up the struggle against social democracy, while inside it a struggle against 'right deviationists' was to be conducted. In consequence, Bukharin was removed from the leadership of the Comintern in April 1929, losing his position on the ECCI Presidium, and a little later his place in the Politburo of the Russian party. He was now accused of 'right deviationism', the offence

---

10 Letter 2 from I. A. Rylsky to the Eastern Secretariat of the ECCI, Shanghai, 4 June 1929; and letter from the Far Eastern Bureau to the Politburo of the CC of the CCP, Shanghai, October 1929, in Leutner et al., eds, *KPdSU(B)*, vol. 3, *1927–1931*, part 1, 700–2 and 784–800, esp. 787–8.

11 Alexander M. Grigoriev, 'The Far Eastern Bureau of the ECCI in China, 1929–1931', in Leutner et al., *Chinese Revolution*, 156–65, at 160.

12 Steve Smith, 'The Curse of Babel: International Communism and the Barriers of Language', unpublished paper, 2017. I thank the author for making this available to me.

13 Letter from the Far Eastern Bureau to the ECCI, Shanghai, 21 November 1929, in Leutner, *KPdSU(B)*, vol. 3, part 1, 818–27, at 825.

14 Ibid.

with which he himself had charged 'former representatives of the ECCI, such as Borodin, Roy, and others' not a year before, at the Sixth Congress of the Chinese Communist Party, held not far from Moscow. He had also accused the Chinese party of 'putschism', a leftist error.[15]

One of those who had to see through the implementation of the new line in China was Gerhart Eisler, of all people, who had earlier been relieved of his party functions in Germany, as a 'conciliator', and sent to Moscow, where he distanced himself from his former comrades. His mission to China was undoubtedly intended as a test, and he found himself recalled and appointed to a post in the Moscow apparatus in 1931. In her memoirs, Rosa Meyer-Leviné (1890–1979) – widow of Eugen Leviné, the executed leader of the Bavarian Soviet Republic, and wife of the ailing Ernst Meyer, one of the leaders of the conciliators, the so-called 'middle group' of the KPD – identifies the political tactics behind it: 'That would help disperse the middle group of the party, who were now called "the conciliators".'[16]

Within the Chinese party, it was Li Lisan (1899–1967), the leader newly appointed by Moscow, who had lived in Paris between 1919 and 1921 and then led the party's trade union work in China, who was responsible for implementing the turn, soon overshooting Comintern policy to the left. As early as June 1929, the ECCI representatives in Shanghai thought it worth communicating their criticisms of his positions to the Eastern Bureau in Moscow: 'Li Lisan turns "left and right" upside down. For [him] everyone's a "rightist"', Rylski reported.[17] Believing revolution to be imminent, Li Lisan had decided to go on the offensive, urging party members to public action in demonstrations and strikes, concentrating the party's work on the proletariat and centralizing party structures. Given the fierce repression, this was an almost certainly suicidal strategy and it led to bitter factional disputes within the party. And it indeed proved to be a disaster, especially in a city like

---

15 Speech by N. I. Bukharin to the First Plenum of the CC of the Chinese CP, Pervomaiskoe, near Moscow, 19 July 1928, in Leutner, *KPdSU(B)*, vol. 3, part 1, 567–8, at 567.

16 Rosa Meyer-Leviné, *Im inneren Kreis: Erinnerungen einer Kommunistin in Deutschland 1920–1930*, ed. Hermann Weber, Cologne: Kiepenheuer und Witsch, 1979, 134.

17 Letter 2 from I. A. Rylski to the Eastern Secretariat of the ECCI, Shanghai, 4 June 1929, in Leutner, *KPdSU(B)*, vol. 3, part 1, 700–2, at 700.

Shanghai, where Communists were targeted not only by the Guomindang but also by foreign police and powerful criminal gangs. There were regular arrests, and many party members resigned or simply melted away.[18]

It also made the work of the ECCI delegation at the Far Eastern Bureau more dangerous. In addition to the external threat, there were also conflicts with the Chinese comrades. The factional struggles in the Russian party, with the stigmatization and exclusion of the Trotskyists and, shortly afterwards, the 'right deviationists', spilt over into every Communist party. Rapid changes of line and shifts in the attribution of blame for supposed political misjudgements made taking political positions dangerous. In addition, the Comintern's new directives in 1929, which called for a sharp upturn in revolutionary activity in what was termed the 'Third Period of capitalism', were not always easy to interpret. Referring to the resolution warning of the dangers of 'right deviation' that the ECCI had sent to the Central Committee of the CCP in October, a Chinese cadre noted that

> While [Zhou Enlai] was discussing the text of the resolution with us, he was very hesitant about how precisely to take it. We returned again and again to the words 'high tide', and even studied the Russian text. Since the Russian original word (*pod'em*) had the connotation of both 'high tide' and 'on the rise', [Zhou] finally decided to translate it as 'rising tide' (in Chinese [gao-zhang]), explaining that the translation 'high tide' ran the risk of being misinterpreted as 'climax' and could easily lead to a repetition of the old putschist line.[19]

Caution, however, was no protection against criticism. For example, the ECCI delegation in Shanghai sent to Moscow a resolution on the decisions of the Tenth ECCI Plenum in which they accused the CCP of opportunism and of 'very often deviating from the Bolshevik line'.[20] At

---

18 On the politics, organizational structure and survival techniques of the Shanghai party after Chiang Kai-shek's coup, see Patricia Stranahan, *Underground: The Shanghai Communist Party and the Politics of Survival, 1927–1937*, Lanham, MD: Rowman & Littlefield, 1998.

19 Cited in Stranahan, *Underground*, 70.

20 Resolution of the Far Eastern Bureau of the ECCI on the Decisions of the Tenth ECCI Plenum, Shanghai, October 1929, in Leutner, *KPdSU(B)*, vol. 3, part 1, 779–84, at 782.

its meeting of 6 December 1929, the Political Bureau of the Chinese party did not let the accusation go unanswered, Li Lisan commenting that 'the Far Eastern Bureau do not yet fully understand the problems in China. These we must explain to them,'[21] while Zhou Enlai accused the bureau of exhibiting a 'conciliationist spirit'.[22]

The conflict escalated to the point that all communication between the two sides was broken off, so that the Far Eastern Bureau only found out about the radical left platform adopted by the Chinese leadership after the fact. With the help of the growing soviet movement in the countryside, the positions lost in the cities were to be won back. Overestimating both the fighting spirit of the workers' and peasants' movement and the effectiveness of partisan warfare, the CCP called on the Red Army to attack the Guomindang-ruled cities and on party and trade union organizations in the towns to strike and to rise in revolt. When the predicted revolutionary wave failed to materialize, the Comintern stepped in. Personnel changes on both sides would bring about political corrections: in October, Pavel Mif was installed as head of the Far Eastern Bureau, while Li Lisan was removed from the leadership of the Chinese party around the turn of 1930/31. He was replaced by the twenty-six-year-old Wang Ming (real name Chen Shaoyu, 1904–1974), a protégé of Mif's and rising star of the Comintern. He stood at the head of the '28 Bolsheviks', the new leadership group made up of students returned from Moscow. A group of Soviet military personnel were also posted to Shanghai for the first time. They were attached to the Far Eastern Bureau, a sign of Moscow's fresh commitment to strengthening party and military in the soviet bases of the countryside.

Smashing of the Comintern Network

The rebuilding of the Chinese party and of the Comintern and Profintern apparatus at the turn of the 1930s was a slow and laborious process. In contrast to the rural areas, which saw the development of the soviet

---

21 Excerpt from the minutes of a meeting of the Politburo of the CC of the CCP, Shanghai, 6 December 1929, in Leutner, *KPdSU(B)*, vol. 3, part 1, 832–9, at 835.
22 Ibid., 836.

movement under Mao Zedong, a movement that relied on peasant guerrilla warfare rather than working-class struggle, the party shrank in the cities. According to a report by 'Robert' (Gerhart Eisler) in August 1930, the CCP had barely 200 members in Hankou, a party stronghold until the 1927 coup, and the red unions, 150.[23] Only with difficulty did the Far Eastern Bureau and the party centre in Shanghai maintain communication with party sections, using a courier network.[24] They had great difficulty in finding reliable people who knew the local languages and would not stick out in the field. What is more, losses were high: 'As a rule, fifty percent of couriers [fall] into the hands of the enemy and are lost to work,' Mif reported to Moscow.[25] One reason for this was the brutal campaign of repression launched by the Guomindang, with the support of the foreign authorities, in 1931, and the greater police powers now available to them in the Shanghai region. For 1931 also saw the Guomindang conclude an agreement with both the authorities of the French concession and the International Settlement Police that allowed Nationalist agents to enter the concessions and make arrests there. The foreign police forces also agreed to assist the Guomindang in every way in their campaign against the Communists. Party members no longer had any refuge: they could be picked up anywhere, at any time.[26]

As if the situation were not already difficult enough, by January 1931 Gerhart Eisler had to leave Shanghai in a hurry, with the police on his tail, though this was only the beginning of a year that would prove catastrophic for the Comintern apparatus. One position fell after another, like dominoes, following the early arrests of a number of key figures. The next twelve months would see the Chinese party decimated, the OMS station in Shanghai exposed and the South East Asian network centred on that city closed down. For the Far Eastern Bureau, with its ECCI delegation and its Pan-Pacific Trade Union Secretariat, it would mean a year-long break from work.[27] The first blow fell on 21 April

23 Letter from B. A. Vasiliev (making reference to two reports of Eisler's) to V. M. Molotov, Moscow, 16 August 1930, in Leutner, *KPdSU(B)*, vol. 3, part 2, 1229–30.

24 Alexander M. Grigoriev, 'The Far Eastern Bureau', 156–65, at 163–4.

25 Letter from the Far Eastern Bureau ('Wilhelm', i.e. Pavel Mif) to the ECCI, Shanghai, 28 March 1931, in Leutner, *KPdSU(B)*, vol. 3, part 2, 1668–88, at 1683.

26 Stranahan, *Underground*, 107–8.

27 On the difficulties faced by the staff of the Pan-Pacific Trade Union Secretariat, in Shanghai in particular, see Josephine Fowler, *Japanese and Chinese Immigrant Activists:*

1931, with the arrest of Gu Shunzhang (1904–1935), head of the special department of the Chinese party's central committee, whose hoodlum looks, regular nightclubbing and occupation as a street magician belied his important security and intelligence role. Gu gave away many names and addresses, resulting in a huge wave of arrests by the Guomindang authorities, who netted cadre as well as ordinary party members; by the end of 1934, party membership in Shanghai had fallen to 450.[28] At leadership level, Gu's betrayal led to the arrest of Xiang Zhongfa (1880–1931, 'Te Sheng'), appointed general secretary of the Central Committee of the CCP by Pavel Mif in 1928, and a member of the ECCI Presidium. Xiang was, however, by then disillusioned and corrupt, and had already been ousted from the party leadership. He immediately testified against the party, a betrayal that did not save him from being murdered by the Guomindang. Other top party leaders were able to flee Shanghai for the soviet zone of Jiangxi in good time, leaving seven of the party's savings books with a representative of the Far Eastern Bureau for safekeeping.

In the meantime, the two Soviet military advisers, who had been in contact with Gu, had hurried away, their homes closed up. The apartment used for the Chinese party's meetings with the Far Eastern Bureau and the OMS was also hastily vacated. In June, the remaining eight or nine foreign staff of the Far Eastern Bureau were recalled, alongside Pavel Mif and his wife 'Lilli', employed by the bureau as a political instructor, and Georgi Bespalov (1904–1967, 'Willi'), who had replaced Alexander Massie at the end of 1929. The Asian staff responsible for translations and courier services, on the other hand, had to remain where they were. The Polish-born Russian Lydia Volynskaya (1901–1937, 'Rosa'), Rylski's wife and technical secretary to the Bureau, left for Moscow on 12 June, taking with her the latest correspondence and a number of files. Rylski himself, whose passport had expired, was able to leave only in August, but succeeded in escaping undetected. The two Americans, Charles Krumbein (1897–1947, 'Stewart', 'Kennedy'), a former student of the International Lenin School, and his wife Margaret Undjus ('Daisy' and 'Alice'), both of whom worked for the Profintern,

---

Organizing in American and International Communist Movements, 1919–1933, New Brunswick, NJ: Rutgers University Press, 2007, 76–83.

28 Stranahan, *Underground*, 122. By mid-March 1927 (before the massacre) membership in Shanghai had climbed to 4,400: Stephen A. Smith, *A Road Is Made: Communism in Shanghai 1920–1927*, Richmond, UK: Curzon Press, 2000, 168.

stayed behind for the time being.[29] By 20 July at the latest, however, they too had arrived in Moscow, together with Zidor Stolyar, the last of the union representatives at the Far Eastern Bureau, who thus brought to an abrupt end his second mission to China (where he had been known as 'Jack' or 'Leon').[30]

On 1 June 1931 came another arrest that again brought a chain of others in its train, paralysing the Shanghai OMS station and its network and causing great alarm in Moscow. It all began in Singapore, where Comintern employee Joseph Ducroux (1904–1980) fell into the hands of the police,[31] an arrest whose consequences would be as devastating for the Comintern as Gu's had been for the Chinese party. The young Frenchman, who had joined the Young Communists at the age of nineteen and been sent to England on behalf of the party in 1924, had been posted to Marseille in 1925, where he supported Roy in sending his newspaper and other Communist literature to India. Since 1926, he had been working on and off for the Comintern in Asia, first among the French sailors and military in Shanghai, as an instructor for the Organization Department of the ECCI. In April 1928, he and the rest of the Far Eastern Bureau were called back to Moscow, where the Youth International made him their India specialist in their Far Eastern Department. He then found employment with the OMS, learnt how to write in code, and made lengthy visits to France. He also contributed to *Inprekorr* under the almost comically banal name of 'Jacques Dupont'. In early 1931 he was sent to India, but found himself unable to sail from Marseille as the British authorities refused him a visa. He travelled instead to Shanghai, via Moscow, adopting the identity of 'Serge Lefranc', a poultry trader. There he had instructions to deliver from Moscow before proceeding to India. Before that, however, he had a number of assignments in South East Asia to complete: establishing contact with the Chinese party group in Singapore, selecting capable comrades for

---

29 Fowler, *Japanese and Chinese Immingrant Activists*, 80 and 231.

30 On the work of the Shanghai office of the Pan-Pacific Trade Union Secretariat, Moscow, 5 September 1931, in Leutner, *KPdSU(B)*, vol. 3, part 2, 1819.

31 Laurent Metzger, 'Joseph Ducroux, a French Agent of the Comintern in Singapore (1931–1932)', *Journal of the Malaysian Branch of the Royal Academic Society* 69:1, 1996, 1–20 (which unfortunately omits some archive references); David McKnight, *Espionage and the Roots of the Cold War: The Conspiratorial Heritage*, London: Frank Cass, 2002, 119–20; Sophie Quinn-Judge, *Ho Chi Minh: The Missing Years, 1919–1941*, Berkeley: University of California Press, 2003, 149 and 184.

training at the KUTV, and making a search in Shanghai and Hong Kong for the missing Comintern instructor Jean Cremet (1892–1973), a Frenchman like him. This last task had been entrusted to him by Alexander Abramovich, Moscow head of the OMS. The Comintern had entirely lost touch with 'the little redhead', as Cremet was affectionately called, as if the earth had swallowed him up.

Cremet's story illustrates both the adventurous and the precarious aspects of a transnational life in the service of the Comintern. It also highlights the difficulty of resigning one's post once privy to the internal secrets of the Comintern apparatus. This was especially the case for those who worked for the OMS. When Margarete Buber-Neumann first undertook a mission for the OMS in the early 1930s, she was aware that she was now 'bound, for better or worse, to a far-reaching underground apparatus and so limited in her freedom of movement, both physical and mental'.[32] For the OMS functioned like a secret service, and its agents knew about the transfers of Comintern funds, the secret codes, the encryption systems, the radio technology, the contact addresses, the safe houses, the intelligence contacts, the channels of communication between Communist parties and Soviet embassies. Cremet had been one of these travellers of the revolution since his conviction *in absentia*, in Paris, in 1927, of industrial espionage on behalf of the Soviet Union; an activity he described in the PCF's newspaper *L'Humanité* (14 May 1927) as no less than the duty of every class-conscious worker in the struggle against the bourgeoisie.[33] Before being sent to China in late 1929, he had worked for the Comintern's Budgetary Commission in Moscow as 'Jean Thibaud', having already travelled halfway around the world under constantly changing identities, with assignments in Berlin, Switzerland, Italy and Czechoslovakia, and likely in Tunisia, China, Norway, Sweden and Denmark as well. In April 1929 he was back again

---

32 Margarete Buber-Neumann, *Von Potsdam nach Moskau: Stationen eines Irrwegs*, Stuttgart: Deutsche Verlags-Anstalt, 1957, 350.

33 Cremet's adventurous life has been reconstructed by two journalists with the help of his daughter: Roger Faligot and Rémi Kaufer, *As-tu vu Cremet?* Paris: Fayard, 1991; new edn: *L'hermine rouge de Shanghai*, Rennes: Les Portes du Large, 2005. The account is somewhat romanticized and details of sources are inadequate, but is more or less correct in its general lines; cf. José Gotovitch et al., eds, *Komintern: L'histoire et les hommes*; *Dictionnaire biographique de l'Internationale communiste en France, en Belgique, au Luxembourg, en Suisse et à Moscou (1919–1943)*, Paris: Éditions de l'Atelier, 2010, with CD-Rom, the biographical entries now also being available on line: maitron.fr.

in Berlin, before travelling to Italy, Belgium and the Netherlands. He arrived in Shanghai in December, via Vladivostok, disguised as 'Raymond Dillen', a Belgian sales representative. There he made secret contact with Chinese, Vietnamese and Japanese Communists, and possibly acted as an intermediary in the purchase and transport of arms. Then, in late 1930 or early 1931, he disappeared during a stormy passage to Hong Kong, leaving the Far Eastern Bureau unable to make contact with him, whereupon they reported him missing to Moscow.[34] In reality, he had quietly sneaked away from his job, a very rare event in the annals of the Comintern's personnel department! The reasons, it seems, were twofold: first, he disapproved of political developments in the Comintern, and, second, he had had enough of the loneliness that came with illegal work. His escape in mid-1931 was then made possible by the blow suffered by the Comintern apparatus in South East Asia, and the help of André and Clara Malraux.[35]

Ducroux, in any case, was unable to find Cremet. In Shanghai, he met the heads of the Far Eastern Bureau and the local OMS station. Security instructions dictated that he stay at a high-class hotel: the Palace Hotel or the Plaza, and if not, the Burlington. This was no guarantee of agreeable accommodations, not in the opinion of the translator Vera Akimova, at least, for whom the Palace Hotel 'was very expensive despite its unattractive exterior, old-fashioned fixtures, and dark, uncomfortable rooms'.[36] To contact the OMS, Ducroux had to dial a telephone number provided (188-24 in 1928) and ask 'Haber' (a pseudonym of Abramovich's) about some goods or other. He was to say that he came from Michel in Paris 'or something of the sort'.[37] This was how Ducroux

---

34 The editors of the documentary collection on the Comintern in China seem to have confused Ducroux with Cremet, who finds no mention: Leutner, *KPdSU(B)*, vol. 3, part 2, 1013 and 1092.

35 Immortalized by André Malraux in *La condition humaine*, his great novel about the Chinese Revolution and the massacre of Communists in Shanghai, Cremet afterwards lived in Belgium, under a false name, employed as an ordinary worker. He did, however, help smuggle weapons to the Republicans during the Spanish Civil War and later organized a resistance network under Nazi occupation.

36 Vera Vladimirovna Vishniakova-Akimova, *Two Years in Revolutionary China, 1925–1927*, trans. Steven I. Levine, Cambridge, MA: East Asian Research Center, Harvard University, 1971, 145.

37 Letter from A. E. Abramovich to I. A. Piatntsky, Shanghai, 14 August 1928, in Leutner, *KPdSU(B)*, vol. 3, part 2, 581–5, 585.

obtained a contact address for Nguyên Ai Quôc (Ho Chi Minh), in hiding from the French police in Hong Kong as 'Mr. Lai', a Chinese businessman. After two and a half years in Guangzhou, in May 1927 Nguyên had made a hasty departure, travelling to Moscow via Hong Kong, Shanghai and Vladivostok. After much journeying about in Europe, he had returned to Asia in 1928, visiting Thailand, India and Shanghai before arriving in Hong Kong in 1930.

That was where Ducroux met Nguyên, who sent him to Saigon and Hanoi to contact the Vietnamese Communists on his behalf, being unable to make the journey himself on account of security concerns. Thanks to the choice of an unconventional route, Ducroux was able to complete his assignment without incident, although the French police had been informed of his presence in Indochina. According to a British police report, he then returned to Hong Kong on a 'Red' (i.e. Soviet) ship, supposedly to have his passport renewed, before arriving in Singapore on 27 April 1931, presenting himself as S. N. Lefranc, the representative of a Paris ironmongery company. As was customary for the Comintern's undercover operatives, he spent the first few days at the best hotel in town before installing himself in 'a good class European boarding-house'.[38] He then rented an office and employed an Indian to do odd jobs for him.[39] He kept in contact with the OMS station in Shanghai by letter and coded telegram, little knowing that he had come to the attention of the police, who were intercepting his mail and paying his assistant to provide them with his outgoing correspondence. After several weeks of round-the-clock observation, they arrested Ducroux on 1 June.

His arrest came as part of an international police operation against Comintern agents and Communist activists in Asia that resulted in a veritable cascade of arrests and a major blow to Communist networks in South East Asia. A collaborative effort by the imperialist powers of Great Britain, France and the Netherlands, this was only the latest example of a long-standing cooperation.[40] The British Secret Intelligence Service

---

38 According to a report from the Director of Criminal Intelligence of 30 November 1931, Public Record Office London, published in Boon Kheng Cheah, ed., *From PKI to the Comintern, 1924–1941: The Apprenticeship of the Malayan Communist Party; Selected Documents and Discussion*, Ithaca, NY: Cornell University, 1992, 59–61.

39 Metzger, 'Joseph Ducroux', 4.

40 With the transnational turn in history and the declassification of police records related to the colonial territories in question, a number of researchers have begun to

(SIS) corresponded with the security services of Singapore, the Dutch East Indies and British India as well as with their Swiss, French, German and Dutch counterparts. There was also a lively exchange of information within the British administration. The SIS worked closely with MI5, the Colonial Office, the Foreign Office and the Shanghai Municipal Police.[41] Ducroux was meeting with two Chinese Communists when the police arrived, and they too were taken in. A police raid on the Singapore headquarters of the Malayan Communist Party only six hours later saw sixteen men and one woman arrested, most of them Chinese. And, four weeks earlier, on 5 May 1931, the French police in Saigon had also managed a spectacular coup, this time against the leadership of the Indonesian Communist Party. Nguyên was arrested in Hong Kong on 6 June, and it was there, rather more than a year later, on 10 October 1932, that the cycle came more or less to a close with the arrest of the Javan Tan Malaka (1897–1949), a former teacher who had been living in Shanghai since 1929, working on setting up in Rangoon a Comintern liaison centre connecting India and Indonesia.[42] For the historian Takeshi Onimaru, the operation eliminated the Comintern's two most important 'regional facilitators': Tan Malaka spoke Indonesian, Javanese, Dutch, English, German, French, Thai, Tagalog and three varieties of Chinese (Mandarin, Cantonese and Hokkien), and Nguyên was almost equally polyglot.[43] Nguyên himself was responsible for liaison between Shanghai and the Communist movements of French Indochina and British Malaya. Such mediators were essential to the work of the Comintern apparatus in the region, for, without them, the network centred on Shanghai could not have existed. To function at all, the Comintern depended on their linguistic skills, their experience of local underground activity and their ability to get comrades to collaborate

---

look at this wave of arrests in institutional and governmental perspective: Christopher Baxter, 'The Secret Intelligence Service and China: The Case of Hilaire Noulens, 1923–1932', in Christopher Baxter et al., eds, *Britain in Global Politics*, vol. 1, *From Gladstone to Churchill*, Basingstoke, UK: Palgrave Macmillan, 2013, 132–52; Anne L. Foster, 'Secret Police Cooperation and the Roots of Anti-Communism in Interwar Southeast Asia', *Journal of American-East Asian Relations* 4:4, 1995, 331–50; Heather Streets-Salter, 'The Noulens Affair in East and Southeast Asia: International Communism in the Interwar Period', *Journal of American-East Asian Relations* 21:4, 2014, 394–414.

41 Baxter, 'Secret Intelligence Service', 136.
42 Onimaru, 'Shanghai Connection', 127.
43 Ibid.

across cultural and political boundaries. They were the bridge-builders. A similar function was served by 'Hilaire Noulens' and his wife, in charge of the OMS station in Shanghai, who were arrested on 15 June.

The police had tracked the couple down thanks to clues found when Ducroux was arrested: two sheets of headed notepaper with a Shanghai post office box number and the telegraphic address 'Hilanoul, Shanghai'. This information led the Shanghai Municipal Police, who were under British control and who worked with the police of the French concession on the case, to an apartment at 235 Szechuan Road, where they found 'Hilaire Noulens' but nothing incriminating. That man's wife, who called herself Madame M. Motte, was arrested at another apartment the same day. The key to yet another residence on the Nanking Road in the International Concession yielded a treasure trove: numerous documents from the Pan-Pacific Trade Union Secretariat, the Far Eastern Bureau and the OMS, together with the details of a good dozen bank accounts, the list of seized items filling thirty-nine closely written pages.[44] With these documents, the police were able to reconstruct much of the Comintern's activity in China and neighbouring countries, including the courier network and the funding that came from Moscow via the WEB in Berlin. They were also able to arrest a further 276 Chinese party members.[45]

The documents found had all ended up in the same place because of the disorganization of the Comintern's Shanghai apparatus caused by Gu's betrayal. The hurried departure of the personnel of the Far Eastern Bureau and the Pan-Pacific Trade Union Secretariat, together with the Red Aid representative, the American James 'Jim' Dolsen (1885–1988, 'Billy'), had left the 'Noulens' couple almost alone in Shanghai.[46] The resulting concentration of activities radically undermined the customary security arrangements and overloaded both of them with work. For the OMS alone, they had to manage eight mailboxes, seven telegraphic addresses, ten apartments, two offices and a sales kiosk,[47] while, at the

---

44 Stranahan, *Underground*, 115.
45 Streets-Halter, 'Noulens Affair', 400.
46 Where not otherwise stated, what follows relies on the written report the two submitted to Dimitrov's secretariat at the Comintern on their return to the Soviet Union: Moscow, 19 September 1939, RGASPI 495/73/77.
47 A list of the addresses, post office boxes and bank accounts operated by the Noulens/Rüegg couple can be found in Takeshi Onimaru, 'Living "Underground" in

same time, ensuring that no connection could be established between the different addresses. They had also to see to the fitting out of the apartments, from the furniture to the decoration of the walls, and engage the domestic staff expected of 'white' foreigners. And, because Shanghai's property market was in the hands of fewer than half-a-dozen firms, they had to use a different identity for almost every address in order to avoid attracting attention.

Conspiracy as an Occupation

Their duties were not light at the best of times. The OMS station was the channel through which almost all communications passed, between the ECCI and the Far Eastern Bureau, the Far Eastern Bureau and the Chinese party, and between the Communist organizations in the Far East and Comintern offices in Western Europe. The Profintern and the MOPR too sent their directives by radio telegraph via the OMS station, these often being encrypted. Coding and decoding were the responsibility of the OMS, which also had to translate all Russian materials into Chinese, for no Chinese comrade was to be given anything in Russian, in order to keep the connection secret. Yet the Russian military advisers, and even some members of the Far Eastern Bureau (such as Mif and Rylski) spoke only Russian. For the Far Eastern Bureau's communications not only with Moscow but also with the Central Committee of the Chinese party (except for the period it spent at the 'Central Revolutionary Base' of Soviet Jianxi in 1933–34) and the Central Committee's Shanghai Bureau, the OMS station used its own radio equipment and its own coders and radio operators. To communicate with the Central Committee in Jiangxi, the less powerful radio station of the CC's Shanghai Bureau was used, which had its own radio operators, coders and translators. Telegrams from the ECCI and the Far Eastern Bureau to the Central Committee of the Chinese party had to be translated from English into Chinese, those in the other direction from Chinese into

---

Shanghai: Noulens and the Shanghai Comintern Network', in Caroline S. Hau and Kasian Tejapira, eds, *Traveling Nation-Makers: Transnational Flows and Movements in the Making of Modern Southeast Asia*, Singapore: National University of Singapore Press, 2011, 96–125.

English. Many were translated twice: first from Chinese to English and then from English to French before being sent on to Moscow, French being the language chiefly used for cipher communications between Moscow and Shanghai in 1933 and 1934.[48]

Even the use of apartments for meetings involved a complex logistics. Public places were too dangerous, but even indoors one had to be careful that no Chinese staff were about, in case they might inform the police. Although foreigners could meet in relative safely, the case of the Noulens showed that they were not immune from arrest. The cooperation recently established between the Guomindang and the foreign security services represented an ever-increasing danger. While the Western police forces had shown interest in Chinese activists only in exceptional cases, and the Chinese, for their part, had ignored foreigners, their new collaboration was especially dangerous to Chinese Communists.[49] Contact with the leading Chinese comrades, threatened by Chiang Kai-shek's 'white terror', was now much more difficult. Direct contacts had to be kept to a minimum and involve the least number of people possible. Otto Braun (1900–1974), a German graduate of the Frunze Military Academy in Moscow, who worked from 1932 to 1933, under the pseudonyms 'Karl Wagner' and 'Li De', as a military adviser and then as an employee and OMS contact at the Far Eastern Bureau in Shanghai, noted in his memoirs that only he and his superior, Arthur Ewert (1890–1959, known in China as 'Harry Berger' or 'Jim') were allowed to meet with the leading Chinese comrades at the secret premises of the Central Committee, which they visited about once a week.[50] 'We were only allowed to enter the house on an agreed sign – for example a lamp on a certain window or a half-drawn curtain in a lighted room and the like.'[51]

---

48 'Einleitung', in Leutner, *KPdSU(B)*, vol. 3, part 1, 55.

49 Wakeman, *Policing Shanghai*, 146.

50 On the adventurous life of Otto Braun, see Frederick S. Litten, 'Otto Braun in Deutschland 1900–1928', *Internationale wissenschaftliche Korrespondenz zur Geschichte der deutschen Arbeiterbewegung* 27:2, 1991, 171–82; Litten, 'Otto Braun's Curriculum Vitae: Translation and Commentary', *Twentieth-Century China* 23:1, 1997, 31–61; and Thomas Kampen, 'Otto Braun auf dem langen Marsch: Die "Chinesischen Aufzeichnungen" und die politischen Hintergründe ihrer Entstehung', *Das neue China* 1, 1993, 42–4.

51 Otto Braun, *A Comintern Agent in China 1932–1939*, trans. Jeanne Moore, London: C. Hurst & Co., 1982, 3.

There they discussed with the secretaries of the Central Committee, 'Bo Gu' (Qin Bangxian, 1907–1946) and 'Luo Fu' (Zhang Wentian, 1900–1976) the acute political and military problems they faced, all the more formidable given the fierce conflict within the Chinese party. 'Both had studied in the Soviet Union and spoke excellent Russian' and Luo Fu also spoke English, 'so we were able to manage without an interpreter'.[52]

Party members known to the police could in any case only venture onto the streets at night, and this was also true of Pavel Mif, former rector of the Communist University of the Toilers of the East, too easily recognizable. As police raids generally took place under cover of darkness, it was otherwise better to hold the meetings during the day. For reasons of security, Chinese comrades were also not to carry any documents of a political nature, which had then to be delivered by special couriers. Handover took place at neutral locations, as couriers were not to know the addresses of the members of the Far Eastern Bureau or other Comintern bodies to whom delivery was made. The transfer of money likewise called for cumbersome security precautions.

Such precautions had been tightened up since the Arcos affair of 1927, when it became known that the British secret services had cracked the Soviet code.[53] Another worrying event was a raid on the Soviet Embassy in Beijing in April 1927, carried out by a Chinese warlord with the approval of the imperialist powers. From then on, the OMS and the Soviet intelligence services were more rigorous in their security measures: no overlap between Soviet intelligence services and foreign Communist parties, either through the recruitment of agents or the provision of logistical support;[54] strict separation between the different apparatuses; reduction to a minimum of contacts between the OMS and Soviet representations abroad.[55] To ensure the flow of funds, the OMS, with the assistance of the KPD, set up a front company in Berlin in 1927, officially owned by Walter Löwenheim (later Lowe, 1896–1977), a

---

52 Braun, *A Comintern Agent in China*, 3.
53 See chapter 6.
54 Jonathan Haslam, *Near and Distant Neighbors: A New History of Soviet Intelligence*, New York: Farrar, Straus and Giroux, 2015, 30.
55 Niels Erik Rosenfeldt, *The 'Special' World: Stalin's Power Apparatus and the Soviet System's Secret Structures of Communication*, vol. 2, Copenhagen: Museum Tusculanum Press/University of Copenhagen, 2009, 231.

member of the German party employed by the Soviet trade representation as an expert on German economic trends.[56]

At the same time, the Shanghai OMS station was reorganized in the wake of the debacle of April 1927. The new head was the long-time OMS staffer and former Comintern emissary Alexander Abramovich ('Albrecht', 'Arno', 'Haber'), who had, in the meantime, been posted to the Soviet embassies in Tallinn and Vienna. His wife, Zelma Bertyn ('Elvira', 1892–?), saw to the encryption, the transfer of money to the Chinese party and the bookkeeping. 'Marin' (the subject of further discussion below) and Paul Rakov (1901–1937), the youngest of the three Rakov brothers, were sent to Shanghai as their assistants.

The new team did not do well, however, their work being hampered by personal feuds. What is more, cooperation between the OMS and the Far Eastern Bureau was poor. In Moscow, Alexander Abramov, operational head of the OMS, soon accused his subordinate Abramovich of incompetence and sloppiness, reporting to Piatnitsky that Abramovich had paid the 'Chinese friends', i.e. the Chinese party, too much, and had had to cut their budget again as a result, causing a great deal of anger and confusion.[57]

Accountable to Piatnitsky, the Comintern's head of finance, for his spending, Abramovich defended himself by reference to the conditions of conspiracy: 'I find it very difficult to meet all the requirements in terms of accounting formalities.' It ought not to be forgotten, he thought, that 'we work after all in a place where conspiracy really means something. I myself introduced receipts, despite all the protests. And we can document all our expenses, with few exceptions. Yet you cannot ask me

---

56 This proved to be a bad choice, as Löwenheim left the KPD that same year and secretly gathered together a group of like-minded people as the Leninistische Organisation, whose goal was to bring about the political renewal of the KPD and to work towards overcoming the split in the workers' movement. From that emerged the Gruppe Neu Beginnen: Jan Foitzig, *Zwischen den Fronten: Zur Politik, Organisation und Funktion linker politischer Kleinorganisationen im Widerstand 1933 bis 1939/40 unter besonderer Berücksichtigung des Exils*, Bonn: Verlag Neue Gesellschaft, 1986; 'Walter Löwenheim' in *Neue Deutsche Biographie* at deutsche-biographie.de (accessed 20 November 2021).

57 A. L. Abramov to I. A. Piatnitsky, Moscow, 3 April 1929, in Leutner, *KPdSU(B)*, vol. 3, part 1, 693–4; see also the letter, from F. J. Kazovskaia [secretary of the Budgetary Commission of the ECCI] to I. A. Piatnitsky, Moscow, 3 April 1929, 694–5.

for half-yearly data or the like, for I have no way of keeping a systematic record.'⁵⁸

Accounting problems of a different kind arose when an employee of the front company went missing with 6,000 dollars. For security reasons, the company had then to be entirely disconnected from the OMS, the operation being entrusted to Hugo Eberlein, the custodian of Comintern funds in Germany and a member of the Comintern's International Control Commission, who was assisted by the Russo-German Friedrich Feyerherd (1897–1937, 'Fritz'), a former employee of the Soviet Embassy in Berlin, who made a special journey to Shanghai in that connection in the autumn of 1928.⁵⁹ July 1929 had seen both Abramovich and 'Marin' ordered back to Moscow, only for them to be sent back to Shanghai in early 1930. This was the situation when 'Marin' took over responsibility for the OMS station in late 1930.⁶⁰ By then, his wife and their son Dmitri had arrived in Shanghai.

Sowing Confusion

In June 1931, then, 'Marin' alias 'Hilaire Noulens' and his wife 'Madame Motte' were arrested. The police found not only the numerous internal documents already mentioned, but also more than a dozen passports, Belgian, French and Canadian, in different names. In the course of the investigation, yet other names they used came to light, notably the supposedly Swiss 'Beuret' and 'Rüegg'. The true identities disguised behind these were never established, but the very confusion that arose regarding them is illuminating, demonstrating on the one hand the

---

58 Letter from A. E. Abramovich to I. A. Piatnitsky, Shanghai, 24 November 1928, in Leutner, *KPdSU(B)*, vol. 3, part 1, 634–9, at 634.

59 Letter from I. A. Piatnitsky to A. E. Abramovich, Moscow, 15 November 1928, in Leutner, *KPdSU(B)* vol. 3, part 1, 633–4; and see also the letter from Abramovich to Piatnitsky, Shanghai, 14 August 1928, 581–5; letter from Abramovich to Piatnitsky, Shanghai, 24 November 1928, 634–9, at 637; excerpt from a letter of F. J. Kazovskaia to Piatnitsky, Moscow, on or before 3 April 1929, 694–5, at 695.

60 His appointment had been suggested by the Far Eastern Bureau, which accused Abramovich not only of incompetence but of 'direct harm' to the work of the party: letter from the Far Eastern Bureau of the ECCI to the Little Commission of the ECCI Secretariat, Shanghai, 20 October 1930, in Leutner, *KPdSU(B)*, vol. 3, part 2, 1307–10, at 1310.

effort made by the Comintern in the early 1930s to obscure the Soviet origins of the two agents concerned, and so minimize any suggestion of Soviet citizens' involvement in Communist subversion abroad, and on the other how effectively the Comintern – in the person of Willi Münzenberg – was able to stage an international campaign that caused a worldwide stir.

It was through their son Dmitri Moiseenko that researchers first learnt that the two arrested in Shanghai were in fact Tatiana Moiseenko-Velikaia (1891–1964) and Jakov Rudnik (1894–1963).[61] They had probably met in 1925, in Vienna, where Rudnik was officially a member of the Soviet Embassy staff until 1927, although actually the head of the OMS station there, one of his duties being to maintain communications with Georgi Dimitrov's Balkan Federation.[62] Elisabeth Poretsky, the wife of a renegade Soviet agent, the Galician-born 'Ignaz Reiss' (in reality Nathan Poretsky), murdered by the NKVD in the environs of Lausanne, also knew him there.[63] The only person to recall him in a memoir, she describes him as not without charm, but highly strung and excitable.[64]

Moiseenko and Rudnik could hardly have come from more different milieux, she coming from an aristocratic background in St Petersburg, while he was the son of a poor Jewish family from near Kiev. She had specialized in mathematics at a girls' high school, while he had received

---

61 It was the Swiss researcher Fritz Nicolaus Platten whom Dmitri Moiseenko first put on the trail, and thus also the present author: F. N. Platten, ' "A Struggle for Life and Death": The Rüegg Affair 1931', *Swiss Journal for History* 41:1, 1991, 52–62. On the basis on this information and aided by the documents that Platten found in Moscow, Frederick S. Litten carried out further research in police files: F. S. Litten, 'The Noulens Affair: Research Note', *China Quarterly* 138, June 1994, 492–512. In the meantime, I too had explored the story, drawing chiefly on Comintern records: Brigitte Studer, *Un parti sous influence: Le Parti communiste suisse, une section du Comintern, 1931 à 1939*, Lausanne: L'Âge d'Homme, 1994, 530–41. My conversations with Dmitri Moiseenko in Moscow and the documentation he had collected and generously made available to me were extremely helpful. Since then, further research has filled out and added detail to the picture. The present study is the first to set the affair in the broader context of the Comintern, its networks and agents.

62 Barry McLoughlin, Hannes Leidinger and Verena Moritz, *Kommunismus in Österreich 1918–1938*, Innsbruck: StudienVerlag, 2009, 104, 119 and 174.

63 Reiss, or 'Ludwig', who had joined the Polish CP in 1919 and soon afterwards began to work for the GRU and then the GPU, had with Sneevliet's help sought to warn Trotsky of the plan to kill him, and had broken publicly with the Comintern.

64 Elisabeth K. Poretsky, *Our Own People: A Memoir of 'Ignace Reiss' and His Friends*, London: Oxford University Press, 1969, 62–3.

a commercial education. Both had joined the Bolshevik Party in 1917. Moiseenko worked first as a teacher and then at the People's Commissariat for Education, before going on to teach at various universities (including a stint in the Department of Economics at the University of Leningrad). She learnt Georgian and Turkish, and in 1923 went to Turkey as a teacher, good camouflage for her work for the Foreign Department (INO) of the GPU. Rudnik too worked for the INO, from 1922 to 1924. At the time of the Bolshevik seizure of power, he had been political commissar of a regiment of the Petrograd garrison and later an officer in the Red Army, and, during the civil war, he had worked for the Cheka at different locations on the front. He was then sent undercover to France, where he was arrested and spent two years in prison. In 1924, he transferred to the OMS. It was during a mission in Vienna, where he used the pseudonym 'Luft', that he also began to use the name 'Marin'; later, in China, he came also to use 'Henri'. Moiseenko for her part called herself 'Henrietta' and 'Koti'.

Immediately upon their arrest, an international exercise was launched to sow confusion about their identities, an effort maintained for years, and indeed decades. The security measures adopted by the Comintern in 1927 provided that all Soviet Comintern agents were in future to be furnished with foreign passports and were not in any circumstances to be identified as Soviet citizens.[65] As intelligence operatives and loyal employees of the Comintern, M. and Mme Noulens – the name used by the authorities, *faute de mieux* – would have had no higher priority than to keep their true nationality a secret. And this was also in their own interest: since the break with the Guomindang, the Soviet Union had no diplomatic representation in China, and citizenship of a democratic, West European polity thus offered better protection. As a result, the OMS station was supposed to be staffed only by people who could pass for West Europeans, as Abramovich, the service's former head had demanded: Germans, French, English, etc., but under no circumstances 'supposed Czechs, Bulgarians, Yugoslavs', only too conceivably Russians with false East European or Balkan passports.[66] The Belgian identities used by the Noulens couple met this requirement, but they soon turned

---

65 Rosenfeldt, *The 'Special' World*, 231.
66 Letter from A. E. Abramovich to I. A. Piatnitsky, Shanghai, 14 August 1928, in Leutner, *KPdSU(B)*, vol. 3, part 2, 581–5, at 585.

out to be false, as the Belgian Foreign Ministry declared. Yet if the two arrestees were not nationals of a state having extraterritorial rights, this meant they were subject to the Chinese courts of the International Settlement, where, under Chinese law, they faced the death penalty. This was a deadly serious game of hide-and-seek.

In the course of the next month, the Comintern machine swung into action. A Swiss identity appeared to be the solution. Since 1926, the local CP had had a contact in the Basel police and residents' registration office who could provide them with official passport application forms, blank passports and even data on passport holders. Depending on what was required, a person could be found whose details were identical or at least similar to those required to figure on a purloined or counterfeit passport.[67] There was also a general expectation that party members would unquestioningly make their own passports available to the organization if they were needed for another comrade. These could then be adapted as required at the OMS's counterfeiting workshops in Moscow, Paris or Berlin. When the Gestapo raided this last in May 1933, they discovered, among other things, genuine stamps and blank passports from Switzerland.[68] It was not then entirely by happenstance that Dimitrov was found to be carrying a passport issued in Basel when arrested. It was with a Swiss passport in the name of Liliane-Edith Bosshardt that Ruth Fischer travelled on a party mission to England in 1924, and Togliatti and his wife used Swiss passports in Italian names when they travelled from Paris to Moscow in June 1937 to receive the instructions for his mission in Spain. On his journeys to France and Spain between 1935 and 1939, the German Franz Dahlem had two Swiss passports in addition to a Danish and a Luxembourg passport. Well-known Swiss Communists who needed to travel incognito also used forged Swiss passports: Jules and Jenny Humbert-Droz, for example, travelled to Spain on the Comintern's behalf in 1931 on a passport in the name of Bauer supposedly issued in Basel.[69]

---

67 Studer, *Un parti*, 190.

68 Siegfried Grundmann, 'Richard Großkopf und die kommunistische Paßfälscherorganisation', *Internationale wissenschaftliche Korrespondenz zur Geschichte der deutschen Arbeiterbewegung* 40, 2004, 423–64; Studer, *Un parti*, 190.

69 Jules Humbert-Droz, *Mémoires*, vol. 2, *De Lénine à Staline: Dix ans au service de l'Internationale communiste, 1921–1931*, Neuchâtel: À La Baconnière, 1971, 455.

In the case of the Noulens, a Swiss couple of good repute with a child of roughly the same age and who lived abroad had to be found. On 3 August, the arrestees were able to inform the authorities that their names were Germain Xavier Alois Beuret and his wife Gabrielle Marthe, both Swiss citizens. M. 'Beuret' was even able to recite their passport number to Patrick Givens, a special branch officer with the Shanghai Municipal Police. This information they had received through their Comintern-appointed lawyer, Dr Friedrich Wilhelm. On that same day, he informed the Swiss consul-general that his clients wished to avail themselves of their supposed Swiss citizenship to avoid being handed over to the Chinese authorities. This move delayed the transfer to Chinese custody of the two 'Belgian Reds', as they were called by the *Shanghai Times* of 4 August, but it was ultimately unsuccessful, for inquiries by the Swiss Federal Police quickly revealed that the real Beuret, a representative of the Chemische Industriegesellschaft Basel, was living with his family in Brussels.[70] The Swiss consul-general, too, had come to the conclusion that something was wrong: these Swiss knew almost nothing about Switzerland and did not understand the dialect of the city they supposedly hailed from! The authorities of the International Concession then declared that the case fell outside their jurisdiction and handed the couple over to the Chinese authorities, a possible precedent carefully noted by the Swiss consul-general, who commented that it showed what Swiss citizens could expect if the extraterritorial jurisdiction were one day to be done away with.[71] The Noulens being accused of an offence against the security of the state in time of war (Japan having embarked on its occupation of Manchuria in September 1931), Chinese law provided that their case fell under military jurisdiction, and they were transferred to Nanjing, 300 kilometres north-west of Shanghai, since 1927 the capital of the Chinese Republic and headquarters of the Guomindang.

Under the aegis of that maestro of propaganda Willi Münzenberg, the Comintern immediately launched an international campaign to save the 'union official and his wife' arrested in China. It was Louis Gibarti (the Hungarian László Dobos) at the Berlin office of the League Against

---

[70] The Swiss Federal Archives in Bern hold several files relating to this incident: E2200.290A#1000/447#1087*, E2200.290A#1000/447#1088*, E2001C#1000/1533#1899*, E4320B#1000/851#150* and J1.217*.

[71] Consul-General in Shanghai to the Swiss Department of Foreign Affairs, 9 July 1932, BAR E2200.290A#1000/447#1087*.

Imperialism who was responsible for the initial coordination, as MI5 would discover.[72] Neither the earliest letters of protest from trade unions nor the appeals in *Inprekorr* named the arrested persons. That changed in mid-September, when the Communist press began to speak of two Swiss, 'Paul and Gertrud Rüegg', a new identity probably organized by Fritz Platten, a Swiss who had emigrated to the Soviet Union in 1923 but who in August 1931 had spent a considerable time in Zurich while engaging in an intensive exchange of coded telegrams with the OMS in Moscow.[73] The new tactic had the advantage that – unlike the 'Beurets' – no inconvenient revelations about their true so-called Rüeggs' place of residence were to be feared. On the other hand, they would now inevitably be labelled Communists. The Zurich-born Paul Emil Rüegg (1898–1942) had been a youthful comrade of Münzenberg's during the First World War and was known to the Swiss authorities as a 'Bolshevik agitator'. Together with his German wife, Gertrude Fischbach (1895–?), he had been living in the Soviet Union for several years.[74]

By October, the Communist press across the world had taken up the new names and Münzenberg's campaign was in full swing. Countless letters of protest from Communist mass organizations (such as the Red Aid) kept up the momentum. As always, Münzenberg had mobilized his contacts to form an international defence committee (chaired by Henri Barbusse) and to lend their signatures to petitions: from Albert Einstein to Paul Klee, Maxim Gorki, John Heartfield, Egon Erwin Kisch and journalist and writer Agnes Smedley, from Walther Gropius and Ludwig Mies van der Rohe (past and present directors of the Bauhaus), to Nicaraguan guerrilla leader Augusto Sandino and Madame Sun Yat-sen (Song Qingling).[75]

The Swiss government were sceptical from the start, and by no means believed in the Noulens' new identity. Yet, so long as any uncertainty persisted, they had to err on the side of caution, and found themselves

---

72 Summary of the MI5 traces up to January 1933, British National Archives, Kew, KV-2-1401 (Gibarti).

73 Platten, 'Ein Kampf', 58–9.

74 The two were arrested in 1937 and Paul Rüegg was later shot. Gertrude Rüegg-Fischbach survived her years in the camps and was able to leave for Germany in the 1950s.

75 Frederick S. Litten, 'Einstein and the Noulens Affair', *British Journal for the History of Science* 24, 1991, 465–7.

obliged to tread all the more carefully when the Communist lawyer Jean Vincent (1906–1989) of Geneva made representations on behalf of Paul Rüegg's mother and news spread in the press that the couple had been sentenced to death. However, when, in late 1931, the Swiss federal prosecutor's office managed to find an old photograph of Paul Rüegg, it became clear beyond doubt that they were dealing with a stolen identity.

The Comintern, for its part, was not ready to give up. As Red Aid Switzerland declared in Basel's Communist daily, the international defence committee did not accept the decision of the Swiss authorities, and had therefore decided to 'send the lawyer appointed in the case to China, to take the matter up there and to undertake Comrade Rüegg's defence directly on the spot'.[76] In reality, the client and organizer of everything was Willi Münzenberg, while the lawyer was the twenty-six-year-old Jean Vincent already mentioned. He travelled to Shanghai via Moscow, while his (first) wife Jacqueline (1906–1997) followed him by the same route in July. She brought with her two new passports, hidden in the cover of a book, though they would not in the end be used. The fact that both travelled armed indicates that their mission was not without danger.[77]

Their journey was in vain. Though Chiang Kai-shek had brought the two prisoners before a civil court rather than a military tribunal (since, according to the Swiss consul-general, it had had to be recognized that the case was not in fact subject to military jurisdiction),[78] foreign lawyers had no right of audience at the Nanjing court where the trial eventually took place on 10 August 1932. The sentences were harsh, 'Hilaire Noulens' being condemned to death, and 'Madame Noulens' to life imprisonment, though the death sentence would be commuted to life imprisonment immediately afterwards.

His efforts to gain the right of audience unavailing, Vincent was ready to return to Switzerland in May, but Münzenberg told him to 'stick with

---

76 Rote Hilfe Schweiz, 'Verstärkt und verbreitert die Aktion zur Rettung von Paul Rüegg und seiner Frau!', *Basler Vorwärts*, 21 January 1932, front page.

77 According to the oral testimony of Jacqueline Zurbrugg, Vincent's former wife, given to the author in Geneva, 30 April 1990.

78 Report of the Swiss Consul-General in Shanghai to the Foreign Affairs Division of the Federal Foreign Ministry, 9 July 1932, BAR E2200.290A#1000/447#1087*.

it'.⁷⁹ When bribery failed, Vincent telegraphed again to Berlin on 7 October 1932 asking for permission to come home: 'Wish to leave October 15 urgently awaiting money. Vincent.'⁸⁰ In early November, Jaqueline and Jean Vincent were at long last able to leave Shanghai.

Vincent had not been alone in his efforts. The Comintern had also mobilized Song Qingling, always prepared to cooperate with the Communists, whose good connections had also allowed her to mediate in other cases. She had brought them both warm clothes, and it was she who had smuggled into prison the information about their new identities as 'Paul and Gertrud Rüegg', or at least bribed a Chinese guard to do it. She had also tried to negotiate their release with Chiang Kai-shek, without success.⁸¹ The Chinese Communist Party, which had withdrawn to the Jiangxi region, was also drawn in, and in July 1932 it made an offer over the radio to swap the prisoners for two missionaries it held. That plan too was unsuccessful.⁸²

The customary propaganda media were also called upon. For the duration of the 'Rüegg Trial' (as Communist idiom would have it from October 1931 on), the ECCI provided the magazine *China Forum* with money from the annual contingency fund, making a payment of 500 dollars, for example, in August.⁸³ The publication

---

79 Letter from Willi Münzenberg, Berlin, to Jean Vincent, Palace Hotel Shanghai, 28 May 1932, BAR J1.217#1991/44#55*.

80 The telegrams between Münzenberg and Vincent were intercepted by the British authorities and forwarded to the Swiss consul. According to the Swiss consul-general's report to the Division of Foreign Affairs of 21 October 1932 it was only then that Vincent received the green light: 'Homeward journey agreed to' – BAR E2200.290A#1000/447#1087*.

81 Report from K. Lesse to the OMS, Moscow, 14 January 1932, in Leutner, *KPdSU(B)*, vol. 3, part 1, 147–61, at 153.

82 Platten, 'Ein Kampf', 61. The Communist daily paper *Basler Vorwärts* reported this offer by the Chinese Soviet government only on 27 November 1932. The response prompted H. C. Woodhead to comment in the *Shanghai Mercury and Evening Post* of 29 November 1932: 'The Chinese government naturally ignored this offer. It cannot make the safety of foreign missionaries and travellers in the interior conditional upon the immunity of communist conspirators who are avowedly working to achieve its overthrow.'

83 Excerpt from the minutes of the meeting of the Political Commission of the Political Secretariat of the ECCI, Moscow, 3 August 1932, in Leutner, *KPdSU(B)*, vol. 3, part 1, 229. Published in English and Chinese, the magazine *China Forum* appeared in Shanghai from 13 January to 13 August 1932 and then from February 1933 to January 1934.

informed its Communist-sympathizing readership about the brutality and excesses of the 'White Terror' directed against Communists and left activists by the Guomindang and the gangster bands, the Communist armies' successes against the Nationalist government, the achievements of the Soviet government in Jiangxi, the Japanese attack on Shanghai in January 1932, and, of course, the Noulens/Rüegg affair.[84]

Improvised Cooperation Between Apparatuses

The arrest of Rudnik and Moiseenko meant that the Shanghai office of the Pan-Pacific Trade Union Secretariat had to close down.[85] The OMS station itself remained unstaffed until early 1932, and documentary exchange between Moscow and the Chinese party was halted. It was Richard Sorge (1895–1944, 'Ramsay') who, in the meantime, took over the liaison function. Ostensibly a newspaper correspondent, he led an ordinary, public life, unlike the two arrested chiefs of station, using his own name and enjoying close relationships with local diplomats and business people, though he had, in fact, been working in Shanghai on behalf of Soviet military intelligence since the winter of 1929–30.[86] Lacking the appropriate experience, he had to take over responsibility for the local *rezidentura* in an emergency.[87] This overlap of roles was a breach of the standard security requirements, even contact between party members and 'neighbours', as the Comintern called those who worked for Soviet military intelligence, being out of the question. Sorge, however, was now linked with Moscow-based OMS staffer Karl Lesse (1894–?), the German former seaman hastily despatched to Shanghai in August 1931, and with Rylski, the only member of the Far Eastern Bureau remaining in the city.[88] Lesse succeeded

---

84 Ruth Price, *The Lives of Agnes Smedley*, New York: Oxford University Press, 2005, 225. The Chinese party responded to the 'White Terror' with a 'Red Terror' (although not on the same scale). So it was that not only traitors and 'provocateurs' but the family of Gu Shunzhang were brutally murdered: Stranahan, *Underground*, 118–21.

85 Resolution of the Executive Bureau of the RILU, Moscow, 5 September 1931, in Leutner, *KPdSU(B)*, vol. 3, part 2, 1819–21, at 1820.

86 Frederick W. Deakin and George R. Storry, *The Case of Richard Sorge*, New York: Harper & Row, 1966.

87 Haslam, *Near and Distant Neighbors*, 60.

88 Following his posting to China, Lesse was appointed chief of the OMS station in Vienna. On him, see his file in the British National Archives at Kew, KV 2/1399; and

in partially restoring the flow of policy documents to the Chinese party, through the German bookshop Zeitgeist, a stopgap until a direct radio connection with Moscow could be re-established.[89] This bookshop on the banks of the Suzhou River, seemingly part of Münzenberg's business empire, was a meeting place for leftist intellectuals and an excellent place for people to leave messages for each other secreted in books.[90] Its manager at that time was the young Irene Weitemeyer (1907–1978), who had studied at an international cadre school in the Soviet Union before going to work for the ECCI and the People's Commissariat for Foreign Trade.[91] It was in Moscow that she had met her Chinese partner.

The real work of rebuilding fell to Rudnik's successor, Nikolai Zedler (1876–1937?), an OMS operative of long standing. He had already done stints in Paris, Brussels, Berlin and Vienna, under the pseudonyms 'Herbert', 'Erwin', 'Kurt' and 'Norsky'. His first task was to restore the links with the Chinese party, the Soviet territories and Korea that had been broken by the exposure of the Noulens couple. He was also expected to re-establish contact with Japan and the Philippines and, if possible, with India and Indochina. To 'legalize' his position – by which the Comintern meant to establish cover for an undercover political operative – he presented himself as a member of the International Music Society and contacted the Shanghai Conservatory and the city's well-known musicians. This led to his finding employment as secretary to a Chinese professor of music who collected ancient Chinese texts on music and theatre. He also organized two performances of Chinese pantomimes, in connection with which he was even interviewed by the American press.[92]

McLoughlin, *Kommunismus*, 385. In Shanghai he probably used the name Oswald Donitz; he came under close observation by the police, prompting his early departure on 25 December 1932: Stranahan, *Underground*, 115.

89 Report from K. Lesse to the OMS, Moscow, 14 January 1932, in Leutner, *KPdSU(B)*, vol. 3, part 1, 147–61, at 150.

90 Chalmers A. Johnson, *An Instance of Treason: Ozaki Hotsumi and the Sorge Spy Ring*, Stanford, CA: Stanford University Press, 1990, 60–1.

91 In the sources, the spelling of the name varies between Weidemeyer, Wiedemeyer and Weitemeier.

92 Report from N. N. Herbert to the International Liaison Department of the ECCI, on his work in Shanghai from 1932 to 1935, Moscow, 29 September 1936, in Leutner, *KPdSU(B)*, vol. 3, part 2, 1306–13, at 1306.

The new head of the Far Eastern Bureau, the German Arthur Ewert mentioned earlier, arrived in September 1932 together with his wife Elise Saborowski, known as Sabo (1886–1939), another employee of the OMS. Ewert was a Comintern veteran.[93] He had lived in Canada in his youth and then returned there on a mission for the Comintern. As a full-timer in the KPD's military apparatus, he was actively involved in preparations for the abortive 'German October' of 1923. He then worked for the ECCI in Moscow, where he was deputy head of the Eastern Secretariat from 1929 to 1931. Ewert's superiors in Moscow were obviously impatient to get things up and running again, and on arriving in Shanghai he found himself asked to submit a plan of work as soon as possible.[94]

In the meantime, Sorge had also had to restore courier communications with Manchuria. Like most of the Germans in his team, he spoke no Chinese, and therefore worked with Chinese who spoke German, having studied in Germany. For security reasons, he could not work with Chinese who spoke Russian, nor, if possible, with anyone who had joined the Communist Party in China. Sorge also kept in touch with the two prisoners – the 'patients' in Comintern terminology – and Vincent the lawyer. He was in contact with Song Qingling, supplying her with the money needed to provide the Noulens with food, legal representation, and, if need be, medical care.[95] It was he, too, who passed money from Moscow on to the 'friends', that is, the Chinese party.[96]

---

93 Hornstein, *Arthur Ewert: A Life for the Comintern*, Lanham, MD: University Press of America, 1993, is unfortunately entirely reliant on the work of others and unreliable in matters of fact. More dependable is Ronald Friedmann, *Arthur Ewert (1890–1959): Der Lebens- und Leidensweg eines deutschen Kommunisten auf drei Kontinenten*, doctoral thesis, University of Potsdam, 2015, available online at publishup.uni-potsdam.de.

94 Directive to Arthur Ewert: To the ECCI Representative Upon Arrival, Moscow, 20 September 1932, in Leutner, *KPdSU(B)*, vol. 3, part 1, 240.

95 Letter from Ramsay (R. Sorge) to 'Mikhail' (Piatnitsky), Shanghai, May 1932, top secret, in Leutner, *KPdSU(B)*, vol. 3, part 1, 201–2 (also published in the journal *Novaia i noveishaia istoriia* [2001], 134–5); report from K. Lesse to the OMS, Moscow, 14 January 1932, ibid., 147–61, at 153–4; Haslam, *Near and Distant Neighbors*, 62.

96 In December 1931 and January 1932 this amounted to $30,000: Telegram from 'Mikhail' (Piatnitsky) to 'Ramsay' (Sorge), for personal attention only, Moscow, 3 May 1932, in Leutner, *KPdSU(B)*, vol. 3, part 1, 196. In 1934, the ECCI budgeted more than $7,400 per month for financial support to the CCP: Telegram from the OMS to N. N.

And it would most likely have been to him that two emissaries from the Intelligence Service of the Fourth Division of the Red Army (or GRU, in the Russian acronym for Main Intelligence Directorate) – one of them the Otto Braun mentioned earlier, as he arrived in post – each delivered $20,000 in May 1932, in order to buy the prisoners' freedom (a technique also employed in other cases).[97]

In addition, Sorge was responsible, behind the scenes, for the publication of the magazine *China Forum*, founded at his suggestion in early 1932. For editor and publisher, he had repeatedly but unsuccessfully suggested Agnes Smedley: 'Instead of which you send us a host of people, some of whom are not very suitable and need another year to get to understand something of the local conditions if ever they learn anything. Why is that? A. [Smedley] would be able to do three times as much in terms of our proposals, which would be three times cheaper.'[98]

In Harold R. Isaacs (1910–1986) Moscow chose another American journalist and China expert who had studied at Columbia University in New York. His extraterritorial status allowed the magazine to be printed in the French sector of the city yet be registered in the United States to evade the Chinese censorship.[99] Isaacs himself, however, did not escape police surveillance. Like many of Shanghai's foreign residents suspected of Communist activities or sympathies, he and his wife, Viola Robinson – a contact of the Noulens couple, according to the police – were kept under close surveillance. In early 1932, the authorities began to open their mail, and in May that year the Shanghai Municipal Police tried to ban the magazine. However, because Isaacs was an American citizen and there was no prohibition on being a Communist in American law, they had to abandon the attempt.[100]

Herbert, top secret, Moscow, 1 July 1934, ibid., 763. Further funding went to the youth federation, the trade unions and International Red Aid.

97 Litten, 'The Noulens Affair', 497. See, for example, the telegram from I. A. Piatnitsky to A. E. Abramovich, Moscow, 6 June 1928, in Leutner, *KPdSU(B)*, vol. 3, part 1, 533, and the letter from I. A. Piatnitsky to A. E. Abramovich, Moscow, 15 November 1928, ibid., 633–4, at 633. There Piatnitsky instructs his colleague to maintain a reserve of $30,000 for purchasing comrades' freedom. For the practicalities and the graduated scale of payments, see Stranahan, *Underground*, 109.

98 Letter from Ramsay (R. Sorge) to 'Mikhail' (Piatnitsky), Shanghai, May 1932, top secret, in Leutner, *KPdSU(B)*, vol. 3, part 1, 201–2.

99 Price, *The Lives*, 224–5.

100 Stranahan, *Underground*, 114–15.

He would edit the 3,500-circulation magazine until it closed in March 1934.[101]

This followed a falling out with the Comintern. Isaacs, who had become sympathetic to Trotskyism, was critical of Comintern policy in both Germany and China. He also rejected the cult of Stalin and refused to put a photo of the Soviet leader on the front page. Conflict with Arthur Ewert, the head of the Far Eastern Bureau, who wanted to take political control of the magazine, was inevitable. Although a very minor episode in the history of the Comintern, it is highly illustrative of the climate of suspicion that spread out from Moscow to afflict the whole of the International, in which everyone soon monitored everyone else. Ewert, who was supposed to ensure the magazine's political purity, was himself under watch. In 1928, he had had to make self-criticism as a 'conciliator' before being entrusted with another role. In China, however, he found himself accused of 'lazy liberal opportunism' and 'a lack of Bolshevik vigilance' by his colleague, the American 'Tom Ryan' (1905–1961).[102] 'Ryan', whose real name was Francis Waldron, and who later became known in the United States as the Communist Party leader 'Eugene Dennis', had clearly been quick to learn the new idiom of 1930s Moscow. In his schoolmasterly reports to headquarters, sent under the pseudonym 'Milton', he accused Ewert of having granted Isaacs too much political freedom. Back in Moscow, he even alleged that Ewert was 'basically' still a 'conciliator'.[103]

After coming into conflict with Isaacs, Ewert himself made several appeals to Moscow, seeking to have Agnes Smedley made editor in his stead. The Comintern authorities did not agree, apparently considering her too politically unreliable, and preferred to close the publication,

---

101 The Comintern in the end contemplated continuing the magazine under Smedley: Excerpt from minute no. 367(B) of the meeting of the Political Commission of the Political Secretariat of the ECCI, Moscow, 3 April 1934, in Leutner, *KPdSU(B)*, vol. 3, part 1, 722–3. This was, however, not possible, first because Isaacs held the rights to the title, and second because Smedley's position in Shanghai had become too dangerous. On the development of Isaacs's politics, see his open letter 'I Break with the Chinese Stalinists', *New International* 1:3, September/October 1934, 76–8, available online at marxists.org. See also Jinxing Chen, 'Harold R. Isaacs' Trotskyist Turn in the *China Forum* Years', *Twentieth-Century China* 24:1, 1998, 31–66.

102 Letter from T. Ryan to the Eastern Secretariat of the ECCI, Shanghai, 3 July 1934, in Leutner, *KPdSU(B)*, vol. 3, part 1, 763–6 and 769–70.

103 Note of a conversation with T. Ryan at the ECCI, Moscow, n.d. [on or before 20 November 1934], in Leutner, *KPdSU(B)*, vol. 3, part 1, 895–904, at 902.

though Smedley, friends with Isaacs, had already been working for the magazine for some time.

A Communist Enclave amid the Foreign Concessions

Agnes Smedley, who had begun to work for the OMS in Berlin in 1927, had been in China since the end of 1928, officially as special correspondent for the *Frankfurter Zeitung*.[104] Her interest in China had been aroused by Münzenberg's campaigns in support of the Chinese Revolution of 1923–27 and her contacts with Chinese activists in Berlin.[105] After stints in Harbin, Shenyang (Mukden), Beijing and Nanjing, she moved to Shanghai in May 1929. More activist than intellectual in her inclinations, Smedley quickly established contacts both with the Chinese party and with Song Qingling, whom she had known in Berlin and who had returned to China in mid-1929. Her circle of acquaintances included Asians as well as Western Communists. Arthur and Elsi Ewert she knew from Germany,[106] and, in Shanghai, she got to know Irene Weitemeyer and those local representatives of Comintern with whom she was as yet unfamiliar, the American Tom Ryan and the German Otto Braun.[107] She soon also found herself working for Richard Sorge, who had got in touch with her, writing reports for him on the role of the United States in China and on American investment in Shanghai. Smedley also acted as a liaison, making her home in the French concession available as a message drop and place of meeting.[108] A young Chinese secretary-translator helped her in finding information.[109] Smedley's extensive network of contacts served Sorge not only to gather intelligence but also in such logistical responsibilities as finding safe

---

104 Agnes Smedley, *Battle Hymn of China*, London: Victor Gollancz, 1944 [1943], 24; Price, *The Lives*, 160.
105 Smedley, *Battle Hymn*, 23–4. See chapter 5.
106 Thomas Kampen, 'Deutsche und österreichische Kommunisten im revolutionären China (1925–1949)', *Jahrbuch für Historische Kommunismusforschung*, 1997, 88–104, at 94.
107 According to Braun, it was Ewert who introduced him to Smedley: Braun, *Chinesische Aufzeichnungen*, 11.
108 Price, *The Lives*, 198–9 and 214.
109 Smedley, *Battle Hymn*, 57.

places to meet, store documents and hiding weapons.[110] She helped recruit discreet new members to Sorge's staff, one of these being 'Sonya', later to be known as Ruth Werner.

'Sonya' was living in Shanghai as a married woman under the name Ursula Hamburger. She had joined the Communist Youth Association at the age of seventeen, the party two years later. Her husband Rolf had taken a job as an architect in Shanghai. To what extent the couple's move to the city was prompted by Moscow's decision in February 1930 to send only non-Russian Communists or sympathizers to Shanghai, members if possible of the liberal professions, is, however, unknown. Once there, they were to get on with their jobs without involving themselves in any illegal work, while also attending to logistical matters for the Comintern. Ruth Werner, as she will be called here (this being the name under which she would publish her memoirs), was, in any event, eagerly waiting to be contacted at last by the party, as she was terribly bored in her role as a wife.[111]

It was through Smedley, whose romanticized autobiography, *Daughter of Earth*, she had read and admired in Berlin, that she met Sorge,[112] and she reports that she accepted his offer to work on behalf of the Chinese Revolution without hesitation.[113] Without informing her husband, she rented post office boxes for Sorge and his deputy, 'Paul', and made her home available to them for secret meetings and for the safekeeping of documents and even weapons. The house was on the Avenue Joffre in the French concession – whose streets were not as handsome or as salubrious as those of the International Settlement, as Lili Körber noted.[114] Chosen with considerations of security in mind, it was ideal for such uses, having two exits and a garden giving on to a number of different streets. Her duties also included gathering information on foreign companies in China and occasional surveillance.

Despite the rules of conspiracy and the dangers attending undercover Communist activity in Shanghai, the Western comrades

---

110 According to the Japanese journalist Ozaki Hotsumi, who would later be indispensable to him in Japan: Price, *The Lives*, 215.

111 Werner, *Sonya's Report*, 32–8.

112 Agnes Smedley, *Daughter of Earth*, New York: Coward-McCann, 1929, reprinted with foreword by Alice Walker, New York: Feminist Press, 2019.

113 Werner, *Sonya's Report*, 41.

114 Körber, *Begegnungen*, 178.

socialized a great deal among themselves. They knew each other, met often and sometimes lived close together. Smedley, who had become close friends with Ruth, soon moved into her neighbourhood, Ruth's husband Rolf seeing to the furnishing of her new home. Arthur and Elsi Ewert, too, lived for a time in the French concession, spending almost a year at 15, route Paul Henry (which, paradoxically, also accommodated a large White Russian community).[115] When the journalist Egon Erwin Kisch ('the Reporter on the Rampage') arrived in Shanghai in the early summer of 1932, he would visit Ruth Werner's house together with Agnes Smedley.[116] The latter also knew Irene Weitemeyer, whom she calls Isa in her memoirs. The same age, and both booksellers by training, they were very close. Irene also enjoyed looking after her friend's baby boy, born in Shanghai in 1931. Ruth would only find out that Irene had had to leave her not yet two-year-old daughter in Moscow for reasons of security when the child died of meningitis. For the same reason, Irene was not allowed to live with her partner while in China.[117]

In distant Shanghai, the prohibition on contact between different apparatuses was apparently even less respected outside working hours. Ruth Werner knew Sorge's entire spy ring, which included the Japanese journalist Ozaki Hotsumi, to whom she was introduced by Agnes Smedley, and a Polish comrade named Grisha, who ran a camera shop for cover.[118] The German-speakers, whether party members, sympathizers or employees of 'the neighbour', would meet for outings and social events.[119] Ruth Werner writes:

> Some of my happiest memories derive from those few occasions when our group did not meet as 'conspirators'. Once in 1932, we gathered in a hotel room: Grisha, Richard, Paul and our dark-eyed, dark-haired host, a vivacious man whom I had not seen before. I called him Fred as the others did . . . Many years later I recognised him on a photo with the caption 'The Hero of Madrid'. It was Manfred Stern. Under the name of General Kléber he had won fame

---

115 Friedmann, *Arthur Ewert*, 278, n.16.
116 Werner, *Sonya's Report*, 86–7.
117 Ibid., 60–1.
118 Ibid., 56.
119 Ibid., 69.

as commander, defender and hero of the Madrid battle front in 1936.[120]

Like the German Otto Braun, the Austrian Manfred Stern (1896–1954, 'Fred') worked for Soviet military intelligence, serving as a military adviser to the Central Committee of the Chinese party. A soldier in the Austro-Hungarian army taken prisoner by the Russians, Stern had fought on the Bolshevik side in the Russian civil war before being sent to Germany to build up the KPD's military-political apparatus, where he played a leading role in launching the ill-fated Hamburg Uprising of 1923. After graduating from the Frunze Academy in Moscow, he was recruited by the Soviet military intelligence, who sent him to New York in 1929 as head of the GRU station there.[121] In China, he was working not only for the GRU but also for the ECCI.[122] He acted as chief military adviser to the CPC, assisted by Braun and Ewert.[123]

Whatever the rules might say, in cosmopolitan Shanghai it was evidently possible for senior cadre of the Comintern and of the Soviet intelligence service to socialize with each other. Breach of conspiracy was a repeated allegation in reports to Moscow. This was the complaint, for example, of Comrade Ryan, himself characterized by a comrade as arrogant and careless:[124] 'Present at the New Year's party, held at the home of Mme Song [Qingling], were Arthur and his wife, Ryan [i.e. the writer himself], Fred, Lincoln and John.' Ryan also noted that 'Lincoln' (whose real name has not been identified) and 'John' (the Russian

---

120 Ibid., 66–7.
121 For his life, see the biography by Walerij Brun-Zechowoj, *Manfred Stern – General Kléber: Die tragische Biographie eines Berufsrevolutionärs (1896–1954)*, Berlin: Trafo Verlag, 2000, which although not very detailed was based on newly available sources.
122 Data from the appendix to Michael Buckmiller and Klaus Meschkat, eds, *Biographisches Handbuch zur Geschichte der Kommunistischen Internationale: Ein deutsch-russisches Forschungsprojekt*, Berlin: Akademie Verlag, 2007.
123 Boris Volodarsky, *Stalin's Agent: The Life and Death of Alexander Orlov*, Oxford: Oxford University Press, 2014, 228.
124 Report by N. N. Herbert to the International Liaison Department of the ECCI on his work in Shanghai from 1932 to 1935, Moscow, 29 September 1936, in Leutner, *KPdSU(B)*, vol. 3, part 2, 1306–13, at 1308. The Yugoslav-American Raymond Baker (1898–?), whose true name was Rudolf Blum and who in 1934–35 worked for the RILU in China, the Philippines and France, also gave Ryan an extremely bad report, describing him as highly inexperienced in conspiratorial matters: Report by R. Baker, Moscow, 9 May 1935, in Leutner, *KPdSU(B)*, vol. 3, part 1, 1004–22, at 1017–9.

Andreev, in reality named Stronsky, 1888–1937/38) were from the neighbour-apparatus, that is, the GRU's Shanghai station, which was also true of 'Fred', i.e. Manfred Stern. The local representative of Soviet news agency TASS was also present. On another occasion, 'at the farewell party for John, held at Lincoln's home, everyone was there, including representatives of the OMS', and the same had happened at a party on 7 November.[125]

Such encounters were indeed dangerous, as Smedley, in particular, was under close surveillance not only by the British but also by the German police. Autumn 1932 also saw the police net tighten around Sorge as well. Alongside Smedley, Harold Isaacs and Viola Robinson, he figured on a list of thirteen suspected Soviet agents drawn up by the Shanghai Municipal Police.[126] Only at the end of the year did Moscow give permission for the departure from China of the man who would later become famous as the 'master spy' who sent militarily crucial intelligence from Japan to the Soviet Union during the Second World War.

Agnes Smedley's letters, much cited by Ruth Price in her study, show that the boundary between political/professional and private relationships was often fluid. Sorge and Smedley became lovers, though the inconstant Sorge soon moved on to 'Sonya', whose marriage to Rolf was ailing. Sorge seems to have been enormously attractive to his contemporaries, as Ruth Werner recalls in her memoirs: 'Richard Sorge was thirty-five years old and I found him just as attractive and good-looking as others have portrayed.'[127] Rosa Meyer-Leviné, who had met him in 1923–24 when she worked at the Frankfurt Institute for Social Research and then again in Moscow, was even more enthusiastic: 'Sorge was in his early thirties, tall, regal and inherently elegant in every movement of his shapely body, a perfect model for classical statuary – Apollo himself.'[128]

That the sexual freedom here described extended also to the women in Communist circles resulted from the influence of an egalitarian feminism, on the one hand, and of the 1920s discourse of sexual reform, particularly widespread in the Weimar Republic, on the other. As lived

---

125 Oral report by Comrade Ryan re. Shanghai, Moscow, 22 December 1934, recorded in shorthand and translated into German by [the Swiss OMS employee] Berta Zimmermann (1902–1937), in Leutner, *KPdSU(B)*, vol. 3, part 1, 916–920, at 920.
126 Stranahan, *Underground*, 114; Haslam, *Near and Distant Neighbors*, 63.
127 Werner, *Sonya's Report*, 39.
128 Meyer-Leviné, *Im inneren Kreis*, 102.

out by Agnes Smedley and Ruth Werner in China, it also reflected not only the personalities of two self-confident women but also the social situation of the foreigner, with its personal isolation and insulation from customary social controls. A friend of the American birth control activist Margaret Sanger and a feminist who herself campaigned for publicly funded birth-control clinics, Smedley had a number of affairs in the United States and in Germany.[129] In a relationship, she was not prepared to sacrifice her personal independence or her professional interests on the altar of housewifely duty. But the place of reproductive labour in everyday life had hardly been taken into theoretical account in the socialist critique of the 'bourgeois' gender order. So long as there was no socialization of housework, there would be a gap between lived reality and the feminist idea of the equal relationship, as Smedley later came to realize in her almost eight-year-long domestic partnership with Virendranath Chattopadhyaya:

> Our way of life was of his choosing, not mine; our home a small edition of that of a great joint family of India. Any Indian who became ill was brought to our home and nursed by me, and on one occasion I had two of them at once . . . I was harassed by domestic difficulties. Hindu and Moslem religious festivals were sometimes celebrated in our home, with dozens of men sitting in a circle on the floor. In the manner of India, no man could be turned away hungry. The cooking and preparation for dinners were therefore endless, and the very walls of our home seemed to be permeated with the odour of curry. Viren thrived on company, but I began to wilt and sink under the complexity and poverty of our life. Everyone understood and loved Viren; few understood me.

Looking back, she was not even sure what she felt about him: 'Whether or not I loved him, I do not really know.'[130]

In China, Smedley not only found reassurance that she was still sexually attractive despite her almost forty years, but also came to realize the importance of the Chinese Revolution for women's emancipation. The pen-portraits of her *Chinese Destinies*, published in 1933, offer a glimpse of the

---

129 Agnes Smedley, *Battle Hymn*, 21; see also Ruth Price's biography of Smedley.
130 Smedley, *Battle Hymn*, 17–18 and 15.

power of Chinese women, but are also marked by an acute sense of how necessary it was to seize the day: 'Across the great historical stage on which the Chinese revolution is being played, appears and reappears the figure of a woman... The woman may speak for herself... It is best that [she] speak quickly, lest tragedy overtake her and silence her tongue forever.'[131]

Unlike Agnes, the fourteen-years-younger Ruth Werner was married and had a child, but she too rejected the traditional life of wife and mother. It was therefore only consistent that she should opt in Shanghai for the role of 'liberal woman with intellectual interests'.[132] Immediately after her son's birth there, she wrote to her brother Jürgen and his wife in Germany: 'I am in heaven over this child and then again appalled how I have succumbed to him. *There is nothing left of me right now*, either for Rolf, or politics, or books, or you. Only the child, and everything else only in relation to the child.'[133] She too was open-minded about sex and relationships. Her three children would all be by different men.[134] Her husband Rolf proved himself equally open-minded when Ruth became pregnant by Ernst, the comrade with whom she worked in Japanese-occupied Mukden in 1934–35, as a radio operator for Soviet intelligence, and when the two of them spent almost two years working for Soviet intelligence in Poland, he was happy to pass off the child as his own.

In Shanghai, while Ruth's relationship with Sorge led to a certain tension between her and her friend Agnes, their differences were chiefly political. Though both worked undercover, they did so in different ways. Smedley was direct and impulsive. She made no secret of her solidarity with the Chinese people and the revolution, even in public, and had fallen out almost immediately with Shanghai's ex-pat community over their attitude towards the Chinese. Smedley was also daring, if not reckless, and did not hesitate to go places not only customarily out-of-bounds to foreign women but also positively dangerous, especially for someone like her, who – as the archives have since revealed – was working for both the OMS and Red Army intelligence.[135] While aware that

---

131 Cited in Price, *The Lives*, 179.
132 Werner, *Sonya's Report*, 47.
133 Ibid., 58; my emphasis.
134 *Auskünfte über Ruth Werner: Festschrift zum 75. Geburtstag*, ed. Joachim Sagasser, Berlin: Verlag Neues Leben, 1982, 148–50.
135 See the documents published by Leutner et al., where it is explicitly stated that Smedley worked for both the Comintern and Red Army intelligence: letter from A.

she was being watched by all Shanghai's different police forces, she undoubtedly overestimated the protection afforded by her extraterritorial status as an American citizen, and responded with vehement indignation to repeated allegations in the press that she was a Communist agent.

Smedley was, however, a difficult colleague, lacking political discipline and rushing into things on her own initiative. In early 1937, Song Qingling complained of her in a letter to Wang Ming: 'With regard to Miss Smedley I wish to say that contrary to repeated instructions she continued to keep up with bad connections, financed them and later asked the party to refund her for all the money she advanced on her own initiatives.'[136] On this, as on many other political matters, the party leadership was divided. Mao Zedong and Zhou Enlai apparently saw nothing wrong with Smedley's propaganda activities, but her independence was too much for the ECCI Secretariat: 'She must not be given the opportunity to present herself as a representative or supposed spokesperson of the Communists.'[137] This lack of discipline lends a certain plausibility to Smedley's repeated claims that she was never a member of a Communist Party, and the early 1930s indeed saw some non-party-members working at the heart of the Comintern apparatus in Moscow.[138] On the other hand, the records show that she was referred to as 'comrade' by the Comintern apparatus that most definitely employed her. Back in Moscow in 1934, after leaving Shanghai for security reasons in May 1933, she was – despite everything – 'assigned' to China by the ECCI, to take over the running of *China Forum*. To avoid suspicion, she travelled via Europe and the United States. Here again, she failed to follow Moscow's instructions,[139] delaying the final leg of the journey until October. In May 1935, however, after developing a plan for a new 'anti-imperialist organ' to replace *China Forum*, she found herself abruptly

---

Ewert to I. A. Piatnitsky, Shanghai, mid-May 1933, in Leutner, *KPdSU(B)*, vol. 3, part 1, 446–7.

136 Letter from Song Qingling to Wang Ming, Hong Kong, 26 January 1937, in Leutner, *KPdSU(B)*, vol. 3, part 2, 1323–5.

137 Telegram from the ECCI Secretariat to the CC of the CCP, Moscow, 19 January 1937, in Leutner, *KPdSU(B)*, vol. 3, part 2, 1319–21, at 1321.

138 Brigitte Studer, *The Transnational World of the Cominternians*, trans. D. R. Roberts, Basingstoke, UK: Palgrave Macmillan, 2015, 25–6.

139 Harvey Klehr, John Earl Haynes and Kyrill Anderson, *The Soviet World of American Communism*, New Haven, CT: Yale University Press, 1998, 188–9.

recalled; her plan had fallen into the hands of the police following the arrest of the head of the Chinese party's Shanghai Bureau, whereupon Manuilsky called for 'those who recommended the employment of such an irresponsible comrade [i.e. Smedley] to be held accountable'.[140]

Ruth Werner, on the other hand, always acted like a well-disciplined party member and adhered to the rules of conspiracy. She therefore participated in the social life of the bourgeois expatriate community, despite finding most of them rather unlikeable, knowing that her behaviour would otherwise draw attention. She also respected, to all appearances, the social distance expected to prevail between Europeans and Chinese. Western Communists could not manifest their solidarity with the Chinese Revolution, nor could they in any way treat as equals the Chinese servants that they like every other ex-pat employed – Ruth Werner, for example, had an 'amah' (a nanny) and a cook, Agnes Smedley a secretary, Ryan a boy and a cook[141] – without attracting unwanted attention. For security reasons, these Communists committed to the abolition of class were obliged to replicate the colonist's relationship to the colonized. When Ruth Werner forgot this, taking in the relatives of her nanny and her cook when the Japanese attacked Chinese Shanghai, she was taken to task by Richard Sorge.[142]

The differences between the two women came to a head over the Noulens's son. While Agnes pampered and indulged the three-year-old 'Jimmy', Ruth thought this a bad thing, and while she would have been happy to adopt the child, as Agnes had suggested, she once again gave priority to the imperatives of conspiracy. Sorge was against it, and she did not want to give up her undercover work. The final rift came when the Noulenses went on a hunger strike and Agnes instantly joined them. When Ruth told her that this would in fact do nothing to help the

---

140 Excerpt from Minute no. 367(B) of the meeting of the Political Commission of the Political Secretariat of the ECCI, Moscow, 3 April 1934, in Leutner, *KPdSU(B)*, vol. 3, part 1, 722–3; excerpt from Minute no. 450(B) of the meeting of the Political Commission of the Political Secretariat of the ECCI, Moscow, 5 May 1935, ibid., 1003–4.

141 Werner, *Sonya's Report*, 74; Smedley, *Battle Hymn*, 57; Oral report by Comrade Ryan re. Shanghai, Moscow, 22 December 1934, recorded in shorthand and translated into German by Berta Zimmermann (1902–1937), in Leutner, *KPdSU(B)*, vol. 3, part 1, 916–20, at 917; report by R. Baker, Moscow, 9 May 1935, ibid., 1004–22, at 1020–1.

142 Werner, *Sonya's Report*, 76.

prisoners, Agnes abruptly ended their friendship.[143] The boy was eventually placed with a non-Communist German family named Holz, where he was called Jakob.[144] In 1935, the Comintern was still undecided as to what to do,[145] only resolving in November 1936 to bring 'Jimmy' to the Soviet Union, where he was placed in an orphanage.

In 1936, nearly everyone mentioned here was recalled from China, leaving behind only Otto Braun and Agnes Smedley. Braun had been deployed to Jiangxi in Soviet China, becoming in 1934 the only European to take part in the Long March. It was not until 1939 that he finally left the country and returned to the Soviet Union. Smedley continued to work as a journalist in China until 1941. Inevitably, the Noulens/Rüegg couple were another exception. The Comintern did not abandon the international defence campaign until 1935, in propaganda terms, at least.[146] It was only in 1937, following the Japanese attack on Nanjing, that the two were conditionally released, alongside many other prisoners whose safety could not be guaranteed. They fled to Shanghai, where they remained in hiding until July 1939,[147] when they were finally able to return to the Soviet Union. They had been waiting since early 1938 for papers to arrive from Moscow, where officials were apparently in no hurry to get them home. After all, the confusion sown about their identity had been successful: the British police had never been able to determine their true nationality.

---

143 Ibid., 91–2.

144 Information provided to the author by Dmitri Moiseenko, Moscow, 21 June 1990. See also Dmitrij J. Moiseenko, Gleb Albert and Bernhard H. Bayerlein, 'Jimmy – Jacob oder Dimitrij? Identitäten eines "Kominternwaisen"', *International Newsletter of Communist Studies Online* 12:19, 2006, 48–52, at incs.ub.rub.de.

145 Excerpt from Minute no. 442(B) of the meeting of the Political Commission of the Political Secretariat of the ECCI, Moscow, 21 March 1935, in Leutner, *KPdSU(B)*, vol. 3, part 1, 983.

146 Kept up in China, somewhat paradoxically, by the 'Trotskyist' Harold Isaacs, and after his departure from Shanghai in 1934 by Sun Yat-sen's widow Song Qingling. Internationally, it had been overtaken as early as October 1932, as a campaigning theme of the League Against Imperialism, by the threat of war: Fredrik Petersson, *Willi Münzenberg, the League Against Imperialism and the Comintern, 1925–1933*, vol. 2, Lewiston, NY: Queenston Press, 2013, 919.

147 They were in fact supposed to report to the police within ten days of being freed: Frank Dikötter, *Crime, Punishment and the Prison in Modern China*, London: Hurst & Co., 2002, 327.

In the spring of 1933, Ruth Werner had been planning to take a holiday and visit her parents, but the Nazi takeover of power in Germany put paid to that. She went instead to Moscow, where she saw not only Agnes, but also Borodin, now editor-in-chief of the city's first English-language weekly newspaper, *Moscow News*, founded by Anna Louise Strong; Liao Huanxing, now adviser to the Eastern Secretariat of the ECCI and secretary of the Chinese party's delegation to the ECCI; and Chatto, now a language teacher in Leningrad. However, she had come to Moscow in a very specific capacity, that is, as a permanently employed agent of the GRU. In that respect, one might say, she represented the fulfilment of Clara Zetkin's demand that women be entrusted not only with legal but also with underground work.[148] She had trained as a radio operator near Moscow before being sent to Mukden in Manchuria and then to Poland. Richard Sorge, too, continued to work for the GRU. After his recall from China, in 1933 he was sent to Japan, again in the guise of a German journalist, where he built one of the most venturesome and effective of twentieth-century intelligence networks, before being arrested by the Japanese in 1941 and hanged in 1944, together with his colleague Ozaki Hotsumi.

For the Comintern's employees, a stint in China was by no means necessarily a prelude to career advancement. Like Borodin, Ducroux was stripped of political functions and assigned to a desk job. After his arrest, he had been sentenced to eighteen months of 'rigorous imprisonment' and afterwards deported to Saigon, where he was again arrested, by the French police, and sentenced to another year in prison. He was finally released in late 1933 and after a brief period of recuperation he reported back to Moscow in January 1934, where he was apparently very coolly received and his report not even discussed. The ECCI Secretariat criticized him for his failure and shunted him off to the Comintern's publishing house. At his request, however, he was allowed to return to France, where he worked for the French party's Éditions Sociales Internationales.

---

148 'Report on Communist Women's Movement', in John Riddell, ed., *To the Masses: Proceedings of the Third Congress of Communist International, 1921*, Leiden: Brill, 2015, 779–95, at 786.

8
Cities of Refuge: Paris, Basel, Zurich, Moscow

In August 1933, Rosa Meyer-Leviné wrote to a Russian woman friend from Paris: 'I'll stay here a year, perhaps two. I'm not sick, Nyura, and there's nothing I need to get over. Regarding my own situation I am as lucid as I was last year, when I suffered so greatly for so clearly understanding the general situation (that the party would not fight). I wasn't wrong either . . .'[1] The KPD had, indeed, collapsed without a struggle. After Hitler's appointment as chancellor on 30 January 1933, a dictatorship was speedily established, one fateful step following another in rapid succession: on 1 February, the dissolution of the Reichstag; on 4 February, suspension of the freedom of the press and freedom of assembly; on 28 February, the signature of the so-called Reichstag Fire Decree, suspending other civil liberties; and on 24 March, the passage of the Enabling Act, suspending the constitution and sidelining parliament while Communist MPs were already in hiding or in preventive custody.

---

1 Rosa Meyer-Leviné, in 'Briefwechsel Pankratova – Rosa Meyer', an appendix to Rosa Meyer-Leviné, *Im inneren Kreis: Erinnerungen einer Kommunistin in Deutschland 1920–1930*, ed. Hermann Weber, Cologne: Kiepenheuer und Witsch, 1979, 317–19, at 319, absent from the English edition: Rosa Leviné-Meyer [sic], *Inside German Communism: Memoirs of Party Life in the Weimar Republic*, ed. David Zane Mairowitz, London: Pluto Press, 1978. Born Rosa Broido, the twelfth child of a rabbi from eastern Poland, then part of Russia, Meyer-Leviné had moved to the Soviet Union following the death of her second husband, KPD leader Ernst Meyer. There she received a pension as the widow of Eugen Leviné, Russian revolutionary and leader of the Bavarian Soviet Republic, but chose to leave for Germany on 26 January 1933, of all times!

Party leader Ernst Thälmann had been arrested on 3 March; Georgi Dimitrov followed on 9 March, accused with others of setting fire to the Reichstag.

The most powerful Communist party outside the Soviet Union collapsed like a house of cards, together with its mass organizations. Consternation reigned among party members, a sense of shock reflected in Manès Sperber's trilogy of novels entitled *Like a Tear in the Ocean*. The protagonist, Dojno Faber, hurries back from Vienna on hearing the news of the National Socialist takeover, pondering events on the train to Berlin:

> 'Germany sleeps', he thought. Immediately he corrected himself: 'Nonsense! For many years this country has forgotten how to sleep peacefully. Tonight decisions are being made, so momentous and so far-reaching that no one man who is making them can evaluate their import. Sixty-five million human beings! If only one million of them realize tonight what must be dome tomorrow, then each hour of the new day will count for years in future history. Everything up to now has just been preparation or practice. In a few hours the real test will come.[2]

But the general strike the party called for did not materialize, and shock at the absence of Communist resistance would be, for Faber, a crucial factor in his disillusionment with the party. At the same time, the brutal repression that now set in tied members ever more closely to the organization, as Sperber observed several decades later in his memoirs.

> Precisely because the underground Communist party was being mercilessly persecuted, its functionaries found it easy to silence the skeptics and critics among the Communist intellectuals and bring them into line quickly. 'In the face of the enemy you don't discuss; you obey your leaders!' This made sense to even the most heretical comrades.[3]

---

2 Manès Sperber, *Like A Tear in the Ocean*, vol. 1, *The Burned Bramble*, trans. Constantine FitzGibbon, New York: Holmes & Meier, 1988, 128.

3 Manès Sperber, *Until My Eyes Are Closed with Shards*, trans. Harry Zohn, New York: Holmes & Meier, 1994, 20.

Rosa Leviné-Meyer reacted no differently. She, too, who had become a Communist critical of Stalin in the Soviet Union, was afraid of burning her bridges, her connection to the party – and the revolution.

If they were to save anything of the organization, or indeed themselves, comrades had no choice but to leave Germany. Willi Münzenberg fled to Paris in late February, part of the first wave of emigration in the wake of the Reichstag fire, which mainly consisted of political activists. The *Inprekorr* editorial team and the staff of the press agency went to Switzerland. Even the Swiss Mentona Moser had to go into hiding, having allowed her name to be used as cover for a number of party businesses. She got away from Berlin only in March: 'I sometimes ran into Red Aid staff on the street. We would pass each other in silence, exchanging only a look, a gesture of the hand, and meet in a side street.'[4] Others, like Ruth Oesterreich – earlier Comrade Thomas's secretary at the West European Bureau, but now a member of the 'Neu Beginnen' group of left Social Democrats – emigrated to Prague; she was followed there by Jakov Reich, Thomas himself, now called Arnold Rubinstein. Many residents of the Laubenheimerplatz artists' colony left Germany that March, or shortly afterwards, among them Ernst and Karola Bloch, Friedel and Alfred Kantorowicz, Gustav Regler and Manès Sperber. Only Susanne Leonhard and her son Wolfgang remained until 1935, she active in the Communist resistance, chiefly as a courier.

The wave of refugees put international solidarity to the test. Germany's neighbours were not terribly keen to take in Communist revolutionaries – 'foreign agitators' in their eyes – and sought to refuse them entry, or expel them as soon as they could. The transnational lifestyle of professional revolutionaries now fell foul of national laws and local police surveillance. From 1935 onward, this would increasingly also be the case in the Soviet Union, where so many revolutionaries had sought refuge, given the lack of alternatives. The safety it had offered now proved to be illusory; the city of Moscow, previously a safe haven for Comintern employees who were persecuted and illegal almost everywhere in the world, had turned into a trap. For, while the general political situation called for all left and democratic forces to work together, what happened was exactly the opposite: an internal offensive against every kind of opposition.

---

4 Mentona Moser, *Ich habe gelebt*, Zurich: Limmat Verlag, 1986, 238–9, quote at 244.

M. N. Roy in uniform (RGASPI).

Ruth Oesterreich in the 1930s (Gedenkstätte Deutscher Widerstand, Berlin).

(confidencial)

C.C. del P.C.E.
Departamento de Cuadros

Valencia 24/1/37.

Estimados camaradas:

La comunicacion que mas abajo citamos ha sido enviada por el Partido Comunista del Brasil a nuestros camaradas de Paris los cuales me han encargado de transmitirla a Uds. a fin de que tomeis las medidas necesarias:

"El teniente Alberto Bezouchet se encuentra actualmente en España. Despues de su salida del Brasil se ha descubierto que Bezouchet ha pasado al trotzkismo. El ha dejado una prueba que es una verdadera provocacion contra la revolucion de liberacion nacional y contra el gobierno español. Si es posible encontrarlo hay que detenerlo y tambien urge notificar todos los camaradas a fin de que no le permitan utilizar el nombre del Partido Comunista del Brasil."

Esta comunicacion me ha sido entregada en Paris el dia 20 de Enero fecha de mi regreso a esta. Me permito indicaros la conveniencia de enviar copia de esta comunicacion a la Comisaria Politica de las Brigadas Intrnacionales.

Con saludos comunistas

Maria

Note dated 24 January 1937, from 'Maria' (Tina Modotti) to the cadre department of the Spanish CP, denouncing the Brazilian Alberto Besouchet (misspelled here as 'Bezouchet'), as suspected of Trotskyism (Arquivo Edgard Leuenroth, University of Campinas, SP, Brazil).

Palmiro Togliatti ('Alfredo') addressing the International Brigades
(Archivio Palmiro Togliatti, Fondazione Gramsci Roma).

This chapter looks at the insecure life and precarious working conditions of Comintern employees in emigration, both political cadre and technical staff, following a number of the actors we have already encountered as they make their escape from Germany: first, Willi Münzenberg and Babette Gross and their collaborators; second, the *Inprekorr* editorial team; and third, the two couples of Heinz Neumann and Margarete Buber and Heinrich Kurella and Charlotte Stenbock-Fermor, who emigrated to the Soviet Union. The focus falls, then, on the cities of Paris, Basel, Zurich and Moscow.

Paris: A Disorganized Effort to Rebuild the Apparatus

Only days before Hitler came to power, Willi Münzenberg, then on a visit to Moscow, had requested that the IAH headquarters be transferred to the Netherlands. The answer he received from the ECCI leadership on 3 February was that he should wait until the organization was banned by the Nazis. He was, however, permitted to make preparations for such an event.[5] Münzenberg thus soldiered on in Germany, even as the danger to him grew with every passing day. As befitted his character, he kept up his political activities and continued to make public appearances. Together with Kurt Grossmann of the Liga für Menschenrechte and the left-liberal writer and lawyer Rudolf Olden, he organized an antifascist event, 'Das Freie Wort' [The Free Word], held at the Kroll assembly rooms on 19 February 1933 and attended by nine hundred participants and a hundred journalists. Among the patrons were such prominent intellectuals as Georg Bernhard and Harry Graf Kessler, while professors Ferdinand Tönnies and Wolfgang Heine addressed the meeting, denouncing the new restrictions on the freedom of the press, freedom of assembly and academic freedom. The meeting was broken up by the police. It was now too late to try and organize resistance on a nonpartisan basis.[6] On 27

---

5 Kasper Braskén, *The International Workers' Relief, Communism, and Transnational Solidarity: Willi Münzenberg in Weimar Germany*, Basingstoke, UK: Palgrave Macmillan, 2015, 231.

6 Dieter Schiller, 'Willi Münzenberg und die Intellektuellen: Die Jahre in der Weimarer Republik 1921 bis 1933', *Jahrbuch für Forschungen zur Geschichte der Arbeiterbewegung* 12:3, 2013, 43–63, at 63; Babette Gross, *Willi Münzenberg: A Political Biography*, East Lansing: Michigan State University Press, 1974, 232–3.

February, Münzenberg addressed an election rally in a small town near Frankfurt. For reasons of security, he did not stay in a hotel that night but rather with a Frankfurt comrade, the secretary of the local IAH branch. There he played cards until two in the morning.[7]

Babette Gross, who had arrived in Frankfurt from Switzerland early in the morning, heard the news of the Reichstag fire from the calls of the newspaper boys. She immediately phoned her home in Berlin, where Münzenberg's secretary Hans Schulz (1904–1988) and his wife Sonja Barofsky were installed to make sure the phone was always answered. The police had already visited the apartment at dawn, looking for Münzenberg. One of the officers had recognized Sonja Barofsky – the daughter of the former Berlin police commissioner Karl Zörgiebel, a Social Democrat – and had taken her aside, murmuring that she and her husband should get away at once, and also warn Münzenberg and Babette Gross. Gross now hurried through Frankfurt to wake Münzenberg's driver, Emil, at his hotel. Together, they intercepted Münzenberg before he arrived at the café where they had all arranged to meet, and they were in the car, travelling towards Darmstadt, when they realized they had to return to Frankfurt to obtain false ID. The quest for a passport demonstrated the strength of comradely solidarity, a young Frankfurt Communist giving his up to Münzenberg without the slightest hesitation. The question now was where to go, for Münzenberg's description had by now been circulated by the police and his photo printed in the newspapers, and it was Babette's sister Margarete's former in-laws who came up with a solution, when the Jewish religious thinker Martin Buber and his wife gave them the address of a university professor friend in the Saarland, then still under League of Nations administration. (It would only be re-incorporated into Germany following a referendum in 1935.) From there, Münzenberg reached France just in time. On 28 February 1933, the premises of the IAH and its newspaper were laid to waste; the next few months also saw the closure and subsequent destruction of the Institute of Sex Research founded by Dr Magnus Hirschfeld, in whose house Babette Gross and Willi Münzenberg rented an apartment.[8]

---

7 His eventful escape is recounted in Gross, *Münzenberg*, 234–9.
8 Bernd Kaufmann et al., *Der Nachrichtendienst der KPD 1919–1937*, Berlin: Dietz, 1993, 279.

Paris had become the refuge of choice, Willi Münzenberg wrote to his old Zurich friend Fritz Brupbacher in May: 'Paris is becoming the city of émigrés. They arrive daily in their hundreds. This is the universal meeting point. So far, about four thousand have arrived.'[9] In this, he was not far off the mark, and the wave of refugees would swell again after the book burnings in May. In August, the Interior Ministry reckoned the number of refugees to be more than 6,300.[10] At the turn of 1936, the historian Ursula Langkau-Alex has estimated, there were 3,000 to 5,500 German Communists in France.[11] Münzenberg also sent Brupbacher greetings from Ruth Fischer and Arkadi Maslow, who had reached Paris by motorcycle, by way of Czechoslovakia, Austria and Switzerland. Life in this city where 'everything . . . was famous', in the words of Manès Sperber, would prove difficult.[12]

> The number of political refugees was constantly on the increase. The small proportion of them with means rented expensive dwellings; lawyers, who were at least officers of the Légion d'Honneur, completed the necessary formalities with the police on their behalf. The rest, however, wanted to work. But the right to work was only bestowed as a special favor, and was far more frequently refused. That was not the worst. By applying for a work permit the refugee made himself suspect of poverty and thus ran the danger of being expelled. Even the managers of the wretchedest buildings were unwilling to let apartments to people who had no definite source of income. So they lived, at far greater expense, in the little hotels, where they occupied the cheapest rooms beneath the eaves.[13]

---

9 Letter from Willi Münzenberg to Fritz Brupbacher, Paris, 15 May 1933, cited in Gross, *Münzenberg*, 243.

10 Gilbert Badia, 'L'émigration en France: Ses conditions et ses problèmes', in Gilbert Badia, ed., *Les barbelés de l'exil: Études sur l'émigration allemande et autrichienne, 1938–1940*, Grenoble: Presses Universitaires de Grenoble, 1979, 11–96, at 18. The word 'refugee' will be used here for all those Communists subject to political persecution and so compelled to emigrate, whatever might have been their legal status.

11 Ursula Langkau-Alex, *Volksfront für Deutschland?*, Frankfurt a. M.: Syndikat, 1977, 42; Langkau-Alex, *Deutsche Volksfront 1932–1939: Zwischen Berlin, Paris, Prag und Moskau*, vol. 1, *Vorgeschichte und Gründung des Ausschusses zur Vorbereitung einer deutschen Volksfront*, Berlin: Akademie Verlag, 2004, 56–7.

12 Manès Sperber, *Like A Tear in the Ocean*, vol. 2, *The Abyss*, trans. Constantine FitzGibbon, New York: Holmes & Meier, 1988, 63. More detailed information is to be found in Langkau-Alex, *Deutsche Volksfront*, vol. 1, 41–51.

13 Sperber, *Like a Tear*, vol. 2, 65–6.

Willi Münzenberg and Babette Gross had better luck. Münzenberg had visited Paris in September 1932, for the congress of the French section of the World Committee against War and Fascism, and had made a number of personal contacts there. Immediately upon arrival, he called at the editorial offices of the illustrated magazine *VU*, known, like the *AIZ*, for its innovative photojournalism. Although not a Communist publication, it was clearly antifascist and pro-Soviet in line. Münzenberg had met its editor, Lucien Vogel, and his daughter Marie-Claude Vogel (1912–1996), who worked for the magazine as a photo-reporter, a few years earlier, in Berlin, when *VU* published a special issue on the political parties of the Weimar Republic. Marie-Claude Vogel – who in 1934 would marry Paul Vaillant-Couturier (1892–1937), editor of the French Communists' daily paper, *L'Humanité*, and later survive imprisonment in a concentration camp as a member of the Resistance – put him in touch with Alfred Kurella, who had started working for Münzenberg in Berlin in 1930 before being posted to Paris by the Comintern in October 1932. Kurella, who was familiar with France from 1924–26, when he headed the PCF's Central Party School, was secretary of the International Committee against War and Fascism; between October 1933 and January 1934, before his recall to Moscow, he also ran Henri Barbusse's magazine *Monde*. Barbusse himself introduced Willi Münzenberg and Babette Gross to influential bourgeois sympathizers. Thanks to these connections, the couple and a number of their staff were successful in claiming political asylum, entitling them to the much coveted French identity card. Initially, Willi and Babette lived at Lucien Vogel's country house, after which they lived, for a time, at least, at the Hôtel Jacob.[14]

Paris was the new centre of antifascist campaigning, where the Comintern concentrated its cadre, sending there many of those who had come to the Soviet Union, among them Arthur Koestler. For Communists, there was no timeout from the struggle, and after a year in Moscow he was told that the leadership of the German section of the Comintern had decided against his staying in Russia, and ordered to go to Paris.[15] Willi Münzenberg took advantage of the influx to expand his

---

14 Sean McMeekin, *The Red Millionaire: A Political Biography of Willi Münzenberg, Moscow's Secret Propaganda Tsar in the West*, New Haven, CT: Yale University Press, 2003, 360, n.27.

15 Arthur Koestler, *The Invisible Writing*, New York: Macmillan, 1954, 153.

circle of close collaborators. The abrupt shift from Berlin to Paris had done nothing to slow down his activity on the cultural front and he remained the great star of the Communist movement. That was the only way he had to deal with the shock of the Nazis' accession to power – a defeat for which the language of the Comintern had no terms. 'It was from Münzenberg I got the answer that was expected, the password,' said Gustav Regler, with a fine sense of the verbal aspect of the party's control over the émigrés: 'Not a defeat, of course, just a strategic retreat.'[16]

Münzenberg set a team to work on *The Brown Book of the Hitler Terror and the Burning of the Reichstag,* founded the World Committee for the Relief of the Victims of German Fascism, and helped set up the Bibliothèque des Livres Brûlés/Deutsche Freiheitsbibliothek (Library of Burnt Books/German Freedom Library). Soon coming to hold some 20,000 works banned, burnt, seized or censored in Germany, this last became an important intellectual centre for Germans in exile, thanks also to its later fusion with the International Anti-Fascist Archive, with its library of 200,000 newspaper cuttings on fascism and antifascism, material accumulated in the course of work on the *Brown Book*.[17] In addition, despite the Comintern's distrust of it as a united front before its time, he remained the éminence grise behind the World Committee Against War and Fascism, the fruit of the World Congress Against Imperialist War held in August 1932.

Münzenberg made up for the loss of the Neuer Deutscher Verlag by purchasing Éditions du carrefour from the Swiss publisher Pierre

---

16 Gustav Regler, *Das Ohr des Malchus: Eine Lebensgeschichte*, Cologne: Kiepenheuer & Witsch, 1958, 210, the relevant passage being omitted from the English translation cited here: G. Regler, *The Owl of Minerva*, trans. Norman Denny, London: Rupert Hart-Davis, 1959.

17 Gilbert Badia, Jean-Baptiste Joly and Jacques Omnès, 'Défense de la culture allemande', in Gilbert Badia et al., *Les bannis de Hitler: Accueil et luttes des exilés allemands en France, 1933–1939*, Paris: Presses universitaires de Vincennes, 1984, 365–78, at 365–7; Dorothée Bores, '"Wir hüten Erbe und Zukunft": Die Deutsche Freiheitsbibliothek in Paris 1934 bis 1939', *Archiv für die Geschichte des Buchwesens* 66, 2011, 1–109; Jean-Michel Palmier, trans. David Fernbach, *Weimar in Exile: The Antifascist Emigration in Europe and America*, London: Verso, 425–30; Dietrich Schiller, *Der Traum von Hitlers Sturz: Studien zur deutschen Exilliteratur 1933–1945*, Frankfurt a. M.: Peter Lang, 2010. See also Kantorowicz's memoirs, in which he suggests that the idea for the Freedom Library was his: Alfred Kantorowicz, *Exil in Frankreich: Merkwürdigkeiten und Denkwürdigkeiten*, Bremen: Schünemann Verlag, 1971, 77.

Gaspard Lévy, which gave him premises and a trading name.[18] Located at 169 boulevard Saint-Germain, and then at 83 boulevard du Montparnasse, the firm published no fewer than fifty-six titles under Münzenberg's ownership, between 1933 and 1938. These addresses also housed the Committee for the Relief of the Victims of German Fascism and Münzenberg's own office, from which he supervised the operations of the German Freedom Library and the International Anti-Fascist Archive.[19] As Manès Sperber recalled, 'In a tiny blind alley that most pedestrians on the boulevard Montparnasse did not even notice, and in a little house that a builder with a taste for parody improvised just for fun, Willi and his people almost effortlessly wove the threads with which they mobilized the free world.'[20] According to Arthur Koestler, Münzenberg 'worked in a large room in the World Committee's premises, but no outsider ever learned about this'.[21] From there, he intervened in a variety of ways to further the struggle against fascism. The German Freedom Library and the provision of aid to comrades in exile or in danger in Germany were political rather than merely charitable or cultural projects, reflecting Münzenberg's thinking about the role of cultural propaganda and his consistent promotion of 'mass organizations', his policy since the early 1920s. By so seeking to address and mobilize Communists and non-Communists alike, he sought to build up the strongest possible front in the battle of ideas, winning new allies in neutral sympathizers and progressive fellow-travellers. The historian Bernhard Bayerlein has suggested the term 'Cultural International' for this sector of Communist activity between the wars, just as important as any of the other 'sympathizing mass organizations for special purposes'.[22] Just as the Comintern's

---

18 Catherine Lawton, 'Les Éditions du Carrefour, rappel d'un passé antérieur', in *Willi Münzenberg 1889–1940: Un homme contre*, proceedings of the international colloquium held at Aix-en-Provence, 26–29 March 1993, Marseille: Le Temps des Cerises, 1993, 173–5.

19 Gross, *Münzenberg*, 255; Koestler, *Invisible Writing*, 198. On Münzenberg's means of control: Liste der Freunde, die in unseren oder mit verbundenen Büros tätig sind, n.d. [December 1936], Archives nationales, Paris, F7/15131, and Liste der Mitarbeiter des Internationalen Antifaschistischen Archivs und der Deutschen Freiheitsbibliothek, ibid.

20 Sperber, *Until My Eyes Are Closed with Shards*, 90.

21 Koestler, *Invisible Writing*, 198.

22 Bernhard H. Bayerlein, '"Cultural International" as Comintern's Intermediate Empire', in Holger Weiss, ed., *International Communism and Transnational Solidarity: Radical Networks, Mass Movements and Global Politics, 1919–1939*, Dordrecht: Brill,

other international organizations were addressed to specific social groups (such as the trade union members of the Profintern), so the 'Cultintern' was addressed to cultural workers.

With his antifascist ventures, Münzenberg was bringing to realization an idea he had first conceived in 1923. Inspired by the example of the Italian immigrants in the USA who had established the Anti-Fascist Alliance of North America, in August 1923 he had formed in Berlin an antifascist committee from which had emerged, in December, the Antifascist World League. This brought together Communists, social democrats, bourgeois progressives and intellectuals of various stripes, pioneering the organizational model that Münzenberg would repeatedly return to. In the late summer of 1924, however, the Comintern's Agitprop Department, under the leadership of Béla Kun, put a stop to the experiment because the danger of fascism had supposedly lessened.[23]

In Paris, Münzenberg again worked with trusted collaborators of long standing. Babette Gross and Sonja Barofsky were employed by the publishing house, while Hans Schulz, a member of the party since 1923 and Sonja Barofsky's husband since 1931, continued as his personal secretary.[24] Another member of his Paris team was the translator Else Lange, who had earlier worked for him in Berlin. They would be joined in September 1935 by Hertha Jurr (née Sommerfeld, 1907–198?), employed as a shorthand typist. In Germany, in 1926–27, she had worked at the national secretariat of the Roter Frontkämpferbund (Red Front Fighters League) and the next year for the Organization Department of the Comintern. In 1930–31 she had been a member of the Communist Party of Germany (Opposition), the KPD-O, but was

---

2016, 28–88. The concept of the 'sympathizing mass organizations for special purposes' originates in a Comintern internal document of 2 June 1926, published in Hermann Weber, Jakov Drabkin and Bernhard H. Bayerlein, eds, *Deutschland, Russland, Komintern*, vol. 2, *Dokumente, 1918–1943*, Berlin: De Gruyter, 2014, 514–23. Ludmilla Stern for her part speaks of 'cultural front organizations' in her *Western Intellectuals and the Soviet Union, 1920–40: From Red Square to the Left Bank*, London: Routledge, 2007. It would, however, be simplistic to think that the non-Communists these were aimed at just allowed themselves to be manipulated.

23 Kasper Braskén, 'The Origins of Communist and Socialist Articulations of Resistance in Europe, 1923–1924', *Contemporary European History* 25:4, 2016, 573–96.

24 Liste der Freunde, die in unseren oder mit verbundenen Büros tätig sind, n.d. [December 1936], Archives nationales, Paris, F7/15131.

subsequently readmitted to the party. She had then worked underground in Germany, until her arrest in December 1934, but then managed to emigrate to England and from there to Paris. In the meantime, she had begun a relationship with another of Münzenberg's trusted collaborators, Louis Dolivet (1908–1989) – known as 'Udeanu', born Ludovic Brecher in Transylvania, who after gaining his doctorate in law from Grenoble in 1931 had been sent by the Comintern to replace Louis Gibarti as Barbusse's secretary in September 1933. The publishing house also employed an accountant and cashier; a non-Communist woman from Alsace who did bookkeeping and shorthand typing, another shorthand typist being Frieda Kantorowicz, the wife of Alfred Kantorowicz, normally an actress, who generally earned for both of them during their exile.

Münzenberg had assembled the World Committee Against War and Fascism in accordance with a tried and tested model: 'No more than 20 per cent of Communists', as many social democrats as possible, and the rest non-party-aligned. Münzenberg succeeded, in Sperber's apt formulation, in convincing the person he wanted to win to his cause 'that he was needed in the great and very difficult struggle'.[25] Well-known figures from the bourgeois-progressive camp served as chairs. The chairman of the World Committee for the Relief of the Victims of German Fascism was Lord Marley, a deputy speaker of the British House of Lords. His counterpart at the World Committee against War and Fascism was the French novelist Henri Barbusse, succeeded on his death in 1935 by Heinrich Mann. They were flanked by numerous personalities from the worlds of politics, culture and journalism. The majority would be social democrats, radicals, sometimes left Catholics, or politically nonaligned, with Communists a small minority. Internal reports reveal, unsurprisingly, that a number of officially non-party figures were Communist Party sympathizers. In the mid-1930s, this was true of three of the twelve members of the council of the World Committee against War and Fascism.[26]

The Communist influence became clearly apparent only at the true core of the organization, at the highest decision-making level. The World

---

25 Sperber, *Until My Eyes Are Closed with Shards*, 91.
26 Namensliste des Weltkomitees gegen Krieg und Faschismus, n.d. [December 1936], Archives nationales, Paris, F7/15131.

Committee's secretariat consisted of five people, and of these Willi Münzenberg and Clemens Dutt were official party members, while the Frenchman René Maublanc, officially politically nonaligned, was a Communist sympathizer. The other two were the German Social Democrat Rudolf Breitscheid and British Labour Party member Dorothy Woodman.[27] The party also dominated at operational level: the administrative manager, the cashier and the majority of the technical staff – telephone operator, typists, secretaries and translators (roles almost exclusively occupied by women) were members of the French or German parties. In accordance with Comintern insistence, effective leadership lay in any event in the hands of Communists: Henri Barbusse and his secretary Louis Dolivet, Alfred Kurella, Bohumír Šmeral and the Frenchman Guy Mérédith Jerram (1896–1951), a member of both the Central Committee of the PCF and of the ECCI, charged by his party in 1930 with leading the fight against Trotskyism. A very similar pattern was to be seen at the World Student Association for Peace, Freedom and Culture, where the secretariat consisted of two party members and a representative of Christian student organizations, while the patrons were well-known academics.[28]

Only the Women's World Committee against War and Fascism was different in this respect, membership of the Communist Party being almost the rule. Officially non-party, its president, the feminist and pacifist Gabrielle Duchêne, had been a fellow-traveller since the late 1920s. Both general secretary Bernadette Cattaneo (1899–1963), secretary of the Syndicat unitaire des employés, a white-collar union, and the former teacher Maria Rabaté (1900–1985), who became secretary of the French national committee in 1935, were both prominent in the leadership of the French party. One of the employees was Hilde Kramer's friend Cilly Vassart, née Geisenberg, born German and French by marriage. In Berlin, she had joined the KPD-O after being expelled from the party for Brandlerite sympathies in 1929, but had subsequently been readmitted. Only the purely cosmetic National Committee was nonpartisan in character, featuring prominent men of different political tendencies,[29]

27 Ibid.
28 Namensliste der Welt-Studentenbewegung für Frieden, Freiheit und Kultur, n.d. [December 1936], Archives nationales, Paris, F7/15131.
29 Namensliste des Weltfrauenkomitees gegen Krieg und Faschismus, n.d., [December 1936], Archives nationales, Paris, F7/15131.

undoubtedly reflecting the fact that few women occupied positions of high public standing.

The secretary of the World Committee for the Relief of the Victims of German Fascism was Münzenberg's close collaborator from Berlin, László Dobos, alias Louis Gibarti, who had already rendered indispensable service in the preparation of the Brussels Congress and the establishment of the League Against Imperialism.[30] It was he who had made contact with Lord Marley, and that without informing him of his Communist affiliation, according to the British secret service.[31] In his different capacities (working not only for the Relief Committee but also for the World Committee against War and Fascism) Gibarti made many journeys abroad, his movements, in fact, being very closely followed by the British secret service.[32] He travelled to the Netherlands in April 1933, presumably in connection with Münzenberg's research on the Reichstag fire trial, which saw Dimitrov and his friends accused of setting fire to the German parliament. It was he, too, who organized Münzenberg's tour of the United States in 1934, which took him to New York, Chicago, Cleveland, Milwaukee, Detroit, Boston, Washington and other cities, as part of the campaign in support of the victims of fascism and for the release of Ernst Thälmann.

In the spring of 1933, though, all attention was on the *Brown Book*, whose success would soon see it followed by a second.[33] In mid-May, Münzenberg told his friend Brupbacher of the good start he had made on his international campaign of denunciation of National Socialism: 'As you know, we are preparing a book about the Hitler government and the Reichstag fire.'[34] 'We' were Münzenberg's trusted confederates, old

---

30 See chapter 5.

31 Memorandum. Subject: Ladilas Dobos, Louis Gibarti, Ladilas Dovosgas, Alfred Feller, available at cia.gov/readingroom. The document is undated, but bears the note 'received from CIA 1/8/49'.

32 See his copious file at the British National Archives in Kew, KV-2-1401 and KV-2-1402.

33 *The Brown Book of the Hitler Terror and the Burning of the Reichstag, Prepared by an International Committee under the Presidency of Albert Einstein, with an Introduction by Lord Marley*, London: Gollancz, 1933, originally published as *Braunbuch über Reichstagsbrand und Hitlerterror: Mit einem Vorwort von Lord Marley*, Paris: Éditions du carrefour, 1933.

34 Letter from Münzenberg to Brupbacher, 15 May 1933, cited in Gross, *Münzenberg*, 243.

and new. The most worthy of notice, perhaps, is the Czech Otto Katz (1895–1952), who wrote under the pen names André Simone (or Simon) and Rudolf Breda, among many others. Born into a wealthy Jewish family, this journalist and aspiring writer (a member for many years of the Russian Association of Proletarian Writers) was a colourful figure, about whom rumours abound in the records of secret services both Western and Eastern.[35] Katz spent his youth among the Bohemian milieux of Prague and Vienna, before moving in 1921 to Berlin, where he frequented artistic circles and worked for the left-liberal periodicals *Montag Morgen* and *Tagebuch*. In 1927 he moved to the Piscator Theatre as administrator. In the Soviet Union to shoot the film *Der Aufstand der Fischer* (based on Anna Seghers's story) for Mezhrabpom, Erwin Piscator would recall Katz's time at the theatre with anger: 'I too fell for his slick self-presentation, which took in almost everyone.' He accused Katz of embezzlement (from publishers Rowohlt) and plagiarism (*Neun Männer im Eis* being not his own work but that of one of the members of the North Pole expedition) and of having the character of a 'fraud, a cheat, a scrounger and a rent boy'. He had even managed to borrow 2,000 marks from Marlene Dietrich that he had never paid back.[36] When the Piscator Theatre went bankrupt, Willi Münzenberg took him on as manager of the Universum-Bücherei. Also a journalist for *Welt am Abend*, *Berlin am Morgen* and the *AIZ*, Katz soon made himself

---

35 The life of Otto Katz with its multiple identities and occupations is recounted in Jonathan Miles, *The Nine Lives of Otto Katz: The Remarkable Story of a Communist Super-Spy*, London: Bantam, 2010, though the tale is somewhat sensationally told, with a focus on his espionage, and without recourse to the Russian archives. The author reports that Katz kept an eye on Münzenberg on Moscow's behalf, relying on the unsubstantiated assertion of Arthur Koestler, *The Invisible Writing*, 210. All in all, Babette Gross paints a rather positive picture of him in *Münzenberg*, 319–23. On the wild rumours about Katz to be found not only in memoirs but also in the files of the American, British and French intelligence services, and the absurd accusations brought against him by the Soviet and Czechoslovak secret police in the Slansky Trial, see Anson Rabinbach, 'Von Hollywood an den Galgen: Die Verfolgung und Ermordung des Otto Katz', *Exil: Zeitschrift für Ideengeschichte* 2:1, 2008 24–35. Against their accusations of espionage, Rabinbach evokes the Comintern's practices of mutual surveillance and report. The account that follows is based on Otto Katz's personal file in the Comintern archives, RGASPI, 495/272/117.

36 Five-page typewritten letter full of complaints, addressed to the Comintern authorities, unsigned, but plainly Piscator's from the contents, Moscow, 15 January 1934, RGASPI, 495/272/117.

indispensable. By late 1930, he was able to move to Moscow as head of the German-language division of Mezhrabpom, so as to escape the German authorities, who held him personally liable for several thousand marks of tax owed by the Piscator Theatre. Initially deputy director, he was soon appointed director of Mezhrabpom-Film. In 1933, Münzenberg brought him to Paris. He employed Katz, like nearly all his close staff, in more than one role, not only as secretary to the World Committee for the Relief of the Victims of Fascism but as editorial assistant and writer at the Éditions du carrefour. For security reasons, Katz did his work in the tiny hotel room he shared with his wife, on a side street off the Rue St Honoré.

He was chiefly occupied, however, by research for the *Brown Book* and the organization of a 'counter-trial' to the Reichstag fire trial (which he later claimed to have been his idea[37]). Gustav Regler, the member of the team given the task of describing the methods of torture employed in the concentration camps, provides in his memoirs a bitterly furious description of his comrades of the day. With Manès Sperber and the young Arthur Koestler, he is one of the three German-speaking Communist writers to have left a literary account of the work on the *Brown Book*. Katz he described as 'a considerable linguist, aged forty-three, with a thin-lipped, hard-bitten face, lined with suffering, that had hitherto been known only to the higher agents of the Comintern, and a tendency to lean his head over on his right shoulder. He was always very neatly dressed.'[38]

Paid by the Comintern via the IAH, this high-powered team of writers also included the journalists Alexander Abusch (1902–1982), Albert Norden (1904–1982) and Rudolf Feistmann (1908–1950). Abusch, formerly editor of the *Rote Fahne*, was responsible for the editing of the text as a whole. Albert Norden, who had been deputy editor of the same paper, wrote the chapters on the international connections of the Nazi party. A journalist on the *Rote Aufbau* in Germany and now editor of the Communist journal *Unsere Zeit* in Paris, Rudolf Feistmann wrote the introductory chapter. Others employed on the project were Alfred Kantorowicz, the journalist and soon writer Bodo Uhse (1904–1963) – a

---

37 André Simone, *Men of Europe: From the Confidential Notes of an International Correspondent*, New York: Modern Age, 1941, 8.
38 Regler, *Owl*, 162

member of the NSDAP until 1930 and so a source of useful insider knowledge – and the art historian, journalist and writer Max Schröder (1900–1958), another recent member of the party (joining in 1932), who, like Kantorowicz had lived in the Berlin-Wilmersdorf 'artists' colony' until 1933.

Their job was to gather as much information as possible about the regime of terror in Germany and its measures against the anti-Nazi opposition. This was intended not only to delegitimize the NSDAP but also to undermine the case against Georgi Dimitrov and his co-defendants. Information for the book came from the Comintern, from German Communists in exile or still in Germany, and from Otto Katz's researches in the Netherlands. As Regler remembered, '[N]ewspapers from all over the world were scrutinised for items of German news. Emissaries who could go without risk were sent into Germany, and every new fugitive we could lay our hands on was invited to visit us and tell us his experiences.'[39]

Münzenberg worked by multitasking, and thanks to the testimony of his collaborators we have some idea of his management style. Here, for example, is Regler, admittedly inclined to a degree of caricature:

> Münzenberg was accustomed to pay brief daily visits to the scene of our labours and grin at the sight of our weary faces . . . He read manuscripts, often tossing them aside after a perfunctory glance, and dictated telegrams, manifestos, and lengthy reports of political meetings. He was as foul-mouthed as a cab driver and as variable in his moods as only a genius can be, at one moment exultant and at the next filled with wrath and melancholy, exaggerating all things, seeing enemies everywhere, and no end to our defeat.[40]

Münzenberg was, no doubt, imperious, but perhaps in the manner of a conductor who pushes the orchestra to give of their very best, or an architect who monitors every aspect of construction and is ultimately responsible for every decision. He both delegated and supervised, a 'benevolent despot', as Koestler put it in his foreword to the German edition of Babette Gross's biography. He went on to say: 'As was

---

39 Ibid., 163.
40 Ibid., 162–3.

customary in the German party, all the staff addressed the boss as "Willi" and "Du" – including the cleaning lady and the chauffeur (who were also party members in emigration). Manners were informal, there were no distinctions of rank or seniority.' Koestler also notes, however, a realistic deference among the 'subordinates': 'The atmosphere among the Münzenberg crowd was a strange mixture of revolutionary comradeship and the jealousy of courtiers . . . Willi was impervious to flattery; nevertheless, out of precaution, we avoided contradicting him or arousing his displeasure, and paid the utmost attention to his moods.'[41]

Produced under great pressure, the *Brown Book* was published by Éditions du carrefour in August 1933 – only six months after the fire and the subsequent arrests – in a printing of some 25,000 (this, however, according to Babette Gross, being the subject of exaggerated rumour in many quarters). Translated into over a dozen languages,[42] the *Brown Book* argued not only that the fire benefited no one but the Nazis themselves, but also that an underground passage ran between the Reichstag and the official residence of its president, Göring, documented in the plans unearthed by Gustav Regler. On the basis of the material assembled, Münzenberg finally developed the highly debatable thesis that the chief defendant, Marinus van der Lubbe, a leftist Dutchman who was not a member of the Communist Party, had been manipulated by the Nazis on account of his supposed homosexuality.

The whole argument rested on 'deduction, guesswork and brazen bluff', according to Koestler, who also worked on the second *Brown Book* in 1934.[43] Yet it seemed plausible and succeeded in convincing countless contemporaries simply on the basis of the facts it presented about the brutality of the Nazi regime. At the counter-trial that opened in London on 4 September with a speech by Sir Stafford Cripps, the accused were found not guilty. Münzenberg, and Katz more especially, had succeeded in gathering together a bevy of eminent lawyers and public figures from different countries who confirmed the theses of the *Brown Book*. 'An unofficial tribunal whose mandate was conferred by

---

41 Arthur Koestler, foreword to Babette Gross, *Willi Münzenberg: Eine politische Biographie*, Stuttgart: Deutsche Verlags-Anstalt, 1967, 10.
42 Gross, *Münzenberg*, 249.
43 Koestler, *Invisible Writing*, 199.

the conscience of the world', as Katz put it in the second *Brown Book*,[44] they had investigated the background to the Reichstag Fire trial, examining documents and questioning witnesses.

The *Brown Book*'s allegations and the not-guilty verdict of the counter-trial, delivered on 20 September, the day before the real trial opened in Leipzig, put the Nazis on the defensive from the start. The effect on international public opinion had been electric. In addition, there was the incredible courage shown by Dimitrov, until then an obscure Comintern official, in challenging Göring in court. He became an international hero overnight. In the end, he and his Communist co-defendants were acquitted, while Marinus van der Lubbe was sentenced to death. (Ernst Torgler would continue to be held in preventive detention until 1935 without the Comintern making any effort to secure his release.) Taking up the theme of '*Dimitrov v. Göring*', Münzenberg immediately embarked on a second *Brown Book*.[45] As historian Kevin Morgan observes, this was 'the first example since Lenin of a Communist to whom a significant international public rallied as if spontaneously'.[46]

While the Comintern did commit money and human resources to the campaign against the Reichstag Fire trial, it had been sparing of its efforts. International Red Aid (IRH) became involved only in the autumn, when it decided to reorganize and reinforce its West European office in Paris, assigning additional cadre to it. It thus sent Vittorio Vidali to be its head, together with his companion, Tina Modotti.[47] Münzenberg, for his part, travelled to Moscow in late July or early August in order to finalize with Béla Kun and Osip Piatnitsky his plans for a propaganda coup against the fascists. Münzenberg himself, however, was after more. He wanted to turn the struggle against fascism into a struggle for freedom, in which the labour movement would be

---

44 *The Reichstag Fire Trial: The Second Brown Book of the Hitler Terror*, ed. World Committee for the Relief of the Victims of German Fascism, London: John Lane/The Bodley Head, 1934, 32, cited in Koestler, *Invisible Writing*, 200.

45 This too was translated into a number of languages in addition to French and English.

46 Kevin Morgan, *International Communism and the Cult of the Individual: Leaders, Tribunes and Martyrs Under Lenin and Stalin*, Basingstoke, UK: Palgrave Macmillan, 2017, 36.

47 Claudio Natoli, 'Tina Modotti: Tra avanguardia artistica e "nuova umanità"', in Paolo Ferrari and Claudio Natoli, eds, *Tina Modotti: Arte e libertà tra Europa e Americhe*, Udine: Forum, 2017, 13–24, at 20.

joined by other democratic and progressive forces (so anticipating the coming shift in Comintern policy, so to speak). The Amsterdam-Pleyel movement under Barbusse, on the other hand, strictly adhered to the Comintern's then current binary line of fascism on the one hand and Communism alone on the other, rejecting any reference to democracy and still describing social democracy as an enemy.[48] It was a matter, as Anson Rabinbach has argued, of establishing antifascism as a political position. The Comintern had until then identified fascism with a whole roster of bogeymen, not only with capitalism and imperialism, but with liberalism, social democracy and eventually anyone outside its own camp. As his personal file reveals, Alfred Kurella, secretary of the International Committee against War and Fascism, was reprimanded by the ECCI for allowing social democrats to be invited to a conference.[49] National Socialist Germany, on the other hand, might still prove a reliable ally, in Stalin's eyes. The campaign was then aimed not only at the global public, but also at the Comintern and Soviet party leaderships, who were to be persuaded to play the antifascist card without regard for diplomatic relations with Germany.[50]

In the end, it was not entirely – or even at all – a matter of saving the defendants' lives. Dimitrov had already been relieved of his functions at the WEB by the ECCI on 3 January 1933, though the reason for this isn't clear.[51] Officially, he was told to concentrate entirely on the

---

48 Claudio Natoli, 'Pour une histoire comparée des organisations communistes de solidarité: Le Secours ouvrier international et le Secours rouge international', in José Gotovitch and Anne Morelli, eds, *Les solidarités internationales: Histoire et perspectives*, Bruxelles: Éditions Labor, 2003, 17–42, at 34.

49 Personal file of Alfred Kurella, RGASPI 495/205/6339, cited in Bernhard H. Bayerlein, 'The Entangled Catastrophe: Hitler's 1933 "Seizure of Power" and the Power Triangle – New Evidence on the Historic Failure of the KPD, the Comintern, and the Soviet Union', in Norman LaPorte and Ralf Hoffrogge, eds, *Weimar Communism as Mass Movement 1918–1933*, London: Lawrence & Wishart, 2017, 260–80, at 274–5.

50 Rabinbach, 'Staging Antifascism', 104.

51 It is said that in 1930 the WEB opened a subsidiary office at 63 rue de la Seine in Paris that served to house instructors from abroad and as a point of contact for couriers: Günther Nollau, *Die Internationale: Wurzeln und Erscheinungsformen des proletarischen Internationalismus*, Cologne: Verlag für Politik und Wirtschaft, 1959, 118. That same address housed the architectural practice of Roger Ginsburger (1901–1981), the head of that office. He joined the party only in 1932, however, making that date more probable for its opening. It may be this office that was expanded and placed under the responsibility of someone else.

Amsterdam-Pleyel movement, which operated under Münzenberg's aegis.[52] It would seem obvious, then, that the Comintern wanted to have someone to keep an eye on a Münzenberg they found too independent. Münzenberg had in fact been having problems with the Comintern for years, and the way it constantly obstructed and held back his work regularly plunged him into depression.[53] By July 1933, however, he could contain himself no longer, writing a letter to Stalin that he had wanted to write 'two years ago . . . then a year ago, then definitely three months ago'.[54] He now set out his criticisms of the way the Comintern worked in a twenty-seven-page typewritten text. 'I write to you because I hope that this account of things will help us review the way our movement works and give hundreds of comrades who are more than eager to work a certain freedom to develop their own initiatives.' For these were smothered and extinguished by 'the weight of the apparatus and the way in which it works'. Münzenberg hoped to 'expose and highlight design faults in the apparatus', and backed up his allegations with examples drawn from his work in the various organizations he had set up, such as the International Workers' Relief, the League Against Imperialism and the Amsterdam anti-war movement. But his criticism also went to fundamentals: the Communists had lost the youth to the National Socialists as a result of their 'extraordinarily extreme, doctrinal, dogmatic, inflexible, immobile and formal propaganda'.

He also described how he had repeatedly been stripped of responsibility for the organizations he had established, criticizing in doing so the

---

52 Marietta Stankova, *Georgi Dimitrov: A Biography*, London: I.B. Tauris, 2010, 103.

53 Ursula Langkau-Alex, 'The Woman in the Background: In Search of Babette Gross and the Others in Münzenberg's Networks in the 1930s', in Bernhard H. Bayerlein, Kasper Braskén and Uwe Sonnenberg, eds, *Globale Räume für radikale transnationale Solidarität/Global Spaces for Radical Solidarity*, Berlin: Internationales Willi Münzenberg Forum, 2018, 387–403.

54 The letter from Münzenberg addressed to 'Dear Comrade', Paris, 20 July 1933, is to be found in his personal file, RGASPI 495/205/7000. Published in *Deutschland, Russland, Komintern.*, vol. 2, 1024–33, it is there said to be addressed to Stalin, which is entirely plausible in view of the contents. Reinhard Müller's suggestion that it was intended for Piatnitsky seems in comparison unconvincing, given the authority its author ascribes to its addressee: Reinhard Müller, '"Das macht das stärkste Ross kaputt": Willi Münzenbergs Abrechnung mit dem Apparat der Komintern und ein Moskauer Drehbuch für den Amsterdamer Kongress 1932', *Jahrbuch für Historische Kommunismusforschung* 2010, 243–65.

personnel policy of Moscow headquarters. Both in the wake of the Brussels Congress and during the development of the Amsterdam anti-war movement, the Comintern apparatus had imposed a new leadership. He was head in name only. 'The *de facto* secretaries were sent without anyone having spoken to me.' He had become, then, 'as a friend there [in Moscow] put it, "one advisor among others", real attention being accorded to other friends [comrades], who were placed in control, in party terms'. The Comintern had in fact set up an 'internal commission' that took effective control of the planning and organization of both the Brussels and Amsterdam congresses.[55] This consisted of a member of the Politburo of the KPD as chair, one representative each of the Communist parties of France, England, Holland, Czechoslovakia and the United States, two representatives from the Profintern, and two members of the planned Soviet delegation. And to cap it all, Münzenberg had been sidelined in favour of the long-time Comintern functionary and regular emissary, the Pole Henryk 'Walecki' (1877–1938, real name Horwitz).

Münzenberg concluded by criticizing the aimlessness and incoherence of political direction from Moscow. Orders were followed by counter-orders, time and time again: '90 per cent of one's energy goes to fending off disruptions, leaving only 10 per cent for actual work.' Finally, Münzenberg also criticized the hierarchization and bureaucratization of the apparatus. He had found only one way of coping with his new situation in exile (and with what remained only implicit, the defeat of the party): 'the most feverish, most intensive work is the only possibility'. He was trying to organize 'the maximum of agitation in support of our German friends' and 'to rally together those who have fled abroad', but felt completely unsupported in this. 'I am trying to set up committees to raise money because no one is lifting a finger and it needs an initial impulse from without.' But what was the reaction of the apparatus? 'Then, after a few weeks, the commissions, the sub-committees, the working parties, the appointed persons and the appointed person's deputies come to the conclusion that it's a good idea, of course, but that it can't be done. Initiative is called for in resolutions, but no one can act upon it but the competent instances.'

---

55 On the Brussels Congress, see chapter 5. On the Amsterdam Congress: Directives to the internal commission on the conduct of the anti-war congress, 6 July 1932, RGASPI, 495/19/32, published in Müller, ' "Das macht das stärkste Ross kaputt" ', 263–5.

No more fundamental critique of the Comintern's bureaucratization and its development into an autocratic apparatus in which people were moved about like pieces on a chessboard had ever been levelled from within the fold of the Comintern, but Münzenberg emphasized that he was not acting factionally and would not in future, either. He did not, in fact, belong to any opposition, and had indeed berated them. In his letter, he bad-mouthed the so-called 'Conciliators', and, in *Der Rote Aufbau* of 15 February 1932, he had described Trotsky as a 'counter-revolutionary fascist'.[56]

Münzenberg called for improvements in 'internal working methods and the way the apparatus relates to individual comrades' and for comrades to be permitted to act on their own initiative. In other words, he wanted more democracy. He did not get it. On the contrary: 1935 saw an inspection of the IAH apparatus in Moscow that led in early 1936 led to the summary dismissal of its senior cadre, and after the Seventh World Congress a liquidator from Moscow, the Swiss Karl Hofmaier, was sent to Paris to wind up the IAH, one of the last of the Comintern organizations not to be headquartered in the Soviet Union.[57] Münzenberg was able to save only the Éditions du carrefour, extracted from the remains of the IAH as a financially self-sustaining entity and run thereafter as an independent company. In April 1936, the Politburo of the KPD issued Münzenberg with a severe reprimand for supposedly having provided confidential party information to the 'democrat' Georg Bernhard, editor of the non-party left-liberal *Pariser Tageblatt*, who was involved in the programmatic discussions of the Paris-based German Popular Front Commission.[58] In late 1936, Münzenberg was relieved of all his functions by the Comintern, his place on the Popular Front Commission he had worked so painstakingly to establish being taken by

---

56 Münzenberg, 'Trotzkis faschistischer Vorschlag einer Blockbildung der KPD mit der SPD', *Der Rote Aufbau: Halbmonatsschrift für Politik, Literatur, Wirtschaft, Sozialpolitik und Arbeiterbewegung* 5:4, 15 February 1932, 147–60. The date of publication is erroneously given as 1933 in *Deutschland, Russland, Komintern*, vol. 2, 1468.

57 On this, see Brigitte Studer, 'Ein Prozess in Rom und seine Wiederholung in Moskau: Der Fall des Schweizer Komintern-Instrukteurs Karl Hofmaier', *Jahrbuch für historische Kommunismusforschung* 1994, 254–74; Gross, *Münzenberg*, 287–8, in which Hofmaier's name is misspelled).

58 'Highly confidential' communication from Albert Müller (i.e. Georg Brückmann) to the Cadre Department, Moscow, 15 September 1936, RGASPI 495/205/7000.

his rival Walter Ulbricht (1893–1973). On 28 October, the ECCI Secretariat took the decision to 'inspect' the Münzenberg apparatus in Paris, which was funded by the Comintern. The task was assigned to Czech Comintern functionary Bohumír Šmeral, a former subordinate of Münzenberg's, who was instructed either to close Münzenberg's publishing houses and solidarity organizations or to take over their management, vetting the staff and purging undesirables. Šmeral was also to get Münzenberg to go back to Moscow again to report, the establishment of a maritime route from Le Havre supposedly having made it possible for this to happen more frequently. Münzenberg, however, claimed to be worn out from overwork, which was why he had already booked a room for a ten-day holiday at the seaside. The real reason he alluded to only cryptically. On his last trip to Moscow, a couple of months before, he observed, the Western press had said he had been arrested.[59] That was not true, but he had certainly been shaken by Radek's arrest while he was there. What is more, he had not been received by Dimitrov – appointed general secretary of the Comintern a year before – or Manuilsky, a clear sign that he had fallen out of favour. He and Babette had also had to wait a long time for the exit visas they needed to return home, which they obtained only with Togliatti's help.[60] It would be their last trip to the Soviet Union.

The flight from Germany in 1933 did not put an end to political conflict over the party line, to conflicts within the apparatus, or to competition for power and influence. An example is offered by the duplication of functions between Münzenberg's International Anti-Fascist Archive and the Institute for the Study of Fascism (INFA). The latter was the result of an initiative by the Communist fraction in the International of Proletarian Freethinkers (IPF), namely the Yugoslav writer Oto Bihalji-Merin (1905–1993; Peter Maros) and the German Comintern functionary Hans Meins (1900–?, alias Jan Jansen, Georg Jacobsen, etc.). Its

---

59 Letter from Bohumír Šmeral addressed to 'Dear Friend', recounting his mission to Paris to close down Münzenberg's organizations and publishing operations, Paris, 17 December 1936, in *Deutschland, Russland, Komintern*, vol. 2, 1290–1.

60 The exit visa applications of 14 and 15 October 1936 submitted to the Liaison Department of the ECCI are signed by 'Ercoli' (Togliatti). The same office, however, also has an application for an entry visa for Babette Gross dated 31 October (RGASPI 495/205/7000). See also Ursula Langkau-Alex, 'Willi Münzenberg im Exil und die Bedeutung der Freundschaft in der Krise der dreißiger Jahre', in Schlie and Roche, *Willi Münzenberg*, 173–94, at 177.

official sponsors, however, were French, among them the Communist Marcel Willard (1889–1956), one of the most prominent lawyers in the French section of International Red Aid and a leading figure in the campaign in support of Dimitrov and Thälmann.[61] The two institutions had come into being at about the same time, pursued the same objectives, and competed for donations and public attention. They also shared the familiar mode of organization: 'Outwardly a bourgeois undertaking' with a 'board of trustees made up of prominent bourgeois figures from France, England, America and the German emigration' with a 'person of distinction' at its head, but the 'real management, of course, in the hands of experienced Communists who are responsible to the Comintern, etc.'[62] While the journalist and publicist Adolf Ende (1899–1951, alias Lex Breuer and Lex Ende) and IPF general secretary Hans Meins – a 'party commissar', in Koestler's eyes – coordinated with the Auslandkomitee, the KPD's Paris-based leadership in exile, Münzenberg evidently dealt directly with the Comintern in Moscow. Vexed by this, the bypassed party leadership wrote to Moscow that 'with his archive, Willi wants to strike a blow against the Institute for the Study of Fascism established by the IPF'.[63] The duplication caused confusion even at the Comintern in Moscow, with Béla Kun, head of the Agitprop Department, mixing up the two institutions in writing to Piatnitsky.[64] Even amid the difficulties of exile, the Communist emigration was riddled with personal quarrels and petty disputes, but it was also pervaded, to grimmer effect, by the struggle against political deviations. Suspicions of sympathy with or membership of opposition groups poisoned the climate and hindered political work not only in France but also Switzerland.

---

61 The INFA has received rather more scholarly attention than has Münzenberg's Anti-Fascist Archive, as not only did Koestler and Sperber work there and write about it, but other German writers such as Bertolt Brecht and Kurt Kläber were also associated with it: Jacques Omnès, 'L'Institut pour l'étude du fascism (INFA)', in Gilbert Badia et al., *Les bannis de Hitler: Accueil et luttes des exilés allemands en France, 1933–1939*, Paris: Presses universitaires de Vincennes, 1984, 185–98; Dieter Schiller, 'Über das Institut zum Studium des Faschismus in Paris 1934/35', *Weimarer Beiträge* 3, 2011, 370–94; Reinhard Müller, 'Über die Gründung des Pariser Instituts zum Studium des Faschismus: Neue Moskauer Dokumente', *Exil* 32:1, 2012, 34–42.

62 Memorandum to the Auslandkomitee of the KPD, signed L. Breuer, Paris, 26 September 1933, published in Müller, 'Gründung', 37–9.

63 Report by 'Rudolf' (Paul Merker) to KPD leaders in Moscow, Paris, 4 December 1933, quoted in Müller, 'Gründung', 35.

64 Müller, 'Gründung', 36.

Basel and Zurich: Precarious Safety

Even before 1933, preparations had been made to transfer the Comintern's publishing operations to the Swiss border town of Basel should the need arise, the associated investment in premises and printing machinery having also been partially safeguarded by arrangements that saw them assigned to Swiss companies. The business of Hamburg's Carl Hoym Verlag (renamed Internationaler Arbeiterverlag in 1927) was thus shifted to Switzerland under the name Buchhandlung A. Müller. Under the management of Fritz Zillig (1894–?), who in Basel used the pseudonyms 'A. Müller', 'Karl Müller', 'Karl Mallaun' and even the cheeky if misspelt 'Jakob Burckardt', Comintern printing orders were placed with Communist printing-houses in the Netherlands, Czechoslovakia and Switzerland, an arrangement that also served to disguise Comintern subsidies to the parties concerned.[65] Münzenberg also benefited from this network, having the newspaper *Unsere Zeit* (formerly *Roter Aufbau*) printed by the Basler Genossenschaftsdruckerei printing cooperative in Basel, the *AIZ* in Prague.

In March 1933, an employee of Münzenberg's named Karl Gröhl (known as Retzlaw from the 1950s on) was made responsible for sales of the *AIZ* in Switzerland. Formerly head of the KPD's illegal apparatus, he had been appointed manager of the Neuer Deutscher Verlag in 1928. That Gröhl was now employed by the Basel subsidiary of Münzenberg's Universum-Bücherei library was a result of the difficulties faced by refugees from the Reich. In Paris, Münzenberg had asked him, in fact, to return illegally to Germany to take care of publishing operations there, believing at the time – so Gröhl says in his memoirs – that all functionaries, with the exception of members of the Central Committee, should return to Germany, as the Hitler regime was beginning to show signs of weakness.[66] Gröhl thus proceeded to Basel and thence to Zurich, calling at cover addresses known to him to ensure that his letters would be forwarded without delay, before going on to Vienna. There he was arrested at the

---

65 Interrogation of Wilhelm Kox by the Gestapo, in connection with the Internationaler Arbeiterverlag, 15 December 1938, Bundesarchiv, DZ, NJ 11, Nr. 2; Studer, *Un parti sous influence: Le Parti communiste suisse, une section du Komintern, 1931 à 1939*, Lausanne: L'Âge d'Homme, 1994, 449–50.

66 Karl Retzlaw, *Spartakus: Aufstieg und Niedergang; Erinnerungen eines Parteiarbeiters*, Frankfurt a. M.: Verlag Neue Kritik, 1972, 367.

Vienna offices shared by the *AIZ* and the Universum-Bücherei and put on a train to Feldkirch, on Austria's border with Switzerland, under police escort. From there he made his way to Zurich, 'like Vienna, a peaceful, petty bourgeois and prosperous city', as it was described not much later by Charlotte Bindel (1909–2008, later Hümbelin by marriage).[67] As his money did not stretch to a hotel room, he stayed at a 'cover address', presumably the home of a party member or sympathizer, until a telegram arrived from Babette Gross telling him to meet her in Basel, where he would find accommodation with the Communist factory inspector Walter Strub (1882–1938), a founder member of the Swiss party. Strub lived with his wife and one of his two sons, both of them party members, in cooperative housing in Riehen. The other son was living in the Soviet Union. Gröhl received a friendly welcome, but as there were other refugees in the house, he had to sleep with a blanket on the floor. (As a cantonal employee, Strub was reprimanded that same year by Basel-Stadt minister Carl Ludwig for his solidarity activity with refugees, and if the Communist Party had not enjoyed considerable support in the city, with a 15 per cent vote, he could well have been in danger of dismissal.)

Babette Gross gave Gröhl three tasks: to set up a non-party refugee support committee, to run the Universum-Bücherei now transferred to Basel, and to look after the distribution of the *Brown Book*, apparently expected to run into the 'millions'.[68] He was given the addresses of Zurich publisher Emil Oprecht and the writer Rudolf Jakob Humm, two left Social Democrats who were involved in aid to refugees aid and open to nonpartisan cooperation. With Oprecht, Gröhl made arrangements for the distribution of the *Brown Book*. Oprecht in turn introduced him to the Italian political refugee Ignazio Silone (1900–1978, real name Secondino Tranquilli), whose antifascist novel, *Fontamara*, he had just published, and which Universum-Bücherei would put at the head of the mail-order list it sent out to members.

This was a decision that took no account of the political orthodoxy of the Central Committee of the Swiss CP. Like the other Communist parties, this had committed itself to the Moscow line in the late 1920s. In 1933, there

---

67 Lotte Hümbelin, *Mein eigener Kopf: Ein Frauenleben in Wien, Moskau, Prag, Paris und Zürich*, Zurich: edition 8, 1999, 237.

68 In addition to the other sources cited, the account that follows is indebted to Retzlaw, *Spartakus*, 369–73.

could be no tolerance of people like Silone, who had been expelled from the PCI in 1931 and since been ostracized as a 'renegade'. Hans Bickel (1884–1961), chair of the Swiss party's literature committee, who himself ran a Communist bookstore in Zurich, ordered Gröhl to leave Switzerland immediately, with distribution of the *AIZ* and the *Brown Book* to be handed over to a Swiss comrade. Bickel, whose son Walter was working in the Soviet Union after studying engineering, and whose other son Ernst was later declared missing in the Spanish Civil War, was supported in this by the Central Committee of the Swiss party, which resolved to boycott the book by the 'traitor and Trotskyist Silone'. When Gröhl showed Bickel's letter to Oprecht, the matter became a public scandal, with the Social Democrat *Berner Tagwacht* of 3 August 1933 running the headline 'A Comrade to Be Expelled from the KPS!' Gröhl then found himself accused by the KPS of 'having publicly slandered our party' by informing a 'well-known officer of the Swiss Socialist Party of an internal dispute'.[69]

Yet not all party functionaries agreed: Hans Märki (1892–1961), manager of the Basler Genossenschaftsdruckerei (whose salary was paid by the Comintern) stood up for Gröhl, suggesting that it was no more than a matter of commercial competition, informing the *AIZ*'s street sellers that Bickel with his so-called Arbeiterbuchhandlung (Workers' Bookshop) was a 'private capitalist', one unhappy, what was more, at not getting the distribution deal for the *AIZ*. On 9 August, Münzenberg intervened personally with a five-page letter from Moscow, in which he called upon the Swiss party to expel Bickel 'for severely damaging the party and mounting a deliberate challenge to the *AIZ* sales operation and its current head Karl Gröhl'. He criticized the Swiss comrades not only for their behaviour but also for the careless and defamatory language they had used throughout. First, he pointed out to the Swiss party that it was 'inadmissible and un-Communist' to speak of IAH employees as 'Münzenbergites', which was the language of the National Socialists. Second, the international fraction leadership at the IAH was not a 'Neumann and Trotsky group', but a responsible Communist leadership politically and otherwise under the direct supervision of the Comintern.[70] Münzenberg did not, however, mention the fact that such

---

69 Letter from the KPS to the KPD, n.d. [late July 1933], RGASPI 495/91/192.
70 Letter from Willi Münzenberg to the Secretariat of the KPS, Moscow, 9 August 1933, RGASPI 495/91/192.

designations as the 'Neumann and Trotsky group' were drawn from the arsenal of Stalinist prosecutors and that the use of such language showed how worryingly poor relationships between comrades had become. The Swiss CP now had to set up a committee of inquiry into Bickel and the whole affair, and while Bickel was not expelled, he was formally reprimanded and removed from the chair of the literature committee. As Münzenberg had demanded, henceforth 'all matters relating to *AIZ* and Universum' were to be 'taken up directly with Münzenberg's representative, Comrade Gross'.[71]

Gröhl had to leave, nonetheless. His presence in Switzerland had become public as a result of the affair, and he received a summons from the cantonal police advising him to relocate his business to another country. This he did. Gröhl was lucky, in that the Basel police were more tolerant of illegal refugees than those of other Swiss cantons, and so did not put a police stamp in his passport that would have barred him from later re-entry.[72]

Switzerland was a difficult place for persecuted German Communists. The local Communist party was weak, then having a significant political presence only in the cities of Basel and Zurich. Official policy, furthermore, was markedly anti-Communist; it was only after the Second World War that the Federal Council agreed to establish diplomatic relations with the Soviet Union. Domestically, the Communists were subjected to severe repression, and from 1932 they were subject to dismissal from federal employment. The Swiss authorities were also extremely reluctant to afford diplomatic protection to Swiss Communists abroad. When Mentona Moser's personal assets in Germany were frozen and afterwards confiscated, the Swiss authorities refused her any diplomatic support because she had promoted Communist propaganda in Germany.[73]

Swiss refugee policy was dominated by the fear of being overwhelmed by immigrants. As early as February 1933, the Federal Prosecutor's

---

71 Letter from Willi Münzenberg to the Secretariat of the KPS, Moscow, 18 August 1933, RGASPI 495/91/192.

72 On Swiss refugee policy from 1933 to 1945, see the report of the government-appointed Independent Commission of Experts: Unabhängige Expertenkommission Schweiz – Zweiter Weltkrieg (UEK), *Die Schweiz und die Flüchtlinge zur Zeit des Nationalsozialismus*, Zurich: Chronos, 2001.

73 The correspondence between Mentona Moser's lawyer and the Swiss authorities forms a thick file: BAR E2001C#1000/1533#1772*; Moser, *Ich habe gelebt*, 225.

Office had thus ordered frontier cantons to keep closer control over the borders, in order to keep out the two categories of refugees considered undesirable, the Jews and the Communists, the latter being seen as a particular threat to internal and external security. Only a few more than a hundred people were recognized as political refugees during the period in question. The rest of the incomers were granted, at best, a precarious 'certificate of tolerance' as an alien without right of residence, and banned from political activity.

Gröhl had not succeeded in establishing a nonpartisan relief committee. There were, though, organizations that aided refugees and public figures who stood up for them. The Swiss writer Rudolf Jakob Humm, whom Babette Gross had recommended to Gröhl, had founded such a committee. Humm had attended the Amsterdam Congress in 1932, and that same year had founded the Neue Russland (New Russia) association, which promoted a positive image of the Soviet Union under the auspices of the All-Union Society for Cultural Relations with Foreign Countries (VOKS in the Russian acronym). This consisted mainly of artists and intellectuals.[74] As Humm told Gröhl, the Swiss authorities had made different groups responsible for the maintenance of their counterparts among the refugees, so that the Schweizerisches Arbeiterhilfswerk (Swiss Workers' Relief Agency) looked after the social democrats, the Swiss section of International Red Aid the Communists, the Schweizerische Israelitische Gemeindebund (Swiss Federation of Jewish Communities) the Jews, and a church aid committee for the Protestant refugees.[75] Responsible for 120 German Communists in March 1933,[76] the Swiss section of International Red Aid had not only to find them accommodation but also to support them financially, most being destitute.

Those employed by the Comintern's news bulletin and its associated telegraphic agency, on the other hand, could rely on their own resources, being paid by the organization.[77] Given the increasing repression in Germany, *Inprekorr* had already been regionalized, with the German edition being published in Basel from 1932 under the title *Rundschau*

---

74 On Das Neue Russland, see Jean-François Fayet, *VOKS, le laboratoire helvétique; Histoire de la diplomatie culturelle soviétique de l'entre-deux-guerres*, Geneva: Georg éditeur, 2014, 281–93.

75 Retzlaw, *Spartakus*, 370–1.

76 Studer, *Un parti*, 439.

77 On the *Rundschau* and RUNA in Switzerland, see also Studer, *Un parti*, 450–66.

über Politik, Wirtschaft und Arbeiterbewegung (Review of Politics, Economics and the Workers' Movement). The English edition had moved to London, the French to Paris, the Czech to Prague.[78] Local comrades served as facilitators, advisers, employees and sometimes frontmen. The official publisher of the *Rundschau*, whose name figured in the local commercial register, was the Basle Communist Otto Schudel. Before returning to Switzerland in 1930, he had worked at the secretariat of the League Against Imperialism and was now news editor, based at the Baseler Genossenschaftsdruckerei on Brunngasse.[79] As he later explained in an interview, he 'edited the articles, the reports that came in, if they still needed it. I also did the page make-up and supervised the publication as a whole.'[80] On the occasion of an employee review in 1937, Julius Alpári spoke highly of him, if somewhat condescendingly: 'From an unremarkable assistant he has developed into an excellent editor. Very loyal and reliable.'[81]

Subscription management and financial administration were now also based in Basel and officially in the hands of Swiss party members. For this purpose, Hans Märki, manager of the Genossenschaftsdruckerei, opened an account and rented a safe deposit box at the Eidgenössische Bank. As the Basel-Stadt police discovered, a great deal of money went through this account, more than 32,000 Swiss francs in July/August 1934 alone. Otto Schudel, for his part, opened an account at the Schweizerische Volksbank (today Crédit Suisse), through which the Comintern subsidies passed on their way to the *Rundschau* and the other editions of *Inprekorr*. In August 1933, around 1,000 Swiss francs were transferred to Willie Clark, the editor of *International Press Correspondence* in London, and 500 francs to Robert Petit ('Bob'), at the head of *La Correspondance internationale* in Paris. A total of 13,419.75 Swiss francs passed through the account over a month.[82] Financial

---

78 Iren Komját, *Die Geschichte der Inprekorr, Zeitung der Kommunistischen Internationale (1921–1939)*, Frankfurt a. M.: Verlag Marxistische Blätter, 1992, 35.

79 *Schweizerisches Handelsblatt* 108, 10 May 1933; Studer, *Un parti*, 451.

80 Otto Schudel, interviewed by Wolfgang Jean Stock, Basel, 28 March 1973, at ifz-muenchen.de/archiv/zs/zs-3035.pdf.

81 Report from Julius Alpári to the Ercoli Secretariat, 'Der Redaktionsstab der Rundschau-Inprekorr-Ausgaben und Tel.Agenturen', Moscow, 9 April 1937, RGASPI 495/12/140.

82 According to an undated report by the Basel-Stadt police, cited in Studer, *Un parti*, 459.

control over the Comintern's publishing operations lay in the hands of Hugo Eberlein (known as 'Daniel Nielsen' in the mid-1930s), a graphic designer and one of the early professional revolutionaries, who thus had oversight of the Communist printing-houses and publishers in Switzerland and neighbouring countries. Banned as an undesirable alien since 1921, however, he was only able to enter Switzerland illegally. His colleague, the German Communist Willy Langrock (1889–1962), long-time director of press and publishing at KPD headquarters, was, on the other hand, a regular visitor to Basel. He was also the unofficial, de facto manager of Imprimmob SA and Diligentia, the two companies established in Switzerland to which interests in the KPD's German printing works had been assigned to save them from the National Socialists. Following a lengthy investigation by the Swiss Federal Prosecutor, Langrock was arrested by the Basel police in February 1935 and expelled to France on 6 March.[83]

Julius Alpári had already fled to Switzerland in late 1932 or early 1933. Most of his Berlin team followed, in dribs and drabs. Irén Komját and Michel Dieschbourg were Alpári's deputies at the *Rundschau*. Together with Fritz Runge, they made up the editorial office.[84] Now called RUNA (for Rundschau-Nachrichten-Agentur), the telegraphic agency had also moved to Switzerland. It was headed by Heinrich Kurella, 'assigned' to Zurich in early March 1933. His partner, Charlotte Stenbock-Fermor, went with the telegraphic agency as translator and typist.[85] The two travelled separately, however. Stenbock-Fermor, smartly dressed, by train, while Kurella – according to Irén Komját's memoirs – crossed the border more adventurously on skis.[86] Fiete Ketzler, who was later able to obtain legal residence thanks to a marriage of convenience, also came from Berlin; the Englishwoman (Ethel) Maud Parlow-Hutchinson moved to Zurich in late summer 1933, her daughter Marka in October that same year.[87]

---

83 On these arrangements, see Studer, *Un parti*, 466–77.

84 Five-page report by Julius Alpári, 'Der Redaktionsstab der Rundschau-Inprekorr-Ausgaben und Tel.Agenturen', Moscow, 9 April 1937, RGASPI 495/12/140, also cited in Studer, *Un parti*, 452.

85 Charlotte Stenbock-Fermor, typewritten political autobiography, Moscow, 2 October 1934, RGASPI 495/205/6433.

86 Komját, *Geschichte*, 35.

87 Official record of interrogation by the Zurich municipal police, June 1934, BAR E4320B#1974/47#412* and BAR E21#1000/131#9282*.

Like the *Rundschau*, the RUNA too was entered on the commercial register, the Zurich Communist Herta Matzinger (1906–1985), Viennese by birth, Swiss by marriage, and a draughtswoman by profession, lending her name as its sole manager; Jenny Humbert-Droz was another authorized signatory. Its registered cooperative capital was 5,000 Swiss francs. The RUNA gathered, selected and distributed news to the different editorial offices: *Correspondance internationale* in Paris, *International Press Correspondence* in London, the *Svetovi Rozhled* in Prague and *Correspondenzia Internacional* in Madrid and Valencia.[88] If need be, it could also be used as a conduit to transmit ECCI political directives to individual parties, and messages also travelled in the opposite direction. In 1933–35, when László Boros (Gibarti) worked for the ECCI press department in Moscow, the *Rundschau* also had a special correspondent in the Soviet Union. Until then, various journalists – though chiefly Boros and Irén Komját – had visited Moscow for longer or shorter periods.

The official members of the RUNA cooperative were a number of Swiss comrades who served as cover for the foreign illegals on the staff. Jenny Humbert-Droz was on the French team, and Theo Pinkus, Kurella's old friend from Berlin, soon joined the German. The agency's registered offices were at Gerbergasse 9, in Zurich, but it also had an undercover office for the illegals not far away, at Hornergasse 12, on the third floor, in the name of the RAPID translation agency. Four or five people worked there every day, compiling the RUNA bulletin and translating the news for the French and English versions. Couriers took these to the official office, where the German-, French- and English-language bulletins were stencil-duplicated and despatched. One presumes that the *Rundschau*'s foreign journalists had likewise used the undercover office to start with. The Gerbergasse building also housed the Arbeiterbuchhandlung on the second floor, and other Communist organizations alongside the *Rundschau* office; 'A whole nest', in the words of the Zurich cantonal police.[89] In February 1934, as evidence of police surveillance mounted, the Swiss comrade who had signed the lease for the illegal office terminated the tenancy, leaving the foreign

---

88 This was the list as of 1937; some titles varied over time.

89 Special report from Detective Iseli to police headquarters, Zurich, 30 June 1933, BAR E4320B#1974/47#412*.

staff to do their writing and translating at home. Orders came by courier. So that their constant typing should be thought unremarkable, *Rundschau* and RUNA journalists and their translators and typists pretended to be writers or scholars. Only Swiss comrades worked at the official office, and it was they who delivered jobs and couriered materials between different individuals.

These complications of working life came on top of the already difficult living conditions faced by political emigrants. As well as the accommodation offered by Swiss party members and fellow-travellers, there were the boarding houses and small hotels in which Comintern employees officially resided as tourists. Alpári and his wife lived for a time in a guesthouse on Ekkehardstrasse in Zurich. When it became evident that the police were on their trail, Alpári moved part of the *Rundschau* editorial team to Lausanne. Dieschbourg had to live semi-legally in Bregenz, across the Austrian border, travelling back and forth. To ensure the link with Zurich, the Czechoslovak Fritz Eichenwald (1901–1941, born Josef Schmitz), would be contacted by letter or phone to take over urgent messages. An engineer, earlier an assistant at the Technische Hochschule in Berlin and now at the Eidgenössische Technische Hochschule in Zurich, Eichenwald, who also belonged to the KPD's illegal apparatus, enjoyed good cover.

Precarity extended from immigration status to housing. In his memoirs, Jules Humbert-Droz speaks of around fifteen people living in illegality in Zurich.[90] Most of the refugees had had to leave everything behind, travelling with only minimal luggage so as not to attract attention. 'At best, you learn from it', Charlotte Stenbock-Fermor wrote to her parents, 'that it makes no sense to own more than you actually need.'[91] She and Heinrich Kurella lived for a time at Zurlindenstrasse 215b, being put up by two neighbouring Communist families with flats on the inner yard, the Kirschbaums and the Kownats; Kurella also lodged for a while with the Humbert-Droz family.[92] With Fritz Eichenwald's help,

---

90 Jules Humbert-Droz, *Mémoires*, vol. 3, *Dix ans de lutte antifasciste, 1931–1941*, Neuchâtel: À la Baconnière, 1972, 352.

91 Cited in Yvonne Hirdman, *Meine Mutter, die Gräfin: Ein Jahrhundertleben zwischen Boheme und Kommunismus; Aus dem Schwedischen von Nina Hoyer*, Berlin: Insel Verlag 2011, 357.

92 Fritz Eichenwald, report to Comrade Müller of the German representation at the ECCI on the arrests in Zurich in June 1934, Moscow, 27 November 1935, RGASPI 495/205/6433.

they then found a small apartment or perhaps a sublet of one or two rooms. In the files of the Swiss Federal Prosecutor's Office, in any event, their address in June 1934 is given as 'c/o Biske, Gladbachstrasse 47', a turn-of-the-century apartment house in a middle-class area.[93] It was, however, often not possible to house a couple or a family together. The Komjáts, for instance, placed their two sons with Dr Fritz Pesch, a left-wing Social Democrat and secretary to Zurich's guardianship authority, but had to live elsewhere themselves. Margarete Buber and Heinz Neumann, ordered back from Spain by the Comintern in November 1933, likewise ended up living apart in Zurich, she at the home of a linoleum-layer and member of the Red Aid in Bleulerstrasse, he with a middle-class family whose son was a Communist.

Despite all the difficulties, a certain routine established itself in tranquil Switzerland. Margarete Buber-Neuman recalled, for example, 'a halfway normal life': 'Almost every morning Heinz picked me up in front of the linoleum-layer's house to go and work with me, his "secretary", in the little room he had in a big detached house just a few streets away.'[94] And Charlotte Stenbock-Fermor wrote to her mother, 'Despite everything, I wouldn't want my life any different, it has meaning and I'm very happy with H.'[95] The price of illegality was, however, exclusion from all public political activity; while exiles were required to join the local Communist party, they could not be active within it.

On security grounds, contact with local activists was to be avoided. This favoured close social relationships among foreign Communists, and, in a small city like Zurich, they were highly dependent on each other. Heinrich Kurella and Heinz Neumann, who had been at daggers drawn in Germany (the one a 'Conciliator', the other a 'party leftist', i.e. a Stalinist), became close friends in Zurich. It was Kurella who first helped Neumann and his partner find accommodation on their arrival.[96] Their partners became friends, too, it would seem. This we learn not from Buber-Neumann's memoirs, in which she says not a word about Charlotte, her 'always elegant friend', but from an intimate pen portrait

---

93 Stenbock-Fermor file, BAR E21#1000/131#9514*.
94 Margarete Buber-Neumann, *Von Potsdam nach Moskau: Stationen eines Irrwegs*, Stuttgart: Deutsche Verlags-Anstalt, 1957, 381.
95 Cited in Hirdman, *Mutter*, 367.
96 Buber-Neumann, *Potsdam*, 380.

she wrote later on.[97] In this way, Buber-Neumann, too, conforms to the pattern of erasing women from the political world.

Given the smaller scale of Swiss society, the foreigners all ended up meeting in the same places: at the leftish Pension Comi, at the homes of the not very numerous left-liberal sympathizers in Zurich, and of those of the local Communists who were willing and able to take in illegal comrades. This resulted in the formation of an identifiable circle of like-minded people – identifiable even to the police. Buber-Neumann admitted, looking back, that the political refugees did not always take security seriously: 'As they became used to illegality, their caution naturally diminished. It became ever more matter of course to meet other émigrés, even comrades from the Swiss Communist Party.'[98] The Neumanns' and Kurellas' wider circle of friends included several married couples whom they knew from Berlin, among them Karola Piotrkowski and Ernst Bloch, with whom Margarete and Heinz spent a few days in the mountains in Graubünden before the others were expelled on 15 September 1934 and moved for a time to Vienna.[99] Another such couple were the Fritz Eichenwald already mentioned and his wife Lissy, still another the German physician and Communist Dr Ernst Ascher (1899–1937?) – who would become Arthur Koestler's brother-in-law in 1935 – and his Zurich-born wife, Elsa, née Brunner. Soon, however, between 1933 and 1934, they would all be expelled from Switzerland for Communist activities. Heinrich Kurella and Heinz Neumann also had dealings with Hans Holm (1895–1981), a 'Conciliator' and former head of Münzenberg's publishing house, who in 1933–34 was encharged by the Comintern with developing Ring Verlag in Zurich as the successor to the Berlin's Verlag für Literatur und Politik – a publishing house that Heinz Neumann would then work for.

As Buber-Neumann says, members of the Swiss party also formed part of the émigrés' circle. Most important to her was Theo Pinkus, a friend from Berlin, followed by the Communist members of the Kirschbaum family, so numerous that they could have formed a party cell of their own. Josef Kirschbaum was a Jewish carpenter who had fled

---

97 Margarete Buber-Neumann, *Die erloschene Flamme: Schicksale meiner Zeit*, Frankfurt a. M.: Ullstein Verlag [1976], 1989, 92–104.
98 Buber-Neumann, *Potsdam*, 382.
99 Karola Bloch, *Aus meinem Leben*, Pfullingen: Verlag Günther Neske, 1981, 93.

Nizhny Novgorod for Switzerland in 1905, and with the exception of Martha all the children he had with his wife Lisa were politically active: Sophie, Vera, Helen, Marie, Benjamin and Annette, the eldest, married to Marino Bodenmann (1893–1964), a journalist and subeditor at the Swiss party newspaper and a longstanding member of the KPS Politburo. Ubiquitous in the Communist life of the city of Zurich, the family took in numerous refugees, and were accordingly kept under police surveillance. Three of the offspring, no longer children but adults by the mid-1930s, worked for the RUNA in one way or another.

Sophie (1912–2002), the youngest daughter, was a shorthand typist. In a 'political autobiography' written after she moved to the Soviet Union (where she worked in the Press Section at the ECCI), she says that she worked at first in the illegal apparatus, 'until the legal one was organized'. That meant taking many precautions. 'After about 2 or 3 months I moved on to legal office operations and was able to circulate more freely again.'[100] Benjamin, the only son, worked for RUNA as an assistant. Helen, married in France to the saddler and trade unionist Isek Tyk (who would die in Auschwitz), served as a courier from late 1932 to the spring of 1934. Mention should also be made of Vera, a courier for the Italian party. Later, in the Soviet Union, acquaintance with her would become a problem for some members of the circle, according to Heinrich Kurella, for she had been expelled from the party for 'Trotskyism' in the early 1930s.

As has been said, the activities of the *Rundschau* and the telegraphic agency were not unknown to the police. They discovered the illegal office and watched it for weeks, but it vanished before they could do anything. They were only able to act after further months of investigation, reflected in a fat file that testifies to frequent exchanges between federal, cantonal and municipal levels.[101]

Although Zurich's city police had long been monitoring the Kirschbaum family's mail, together, more recently, with that of Maud and Marka Parlow, it was an entirely chance event that gave them their first concrete lead. In January 1934, the police learned of the existence of a 'Ch. (or Cl.) Stenbock, Zurlindenstrasse 215b, Zürich 3', from a

---

100 Political autobiography of Sophie Kirschbaum, submitted to the International Control Commission, Moscow, 21 October 1936, RGASPI 495/274/58.
101 BAR E4320B#1974/47#412*.

'foreign money order form thrown into the rubbish on account of ink blots', as Detective Hüni reported.[102] Charlotte, whose name it was on the money order, had wanted to send 40 Swiss francs to her mother in Leipzig. But this was only an initial clue. As yet, the police knew nothing more: 'I have not yet determined whether the person Stenbock exists or whether it is cover for a member of the Kirschbaum family', Hüni went on to say.

On 7 June 1934, Charlotte Stenbock-Fermor was finally arrested on suspicion of Communist activity, at her home at Gladbachstrasse 47. Seven lever-arch files, a typewriter and a small notebook with poorly anonymized names were seized. Heinrich Kurella the police did not find, because, unlike his partner, he was not registered, and the police didn't know he was living there, leaving him to escape the apartment unnoticed with his landlady's help. This left Fritz Eichenwald, come to deliver a message from 'Comrades Stein' (Irén and Aladár Komját) at the *Rundschau*, to fall into the police trap. That same day, the police arrested the two Parlows, mother and daughter. All four were expelled as a danger to the internal and external security of the state. While the Parlows were able to travel to England, Charlotte Stenbock-Fermor and Fritz Eichenwald were deported to Austria, she going on to Prague, he remaining in Vienna for the time being. He would emigrate to the Soviet Union, in March 1935, only after his appeal against expulsion had been rejected by the Swiss Federal Prosecutor's Office.

This blow against the RUNA was a warning. From then on, the agency worked with a reduced staff and employed only Swiss Communists, the police authorities being unable to take action against them because the Swiss Communist Party was legal at the time.[103] Arriving in Moscow, Fritz Eichenwald attributed the uncovering of part of the RUNA-*Rundschau* apparatus to a number of weaknesses: disregard of the elementary rules of conspiracy; overconfidence in the tolerance of the Zurich city police, which was under Social Democrat leadership; and the lack of an 'an organizer, a technician of illegality' capable of holding

---

102 Report by Detective Hüni, Zurich city police, 8 January 1934, BAR E4320B#1974/47#412*.

103 The RUNA would in fact increasingly lose importance relative to the Agence France-Monde in Paris and Nordisk-Press in Scandinavia.

'staff to the strict discipline and the rules of conspiracy that must be adhered to under conditions of illegality'.[104]

Yet the police scored only a limited success, much to their chagrin. The Federal Prosecutor's Office did indeed conclude that 'concealed within the Runa is a vigorous intercommunication between Communist agents operating undercover and internationally, who, through their press service, contribute to the propaganda efforts of the Communist International',[105] and they had been able to draw up a list of some forty names. Yet most of these were Swiss citizens or resident abroad or had otherwise proved impossible to lay hands on.[106] The reason was that '[RUNA] correspondents and staff actually in Zurich use only their first names, in accordance with Communist Party instructions for work in illegality. Over the period of surveillance, more than twenty first names came to light, only half-a-dozen of which could be identified, most of them the aliases of well-known Zurich Communists.'[107] Nor did a raid on the Arbeiterbuchhandlung on 17 July 1934 yield anything concrete. The police were unable to track down the Alpáris or the Komjáts, and were equally unable to lay hands on Hugo Eberlein ('Ernst'), although they knew that he regularly visited Switzerland illegally, together with his 'secretary Lisette Gil' (in reality his partner Charlotte Scheckenreuter, 'Lotte Reuter', 1909–1982).[108] When Michel Dieschbourg was arrested in Lausanne in April 1935, the police were ignorant of his role. And

---

104 Fritz Eichenwald, report to Comrade Müller of the German representation at the ECCI on the arrests in Zurich in June 1934, Moscow, 27 November 1935, RGASPI 495/205/6433.

105 Report of the Swiss Federal Prosecutor's Office to the Federal Department of Justice and Police re. Expulsion of Parlow and others, Bern, 20 June 1934, BAR E21#1000/131#9282* and BAR E21#1000/131#9514*.

106 List of significant persons in the circle around Runa-Zurich (Rundschau-Nachrichten-Agentur), n.d., BAR E4320B#1974/47#412*.

107 Swiss Federal Prosecutor's Office re. Expulsion of Parlow and others, Bern, 20 Juni 1934.

108 Report by the Zurich cantonal police, 6 June 1933, BAR E4320B#1974/47#412*. Eberlein and 'Lotte Reuter' were arrested by the French police in Strasbourg in October 1935. On their expulsion, they went to the Soviet Union. On their fate, see Ruth Stoljarowa and Wladislaw Hedeler, '"Deine Liebe zu unserer Sache hat dir wenig Freude und viel Leid gebracht": Die junge Kommunistin Charlotte Scheckenreuter als Mitarbeiterin und Frau Hugo Eberleins in den 1930er-Jahren, aufgezeichnet nach den Akten in Moskauer Archiven', *Jahrbuch für Forschungen zur Geschichte der Arbeiterbewegung* 1, 2008, 5–35.

when the Federal Prosecutor's Office claimed in July that they would be able to arrest Heinrich Kurella in Davos, he had long been in Moscow, where the pregnant Charlotte Stenbock-Fermor would arrive in late August. After almost fifteen months in Switzerland, Kurella had been recalled 'to work in Cde. B. Kun's commission', as he states in the party autobiography written after reaching the USSR.[109] Increasing repression in Switzerland did, however, lead the ECCI to move the *Rundschau* office to Paris in 1935.

On Saturday, 8 December 1934, the Zurich police did strike lucky again. At 10:30 a.m. that day they managed to arrest Heinz Neumann at the home of the Wettler family, at Wonnebergstrasse 69 in the middle-class neighbourhood of Seefeld, where he rented a room for 35 francs a month. Only the son, a Communist, knew who he really was. Two detectives from the city police had called to check the identity of the Karl Bieler registered at that address, and when Neumann reacted nervously they had become suspicious and searched his attic room. 'Else Henk', that is, Margarete Buber, who had spent the night there, against all the rules, managed somehow to sneak away. 'From the notes, memoranda and so forth lying about, it was clear that the man holding himself out to be BIELER was intensively engaged in working against the present German government', the police report recorded. 'The so-called BIELER was arrested by us because we suspected that this was not his real name.'[110]

The police had apparently known that Neumann was present in Switzerland, but not his whereabouts. It was not until they arrived at the police station that they found out his real name. So it was again a mere fluke – followed by what seems at first sight to have been a surprisingly inept reaction on the part of a long-standing party and Comintern functionary like Neumann – that had led to his arrest. It is clear from Margarete Buber-Neumann's memoirs that the lapse of the overnight stay was not the result of any naivety regarding the policing of Social Democrat–governed Zurich.[111] On the contrary, both of them had

---

109 Hand-written political autobiography, Moscow, n.d. [1934 or 1935], RGASPI 495/205/6202-2. The reference is presumably to the Commission for the Struggle Against War, Fascism and Social Democracy.

110 Report to the Zurich police inspectorate, 10 December 1934, BAR E4320B#1978/121#48*.

111 Buber-Neumann, *Potsdam*, 382.

reckoned on the possibility of arrest. More likely it had to do with Neumann's frame of mind at the time. He who, with Thälmann and Hermann Remmele, had pushed the KPD's ultraleft course had in 1931 strongly opposed Thälmann's and Stalin's policies for being soft on the National Socialists. In 1932, he found himself relieved of his party functions and posted to Moscow. That same year, he was assigned to Spain as an instructor with the Comintern delegation sent there to bring the faction-riven Spanish party into line with Moscow. This was a test of loyalty. Margarete was allowed to follow him there only in January 1933. Neumann's position in the Comintern worsened again when in November 1933 a letter was discovered that he had written seven months earlier. In it, he asked his comrade Remmele to continue the factional struggle against the passivity of the KPD leadership.[112] 'Octavio', as he was called in Spain, was then shunted off to Switzerland. Without any official political role or mission, without any regular income, he got by working for Ring Verlag. In this he was assisted by Margarete Buber-Neumann. As she would later write in her party autobiography: 'In Switzerland ... [I] did technical work for the KI-Verlag without being formally employed.'[113]

Self-criticism proved insufficient to return Neumann to a position of responsibility. In a statement of early 1934, recognizing his 'political errors', he declared his full support for the resolutions of the Thirteenth (and most recent) ECCI Plenum of December 1933, according to which the German policy partly responsible for the rise of the National Socialists was entirely correct. He further declared that the KPD was organizing 'the masses for the decisive struggle to overthrow the Fascist dictatorship', a claim very far from the truth. Last but not least, he asked to work again for the Comintern: 'Given the seriousness of my errors, I am aware that it is only through their swift and just correction through practical work that I shall be able to prove myself worthy of collaborating as a party member, under the banner of Lenin and Stalin, in the struggle for the cause of the Communist International.'[114] His self-abasement was unavailing.

---

112 Written in Spain on 7 March 1933, the letter to Hermann Remmele is published in *Deutschland, Russland, Komintern*, vol. 2, 963–4.
113 Political autobiography of 22 September 1936, RGASPI 495/205/1612.
114 Statement by Heinz Neumann, addressed to Cdes Piat[nitsky] and Manu[ilsky], Amsterdam, 14 January 1934, published in *Deutschland, Russland, Komintern*, vol. 2, 1065–7.

This side of the Comintern remained invisible to the Swiss police. They saw only the contacts and political doings of a stateless German Communist, described as '174.5 cm tall, medium stature, blue eyes, black-brown hair, clean-shaven, oval face, full, somewhat brownish teeth, speaks German, French and English'.[115] He also spoke a little Russian and Spanish, he told the Zurich city police, and was in the process of learning Japanese. The Federal Prosecutor's office, which had kept a file on him since 1920, mistakenly believed Neumann to be the author of *Der bewaffnete Aufstand: Versuch einer theoretischen Darstellung* [Armed Insurrection: An Attempt at a Theoretical Presentation] supposedly published in Zurich in 1928. He was therefore thought to be a 'theoretician of Communist insurrection'. Behind the pseudonym 'A. Neuberg' under which the book had appeared was in fact a group of authors working under the direction of the Comintern's Agitprop Department. Neumann was not one of them, although the report on the Canton Uprising that he had written for the Comintern had served as source material.[116]

For the police, then, he represented the very type of the perpetually mobile, professional revolutionary operating under cover, an impression supported by his constant travel, false papers, pseudonyms and illegal border-crossings. They meticulously reconstructed his movements: On 9 January 1934, he had stayed at the Hotel Touring in Zurich, together with his wife, Else Henk; on 11 January, alone, at the Hotel Metzgerbräu; on 12 January, without wife, at the Hotel Touring again; on 24 April, alone, at the Gasthof zum Goldenen Schäfli. When questioned, he said that he had spent the intervening period, till March, in France. He had in any event regularly visited Paris for three or four days (in May, June, August, October and November). He must have crossed the border each time under a false a name, as he had been arrested by the police as a representative of the KPD attending the Second Congress

---

115 This and what follows draws on the police file on Heinz Neumann and Margarete Buber-Neumann, BAR E4320B#1978/121#48*.

116 The book was published in several languages. Its authorship was revealed in 1970 by one of the writers involved: Erich Wollenberg, 'How We Wrote *Armed Insurrection*', at versobooks.com. It was later translated into English as A. Neuberg, Tukhachevsky, Ho Chi Minh, Piatnitsky and Wollenberg, *Armed Insurrection*, trans. Quintin Hoare, London: NLB, 1970. On the Canton Uprising and Neumann's role in it, see chapter 6.

of the PCF in 1921, and banned from France for life. The Swiss authorities also discovered that Neumann was not financially supported by his father as he had stated when he registered in Switzerland:[117] it was in fact his party friends in Paris who sent him 300 to 350 Swiss francs a month, plus travel expenses. As he explained to the police, this was enough for him to live on, since he kept a very modest household. Given the dozen manuscripts and articles of his the police had found and seized, he also admitted that he wrote for the theoretical journal *Die Kommunistische Internationale* and was paid for that. For the Swiss authorities, there could be no doubt regarding Neumann's political convictions or his connection with Communism (confirmed by his having been a member of the Swiss party since 2 March 1934, as Detective Hüni was informed by the city police). On 21 December 1934 the Swiss government issued Neumann with an expulsion order on the grounds of his endangering the internal and external security of the state.

In the meantime, Swiss Red Aid had launched a campaign to save Heinz Neumann, which quickly gained the support of the entire left. In her memoir, Margarete Buber-Neumann doubts that this was helpful. Without the support campaign, Neumann could have been discreetly deported to France.[118] However, due to the publicity generated by the campaign, the Nazi government heard about it and requested his extradition. Red Aid, which had an international legal network to support political prisoners, found him a lawyer, a Maître Jaeglé of Strasbourg, who was not, however, accepted by the Swiss authorities,[119] and a Swiss lawyer eventually took on his defence. Luckily for Neumann, the Swiss refused the German government's request for his extradition on the grounds of 'intellectual authorship' of the murder of two police officers, yet until a country of asylum could be found, he would remain in

---

117 Having stated that he was working on a book on Kant and Hegel, he had been granted a one-year residence permit: Margarete Buber-Neumann, *Kriegsschauplätze der Weltrevolution: Ein Bericht aus der Praxis der Komintern 1919–1943*, Stuttgart: Seewald Verlag, 1967, 403.

118 Buber-Neumann, *Potsdam*, 390.

119 Heinrich Rothmund, head of policing at the Federal Department of Justice and Police to the management of Regensdorf Prison, Bern, 16 January 1935, BAR E 4320 (B), 1978/121. On the International Red Aid's network of lawyers, see Frédérick Genevée, 'L'Association juridique internationale, 1929–1940)', in Gotovitch and Morelli, *Les solidarités*, 101–12.

custody in Regensdorf prison.[120] It was six months before Neumann was finally able to leave Switzerland, having been granted asylum in the Soviet Union when both Austria and France proved unwilling to take in a notorious Communist. Willi Trostel (1894–1942), the head of Swiss Red Aid, whose salary was paid by Moscow, saw to the application and this time received a favourable response. The Soviet Union granted asylum only if there was a risk of death or life imprisonment. Margarete Buber-Neumann (in the guise of the Luxembourgish Else Brand) and Heinz Neumann made their way 'over there' or 'home', as the Comintern-speak of the 1930s had it, by Soviet steamer from Le Havre.

On their way to Leningrad, Margarete told Neumann of the suicide of his friend Besso Lominadze in December 1934, news of which she had been given in Paris by Otto Katz, just back from the Soviet Union.[121] The two of them had known each other not only at the Comintern in Moscow, but also in Germany in 1925–26, where Lominadze had been sent on party work and Neumann was the only member of the German leadership to speak Russian. In 1927, they had been in China together as Comintern representatives. Heinz's reaction disconcerted her: he was disinclined to believe in suicide and expressed 'gloomy suspicions' about coming arrests.[122] They arrived in Leningrad in June 1935. This was the third time Margarete Buber-Neumann had come to the Soviet Union, having first visited in 1931 as delegate of the Tiez department store cell, and then again, as Heinz Neumann's wife, from June 1932 to January 1933. It would be the last.

Moscow: Caught in the Trap

In Moscow, Margarete and Heinz Neumann were met by an OMS chauffeur who, to their great astonishment, conveyed them to the Hotel Lux and even booked them into a sizeable room, 'elegantly furnished by Moscow standards'.[123] Position in the Comintern's political hierarchy, formal or informal, was generally reflected not only in living standards

---

120 Buber-Neumann, *Kriegsschauplätze*, 415.
121 Ibid., 416.
122 Buber-Neumann, *Potsdam*, 400–1 and 406–7.
123 Ibid., 409.

and special privileges but also in a spatial pecking order. That the ostracized Heinz Neumann should find himself in the Hotel Lux, of all places, and in a spacious room, could only be a misunderstanding. Their friends Charlotte Stenbock-Fermor and Heinrich Kurella lived nearby, in room 87 at the Soyuznaya Hotel, similarly centrally located, in Gorky Street (Ul. Gor'kogo), but reserved for less important Comintern employees. (Tina Modotti and Vittorio Vidali, for example, had lived in the same hotel for a while before their transfer to Paris in August 1933.)

Heinz Neumann's status as a deviationist was, however, soon made clear in his political marginalization. Unlike Heinrich Kurella, who worked as a journalist at the telegraphic agency, part of the ECCI's Press and Radio Service, under the Czechoslovak Bedrich Geminder (1901–1952, 'G. Friedrich'), Neumann was not given a Comintern post and had instead to earn his living as a translator for the Foreign Workers Publishing House. As he was employed only on a freelance basis, he worked in their room at the Lux. And as Grete could not find a job, she worked as his 'secretary'. Charlotte Stenbock-Fermor's situation was somewhat better, though even she found only precarious employment.

That changed for her in the early summer of 1935, when Mikhail Kreps (1895–1937), head of the Press Section, hired Charlotte to prepare an exhibition about the Comintern, on account of her language skills. The Seventh World Congress of the Comintern was to take place from 25 July to 21 August, at which the new 'Popular Front' line was to be introduced and celebrated with great pomp. Margarete's sister Babette and her brother-in-law Willi Münzenberg travelled from Paris. Sophie Kirschbaum, too, had by now left Switzerland for Moscow, where she was working as a typist in the Press Section. The city of Moscow was especially spruced up for the occasion, and the first metro line began operation two months before the opening of the congress. Jules Humbert-Droz, attending as a delegate for the Swiss party, wrote enthusiastically to his wife Jenny:

> The Lux is sparkling, completely renovated, new furniture, a sign of new times. Moscow entirely transformed, buildings demolished, whole neighbourhoods razed to the ground and replaced with vast edifices . . . The House of the Unions, where the Congress is taking place, now looks like a hovel beside the two palatial hotels

that have replaced the little shops. In sum, a sense of real strength, of rejuvenation.[124]

In the countryside, however, he went on to say, everything was the same as ever.

In 1935, Stalin's great slogan was 'Life is better, comrades, life is happier!', an observation flatly contradicted in the experience of the foreign Communists. The murder of Kirov had seen the mood in the Soviet Union darken. In December 1934, Stalin's former allies Zinoviev and Kamenev had been arrested and sentenced to five years imprisonment, increased to ten the following year. The call for 'vigilance' against 'oppositionists' and 'hostile elements' now required all party members to watch out for every critical utterance, their own included. Invited to the USSR by the VOKS, the Hungarian writer Ervin Sinkó kept a diary of the two years he spent in Moscow. On 21 June 1935, he was at the Lux and going on about the stupidity of the Stalin cult when he found himself quickly pulled away from the radiator: 'So is it true? Even in the Lux, which is reserved for the guests of the Comintern, these people themselves consider that there might be listening devices in the heating system.'[125] Already in late 1934 the Hungarian journalist and sinologist Lajos Magyar (1891–1940) had been arrested. This former deputy head of the Eastern Secretariat, employed at the Soviet consulate in Shanghai from 1928 and politically active on the Comintern's behalf in Berlin, Paris and Prague from 1932 to 1934, was accused of 'Zinovievite' sympathies and sentenced to imprisonment. This was the first time a foreigner employed by the Comintern had been prosecuted for his supposed political beliefs.[126] The purge then beginning was not directed only at people: whole organizations seen as overly independent were dissolved. The first to go was the IAH, wound up by the Swiss Karl Hofmaier on the instructions of Nikolai Ezhov, Stalin's special

---

124 Humbert-Droz, *Dix ans*, 130.
125 Ervin Sinkó, *The Novel of a Novel: Abridged Diary Entries from Moscow, 1935–1937*, ed. and trans. George Deák, Lanham, MD: Lexington Books, 2018, 104.
126 The case and its consequences for the Comintern are documented in William J. Chase, *Enemies Within the Gates? The Comintern and the Stalinist Repression, 1934–1939*, the Russian documents trans. Vadim A. Staklo, New Haven, CT: Yale University Press, 2001.

emissary, soon to be head of the NKVD, its Moscow office being closed in the summer of 1935, and the Paris headquarters that autumn.

Neumann was not alone in feeling obscurely uneasy. In the summer of 1935, this was no more than a mood, with little to go on but a few signs here and there. As Sinkó noted in his diary the night after the incident at the Lux: 'I have noticed in the last few days here and there that people pronounce a name, and everyone raises their eyebrows: silently, but all the more significantly. I finally realized today what is going on. There are rumours, albeit, so far unverifiable ones, of some kind of unusually large-scaled "purge".'[127] Precisely because no one knew exactly what was going on, such rumours spread quickly and fear soon became general, even affecting personal relations as the foreign Communists became increasingly cautious.

Heinz Neumann, who described himself as a 'professional revolutionary' on the questionnaire he filled out on 23 October 1935, but who still bore the stigma of factionalism and deviation from the line, found himself cut by comrades at the Lux. Only a few friends came by, of whom Heinrich Kurella was one. 'For Heinz,' writes Margarete, 'who loved a friendly get-together more than anything else, it was a very hard blow.'[128] Hardly had the couple arrived, indeed, than Wilhelm Pieck had sought to have them thrown out of the Lux.[129] On top of the atmosphere of mutual distrust, there was a general sense of uncertainty about what life held in store. In early 1935, Charlotte Stenbock-Fermor had an abortion, despite having looked forward to the child in her letters to her mother. In March 1935, however, she wrote to her: 'Two or three years ago, I would still have liked to have children, despite everything – but now? Who knows where I will be next year? Besides, I couldn't drag the poor unfortunate creature about with me everywhere.'[130] She, at least, was able to have it done before the political campaign against legal abortion began in early summer that year. As Ervin Sinkó and many other foreign party members discovered with astonishment and horror, the Soviet Union, of all places, was going to backtrack on the right they had

---

127 Sinkó, *Novel of a Novel*, 105.
128 Buber-Neumann, *Potsdam*, 411.
129 Ibid., 409.
130 Hirdman, *Mutter*, 387.

insistently demanded for women in the West: 'Now I am totally confused. I couldn't believe my eyes when I saw a huge article in *Pravda*. It was about the necessity of abolishing the rights of Soviet women to medical intervention for the termination of unwanted pregnancies.'[131]

The year 1935 also saw growing pressure on political emigrants and foreign Comintern staff to take Soviet citizenship. Heinrich Kurella, now called Albert Schief, was not at all sure what he and Charlotte should do this regard. To be on the safe side, he asked the KPD's representation at the ECCI at the end of November. He marked his enquiry for the attention of 'Cde. Müller' (1903–1942, in reality Georg Brückmann), who had been the Germany specialist at the Cadre Department for only a month. Müller in turn asked Wilhelm Pieck, who agreed with him that they should take Soviet citizenship. Before they could do that, however, Heinrich and Charlotte had to join the Soviet party. Communists had indeed been expected to join the party of their place of residence ever since the adoption of the Twenty-One Conditions for Admission to the Comintern in 1920, political emigrants explicitly included. In the 1920s, the requirement had not been rigorously enforced, as witnessed by the foreign Comintern employees in Moscow. Jules Humbert-Droz, for example, had remained a member of the Swiss party throughout his ten years as a Comintern official. Now, in the mid-1930s, the transfer of membership had become an elaborate bureaucratic process, inquisitorial in character.[132] The Comintern's Cadre Department, established in 1932, carried out extensive investigations, making detailed inquiries. Information from party questionnaires, political autobiographies, responses to inquiries and the minutes of meetings and discussions were distilled into a 'characterization' that resulted in a recommendation. If there were any suspicion, the Comintern's International Control Commission (ICC) would be called in.

When Grete Buber had applied to be transferred during her second stay in the Soviet Union, in 1932, there had been no problem. On 7 June, the KPD secretariat sent her party registration card to Moscow, with a

---

131 Sinkó, *Novel of a Novel*, 80.
132 The process is described in detail in Brigitte Studer, *The Transnational World of the Cominternians*, trans. D. R. Roberts, Basingstoke, UK: Palgrave Macmillan, 2015, 82–7.

recommendation for transfer.[133] In August, Wilhelm Florin (1894–1944), then the KPD's representative at the ECCI, sent it on to the transfer commission at VKP(b) headquarters, and she was made a member of the Soviet party shortly thereafter. Tina Modotti's transfer in 1931, too, had taken only a few months.[134] In 1935, though, the matter was more complicated. Buber applied, under her married name of Grete Neumann, on 21 December 1935. On 22 July 1936, 'Fritz Weber' (1896–1945, in reality Heinrich Wiatrek), the German representative at the ECCI, wrote saying that 'the political autobiography on the back of the questionnaire does not provide information on all matters'. She should therefore submit a new, 'quite detailed' autobiography 'with more precise information about social origin, membership of youth organization and party, employment history, all posts held in the party with dates, views on internal party debates, as well as your activities during your time in the Soviet Union'. Furthermore, she should name at least two comrades (though not Comrades Pieck or Florin) who were 'in the SU' and in a position to testify to 'work actually done for the party in the Potsdam and Berlin organization'. On 17 September he wrote again: 'We take this opportunity to draw to your attention the fact that in your questionnaire of 21 November 1935 you state that you have been a member of the party since 1926, whereas according to the registration card from the Central Committee you have only been a member of the party since 1 September 1927, and await an explanation.' She responded to these various demands on 22 September, submitting a four-page, typewritten CV. She still claimed to have joined the party in 1926 and made no comment on the discrepancy. As requested, she stated her position on matters of debate, and as the wife of Heinz Neumann (even if the marriage was 'not legally registered', as she explained), she had of course to comment on his political positions in 1932–33.

> In 1932–33 I was a member of the Neumann group for whose sectarian and factional errors I am jointly responsible. Although I did not take an active part in the debates of the time, I agreed with Cde. Neumann's erroneous views ... On realizing the erroneous and

---

133 This and what follows are drawn from her personal file, RGASPI 495/205/1612.
134 Letter from the German representation at the ECCI to the Transfer Commission of the CC of the AUCP(b), Moscow, 8 January 1931, RGASPI 495/221/1605.

anti-party character of those views in 1933, I learned the lessons from my error and adhered firmly to the standpoint of the party line in all political and intra-party matters. In discussions with Cde. Heinz Neumann in the spring of 1933 I sought to persuade him to correct his deviations and to return completely to the party line.

Her brief period of political sympathy with Neumann, however, had been her only 'deviation from the party line'.

No one would have believed her had she denied membership of the 'Neumann group'. In the Comintern, too, with few exceptions, women were simply assumed to identify politically with their husbands. In the very last sentence of her statement, she also conveyed the idea that her husband was now completely back on the correct line again. It did not help, however. In January 1937, after the KPD representative had asked a number of comrades for further information on her without turning up anything doubtful, the issue of transfer was 'put on temporary hold'. Then, on 21 June 1938 – according to the chronology attached to Grete Neumann's Comintern cadre file – a brief, pencilled note was added to that last document: 'Arrested'.

This dramatic development is typical of the experience of foreign Communists during the Great Terror of 1936–38. Any suspicion of political opposition was cataclysmic in its consequences. The experience of Heinz Neumann, who had arrived in the Soviet Union already bearing the stigma of opposition, exemplifies this road to Calvary, one he did not travel alone. Asked in the questionnaire of 23 October 1935 whether he had 'participated in groups or factions within the party', he answered: 'Neumann group 1932–33, erroneous sectarian politics, factional work'. Denial was out of the question. But it was not enough, and on 17 November 1935 the ICC issued him with a formal reprimand 'for anti-party discussions'.[135]

The volume of cases dealt with by the ICC over the years shows a rising trend and it more than triples from 1933 to 1935, rising very dramatically in that last year to 231.[136] The first Moscow trial also

---

135 Report on the transfer of Comrade Heinz Neumann, Moscow, 29 November 1936, RGASPI 495/205/6185.
136 Confidential: Total numbers of party members brought before the ICC each year, Moscow, 8 February 1936, RGASPI 495/20/811.

marked a drastic change in the way oppositionists in general and foreign Communists in particular were dealt with. On 15 August 1936, the Soviet public prosecutor's office announced the launch of a case against a 'Trotskyite-Zinovievite terrorist centre', and even before the trial had begun, resolutions from party and workplace meetings called for the highest penalty to be imposed on the accused. Konrad Mayer (1903–1983), the Swiss party's representative in Moscow, was equally sure of the coming verdict. Two days before the trial, he wrote to a friend in Switzerland that the trial was 'of far-reaching importance', as 'the death sentence ha[d] never been passed on a member of the opposition' and it was now going to happen.[137] In this context, the appeal for vigilance issued after Kirov's assassination – since early 1936 already more specifically directed against political emigrants, i.e. foreign Communists, as possible 'spies and saboteurs' – took on a new and even more troubling aspect. For among the defendants were some who had been members of the German party. Everyone was now a suspect, and not only party and Comintern authorities but ordinary party members were under an absolute duty to follow up on every hint, no matter how small, and to report the person concerned if need be. From now on, the carrousel of accusations would turn faster and faster, the accusations themselves growing wilder and wilder.

As early as 4 September 1936, Heinz Neumann had had to explain himself before the ICC. His three-page, closely typed statement provided the further information requested about his 'position on the internal party issues of the VKP(b)'. In it, he distanced himself from the Trotskyist opposition on the one hand and the 'Zinovievites' and the Bukharin group on the other. However,

> of the Lominadze group I have to say that I was on friendly terms with W. Lominadze, both personally and politically, so long as he was actively fighting against deviationists and oppositionists in the Comintern and the CPSU [sic] ... When Lominadze first began to depart from the line in 1929, alongside Schatzkin and Sten ... I immediately turned against him and informed the leading comrades of the CPSU, in the presence of comrade Thälmann.

---

137 Handwritten letter from Konrad Mayer to 'Dear Friend', Moscow, 17 August 1936, published in Studer, *Un parti*, 592–3.

In conclusion, he emphasized that

> during the whole period of my error on the German question, no matter how serious my sectarian deviations or how inexcusable the factional struggle I waged, I never faltered for a moment on the questions of Stalin's policy on the Comintern line and of ruthless struggle against all Russian and international opposition groups.[138]

Here, he was trying to draw a distinction between opposition to the German party leadership (Thälmann) and opposition to Stalin. But by 1 October the ICC had received (presumably from the German party leadership) a nine-page document describing in detail Neumann's relationships with a number of defendants in the first Moscow trial. And, on 8 October, the Politburo of the KPD sent a written response to Neumann's statement. Extremely sharply worded, this accused Neumann of 'barefaced deception' and 'duplicity and hypocrisy of the worst kind'. He had made no mention of the letter he sent to Remmele in February 1933 in which he sought 'to bring about a split in the KPD'.[139] And with the 'trick' of distinguishing between the policy of the KPD and the questions of the Comintern line and of Stalin's policy, Neumann was seeking once again 'to deceive the comrades'. In closing, it threatened to bring the question of Neumann's party membership to the ICC. Not much later, the KPD's own transfer commission declined to take a decision on his transfer to the Soviet party.

Quite different, apparently, was the case of Kurella, who was not known to have taken an oppositional stance. He wrote the required political autobiography on 8 July 1936 – by when he had abandoned the pseudonym Albert Schief for Albert Palva – and just over a month later, on 17 August, the German commission recommended his transfer.[140] He apparently felt it necessary, however, to further demonstrate his loyalty to the party by providing the Cadre Department with information on some of the German Communists accused in the first Moscow trial, writing on 24 September: 'I believe the following information may

---

138 This, and what follows, is drawn from Heinz Neumann's personal file, RGASPI 495/205/6185.
139 Underlined in the original.
140 What follows is drawn from Kurella's personal file, RGASPI 495/205/6202-2.

perhaps be of use to you in the struggle against the Trotskyist terrorists and the Gestapo.' One can only speculate on his motives. Did he really credit the allegations against them? What would seem in retrospect a very naïve belief could have seemed plausible at the time. Paradoxically, the confessions might have seemed so extraordinary as to exclude the possibility of fabrication.

The move proved counterproductive. Only a month later, on 25 October 1936, he had to write a report to the ICC on all the Trotskyists he had ever known. As a Comintern functionary and a long-standing member of the German party, he naturally had of course known the defendants at the Moscow trial: David, Emel, Jurin-Berman and Süsskind. But having already spoken of them, Kurella was now expected to denounce others. He responded in a way that would endanger no one directly, naming only people who were abroad, beyond the immediate reach of the NKVD: Bernhard von Brentano and Silone, whom he had met in Switzerland, and Vera Kirschbaum, 'who used to be an active Trotskyist in the Italian Communist Party', with whom he had 'hardly ever spoken a word', and finally a comrade he had met in Prague.

For the ICC, these denunciations were insufficient, and on 27 November he found himself having to write a new letter. This time, he adopted a different language, using such stereotyped formulations as 'get behind his mask', 'exposing the whole milieu', 'learn from one's mistakes' and 'work systematically on myself'. These he had learned from his party group and their hours-long, even days-long, discussions about each of the comrades and their relationships with each other: his 'case' was dealt with on 28 September, together with three others, including that of Sophie Kirschbaum.[141] A little more than a page long, Kurella's typewritten letter concerned his acquaintance with Heinrich Süsskind. He began 'with the observation that I am well aware that I allowed myself to fall into serious error in having dealings with Süsskind over a period of some 6 weeks'. Particularly serious was the fact 'that I did not know how to get behind his mask'. Kurella drew two conclusions from the mistakes he had made. First, that he should now 'assist the party . . . by exposing the whole milieu around Süsskind'; an attachment to the letter summed up what he knew. Second, that he should 'further

---

141 Kurella's personal file includes a transcript of the meeting, which extends to sixty-four typewritten pages.

assist the party' by 'working systematically on myself . . . so that I shall in future be able to actively assist the party to expose every enemy'. Thanks to the 'educational work' of his party group, he had already made a serious beginning, and now hoped to develop the vigilance that was 'one of the most important duties of every party member today'.

Despite these declarations, Kurella was called to appear before the ICC on 3 December. There he repeated what he had written about Süsskind. According to the transcript, he also admitted 'that Neumann had had a great influence on him'. They had become close friends. He added that Neumann and Süsskind were interesting people, 'they made you think'. Questioned by the ICC, Kurella stated that he had also befriended Neumann 'because he [Neumann] was completely isolated'. The transcript records that the questioning made Kurella cry and that he subsequently left the room where the interview had taken place. In their conclusions, the party officials declared him to be 'insincere'. Not a week later, 'Albert Müller', known as 'Cadre-Müller', sent a report to the ICC. In it he listed twenty-four people who had regularly visited Heinz Neumann. (As we know today, the 1930s saw lists of those expelled from the party and other 'doubtful persons' regularly sent to the NKVD,[142] this not infrequently being followed by arrests.) Among them was Charlotte Stenbock-Fermor, who had apparently done so eighteen times between 11 March and 27 October. From this, 'Müller' concluded that Heinrich Kurella had to 'know more about the goings-on around Heinz Neuman than he has yet said'. On 14 December, Kurella thus had to send the ICC a list of all the people he had met at Heinz Neumann's or with whom Neumann had been seen in Zurich. He followed this on the 22nd with a list of the subjects that he and others had discussed with him. This ran to more than three pages, but made no mention of any criticism of the party line. On 30 December 1936, Kurella's case again came up for discussion at the ICC, and, on 2 January 1937, he provided further explanations, going into detail about Neumann's 'attitude to the KPD

---

142 From 1933 onward, according to Friedrich Firsow, 'Die Komintern und die "Grosse Säuberung"', in Michael Buckmiller and Klaus Meschkat, eds, *Biographisches Handbuch zur Geschichte der Kommunistischen Internationale: Ein deutsch-russisches Forschungsprojekt*, Berlin: Akademie Verlag, 2007, 361–77, at 365. Such lists are to be found at RGASPI in fonds 546/1/378, 379 and 420. The appointment of 'Moskvin', i.e. Meer Abramovich Trilisser (1883–1941) as a Comintern secretary in 1935 saw an NKVD officer given a powerful and prominent place in the ECCI apparatus.

and the ECCI'. There he says that Neumann 'certainly sees his errors, but rather than repeatedly declaring that he has recognized them, he in the end would prefer to have the opportunity to prove in practical political work that he has done so, not in words only but also in fact'. He also noted that Neumann had written to Stalin asking him to intervene. In closing, Kurella analysed his own 'errors' in terms of the increasingly dominant understanding of due vigilance, according to which 'errors' and even suspicions had to be proactively reported. 'I must emphasize at this point that <u>I did not withhold</u> these facts from the party.'[143] He had, however, not informed them spontaneously. A 'second criticism that I must make of myself is more serious'. He had indeed reported his doubts regarding Neumann's attitude to the party when 'prompted by others', but had not drawn the practical conclusions. Now, however, he had acted: 'I can inform you that I broke off all contact with Neumann on 31 December 1936.' This again was insufficient, and on 6 January Kurella wrote another letter to the ICC, 'about people whom I met in the course of my work for the party or the youth organization in different places, whose attitude to the party struck me as hostile or suspicious to one degree or another'.

The last of Kurella's contributions to the file is a ten-page typewritten submission to the ICC dated 6 March 1937. It begins with a confession: 'I told only a fraction of the truth about my relationship with Neumann, about what I knew of Neumann's political position and activities and about my own relationship with Neumann and my own political position.' As well as much repetition of things said earlier, this rambling and clumsily written statement contains the admission that Kurella had 'belonged to the Neumann faction'. 'Due to my own political volatility and under Neumann's influence, I became a member of Neumann's faction, effectively taking up a position hostile to the KPD leadership and the Comintern.'

The rest of the file consists of institutional documents. The Cadre Department reports that Kurella and Charlotte Stenbock-Fermor stopped living together in January 1937. By her own account (echoed in this by Margarete Buber-Neumann), Charlotte was able to travel abroad, sent by the NKVD to infiltrate Trotskyist groups.[144] Evidence supporting

---

143 Underlined in the original.
144 Buber-Neumann, *Flamme*, 92–104.

this is to be found in Stenbock-Fermor's personal file,[145] which includes a half-sheet of paper dated 23 July 1937 alluding to her work and to information about her to be obtained 'from the relevant authorities' (almost certainly meaning the NKVD, whose name customarily goes unmentioned in Comintern documents). Furthermore, a list dated 19 September 1937 seems to represent a series of code numbers with their meanings, certainly suggesting such activity: '59. GPU mission; 60. Anna; 61. Michael; 62. Riva; 63. a German passport; 64. obtain passport; 65. the Russian visa; 66. GPU, 67. 300 dollars; 68. address in M.; 69. Trotskyite circles; 70. friend of the GPU; . . .'[146]

A little later, a memorandum was circulated between the Cadre Department, the ICC and the NKVD stating that Kurella was now in a relationship with the Swiss-born Pole Wanda Brońska (1911–1972) (daughter of the Old Bolshevik and former Soviet ambassador in Vienna Mieczysław Broński, and stepdaughter of Stefan Bratman-Brodovsky, former Soviet ambassador in Berlin and then Soviet ambassador to Latvia) and wanted to go on a two-month holiday with her. At the Cadre Department's suggestion, Kurella was dismissed from his post at the Press Section on 23 May 1937. His new partner, Wanda Brońska, who also worked there as an editor at the telegraphic agency, had already been dismissed on 23 April. On 8 June, Kurella was again questioned by the ICC and subsequently expelled from the party. On 11 June a Cadre Department employee sent to the NKVD a list of the people named by Heinrich Kurella. On 15 June, she followed this up with a further communication regarding the Kurella affair, according to which Kurella's former wife, Charlotte Stenbock-Fermor, had 'turned up among the Trotskyite groups' in Copenhagen in January, having left Moscow without the party's permission. Questioned by the German party, she had said that she was working among the 'Trotskyites' 'on behalf of the Russian authorities' (i.e. the organs of the Soviet state), but her claims had been lent no credence.

In July, Kurella was arrested. In October, he was shot. Neumann was executed a month later, towards the end of November. On 20 June 1938, Margarete Buber-Neumann was arrested and, like Wanda Brońska, sentenced to forced labour. In February 1940, she would be extradited to

---

145 Personal file, RGASPI 495/205/6433.
146 On this, see also Hirdman, *Mutter*, 444–9.

Germany. By mid-1937, of Heinz Neumann's circle, Ernst Ascher, Fritz Eichenwald, Hermann Remmele, Hugo Eberlein,[147] Betty Schönfeld, Ernst Ottwald (regarding whom Willi Bredel had written to the Cadre Department, saying that he had embarked on a relationship with Charlotte Kurella, wife of Comrade Heinrich Kurella[148]), Hilda Duti and her ex-husband Arno Vartanjan were all in custody, to name only some. According to an estimate by Paul Jäkel (1890–1943, 'Jan Dietrich'), responsible at the ECCI for the care of German political emigrants, over 70 per cent of KPD members in the Soviet Union had been arrested by April 1938.[149] Given that there are believed to have been some 4,000 political emigrants in the USSR, this would represent something in the region of 2,800 people.[150] Within the ECCI apparatus itself, the party organization shrank by more than half between 26 January 1936 and 1 April 1938, 181 remaining out of 394; arrests also took place in the Comintern-affiliated organizations and at the cadre schools.[151]

With the Nazi seizure of power, there vanished one of the last countries in Central Europe to still show a certain, albeit ever-decreasing tolerance of international Communist activity, a development the Comintern had not adequately prepared for, if at all. Even afterwards, there was no official revision of its astonishingly uncomprehending analysis, which held that the KPD had not suffered defeat and that National Socialism's accession to power was no more than a temporary setback. In terms of Stalin's foreign policy, the Comintern was an irrelevance. Münzenberg and other members of the Comintern apparatus were left to make their way to safety as best they could, as the constantly mobile transnational

147 His partner Charlotte Scheckenreuter was arrested a year later, on 19 June 1938. She found herself in such dire poverty after her release in January 1939 that she decided to return to Germany.
148 Willi Bredel, 'Bericht über Ernst Ottwalt an die Kaderabteilung der Komintern, Nov. 1936', *Europäische Ideen* 79, 1992, 6–10.
149 'Dietrich' to the CC of the KPD and the German representation at the ECCI, Moscow, 29 April 1938, RGASPI 495/292/101.
150 On the German emigration, see Carola Tischler, 'German Emigrants in Soviet Exile: A Drama in Five Acts', in Karl Schlögel, ed., *Russian–German Special Relations in the Twentieth Century: A Closed Chapter?* Oxford: Berg, 2006, 77–97. On the chain reaction that saw one arrest lead to another, see Alexander Vatlin, *'Was für ein Teufelspack': Die deutsche Operation des NKWD in Moskau und im Moskauer Gebiet 1936 bis 1941*, Berlin: Metropol Verlag, 2013.
151 Firsow, 'Die Komintern', 376.

agents of the Comintern became involuntary migrants. Those Comintern officials who had laid the groundwork for shifting news and publishing operations to neighbouring counties had been rather more far-sighted, but much remained to be improvised when 1933 actually happened. Comintern employees depended on the support of local comrades, a solidarity that suffered, in the case of Switzerland, from the weakness of the national party and the smallness of the left-wing world, which made it all the easier for the police authorities to monitor their activities.

For political emigrants, exile meant the loss of belongings and a life of cheap hotels with often hardly enough the money for food, while illegality imposed a permanent vigilance against the local police and Gestapo spies. Yet it was not, on the whole, the difficulties of life that led them to serious doubt and uncertainty, but internal party conflict and the ambiguity and confusion of the Comintern's political line. The struggle against oppositionists, against Trotskyists and Conciliators, generated an atmosphere of mutual suspicion and accusation, poisoning relationships among the comrades in Paris, Basel and Zurich, as it did in other places of refuge not considered here, such as Prague, Amsterdam and Copenhagen. The long arm of the Comintern – of Stalin's Soviet Union – also extended to the West. So it was that in December 1936, the ECCI stripped Münzenberg of control over every organization directly subordinate to or financially supported by the Comintern.[152]

In the Soviet Union, the country in which most German Communists – like their Hungarian, Polish, Indian and Chinese predecessors – had thought to find refuge, the consequences of such suspicion were even more serious. One single critical remark could prompt a wholesale recasting of one's actions, of one's past, present and future. Arrests, banishments and executions cut a swathe through the ranks of Comintern employees. An atmosphere of fear and mutual distrust pervaded the Lux, where, according to an official list, 83 of the Comintern staff occupying the hotel's 350 rooms had been shot.[153] The others would

---

152 Documenting the many allegations made against him, Münzenberg's personal file attests to the distrust in which he was held by the organs of the Comintern from the mid-1930s on, RGASPI, 495/205/7000.

153 Wladislaw Hedeler, 'Die Präsenz staatlicher Gewalt inmitten einer urbanen Umwelt: Das Beispiel Moskau', in Karl Schlögel et al., eds, *Mastering Russian Spaces/ Raum und Raumbewältigung als Probleme der russischen Geschichte*, Munich: R. Oldenbourg Verlag, 2011 199–252, at 214.

wake up in the morning to discover doors newly sealed by the NKVD. Many committed suicide. Heinz Neumann had considered this after finally completing the translation of the official record of the first Moscow show trial.[154] Against this background, the revolutionary movement that emerged in Spain in the summer of 1936, out of the struggle against the Franco putsch, appeared to offer new political hope. Many Communists asked to be sent to Spain as volunteers.[155] Heinz Neumann himself made such a request to Manuilsky on returning from his holiday in Crimea, to no effect. And when, against all common sense, Babette Gross and Willi Münzenberg travelled to Moscow again in October 1936, it was because they wanted to press the Comintern and the Soviet Union to help Spain, with 'arms, money, people'.[156]

---

154 Buber-Neumann, *Potsdam*, 447.
155 Not only foreign Communists, but also ordinary Soviet citizens: Gleb Albert, '"To Help the Republicans Not Just by Donations and Rallies, but with the Rifle": Militant Solidarity with the Spanish Republic in the Soviet Union, 1936–1937', *European Review of History / Revue européenne d'histoire* 21:4, 2014 501–18; Jochen Hellbeck, *Revolution on My Mind: Writing a Diary Under Stalin*, Cambridge, MA: Harvard University Press, 2006, 92–3; Daniel Kowalsky, *Stalin and the Spanish Civil War*, New York: Columbia University Press, 2004, chapter 12, electronic publication available at gutenberg-e.org.
156 Buber-Neumann, *Potsdam*, 452.

9

The Last Big Mission: Barcelona, Madrid, Albacete, Valencia

Immediately upon returning to Paris from Moscow, Münzenberg set about organizing material aid and propaganda support for Spain, the new flashpoint and therefore focus of revolutionaries' attentions. According to Koestler, the Spanish Civil War had 'become a personal obsession' for Münzenberg,[1] who wanted devote the organizational savoir-faire he had acquired over twenty years of activism to the Republican cause. In late July 1936, he set up a war relief committee in support of Republican Spain that established residential homes for Spanish refugee children in France. In August, he sent his earlier collaborator, Koestler, who still had an old press card, behind the Franquist lines in the guise of a newspaper correspondent, to collect evidence of German and Italian involvement. As he explained in his *Propaganda als Waffe* [Propaganda as a Weapon], published in 1937, propaganda for socialists was a matter of elucidation, of research and education, while, for the National Socialists, it was the manipulation of opinion.[2] In October, Münzenberg and Julio Alvarez del Vayo, foreign minister of the Spanish Republic, set up the Agence Espagne press agency in Paris, entrusting its management to Otto Katz.[3] Münzenberg

---

1 Arthur Koestler, *The Invisible Writing*, New York: Macmillan, 1954, 333.
2 Willi Münzenberg, *Propaganda als Waffe*, Basel: Universum-Bücherei, 1937, 10–12.
3 Otto Katz himself left Münzenberg out of the story, claiming to have been recruited to the post by Del Vayo: André Simone, *Men of Europe: From the Confidential Notes of an International Correspondent*, New York: Modern Age, 1941, 17.

already knew del Vayo, a member of Spain's PSOE but close to the Communists, from Berlin in the early 1920s. They had come into contact again in Paris and the Spaniard had invited Münzenberg and Babette Gross to Madrid and then to Málaga for Christmas 1934.

Franco's coup against the democratically elected government of Spain mobilized left and progressive circles around the world. This huge, transnational wave of solidarity was prompted not only by identification with the social forces and the political goals represented by the Republic, but also, and most importantly, by the recognition of Spain as a crucial battleground in the struggle against fascism in Europe, after the Nazis' accession to power in Germany, the suppression of the Asturian workers' revolt in 1934, and the Italian invasion of Abyssinia in 1935. Internationalism took a great variety of practical forms. Gustav Regler, whose experiences in Spain inspired his novel *The Great Crusade* (first published in an English translation in 1940), tells in his autobiography how in September he, Kurt Stern (1907–1989) and Louis Aragon (1897–1982) received the first donations sent to Madrid by the International Association of Writers for the Defence of Culture (Regler was secretary of its German section): a small truck, a printing press, a film projector and a number of rolls of film, which the journalist and writer Ilya Ehrenburg (1891–1967) had arranged for the Soviet section to pay for.[4] Ehrenburg was working in Paris as special correspondent for the Soviet government newspaper *Izvestia*, but in late August he had visited Catalonia on his own initiative.

The impulse to help Spain in its hour of need was spontaneous, but soon took on organized form, not least through the efforts of the Comintern and the Soviet Union. For the Comintern, the Spanish Civil War represented its last and most significant major operation. For more than two years, it concentrated all its forces on Spain: every party and every affiliated organization mobilized, and that all the more effectively for the impulse coming not just from above, but also from below, from ordinary party members. Solidarity campaigns were set up in every country, social forces organized to provide assistance in the way of money, food and medical staff. The longer the war went on, the greater the numbers of people required to set up and operate the structures that

---

4 Gustav Regler, *The Owl of Minerva: The Autobiography of Gustav Regler*, trans. Norman Denny, London: Rupert Hart-Davis, 1959, 271–2.

cared for wounded soldiers and evacuated civilians, children most notably among them. From September 1936, it additionally involved the recruitment in each country of volunteers for the International Brigades, provided by the Comintern with money for travel and contacts for each stage of the journey. To manage the process, the Communist parties of a number of countries set up a transnationally coordinated apparatus, whose activities had to be kept secret for reasons of security. It was also necessary to institute a screening process, to exclude not only police spies and provocateurs but also those whom the Communists believed to be politically unreliable. And then, in Spain itself, the infrastructure had to be established to receive, accommodate, train and deploy this corps of volunteers.

Though largely paralysed by the repression that had begun in 1935, the Comintern apparatus in Moscow had been on high alert since the outbreak of war, the first six months in particular seeing the Secretariat meet frequently to discuss the question of Spain.[5] In 1938, however, interest began to decline significantly, and the Japanese invasion of China would then bring the situation in the Far East very much to the fore again. Dimitrov, the general secretary – irreverently called *dios* or 'God' by the Spanish Communists – followed events with great attention, reflected in a voluminous flow of coded telegrams between Madrid and Moscow.[6] As evidenced by his diary and correspondence, Dimitrov regularly checked that he had Stalin's backing, if sometimes only after the fact and without accepting every suggestion.[7] The

---

5 The opening of the Russian archives was followed by the publication of a number of important works on the Comintern and the Spanish Civil War, casting light on many details. Worth particular mention here are the monographs by Antonio Elorza and Marta Bizcarrondo, *Queridos camaradas: La Internacional comunista y España, 1919–1939*, Barcelona: Planeta, 1999; and Frank Schauff, *Der verspielte Sieg: Sowjetunion, Kommunistische Internationale und Spanischer Bürgerkrieg 1936–1939*, Frankfurt a. M.: Campus, 2004. These did not effect any fundamental revision, unless in revealing that not only the Comintern's and the Soviet Union's capacities for influence and control but also that their activities of political represssion had been considerably less than has long been supposed. During the thirty-three months of the Civil War, the ECCI Secretariat met on twenty-two occasions to discuss Spain, fourteen during 1936, five in 1937 and three in 1938, while in 1939 the subject was discussed only after the war was over: Schauff, *Der verspielte Sieg*, 117.

6 See Fridrikh I. Firsov, Harvey Klehr and John Earl Haynes, *Secret Cables of the Comintern, 1933–1943*, New Haven, CT: Yale University Press, 2014.

7 See Georgi Dimitroff, *Tagebücher 1933–1943*, vol. 1, ed. Bernhard H. Bayerlein, trans. Wladislaw Hedeler and Birgit Schliewenz, Berlin: Aufbau-Verlag, 2000; and also

second member of the ECCI Secretariat closely involved was Dmitri Manuilsky, responsible for the Latin countries and their colonies and also for the Cadre Department. Manuilsky was Stalin's man in the Comintern and its link with the Politburo of the Soviet party. A third was 'Moskvin' (Meer Abramovich Trilisser, 1883–1941), a long-time Chekist and officer of the GPU elected to the ECCI Presidium in 1935 and made responsible for both the International Liaison Department and the Comintern's finances. It was an appointment that underlined the links between the Comintern apparatus and the Soviet party and the NKVD. Until his arrest in November 1938, Moskvin was responsible both for overseeing the Spanish Communist Party and for the flow of Comintern funding to Spain. In the persons of André Marty and Palmiro Togliatti, likewise members of the ECCI Secretariat, the Comintern also sent two of its highest-ranking cadres to Spain, together with two of Manuilsky's closest collaborators, the Hungarian Ernö Gerö ('Pedro', 1898–1980) and the Bulgarian Stojan Minev ('Stepanov', 'Moreno'), both well-travelled emissaries of long standing, with experience of illegal work in Barcelona and Madrid.[8]

The Comintern had not sent such a numerous and high-powered team of professional revolutionaries abroad for any length of time since the ill-fated German revolution of 1923. This it did despite having a number of advisers already in Spain before the coup, some of them there for months, others for years. Dozens more middle- and lower-ranking Comintern employees would now be sent to Spain, accompanied and supported by many cadres from the national Communist parties, many drawn from the large reservoir of party leaderships driven into emigration. Beside these foreign Communists there were Soviet military advisers and other specialists transported to Spain along with the weapons and other matériel as part of the secret Operation X, together with embassy staff, translators and interpreters, assistants of all sorts and, last but not least, GRU agents and high-ranking NKVD officials[9] – amounting all in all to about 2,200

Alexander Dallin and Friedrich Firsov, eds, *Dimitrov and Stalin, 1934–1943: Letters from the Soviet Archives*, New Haven, CT: Yale University Press, 2000.

8 On Gerö, see György Borsányi, 'Ernö Gerö: Aus dem Leben eines Apparatschiks', *Jahrbuch für Historische Kommunismusforschung*, 1994, 275–80.

9 On the most famous yet at the same time unknown NKVD agent, see Boris Volodarsky, *Stalin's Agent: The Life and Death of Alexander Orlov*, Oxford: Oxford University Press, 2014.

Soviet personnel.[10] They travelled back and forth among the cities of Spain, between Madrid and Barcelona, and between the temporary seat of government in Valencia and the military training camp at Albacete.

This chapter looks at a number of Comintern employees and officials, some charged with establishing the transnational infrastructure to convey volunteers to Spain, and others with carrying out propaganda or providing military or 'humanitarian' assistance in Spain itself. Though these two spheres were organizationally separate, they were connected in many ways and also overlapped in personnel. What were the duties, the working lives and everyday realities of these emissaries of the Comintern, who had to adapt very quickly to the paradoxical if not contradictory political expectations laid upon them? On the one hand, the mid-1930s turn to the Popular Front policy brought the demand to open up to other, left-wing and progressive bourgeois forces, a process not without its ambivalences, as illustrated by the case of International Red Aid; on the other, the first Moscow show trial prompted the export to Spain of Soviet practices of vigilance and the systematic suspicion that went with them. The chapter begins with an overview of the emergence of Spain as a distinct field of action for the Comintern, together with some consideration of the explosion of international solidarity in the summer of 1936.

Advent of the Comintern Representatives

Spain's civil war, which lasted 984 days, saw the country become for antifascists worldwide both the symbol and the concrete locus of a decisive battle. Having first emerged on the horizon of attention of the Comintern and its affiliated organizations in the early 1930s, Spain moved in 1936 from periphery to centre, becoming for the next three years the most important arena of action for a host of people working for the Comintern, the Profintern, the Youth International and International Red Aid, as also for numerous Soviet advisers and

---

10 See chapter 12 of Daniel Kowalsky, *Stalin and the Spanish Civil War*, New York: Columbia University Press, 2004, electronic publication at gutenberg-e.org.

technical specialists, the Spanish party – the Partido Comunista de España (PCE) – serving as their organizational base.

Founded in 1919–20 by Mikhail Borodin, M. N. Roy and 'Jesús Ramírez' as they passed by on their way from Mexico to Moscow, and operating in clandestinity, this small Communist party had for a long time led only a shadowy existence. Political events since 1931, however, had seen it come to play a key role on both the domestic and the international stage. With the proclamation of the Second Republic and the repeated revolutionary uprisings by anarchists and peasants' and workers' organizations, its membership increased rapidly. With this growth and further revolutionary developments in Spain came the Comintern emissaries.[11]

It began in 1931 with a large (six-member) Comintern and Profintern delegation headed by Victorio Codovilla, the Italian-Argentinian who had fought the supposed 'rightist threat' in Latin America in 1929. In Spain, he was called 'Medina' or 'Luis/Louis', and also 'Tomas' in the coded telegraphic correspondence with the ECCI after 1934. Since the Comintern had no experts on Spain in 1931, Codovilla was accompanied by Latin America specialists, these being the two Swiss, Humbert-Droz and Woog (though the latter was soon arrested and expelled from Spain).[12] Four of the remaining five members of what Humbert-Droz described as a thoroughly

---

11 On the relationship between the Comintern and the PCE, see Antonio Elorza, 'In the Shadow of God: The Formation of the Comintern's Spanish Policy', in Mikhail Narinsky and Jürgen Rojahn, eds, *Centre and Periphery: The History of the Comintern in the Light of New Documents*, Amsterdam: Internationaal Instituut voor Sociale Geschiedenis, 1996, 237–45; Elorza and Bizcarrondo, *Queridos camaradas;* Tim Rees and Andrew Thorpe, eds, *International Communism and the Communist International 1919–1943*, Manchester: Manchester University Press, 1998, 143–67; the trilogy by Ángel Viñas, *La soledad de la República, El escudo de la República* and *El honor de la República*, Barcelona: Crítica, 2006–2008; and Fernando Hernández Sánchez, *Guerra o revolución: El Partido Comunista de España en la Guerra Civil*, Barcelona: Crítica, 2010. See also the memoirs of Enrique Castro Delgado, 1907–1965, member of the CC of the PCE and after 1939 the PCE's representative in the Soviet Union, who would, however, become a virulent anti-Communist after his expulsion from the party in 1944: Delgado, *Hombres made in Moscú*, Barcelona: Luis de Caralt, 1963.

12 On the Comintern's Latin America specialists, see Jürgen Mothes, *Lateinamerika und der 'Generalstab der Weltrevolution': Zur Lateinamerika-Politik der Komintern*, Berlin: Karl Dietz Verlag, 2010.

underemployed delegation soon left as well, leaving only Codovilla behind.[13] There then followed a steady succession of new emissaries. Humbert-Droz, who spoke some Spanish, was the first to return to Spain, accompanied by the German Walter Stoecker and the Pole Leon Purman ('Andrés', 1892–1933). Humbert-Droz's wife, Jenny, served as typist, and also coded and decoded the often very lengthy telegrams. To give her a break from this routine work, whose tedium he would decry in his memoirs, the two of them decided to inspect the Communist organizations of Andalusia, a pretext, it seems, for sightseeing and a number of enjoyable excursions.[14]

The delegation's mission to Spain had in fact a very different side, as witnessed by Humbert-Droz's reports to Moscow. To his mind, the crisis in the Spanish party was entirely the result of the incapacity of its general secretary, José Bullejos (1899–1973). An opinion echoed by Purman in a *spravka* or informational note of 30 April 1932 describing him as 'a person without political character', completely dependent on Gabriel León Trilla (1899–1945), the PCE representative in Moscow.[15] In the summer, the delegation summarily unseated both: Bullejos was called to Moscow for 'talks', where the ICC accused him and Trilla of having formed an 'anti-party group'; both were expelled and a new party leadership installed.[16]

Under the supervision of the Comintern delegation, a new Spanish party leadership was formed, drawing on provincial politicians. The secretariat now consisted of seven members and met weekly. To this was

---

13 Jules Humbert-Droz, *Mémoires*, vol. 2, *De Lénine à Staline: Dix ans au service de l'Internationale communiste, 1921–1931*, Neuchâtel: À La Baconnière, 1971, 412 and 419. Also members of the delegation were Octave, Jacques Duclos and Maria Anne Rabaté, though Humbert-Droz makes no mention of the latter.

14 Humbert-Droz, *De Lénine*, 457; at 403–63, Humbert-Droz gives a very extensive account of the mission to Spain.

15 'Characterisation' on the CD-Rom of data accompanying Michael Buckmiller and Klaus Meschkat, eds, *Biographisches Handbuch zur Geschichte der Kommunistischen Internationale: Ein deutsch-russisches Forschungsprojekt*, Berlin: Akademie Verlag, 2007. See also the letter from Humbert-Droz to his wife, Jenny, in Humbert-Droz, *De Lénine*, 445: 'Bullejos, who offers the analysis of Spain wished for by Trilla and his master'.

16 Following his self-criticism, Trilla was readmitted during the Civil War. He would meet a tragic end, being killed in Madrid in 1945, as a supposed 'provocateur', on the orders of the party leadership.

attached a technical secretariat operating in illegality.[17] Among the new leaders were José Díaz (1895–1942), a general secretary who would be loyal to the Comintern line, and Dolores Ibárruri (1895–1989), editor of the party newspaper *Mundo Obrero* since 1931, who was made a member of the Politburo and chair of the PCE's women's commission, though only after a detailed self-criticism in which she distanced herself from Bullejos in a symbolic ritual of submission. They were joined by Lenin School graduates Jesús Hernández (1907–1961), Vicente Uribe (1902–1961) and Manuel Hurtado (1902–?), all of whom came from very lower-class social backgrounds and had only completed elementary school. This was the leadership that would rise to international prominence in the Civil War.

Codovilla remained the party's authoritarian éminence grise, still in place in July 1936, when the rebel generals under Franco's leadership carried out their coup in Spanish Morocco, an event he misjudged completely. His reports from Madrid to Moscow were soothing: the Republic was in no danger.[18] In fact, the workers had armed themselves immediately and put down attempts at insurrection in Barcelona and Madrid. The revolutionary enthusiasm even extended to the Catalan Communists, who on 23 July 1936, without the knowledge of the national party leadership and 'against the instructions received', had united with the Socialist Party of Catalonia to form the PSUC, as Codovilla and Díaz had somewhat ruefully to report to Moscow.[19] Before the end of the month, Germany and Italy had begun delivering aircraft to the rebel government in Burgos. Seeking to avoid the conflict's becoming international, the bourgeois-democratic states of France and Great Britain set up a Non-Intervention Committee, joined by Germany, Italy and the Soviet Union among others. If the legal Spanish government could expect no support from other states, the left, on the other hand, was quick to mobilize.

---

17 Elorza and Bizcarrondo, *Queridos camaradas*, 171–2.
18 Elorza, 'In the Shadow', 242.
19 Report by Díaz and 'Luis' to Dimitrov, 30 July 1936, published in Ronald Radosh, Mary R. Habeck and Grigory Sevostianov, eds, *Spain Betrayed: The Soviet Union in the Spanish Civil War*, New Haven, CT: Yale University Press, 2001, 17–18, at 17.

Solidarity with the Spanish Republic... and the Revolution

The worldwide wave of antifascist solidarity with the democratically elected government of the Republic crossed party lines on the left and embraced not only the Western democracies but also the Soviet Union (where it could be said to have been even stronger). The pro-Soviet American journalist Louis Fischer, who shuttled back and forth between Moscow and Madrid during the Civil War, remarked on the enthusiasm of the Soviet population: 'Moscow lived in Spain. Everybody talked Spain.'[20] Fischer was not a member of the party, but he was so close to the Soviet government that once, visiting Moscow in late December 1936, he gave the head of the GRU an oral report on the Spanish situation.[21] For Communists and social democrats, anarchists, anti-Stalinist Marxists and Trotskyists, Quakers and pacifists, and for many liberals, left and not-so-left, the battle against the Nationalist rebels represented the last chance to stop the spread of fascism in Europe. Countless meetings were held, appeals drafted and published, money raised. Support for the Republicans found bodily expression in Spain and moral and material at home. The list of prominent journalists, writers, intellectuals, artists and photographers who travelled to Spain is long, many of their names still famous. From France came André Malraux, winner of the Prix Goncourt in 1933, who had moved decisively closer to both the Communists and the Soviet Union over the first half of the decade. He hurried to Spain without delay, mustering a squadron of pilots under his own command, though he himself knew neither how to fire a weapon nor fly a plane. In 1934, he had travelled to Moscow with his friend Ilya Ehrenburg to attend the first All-Union Congress of Soviet Writers, though he was there somewhat critical of the Socialist Realism already adopted as official doctrine. The following year, he was one of the headline speakers at the high-profile International Congress of Writers for the Defence of Culture held in the 3,000-seat auditorium of the Mutualité in Paris, which led to the establishment of the International Association of Writers for the Defence of Culture,[22] its title reflecting the

---

20 Louis Fischer, *Men and Politics*, London: Cape, 1941, 403, cited in of Kowalsky, *Stalin*, chapter 4.

21 See the shorthand record of the conversation in Radosh, *Spain Betrayed*, 108–20.

22 The speeches and other contributions to this congress are reproduced in Sandra Teroni and Wolfgang Klein, eds, *Pour la défense de la culture: Les textes du Congrès*

Communists' new political theme of the defence of humanism and of the shared cultural heritage.²³

The initiative for the creation the International Association apparently came from Henri Barbusse, but the actual organization of the congress was left in the hands of the German writer and poet Johannes R. Becher (1891–1958), earlier an Expressionist but now committed to Socialist Realism, who was able to mobilize many French colleagues. Also involved in the preparations were Ilya Ehrenburg and Mikhail Koltsov (1898–1940), a journalist and the head of the foreign department of the Soviet Writers' Union, a cultural functionary who not only had close links with Soviet state security (i.e. the NKVD), but is said to have directly collaborated with them in connection with Spain. The Danish historian Niels Erik Rosenfeldt, who has devoted many years to meticulously tracing the secret apparatuses undergirding Stalin's power, also describes him as a special correspondent, that is, a direct informant of Stalin's.²⁴ The American historian Daniel Kowalsky, on the other hand, who has also researched in the Russian archives, describes Ehrenburg as a 'Stalinist agent', but Koltsov only as a journalist who produced Soviet-slanted reports.²⁵

Regler, Koestler, Aragon, Stern (who, like Regler, became a political commissar with the International Brigades), Ehrenburg and Malraux were not the only writers drawn to Spain. Among the best-known members of this 'international battalion of bespectacled volunteers', as Koltsov dubbed them,²⁶ were the Soviet-friendly Ernest Hemingway, who wrote about his experiences in the novel *For Whom the Bell Tolls*, and George Orwell, who arrived under the auspices of Britain's

---

international des écrivains, Paris, juin 1935, Dijon: Éditions universitaires de Dijon, 2005.

23 Bernhard H. Bayerlein, 'Von der Roten Literaturinternationale zu Stalins Hofschreibern? Arbeitsmaterialien zu den Schriftstellerinternationalen, 1919–1943', *International Newsletter of Communist Studies Online* 15:22, 2009, 202–10.

24 Niels Erik Rosenfeldt, *The 'Special' World: Stalin's Power Apparatus and the Soviet System's Secret Structures of Communication*, vol. 2, Copenhagen: Museum Tusculanum Press, 2009, 354.

25 Daniel Kowalsky, *Stalin*, chapter 2, n.26. The author, however, provides no evidence for either assertion.

26 Michael Kolzow, *Spanisches Tagebuch*, 3rd edn, Berlin: Militärverlag der Deutschen Demokratischen Republik, 1986, 531.

Independent Labour Party and whose *Homage to Catalonia* (1938) offers a critical account of the Communists' repression of the POUM and the disempowerment of the CNT-FAI following the May 1937 events in Barcelona.[27] Another who wrote about the conflict, in *Spain in Arms* (1937), was the American journalist and long-time fellow-traveller Anna Louise Strong, married to Comintern employee Joel Shubin (1888–1942) since the early 1930s.

Spain attracted filmmakers too. Just a month after the outbreak of war, the Soviet Politburo allowed Roman Karmen and Boris Makaseev to travel to Spain. Footage of theirs was used in the propaganda film *España 1936*, produced by Luis Buñuel on behalf of the Republican government, in association with the French Communist Party. The documentary filmmaker and Communist Joris Ivens (1898–1989) came from the Netherlands and shot the film *The Spanish Earth* (1937) from a script by Ernest Hemingway and John Dos Passos. This was officially funded by the Spanish government, unofficially by the Soviet Union. Orson Welles, Jean Renoir and Lilian Hellman were also involved. Based on André Malraux's novel *L'espoir* (*Man's Hope*) and directed by Boris Peskine and Malraux himself, the feature film *Sierra de Teruel*, shot in 1938, offers a highly realistic portrayal of an episode from the war.

There were also hundreds of war correspondents, almost a thousand all told.[28] As has already been noted, Ilya Ehrenburg was there for *Izvestiia* and Mikhail Koltsov ('Friedland') for *Pravda*, also writing for *Inprekorr* on the side. Koltsov came with his wife, the German writer Maria Osten (1908–1942), who had lived in Moscow for a year and then, from 1933, in Paris, as correspondent for Moscow's *Deutsche Zentralzeitung*, for which she now worked in Spain. John Dos Passos, Josephine Herbst, Louis Fischer, W. H. Auden, Stephen Spender, Cyril Connolly, Antoine de Saint Exupéry and Paul Nizan were also there. They worked for newspapers such as the daily *Ce Soir*, founded by the PCF in March 1937, which sent eighteen journalists and photo-reporters, among them Otto Katz (as André Simone) and Arthur Koestler. The

---

27 On this see, for example, Manfred Lentzen, *Der Spanische Bürgerkrieg und die Dichter: Beispiele des politischen Engagements in der Literatur*, Heidelberg: Winter, 1985; and on the cultural and propaganda war more generally, Stanley G. Payne, *The Spanish Civil War*, Cambridge: Cambridge University Press, 2012, 160–8.

28 Paul Preston, *We Saw Spain Die: Foreign Correspondents in the Spanish Civil War*, London: Constable, 2008.

bourgeois press also had its representatives in Spain. Martha Gellhorn, who would marry Ernest Hemingway a few years later, reported for the American magazine *Collier's*, and Hemingway himself for the North American Newspaper Alliance, a press syndicate established by a number of major American and Canadian publications. Kim Philby (who had joined Münzenberg's World Committee for the Relief of the Victims of German Fascism in 1933 and who would later become famous as a Soviet-British double agent) reported first as a freelancer and then for Britain's *Times*. Apart from Koestler, he was probably the only Communist to report from the Nationalist side, and certainly the only one to be awarded a military decoration by Franco.[29]

In war, very few play straight. No one knew this better than the shrewd Otto Katz, head of the Agence Espagne. According to the British journalist Claud Cockburn (1903–1981), who reported on Spain, under the name Frank Pitcairn, for the CPGB's *Daily Worker* and the *Inprekorr/Rundschau* stable, the consistently 'stagy' Katz persuaded him that they should publish a fake story.[30] The supposed anti-Franco revolt in the Moroccan city of Tetuán, which in those days still belonged to Spain, was intended to convince Prime Minister Léon Blum that the Republican cause was not yet lost, and so to close his eyes to another delivery of Soviet arms via France. The two thus feverishly put together a report about Moorish soldiers who, sickened by the war, had risen up in rebellion alongside civilian victims of colonial oppression and Spanish anti-fascists. Having no idea of the local geography, the two journalists turned to the city plans in the travel guides. Without any indication of heights, and not wishing to stage a shoot-out on a long street where opposing forces might not be able to see each other on account of some 'great hump in the middle', they opted to set events on 'very short streets and open squares'. 'In the end it emerged as one of the most factual, inspiring and yet sober pieces of war reporting I ever saw, and the night editors loved it.'[31] All the newspapers carried the report, and their goal of nudging Blum to forbearance regarding the weapons was apparently achieved.

---

29 On Philby's recruitment as a Soviet spy in 1934, see Christopher Andrew, *The Defense of the Realm: The Authorized History of the MI5*, London: Penguin, 2010, 168–9.

30 Claud Cockburn, *Crossing the Line, Being the Second Volume of Autobiography*, London: MacGibbon & Kee, 1958, 27–8.

31 Ibid., 28.

The Spanish Civil War was indeed a media war for both sides, much of it fought by photojournalists,[32] among the most notable being Gerda Taro (real name Gerta Pohorylle), run over by a tank, at the age of twenty-seven, at the Battle of Brunete in July 1937, Robert Capa (actually Endre Ernö Friedmann), responsible for the iconic image *The Falling Soldier*, and David Seymour, nicknamed 'Chim'. The three of them would later achieve legendary status, Taro and Capa as a couple. They worked mostly for left, republican or Communist clients such as *Ce Soir*, Agence Espagne, *Regards*, *Vu*, *L'Humanité*, and *Volks-Illustrierte* magazine (successor to the *AIZ*, produced in Prague until 1938). In 1938, Capa also worked for Münzenberg's oppositional *Zukunft*, as well as for *Time* and other bourgeois publications. In addition, many less well-known photographers also reported on events, such as the Swiss Paul Senn, who, working for the *Zürcher Illustrierte*, accompanied an aid convoy to Spain, or Walter Reuter, who documented the 'Despedida', the farewell ceremony for the International Brigades held in Barcelona in October 1938. The effect of their images in popularizing the Republican struggle and strengthening international solidarity cannot be overstated.[33]

It was not just professional employment of one kind or another that brought people rushing to Spain in the summer of 1936. Even before the formation of the International Brigades, many volunteers travelled there on their own initiative to join the militias that were hastily set up by the anarchist CNT-FAI, the POUM and the PSUC.[34] German and Italian antifascists in exile, emigrant Spaniards, and also anarchist, left social democratic and Communist workers from France, Belgium, Portugal, Switzerland and Eastern Europe poured into Spain. Others had come to Barcelona to take part in the Spartakiad, the antifascist counter-event to the Berlin Olympics, due to open on the evening of 17 July 1936, and then stayed in Spain after the coup.

This was the case of Clara Ensner of Switzerland. Her partner, Paul Thalmann of Basel, who after studying at a Comintern cadre school in

---

32 Josep M. Solé and Joan Villarroya, *Guerra i propaganda: Fotografies del Comissariat de Propaganda*, Barcelona: Viena/Arxiu Nacional de Catalunya, 2006.

33 François Fontaine, *La guerre d'Espagne: Un déluge de feu et d'images*, Paris: BDIC/Berg International, 2003.

34 The Partido Obrero de Unificación Marxista (POUM) was a Marxist party formed in 1935 by the fusion of the Trotskyist Izquierda Comunista (Communist Left) and the Bloque Obrero y Campesino (Workers' and Peasants Bloc).

Moscow had found himself expelled from the party in 1929 on account of his oppositionist sympathies, came to join her a few days after the coup. He arrived to find the city in a state of revolutionary euphoria:

> A dense mass of people filled the street [La Rambla], militia uniforms predominating (simple blue overalls, coloured caps). Allegiance could be identified by the colours of flags, caps or armbands. Black and red, the anarchist colours, were by far the most prevalent. Lorries and private cars carrying militiamen armed to the teeth hurtled along the streets at reckless speed. In front of party and trade union offices, primitively armed military units formed up to march to the front. Every departing detachment was enthusiastically cheered by the public. Chants, speeches, and news announcements rang through the air from half a dozen loudspeakers. Everything looked terribly martial and yet somehow good-natured.[35]

When Thalmann found his partner, she was preparing to leave for the front with an anarchist militia. The revolutionary movement had also shaken up the traditional gender order. This was readily apparent in the fact that it was now socially acceptable for women to wear trousers and overalls – itself significant as both a material and a symbolic emancipation – but more important yet was their being able bear arms as members of the militias.

It is more than likely that Thalmann, who published his memoirs in 1973, had earlier read George Orwell, who had described the atmosphere in Barcelona in very similar terms:

> Practically every building of any size had been seized by the workers and was draped with red flags or with the red and black flag of the anarchists . . . Down the Ramblas, the wide central artery of the town where crowds of people streamed constantly to and fro, the loudspeakers were bellowing revolutionary songs all day and far into the

---

35 Paul Thalmann, *Wo die Freiheit stirbt: Stationen eines politischen Kampfes*, Olten and Freiburg im Breisgau: Walter Verlag, 1974, 129–35, quote at 134–5.

night ... Practically everyone wore rough working-class clothes, or blue overalls, or some variant of the militia uniform.[36]

Whether the one influenced the other or not, photographs, newspaper articles and the accounts put about by the people and organizations involved all conveyed the same sense of revolutionary enthusiasm. In this respect, the PCE was no exception. In the early months following the Nationalist rebellion, members of the Communist party occupied factories and other buildings alongside anarchists and socialists, joined them in forming autonomous collectives, and set up their own militias. At the same time, in accordance with the Comintern's new popular front policy, the party backed the restoration of the Republic, i.e., the bourgeois state, and with that the social status quo[37] – a contradictory compromise position it shared with the left-Socialists whose consequences would prove fateful.

Recruitment and Conveyance of Volunteers

At the forefront of international historical memory stand those who travelled to Spain to support the Republic in battle. Countless images document the 35,000 or so volunteers, some 500 of them women, who came from fifty-four different countries. Of these, some 31,000 belonged to the International Brigades. Historians have tallied their numbers, analysed their social characteristics, unearthed their biographies and explored their experiences,[38] and we shall not be concerned here to tell

---

36 George Orwell, *Homage to Catalonia*, Harmondsworth, UK: Penguin Books, [1938] 1975, 8–9.

37 A line decided on by the ECCI Secretariat at its meeting of 23 July 1936: Schauff, *Der verspielte Sieg*, 125.

38 Most studies have been undertaken on a national basis, and there is no room here for even a half-way-comprehensive bibliography. For an overview, see Manuel Requena Gallego, ed., 'Las Brigadas internacionales', *Ayer: Revista de Storia Contemporánea* 56:4, 2004; and for a survey of the literature, Manuel Requena Galego and M. Lourdes Prades Artigas, 'Las Brigadas internacionales', *Studia Historica: Historia Contemporánea* 32, 2014, 181–95; as well as Stéfanie Prezioso, Jean Batou and Ami-Jacques Rapin, eds, *Tant pis si la lutte est cruelle: Volontaires internationaux contre Franco*, Paris: Syllepse, 2008. On the experiences of Communist and more especially English-speaking volunteers, see Lisa Kirschenbaum, *International*

this story – or stories – again. What interests us rather, in keeping with the theme of the book as a whole, is the work of the Comintern and its agents in creating the structures and the logistical networks necessary to recruit volunteers and bring them to Spain.

The Comintern was late in deciding to provide this kind of military assistance and had been preceded into the field by other political formations and indeed by individuals who hadn't waited to be organized before volunteering. The anarchist organizations – the CNT and the FAI – and Catalan parties the POUM and the PSUC had formed the first military columns. The first groups from abroad were often organized by individuals, among them a member of the antifascist Italian organization Giustizia e Libertà and the German Communist Hans Beimler (1895–1936), who, by July, had already mobilized a group of sixty German émigrés. In his memoirs, Herbert Wehner, alias 'Kurt Funk' (1906–1990), a member of the KPD leadership, says that it was Willi Münzenberg who negotiated their entry with Luis Araquistáin, the Spanish ambassador in Paris.[39] In early August, the KPD called on its members in emigration to enlist in Spain.[40] That same month, about thirty young Communist volunteers left Switzerland on their own initiative, but got stuck in Paris for lack of money to continue their journey. The Swiss Otto Brunner (1896–1973), a member of the KPS secretariat, who happened to be in Paris after a short trip to Moscow, sent a telegram to his colleagues at home requesting assistance for them.[41] As no official policy on recruitment had yet been adopted, the leadership declined and ordered them to return home immediately, though not all

---

Communism and the Spanish Civil War: Solidarity and Suspicion, Cambridge: Cambridge University Press, 2015.

39 Herbert Wehner, *Zeugnis*, Cologne: Kiepenheuer & Witsch, 1982, 177. Wehner himself takes credit for the mobilization of the first group of volunteers, also inflating their number to a hundred.

40 This appeal by the CC of the KPD appeared in the German emigrant press after 7 August 1936. On the KPD in the Spanish Civil War, see Patrick von zur Mühlen, *Spanien war ihre Hoffnung: Die deutsche Linke im Spanischen Bürgerkrieg 1936 bis 1939*, Berlin: J.H.W. Dietz Nachf., 1985, 145–7, and Michael Uhl, *Mythos Spanien: Das Erbe der internationalen Brigade in der DDR*, Bonn: Dietz, 2004, 65–6. See also Willi Bredel, *Spanienkrieg: Zur Geschichte der 11. Internationalen Brigade*, vol. 1, Berlin: Aufbau Verlag, 1977, 19.

41 Telegram to Zurich from Otto Brunner in Paris, 4 August 1936, in Brigitte Studer, *Un parti sous influence: Le Parti communiste suisse, une section du Komintern, 1931 à 1939*, Lausanne: L'Âge d'Homme, 1994, 491.

of them did. This did not, however, put a stop to the activities of Hans Anderfuhren (1893–1973), a metalworker and a member of the Swiss party's central committee, who since early August had himself been organizing volunteer groups on his own initiative.

According to Giulio Ceretti ('Pierre Allard' and many other pseudonyms, 1903–1985), there was also pressure to organize volunteer detachments from Spanish migrants in France. He says that at the 3 rue Montholon offices of Main d'Œuvre Immigrée (MOI), the PCF's organization for foreign workers, he was almost overrun by deputations demanding that the French party send men with a knowledge of weapons to Spain.[42] Ceretti, who owed his rise through the apparatus to his struggle against the Trotskyists in 1928–30, would soon take over the presidency of the Paris-based Comité International de Coordination de l'Aide à l'Espagne Républicaine (CICAER – International Committee of Coordination and Information to Aid Republican Spain). Besides this, of course, he had more important but less public responsibilities as the head of the PCF's secret financial and commercial operations. He was thus in close contact with Eugen Fried (1900–1943), since 1930 the Comintern's all-powerful envoy to the PCF.[43] In 1937, Ceretti also became responsible for the management of shipping company France-Navigation, set up by the Comintern, as part of Operation X, to carry weapons purchased in the Soviet Union or elsewhere to Spain.[44]

The initial reluctance of the Comintern and its member parties to intervene militarily in the Spanish conflict can be explained by the hesitancy of Stalin, who wished to come to an understanding with the Western powers and so joined the non-intervention pact with France

---

42 Giulio Ceretti, À l'ombre des deux T. 40 ans avec Palmiro Togliatti et Maurice Thorez, Paris: Julliard, 1973, 165–7.

43 For the life of Eugen Fried, a Jew belonging to the ethnic Hungarian minority incorporated into Czechoslovakia in consequence of the Treaty of Versailles and who would be killed by the Gestapo in Brussels in 1943, see Annie Kriegel and Stéphane Courtois, Eugen Fried: Le grand secret du PCF, Paris: Seuil, 1997.

44 On Soviet weapons deliveries, see the monumental work of José Ángel Sánchez Asiaín, La financiación de la Guerra Civil Española: Una aproximación histórica, Barcelona: Grupo Planeta, 2014, and Yuri Rybalkin, Stalin y España: La ayuda militar soviética a la República, Madrid: Marcial Pons Historia, 2007; also Kowalsky, Stalin, chapters 9 and 10, and – with due caution – Ceretti, À l'ombre, 165–80.

and Great Britain.⁴⁵ Passed on 3 August 1936, the first Comintern resolution on Spain called only for the collection of medical supplies, food and gold, the purchase of ambulances and the despatch of medical volunteers. The policy of non-intervention attracted criticism within the ranks of both the Comintern and the Soviet party, however, with Willi Münzenberg and Karl Radek being among its most prominent opponents. It was not until 14 September 1936 that Stalin decided to approve the supply of weapons as requested by the Republican government, and only on 18 September did the ECCI decide to send volunteers with military experience,⁴⁶ their recruitment falling to the French and Italian parties. The decision to form the International Brigades was communicated to the heads of the Communist parties not present in Moscow at a meeting in Paris shortly afterwards.⁴⁷

The Comintern and the PCF had already sent observers to Spain. One was Vital Gayman (1897–1985), a Frenchman of Russian-Jewish extraction who had gained military experience in the First World War, who travelled to Madrid in mid-August 1936. He was followed not long after by Jules Dumont (1888–1943), a former career officer who had been sent to Ethiopia by the ECCI in 1935 as military adviser to Haile Selassie. In Spain, Dumont immediately began organizing a French unit and on the formation of the International Brigades he took command of the 'Commune de Paris' battalion of the First Brigade.⁴⁸ Already in Spain was Vittorio Vidali, appointed a military adviser to the PCE, who had managed to catch the last flight from Paris to Madrid on 17 July. Posted there with him, as his 'assistant for international affairs', was the Lithuanian Iosif Grigulevich (1913–1988), an agent of the NKVD.⁴⁹

---

45 Ángel Viñas, 'La decisión de Stalin de ayudar a la República: Un aspecto controvertido en la historiografía de la Guerra Civil', *Historia y Política* 16, 2006, 65–108, and on the democratic states, Viñas, *La soledad*.

46 Daniel Kowalsky, 'The Soviet Union and the International Brigades, 1936–1939', *Journal of Slavic Military Studies* 19, 2006, 681–704, at 687; and Rémi Skoutelsky, *L'espoir guidait leurs pas: Les volontaires français dans les Brigades internationales, 1936–1939*, Paris: Grasset, 1998, 53. On the ECCI's first meeting on Spain following the coup, see also E. H. Carr, *The Comintern and the Spanish Civil War*, London: Macmillan, 1984, 20–22.

47 Jules Humbert-Droz, *Mémoires*, vol. 3, *Dix ans de lutte antifasciste, 1931–1941*, Neuchâtel: A La Baconnière, 1972, 178.

48 As political commissar with the Francs Tireurs et Partisans (the Communist armed Resistance), Dumont would be shot by the Germans on 15 June 1943.

49 Patrick Karlsen, *Vittorio Vidali: Vita di uno Stalinista (1916–56)*, Bologna: Il Mulino, 2019, 163, 173 and 188.

That same August, Comintern secretary André Marty, who could read and understand Spanish, visited the Irún front in the Basque Country on a mission for the ECCI.[50] Just one day after the ECCI Secretariat's decision to form the International Brigades, at a meeting he did not attend, Marty was asked to draw up an operational plan.[51] Under various designations – ultimately as inspector-general – Marty subsequently assumed political control over the Brigades.[52]

To ensure that volunteers from abroad reached the base at Albacete, special arrangements had to be made for their movement, as many countries prohibited travel to Spain or refused the necessary transit visas. Switzerland, for example, had already criminalized participation in the fighting on 14 August 1936, while France, the country through which all volunteers had to pass, was bound by the Non-Intervention Agreement. Though customs officials might initially have turned a blind eye, had they antifascist sympathies, this possibility vanished in February 1937 with the official closure of the border. Yet even this did not completely bar passage, for on the one hand the volunteers could not infrequently count on the solidarity of much of the French population, and on the other, the Communist organizations had created a 'Spain apparatus' for the illegal conveyance of volunteers. This was run by the PCF and the leadership in exile of the PCI, who together formed the 'Paris Committee' with its headquarters at 120, rue La Fayette.

There was also a recruiting centre in Paris, located at the former headquarters of the Communist trade union confederation (which had fused with its social democratic counterpart under the Popular Front), at 7, avenue Mathurin Moreau, also home to International Red Aid, which had opened offices in Paris in response to the flood of refugees from Germany. Located on the rue de Chabrol near the Gare de l'Est, the technical back-office for the whole operation was led by the Pole Karol Swierczewski (1897–1947, known as 'Walter') until December 1936, when he took over command of the Fourteenth

---

50 According to Marty's party autobiography of 28 October 1931, his knowledge of languages also extended to English (active) and Italian (passive): RGASPI 495/270/9053.

51 Pelai Pagès i Blanch, 'Marty, Vidal, Kléber et le Komintern: Ce que nous apprennent les archives de Moscou', in Prezioso, *Tant pis*, 85–100, at 86–7.

52 Claude Pennetier, 'Thorez-Marty: Paris-Moscou, Moscou-Paris', in Narinsky and Rojahn, *Centre and Periphery*, 203–17.

Brigade ('La Marseillaise') in Spain. Swierczewski, who had spent five years at a 'military-political school' in the Soviet Union, was one of the few the Comintern sent to Spain with any military training. To their surprise and frequent dissatisfaction, volunteers in Paris had to hand over their money, and sometimes their passports; if not, the latter would be confiscated after the border had been crossed. They would subsequently be used by the Spanish and Soviet secret services.[53] At the avenue Mathurin Moreau recruiting centre, volunteers would also be tested for political reliability by representatives of the relevant nations. Josip Broz (1892–1980), the future Marshal Tito, was responsible for a time for dealing with those from the Balkans,[54] taking over the name 'Walter' from his predecessor Swierczewski. The screening system as a whole was under the direction of the Frenchman Maurice Tréand (1900–1949), responsible since 1933 for the establishment and development of the PCF's Cadre Commission. He called himself 'Le Gros' or 'Legros'.

Having cleared this hurdle – not then as tricky as it would later become – the volunteers would pass into the care of Red Aid in the rue de la Grange-aux-Belles, where they were usually looked after until their departure by female party members with Comintern experience. Charlotte Hümbelin of Vienna, then still Bindel, had previously worked as a courier between Vienna, Prague and Moscow for Austria's Young Communists, and as an editor at the Comintern's Foreign Workers' Publishing House in Moscow. In 1936, her party sent her to Paris, where she 'was to find a job to do'.[55] As 'Jana Wagnerowa', she was responsible for welcoming volunteers from Austria and Czechoslovakia and looking after them until they continued their journey:[56]

---

53 On the use made of the passports, see Andreu Castells, *Las Brigadas internacionales de la guerra de España*, Barcelona: Ariel, 1974, 63, and also the memoirs of Herbert Crüger, *Verschwiegene Zeiten: Vom geheimen Apparat der KPD ins Gefängnis der Staatssicherheit*, Berlin: Linksdruck, 1990, 101, and Walter G. Krivitsky, *In Stalin's Secret Service: An Exposé of Russia's Secret Policies by the Former Chief of the Soviet Intelligence in Western Europe*, New York: Harper Brothers, 1939, 112.

54 Rémi Skoutelsky, 'Le rôle du Parti communiste français dans l'organisation des Brigades internationales', in Prezioso, *Tant pis*, 53–70, at 59.

55 Lotte Hümbelin, *Mein eigener Kopf: Ein Frauenleben in Wien, Moskau, Prag, Paris und Zürich*, Zurich: edition 8, 1999, 241.

56 Hümbelin, *Mein eigener Kopf*, 243.

I received my fellow Austrians and also the Czechs, taking whatever money they had on them to put it into a common fund, and providing them with pocket money and first instructions. They had to fill out questionnaires and give a brief account of their background and their views.

Charlotte Bindel accommodated the *Spanienfahrer*, the 'Spainward travellers', as they were known – 'up to ten Austrians or Czechs a day' – in a hotel she described as 'shabby', the rooms offering no comforts but an iron bedstead and a wash basin.[57]

The Communist organizations in Paris set up nursing courses for the numerous women emigrants from Germany, Hungary, Poland, Yugoslavia and Austria.[58] Usually held in the evenings and at weekends, they were delivered under the supervision of experienced doctors. Whether any of the few female volunteers whose service in combat units has been documented ever passed through the Paris recruitment centre is unknown, but it seems unlikely. Even if there was, at first, no explicit prohibition, the most important criterion for enrolment in the International Brigades was experience of weapons and warfare – a requirement by no means met by all male recruits, however – followed by medical knowledge. Most female volunteers probably travelled to Spain on their own, or happened to be there already, like Clara Ensner. It was, in fact, the anarchists and the POUM who tended to accept women into their units on an equal footing with men, while the Communists pressed as early as October 1936 for the transformation of the militias into a disciplined people's

---

57 Ibid., 244–6.

58 Among them the Austrian Communists Anna Peczenik and Gundl Herrnstadt-Steinmetz: Irene Filip, 'Anna Peczenik: Biographische Skizze einer Spanienfreiwilligen und Widerstandskämpferin', in *80 Jahre Internationale Brigaden: Neue Forschungen über österreichische Freiwillige im Spanischen Bürgerkrieg*, Vienna: Dokumentationsarchiv des österreichischen Widerstandes, 2016, 43–63, at 51. And on the Yugoslavs, Ksenija Vidmar Horvat and Avgust Lešnik, 'The Spanish Female Volunteers from Yugoslavia as Example of Solidarity in a Transnational Context', in Bernhard H. Bayerlein, Kasper Braskén and Uwe Sonnenberg, eds, *Globale Räume für radikale transnationale Solidarität/Global Spaces for Radical Solidarity*, Berlin: Internationales Willi Münzenberg Forum, 2018, 121–41. On foreign women volunteers more generally, see Magdalena Rosende, 'L'engagement féminin international en Espagne', in Prezioso, *Tant pis*, 399–418, and Ana Martínez Rus, 'Mujeres y Guerra Civil: Un balance historiográfico', *Studia Historica: Historia Contemporánea* 32, 2014, 333–43.

army, modelled on the Red Army, in which women had no place as combatants.[59]

In the Brigades, then, women were from the beginning assigned to sanitary, logistical, administrative and occasionally journalistic tasks. This is reflected in the party autobiographies of two Swiss women, Anny Brunner and Berta Bickel, both of whom had wanted to fight. As the barely twenty-three-year-old Basel hairdresser Anny Brunner explained in her awkward written German, 'I was not permitted to go to the front with a rifle. First, the many men hanging about here need rifles, they said.'[60] When all women were ordered away from the front line in February 1937, Anny Bruner had to go to Barcelona, where she worked as a nurse. Bert(h)a Bickel-Schuler – whose husband Ernst Bickel (1908–1938?), one of a family of Zurich Communists, was political commissar of the 'Thälmann' battalion of the Second Brigade – was assigned to International Red Aid as an auxiliary nurse and hospital laundress. This she refused, making a formal protest. She also complained of the attitude of André Marty, legendary even then for his misogyny, who had decreed that there be 'no women and no adventure-seekers' in the Brigades.[61]

For most volunteers, however, Paris was not the first hurdle, for they had first to get to France, for the most part illegally. To assist with this, the Communist Party mobilized activist networks, developing them where necessary. In the *départements* of the Nord and the Pas-de-Calais, they saw to volunteers from Belgium, and in the port of Le Havre to the hundreds of Americans who arrived there from 1937 onward.[62] Volunteers from Eastern Europe had to travel through Switzerland, being barred by both Germany and Italy, both aligned with Franco.

In Switzerland, as in France, the management of volunteer transfer was confided to current or former Comintern officials known to be

---

59 As Nash has shown in her standard work on the subject, the positive image of the *miliciana* took on an increasingly negative coloration from the autumn of 1936, under the influence of a deliberate political campaign: Mary Nash, *Rojas: Las mujeres Republicanas en la Guerra Civil*, Madrid: Taurus, 1999, an expanded edition of a work first published English: Mary Nash, *Defying Male Civilization: Women in the Spanish Civil War*, Denver: Arden Press, 1995.
60 Party autobiography of Anny Brunner, date illegible, RGASPI 545/6/1481.
61 International Brigade personal file on Bert(h)a Bickel, RGASPI 545/6/1478.
62 Skoutelsky, *L'espoir*, 121.

politically reliable.⁶³ The man in charge of it all was Edgar Woog, a long-standing Comintern emissary known by the names 'Enrique Martin' and 'Alfred Stirner'. As well as having been an instructor in Spain from autumn 1930 to July 1931, he had several times served as a Comintern representative in Mexico (in 1921–22, 1927 and then again in 1928–29). Woog had also worked at the WEB in Berlin and in various departments of the ECCI apparatus, mainly in the Latin Secretariat. From 1932 to 1934, he had also lectured on 'party building' at Moscow's Communist University of the Toilers of China. In October 1935, Woog had finally been allowed to return to Switzerland, having been told in late 1933 that he could go after the Seventh World Congress, which had then been postponed over and over again.⁶⁴ Joint head of the Swiss apparatus in Spain was Karl Hofmaier, sixteen years in the service of the Comintern (including seven in prison in Italy). Posted to Switzerland in 1935 to bolster the party leadership, he had proved his loyalty in seeing to the closing down of Münzenberg's International Workers' Relief in Paris and Moscow. Woog and Hofmaier were believed by the Comintern to have the know-how necessary for such a delicate and important mission. They were familiar with the techniques of undercover work, the criteria of cadre evaluation and the system for the secret transfer of funds. On his return, Woog was also made responsible for setting up the Swiss cadre commission.

While Hofmaier was tasked with building up the Swiss network, in August 1936 Woog travelled to Spain. He spent a good month in Madrid and Barcelona, where he met members of the PCE and PCF leaderships as well as Maurice Tréand, head of the French party's cadre department and its volunteer recruitment apparatus. By 4 September, he was back in Switzerland, though he left for Spain

---

63 For the Swiss element of the 'Spain apparatus' I rely extensively on Studer, *Un parti*, 479–527. As a result of carelessness on Anderfuhren's part, the Swiss Federal Prosecutor's Office, which was pursuing more than a half-dozen party officials, discovered a good deal about the KPS and Comintern structures involved in assistance to Spain. In addition, independent volunteers returning from Spain tended to be very talkative. All Swiss volunteers known to the police were sentenced either to imprisonment and/or to a temporary deprivation of civil rights.

64 Letter from 'Stirner' to Piatnitsky for the attention of the Political Commission of the ECCI, Moscow, 18 December 1933, and decision of the Political Commission of 27 December 1933, RGASPI 495/274/6-I.

again on the 9th; on the 15th he travelled to the Soviet Union via Prague.[65]

The Swiss party's recruitment campaign only really got off the ground in October 1936, after Woog had come back from Moscow and Jules Humbert-Droz, the third of the senior cadre involved, from Paris. Discreet contact with trusted figures in Switzerland was now officially assigned to Hans Anderfuhren, while the men from the Comintern worked only in the background. For reasons of security, in both France and Switzerland, directives were communicated to local section leaders only orally. Wherever possible, one person was appointed (usually a Communist but not necessarily a local party leader) whom volunteers could approach and who would provide them with the necessary contact addresses. Woog and Hofmaier saw to the money and the necessary papers. Volunteers from Switzerland, Austria, Czechoslovakia and elsewhere were smuggled across the border in small groups, to be received by French comrades and thence conveyed to Paris. The border would be crossed from Basel to Saint-Louis, from Geneva to Annemasse, or from Le Locle to Morteau. However, volunteers coming from the east had first to negotiate the Austrian–Swiss border, where from late 1936 at the latest the officials of both countries made strenuous efforts to block the passage of any volunteers for Spain. In August and September 1937 alone, Austrian customs stopped 93, among them 28 Yugoslavs, 7 Czechs, 3 Germans, 2 Italians and 2 Hungarians. On the other hand, at least 250 managed to make their way from Vienna to Paris via Basel between October 1936 and March 1937.[66]

After screening at the recruitment centres in Vienna and/or Prague, the volunteers were vetted again in Switzerland, the aim each time being to exclude not only Gestapo agents and provocateurs but also adventure-seekers and, increasingly, Trotskyists, the struggle against whom had come to be seen, since the first Moscow Trial, as an integral part of the battle against fascism. The Swiss party were not the only ones involved in this: both the Austrian and the German parties had a reception centre in the Swiss city of St Gallen, staffed in part by officials

---

65 After a short visit to Paris, in January 1937 he travelled again to Moscow, and yet again, for the last time, in October that same year.

66 Brigitte Galanda et al., *Für Spaniens Freiheit: Österreicher an der Seite der Spanischen Republik 1936–1939. Eine Dokumentation*, Vienna: Österreichischer Bundesverlag, 1986, 48–9, 69–73 and 99.

specially sent from Paris, which not only provided volunteers with board and lodging but vetted them politically. Identifying signs were discreet pins and, of course, passwords. These were changed regularly: for a time, volunteers seeking contact with the network had to ask for Peter's German-French dictionary at the party bookshop in Zurich. True names were never used by members of the 'Spain apparatus', only first names and pseudonyms. The groups would find out where they were going next only at the last minute, and, as a further security measure, every volunteer would be allocated a number that had to be given on arrival in Paris. Should a number go missing or be delayed, the apparatus was immediately informed that there might have been an arrest or some other problem and would reorganize the network accordingly.

For each convoy of volunteers, a list would be drawn up, giving not only surname and forename but also age, place of residence, occupation and former military rank, if any. It also noted whether the person concerned had a passport. The lists had to be signed by a party official before departure, and the group leader would show it and have it stamped at every stage. With the growing professionalism of the operation, the Comité International d'Aide au Peuple Espagnol eventually issued a form (probably in 1937) on which the biographical data were to be entered, which local committees then sent to the Paris Secretariat, where all would be held on file.

In Paris, volunteers would be vetted yet again. In 1937, Herbert Wehner – who in Paris had charge of the groups of exiled KPD members in northern France – explained to the Cadre Department in Moscow, as laconically as any accountant, that 'intakes from Luxembourg, Holland, Belgium and Scandinavia were first checked there, and then again in Paris'.[67] In fact, the KPD and its *Abwehrmann* or counter-intelligence officer, as the party official responsible for preventing infiltration was called, had first set up its own vetting commission in Paris. This, however, was soon merged with the French commission under Tréand. A member of the KPD leadership in exile, Siegfried Rädel ('Sachs', 1893–1943), was made responsible for screening the Germans after being deported to France following his arrest in Switzerland in October 1936.

---

67 Answers to questionnaire, filled out in Moscow on 30 August 1937, published in Reinhard Müller, *Die Akte Wehner: Moskau 1937 bis 1941*, Berlin: Rowohlt, 1993, 296.

A certain pragmatism proved essential in recruitment. Criteria such as knowledge of weapons, war experience, technical expertise, sex (male), age (young to middle-aged) or marital status (single) were not always insisted upon, either because the growing number of volunteers could not be processed quickly enough, or because the inequality between the two warring parties was such that any help was welcome.[68] In matters of 'vigilance' against Trotskyism, too, it took some time for the process to take hold, and the criteria for what constituted a 'Trotskyist' were furthermore somewhat unclear. Anarchists too were excluded, though social democrats would be tolerated under the Popular Front policy.

Those who joined the convoys directly in Paris had to report to the offices of the CGT at 163, boulevard de l'Hôpital in the 13th arrondissement. From Paris, volunteers then generally travelled by train, either directly to the Spanish border or to Marseille, where they would take ship for Spain – a route that became dangerous with the imposition of the naval blockade. In the spring of 1938, the *Ciudad de Barcelona*, the passenger vessel that carried the most volunteers, was sunk with the loss of many lives. Harry Fisher, a member of America's Young Communist League, took the train. In Perpignan, his group of around thirty volunteers was met by a person who led them to a number of taxis on the outskirts of the town. After a while, they had to continue on foot, crossing the Pyrenees with the help of a Frenchman, 'a smuggler by trade'. The route was arduous, passing through snow and ice, but when they reached the Spanish border near Figueras, they broke out in joy: 'We raised our clenched fists and shouted ¡Viva España! We began to sing "The Internationale", quietly, a little self-consciously at first, then louder and louder.'[69]

Establishment of a Military Base in Albacete

Harry Fisher was a late arrival. In the hope that Italy and Germany would withdraw their troops, the Communist parties, in consultation

---

68 Skoutelsky, *L'espoir*, 119.
69 Harry Fisher, *Comrades: Tales of a Brigadista in the Spanish Civil War*, Lincoln: University of Nebraska Press, 1998, 16–26, quote at 26.

with the Spanish government, stopped recruiting volunteers in the summer of 1938, and in the autumn the International Brigades were disbanded.[70] By then, the Comintern and the PCE had built up a full-fledged military base in Albacete, complete with arms depots, instruction centres, training schools for officers, NCOs and political commissars, medical services, billets, canteens and a postal censorship unit. Staff and volunteers together could number up to 4,400.

Control of the base lay in the hands of experienced Comintern officials and Red Army cadre. At their head was André Marty, a former naval officer who still retained the aura he won as a hero of the Black Sea Mutiny of 1919. In 1931, he had joined the Comintern leadership on the strength of his role in the elimination from the PCF of the supposedly oppositional 'Barbé-Celor Group', and he had been elected to the Presidium and appointed ECCI secretary for the English-speaking countries following the Seventh World Congress in 1935. In that role, he was also responsible for leading the work of the Communist fraction in International Red Aid.[71] From the beginning, he had been one of the Comintern's most trusted representatives in Spain.

The political leadership of the base, theoretically an appurtenance of the PCE, Marty shared with two other Comintern employees of long standing. An engineer by training, the Italian Luigi Longo (1900–1980) was like Marty a member of the Central Political Commission, yet not his equal in the Moscow hierarchy, which may explain why Marty always presented himself as the most senior figure at Albacete. Longo had been involved in establishing the base and, in December 1936, he participated in the defence of Madrid. He was made political commissar of the Twelfth International Brigade that same month, and, not long after that, appointed inspector-general of the International Brigades with the rank of divisional commissar. 'Gallo', as he was most frequently known, had lived in exile since 1926, first in France and then in Moscow. Once a member of the ECCI's Organizational Bureau, in 1932 he became a candidate member of the ECCI Presidium; he was

---

70 Skoutelsky, *L'espoir*, 139.
71 See the minutes of the meeting of the ECCI Secretariat, Moscow, 2 October 1935, published in Brigitte Studer, 'Die Kominternstruktur nach dem 7. Weltkongress: Das Protokoll des Sekretariats des EKKI über die Reorganisierung des Apparates des EKKI, 2. Oktober 1935', *Internationale wissenschaftliche Korrespondenz zur Geschichte der deutschen Arbeiterbewegung* 31:1, 1995, 25–53, at 35.

also the PCI's representative in Moscow from 1933 to 1935. The third man in the political leadership of the base was the German Franz Dahlem, who had been a journalist at *Inprekorr* in its earliest years, before moving over to *Rote Fahne*, and for many years a member of the Central Committee and Political Bureau of the KPD. On going into exile, he lived in Paris and then Prague before returning to Germany, illegally, for six months in 1934, and then leaving again for Paris, where he was a member of what was called the operational leadership in exile of the KPD alongside Walter Ulbricht. In 1935 he was made a candidate member of the ECCI. In Spain, he was the KPD's representative to the PCE and the head of the counter-intelligence and enemy affairs department of the KPD.[72]

The base commandant was the long-serving PCF official Vital Gayman, who, unlike the other two, had only spent a brief time in Moscow, in the early 1930s. His responsibilities were the organization of combat units, the selection of officers and the general administration of the base. He worked so closely with his superior, Marty, that Manfred Stern ('General Kléber', hailed by the press as the 'hero of Madrid'), at daggers drawn with both 'Vidal' and Marty, called him Marty's 'evil genius'.[73]

A fact generally ignored in the scholarship is that a good many of these leadership figures were accompanied in Spain by their partners.[74] Dahlem, whose wife and son had remained in the Soviet Union, was an exception. Marty and Gayman, on the other hand, lived in Albacete with their wives. Longo's wife, too, was in Spain. Like their husbands, these women did jobs of great importance for the Republican side. Vital Gayman's young wife, Jacqueline Bureau (1913–2005), then only

---

72 Werner Abel, 'Die versuchte Neutralisierung der "Münzenberg-Kreise" durch die KPD-Abwehr im republikanischen Spanien', in Bayerlein, *Globale Räume*, 467–93, at 469 and 474. According to Volodarsky, Dahlem was in direct contact with the NKVD: Volodarsky, *Stalin's Agent*, 248.

73 On 14 December 1937, under the name 'M. Fred', Kléber drew up an extremely detailed report on his fifteen months in Spain, in which he describes his conflicts with other military and political 'advisers'. This can be found in Radosh, *Spain Betrayed*, 295–368, quote at 324.

74 This is exemplified by the two standard works, Burnett Bolloten, *The Spanish Civil War: Revolution and Counterrevolution*, New York: Harvester Wheatsheaf, 1991, and Hugh Thomas, *The Spanish Civil War*, London: Penguin Books, 2003, both first published in 1961.

twenty-three years old, set up the Albacete base's pharmaceutical service. Marty's first wife, Pauline Taurinya (1898–1993), a party member since 1923 and a liaison agent with the OMS in Moscow from 1932 to 1934, organized the emergency medical service in Albacete, before taking on responsibility for the administration, inspection and possibly also the political surveillance of the International Brigades' hospitals.[75]

Such surveillance was undoubtedly the business of Marty's second wife, the Parisian Raymonde Lefebvre (1912–2009), in her formal employment at least. Marty and Lefebvre began an affair after Pauline Taurinya had left her husband for a Spaniard while in Albacete. Raymonde Leduc, as she still was from a previous marriage, came to Spain as a volunteer in February 1938, offering her services to the PCE. She was employed as a typist in the International Brigades' cadre department, in which role she also acted as secretary to André Marty. As a former Comintern employee who had in the ECCI's translation department in Moscow, she knew how Communist cadre policy worked.

Longo's Turinese wife Teresa Noce (1900–1980) was another who had earlier worked for the Comintern in Moscow. A child seamstress before finding work as a machinist at Fiat, she had been born into great poverty. Fleeing fascism, she and her husband had gone to Paris, where they became members of the PCI leadership in exile. After attending the Lenin School in the late 1920s, she worked for the Executive Bureau of the Profintern from 1932 to 1934. She then returned to the political front line in Paris, where under the name 'Estella' she edited the Italian party newspaper *Il Grido del Popolo* (The Cry of the People) and women's monthly *La Voce delle Donne* (Women's Voice). She was also active in recruiting volunteers after the outbreak of the Spanish Civil War. At her husband's suggestion, she went to Spain in 1936 to edit *Il Volontario della Libertà* (Volunteer of Freedom), the newspaper of the Italian brigadistas. In her memoirs, she retrospectively explains the invitation by the sexual division of labour: she was brought to Spain 'because I was a

---

75 Antonio Ramirez Navarro, 'Pauline Taurinya, la mujer que abandonó a André Marty', in Josep Sánchez Cervelló and Sebastián Agudo Blanco, eds, *Las Brigadas internacionales: Nuevas perspectivas en la historia de la Guerra Civil y del exilio*, Tarragona: URV, 2015, 499–514, at 505.

woman and the men had to fight. This principle we would have adhered to even if the comrades from other countries did not.'[76] Despite her acceptance of the supposedly natural gender order (an order evidently not unchallenged by other party members), Noce did not reject a new role in Spain on grounds of maternal responsibility. As she recalls, she explained the situation to her son, who was barely seven, and he gave his consent to her new assignment. What he did not understand, however, was that his father, who was a Communist, 'and so against war, was going to war in Spain'.[77]

It was an Italian comrade, Olga Donini, who had a son of about the same age, who took in little Puccio. Nor did Noce go to Spain to be with her husband. She went first to Barcelona, where she met Ernö Gerö, the Comintern adviser who had been there since the start of the war, whom she knew from the Lenin School. It was not the first time this Comintern instructor of long standing, who spoke both Castilian and Catalan, had been in Spain, as Gerö had already been a member of the ECCI delegation in Spain from October 1933 to August 1934. Noce then drove to Valencia by car, 'because trains no longer ran in Spain' (there were some, in fact, but few). Valencia, the city to which the Popular Front government had escaped during the Battle of Madrid, and which was therefore bursting at the seams, was also home to the German and French editions of the Brigades' newspaper. 'To accommodate the editorial offices and to have somewhere to live, the Germans had requisitioned a beautiful apartment in a modern palazzo, the owners of which had gone over to the rebels.' She decided to occupy the living room, 'which the Germans used only to smoke and to play cards in the evening'. There she worked and slept.[78] In Valencia, too, she immediately met acquaintances from Moscow, among them Codovilla and his wife Itala, an old friend, whose home was frequented by the leaders of the Spanish party, that is, José Díaz and Dolores Ibárruri, and countless Comintern officials posted to Spain. While in Valencia, Noce finally met up with her husband, but only for two days before he returned to the front. She herself left soon afterwards for Madrid, where the newspaper was printed and now also edited, so as to be closer to the fighters at the front, a move, she notes

---

76 Teresa Noce (Estella), *Rivoluzionaria professionale*, Milan: la Pietra, 1974, 187.
77 Noce, *Rivoluzionaria*, 187.
78 All quotes, Noce, *Rivoluzionaria*, 189.

maliciously, that had been resisted by her German and French colleagues and comrades, who had not wanted to leave the tranquillity of Valencia. It was an eventful journey, marked by detours and breakdowns, and they did not arrive at International Brigade headquarters on Calle Velázquez until late at night.

Marked by war and bombardment, Madrid was cold, hungry and plagued by mice. Located in a 'majestic palazzo' that had apparently belonged to a duke, her room was overrun with them.[79] Memoirs such as Teresa Noce's testify not only to the precarious living conditions and the great mobility of those posted to Spain by the Comintern, but also to the improvisation that attended their work. Those charged with some task had to find their way about an unfamiliar environment under conditions of war, as often as not having to create their own workplaces as they moved from one place to another. Hierarchies and decision-making processes were not only difficult to grasp but also frequently confused and contradictory. Teresa Noce herself was at first unclear as to what institution she was attached to: was it the Brigades' military base at Albacete, the agitation and propaganda department of the Republican army, or even the Spanish Communist Party? It turned out to be, in effect, all three. She was in contact with all of them and received material and communications from each.[80]

Our final example of Comintern women's involvement in Spain is Lise Ricol (afterwards London, 1916–2012). The daughter of Spanish migrants who had grown up in a Communist miner's family near Le Creusot, she had, like her brother and sister, become involved in the Young Communists at an early age. She had worked for two and a half years as a typist in the Comintern's translation department, where she met her new partner, Arthur London (1913–1986), who worked for the Czechoslovak delegation at the Communist Youth International. On returning, now pregnant, to Paris in the late summer of 1936, she worked briefly for Giulio Ceretti before André Marty took her on, in October, as a secretary and interpreter for Albacete. Initially, her work was not particularly varied. As she recalls in her memoirs, she and another woman comrade 'spent their days typing out organizational plans for the base, service orders, minutes of meetings of the General Staff,

---

79 Ibid., 193.
80 Ibid., 189.

correspondence with the Spanish military and civil authorities and the Spanish Relief Committee'.[81]

The Communist organizations reproduced and institutionalized the traditional sexual division of labour. Women serving with the International Brigades were employed in the rear as paramedics, doctors, nurses and ambulance drivers, as (mostly improvised) social workers, as secretaries, translators and interpreters to the general staff, as journalists and censors in the press service, as liaison agents and couriers, and as cooks, librarians and postal assistants, but not ever as combatants. These activities were as indispensable to warfare as was the fighting, but less highly valued, either then or in the later historiography. Women's experiences were diverse, but they were, on the whole, granted less responsibility than the men. Despite this general confinement to 'women's tasks', there were exceptions, as illustrated in the following section by the case of Tina Modotti, the de facto if not the de jure head of International Red Aid in Spain.

(Proto-)Humanitarian Aid

The first of the international Communist organizations to arrive in Spain was International Red Aid, whose involvement had begun with the 'Asturian October' of 1934. That failed uprising against the right-wing government brought many refugees to France, while, in Spain, itself thousands of insurgents and their families suffered under the ensuing persecution. Close cooperation was established between the Spanish and French sections of the organization.[82]

---

81 Lise London, *Le printemps des camarades*, Paris: Seuil, 1996, 253.

82 Laura Branciforte, *El Socorro Rojo Internacional (1923–1939): Relatos de la solidaridad antifascista*, Madrid: Biblioteca Nueva, 2011, 195, written, however, without recourse to the Russian archives. On the history of the Communist aid organizations see also Nikolaus Brauns, *Schafft Rote Hilfe! Geschichte und Aktivitäten der proletarischen Hilfsorganisation für politische Gefangene in Deutschland (1919–1938)*, Bonn: Pahl-Rugenstein, 2003, and Claudio Natoli, 'Pour une histoire comparée des organisations communistes de solidarité: Le Secours ouvrier international et le Secours rouge international', in José Gotovitch and Anne Morelli, eds, *Les Solidarités internationales: Histoire et perspectives*, Brussels: Editions Labor, 2003, 17–42. On the role of the MOPR in the Soviet Union, see Gleb Albert, 'The USSR Section of International Red Aid (MOPR): The Institutionalisation of International Solidarity in Interwar Soviet Society',

Since the summer of 1933, International Red Aid's Paris office had come to serve as its European headquarters. The National Socialists' rise to power in Germany had presented the organization with an enormous challenge, for not only was there a great increase in the number of political prisoners to be looked after, but there was also much more to do in the way of support campaigns, notably for Dimitrov and Thälmann. Elena Stasova, the Moscow-based head of the MOPR (as International Red Aid was known in its Russian acronym), despatched the somewhat ill-matched couple of Vittorio Vidali and Tina Modotti to Paris to set up the new office.[83] Both came from working-class backgrounds in northern Italy, but they were miles apart in culture.[84] They had met in Mexico City in the late summer of 1927, where Vidali the professional revolutionary had been sent, under the name 'Jorgé Contreras', as the representative of Red Aid's Moscow headquarters. Modotti, who apparently joined the party thanks to him,[85] was a member of the League Against Imperialism and of the Caribbean Anti-Fascist Committee in Mexico City. They only became a couple (without ever being married) in Moscow, when they were both working for the Executive Committee of International Red Aid.[86] While Modotti still fascinates today, for her career and her talent as a photographer, for her beauty, her sexual freedom and her glamorous life among the avant-garde Communist and left-progressive artistic

---

in Holger Weiss, ed., *International Communism and Transnational Solidarity: Radical Networks, Mass Movements and Global Politics, 1919–1939*, Dordrecht: Brill, 2016, 89–129.

83 Claudio Natoli, 'Tina Modotti: tra avanguardia artistica e "nueva umanità"', in Paolo Ferrari and Claudio Natoli, eds, *Tina Modotti: Arte e libertà tra Europa e Americhe*, Udine: Forum 2017, 13–24, at 20, the author relying here on the minutes of the meeting of the Secretariat of the Executive Committee of the International Red Aid in the Comintern archives in Moscow, and Karlsen, *Vittorio Vidali*, 150.

84 See the answers given in the party autobiographies to be found in their personal files in the Comintern archives: Modotti, 27 January 1932, in English, the answers to the questionnaire also being translated into Russian, RGASPI 495/241/40; Vidali, autobiography, in Italian, 26 January 1932, RGASPI 513/2/36.

85 Vidali's role in Modotti's political education is discussed in Karlsen, *Vittorio Vidali*, 113–16.

86 Modotti came to Moscow from Berlin in October 1930, as an employee of the MOPR: letter from D. V. to 'Dear Comrades' [KPD], Moscow, 29 October 1930, RGASPI 495/221/1605.

circles of 1920s Mexico,[87] Vidali is suspected by scholars of having been an NKVD agent.[88]

As has been said, Modotti worked at International Red Aid in Paris from 1933 to late 1934, during which time she used a Costa Rican passport and the matching pseudonym 'Kostarikas', though she may perhaps have used in Paris one or more of the pseudonyms she would use in Spain: 'Julio Antonio', 'Maria Cortes', 'Magda Toledo' and 'Carmen Ruiz Sanchez'.

International Red Aid's European headquarters was then to be found at the offices of its French section, the Secours Rouge. Employed there were Jean Chauvet (1903–?, 'Jean Léar'), a full-timer with the SR since 1928 and its secretary from 1932, and Marcel Cordier (1895–?), a hairdresser by profession, responsible since 1923 for building up the French section. Modotti knew both from Moscow: Chauvet as a delegate to Red Aid's first world congress in 1932, which she had helped organize; Cordier as secretary to Red Aid's executive committee in Moscow when she was also working in the Soviet capital. The two Frenchmen formally represented the organization, while Modotti and Vidali concerned themselves with the illegal apparatus, supplying funds and instructors to its West European structures, smuggling refugees out of Germany,

---

87 Numerous variably well-documented biographies of Modotti have been published. Drawing on both oral history and original sources, yet not entirely satisfactory as scholarship are Christiane Barckhausen, *Auf den Spuren von Tina Modotti*, Kiel: agimos, 1996, almost unchanged from the edition of 1987; Christiane Barckhausen, ed., *Tina Modotti: Leben – Werk – Schriften*, Kiel: agimos, 1996; Patricia Albers, *Shadows, Fire, Snow: The Life of Tina Modotti*, New York: Clarkson Potter Publishers, 1999; Letizia Argenteri, *Tina Modotti: Between Art and Revolution*, New Haven, CT: Yale University Press, 2003. See also Ferrari and Natoli, *Tina Modotti*. Focussed mainly on her photographic career is Mildred Constantine, *Tina Modotti: A Fragile Life*, San Francisco: Chronicle Books, 1993 [1975]. Romanticized and sometimes entirely fictional are Pino Cacucci, *I fuochi, le ombre, il silenzio: La fragil vida di Tina Modotti*, Bologna: Agalev Edizioni, 1988; and Elena Poniatowska, *Tinisima*, trans. Katherine Silver, New York: Farrar, Strauss and Giroux, 1996. And finally, Vidali's own portrait of Modotti, written only after she had attained iconic status as a photographer: Vittorio Vidali, *Ritratto di donna: Tina Modotti*, Milan: Vangelista, 1982; and his own autobiography, Vittorio Vidali, *Comandante Carlos*, Rome: Editori Riuniti, 1983.

88 For example, by Thomas, *The Spanish Civil War*, edn of 1965, 581 (though absent from the most recent edition cited elsewhere), and Paul Preston, *The Spanish Holocaust: Inquisition and Extermination in Twentieth-Century Spain*, London: HarperPress, 2012, 353.

organizing fundraising and providing courier services for Moscow.[89] While based in Paris, Modotti travelled abroad several times as a Comintern emissary, such as in 1933, as a member of an International Red Aid delegation to Spain, where she was arrested and deported. In addition to many other tasks, Modotti, under the name 'Renée', was apparently also one of the organizers of the International Congress of Women against War and Fascism, held in Paris in August 1934.[90] At the end of that year, she returned to Moscow as MOPR's Latin America specialist, a position she took over from Vidali when he was again posted abroad, including some time as OMS emissary in Berlin.[91] As the in-house expert, she was expected not only to have a detailed knowledge of the politics of the countries she was responsible for, but also to give presentations at meetings of the Political Commission of the ECCI.[92]

In 1935 came a new mission in France. Her task, as envisaged in a note written by Malke Schorr (1885–1961) – the daughter of an Orthodox Jewish family in then-Austrian Eastern Galicia, a member of International Red Aid's executive since March 1927 and head of the Paris office since May 1934 – would be both organizational and technical: 'Obtaining and checking the addresses, technical liaison with the sections and the Executive Committee, securing apartments for committee meetings and other gatherings, records and the like.'[93] Modotti travelled to Paris on a false passport in the name of 'Maria

---

89 Nikolaus Brauns, *Schafft Rote Hilfe! Geschichte und Aktivitäten der proletarischen Hilfsorganisation für politische Gefangene in Deutschland (1919–1938)*, Bonn: Pahl-Rugenstein, 2003, 282.

90 The pseudonym is given in Patricia Albers, *Shadows*, 273. On the congress, see Christine Bard and Jean-Louis Robert, 'The French Communist Party and Women 1920–1939: From "Feminism" to Familialism', in Helmut Gruber and Pamela Graves, eds, *Women and Socialism – Socialism and Women: Europe Between the World Wars*, New York: Berghahn Books, 1998, 321–47, at 329–30 (without, however, any mention of Modotti).

91 Vittorio Vidali, *Missione a Berlino*, Milan, Vangelista Editori, 1978; and Karlsen, *Vittorio Vidali*, 153. Vidali's protectress Stasova also worked for the OMS; on this, see the personal data on the CD-Rom accompanying Buckmiller and Meschkat, *Biographisches Handbuch*.

92 Material on the production plan consultation with the specialist advisers of the regional secretariats, Moscow, 4 December 1932, RGASPI 495/18/945.

93 Note dated 3 November 1935 in the papers of Wilhelm Pieck, SAPMO, cited without an archive reference in Barckhausen, *Auf den Spuren*, 311.

Pidal', and with a courier mission from the OMS. Mentona Moser – the Swiss heiress whose assets had been seized in Germany – was also in Paris in 1935, working at the International Red Aid office. Modotti would not stay long in the French capital, however, for the victory of the Popular Front in the Spanish elections of February 1936 soon saw her posted to Spain.

Two days after the military uprising in Spanish Morocco on 17 July, Tina Modotti returned to Madrid from Granada,[94] just in time to receive an order, addressed to her and the Spanish comrade Matilde Landa (1904–1942), with whom she would later work closely, to reorganize the commandeered Hospital Obrero in the Cuatro Caminos district to receive wounded militia officers. There she again met with Vittorio Vidali, who had been active in Spain, with occasional interruptions, since late 1934, at first under the name of 'Don Manuel Prieto Lopez'. Co-opted onto the Executive Committee of the Socorro Rojo as the representative of International Red Aid's Moscow headquarters in September 1935,[95] in early 1936 he found himself permanently posted to Spain, thanks to his protectress Elena Stasova, just as the terror against party members picked up speed in the Soviet Union.[96] With this, he also transferred his membership from the Soviet to the Spanish party. Now, as 'Carlos Contreras', he was political commissar of the Fifth Regiment, the militia regiment established in all haste by the PCE and forerunner of the International Brigades, whose headquarters were also in Cuatro Caminos. Vidali had no war experience, but he had been a member of the 'Red Guard' in Trieste 'for a week', as he reported in a party autobiography, adding that this organization, formed by a group of young people 'without a clear idea as to what it was, whether for defending the newspaper and socialist cooperatives from attack or fighting the 'National Guard' of the Italian nationalists. After that, he had been one of the

---

94 Laura Branciforte, 'Tina Modotti: Una intensa vida entre Europa y América', *Studia Historica: Historia Contemporánea* 24, 2009, 289–309, at 298. Branciforte does not, however, allude to the fact that Modotti was already active before the Spanish coup.

95 Branciforte, *El Socorro Rojo*, 193.

96 Typewritten memorandum from Stasova to 'Müller' (aka Boris Melnikov), head of the OMS liaison service since November 1935, 13 December 1935, RGASPI 495/221/3776, vol. 1. See also Karlsen, *Vittorio Vidali*, 161, and on Vidali's role in Spain, 163–229.

organizers of a 'red stewarding service' equally ambivalent in its objects.⁹⁷

In Spain, Modotti found herself overwhelmed with work. Her task was not only to help set up a medical service and to procure the necessary food, but also to guide the Spaniards in transforming the Socorro Rojo into a mass organization.⁹⁸ On 1 August 1936, the MOPR executive set up a special commission on Spain, and from then on aid to Spain appeared on the agenda of every meeting of secretariat or presidium.⁹⁹ Taking the form not only of medical and psychological assistance but also of material and financial support, this aid was no longer provided only to Communists but was extended in principle to the Republican side as a whole, in accordance with the Comintern's adoption of the Popular Front policy in 1935.¹⁰⁰ By 1936, International Red Aid had also absorbed the national sections of Münzenberg's Workers' International Relief, when the latter was dissolved by the ECCI. (The two organizations already collaborated, if not always smoothly, and in the summer of 1935 Münzenberg had gone to Spain with Malke Schorr to set up a joint operation.)

The opening to other political forces had not been easy for Red Aid. At the Comintern's Seventh World Congress in 1935, it was heavily criticized by Dimitrov for its 'sectarianism, burocracy [sic], inadequate methods and forms of work'. That at least was the summary offered by

---

97 Twelve-page party autobiography of 'Jorgé Contreras' (the pseudonym Vidali used in Mexico, Russified in the Soviet Union as Georgi Ivanovich Kontreras, though known as 'Carlos Contreras' in Spain), in Italian, Moscow, 28 January 1932, echoed in the undated party autobiography headed 'Biografia', both RGASPI 513/2/36.

98 Barckhausen, *Auf den Spuren*, 349.

99 Anatolii I. Avrus, 'MOPR i natsional'no-revoliutsionnaia voina v Ispanii' [MOPR and the National-Revolutionary War in Spain], in A. A. Makarenko and V. A. Vraddi, eds, *Massovye dvizheniia solidarnosti: Traditsii i sovremennost'* [Mass Movements of Solidarity: Their Traditions and Present], Kiev: Naukova dumka, 1983, 86–97, at 88–9.

100 Thomas, *Spanish Civil War*, 302–3 (here again the 1965 edn). The notion of 'proto-humanitarian' is from Axelle Brodiez, *Le Secours populaire français, 1945–2000: Du communisme à l'humanitaire*, Paris: Presses de Sciences Po, 2006, 37–9, who points out that International Red Aid did not abandon a class-centred for a more universal conception of its role until after the Second World War, though the French section changed its name from *Secours rouge* to *Secours populaire de France* in the autumn of 1936.

Vittorio Vidali in a lengthy, English-language letter to Elena Stasova, in which he gave his thoughts on the future of the organization.[101] The criticism seems to have been taken as a personal attack by Stasova, leading Vidali to respond, in typical Communist fashion, that 'personal feelings, matters of formality, etc., don't play a role in the solution of this problem'. It was an issue of importance, and it was therefore necessary to modify the organization's constitution and mode of operation in accordance with the lines adopted at the World Congress and the subsequent MOPR Plenum. To this end, Vidali recommended that his mentor Comrade Stasova – his institutional superior, more than thirty years his senior, and considerably more politically experienced – should, without delay, publish an article in the Communist press, recognizing the new line to be correct. However, he warned, it was essential that International Red Aid not be turned into a 'committee movement'. The Communists were in no way to lose political control! He was not alone in feeling this: as Codovilla reported to the Latin Secretariat in Moscow on 16 June 1935, the goal was 'to make the Socorro Rojo one of the great popular organizations of the country' on the basis of a 'united front from below', yet its political direction would still be determined by the party through the involvement of members 'Carlos' (Vittorio Vidali), 'Ricardo' (presumably Octave Rabaté, 1899–1964), Dolores Ibárruri, José Díaz and himself.[102]

Throwing everything it had into support for the Republican cause, Red Aid grew enormously in both France and Spain. In France, membership almost quadrupled between 1934 and 1937, to reach 150,000. Growth in Spain was even more impressive, the Spanish section exceeding 350,000 or even 500,000 members in 1937, depending on the source, and reaching 900,000 by 1939.[103] Donations likewise multiplied,

---

101 Vittorio Vidali to 'Dear comrade Stassova', 8 December 1935, RGASPI 513/2/36.

102 Acta de las decisiones relativas a la linea politica, las actividades y las tareas de los Comités de Ayuda a Espana [Minute of decisions on the political line, activities and tasks of the Aid to Spain Committees] RGASPI 539/3/665, cited in Elorza and Bizcarrondo, *Queridos camaradas*, 230.

103 The figure of 350,000 for 1937 is given by Leonid Babichenko, 'The International Red Aid', unpublished paper, international conference on the History of the Communist International held at IISH, Amsterdam, in 1992, 9, while a PCE report speaks of 517,000 members: Radosh, *Spain Betrayed*, 405. The difference may be explained by the dates the statistics were compiled. This impressive growth may have been due, at least

collections rising from 950,000 francs in 1935 to more than 3 million in 1936 and over 4 million in 1937.[104]

The greatest financial and material support, however, came from the Soviet Union, where the state mobilized the people.[105] In comparison, financial aid from the Socialist International was extremely meagre,[106] and Red Aid therefore had a de facto monopoly on donations to Spain, giving it a corresponding influence in the united front organizations it formed with social democratic and non-party forces.[107] An excellent example is the non-party, though Red Aid–initiated, coordination committee, CICAER, which emerged from the great international conference on Spain organized by the World Committee Against War and Fascism and held in Paris on 13 August 1936.

It was this committee that suggested the creation of the Centrale Sanitaire Internationale, an international medical relief organization that would soon count twelve national sections and enjoy the official recognition of the Republican government. Until then, International Red Aid had been responsible for the coordination of medical assistance, while also being the most important source of a support to the Republican government in its reorganization of the health system. The local hospitals had relied chiefly on the nuns, who were no longer welcome, and who were indeed persecuted and attacked, and the Spanish Red Cross had sided with the rebels. As the Bulgarian Communist physician Tsvetan Kristanov (1898–1972, 'Dr Oscar Telge', the head of the International Brigades' medical service) noted dryly: 'It must be said that, with few exceptions, the Red Cross has failed as a relief organization.'[108]

---

in part, to pressure from above, for 80 per cent of the members of the Fifth Regiment (whose political commissar was Carlos Contreras) were also members of Red Aid: Avrus, 'MOPR', 96.

104 Brodiez, *Le Secours populaire français*, 39; Babichenko, 'The International Red Aid', 9.

105 Kowalsky, *Stalin*, chapter 4.

106 Elorza and Bizcarrondo, *Queridos camaradas*, 229. There exists, to my knowledge, no comparative international survey of Spanish relief activities, though the volume of more-or-less nationally focussed studies is almost unmanageable. One of these, looking at Switzerland, is Sébastien Farré, 'Mobiliser, unir, sauver: L'aide humanitaire durant la Guerre civile espagnole', *Cahiers de l'AEHMO* 23, 2007, 69–84.

107 Elorza and Bizcarrondo, *Queridos camaradas*, 230.

108 Dr Oscar Telge, introduction to Gusti Jirku, *We Fight Death: The Work of the Medical Service of the International Brigades in Spain*, Madrid: Rivadeneyra, 1937, 7–9,

By early 1937, Red Aid's Comisión Nacional de Sanidad had set up 275 hospital facilities in requisitioned hotels and other buildings, and with the help of Canadian doctor Norman Bethune had established mobile blood transfusion units to serve the front.[109] While money collected was chiefly spent on medical assistance – the provision of doctors, nurses and medical supplies – it was also used in a number of other ways, for Red Aid also saw to the evacuation of the civilian population from zones occupied by Franco's troops, raised funds for refugees, established day nurseries, provided support to the families of those who died in combat and helped sustain links between front and rear,[110] notably in maintaining and controlling postal communications, with its distribution centre and censorship office in Albacete. Another area of work was the establishment and operation of residential homes for Spanish children in other countries, such as Belgium, Britain, France, Norway, Switzerland and the United States.[111]

Modotti coordinated all these activities. Her first headquarters were in Madrid, at the Socorro Rojo's offices on the Calle Velázquez, at the corner with Padilla. In December 1936 (a month after the Republican government had moved there), Modotti and Landa also opened an

---

at 8. Also published in Spanish, French and German, this copiously illustrated sixty-page brochure was the work of the Bukovina-born Austrian Communist journalist and writer Augustina 'Gusti' Jirku (1892–1978, née Mayer, afterwards Stridsberg), also the author of *Wir Kämpfen Mit! Antifaschistische Frauen vieler Nationen berichten aus Spanien*, Barcelona: Ayuda Medica Extranjera, 1938. Earlier employed by the Young Communist International in Moscow, she was now working for the medical service's press department. Jirku and her daughter would later act as Soviet spies.

109 Report on the Plenum of the Spanish section of Red Aid, 7–8 February 1937, and accompanying article, C. Contreras, 'Las tareas fundamentales de Socorro Rojo Español', *Ayuda*, 16 May 1937, cited in Branciforte, *El Socorro Rojo*, 232. See also Avrus, 'MOPR', 94. On Bethune's relationship to Communism and to the Spanish Civil War, see Andrée Lévesque, 'The Transnational Experience of Some Canadian Communists', in Oleksa Drachewych and Ian McKay, eds, *Left Transnationalism: The Communist International and the National, Colonial, and Racial Questions*, Montreal: McGill-Queen's University Press, 2019, 183–203, at 184, 186 and 195; see also Paul Weil, 'Norman Bethune and the Development of Blood Transfusion Services', in David A. E. Shepard and Andrée Lévesque, eds, *Norman Bethune: His Times and His Legacy/Son époque et son message*, Ottawa: Canadian Public Health Association, 1982, 177–80, at 178, and Hazen Sise, 'The Vivid Air Signed with His Honour: In Memory of Norman Bethune', in Shepard and Lévesque, *Norman Bethune*, 162–9, at 166–7.

110 Natoli, 'Pour une histoire comparée', 42.

111 Babichenko, 'The International Red Aid'.

office at 1, calle Montornés in Valencia, International Red Aid's new Spanish headquarters.[112] On party orders, the president of the Spanish section, the writer Isidoro Acevedo (1867–1952), originally a typesetter and one of the founders of the PCE, had already been taken to safety there in October, as Madrid was bombarded.[113] In 1937, the headquarters made its final move to 615, calle Cortéz in Barcelona. Like other foreign advisers, Modotti shuttled back and forth between the different cities, depending on the course of the war and her varying duties. She was constantly on the move, being responsible, after all, for ensuring that deliveries of food really reached their destinations – no easy task in the chaos of the civil war with its always shifting fronts.[114] She also wrote numerous articles, mostly on women and children as victims of the war, for the Red Aid weekly newspaper, ¡Ayuda! Semanario de Solidaridad del Socorro Rojo Internacional, whose operation she supervised. Modotti used various pseudonyms, among them 'Maria' (a name she had already used in Moscow, in a variety of combinations), 'Carmen Ruiz' and 'Vera Martini'.[115] Last but not least, she was also responsible for the administration of the relief funds from abroad that International Red Aid received. A report by the Socorro Rojo's national executive committee states that these amounted to 1.4 million pesetas over the years 1934 to 1938, of which, as has been noted, well over half came from the Soviet Union.[116]

Modotti had the status of an official representative of International Red Aid and so many diplomatic responsibilities. She was also, as 'Rafael' (presumably Jesús Hernandez) put it in a report in 1938, 'la principal dirigente efectiva' – the chief leader in reality.[117] Modotti's language skills were useful in all of these capacities. She was fluent in Italian, Spanish and English, both spoken and written. She had picked up a little German as a small child when her family lived for a time in Carinthia, and French while working for Red Aid in Paris. At the Congreso de la

---

112 The address comes from an interview with the Argentine Communist Fanny Edelman, who worked in Spain as a Red Aid volunteer: Stella Calloni, 'Fanny Edelman, 70 años de militancia', La Jornada, 27 September 2004, on line at jornada.com; Branciforte, El Socorro Rojo, 235, relies on the same source.

113 As he notes in his party autobiography: Branciforte, El Socorro Rojo, 235.

114 Ibid., 238.

115 Ibid., 229; Branciforte, 'Tina Modotti', 295.

116 Branciforte, El Socorro Rojo, 242.

117 Handwritten report on Tina Modotti ('Maria') by Rafael, in Spanish, 25 January 1938, RGASPI 495/241/40.

Solidaridad held in Madrid on 23–24 July 1937, Modotti represented the Comisión de Solidaridad Internacional, the umbrella organization for all the solidarity campaigns, then based in Valencia, the acting capital. In August, she received two delegations from France in Valencia and Madrid, and in December another foreign delegation in Barcelona.[118]

Modotti had earlier represented International Red Aid at the Second International Congress of Writers for the Defence of Culture, which opened in Valencia on 4 July 1937, before continuing in Madrid, Barcelona and Paris. The opening speech was given by the recently appointed Socialist prime minister Juan Negrín, whose government included Communists. The congress was attended by delegates from twenty-seven countries, among whom were the Spaniards Rafael Alberti and María Teresa Léon – the latter received by Stalin in Moscow that March – the Germans Anna Seghers and Egon Erwin Kisch, the Britons Stephen Spender and Silvia Townsend Warner (who, with their colleague and companion Valentine Ackland, had travelled illegally to Spain), André Malraux and Tristan Tzara from France, the Chilean Pablo Neruda, the Cuban Alejo Carpentier, Hans Mühlestein from Switzerland, the Americans Louis Fischer and Anna Louise Strong, and the Russians Ilya Ehrenburg and Mikhail Koltsov, as well as photographers Gerda Taro and Robert Capa – these being only a few of the well-known figures present.[119]

Koltsov was in his element. He orchestrated the debates, drove groups of congress participants about in his car and gave political instruction to what he considered to be the unworldly writers.[120] Between fascists and

---

118 Branciforte, 'Tina Modotti', 304–5; Branciforte, *El Socorro Rojo*, 239–42.

119 On the course and proceedings of the congress, see Manuel Aznar Soler, ed., *Il congreso internacional de escritores para la defensa de la cultura (1937)*, 3 vols., Valencia: Generalitat Valenciana, 1987. A critical account of the Soviet instrumentalization of writers is Robert S. Thornberry, 'Writers Take Sides, Stalinists Take Control: The Second International Congress for the Defense of Culture (Spain 1937)', *The Historian* 62:3, 2000, 589–605. Unmentioned in congress proceedings or participants' memoirs, Modotti's presence is registered in nearly all biographies, e.g. Poniatowska, *Tinisima*, 281–8 (though without any source given), and also in Branciforte, *El Socorro Rojo*, 239–40. Except for Anna Seghers, the women attending, a small minority, are hardly mentioned in either contemporary newspaper reports or the memoirs of the men and women (!) who were there: Allison Taillot, *Les intellectuelles européennes et la guerre d'Espagne: De l'engagement personnel à la défense de la République espagnole*, Paris: Presses universitaires de Paris Ouest, 2016, 218–24.

120 On literary unworldliness, see Koltsov's comments on the swaddled writers' ignorance of the realities of the war, and more especially on the 'short-sighted' Anna

antifascists there was an insurmountable divide, he declared in a Spanish-language lecture, there was no in-between. Everyone was welcome in the struggle against fascism: 'Republicans, anarchists, Marxists, Catholics and non-party people'. Only the Trotskyists had no place, it would seem, and alongside them André Gide, who had just published *Retouches à mon Retour d'URSS*, his second book about the Soviet Union, much more critical and better documented than the first.[121] Given it by a congress participant a few days earlier, Koltsov described it as 'entirely blatant Trotskyist slander and abuse'.[122] Criticism of the Soviet Union, he made clear in his speech, had no place in the antifascist ranks.

Security and Surveillance in Spain

Koltsov's comments came after two of the three Moscow Trials had already taken place, with such prominent figures as Zinoviev and Radek in the dock, and two months after the revolutionary uprising in Barcelona had been violently suppressed by the Communists. There was scarcely any criticism heard at the congress, however, as the extreme polarization of politics encouraged the concealment of differences in favour of unity. No one in the Republican camp – hardly anyone, at least – wanted or was able to oppose the Soviet Union. Not only because it was the only country that provided Spain with urgently needed military aid, but also because the Communists had succeeded in hegemonically identifying antifascism with a pro-Soviet stance. In France, for example, even the influential Ligue des droits de l'Homme (Human Rights League) remained largely silent about the Moscow show trials. Not so the Communist organizations, which very much adopted the prosecutors' view and loudly and publicly defended the verdicts.[123] A mass

---

Seghers, who, apparently, had a wonderful conversation with Negrín over a meal but had no idea at all who he was: Michael Kolzow, *Spanisches Tagebuch*, 3rd edn, Berlin: Militärverlag der Deutschen Demokratischen Republik, 1986, 528–30.

121 André Gide, *Back from the U.S.S.R.*, trans. Dorothy Bussy, London: Secker and Warburg, 1936.

122 Kolzow, *Spanisches Tagebuch*, quotes at 526 and 534–5.

123 Fréderick Genevée, 'Solidarité internationale et procès de Moscou', in Jean Vigreux and Serge Wolikow, eds, *Cultures communistes au XXe siècle: Entre guerre et modernité*, Paris: La Dispute, 2003, 103–14, at 113–14.

organization like Red Aid was not exempt, and in the aftermath of the second show trial of January 1937 one could read in the French section's magazine, *La Défense*, that 'The Central Bureau of the Secours Populaire congratulates the Soviet judicial system on the vigilance it has shown'.[124] And a little earlier, in November 1936, the same magazine had spoken of 'the POUM spies'.[125]

Following the First Moscow Trial, the POUM, considered to be Trotskyists, had become the Comintern's worst bugbear. As early as mid-1936, as preparations were being made for the trial, *Inprekorr* had launched a fierce campaign against the Catalan party.[126] That the POUM then publicly denounced the execution of Kamenev, Zinoviev and other Old Bolsheviks only confirmed its counterrevolutionary role. But it was only in the wake of the Barcelona uprising of May 1937 that the call to 'liquidate' these 'traitors' and 'fifth columnists' became more than metaphorical in Spain.[127] The POUM was banned, its leader, the former Communist Andreu Nin (1892–1937), murdered, and many others imprisoned, as the left-Socialist prime minister, Largo Caballero, open to compromise, was replaced by the right-Socialist Negrín, more closely allied with the Communists and sympathetic to their centralizing impulses. With the repression, the cooperatives and other initiatives that had emerged in Catalonia with the revolutionary collectivization of land and industry were dismantled.

Such militias as still existed were integrated into the People's Army of Catalonia. The POUM leaders were put on trial in October 1938, charged with treason and espionage. The Spanish judiciary, however, despite what is often claimed, was not in thrall to the Soviets: the prosecution failed and the defendants were acquitted. Andreu Nin, who had worked for the Profintern in Moscow from 1925 to 1930 and there been won over to Trotsky's Left Opposition, had been kidnapped and killed

---

124 *La Défense*, 19 February 1937, cited in Brodiez, *Le secours populaire*, 37.

125 *La Défense*, 4 November 1936, cited in Brodiez, *Le secours populaire*, 37.

126 Antonio Elorza, 'Stalinisme et internationalisme en Espagne, 1931–1939', in Serge Wolikow and Michel Cordillot, eds, *Prolétaires de tous les pays, unissez-vous? Les difficiles chemins de l'internationalisme (1848–1956)*, Dijon: Éditions universitaires de Dijon, 1993, 192–200, at 199.

127 Though there had already been murders and executions of traitors and supposed traitors or fifth-columnists on the Republican side: Preston, *The Spanish Holocaust*; and Julius Ruiz, *The 'Red Terror' and the Spanish Civil War: Revolutionary Violence in Madrid*, Cambridge: Cambridge University Press, 2014.

following his arrest in June 1937. Behind this act, as we know today, was the NKVD, and more particularly Alexander Orlov (1895–1973, in reality Leiba Feldbin, who called himself Lev Nikolsky from 1920) and his staff. Ostensibly a member of the Soviet diplomatic corps in Madrid, Orlov had been sent to Spain in the late summer of 1936. In the spring of 1937, he was promoted to chief resident officer in Spain, charged now with clearing the Popular Front of Trotskyists and other oppositionists.[128] Many rumours have circulated over the years regarding Nin's murder and the disappearance of other prominent critics of Stalin. According to the historian Boris Volodarsky, who has looked in detail at the NKVD's activities in Spain, Nin's killing should undoubtedly be attributed to the sinister but relatively ineffective Orlov. He does, however, deny that Spain saw large-scale Stalinist purges, the murder of political dissidents having been far less common than suggested by some of the wilder speculation. Volodarsky estimates that there may have been around twenty such killings, and says that there were in fact no more than ten NKVD officers operating in Spain,[129] though these were, of course, supported by volunteer agents and informants from other countries.

Spain did no doubt see a proliferation of intelligence networks and political surveillance agencies, varying in sophistication and often unclear or multiple in their allegiance, be it to the Republican government in Valencia, the PCE, the KPD, the Comintern, the Communist-dominated PSUC or the Soviet state apparatus. Nor were their powers always clearly defined.[130] In Albacete, for example, there had been a cadre commission almost from the very beginning, such as had been

---

128 On Orlov's activities in Spain, see Volodarsky, *Stalin's Agent*, 214–91. Other works also draw a clear line between the practices of the Soviet secret police and those of the civil police in the Spanish Civil War, among them a comparative study by José M. Faraldo, *La redes del terror: Las policías secretas comunistas y su legado*, Barcelona: Galaxia Gutenberg, 2018, 138–43.

129 Volodarsky, *Stalin's Agent*, 218.

130 The organs of surveillance established in Spain by the Comintern and the individual Communist parties have been much studied by German scholars, not least because the KPD and German Communists played a central role in them: Zur Mühlen, *Spanien war ihre Hoffnung*, 164–204; and Peter Huber and Michael Uhl, 'Politische Überwachung und Repression in den Internationalen Brigaden (1936–1938)', *Forum für osteuropäische Zeit- und Ideengeschichte* 5:2, 2001, 121–60. See also the standard work: Skoutelsky, *L'espoir*, 236–246 and 251–63.

established in the Soviet party in 1922, in the Comintern in 1932 and in the PCF in 1933, even if its functioning left something to be desired. In the context of the International Brigades, it fell to the cadre commission to select from among the volunteers those who could be entrusted with positions of military or political leadership. But, as André Marty reported to the Comintern in March 1937, it was also concerned to 'identify provocative elements' that might have crept into the Brigades.[131] This intermixture of security and surveillance, the fusion between the assessment of personal qualities (in terms not only of military aptitude but of political work and political and personal conduct), the monitoring of political conformity and the uncovering of spies and provocateurs, fuelled an atmosphere of mutual distrust and suspicion. All the more so as with the Moscow Trials and Stalin's policy of eliminating his former comrades, a realistic fear of the 'fifth column' became infused with Soviet paranoia.[132] Subversion and betrayal were supposedly ubiquitous. Even Franz Dahlem, head of the Brigades' political commission, noted in a private observation of 1937 the existence of an 'arrest psychosis' resulting from the general 'espionage psychosis'.[133] Over time, each Communist party represented in Albacete came to have its own cadre bureau, leading to continuous disputes, at least until the centralization of cadre functions at the PCE's Comisión de Extranjeros (Foreigners Commission) in Valencia, in 1938. The chair of this new commission, responsible for the transfer of foreign Communists to the Spanish party, was the ubiquitous André Marty.[134]

Alongside this were other parallel apparatuses exercising sometimes self-attributed police powers.[135] Especially notorious was the Servicio Alfredo Herz, informally named after its German director Alfred Herz, which operated as part of the Servicio Extranjero del PSUC, officially responsible for the intake of foreign volunteers at the Hotel Colón on Barcelona's Plaça de Catalunya. One of those employed by the Servicio

---

131 Report by André Marty, Albacete, 4 March 1937, cited in Huber and Uhl, 'Überwachung', 135.

132 Javier Cervera, *Madrid en guerra: La ciudad clandestina, 1936–1939*, Madrid: Alianza Editorial, 2006.

133 Huber and Uhl, 'Überwachung', 135.

134 Transfer to the party of the member's place of work or residence was required by rule.

135 The government's intelligence service, the SIM, is not to be confused with the International Brigades' military intelligence service of the same name.

Alfredo Herz was Erzsébet Fazekas (1900–1967), the wife of Ernö Gerö, the Comintern's representative in Catalonia and a draughtswoman and a teacher by profession who had worked for the Comintern apparatus for years, including a long period in France under the name 'Maria'.[136] Both organizations, and also the government intelligence service, the Departamento Especial de Información del Estado (DEDIDE), had been set up by Comintern and NKVD cadre and all had ties with the Catalan police. In 1937, the newly appointed Negrín government created the Servicio de Investigación Militar (the Military Investigation Department, SIM), which should have brought about a separation of policing from cadre policy, but the government soon lost control of the SIM and its various branches. In reality, the PCE's Comisión de Extranjeros and the SIM exchanged information.

So it was that the expertise in the collection and handling of data on party members that the Comintern had developed over the years, for purposes both administrative and political, was turned to political repression in Spain. The information collected via numerous questionnaires and party autobiographies was collated in card indexes, 'characterizations' and files. Originally gathered for the selection and assessment of party cadre, the data might also provide indications of political nonconformity.[137] In the Spanish Civil War, in addition to the questionnaire filled in on applying to transfer to the PCE (of which there were shorter and longer versions, sometimes extending to sixty-five questions) and the characterizations and evaluations produced by the cadre commissions, there was also a questionnaire for joining the International Brigades and a 'leaving certificate' intended for the member's home party.[138] The typed 'characterization' gave concise information on the subject's family background and political and professional career, together with a political and personal evaluation. In some, categorizations were entered by hand, in capitals, as in the case of the Swiss volunteer Alfred Kuerzi: 'TROTSKYITE'.[139] The leaving certificate used a

---

136 Abel, 'Die versuchte Neutralisierung', 474.

137 On the Comintern's bureaucratic practices of political control, see Brigitte Studer, *The Transnational World of the Cominternians*, trans. D. R. Roberts, Basingstoke, UK: Palgrave Macmillan, 2015, 73–89.

138 In the summer of 1939, this material was shipped to Moscow via France and can now be consulted, arranged by nationality, at RGASPI, Fonds 545, Opis 6.

139 Characterization, Alfred Kuerzi, RGASPI 545/6/1491.

six-fold evaluation that ranged from 'good antifascist (socialist, non-party or similar) though not Communist', 'requires further political education', 'good party member' and 'organizer, agitator or similar' to 'enemy (Trotskyite, *agent provocateur* etc.)' and 'déclassé element (deserter, disorganizer), to be countered and denounced'.[140]

Cadre commission evaluations were not without consequences. When Vittorio Vidali was to be awarded a decoration, the cadre commission was consulted first. Reporting in Moscow on 7 March 1937, André Marty had been full of praise for 'Comandante Carlos', 'one of the best military leaders'.[141] In February 1938, 'Comrade Carmen' was instructed by 'Comrade Jelesoff' to compile information on 'Carlos Contreras'.[142] 'Carmen' was Carmen Martínez Cartón (1905–?), secretly an OMS employee and actually a German called Ruth Kahn. She had been sent to Spain in 1934 by the Young Communist International, as an adviser to Santiago Carrillo (1915–2012), and had gained Spanish citizenship through her marriage to Comrade Pedro Martínez Cartón (1905–?), who had briefly worked for the Profintern in Moscow in 1933. But Carrillo did not like her, criticizing her for her 'Prussian demeanour' and even managing to have her sent back to Moscow. However, in January 1937, by then pregnant, she was able to return to Spain, where she gave birth to her child. Cartón was then appointed head of the Comisión de Extranjeros of the PCE.[143] In his slightly ungrammatical German, 'Jelesoff' (perhaps Capt. Jelesov of the International Brigades) asked for the 'surname and forename under which he [Vidali] is registered at the Big House [Comintern HQ]'. The information, he added, was 'requested of us by a special organ'. First, however, it would be submitted to the Central Committee or the Military Commission of the Central Committee of the PCE 'for review and evaluation', 'before we pass it on'. 'Jelesoff' also asked her to inform comrade 'Alfredo', i.e. Togliatti, that he had already collected various items of information 'on the list he gave me'. Not long afterwards, the Comisión de Extranjeros,

---

140 This from the certificate of Pierre Jacquart, RGASPI 545/6/1490.

141 André Marty, report at a meeting of the Secretariat of the Comintern, 7 March 1937, in Radosh, *Spain Betrayed*, 141–6, at 142 (from a shorthand record of the discussion).

142 Handwritten letter of 18 February 1938 in the personal file of Vittorio Vidali, RGASPI 495/221/3776, vol. 1.

143 Abel, 'Die versuchte Neutralisierung', 487–9.

the PCE's cadre commission for foreigners, forwarded a recommendation received from the party organization in Albacete regarding the planned award to 'Contreras'. It was unfavourable. 'In our opinion, this proposal is out of the question, as Comrade Carlos has never commanded a military unit or taken part in the actual fighting. While we in no way underestimate his organizational work in the Fifth Regiment, we do not believe it right to propose that Comrade Carlos be awarded a decoration for valour at the front.'[144] Vidali remained undecorated.

Such a report also had consequences for Berta Bickel, who was excluded from the International Brigades and expelled from Spain 'for disruption to the advantage of the enemy'.[145] The allegations in her case, however, were gendered in nature. She had come to Spain in a convoy, 'contrary to the express prohibition, that no women, except doctors or qualified nurses, be admitted to our ranks'. In addition, she 'continually refused to do any work'. It was also noted that she associated with 'dubious elements' and 'suspect individuals' and wandered the streets at night.[146] On her return to Switzerland, Berta Bickel was expelled for 'indiscipline' by the KPS, which had received the report from Spain. The party had also refused her the press pass that her husband, Ernst Bickel, had applied for so that she could stay in Spain. Berta's letters were intercepted, copied and later deposited in her personal file in Moscow. In February 1938, Ernst Bickel, who had been in Spain since November 1936, applied for discharge from the International Brigades.[147] In a later characterization, he is also tarred by association with the markedly elastic term 'Trotskyite'. The German author simultaneously criticized the KPS, claiming that the POUM business had revealed 'the work of various party bodies [to be] very

---

144 Comisión para extranjeros to the Secretariat of the CC of the PCE, Barcelona, 22 February 1938, RGASPI 495/221/3776, vol. 1.

145 International Brigades, Base Headquarters, Albacete, 17 February 1937, RGASPI 545/6/1478.

146 Characterization of Berta Bickel, from I. B. Base, undated, RGASPI 545/6/1478 and International Brigades, Base Headquarters, Albacete, 17 February 1937, RGASPI 545/6/1478. This misogynistic style of judgment is also to be found in the cases of other women: see Renée Lugschitz, 'Pressebüro und Zensur im Spanischen Bürger*innenkrieg: Reporterinnen zwischen Journalismus, Propaganda und Überwachung', ÖZG 27:3, 2016, 160–71.

147 Ernst Bickel to Base Commandant 'General Gomez' (Wilhelm Zaisser, 1893–1958), Albacete, 5 February 1938, RGASPI 545/6/1479.

superficial'. 'Trotskyites now in custody in Barcelona' for example, had 'received papers to come to Spain from Swiss party officials'.[148] Ernst Bickel was reported missing in March.[149]

Lists of deserters and other 'destructive elements' were also circulated. On one, the Swiss Raymond Kamerzin was described as 'espia' – a spy.[150] When the twenty-two-year-old Kamerzin travelled to Spain in early 1938, Swiss party secretary Karl Hofmaier notified the French cadre commission in Paris that Kamerzin was 'in the service of the anti-Communist alliance of former Federal Councillor Jean-Marie Musy and Genevan National Councillor Aubert', which worked with the German Gestapo and Italy's OVRA. He added, 'You will naturally understand how important it will be for our friends to keep an eye [on] Kamerzin.'[151] His French correspondent passed the information on to both Spain and Moscow. Six months later, on returning from his July 1938 trip to Barcelona, where he met André Marty, Luigi Longo and other leading Communists, Jules Humbert-Droz, as a member of the Swiss cadre commission, confirmed to Moscow that Kamerzin was indeed not trustworthy.[152] The young Swiss never came home, and his fate remains unknown today.

Other volunteers were more fortunate, among them the Swiss couple Clara and Paul Thalmann, also the subjects of intelligence circulated transnationally between Spain, the national party leadership and Moscow. After he had published a pamphlet entitled *Für die Arbeiter-Revolution in Spanien* (For the Workers' Revolution in Spain) under the name 'Franz Heller', in Basel, in late December 1936, and then smuggled it into Catalonia, Paul Thalmann and his wife found themselves arrested in Barcelona following the May Events. In his pamphlet, Paul had

---

148 Typewritten note re. Berta Bickel, undated, with handwritten marginal annotation, 'Swiss', RGASPI 545/6/1478.

149 It is not known whether he was liquidated by his comrades or captured by the Nationalists. See Studer, *Un parti*, 511–12, 522–3 and 622, and Nic Ulmi and Peter Huber, *Les combattants suisses en Espagne républicaine (1936–1939)*, Lausanne: Antipodes, 2001, 199–201.

150 List of fifty-five Swiss (mostly deserters), RGASPI 545/6/1477.

151 Letter from Karl Hofmaier to 'Mon cher' (Maurice Tréand), 19 February 1938, RGASPI 545/6/1489, also in Kamerzin's personal file at the ECCI, 495/274/204.

152 Letter from Jules Humbert-Droz to Georgi Dimitrov, 20 August 1938, RGASPI 495/74/ 561. On the trip to Spain, see Humbert-Droz, *Dix ans*, 335–7 and 345–6.

critically welcomed the POUM's programme and accused the 'Stalinists' of betraying the revolution. It was the KPS that communicated the true identity of the author to Spain. The Catalonian Guardia de Asalto took the Thalmanns to a prison not far from the port, located in a former private house in the Portal de l'Àngel. There, Paul Thalmann says in his memoirs, they were interrogated separately by a group of foreigners, mostly Germans, who nonetheless presented themselves as a 'Spanish court'. Among them was a man Thalmann referred to as the 'boxer', on account of his nose,[153] whom scholars have since identified as 'Orlov'.[154] Neither of the Thalmanns said anything about the Trotskyist networks about which they were repeatedly questioned. After a few weeks, they were transferred to a larger and significantly less comfortable prison housed in the former convent of Santa Ursula in Valencia. After more than ten weeks in detention, and in response to pressure from the Socialist International, the two were eventually freed by Spanish government officials, to leave Spain in mid-September.

Hardly any Comintern employees or party members doubted the truth of the claim that 'Trotskyists' were enemies of the party, and even 'agents of fascism', as the ECCI Presidium declared on 28 December 1936. ECCI staffer 'Stepanov' ('pedantic and incompetent', in Humbert-Droz's opinion) readily applied this designation to the POUM immediately on his arrival as political adviser to the Central Committee of the PCE in early 1937.[155] It was a 'fascist organization of provocateurs, spies, bandits and murderers'.[156] Yet Ernö Gerö, who worked for the PSUC in Barcelona, had been much less harsh in his judgement when recognizing that a place for the 'semi-Trotskyist POUM' in Catalonia's government was simply the price to be paid for ending the chaos that reigned there.[157]

The repression against the POUM, which in 1937 had 300,000 members, was not just copied from the Soviet playbook on Stalin's orders. The sense that Trotskyists were hostile elements and even mortal enemies was by now deeply rooted in Communist thinking, planted there on Trotsky's expulsion from the Soviet party, and nourished since

---

153 The story of their arrest is told in Thalmann, *Wo die Freiheit stirbt*, 204–39.
154 Volodarsky, *Stalin's Agent*, 265.
155 Humbert-Droz, *De Lénine*, 445.
156 Cited in Elorza and Bizcarrondo, *Queridos camaradas*, 371.
157 Ibid., 363.

by the Show Trials in Moscow.[158] When Vittorio Vidali reflected in his long letter to Stasova on the possibilities of Communist organizations' new openness to other political forces following the Seventh World Congress, he warned 'that it will be very easy for the enemies (the Trotzkites [sic], Anarquistas) to use the International Red Aid or the new organization against the Soviet Union'.[159] The longer the war wore on, the deeper became the rift on the Republican side between political forces like the CNT-FAI and the POUM, who wanted to win the war through revolution, and those, like the Communists, who wanted to win the war first and leave the revolution till afterwards. And, if old conflicts had not been resolved by the turn to the Popular Front, they were then revived and exacerbated by the Moscow Trials.

Cadre policy and its multipurpose blurring of the boundaries between administrative data collection, individual evaluation, the monitoring of political conformity and police surveillance, had become part of party members' life by the mid-1930s at the latest, and those who had travelled to the Soviet Union and anyone who had worked for the Comintern were already long familiar with its bureaucratic practices. To be called to work in the area of cadre control was a sign of trust on the part of the organization. It thus came as a great relief to Lise London to find that she was allowed to work for the cadre department in Albacete, and afterwards, with her husband, with military intelligence both there and in Barcelona after the closure of the base.[160] Earlier, in Valencia, where she first recovered from her miscarriage, and lodged with Comrade Carmen Martinez Cartón and her young son, she had worked as a courier for 'Pablo', the 'blond Italian'. This was very likely Carlo Codevilla (1900–1950), a man of the illegal apparatus and the OMS, who served the ECCI as an informer regarding the official Comintern representatives in Spain and someone with whom London did not get on.[161]

Whether this was because she had a personal dislike of 'Pablo', who had tried to seduce her in Moscow, or was bored with coding, or harboured a deeper aversion to the activities of the OMS she does not

---

158 On the adoption of this interpretative schema by volunteers in Spain, see Kirschenbaum, *International Communism*, 137–44.
159 Vittorio Vidali to 'Dear comrade Stassova', 8 December 1935, RGASPI 513/2/36.
160 London, *Le printemps*, 268–71.
161 Codevilla's role as an informant is touched on in Firsov et al., *Secret Cables*, 15.

say in her memoirs. Nor do they indicate to what extent she knew how closely tied, by then, were the OMS and the NKVD, in terms of both personnel and operations.[162] As a former Comintern employee and someone who had worked for Ceretti, she was one of the narrow circle of party members who knew something of the organization's secret life.

The flow of information was fed not only by the increasing interdepartmental traffic of the 1930s but also by the goodwill of individual party members. When Tina Modotti was briefly in Paris in early 1937, the PCF provided her with information 'from Brazilian comrades' to be passed on to the cadre department of the PCE, and Modotti duly informed them:

> Lieutenant Alberto Bezouchet [Besouchet, in fact] is now in Spain. Following his departure from Brazil it was discovered that Bezouchet had turned Trotskyite. He left proof, a true provocation against the revolution of national liberation and the Spanish government. If he can be found, he must be arrested, and it is urgent that all comrades be notified so that he will not be able to speak in the name of the Communist Party of Brazil.

She added that it would be best 'to send a copy of this communication to the Political Commissariat of the International Brigades'.[163] She signed off, 'with Communist greetings', as the representative of International Red Aid. What exactly happened as a consequence of this message, we do not know. The twenty-five-year-old Alberto Besouchet, a member of the party since 1933, was the first Brazilian to

---

162 London, *Le printemps*, 287–312. As already noted, 'Moskvin' at the head of the OMS represented a direct personal link between the two.

163 'Maria' to the Cadre Commission of the CC of the PCE (Departamento de Cuadros, CC del PCE), Valencia, 24 January 1937, Arquivo Edgard Leuenroth (Universidade Estadual de Campinas, Campinas, SP, Brazil) IC 1447. I thank Dainis Karepovs for sending me this document and others from RGASPI's holdings on the Brazilian CP, and also Dr Victor Strazzeri for having put me in touch with him. See Dainis Karepovs, 'O caso Besouchet, ou o lado brasileiro dos processos de Moscou pelo mundo', *O Olho da História* 12:9, 2006, and also 'The Fate of the First Brazilian Brigadist in Spain: A Biographical Note about Alberto Bomilcar Besouchet', *International Newsletter of Communist Studies Online* 9:16, 2003, 52–6, available at kommunismusgeschichte.de. Citing Karepov, the communication is also discussed in Albers, *Shadows*, 301–2 (with a questionable translation) and Argenteri, *Tina Modotti*, 175.

volunteer in Spain. He left a letter for his comrades that used such phrases as 'proletarian world revolution', which by then no longer accorded with the Communist line and were hence characterized as 'Trotskyite'. What is more, in November 1936 the letter was published by *Comunista Internacionalista,* the official organ of the Trotskyist organization in Brazil. Besouchet travelled to Antwerp on a Cuban passport, arriving in December before going on via Paris and Perpignan to Spain. He never returned home, nor did his name appear on any list of Brazilian volunteers when the International Brigades were disbanded in late 1938. Apolônio de Carvalho, another Brazilian volunteer and a fellow graduate of the Realengo military academy in Rio, recalls in his memoirs that Besouchet was 'killed in cowardly fashion' in late 1938, but does not say by whom.[164]

Fatigue and Conflict among the Comintern Advisers

By May 1937, the romantic phase of the civil war had definitively come to an end. The supply situation was dire, children were undernourished. In July 1937, after the Battle of Brunete, the rebels occupied two-thirds of Spain. The big cities remained in government hands, but the country was cut in two. The Republican side was politically divided as well. Largo Caballero soon came to be seen as a traitor by the Communists. PCE General Secretary José Díaz was seriously ill and hardly able to take part in Central Committee meetings. Even within the Communist camp, there were severe differences, uncoordinated interventions, institutional rivalries and innumerable personal quarrels, while the activities of the NKVD were generally beyond the control of the Comintern's representatives, as illustrated by the following example.

The kidnapping of Mark Rein, a Russian-born member of the German Young Socialists, in Barcelona in April 1937, led the Socialist International to make a protest to the Comintern.[165] Dimitrov therefore thought it 'politically expedient' to instruct 'Stepanov' (Stojan Minev),

---

164 Apolônio de Carvalho, *Vale a pena sonhar,* Rio de Janeiro: Rocco, 1997, cited without page reference in Karepovs, 'The Fate of the First Brazilian Brigadist in Spain', n.36.
165 Zur Mühlen, *Spanien war ihre Hoffnung,* 192–9; Volodarsky, *Stalin's Agent,* 247.

his man on the spot, to look into the case and 'prevent any irresponsible action against Rein', seemingly unaware that his kidnapping was the work of NKVD agents, as would be his later murder. Minev replied to the coded telegram three weeks later, saying that 'the case is very complicated' and that Spanish party organs had been told nothing. Both the PCE and the Comintern were completely in the dark, so it had to have been the NKVD. Unwilling to say so explicitly, Minev ventured that it involved 'other organs', though he could not 'explain to you in a telegram or letter what is a mere supposition'.[166]

In the face of all these problems, the Comintern now sought to play its best card. After months of hesitation, in July 1937 it despatched Dimitrov's deputy, Palmiro Togliatti, to Spain. Given the complex and conflict-ridden situation, it needed the intervention of a highly capable and senior official who could assess the situation and evaluate the work of the Comintern advisers, a task that could no longer be done at a distance. On his way to Spain, however, Togliatti had another mission to fulfil, joining Pedro Checa (1910–1942), organizational secretary of the PCE, in Annemasse to negotiate aid for Spain with the Socialist International[167] – one reason why Dimitrov had asked Minev to find out about Mark Rein.

Once in Spain, Togliatti ('Alfredo') set to work immediately, informing himself about the political and military situation and speaking with the Comintern advisers. Although he was in Spain unofficially, as Stalin had instructed, his presence could not be kept secret for long. He found himself in a 'position . . . politically erroneous and dangerous', as he complained in one of his first reports, before moving on to the political situation.[168] On that, he was not very sanguine, taken all in all. He saw advantages in Caballero's replacement by Negrín, in terms of both the war and the influence of the Communist Party, but the illegal activity of the Trotskyists and anarchists, who called the Negrín government a 'gobierno de la

---

166 The coded telegrams of 9 and 30 July 1937 are published in part in Friedrich Firsov, 'Geheimtelegramme der Komintern im Spanischen Bürgerkrieg', *Forum für osteuropäische Ideen- und Zeitgeschichte* 3:1, 1999, 81–114, at 96.

167 See his report of 8 July 1937 in Palmiro Togliatti, *Escritos sobre la guerra de España*, Barcelona: Critica, 1980, 121–5.

168 Report of 30 August 1937, in Togliatti, *Escritos*, 126–42, quote at 129. There are also extracts from the report in Firsov et al., *Secret Cables*, 74.

contrarrevolución' – a government of the counter-revolution – posed a danger. Furthermore, the Republican camp's internal struggles had worsened, not least because the Communists' growing influence was meeting with resistance from parts of the Socialist Party and the CNT. The PCE's plan to openly strive for hegemony over the government would now be implemented in a completely improvised and disorderly fashion, and moreover could only increase the political difficulties. He also criticized the weakness of the party's cadres, most being young and inexperienced. Togliatti was also unsparing in his judgement of the methods of work of the party leadership in Valencia, criticizing the aimlessness of their approach and their disconnection from the situation on the ground.

> The leading comrades spend entire days debating with each other and with different people working in the ministries, the army, and so on. It is a permanent meeting that proceeds without a plan, during which lots of decisions are taken, but without anyone then bothering to see if they have been implemented. All the leading comrades are tired, worn out by overwork, unwell. That too is a result of the way they operate.[169]

It was not enough, he concluded, to decide things among a closed circle at party headquarters without reference to or feedback from actors in the field. An effective process required permanent confrontation with practice. There had to be rational, retrospective assessment of actions, of how they were conceived and the goals they were meant to serve. You had to know whether resolutions had been acted upon and whether this had had the results expected. The PCE leadership was far from capable of this, in Togliatti's view.

Nor was there much positive to report on the military front. In Albacete, he met briefly with 'Kléber' (Manfred Stern), who apparently told him of the numerous personal conflicts between the military advisers.[170] Togliatti also found that casualties among the International Brigades had been very high, with almost half the foreign volunteers lost

---

169 Report of 30 August 1937, in Togliatti, *Escritos*, 140–1.
170 Report by 'M. Fred' (Stern) of 14 December 1937, in Radosh, *Spain Betrayed*, 351.

in one way or another: 2,658 killed, 3,287 wounded, 1,500 evacuated, 696 'missing'. It was no wonder they were demoralized and wanted to go home.[171]

As well as inspecting Albacete, Togliatti evaluated the Comintern advisers posted to Madrid, Barcelona and Valencia. His opinion of Codovilla's methods of work was particularly negative. He had to 'stop being the workhorse of the entire Central Committee, hand over operational work to the Spanish comrades, and stop being the man without whom no one does anything and no one knows what to do'. And, whereas he had previously complained about the immaturity of Spanish party cadre, he now said that the Spanish comrades had since grown up and ought to be standing on their own two feet.[172]

In this, Togliatti only confirmed what André Marty had previously reported, when, shortly after his arrival in Madrid, he noted in a coded telegram to Manuilsky and Moskvin that he was truly astounded by the way Codovilla was behaving: 'There is no other term than big boss. He does everything himself. From nine o'clock in the morning in Gil Robles' former office (the PCE's headquarters is in the CEDA's old building), he receives people and deals with everything himself.'[173] The ECCI Secretariat had responded with the instruction that 'Comrade Luis should at all costs avoid replacing the General Secretary of the Spanish CP' – an injunction that evidently went unheeded.[174] On many other matters, Marty and Togliatti disagreed. While the slightly paranoid Marty blamed the poor morale of the International Brigades on 'provocative, hostile elements', Togliatti identified the problem more concretely as the lack of leadership from the PCE, which paid scarcely any attention to

---

171 Report by Togliatti to the International Brigades, 29 August 1937, cited in Firsov et al., *Secret Cables*, 103–4. Later research has confirmed the elevated casualty rate in the International Brigades: Skoutelsky, *L'espoir*, 334–6, which also highlights the exceptionally high price paid by the Spaniards who fought among them.

172 Report of 30 August 1937, in Togliatti, *Escritos*, 141–2.

173 André Marty, notes on the PCE, RGASPI 495/10a/209, 14 October 1936, cited in Antonio Elorza, 'Stalinisme et internationalisme en Espagne, 1931–1939', in Wolikow and Cordillot, *Prolétaires de tous les pays,* 192–200, at 196. Also in Radosh, *Spain Betrayed*, 35–40 (in an unsatisfactory translation). The CEDA was the Confederación Española de Derechas Autónomas (Spanish Confederation of Autonomous Rights), an alliance of Catholic and right-wing parties under José María Gil-Robles.

174 Cited in Firsov, 'Geheimtelegramme', 86.

them.¹⁷⁵ In his reports, Togliatti was also critical of Marty's leadership within the International Brigades, so succeeding in having him placed beneath his authority.¹⁷⁶

In mid-September, there had, in Togliatti's opinion, been no improvement in the work of the advisers. He informed Dimitrov and Manuilsky that 'Uribe, Dolores, Hernandez and Giorla are perfectly capable of leading the party on their own'.¹⁷⁷ The advisers only disoriented the party, setting it on 'a wrong path, either by the fabrication of improvised and erroneous theories, or by an uncalled-for political nervousness that, in combination with the nervousness of the Spanish comrades, has gradually undermined the party's tactics'.¹⁷⁸ A criticism in connection with which Togliatti explicitly referred to L. ('Luis', Codovilla) and to 'Pedro' (Gerö, with whom he had worked in the early 1930s as a member of a Comintern delegation in France). The advisers thought the Spanish comrades 'worth nothing' and that one could do things better or more quickly oneself. Referring to Codovilla, he observed that if L. couldn't 'change his working methods, he shouldn't come back'.¹⁷⁹ As would afterwards be noted in Codovilla's personal file, Togliatti also charged him with specific tactical errors: by maintaining independent contact with the other political parties, he had disowned the PCE leadership and aroused distrust of the Spanish party. He concluded with a negative judgement on L.'s character, describing him as 'selfish and ambitious'.¹⁸⁰ Togliatti did not have the power to dismiss Codovilla himself, but, together with 'Stepanov', he succeeded in getting him out of the way. Ordered with Pedro Checa to report to Moscow in September 1937, Codovilla was allowed to return to Spain, but not as adviser to the PCE. He was instead to head a special commission that was to organize an

---

175 Report by Togliatti to the International Brigades, 29 August 1937, in Radosh, *Spain Betrayed*, 254–5. On the characterization of Marty as paranoid, see Skoutelsky, *L'espoir*, 253.

176 Pennetier, 'Thorez-Marty', 212.

177 Meaning Vicente Uribe (1902–1961), Dolores Ibárruri, Jesús Hernandez (1907–1961) and the Catalan Luis Cabo Giorla (1906–1975).

178 Report by Togliatti to Dimitrov and Manuilsky, 15 September 1937, in Togliatti, *Escritos*, 143–50, at 144.

179 Ibid.

180 Characterization of Codovilla by the Bulgarian Georgi Damyanov ('Belov', 1892–1958), head of the ECCI Cadre Department, 1943, cited in Firsov, 'Geheimtelegramme', 108.

international campaign to gain support for the Spanish Republic and to recruit more volunteers.[181]

Now followed by a flight rather than a long train or boat journey, the 'invitation home', as the order to report to Moscow was called in Comintern language, was deployed ever more frequently from the mid-1930s on, as a means both of gaining information and of exerting political control, especially as large-scale meetings with non-Soviet comrades (such as the ECCI Plenums) had been abandoned. Long-distance communications were, in any event, too insecure and too slow, a letter to Moscow taking up to a month. One thus sees Franz Dahlem flying to Moscow in December 1937, and Togliatti in mid-1938, to give but two examples. During the Spanish Civil War, an oral report in Moscow also compensated for the weaknesses of telegraphic communication, which, despite the installation of a radio transmitter/receiver on a Madrid rooftop in 1933 had become increasingly scrambled and sometimes completely interrupted as the war went on.

In October 1936, for example, Ernö Gerö complained to Manuilsky, his former boss in Moscow, that he had not received any instructions. On the occasion of the May Events in 1937, of all times, 'Stepanov' had no reply from Moscow for several weeks.[182] And, when indeed the communications worked, Moscow's instructions might still prove unworkable. Stalin's absurd proposal to call new elections in the autumn of 1937 was as usual rubber-stamped by Togliatti and the Politburo of the PCE, but was subsequently allowed to sink without a word by anyone. Directives might also come to nothing because they ran completely counter to the thinking of local actors, as for example in February 1938, when Stalin demanded that the Spanish Communists leave government just as the latter were contemplating the formation of a purely Communist/trade-union administration.[183] Given the catastrophically deteriorating situation on both the military and foreign policy fronts, however, neither plan in fact came to anything.

* * *

---

181 Ibid., 107–8.
182 Elorza, 'In the Shadow', 243; and Elorza and Bizcarrondo, *Queridos camaradas*, 122.
183 Firsov, 'Geheimtelegramme', 110–12.

The many apparatuses active in Spain (the Comintern and its affiliated organizations, party representations, the Soviet diplomatic corps, the GRU and the NKVD) did not in any way resemble the well-oiled machine often invoked in discussions of the Comintern. Some actors were familiar neither with the country nor with its cultures or languages. Most were professional political cadres of long experience, but they found themselves in an unfamiliar situation, amid a civil war in which their own camp was riven by deadly political conflict. So where were the enemy to be found? Only on the side of the Nationalist rebels and their fifth column? Or also on one's own side, in the shape of Trotskyists, anarchists and left Socialists? What could it mean, this war between the struggle against fascism and the struggle for social revolution, between defending the Republic and defending the interests of the Soviet Union?[184] (This last option being an unconditional must for not only Soviet but all Communist cadres.) Although the Communists had the advantage over other forces in terms of their organizational capacity, discipline and determination, they had, in practice, to improvise in a difficult situation. It is therefore hardly a surprise that personal conflict and mutual criticism prevailed at many levels: between Marty and Dahlem on the Central Political Commission of the International Brigades; between Marty and 'General Emilio Kléber' (Stern), commander of the Ninth Brigade, in the military; between Togliatti and the other Comintern advisers; and so on.

It cannot be denied that Comintern staff sent to Spain, from highest cadre to the lowest employee, were willing to risk danger. In return, their work as professional revolutionaries, which in many cases had degenerated into bureaucratic routine, regained historical significance in their own eyes. A Republican victory also promised revenge for their defeat by fascism in Italy and Germany and by repression and 'White terror' in China, Mexico, Brazil, Argentina, Hungary, Yugoslavia and elsewhere.

This hope, however, would be disappointed. The left lost the war. Around a hundred Comintern officials died on the battlefield or in the Francoist repression that followed. Many of those who survived lost their belief in the Communist cause, while many of those who returned

---

184 On the differing understandings of the war on the Republican side, see Xosé-Manoel Núñez and José M. Faraldo, 'The First Great Patriotic War: Spanish Communists and Nationalism, 1936–1939', *Nationalities Papers* 37:4, 2009, 401–24.

to the Soviet Union would fall victim to Stalin's purges. Ordered back to Moscow in October 1937, Manfred Stern was given a job as military adviser to Otto Kuusinen, ECCI secretary and Stalin loyalist. Yet, on 23 July 1938, this man who had worked on behalf of the Comintern in the German, Chinese and Spanish revolutions was arrested at the Hotel Lux and sentenced to fifteen years of forced labour. He died in a prison camp in 1953, his sentence having been extended by ten years in 1945. Mikhail Koltsov, recalled to Moscow in the late summer of 1938, was arrested that same year and executed in February 1940. His wife, Maria Osten, who, despite his arrest, had followed him to Moscow and taken Soviet citizenship there, was arrested in 1941 and shot as a spy a year later.

Willi Münzenberg, who had gradually become an anti-Stalinist in the wake of the Moscow Trials and now sought to build a new left with his magazine *Die Zukunft* [The Future], refused to accept yet another 'invitation' to Moscow. On 6 March 1939, the Central Committee of the KPD expelled him from the party, and thus from the Comintern, officially because he had not complied with the request to 'take a public stand against the Trotskyist spies and against the crimes of the POUM'.[185] He would die a mysterious death in late June 1940, following his escape from internment by the French authorities as the Germans invaded France. Otto Katz, for his part, had already been removed as head of the Paris-based Spanish Republican news agency Agence Espagne in 1938, when the Central Committee of the PCE declared him to be 'an anti-party element', very likely on account of his closeness to Münzenberg.[186] This despite his being described as 'disciplined' by Franz Dahlem, representing the Central Committee of the KPD, following 'a nine-month-long examination' prompted by that relationship.[187]

In early 1939, the last Comintern advisers and other staff withdrew from a Barcelona under bombardment, the final refuge of the Republican authorities. When the first Nationalist tanks entered the city that January,

---

185 In October 1936 the ECCI Secretariat inspected Münzenberg's apparatus in Paris and in March 1938 sent Bohumír Šmeral to wind up what remained of his Paris-based operations.

186 Brief note on Otto Katz (Simon), in Spanish, 2 July1938; *spravka* (informational note) on Otto Katz, 15 November 1948, RGASPI 495/272/117.

187 Franz Dahlem of the Secretariat of the CC of the KPD, to the CC of the French Communist Party, 26 July 1938, RGASPI 495/272/117. Six months later, however, Walter Ulbricht gave a negative characterization of Katz.

Togliatti had to go into hiding before fleeing to Moscow. His visit of inspection had turned into an eighteen-month stay. Tina Modotti crossed the Pyrenees on 8 February 1939, with Vidali and a column of refugees. She then returned, via Paris and the United States, to Mexico City, where, on 5 January 1942, she would die of heart failure on the way home from an evening with friends – the German photographer Lotte Jacobi and the Swiss Communist architect Hannes Meyer (1889–1954), a former director of the Bauhaus. André Marty, entrusted by the Comintern with the demobilization and evacuation of the International Brigades, had already returned to Paris in November 1938. On 18 August 1939, he flew via Stockholm to Leningrad, five days before the signature of the Hitler-Stalin Pact – the treaty that in one fell swoop undermined years of efforts by the European left to build a culture of antifascism.

Left distrust of the Communists was now rekindled. Already during the Spanish Civil War, there had been speculation about political liquidations and the role in them of Comintern and Soviet agencies, and the Cold War installed a climate of almost obsessional suspicion in the West, reflected in the work of many historians. Many rash claims have been made in both the popular and the scholarly literature, often without any evidence, notably in the case of Vittorio Vidali. It has been said, for instance, that Vidali and Ernö Gerö were directly involved in the brutal murder of Andreu Nin.[188] Vidali is also suspected of the murder, on 10 January 1929, in Mexico City, of Modotti's lover, the Cuban Julio Antonio Mella, with Modotti herself, perhaps, an accomplice.[189] And

---

188 On Vidali, see above, and on Gerö: Pierre Broué, *Histoire de l'Internationale communiste, 1919–1943*, Paris: Fayard, 1997, 697.

189 In a text apparently written in Moscow in early 1932 for publication in Red Aid newspapers, Modotti claimed that the murder had been procured by the Cuban dictator Machado, to escape whom Mella had fled to Mexico: Tina Modotti, 'Neues Licht auf die Ermordung Julio Antonio Mellas am Vorabend des dritten Jahrestages', composed in English in early 1932, published with no further indication of source in Barckhausen, *Tina Modotti: Leben*, 67–8. The historian Pierre Broué doubts this, asking whether the murderer might not have been Vidali and claiming that Mella had joined a group of Left Oppositionists, been accused of Trotskyism and so expelled from the party: Broué, *Histoire*, 500–3. However, Broué provides no evidence, and nor does Pino Cacucci, who also claims that Modotti was Vidali's accomplice, consulted here in the German translation: Cacucci, *Tina Modotti: Ein brüchiges Leben in Zeiten absoluter Gewissheiten*, Frankfurt: Verlag Neue Kritik, 1989, 160–2 and 165–7. Both suspect him of involvement in the assassination of Trotsky, concluding from this that he could be entrusted with anything.

some have seen the hand of Vidali or some other Communist agent in Modotti's sudden death at barely forty-six years old.[190]

Such suspicions draw on both fact and fantasy. They are certainly nourished by the Stalinist practices associated with relentless struggle against a supposed enemy, whether in rhetoric and propaganda, in mutual suspicion and denunciation, or in the physical elimination of political opponents, as in the Great Terror in the Soviet Union, or, more especially, in the liquidation of enemies abroad by agents of the NKVD. In Vidali's case, the current state of research allows no such conclusions to be drawn. There is no evidence for the claim that the NKVD agent called 'Mario', who played a role in Trotsky's murder in Mexico, was Vidali, as some authors have suggested, and a claim others have also found implausible. The only thing that is certain is that Vidali, in the defence of Madrid, gained a reputation for being implacable in the struggle against the fascists and had all suspected 'fifth-columnists' shot. It is also clear that as head of the Fifth Regiment he worked alongside the NKVD agent Grigulevich and also had contact with Orlov. It is therefore quite possible that, as a loyal and disciplined and party member, he would have put himself at the disposal of the NKVD had the latter asked for help.[191] But, if we are ever to unequivocally separate fact from fiction, historical truth from Cold War fantasy, in this and other such cases, we can only await the opening of the KGB archives.

---

190 Cacucci, *Tina Modotti*, 165–7. An account of the genesis of these allegations – or 'myths' – can be found in Karlsen, *Vittorio Vidali*.

191 Volodarsky, *Stalin's Agent*, 360, 365–6 and 598–9; but compare Karlsen, *Vittorio Vidali*, 188–90.

10

Conclusion: A Life with Bags Packed

The revolutionary travellers of the Comintern – the men and women whose lives we have examined here – each played their part in a many-sided venture, one of the greatest collective experiments of the twentieth century. They developed a political practice in transnational space. Their personal commitment saw them start life afresh in one place after another, whether escaping the police or simply moving on at their employer's behest. An internationalism not only theoretical but practical thus combined with repression and persecution to generate what can be called transnational life-courses, spinning a variably dense web of clandestine activity across the world. As Comintern employees, they carried out lengthy missions abroad, accepted long-term postings far from either Moscow or the countries of their birth. They uprooted themselves continually, moving on after months or years, in the hope of nourishing or supporting revolutionary movements or participating in revolutionary events, while everyday work likewise saw them constantly travelling, to a rendezvous, a meeting, an international conference. They covered vast distances, both geographical and cultural, changing names, deploying countless aliases, disguising themselves as writers, journalists, commercial travellers . . . They travelled with false passports and double-bottomed suitcases. Living often in illegality and in hiding from the authorities, they attended 'conspiratorial' gatherings and communicated through encrypted telegrams and despatches smuggled across borders by secret couriers. By any standard, this was far from an ordinary way of life, and their lives, too, were sometimes extraordinary. The boundaries they ignored or flouted were more than lines on a map, and for the bourgeois world, Moscow's emissaries were 'foreign agitators', the hostile Other personified.

Conditions, Duties, Job Requirements

If they were to fulfil their tasks, that is, to provide foreign parties with political guidance and technical support, and so to live up to their own aspiration to revolutionary leadership, they needed skills both practical and intellectual. They had to be flexible and adaptable, diplomatic and determined. Roy and Borodin, for example, who were in China with official permission, needed not only writing skills and effective working habits but also the ability to marshal an argument, to think logically, to acquire knowledge quickly, to orient themselves in and adapt to a new situation, together with a talent for organization and forcefulness in debate. To understand the situation in the field, they had only the local and foreign press and the testimony of domestic leaderships. Without being able to speak the language, they then had to convince their Chinese comrades of the correctness of the political line – a labour of persuasion they undertook against a generally confused political and military background and in competition with each other. The knowledge newly gained had to be summed up in reports, expenses recorded and submitted, work plans drawn up, and above all, their superiors in Moscow, 6,000 kilometres away, had to be informed of the steps they proposed to take, in order to obtain their approval, even if that often came late. It needed a great deal of tactical skill, and a good dose of bluff should someone like Willi Münzenberg want to present headquarters with a fait accompli.

Knowledge alone was not enough: a certain savoir-faire was also required, this presenting a particular challenge abroad. Neither the leadership of the 'brother party' nor social reality could be simply controlled from above, ordered into alignment with a political programme. Communist parties did not always welcome Comintern emissaries with open arms. They were, often enough, met with suspicion, and even resistance to any outside interference in party affairs. While Comintern emissaries came to their discussions with local leaderships armed with the authority of the Moscow Centre (or its regional representations, such as the WEB) and with that the power to dismiss entire party leaderships and set a new political course, this could leave a divided and weakened party leadership with half the membership gone. In China, both Roy and Neumann made decisions catastrophic in their consequences.

The larger the Comintern delegation and the more important the mission, the more likely that conflict and competition between its members would be added to individual weakness and error and the intrinsic imponderables of the situation, especially as every decision taken in the field had to take into account the balance of power in Moscow, the fierce political struggle that raged in Soviet Union through the 1920s. The Stalinist culture of distrust, not to say suspicion or even paranoia, increasingly corroded interpersonal relationships, as evidenced by the letters of mutual blame and accusation sent to Moscow headquarters by Comintern delegates posted to unfamiliar environments abroad. Political reports not infrequently turned into denunciations of colleagues, increasingly concerned not only with personal differences but with allegations of political deviation. The Spanish Civil War saw Palmiro Togliatti sent to Spain to oversee the other Comintern representatives, to identify their political inadequacies, tactical errors and weaknesses of character and to intervene accordingly. This was not, however, the only case in which it was unclear to the authorities in Moscow whether political failure was the result of personal incompetence or of an unwillingness to implement the line. More and more often, they suspected political sabotage.

Work abroad required rigorous security precautions, so it was not only the local police who were to be kept in the dark about Comintern employees' arrival but also, if possible, the rank-and-file membership of the party in question. They had, therefore, to be extremely discreet: although they had to investigate the local situation and bring their powers of persuasion to bear on local party leaders, they were not to attract attention in doing so. This, in turn, meant as regular as possible a daily routine. 'Noulens/Rüegg', the OMS station chief in Shanghai had to go to his office on the Szechuan Road at a number of fixed times each day, to await a visit from his Chinese comrades, and, at other times, to a second office on the Nanking Road. Sent to Berlin with Dmitri Manuilsky to set up the WEB, Jules Humbert-Droz wrote to his wife in Moscow that he found himself bored to death by always following the same routine.

In practice, even the most sophisticated security regulations were unavailing. When the highly secret OMS station in Shanghai was exposed, together with its extensive network in East and South East Asia, Richard Sorge had to step in as the man in the middle. This was a most dangerous breach of the rules of conspiracy: under no circumstances was an employee of the Soviet military intelligence apparatus supposed to take on such an important Comintern role. Sometimes, it was simple carelessness that saw illegals apprehended: just after the Reichstag fire, as the Berlin police were frantically looking for the suspected arsonist Van der Lubbe, Georgi Dimitrov, unruffled, met his two Bulgarian comrades for dinner in a busy restaurant on the Potsdamerstrasse, only to have a suspicious waiter call the police on the three 'Russians'.

Personality Types, Career Opportunities and Cadre Policy

The image of the Comintern workforce that comes most readily to mind tends to the monochromatic – a disciplined body of men devoted to Stalin's Soviet Union – but first impressions can be deceptive. Communists never formed a uniform class, not even in the second half of the 1930s, when Stalin had arrogated all power to himself. The Comintern employees whose lives we have followed here, from the revolutionary hub that was Berlin in the twenties, through the translocal anticolonial networks and preparations for revolution in China, to the Spain of the Civil War, were diverse in sex, age, social origin and nationality, even if Europeans, and middle-aged men at that, clearly held most posts of responsibility while women were, on the whole, confined to auxiliary roles. The world of the professional revolutionaries was indeed characterized by division of labour and internal stratification, with superiors and subordinates. In Berlin, Borodin had the young and enthusiastic Hilde Kramer as his private secretary, while Willi Münzenberg employed a whole team.

There were exceptions, however. Communist agents, who for the historian Karl Schlögel represent a cultural type all of their own, were not exclusively male,[1] and his sketch of the cosmopolitan agent of Soviet power who gathers intelligence not for money but for the cause fits the women as well. Ruth Werner, a spy who rose to the rank of colonel in the Red Army before eventually turning children's author, followed up her posting to Shanghai with stints in Japanese-occupied Manchuria, in Poland and in Switzerland, before moving to the UK in late 1940, where, among other things, she ran a string of nuclear spies. In general, however, women were rarely able to convert activist into political capital, that is, to convert political experience on the ground into institutional recognition and official roles. Tina Modotti came very close to it in Spain, yet remained only the de facto leader of International Red Aid, rather than its appointed head, officially recognized as such.

In most cases, women served as indispensable assistants, working in the background, often, like Luise Geissler and Margarete Buber-Neumann, as secretary to partner or husband. It was they who were chiefly responsible for the logistical tasks without which the Comintern's representatives, usually operating in illegality, would have been unable to function. It was Jenny Humbert-Droz, for example, who painstakingly coded and decoded the encrypted telegrams through which the Comintern's emissaries in Spain communicated with Moscow in the early 1930s. Despite its ostensible commitment to the equality of the sexes, the Comintern was no different to inter-war civil society in simply not considering women fit for leadership or political responsibility, the few exceptions only proving the rule. A mere theoretical commitment to sexual equality was not enough to refashion the gender order with its conventional practices and representations.

Over time, however, one does see a change in personality type, or if not exactly that, a narrowing of range, as characters like Jakov Reich – the combination professional revolutionary, Jewish intellectual and social adventurer who lived many lives in one – become increasingly rare. There were two reasons for this. First, the Comintern apparatus became increasingly professionalized as the improvisation of the early years gave way to a mode of administration based on the division of labour, the longer time frame implied by the ebb of the revolutionary tide seeing a premium placed on bureaucratic control. As the

---

1 Karl Schlögel, *Das russische Berlin: Ostbahnhof Europas*, Munich: Hanser, 2007, 317–23.

organization's chief financial officer, Osip Piatnitsky clamped down on the casual treatment of assets characteristic of Reich, whose bookkeeping can, at best, be described as rudimentary, and who had failed to change the Comintern's German marks in good time in the face of the Weimar hyperinflation, incurring immense losses. Regular working hours became the norm for the Comintern apparatus in Moscow, and political and administrative conformity increasingly determined the possibility of advancement. Second, the establishment of the Cadre Department in 1932 saw the creation of a human resources administration of a distinctive kind, which now systematically collected and evaluated biographical data on the Comintern's employees, hitherto only incidentally recorded. With this, political conformity became a central criterion for appointment, assignment and promotion, one that in the mid-1930s became far more stringently applied, and that in two senses. On the one hand, the long arm of Moscow now extended beyond the confines of the Soviet Union: Willi Münzenberg's apparatus in Paris was dismantled by a liquidator and its personnel screened by Comintern representative Bohumír Šmeral, with those insufficiently reliable being dismissed; the RUNA, too, shared the same fate, Julius Alpári and Jules Humbert-Droz spending a whole day in December 1936 on what they called a 'spring clean' of RUNA employees. And, for Comintern staff within the Soviet Union itself, of course, the First Moscow Trial in the summer of 1936 saw the notion of 'cleansing' or 'purge' take on an altogether more sinister colouration, implying the possibility of their physical elimination.

Violence and Imprisonment

Police surveillance, arrest, deportation, persecution, flight, exile and even death counted among the 'normal' experiences of professional revolutionaries, and questions about arrest and imprisonment soon found their way into the successive versions of the Comintern questionnaire. They also shaped the Communist worldview, as illustrated by Tina Modotti's description of her political commitments, as she declared herself against 'the intolerable exploitation of the workers of the countries of South America and the Caribbean', against 'bloody revenge on peasants who fight for their land, the torture of imprisoned revolutionaries, armed attacks on street rallies and unemployed marches'.[2] The experience of prison was shared by Comintern agents across the world. Arrested in 1932, Chen Duxiu spent five years in a Guomindang prison. Jenny Humbert-Droz was held in custody for several days in October 1939, as the Swiss authorities searched what was left of the RUNA's offices following the outbreak of war. Her husband, Jules, for his part, had spent more than four months in custody in late 1937 and early 1938 before his acquittal on a charge of having established a recruiting centre for Spanish volunteers. After a brief arrest, the Communist student leader Julio Antonio Mella fled Cuba in the face of the Machado dictatorship's threats to his life, only to be killed in Mexico, where he had thought to find refuge. Eugen Fried, the Hungarian-speaking Jew from Slovakia who was, in the 1930s, the long-serving Comintern emissary in Paris, spent several years in Hungarian and Czechoslovak prisons in the 1920s. Dimitrov, like other comrades, served time in prison before his arrest in 1933, though conditions under the Nazi regime were worse than in Sofia in 1918, being permanently handcuffed for the first five months and also denied daily exercise. Arthur Ewert and his Polish-born wife Elisabeth Saborowski were both severely tortured in Brazil, before she was expelled into the hands of the Gestapo, to be killed in Ravensbrück. Her husband went mad and spent the rest of his life in psychiatric institutions after being amnestied in 1945. Active in the resistance during the war, as anti-Stalinists outside the ambit of the Comintern, Ruth Oesterreich and Hendricus Sneevliet were both executed by the Nazis, she by guillotine, he by firing squad. Arrested by the Gestapo in Paris in 1940, together with Hans Glaubauf, Julius Alpári died in Sachsenhausen after months of confinement in a darkened cell; Glaubauf was shot for high treason in 1942. Tiemoko Garan Kouyaté was also murdered by the Nazis, and Eugen Fried was likely another of their victims, though the exact circumstances of his death in Brussels in 1943 remain unclear, and it is possible that he was killed by the NKVD. The Spaniard Matilde Landa, Tina Modotti's colleague in Red Aid, committed suicide while in Francoist custody, while Richard Sorge was hanged in Japan in 1944 after the Soviet Union refused the offer of an exchange of agents.

---

2 Maria, 'Die IRH in den Ländern Südamerikas und der Karibik', *Internatsionalnyi Maiak* [International Beacon, the magazine of the MOPR], 1934, reprinted in Christiane Barckhausen, ed., *Tina Modotti. Leben – Werk – Schriften*, Kiel: agimos, 1996, 89–90.

Conversely, a willingness to use violence against others was at least a foreseeably necessary aspect of the Communist way of life, if only because a violent seizure of power was contemplated. Political commitment meant a life-and-death struggle against capitalism: Comintern employees expected repression from the enemy and were not squeamish about countering in kind. Although individual political violence was no part of the programme, Communists and Nazis engaged in regular street battles under the Weimar Republic. During her apprenticeship not far from Moscow, Ruth Werner learnt not only how to encode and to operate a radio transmitter but also how to handle explosives. And, with the Stalinist terror of the 1930s, violence came to be directed at the party's own members. While this fell mainly within the purview of the Soviet secret services (who might sometimes be assisted by comrades, as in the case of 'Ignaz Reiss'), Willi Münzenberg was likely killed by Communists on his escape from internment in France in 1940, though this is far from having been conclusively established.

In an age of growing nationalism, the internationalists of the Comintern increasingly found themselves harried by matters of nationality. Denial of residence and deportation on grounds of illegal entry, statelessness or political undesirability were the lot of many Comintern employees. Modotti and Vidali were expelled from Mexico (and he, later, also from the USA). Luise Geissler, who lost her German citizenship through marriage to a Swiss, found herself deported to Switzerland in the wake of the Bavarian Soviet Republic. M. N. Roy's life (shared at first with Evelyn Trent) was an uninterrupted series of deportations and escapes from arrest, prompting him to complain in 1925 that 'the British police have not left me in peace, even in my exile. They have pursued me step by step, from one country to another, from Java to Japan, from China to the Philippines, to America, to Mexico and through most of the countries of Europe.'[3] When he finally returned to India, after breaking with the Comintern, he was very soon arrested and spent almost six years in prison. There were also those persecuted by their own

---

3 Letter from Manabendra Nath Roy to the French Ligue des droits de l'Homme et du citoyen protesting his expulsion from France, Luxembourg, 1 February 1925, appended to Evelyn Roy, 'Indian Political Exiles in France', *Labour Monthly* 7:4, April 1925, 205–10, at 210, also available at marxists.org.

governments on account of their political affiliation, leading to the revocation of citizenship – the fate chiefly of Germans under National Socialism.

Those arrested or imprisoned did, however, benefit from the solidarity of their comrades. Whenever possible, International Red Aid provided them with money, clothes, food, newspapers and books, forwarded mail, maintained contact with families and arranged legal representation, tasks that in accordance with the sexual division of labour fell largely to women. The Spanish Civil War saw the volume of such work expand many times over. In the case of prominent prisoners, or those who exemplified a cause, the Comintern and the other Communist organizations also mounted broad international solidarity campaigns, with countless letters of protest, petitions, meetings and newspaper articles. This was notably the case for the 'Noulens/Rüegg' couple in China and Heinz Neumann in Switzerland.

The experience of prison could sometimes also serve as a spur – that, at least, is what Jules Humbert-Droz felt when imprisoned in the Santé in Paris in 1928, as he described in a letter smuggled out to his wife:

> Prison is, in the end, an excellent school of revolution, from which one's faith and revolutionary energy emerge reinvigorated. A wonderful bath of hatred – one becomes wicked, but with that good hatred, that sacred cruelty that forges the revolutionary spirit. After so many years spent in bureaucratic work, just as I began to turn to fat, both physically and morally, this imprisonment represents an excellent cure.[4]

Political Commitment: Gains and Losses

Political failure and the many adversities of everyday life posed a recurrent threat to professional revolutionaries' self-belief. The Comintern's own major offensives and those in which it engaged as an ally – the German Revolution of 1923, the Chinese Revolution of 1926–27 and the defence of the Spanish Republic in 1936–39 – all ended in patent defeats.

---

4 Jules Humbert-Droz, *Mémoires*, vol. 2, *De Lénine à Staline: Dix ans au service de l'Internationale communiste, 1921–1931*, Neuchâtel: À La Baconnière, 1971, 299.

At such moments, Comintern employees' perpetually precarious and unsettled existence made clear the cost of their political commitments, not infrequently leading to a personal crisis. Of the non-Soviet delegates to the Second World Congress in 1920, only two-fifths were still Communists in 1933; and when it was dissolved in 1943, only a quarter.[5] Of the foreign delegates to the 1920 Congress who have featured in this account, not one was left when the Comintern was dissolved. They had either been expelled, left the party, died of natural causes, or been killed.

Those who did stay might have a political faith immune to all difficulties; they could equally well be political opportunists; or it might be that they had already invested so much that giving up only made the sense of failure worse. In any event, a capacity to tolerate frustration was a must. As a regional specialist at International Red Aid headquarters in Moscow, Tina Modotti spent her days immersed in Latin American newspapers and magazines, drawing systematic conclusions from what she read and occasionally reporting to the Political Commission of the ECCI.[6] While such analytical work could be intellectually stimulating, even challenging, especially for those with limited schooling, it also required the ability to indefinitely postpone the prospect of revolutionary overthrow. Such deskwork only made sense when one's own activity could be seen as part of a larger scheme of things.

With the retreat of the revolutionary horizon, however, the upwelling of utopian expectations threatened to collapse into bureaucratic routine. Many sources thus give expression to the sense of boredom that gradually came to pervade the daily work of Comintern officials, at Comintern headquarters in Moscow more particularly. To escape it, some tried to get sent back to their own parties. Edgar Woog made several such attempts. Fed up with his job maintaining the party's statistical records, he wrote to Osip Piatnitsky and the Political Commission in 1933, stressing how long he had worked for the Comintern: 'I left Switzerland in late 1918, worked for 3 years in Mexico and since 1922 in the ECCI apparatus.'[7] It was not until 1935, after more than sixteen years as a

---

5 John Riddell, ed., *Workers of the World and Oppressed Peoples, Unite! Proceedings and Documents of the Second Congress, 1920*, vol. 1, New York: Pathfinder, 1991, 9.

6 Material on the production plan consultation with the specialist advisers of the regional secretariats, Moscow, 4 December 1932, RGASPI 495/18/945.

7 Letter from 'Stirner' (E. Woog) to Piatnitsky, for the attention of the Political Commission, Moscow, 18 December 1933, RGASPI 495/4/274.

professional revolutionary, that he was finally allowed to return to Switzerland, though he had to leave behind the Russian wife he had only recently married, who was not granted an exit permit. Siegfried Bamatter was another Swiss who made several attempts to give up his post in the Comintern apparatus. It was only in 1930 that he succeeded in getting himself sent home to work for the Swiss party, when that found itself in serious crisis – only to be recalled to Moscow in 1932, when Humbert-Droz returned to Switzerland to join the party leadership. It was in Moscow that he died in 1966. Others, such as Charlotte Stenbock-Fermor or Vittorio Vidali, asked in vain for permission to attend a cadre school.

Yet the Comintern's record of failure, so obvious in retrospect, only obscures the complexity of the experience of the actors themselves, as the former Communist Manès Sperber bitterly observed: 'Oh, the petty wisdom of survivors who see in endeavours that failed only the failure itself and who can so easily discover the causes.'[8] Such a simplistic approach loses sight of the great sense of group cohesion created by shared goals and beliefs and by the Comintern itself as an institution, with its shared language, rules and practices, its networks of cooperation and solidarity. In the Comintern, revolutionaries found not only a sense of community but also a way of explaining social reality and a political space within which to act on their concerns. The Comintern was a way of living the world. 'The Comintern was intended to, and very largely did, give the movement immunity against the terrible collapse of its ideals,' as the British historian Eric Hobsbawm noted on the basis of his own experience.[9]

For convinced internationalists, one key to their commitment was the opportunity the Comintern offered to live their internationalism to the full. In her novel *Die Gefährten* (The Companions, 1932), the Communist writer Anna Seghers treats internationalism chiefly as the idea, the awareness, that others elsewhere want and do the same things. But if ideas are to be shared, then go-betweens and channels of communication are required. As we have seen here, the Comintern employees

---

8 Manès Sperber, *Wie eine Träne zum Ozean: Romantrilogie* (Munich: dtv, 1983), 226.

9 Eric Hobsbawm, 'Problems of Communist History', in Hobsbawm, *Revolutionaries: Contemporary Essays*, New York: Pantheon, 1973, 3–10, at 5.

who travelled the world on political missions made such internationalism a reality through their own activity, living their internationalism as action. The networking of the like-minded was, for them, a connection with particular comrades in struggle, while every individual situation gave rise to an internationalism specific to its time and place that was equally the creation of specific actors. Willi Münzenberg, who never travelled to Asia or to any colonial territory – his only journey outside Europe being to the United States in 1934, as part of the campaign in support of Ernst Thälmann, imprisoned by the Nazis – and who thus travelled all the more often to the Soviet Union, created through his working contacts with Chinese, Indian, African and other anticolonial activists an extensive transnational network against imperialism, colonialism and racism. With a keen political sense, he knew how to bring existing forces of political resistance together to transform them into new movements, bigger and stronger.[10]

The Comintern thus offered its employees a distinctive lifeworld, membership of a community bound together by shared goals and reinforced by common action in a generally hostile environment. Pervaded by a dense network of acquaintances, friendships, love affairs and enmities, the world of the inter-war Communists can be compared to a widely ramifying extended family: unless you turned your back on it entirely, you somehow always belonged.

As we have seen, the lives of the internationalists considered here were in many ways intertwined. Thanks to their transnational way of life, their paths crossed again and again in different places around the world. The most important occasions of encounter were the regular international congresses and the periodic meetings with the Comintern apparatus in Moscow. In the language of the Comintern, 'going home' or 'over there' meant, significantly, going to Moscow. One-off events,

---

10 Münzenberg did not act alone, but his energetic activism and the resources he commanded in the way of organizations, publications and personnel made him a central figure. Other activists, treated only marginally here (such as the Black Communist intellectuals and activists scattered across countries and continents who were involved in the development and definition of a distinctive internationalism that linked antiracism, anticolonialism and antifascism at the time of the Spanish Civil War) also deserve mention but could not call on the same institutional resources. See David Featherstone, 'Black Internationalism, International Communism and Anti-Fascist Political Trajectories: African American Volunteers in the Spanish Civil War', *Twentieth Century Communism* 7, 2014, 9–40.

such as the Brussels Congress of 1927, might also bring a good number of the 'usual suspects' together. The experience of collective enthusiasm they offered made such events engines of mobilization. Cities, too, served as meeting places, notably Berlin, a key hub in the Comintern's international network and an obligatory point of transit for the great majority of those travelling to or from Moscow. And, finally, the revolutionary hotspots of the inter-war years, such as China and Spain, also drew in and drew together numbers of Comintern employees.

These recurrent encounters resulted in friendships and enmities and also the formation of couples and sometimes oppositional groups. Personal relationships were put to the test by the difficulties and vicissitudes of life in the service of the Comintern. Lifelong relationships were unusual, even if they did indeed happen, as witness Jenny and Jules Humbert-Droz and Babette Gross and Willi Münzenberg. Friendships could survive expulsion or exile. Münzenberg continued to associate with Fritz Brupbacher, expelled from the party in February 1933 for his anarchist inclinations, while their women, Babette Gross and Paulette Brupbacher-Raygrodski, continued to meet and wrote regularly to each other, the one in Berlin and afterwards Paris, the other in Zurich. But friendships also turned into enmities. This is what happened, for example, between Jules Humbert-Droz and the Bulgarian Stojan Minev, as is clear from Humbert-Droz's detailed letters to his wife, Jenny. When he was found guilty of 'right opportunism' by the ECCI Presidium in late 1928, Minev, his deputy in the Latin American Secretariat, took the side of the authorities, bringing an end to the trust and friendship that had hitherto existed.

Stalin and the Transformation of the Comintern

The conflicts within the Comintern, not only those over the political line but others over many tactical questions, cannot be understood without reference to Stalin and the Soviet party, but they did not simply and exclusively derive from the clash between the interests of Soviet foreign policy and those of the world revolution, as there is sometimes a tendency to suggest. They also arose from the difficulty of analysing and interpreting the complex sociopolitical realities of the transnational spaces in which the Comintern's representatives acted and then of formulating and implementing appropriate tactics. As witnessed by the relationship between Minev and Humbert-Droz, there were also conflicts over influence, jobs and power within the Comintern hierarchy, though these in turn hinged on the 'correct' political position, that is, the majority position for the time being. A young, up-and-coming generation did not hesitate to use the ultraleft turn of the late 1920s as means of furthering its career ambitions. The history of the Comintern from the point of view of its actors is thus also a history of opportunism and moral courage, of competition and repression. Actors' agency and capacity are an indispensable element in historical analysis, but equally important are the changes in their field of action and the associated alteration or reduction in room for manoeuvre. The increasing ascendancy of Stalin and the Soviet party, whose pre-eminence had been assured from the start, saw a transformation of the Comintern. The activists who travelled to Moscow in 1920 saw Soviet reality through the lens of their own expectations of the revolution. They were by no means ignorant or imperceptive, but they were prepared to turn a blind eye or two to the problems, wishing to give the young revolution and its state a chance. Furthermore, 1917 marked the onset not only of a revolutionary wave but also of a counter-revolutionary, anti-Communist movement that swelled first from 1917 to 1922–23 and then again in the 1930s, against which the Soviet Union seemed to be the only bulwark. Under the power of this fact, the political pre-eminence of the Soviet Union turned into a Soviet domination of politics. A clear reflection of this was the rapid rise of the Russian language within the cosmopolitan Comintern apparatus, which saw the Hungarian Béla Kun complain at a meeting in November 1925 of a decline in its 'international atmosphere'. 'There is a process of de-internationalization going on in the Comintern. Even the signs are in Russian,' he declared, adding that he was not alone in thinking so.[11] In fact, after the Fifth World Congress of 1924, Russian became increasingly prominent in the everyday life of the Comintern, alongside its official language, German. Mastery of Russian now became the key to a career in international Communism, more especially as adoption of the language might be accompanied by political adaptation.

---

11 Minute of the consultation of the various departments on improving the work of the apparatus, 30 November 1925, RGASPI 495/46/3.

Heinz Neumann offers an example. He and other Young Turks lined up behind Stalin, not Trotsky or Bukharin, in the intra-Russian factional struggles that also embroiled the Comintern. However, the 'Russian model' very early came to be based on a political practice conceivably counterproductive for a revolutionary organization. Instead of giving Comintern agents a free hand to adapt their activist know-how to the particular political situations they confronted, it was expected that the model of the October Revolution be copied elsewhere. This proved to be a fatal error in the German Revolution of 1923.

More immediately relevant to the everyday practice of the Comintern's representatives, of course, was the expectation of a disciplined and unprotesting compliance with instructions from the centre. Accepted in theory by all Comintern employees, the obligation was repeatedly ignored in practice, either because compliance was impossible, for any number of reasons, or because a political organization is not in the end an army and political decisions are never immune to contestation. Even Heinz Neumann, a Stalin loyalist, found himself in 1932 in (covert) opposition to the Comintern's policy of rapprochement with National Socialism. With Stalin's ascendancy from 1924 on, however, the interests of the Soviet Union became ever more dominant and the Soviet party came increasingly to set the political line. Free discussion died out, and by the mid-1930s dissent had been criminalized. The Seventh World Congress of 1935 represented, in reality, no more than 'a masquerade of unity' – a criticism that Leon Trotsky had already levelled at the theatrical representations of consensus that accompanied the Second Congress in 1920.

Employment by the Comintern allowed ever less room for criticism or dissent – 'voice' in Albert Hirschman's terminology.[12] Unlike the firms investigated by Hirschman, the Comintern recognized no right to give up one's employment, as shown by the case of Edgar Woog. 'Exit' could only mean a break with international Communism, a step that many shied away from, and one that would, in any event, become impossible in the Soviet Union. With the Terror, even a request to resign from the apparatus became unthinkable, while dismissal came hand in hand with arrest. When the social technology of preventive repression was

---

12 Albert O. Hirschman, *Exit, Voice and Loyalty: Responses to Decline in Firms, Organizations and States*, Cambridge, MA: Harvard University Press, 1970.

turned on the Comintern, not all foreign Communists managed to react 'competently' to the situation.

Escape from the machinery of repression was often enough a matter of chance or luck. As no one's biography was free of moments of doubt or criticism, no one was above suspicion, and everyone had thus consorted with suspects, convicted or otherwise. Julius Alpári, accused by the Comintern Cadre Department of having ties to the disgraced Radek, could undoubtedly be glad that he did not go back to the Soviet Union in the 1930s, even if this gained him only a few more years of life. The history of the Comintern is also the history of the elimination of opposition movements and their real or supposed members. Despite all its own politico-semantic vicissitudes, Stalin's Comintern wanted a movement freed of all contradictions, preferring political unity over diversity regardless of the human cost.

The Dead on Leave: The Great Massacre

'We Communists are all dead men on leave': Eugen Leviné's declaration before the German counter-revolutionary court that would sentence him to death in 1919 now took on a bloody reality in the Soviet Union, of all places in the world. The years of the Great Terror of 1936 to 1938 not only decimated the colony of foreign Communists in Moscow but also cost Russian Comintern employees their lives or freedom. Heinrich Kurella and Heinz Neumann were both shot in 1937. Kurella's companion, Charlotte Stenbock-Fermor, managed to escape to Denmark on an assignment for the NKVD, before making her way to Paris to see Heinrich's sister; Margarete Buber-Neumann, also arrested, would be handed over to the Nazis in 1940. She survived the Ravensbrück concentration camp. Virendranath Chattopadhyahya (Chatto) and Abani Mukherji were arrested and shot in 1937. Liao Huanxing was sentenced to labour camp in 1938, remaining there until 1949. Béla Kun was shot in 1938, as was Osip Piatnitsky.

Of the 320 or so Comintern employees mentioned by name in this book, nearly a third died a violent death. The majority of them – 58 people – perished in the Stalinist purges before 1945; four others were murdered by Stalin's henchmen, or by their own comrades, outside the Soviet Union; and two committed suicide in the Soviet Union. Rather fewer – 17 people – died at the hands of the Nazis. Four Chinese died as a result of Guomindang repression. Two people were executed in Japan, two killed or driven to suicide by the Francoists, while one person died in the Spanish Civil War and another went missing. Of the remaining two, one committed suicide due to illness and the other was murdered by an unknown person. Only six of the group died violently after 1945: one in the Gulag, two following the Slansky Trial (these being Otto Katz, the 'Trotskyite-Titoite Zionist' who had returned to Prague from Mexico in 1946 in order to help build socialism, and Bedrich Geminder, head of the Press Section at the Comintern until 1943 and head of the International Department of the Czechoslovak CP after the war), one was executed by the Dutch colonial power, one died from acts of war, one in an accident.

Aftermath

After 1938, the future-oriented time of the Communists came to a halt. With Franco's victory in Spain, Fascism's spread through Europe seemed unstoppable. The publication of the *Short Course*, in preparation since October 1934 and approved by the Central Committee of the CPSU(B) in 1938, marked a further ideological tightening.[13] The German-Soviet Non-Aggression pact of August 1939 saw the Workers' Fatherland ally itself with the arch-enemy whom the Comintern agents considered here had devoted years of their lives to fighting.[14] One can well imagine what they might have felt on hearing a newspaper vendor sing in Berlin:

Es war einmal ein Kommunist,
der wusst' nicht, was ein Nazi ist,
da ging er in ein braunes Haus,
da kam er ohne Knochen raus! Hahahaha![15]

---

13 On the so-called *Short Course*, which would be translated into twenty-six languages, see David Brandenberger and Mikhail V. Zelenov, eds, *Stalin's Master Narrative: A Critical Edition of the History of the Communist Party of the Soviet Union (Bolsheviks), Short Course*, New Haven, CT: Yale University Press, 2019.

14 On this, see Bernhard H. Bayerlein, ed., with the assistance of Natalja S. Lebedewa, Michail Narinski and Gleb Albert, *'Der Verräter, Stalin, bist Du!': Vom Ende der linken Solidarität; Sowjetunion, Komintern und kommunistische Parteien im Zweiten Weltkrieg 1939–1941*, Berlin: Aufbau Verlag, 2008.

15 Reported by Gustav Regler in *Das Ohr des Malchus: Eine Lebensgeschichte*, Cologne: Kiepenheuer & Witsch, 1958; in English, *The Owl of Minerva: The*

The fall of France saw the Comintern's representatives lose one of the few countries – Norway, Sweden and Denmark being the others – that still offered them a reasonably safe haven on the continent of Europe. A number of senior party figures found refuge in the Soviet Union, now over the worst wave of the repression, among them Dolores Ibárruri and her two children; Maurice Thorez and his wife, Jeanette Vermeersch; Palmiro Togliatti and his then wife, Rita Montagnana; and Walter Ulbricht and his (second) long-term partner, Lotte Wendt, née Kühn, an employee of OMS. All loyal to Stalin's Soviet Union, they were able to return to leadership posts in their national parties after the war, Ibárruri in the Spanish party in exile, Thorez in France, Togliatti in Italy, Ulbricht in the GDR, while the party leaders and Comintern employees who had actually struggled against the Nazi occupation were relegated to the second rank. The early years of the war, relatively neglected in Comintern scholarship, saw the policy of neutrality vis-à-vis Nazism provoke great disorientation among the membership and prompt many resignations, though the party as a whole retained its discipline. Individual party members, on the other hand, turned back to antifascist activity even before the German invasion of the Soviet Union in the summer of 1941.[16] The Yugoslav Communists launched their resistance immediately upon the German attack on their country in April 1941, in defiance of the prevailing Comintern line. In other countries, too, most notably France, Communists joined the Resistance (albeit individually or in small groups) without waiting for instructions – among them Irén Komját, who survived to return to Hungary in 1945.

Autobiography of Gustav Regler, trans. Norman Denny, London: Rupert Hart-Davis, 1959, 159: 'A Communist, the silly tyke / Didn't know what Hitler's boys were like. / In a brown house he showed his head / And now the bastard's good and dead! / Ha ha ha!'

16 On this see the documentary collection by Natal'ia Lebedeva and Mikhail Narinski, eds, *Komintern i Vtoraia Mirovaia Voina* [The Comintern and the Second World War], 2 vols, Moscow: Pamiatniki Istoricheskoi Mysli, 1994, 1998; Bernhard H. Bayerlein, Mikhaïl Narinski, Brigitte Studer and Serge Wolikow, eds, *Moscou – Paris – Berlin. Télégrammes chiffrés du Komintern (1939–1941),* Paris: Tallandier, 2003. On the resistance in Belgium, José Gotovitch, *Du rouge au tricolore: Les communistes belges de 1939 à 1944; Un aspect de l'histoire de la Résistance en Belgique,* Brussels: Éditions Labor, 2018; on Yugoslavia, Geoffrey Swain, 'Tito and the Twilight of the Comintern', in Tim Rees and Andrew Thorpe, eds, *International Communism and the Communist International 1919–1943,* Manchester: Manchester University Press, 1998, 205–21.

Conclusion: A Life with Bags Packed

Stalin's dissolution of the Comintern in 1943 in no way meant the end of Communism as a cause that could still move many. It did, however, mark the end of a world-historical experiment, the attempt to bring about a global revolution through the intervention of a relatively small group of professional revolutionaries who devoted all their time and energy to the job – or better, vocation. The history of the first half of the twentieth century cannot be understood without the history of the Comintern, a unique global and transnational network that established bases across the world: in Berlin, Paris, London and Stockholm, in Basel and Zurich, in Shanghai, Guangzhou and Singapore, in Mexico, Montevideo and Mumbai, in Madrid, Barcelona and Albacete. It supported movements of emancipation and gave a voice to the oppressed: the working class, women, Blacks, the peoples of the colonies, the victims of imperialism. The global solidarities created in the face of constant fragmentation and erosion only emerged thanks to the tireless commitment of individuals. The agents of the Comintern show how far political commitment can go, in terms of the willingness not only to devote one's life to a cause but also to justify means by ends. They put into worldwide circulation a whole repertoire of new political practices (prompting, too, a proliferation of counter-practices, including cross-border police cooperation). Although they always needed local assistance in gaining entry to other cultures and other political milieux, they were the bearers of a certain idea of justice, its propagators through space and time. And finally, they show us, in their own sphere, that globalization is always the work of people, and that the Comintern was the work of all its members, and not merely the instrument of a Lenin or a Stalin.

A Brief Epilogue: The Survivors

Hilde Kramer, who had joined the KPD-Opposition in 1929, had a very difficult life in Germany after 1933. It was only when the British consulate recognized her Soviet marriage to Edward Fitzgerald and with it her status as a British subject that she and her son Desmond were able to leave for the UK in 1937. Edward, who left Germany shortly after the Nazi takeover, moved first to Paris and then to London before installing himself (illegally) in Amsterdam in 1935. The two lived apart. From London, Kramer wrote about the situation in Germany for the Paris-based newspaper of German left social democratic party the SAPD, founded in 1931 and now in exile. She found work as a secretary for various companies and was active in the Labour Party. During the war she worked for social scientist Richard Titmuss, and in 1954 she (under the surname Fitzgerald) and Sheila Ferguson published an official study on the gender aspects of wartime social welfare, *Studies in the Social Services: History of the Second World War*. She died on 17 February 1974, in Otley, near Leeds.

Faced with political stalemate and the difficulties of gaining a living in Germany, **M. N. Roy** returned to India in 1930. There, in a trial behind closed doors, he was convicted and sentenced to twelve years' imprisonment (reduced to six on appeal) for his alleged role in the 'Kanpur Communist Conspiracy' of 1924. He was supported during this time by his second wife and third long-term partner, Ellen Gottschalk, like him a member of the KPD-O. With Roy's first wife, Evelyn Trent

– now back in the United States and working as a journalist – she organized international protests against Roy's imprisonment by the British colonial authorities. On his release from prison in 1936, Roy joined the Indian National Congress, whose policies he had fiercely rejected in the 1920s, though his attempts to radicalize the party were unsuccessful. In 1940, following a major controversy over support for Great Britain and France against the Nazi enemy, he resigned and turned his League of Radical Congressmen into an independent party. Gottschalk, a Jew who had fled to Paris on the Nazi takeover of power, had joined Roy in India on his release, and they married that same month. In the years that followed, Gottschalk supported Roy in the political struggle for Indian independence. Roy, a prolific writer, increasingly distanced himself from Marxism, developing a philosophy he called Radical Humanism, a bridge between Communism and liberalism. He died on 25 January 1954 in Dehradun in northern India. Ellen Gottschalk Roy was murdered in 1960, in unresolved circumstances.

Jakov Reich, 'Comrade Thomas' – who called himself Arnold Thomas Rubinstein from the late 1920s on – emigrated to Prague within weeks of the Nazi seizure of power, together with **Ruth Oesterreich** and their daughter Ruth. The couple had joined the KPD-Opposition in 1929. Rubinstein's possessions, a total of thirty-two boxes of books and papers, were seized, but released and sent to Prague following the somewhat surprising intervention of the Soviet embassy. When his application to join the German Social Democratic Party in Exile (SOPADE) was rejected in 1934, he withdrew from politics. Until 1938, he worked in the Russian history archive of the Ministry of Foreign Affairs in Prague, though on what basis is unclear. Some time in the mid-1930s, it seems, he met the psychoanalyst Annie Pink, the divorced wife of Wilhelm Reich, whom he married in 1938 and with whom he emigrated to the USA, together with their two daughters. His other daughter stayed with her mother, Ruth Oesterreich, and Rubinstein did not succeed in bringing them to the United States. As has been said, Oesterreich, involved in the anti-Nazi resistance in Brussels, was executed at Berlin's Plötzensee prison on 25 June 1943. After Trotsky's assassination in 1940, Rubinstein, who was close to him, feared for his own life. Taking American citizenship as Arnold Thomas Rubenstein, he avoided all mention of his past with the Comintern. He died in New York on 15 March 1955; his papers, including unpublished manuscripts on the history of the Russian

Revolution and the Soviet Union, are held by the Raymond H. Fogler Library at the University of Maine.

Babette Gross (née Lisette Babette Thüring), left the KPD in 1937 when her partner Willi Münzenberg came into increasing ideological conflict with the Comintern. In 1940, she was interned for a time at Gurs in southwestern France. After waiting in vain for Münzenberg, killed following his own escape from internment, she made her own escape in accordance with their joint plan, travelling via Portugal to Mexico, where she made her living as a secretary. After the war, she returned to Germany and co-founded the *Frankfurter Allgemeine Zeitung*. In 1967, she published an extensive and well-documented biography of Willi Münzenberg. Gross died in Berlin on 8 February 1990. The two sisters, Babette Gross and Margarete Buber-Neumann, remained in touch throughout their lives. After Heinz Neumann's arrest during the Great Terror, Buber-Neumann shared the fate of the wives of those arrested, namely unemployment and impoverishment, and Gross tried to send her money, clothes, and a passport. In June 1938, Buber-Neumann herself was arrested. Sentenced to forced labour, she was sent in 1939 to the Karaganda camp in Kazakhstan. In February 1940, in the wake of the Hitler-Stalin Pact, she was deported to Germany together with thirty other prisoners, and entered the Ravensbrück women's concentration camp in August 1940. There she became close friends with Milena Jesenská (friend and translator of Franz Kafka), a fine biography of whom she published in 1963. Buber-Neumann was released shortly before the liberation of the camp by the Red Army and after the war lived in Frankfurt, as did her sister. Having become a well-known writer and speaker against totalitarianism, she died on 6 November 1989.

Jules Humbert-Droz visited Moscow for the last time in the summer of 1938 and received an exit permit only after agreeing to write an article against Bukharin on his return to Switzerland. He was removed from the leadership of the KPS during the Second World War, after criticizing what he saw as its sectarianism, and, in 1943, both he and his wife, Jenny, were expelled from the party. Both then joined the Social Democratic Party of Switzerland (SPS), with which they had earlier advocated a fusion, rising relatively quickly to positions of responsibility. Jules became national secretary of the SPS in 1947, a position he held until 1959, while Jenny was elected president the Zurich branch of its women's organization in 1953. Jules would play a leading role in the movement against Switzerland's adoption of nuclear arms, while Jenny campaigned on women's suffrage and consumer protection. In 1959, the couple returned to La Chaux-de-Fonds. Jules died on 16 October 1971, Jenny on 4 January 2000, at the age of 107. In her final years she tended to her husband's extensive archive of Comintern papers, deposited at the municipal library of La Chaux-de-Fonds.

Charlotte Stenbock-Fermor (née Schledt), a countess by her first marriage, emigrated to Moscow together with her partner, Heinrich Kurella, in 1934. The evidence suggests that she was able to escape the terror thanks to an assignment from the NKVD, being sent to Copenhagen to spy on Trotskyists in German émigré circles. How well she did her job, if at all, is not known. Arriving on 17 February 1937, she was identified by the Danish police the day after, possibly on account of her forged German passport, a few days past its expiry date. Stenbock-Fermor was, however, able to stay in Denmark until she obtained an entry visa for France in July 1937. Before her expulsion from that country two years later she met her future husband, the Swede Einar Hirdman, at a cultural event at the former Cistercian abbey in Pontigny in Burgundy. After the war, Charlotte Hirdman became involved in the Swedish social democratic labour movement. She died in Stockholm in February 1966.

Agnes Smedley went to Moscow on leaving Shanghai in May 1933, but soon returned to China as a journalist for German, British and American newspapers, reporting from close at hand on the Chinese civil war and the war against the Japanese occupiers. With Edgar Snow, she was one of the few war correspondents in direct contact with Communist leaders such as Mao Zedong and Zhu De. Her application to join the Chinese Communist Party was rejected, however, as she was thought to be too undisciplined. Having moved back to the United States in the 1940s, in 1947 she found herself suspected of espionage as the Cold War set in. She escaped to Great Britain, where she died on 6 May 1950, following a surgical operation. Her ashes were buried the following year in the Babaoshan Revolutionary Cemetery in Beijing, in recognition of her contribution to the struggle.

On leaving Berlin with her son in 1933, **Mentona Moser** moved first to Morcote in Italian-speaking Switzerland. She continued to work for the Comintern, serving in 1934–35, for example, as a courier for

International Workers' Relief, carrying money between Moscow, Vienna, Zurich and Paris (where she worked illegally for International Red Aid in 1935). She spent the war and the immediate post-war years in Zurich, virtually penniless because her considerable private assets in Germany were frozen and later seized; she lived on social assistance as a boarder at the Café Boy, a left-wing cooperative hostel. She remained a member of the Swiss party even during its period of illegality and joined its successor, the Swiss Party of Labour, on its foundation. Moser moved to the GDR in 1950, invited by its first president, Wilhelm Pieck, and died in East Berlin on 10 April 1971.

Ruth Werner was another who ended up in the GDR. Invited in 1933 to attend a six-month course for spies, in Moscow she met again with Agnes Smedley, Borodin and Liao Huanxing. After training as a radio operator, she was sent – together with her son and another GRU employee – to Shenyang (Mukden) in Manchuria, where she regularly transmitted coded messages to the Soviet Union. After another course in Moscow, in 1935, she was sent on an undercover mission to Poland, together with her husband, Rolf Hamburger, who had now joined the party. Her daughter, fathered by her GRU colleague in China, would be born in Warsaw. In 1938 she was posted to Switzerland, where she worked as part of the Rote Drei (Red Three) spy ring from her home in Caux, above Montreux. Through this, she met Leon (Len) Beurton, an English Communist who had fought in Spain, whom she married and with whom she moved to Britain in 1940. There, she sent the Soviet Union important information on the construction of the atom bomb. In January 1950, when her informant – the nuclear physicist Klaus Fuchs – was exposed, she fled to the GDR, to settle in East Berlin, where she worked for different government departments before embarking, in 1954, on a career as a novelist and children's writer. She died on 7 July 2000.

One of Münzenberg's closest collaborators, the very well networked **Louis Gibarti** (real name László Dobos) went to the United States in 1934 to promote the campaign for the release of Ernst Thälmann and to organize the counter-trial to be staged in New York by the World Committee for the Relief of the Victims of German Fascism. He remained there, where he published the antifascist newspaper *Volksecho*, until May 1938, when he returned to France. When Münzenberg was expelled from the party, Gibarti resigned in protest. He then wrote for

Münzenberg's newspaper, *Die Zukunft,* and in 1939 became editor of *Paris-Soir.* In 1941, he fled across the border to Spain in order to avoid extradition to Germany. Arrested in Spain, Gibarti spent twenty-seven months in Spanish prisons and camps, and was able to return to Paris only after the end of the war. In 1947, he obtained a post at UNESCO. An anti-Stalinist, he served as an informant for the FBI during the Cold War. In 1955 he renewed contact with Jawaharlal Nehru, whom he knew from the time of the Brussels Conference and who had meanwhile become prime minister of India, and, in June that same year, he published an interview with him in the newspaper *Le Monde diplomatique* in connection with the Bandung Conference. Gibarti died in 1967.

Elena Stasova, who had left Germany only reluctantly in 1925, joined Stalin's personal secretariat in 1926, becoming one of his confidential advisers on Comintern affairs. In 1927 she was also appointed head of International Red Aid (MOPR), a position she held until 1938. From 1930 to 1934, Stasova was also a member of the Central Control Commission of the CPSU, and from 1937 to 1943 a member of the Comintern's International Control Commission. Having retired in 1946, in 1948 she received a 'severe reprimand' from the Central Committee of the CPSU for 'praising' Nikolai Bukharin, executed in 1938. She died in Moscow on 31 December 1966.

Following his acquittal, **Georgi Dimitrov** arrived in Moscow in February 1934, receiving a triumphant welcome. Having in mind for him a new role as the public face of the Comintern, Stalin asked him to draw up proposals for its reform. His rise was rapid: on 29 April, he was co-opted as a member of the Political Secretariat of the ECCI, becoming head of the Central European Secretariat, and, on 23 May, he was made a member of the Presidium. He was elected general secretary of the Comintern at its Seventh World Congress in the summer of 1935, where he gave the key speech that announced the turn to the Popular Front policy. By then, he had married and had a son, who would, however, die of diphtheria during the war, barely seven years old. He had also adopted the daughter of a Chinese party leader, a not uncommon practice among party members. After Moskvin's arrest in December 1938, he also had to assume responsibility for the OMS and the administrative management of the ECCI Secretariat. As can be seen from his diary, he found his position as head of the Comintern very difficult as the Terror took its toll among his staff and he took refuge in drink. In 1946, Stalin's loyal companion returned to Bulgaria after twenty-two years of exile, to take over the party leadership there. He would die on 2 July 1949 in a sanatorium near Moscow, after Stalin invited him to the Soviet Union for a discussion of relations between Bulgaria and Tito's Yugoslavia.

After the end of the Spanish Civil War, **Vittorio Vidali** returned to Mexico, together with his partner Tina Modotti, who would die of heart failure in 1942. A member of the leadership of the Mexican party and a loyal Stalinist, in March 1941 Vidali was arrested by the Mexican police in connection with the murder of Trotsky, though nothing was proven against him. In 1943, he married a Mexican woman, with whom he had a son, and in 1947 he returned to Europe, to his hometown of Trieste. There he became general secretary of the Communist Party of the Free Territory of Trieste, and in 1949 he was elected a city councillor. After Trieste's reunification with Italy in 1954, he rose within the Italian party, becoming a member of the Central Committee of the PCI and in 1958 a parliamentary deputy and then a member of the Italian Senate from 1963 to 1968. He died in Trieste on 9 November 1983.

Index

Abdelkader, Hadj Ali 201, 202
Abramov, Alexander 117, 295
Abramovich, Alexander 108, 109, 287, 288, 295, 296, 298
Abusch, Alexander 334
Acevedo, Isidoro 418
Ackland, Valentine 419
Akimova, Vera Višnjakova 247, 253, 255, 261, 288
Alberti, Rafael 419
Alexandrescu, Peter 42
Alpári, Gyulá Julius 17, 142, 144–6, 149, 150, 152, 154, 155, 157, 171, 227, 349, 350, 352, 357, 446, 447, 456
Alvarez del Vayo, Julio 378
Amsterdam, Saul 10, 46, 81, 131, 197, 203, 233, 247, 339, 340, 348, 359, 376, 383, 415, 460
Anderfuhren, Hans 394, 401
Andreev, Stronsky 313
Appel, Jan 50,
Aragon, Louis 379, 387

Araquistáin, Luis 393
Arnot, Robert Page 273
Ascher, Ernst 354, 375
Åsen, Augusta 71
Auden, W. H. 388

Balabanova, Angelica 42, 62, 63, 100
Baldwin, Roger 215, 220
Bamatter, Siegfried 50, 132, 150, 183, 451
Barbé, Henri 130
Barbusse, Henri 164, 202, 215, 222, 301, 326, 330, 331, 338, 387
Barofsky, Sonja 324, 329
Barthel, Max 44, 55, 71
Beals, Carleton 223
Becher, Johannes 174, 387
Becher, Lilly, see Korpus, Lilly
Beimler, Hans 393
Benario, Olga 135
Bernhard, Georg 323, 341
Bertyn, Zelma 295

Berzin, Jan 106
Besouchet, Alberto 430, 431
Bespalov, Georgi 285
Bickel, Ernst 346, 426, 427
Bickel, Hans 346, 347
Bickel-Schuler, Berta 399, 426, 427
Bilé, Joseph Ekwe 187, 236–8
Bindel, Charlotte, see Hümbelin, Charlotte
Bloch, Ernst 168, 322, 354
Bloch, Karola 168, 169, 322
Bloch, Rosa xi, 100
Blum, Léon 312, 389
Bodenmann, Marino 355
Bordiga, Amadeo 66, 68
Borodin, Mikhail 17, 42, 46, 78, 109, 160, 225, 228, 244–7, 249, 250, 253, 255–7, 260–2, 264–7, 277, 281, 319, 383, 442, 444, 464
Boros, László 142, 146, 351
Brandler, Heinrich 122, 123, 129, 152, 273
Bratman-Brodovsky, Stefan 374
Braun, Otto 135, 293, 294, 307, 309, 312, 318
Braunthal, Bertha 146
Brecher, Ludovic, see Dolivet, Louis
Brecht, Bertolt 158, 177, 186, 210, 343
Breitscheid, Rudolf 331
Bringolf, Walther 44, 46, 49, 52, 58
Brockway, Fenner 216, 217
Broido, Rosa, see Meyer-Leviné, Rosa
Brońska, Wanda 374
Bronski, Mieczyslaw 374
Bronstein, Lev, see Trotsky, Leon
Browder, Earl 251, 252
Broz, Josip 397

Brunner, Anny 399
Brunner, Otto 393
Brupbacher, Fritz 46, 123, 152, 169, 170, 183, 325, 332, 453
Brupbacher-Raygrodski, Paulette 453
Brutzkus, Berta 110
Bryant, Louise 44, 100
Buber, Martin 144, 153, 154, 172, 323, 324, 353, 358, 366, 367
Buber-Neumann, Margarete 17, 144, 146–50, 152, 153, 155, 167, 169, 176, 177, 180, 181, 184, 218, 228, 271, 287, 353, 354, 358–62, 365, 373, 374, 377, 445, 456, 462
Bullejos, José 384, 385
Buñuel, Luis 388
Bureau, Jacqueline 405

Caballero, Largo 421, 431, 432
Cachin, Marcel 44, 51, 55–8
Cai, Hesen 245
Capa, Robert 224, 390, 419
Carpentier, Alejo 419
Carrillo, Santiago 425
Cattaneo, Bernadette 331
Ceretti, Giulio 394, 408, 430
Chattopadhyaya, Virendranath 17, 47, 213, 314
Chauvet, Jean 411
Checa, Pedro 432, 435
Chongxi, Bai 257
Clark, William 146, 349
Cockburn, Claude 389
Codevilla, Carlo 429
Codovilla, Victorio 127, 151, 383, 384, 385, 407, 415, 434, 435
Cohen, Rose 227
Connolly, Cyril 388

Cordier, Marcel 411
Cremet, Jean 287, 288
Cripps, Stafford 336
Crispien, Arthur 51, 52, 65, 66

Dahlem, Franz 142, 299, 405, 423, 436–8
Díaz, José 407, 415, 431
Dieschbourg, Michel 147, 350, 352, 357
Dietrich, Marlene 333
Dimitrov, Georgi 15, 129, 133, 137–9, 143, 150, 152, 159, 167, 170, 178, 182, 291, 297, 299, 321, 332, 335, 337–9, 342, 343, 380, 385, 410, 414, 427, 431, 432, 435, 444, 447, 465
Dittmann, Wilhelm 51–3, 65, 66
Dobos, László 231, 232, 300, 332, 464
Dolivet, Louis 330, 331
Dolsen, Jim James 291
Dombrowski, Dora 225
Donini, Olga 407
Doriot, Jacques 130, 198, 199, 235, 251, 252, 255, 256, 262
Dos Passos, John 388
Duchêne, Gabrielle 215, 220, 331
Duclos, Jacques 130, 384
Ducroux, Joseph 286, 288–91, 319
Dumon, Jules 395
Duncker, Käte 186, 187
Duti, Hilda 375
Dutt, Clemens Palme 199, 203, 331
Dutt, Rajani Palme 199
Dutt, Salme 199

Ebenhoech, Frieda 168
Eberlein, Hugo 6, 133, 296, 350, 357, 375

Eichenwald, Fritz 352–4, 356, 357, 375
Einstein, Albert 186, 214, 222, 301
Eisler, Elfriede 112
Eisler, Gerhart 158, 210, 279, 281, 284
Eisler, Hanns 158, 186, 210
el Bakri, Mazhar Bey 218
el-Krim, Abd 230
Ende, Adolf 343, 457
Ensner, Clara 390, 398
Evans, Ernestine 87, 96, 121
Ewert, Arthur 293, 306, 308, 309, 311, 312, 315, 447
Ezhov, Nikolai 364

Fazekas, Erzsébet 424
Feistmann, Rudolf 334
Ferguson, Sheila 460
Feyerherd, Friedrich 296
Fimmen, Edo 222, 229, 230
Fischbach, Gertrude 301
Fischer, Louis 386, 388, 419
Fischer, Ruth 64, 106, 112, 116, 153, 158, 172, 299, 325
Fisher, Harry 403
Fitingov, Roza 87
Fitzgerald, Edward 147, 148, 154, 167, 172, 460
Florin, Wilhelm 367
Ford, James 236
Franco, Francisco 377, 379, 385, 389, 392, 399, 417, 457
Fried, Eugen 152, 394, 447
Friedländer, Paul 147
Friedmann, Endre Ernö, see Capa, Robert
Frossard, Louis-Oscar 51

Fuchs, Eduard 49, 117, 464
Fürstenberg, Jakub 105

Gandhi, Mahatma 214
Garvey, Marcus 220, 221
Gaspard Lévy, Pierre 327, 328
Gayman, Vital 395, 405
Geisenberg, Cilly 123, 172, 331
Geissler, Luise 165, 166, 169, 245, 251–3, 255, 267, 272–4, 445, 448
Gellhorn, Marta 389
Geminder, Bedrich 363, 457
Gerö, Ernö 381, 407, 428, 435, 436, 439
Gibarti, Louis 213, 227, 231–3, 300, 330, 332, 351, 464, 465
Givens, Patrick 300
Glaubauf, Hans 146, 148, 447
Glaubauf, Mireille 146
Gohl, Max 155
Goldenberg, Aron 50
Gorki, Maxim 301
Gottschalk, Ellen 164, 273, 460, 461
Gottwald, Klement 130
Gramsci, Antonio 113, 114, 142, 143
Grigulevich, Iosif 395, 440
Gröhl, Karl 113–15, 122, 123, 344–8
Gropius, Walter 301
Gross, Babette 17, 105, 109, 117, 120, 167, 169–71, 176, 177, 180, 187, 206, 215, 216, 218, 226, 229, 230, 323–6, 328, 329, 332, 333, 335, 336, 339, 341, 342, 345, 347, 348, 377, 379, 453, 462
Gruen, Josef Pepi 146
Gruzenberg, Mikhail, see Borodin, Mikhail

Gumede, Josiah Tshangana 215, 218, 237
Gyptner, Richard 129, 136, 138, 150, 152

Hadj, Messali 201, 202, 216
Hardy, George 279
Heartfield, John 174, 186, 301
Heckert, Fritz 130
Heimo, Mauno 124
Heine, Wolfgang 323
Hellman, Lilian 388
Hemingway, Ernest 387–9
Herbst, Josephine xiii, 16, 110, 111, 117, 135, 388
Hernández, Jesús 385, 418, 435
Herzog, Jakob 67, 109
Hikmet, Nâzım 13, 14
Hirdman, Einar xiii, 146, 154, 173, 352, 353, 365, 374, 463
Hirschfeld, Magnus 169, 170, 324
Hitz, Christian 198, 274
Hodann, Max 170
Hoernle, Edwin 186
Hofmaier, Karl 182, 341, 364, 400, 401, 427
Holm, Hans 354
Hölz, Max 179
Horwitz, Henryk 340
Hümbelin, Charlotte 345, 397
Humbert-Droz, Jules xi, 9, 17, 42–3, 46, 48, 49, 63, 66, 68, 97, 99, 114, 119, 123, 125–8, 150–2, 181, 299, 352, 363, 366, 383–4, 401, 427, 444, 446, 449, 451, 453, 454, 462–3
Humbert-Droz, Jenny 47, 97, 98, 126, 128, 299, 351, 363, 384, 445, 447, 453, 462–3

Humm, Rudolf Jakob 345, 348
Hurtado, Manuel 385

Ibárruri, Dolores 385, 407, 415, 458
Isaacs, Harold R. 254, 257, 259, 260, 266, 269, 307–9, 313, 318
Itschner, Hans Heinrich 181, 183, 212, 213
Ivens, Joris 388
Ivošević, Ljubica 167

Ja'far Javadzadeh, Mir 83
Jacobi, Lotte 439
Jahnke, Franz 158
Jäkel, Paul 375
Jansen, Jan 83, 97, 342
Jerram, Guy Mérédith 331
Jesenská, Milena 462
Jirku, Gusti später Stridsberg 416
Jordi, Fritz 111
Jordi, Hans 111
Jung, Franz 18, 50, 223
Jurr, Hertha 329

Kaetzler, Fite 149
Kaetzler, Gabriele 149
Kahn, Ruth, see Martínez Cartón, Carmen
Kai-shek, Chiang xiv, 246, 248, 250, 253, 256–9, 272, 293, 302, 303
Kamenev, Lev 364, 421
Kamerzin, Raymond 427
Kantorowicz, Alfred 168, 322, 330, 334, 335
Kantorowicz, Friedel 168, 322, 330
Karmen, Roman 388
Katayama, Sen 219

Katz, Otto 333–7, 362, 378, 388, 389, 438, 457
Kessler, Harry Graf 268, 323
Kirschbaum (Family) 354–6
Kisch, Egon Erwin 186, 301, 311, 419
Kivilovich, M. M. 133
Klee, Paul 301
Knorin, Wilhelm 129
Koestler, Arthur 158, 168, 177, 180, 326, 328, 333–7, 343, 354, 378, 387–9, 480–2
Komját, Aladár 146, 150, 154, 155, 171, 184, 353, 356, 357
Komját, Irén 142, 145, 146, 171, 226, 350, 351, 353, 356, 357, 458
Kopp, Victor 50
Korpus, Lilly 174
Korsch, Karl 184, 268
Kouyaté, Tiemoko Garan 220, 236, 238, 447
Kracauer, Siegfried 210
Kramer, Hilde 17, 41, 42, 44, 48, 49, 53–5, 57, 61–3, 69, 71, 72, 77, 78, 102, 109, 110, 115, 116, 121–3, 147–9, 167, 172, 331, 444, 460
Kreps, Mikhail 363
Krueger, Ani 167
Krumbein, Charles 285
Kuczynski, Ursula 17, 131, 278
Kuerzi, Alfred 424
Kun, Béla 83, 116, 175, 329, 337, 343, 358, 454, 456
Kurella, Alfred 125, 173, 174, 326, 331, 338
Kurella, Heinrich 17, 125, 146, 149, 153–6, 168, 173, 174, 323, 350, 352, 356, 358, 363, 365, 366, 370–5, 456, 463

Kuusinen, Aino 131, 135
Kuusinen, Otto 9, 128, 183, 206, 272, 438

La Guma, James 215, 237
Landa, Matilde 413, 417, 447
Lange, Else 329
Langrock, Willy 350
Lansbury, George 214, 215, 218, 222
Laurat, Lucien 49
Lefebvre, Raymonde 406
Lenin, Vladimir 3, 6, 10, 16, 18, 26, 31, 41, 44, 51, 60, 64, 67–9, 76, 78–80, 82, 84, 87, 108, 111, 112, 130, 131, 178, 238, 262, 263, 285, 337, 359, 385, 406, 407, 459
Léon, María Teresa 419
Leonhard, Susanne 168, 322
Leonhard, Wolfgang 168, 322
Lesse, Karl 303–6
Levi, Paul 9, 19, 49, 50, 117
Levien, Max 166
Lominadze, Vissarion Besso 131, 218, 269, 270, 271, 362, 369
London, Arthur 408
Löwenheim, Walter 294
Lubbe, Marinus van der 336, 337, 444
Lubieniecki, Jan, see Rylski, Ignacy
Ludwig, Carl 186, 297, 301, 345
Lukács, Georg 143
Luxemburg, Rosa 7, 113, 133, 142

Machado, Gerardo 215, 439, 447
MacManus, Arthur 233
Magyar, Lajos 364
Makaseev, Boris 388
Malaka, Tan 290

Malraux, André 247, 258, 288, 386–8, 419
Malraux, Clara 288
Mann, Erika 274
Mann, Heinrich 330
Mann, Tom 251
Märki, Hans 346
Marley, Lord 330, 332
Marteaux, Albert 222
Martínez Cartón, Carmen 425, 429
Martínez Cartón, Pedro 425
Martins, Carlos Deambrosis 215
Marty, André 381, 396, 399, 404–6, 408, 423, 425, 427, 434, 435, 437, 439
Maslow, Arkadi 325
Massie, Alexander 279, 285
Mattar, Ahmed Hassan 225, 230–2
Matzinger, Herta 351
Maublanc, René 331
Maxton, James 222, 229
Mayer, Konrad 12, 369, 416
McKay, Claude 11, 76, 417
Meins, Hans 342, 343
Mella, Julio Antonio 215, 439, 447
Meyer, Ernst 24, 50, 281, 320
Meyer, Hannes 186, 439
Meyer-Leviné, Rosa 24, 281, 313, 320, 322
Mickiewicz, Olga 279
Mif, Pavel 255, 283–5, 292, 294
Minev, Stojan 49, 130, 381, 431, 432, 453, 454
Misiano, Francesco 176, 179–83, 209
Modotti, Tina 17, 135, 136, 175, 215, 223, 224, 229, 337, 363, 367, 409–14, 417–19, 430, 439, 440, 445–8, 450, 466

Moiseenko-Velikaja, Tatiana 297
Montagnana, Rita 458
Moor, Carl Vital 112
Moser, Mentona 156, 185, 322, 347, 413, 463, 464
Mühlestein, Hans 419
Mühsam, Erich 41
Mukherji, Abani 47, 48, 88, 90, 162, 456
Münzenberg, Willi 11, 16, 17, 42–4, 46, 48–53, 55, 56, 71, 105, 108, 109, 117, 120, 121, 125, 130, 141, 147, 158, 167–71, 174–85, 187, 191, 204–6, 208–19, 221–40, 297, 300–3, 305, 309, 318, 322–37, 339–44, 346, 347, 354, 363, 375–77, 378, 379, 389, 390, 393, 395, 398, 400, 414, 438, 442, 444, 446, 448, 452, 453, 462, 464, 465
Murrik, Salme, see Dutt, Salme
Murphy, John Thomas 44, 50, 70, 217, 220, 221, 247
Musy, Jean-Marie 427

Narbutabekov, Taspolad 90
Nasonov, M. N. 250
Negrín, Juan 419, 421, 424, 432
Nehru, Jawaharlal 215, 229, 235, 269, 465
Neruda, Pablo 419
Neumann, Heinz 130, 144, 149, 150, 153, 154, 169, 172, 263, 269–71, 323, 346, 347, 353, 354, 358–363, 365, 367–70, 372–75, 377, 443, 449, 455, 456, 462
Nguyên, Ai Quôc 187, 201, 202, 261, 289, 290

Nicolaevsky, Boris 104, 105
Nin, Andreu 421, 422, 439
Nizan, Paul 388
Noce, Terese 406–8
Norden, Albert 334

Oesterreich, Ruth 113, 115, 121–3, 167, 322, 447, 461
Olden, Rudolf 323
Oprecht, Emil 345, 346
Orlov, Aleksandr 312, 381, 422, 428, 440
Orluk, Fanni 253
Orwell, George 387, 391, 392
Osten, Maria 278, 279, 388, 438
Ottwald, Ernst 375
Ozaki, Hotsumi 305, 310, 311, 319

Padmore, George 236, 238
Parlow-Hutchinson, Maud 146, 350
Pauker, Ana 135
Pavlovich, Mikhail N. 94
Pesch, Fritz 353
Peskine, Boris 388
Petit, Robert 142, 349
Petrie, Sir David 77, 160, 194, 199, 202
Petrovsky, David 227, 233
Philby, Kim 389
Phillips, Charles Francis 42, 45, 219, 246
Pieck, Wilhelm 116, 208, 365–7, 464
Pink, Annie 461
Pinkus, Theo 158, 173, 351, 354
Piscator, Erwin 185, 186, 333, 334
Platten, Fritz 166, 297, 301, 303
Pogány, Jószef 234, 270
Popov, Blagoi 133

Poretsky, Elisabeth 297
Poretsky, Nathan 297
Prestes, Luís Carlos 135
Prohme, Rayna 252, 254, 255
Protazanov, Jakov 182
Pudovkin, Vsevolod 182
Purman, Leon 384

Qingling, Song 222, 301, 303, 306, 309, 312, 316
Quelch, Tom 83

Rabaté, Maria 331
Radek, Karl 42, 54, 60, 64, 68, 72, 83, 95, 100, 111–14, 120, 140, 179, 243, 268, 342, 395, 420, 456
Rákosi, Mátyás 9, 166
Rakov, Paul 295
Rakov, Werner 113, 114, 121
Raskolnikov, Fyodor 235
Razumova, Anna 135, 200
Reed, John 4, 42, 43, 45, 51, 53, 68, 71, 76, 77, 83, 84, 91, 94, 100
Reese, Maria 172, 185
Regler, Gustav 156, 168, 322, 327, 334–6, 379, 387, 457
Reich, Jakov 17, 47, 49, 104–22, 140, 167, 322, 445, 446, 461–2
Reich, Wilhelm 186, 461
Rein, Mark 339, 431, 432
Remmele, Hermann 130, 137, 179, 185, 271, 359, 370, 375
Renn, Ludwig 186
Renoir, Jean 388
Reuter, Walter 357, 390
Ricol, Lise 408
Robinson, Viola 307, 313
Rolland, Romain 214

Rosmer, Alfred 44, 45, 52, 53, 56, 60, 68, 80, 81, 83, 84, 91, 97, 268
Roy, Evelyn Trent 1, 2, 17, 42, 46, 47, 62, 78, 87, 99, 142, 159–64, 190, 202, 203, 448, 460, 461
Roy, Manabendra Nath 1–3, 17, 42, 46–8, 50, 53, 57, 62, 77–80, 84–90, 95–7, 99–101, 142, 159–66, 169, 183, 184, 188, 189, 190, 193–5, 197–9, 201–3, 228, 229, 233–5, 239, 241, 242–6, 251–3, 255–7, 260–74, 277, 281, 286, 383, 442, 443, 448, 460, 461
Rudnik, Jakov 297, 298, 304, 305
Rüegg, Paul Emil 291, 296, 297, 301–4, 318, 443, 449
Rühle, Otto 223
Runge, Fritz 146, 150, 154, 350
Runge, Marie 146
Rylski, Ignacy Jan Lubieniecki 279, 281, 285, 292, 304

Sabiani, Simon 193, 194
Saborowski, Elise 306, 447
Sadoul, Jacques 50
Safarov, Georgij 84, 87
Saint Exupéry, Antoine de 388
Saklatvala, Shapurji 162, 203, 237
Sandino, Augusto 204, 223, 224, 301
Sanger, Margarete 314
Scheckenreuter, Charlotte 357, 375
Scheller, Hans Walter 165
Schönfeld, Betty 375
Schorr, Malke 412, 414
Schramm-Ehrlich, Marie 135
Schröder, Max 335
Schudel, Otto 224, 349
Schüller, Richard 129, 150

Schulz, Hans 324, 329
Seghers, Anna 210, 226, 271, 333, 419, 451
Selassie, Haile 395
Semard, Pierre 137
Senghor, Lamine 201, 202, 215–21, 236
Senn, Paul 390
Serge, Victor 44, 58, 59, 62, 69, 106, 142, 143, 145, 167, 198, 199
Serrati, Giacinto Menotti 65, 66
Seymour, David 390
Shafiq, Mohammad 88
Sheean, Vincent 254, 255, 259, 261, 264, 265
Silone, Ignazio 345, 346, 371
Singh, Brajesh 272
Sinkó, Ervin 150, 364
Smedley, Agnes 17, 89, 161–3, 213, 229, 301, 307–11, 313–18, 463, 464
Šmeral, Bohumír 130, 238, 331, 342, 438, 446
Sneevliet, Henk 42, 78, 79, 84, 161–5, 203, 242, 249, 277, 297, 447
Snow, Edgar 278, 463
Sokolnikov, Grigory 84, 87
Sorge, Richard 304, 306, 307, 309–11, 313, 315, 317, 319, 444, 447
Souvarine, Boris 119, 142, 143, 198, 268
Spender, Stephen 388, 419
Sperber, Manès 2, 3, 29, 168, 321, 322, 325, 328, 330, 334, 343, 451
Stalin, Josef ix, 8, 10, 11, 16, 26, 31, 32, 39, 42, 49, 61, 64, 65, 82, 103, 106, 108, 112, 113, 117, 120, 122, 129–31, 133, 140, 142, 151, 153, 154, 174, 177, 245–7, 249, 258, 261, 264–6, 268–72, 294, 308, 312, 322, 337–9, 359, 364, 370, 373, 375–7, 380–2, 386, 387, 394, 395, 397, 405, 416, 419, 422, 423, 428, 431, 432, 436–8, 440, 444, 453–9, 465, 466
Stasova, Elena 17, 82, 94, 107, 116, 118, 119, 121, 122, 410, 412, 413, 415, 429, 465
Stenbock-Fermor, Charlotte xiii, 17, 146, 149, 168, 173, 323, 350, 352, 353, 356, 358, 363, 365, 372–4, 451, 456, 463
Stern, Kurt 379, 387
Stern, Manfred 311–13, 405, 433, 437, 438
Stoecker, Walter 233, 384
Stoljar, Zidor 252
Strong, Anna Louise 7, 103, 150, 179, 207, 211, 249, 266, 267, 319, 388, 419
Strub, Walter 345
Sulzbachner, Fritz 46, 222–4
Swierczewski, Karol 396, 397

Tanev, Vasil 133
Tanner, Jack 68, 219
Taro, Gerda 224, 390, 419
Tasca, Angelo 114, 123
Taurinya, Pauline 406
Thalheimer, August 113, 117, 129, 142, 154
Thalmann, Paul 109, 223, 390, 391, 427, 428
Thälmann, Ernst 130, 137, 152–4, 179, 185, 271, 321, 332, 343, 359, 369, 370, 399, 410, 452, 464

Thorez, Maurice 394, 458
Titmuss, Richard 460
Tobler, Max 215
Togliatti, Palmiro 15, 96, 127, 130, 183, 299, 342, 381, 394, 425, 432–7, 439, 443, 458
Toller, Ernst 185, 215, 274
Torgler, Ernst 337
Trilisser, Meer Abramovich 372, 381
Trilla, Gabriel León 384
Trostel, Willi 215, 362
Trotsky, Leon 3, 18, 31, 52, 54, 60, 61, 64, 69, 74, 87, 111, 120, 121, 123, 198, 247, 258, 268, 341, 346, 347, 421, 428, 440, 455, 461, 466
Tyk, Isek 355
Tzara, Tristan 419

Uhse, Bodo 334
Ulbricht, Walter 15, 96, 341, 342, 405, 438, 458
Ulyanov, Vladimir, see Lenin, Vladimir
Undjus, Alice Margaret 285

Vaillant-Couturier, Paul 326
Vallentin, Maxim 158
Van der Rohe, Ludwig Mies 301
Vandervelde, Emile 214
Varga, Jenö Eugen 61, 125, 226, 227
Vartanjan, Arno 375
Vassart, Albert 172, 173, 331
Vermeersch, Jeanette 458
Vidali, Vittorio xiii, 17, 224, 363, 395, 410–15, 425, 426, 429, 439, 440, 448, 451, 466
Vincent, Jacqueline 302
Vincent, Jean 302, 303
Vogel, Lucien 326
Vogel, Marie-Claude 326
Vogeler, Heinrich 168
Vogeler, Marieluise 168

Waldron, Francis 308
Warszawski, Mieczyslaw 117
Wehner, Herbert 96, 104, 105, 114, 119, 120, 393, 402
Weitemeyer, Irene 305, 309, 311
Welles, Orson 388
Wendt, Lotte 458
Werner, Ruth, see Kuczynski, Ursula
Wiatrek, Heinrich 367
Wilde, Grete 135
Wilhelm, Ernst 51, 52, 109, 116, 129, 186, 208, 212, 255, 284, 300, 344, 365–7, 412, 426, 461, 464
Wilkinson, Ellen 215, 220
Willard, Marcel 343
Wittfogel, Karl August 186, 210, 215, 219, 226, 238
Wolf-Ferrari, Frieda 168
Woog, Edgar 132, 150, 383, 400, 401, 450, 455

Zedler, Nikolaj 305
Zedong, Mao 225, 262, 271, 275, 284, 316, 463
Zhang Wentian 294